S0-BRF-554

20,000 Dreams

20,000 Dreams

Discover the real meaning of your dream life

MARY SUMMER RAIN

Illustrated by Ivan Hissey

THUNDER BAY
P·R·E·S·S
San Diego, California

CONTENTS

Demystifying Dreams

Throughout time, dreams have held a deep fascination for people the world over. The mystery of dreams and what those vividly colorful visions are meant to convey have had an enrapturing effect on us since the time of the ancients when nearly every culture had a wise woman, oracle, or gifted member of the community who was revered as the one possessing enigmatic wisdom into dream insight. Normally, for the ordinary dreamer of today, the nightly ebbing and flowing of the endless tide of seemingly unrelated images most often present a confusing influx of nonsensical visuals which, more times than not, leave the individual to ponder what they all meant.

Dream fragments

Some dreamscape images can be so vivid that they remain strongly imprinted in the forefront of the dreamer's mind for hours or days at a time. These exceptionally vibrant fragments call to the consciousness for attention. They refuse to be ignored, put aside, or regarded as irrelevant. They have a way of rudely intruding on our thoughts and unexpectedly reappearing before our mind's eye at the most inopportune times during our daily routine. They continually strive to catch our eye or bend our ear toward their whispered message in an attempt to get in our face and say, "Hey! This is really important! You need to know about this! You need to give this attention!"

And what do we do about it? We shake our heads as though we're dislodging a fallen autumn leaf from our hair. Or we mentally swat at it as though trying to wave a pesky mosquito from our face. Why? Because we haven't a clue as to what the stubborn dream visual means, and it's now becoming nothing more than a bothersome irritation we want to be rid of. Ignorance will view the pesky dream fragment as a nuisance; insight will perceive it as a blessing to be counted.

Ignorance is easy when it comes to shunning dreams, but insight can be just as easy when one is interested in dissipating the mystery of every dreamscape's intended message. A cursory

Dreams of technology are usually linked with progress, which may have good and bad attributes.

scan through the pages of this book will illustrate the fact that every single thing we encounter, see, experience, touch, or have even a rudimentary knowledge of can become critical elements appearing in our dreams. Clearly, no object is too outlandish, rare, or ridiculous to include in a dream symbology volume such as this. It needs to be as comprehensive as possible to serve as an effective interpretive tool. For example, if someone dreamed of the Tin Man in *The Wizard of Oz*, the dreamer is going to be needing an interpretation for the Tin Man. Therefore, dream interpretation books should fully embrace as many elements of our world as possible. Otherwise, the reference volume remains incomplete and falls short of adequately providing the questing dreamer with the required tools for arriving at insightful interpretations. Keeping this in mind, and realizing that our world's vocabulary has grown by leaps and bounds with the technology explosion and other contributing factors such as recently popularized slang, these new terms have been included for the purpose of providing a more comprehensive reference volume of symbols that fully embraces a current view of our daily realm of experience. A well-rounded interpretation can't be reached if key pieces are missing from the puzzle. And, quite frequently, some of a dream's most revealing elements are quietly represented on the smallest puzzle fragments. Every piece has value. Every piece holds a precious clue. Every symbolic piece plays an integral part in serving the message as a whole. Every piece, no matter how small or insignificant it may initially appear, is in the dream for a reason and requires our attention. Every piece refines and sharpens the clarity of the dream's overall message.

The key to interpretation

The master key to unlocking the door to insightful dream interpretation is knowing that a multitude of dream elements can be grouped into various categories, each having an associative, generalized meaning. Once these foundational, associative themes are understood, they quickly coalesce to meld into an overview image that, in turn, clearly converts to a simplistic, bottom-line message. Simplicity is the ultimate goal to any dream interpretation. Though myriad elements usually comprise each and every dream, they can be poured into the interpretive funnel and quickly distilled into a single, pure idea. And that singular idea will be the main message of the dream. Normally, dreams are examined by laboriously attempting to look at each fragment individually and trying to attach a meaning to it. Yet that labor-intensive

Cars relate to the physical state of one's body.

Keys to Dream Interpretation

Normally dreams are examined by looking at each fragment and trying to attach a meaning to them individually. Yet that method is working without the keys of insight. The key here is that dream elements can be grouped into themes or categories. It's the category that carries the generalized meaning of the fragment.

Sample dream categories & generalized meanings

Category	Meaning
Air	One's thoughts/the mind
Canines	Friends
Christmas	Spirituality
Clothing	How one chooses to outwardly present oneself
Colors	Emotions and personality traits
Death	Waning/fading away or loss of energy rather than actual death
Elections	Freedom of speech
Explosives	Volatile relationships or situations
Eyes	Personal perception; worldview
Fabric	One's nature or personality
Fear	Variety of personal insecurities
Flowers	One's attitudes or natural talents
Hair	Thoughts
Marine life	Spiritual attitude
Murder	Symbolic death of plan or relationship
Musical sounds	Call for attention
Patterns	Type or level of a situation's condition
Rings	Bonds or clues to character
Season	Timing: current phase of a real-time situation or life condition
Vehicles	The physical body
Water	Spiritual concepts

method often proves unfruitful because it's working without the keys of insight. Remember, the key here is that dream elements can be grouped into themes or categories. It's the category that carries the generalized meaning of the fragment element. For example, the key insight for a dog in a dream is to know that the entire category of canines is directly associated with friends. A dog will nearly always point to a friend. Another example of a key category insight is that of vehicles. Vehicles are directly associated with one's physical body. For example, dirty headlights would mean that one's eyes aren't seeing something in its entirety. The message is that better lighting needs to be shed on the issue. A windshield would therefore represent the viewpoint (eyes and mind) through which perspectives are formed. Was the windshield tinted? That would indicate a colored perspective based on bias. An unadulterated perspective requires an unobstructed view free of all cracks, coloring, slant, and so on.

Dogs are a dreamscape symbol that always refer to one's friends and those one is closely associated with.

The thematic associative insight for fear is related to one's unique type of personal insecurities and how they adversely affect life perspectives and, ultimately, subsequent behavior. The insight key for hair is knowing it's associated with one's thoughts. Was the hair disheveled? If it was, then the message reveals unorganized thought. Braided? This particular dream element points to one's twisted or convoluted thought process, or that aspects of a specific issue are being entangled together instead of being kept separated.

The key insight for eyes is a revelation of one's personal perception, how one looks at life and its multifaceted elements. The key to clothing reveals the insight into how one chooses to outwardly present oneself. The key insight into patterns will relate to a type or quality of a situation's current condition, whether it's complex or interconnected with other aspects. Each of the various types of fabric are associated with one's nature and personality. And the key to flowers is their association to one's natural talents, the blessings that have been bestowed on us. Water will always have spiritual connotations. Air represents the mind, specifically one's thoughts. The above-mentioned symbols and their interpretive keys are but a few examples of the common dreamscape fragments that manifest in our dreams and the insightful keys that associate them with a specific category. The more one becomes familiar with dream fragments and expands his or her knowledge of the various insight keys, the easier interpretation becomes. Buildings, occupations, animals, weather, geology, and all of the other thematic categories carry their own key insight related to their specific, associative meanings and, with routine familiarization, the dreamer will soon have the knack for quickly distilling all of the many separate elements into a simple, one-line message. Many times, that message will be effectively reduced to just a few words or a phrase, perhaps to just a strong feeling or rightness about an awake-state issue or situation. Interpretation, when it comes, will appear as an instantaneous knowing. The message will be pointedly clear and concise.

Flowers refer to a person's natural talents that will blossom as they are used.

Recurring dream symbols

A unique aspect to dreams is that of the continually recurring one. It's not only bothersome as it perpetually chisels away at our efforts to concentrate on other thoughts, but it also purloins our ability to focus on any other task at hand. The repetitive dream can be insidiously determined as it relentlessly burrows its way beneath the dreamer's skin and becomes an itch that never sees relief until it's given due attention. It's persistent because it demands to be heard. It resolutely remains committed to its steadfast objective of enlightening the dreamer to a critically important message.

The recurring dream will not tolerate being ignored, nor will it take "no" for an answer. It will not be intimidated into silence by the dreamer's efforts to force denial of it. It will not accept a failed mission. It knows it can outlast our best efforts to ignore it. It knows it and, therefore, mulishly continues to doggedly stay its course until it wins. And it will win. It will, in the end, claim victory because it knows that a continually recurring anything in one's life becomes more than the casual coincidence.

The recurring dream will haunt its subject until it mutates into a mildly esoteric event that demands much more than a cursory nod of recognition to make it vanish. And for the afflicted dreamer who is swiftly becoming weary with frustration, the situation becomes so intolerable, he or she finally relents. The dream, satisfied that the dreamer has closely examined the contents of the recurring dream and has accurately acknowledged its message, fades to black and never again shows its face.

The significance of color

Colors in dreamscapes carry far more importance than simply providing a technicolor experience. The overall visual presentation comes equipped with its own interpretive key—that of one's perceptual intensity—or lack thereof, as the case may be.

Brilliantly bright colors will represent the intense strength of the dreamer's unique perspectives: a passion, if you will. Conversely, a wash of dull and faded hues indicate a lack of individual expression that may border on indifference and a noncommittal attitude. A colorless dream presenting itself in shades of gray indicates the dreamer's lack of clarity regarding a life issue, condition, or situation.

Colors are very revealing because they represent a dreamer's emotions and personality traits.

Monochromatic colors reveal the dreamer's habitual way of viewing life through a particular personal perspective. This, of course, indicates impaired perception. The specific colors of dreamscape elements are important to recall because they lend additional clues to the overall message. Their colors are never random. Rather than the dream itself presenting the various arrays of color, their specific presentation reveals how we, ourselves, are currently coloring our world. An object with a swirl of colors suggest a perspective that is based on two or more personal opinions or ideologies. A nondescript color—one that appears to be an undefinable blend of several different colors—alludes to a questionable or unclear perspective. Crisp and sharp colors signify a well-defined perspective, while blurred and opaque colors denote a cloudy perspective or perception.

The role of the seasons

The seasons are frequently prominently displayed in dreamscapes and, though they appear to represent a specific time of year, the seasonal interpretive key signifies the current phase of a real-time situation or life condition. This phase will indicate one of the following four options:

- Spring applies to new beginnings: the start of a situation, plan, or relationship.
- Summer represents a phase in full swing.
- Fall denotes the time to wind down and perhaps tie up loose ends.
- Winter symbolizes a resting phase for the purpose of rejuvenation and contemplation.

The dream's particular season provides the key for timing. It literally reveals the right timing for initiating new ideas and points to the best time to bring about conclusions. Although the season is often overlooked when recalling dream elements, it remains a vital aspect to correct interpretation.

Foretelling the future

Previewing a future event in one's dreams happens quite frequently without the dreamer ever being aware of what has transpired during the night. Recognition may come at a later date when the dreamer experiences that odd sensation of déjà vu after witnessing or hearing about a particular event.

If the dreamer remembers dreaming about the event, then the recognition of having a premonition will come on swift wings. Most often, the familiar wave of déjà vu is generated by an individual having a premonition in a past dream and then forgetting about it until the event happens in real time.

Of course, déjà vu also has other causal factors such as the recurrence of a past-life experience; however, the sensation is normally brought about by a subconscious dream memory that has been sparked within the consciousness. These premonitions are usually associated with a particular name or number that may or may not hold current meaning for the dreamer. Yet recognition comes after the dream name and number crosses the dreamer's path in the awake-state reality. And this is the underlying reason why it is imperative to write these down as soon as one awakes.

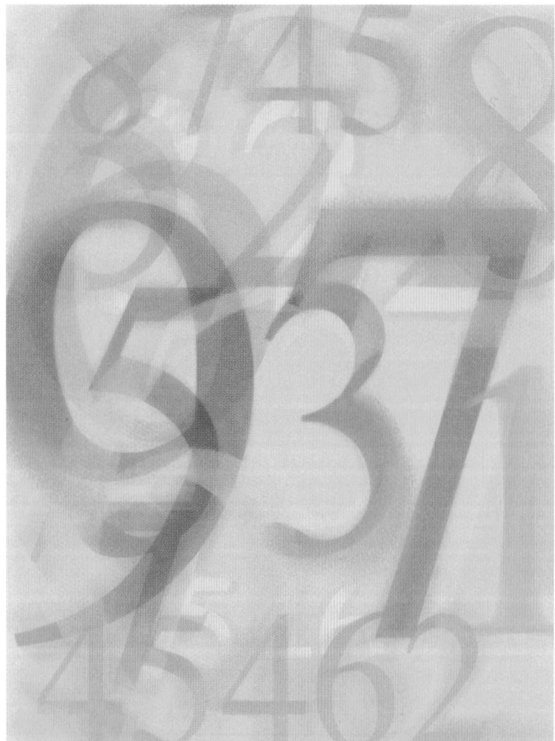

Numbers, like names, are often of critical importance when remembering dreams and may have a myriad of meanings.

Names and numbers

Names and numbers can be so prominent in a dream that they literally pop out of the background like a visual in a 3-D movie. A name is most frequently the name of someone the subconscious is attempting to draw attention to. Numbers have a multitude of diverse meanings. Oftentimes, a name or number will be the only element that a dreamer vividly recalls upon awaking. This fact alone serves to underscore their critical importance and, although the dreamer may have no conscious awareness or recognition of the displayed name or number, their importance will become evident at some future point in time.

Naturally, it's always wise to immediately write these down, because even though the dreamer is convinced that they'll be remembered, they rarely are. They have a habit of fading back into the Land of Lost Dreams.

Dreams of death

Death in dreams can be a confusing—and sometimes completely terrifying—issue for many dreamers, and these dreamers may well be consumed with worry and anxiety over an event that has been seriously misinterpreted as an upcoming death of a friend or loved one, possibly even oneself. However, the symbology for this final event is only very rarely associated with a actual, real-time physiological demise but rather stands for termination and finality. Dreaming of death is very unlikely to specifically point to a physical death but instead is a representation of a variety of different forms of wilting or fading away. These various forms are related to other aspects in a person's life, such as a waning energy level, a loss of optimism, a sudden drop in perseverance or fortitude, plans or goals that one is severely losing interest in, a spirit that is losing its spark, and so on. Frequently a dream of death will be generated by the dreamer's actual fear of the event.

Fears and phobias represent the dreamer's personal insecurities and a lack of self-confidence.

Nightmarish visions

A dreamer's innermost fears are often expressed through nightmarish visions. These fears are often the generating subconscious impetus for dreams associated with those elements the dreamer experiences most anxiety over in his or her awake-state hours. For example, if a woman continually spends her days fearing that her young child will die in a car accident and holds onto that anxiety during her waking hours, this conscious focus on a negative event will be seared into the mind and, during sleep, will exhibit itself by way of dream symbols. In her dream, the mother sees her child being injured or killed by a passing vehicle. Now she is sure the child is going to soon pass from her world. But that is simply not the case. The mother's anxiety is simply expressing itself through her subconscious during the sleep state. The dream event didn't come as a warning that her child was about to die, but rather as a strong advisement to stop worrying so much about something that may never happen during the mother's lifetime.

A death dream that actually forecasts a future physical demise will normally present itself in such a way that the visuals include names, numbers, dates, and funereal accoutrements, such as a cemetery, a specific headstone that is readable, a hearse, a death announcement bordered in black, and so on.

Guide to interpretation

Utilizing the simple interpretive keys to ferret out a dream's message is only half of the process. Interpretation springs to life through the additional application of logic or common sense. Although many dreams appear hopelessly tangled, there will still be logic to them. It's logical that the color black will represent waning energy or interest, depression, or death. There is a reason for how the condition of a road is portrayed. If it's serpentine, then it means that one isn't taking the most direct route to achievement or attainment, which is logical.

If the dreamer is depicted standing out in the rain and shivering, then the message would be a literal indication that one hasn't been using good sense lately, or hasn't the common sense to come in out of the rain, which is also logical.

A school will naturally be associated with learning. If it's an elementary educational institution, then this logically points to a need for the dreamer to get the "basics" of an issue or situation—some foundational information is missing. The same logic applies to a university and would indicate a strong advisement to expand one's knowledge on a specific issue. All of these symbols and interpretations are nothing more than plain common sense and carry no esoteric meaning to them.

Lastly, the final clue to the interpretation of a dream comes from the dreamer's emotional reception of it upon awakening. The initial reactive response is frequently accompanied by the sudden onset of marked physiological effects such as the heart pounding against one's rib cage, sweating, the spine-tingling sensation of déjà vu, feeling somewhat awestruck, and so on. These emotional and physiological responses are important. They mark the final element of the dream and serve to make an unforgettable and lasting impression on the dreamer.

The realm of inner knowingness

Dreams are not created in the mysterious depths of an individual's imagination. Dreams are not random images that are idly drifting about the ether waiting to be drawn into the slumbering consciousness of a dreamer.

In fact, dreams are free-flowing messages from within our own realms of inner knowingness, and they come to guide our consciousness toward the ultimate goal of evolving into the spiritual people we were meant to be. This book, then, is warmly offered to you as a helpful tool for gleaning optimum insights found nowhere other than . . . in your dreams.

Dreams are not random images; one can gain insights into the issues in one's life through dream symbols.

Chapter 1

Animals, Insects, Birds & Reptiles

These symbols generally point to personality traits and character qualities. They will often reveal unique clues to gaining invaluable information lying just beneath the surface of a situation or an issue.

Domestic & Farm Habitats

Aviary warns against confining one's spiritual talents or knowledge.
Birdhouse signifies noble and high ideals that are held to and take precedence (kept close to home).
Bird nest is representative of ingrained character traits and thought processes. What was the condition of the dreamscape nest? If it was high up in the top of a tree, the dream symbol will relate to one's thought process. If it was lower on the tree toward the ground, it will relate to one's emotions.
Brooder house symbolizes a wealth of new ideas; multiple plans for new beginnings.
Burrow indicates trepidation; escapism; attempts to hide from something.
Cage pertains to an aspect that prevents the exercise of one's freedoms or rights. This may even refer to oneself.
Caged birds refer to suppressed emotions.
Chicken coop signifies the self-confining aspects of insecurities.
Coop See cage.
Corral denotes personally controlled or confined aspects. May indicate a need for some type of containment.
Hornet's nest is representative of a troublesome situation or relationship.
Hutch (rabbit) warns against confining or hiding one's more innocent qualities for fear of ridicule.
Kennel implies a confining relationship.
Lair connotes the special place one goes to rest and recuperate from the stress and commotion of daily life.
Nest denotes a security factor and will imply insecurity.
Pen (enclosure) illustrates confinement, usually self-generated.
Perch See roost.
Pigpen connotes willful disorder and one's concern over it. It may also reveal a lack of self-respect.
Pigsty See pigpen.
Roost refers to a temporary rest period.
Stall (animal) See stable.
Stockade See corral.
Stockyard See corral.
Sty See pigpen.

Wildlife Habitats

Aerie signifies high philosophical thought.
Anthill represents order and/or cooperation toward the common good.
Apiary refers to an industrious nature.
Crow's nest cautions one of the need for a better view of something; wider perspective required; greater wisdom.
Dovecote typifies a contentment with self and surroundings.
Rabbit hole See black hole.
Snake pit exemplifies a highly dangerous situation, relationship, or belief.
Warren (rabbit) is most often representative of the quiet endurance of one's personal pain in life.

Animal Sounds

Bark represents a warning or greeting from a friend.
Bay See howl.
Birdcall is a call to think more deeply and follow ideas and concepts as far as they can possibly go.
Birdsong is usually associated with a light heart; inner joy and acceptance.
Howl relates to desolation; despair; loneliness.
Quack (sound) represents a swindler; fraudulence.

Animal Anatomy

Antler alludes to one's personal defense mechanisms; a method of body language.
Bear claw stands for a desire to maintain control of one's life.
Carapace signifies one's defenses; an ability to remain sensitive within a hardened society.
Claw warns of an attitude that goes against nature; a clawing toward something; a struggle.
Fang represents vicious and cutting speech.
Feather stands for a free-spirited thinker; applies to an open and expanding intellect; deep wisdom.
Gizzard corresponds with an aid to acceptance.
Guard hair indicates one's personal first defenses.
Hackles indicate one's position of defensiveness.
Hindquarter usually refers to concluding aspects; nearing an ending or closure.
Hoof implies a difficult situation or pathway.
Horn See antler.
Horsehair signifies a coarse personality covered with a sleek veneer.
Horseshoe represents superstition; a belief in charms.
Ivory corresponds to the value of one's relationships. Recall what the ivory was shaped as.
Mane relates to cleverness.
Muzzle (snout) suggests sensory insights.
Paw (pet's) portrays encouragement and loyalty of a friend.
Pelt (animal skin) represents an essence bond with the animal. See specific animal type.
Pineal eye (a sensory structure capable of light reception in some reptiles) constitutes one's inherent knowledge; insights.
Proboscis points to self-assuredness.
Rabbit ears (antennae) relate to awareness; one's personal antennae.
Rabbit's foot denotes a belief in luck rather than in oneself.
Rack See antler.
Skin See pelt.
Tail (of pet) signifies a friend's attitude. Recall if the tail was wagging, hanging down, held up, and so on.
Talon represents control of one's potential aggressiveness.
Tusk pertains to natural defense mechanisms.
Udder alludes to a nourishing factor in one's life.
Viscera refer to the internal workings or hidden elements of an issue.
Whiskers (animal) allude to awareness; acute sensitivity.
Wings emphasize one's personal freedoms.

see also
• Living Creature Phobias *p. 153*
• Animals & Wildlife *p. 262*

Mammals

Skunk can indicate that one needs to protect oneself from something.

Aardvark represents a tendency to hide from problems; escapism; denial.
Alpaca See llama.
Anteater signifies a disruptive nature coupled with mental focus.
Armadillo stands for one's personal defense mechanisms.
Badger stands for a nagging personality, usually one who interferes in another's life.
Bat means the use of spiritual intuition in all aspects of life.
Bear characterizes an overbearing personality, relationship, or situation. Often points to the source of a dreamer's stress.
Black bear is a very dangerous person linked to the dreamer.
Bunny See rabbit.
Camel connotes tenacity and perseverance.
Coon See raccoon.
Cottontail See rabbit.
Duckbill See platypus.
Ferret typifies attitudes or responses tempered with a sense of humor. May also indicate a need to do some further investigative work.
Fisher (animal) means honesty.
Fox connotes cunning; shrewdness.
Giraffe warns against meddling in the affairs of others.
Goat warns against a voracious intake. This could refer to information, self-consumption, etc.
Grizzly bear denotes a self-absorbed personality.
Hare See rabbit.
Hedgehog See porcupine.
Ibex See goat.
Jackrabbit See rabbit.
Koala See bear.
Llama will correspond to one who has the capability of easing another's burden.
Mammal will be associated with behavioral elements. See specific type.
Marten symbolizes inquisitiveness; curiosity.
Meerkat denotes cooperation; commitment; community minded.
Mink (animal) pertains to cleverness.
Mongoose represents a quick wit and acuity in respect to perceiving deception.
Mountain goat connotes a determined effort to persevere; tenacity.
Otter implies the recognition of inner joy generated by spirituality.
Panda will reveal a friend with ulterior motives.
Pika (tailless hare) applies to quick thinking.
Platypus signifies an ability to incorporate spiritual elements such as beliefs and talents into one's daily life.
Polar bear relates to spiritual aloofness or an overbearing spiritual attitude. This symbol may point to the hidden aspects of oneself and points to a need to look at one's subconscious motives.
Polecat See skunk.
Porcupine stands for a tendency to utilize subconscious defense mechanisms to obtain personal desires and goals, and is usually a strong warning to stop manipulating others. It also means an instinctive reaction to bristle and hide from new ideas, relationships, or situations.
Porcupine quill illustrates personal defenses.
Rabbit represents an obsessive preoccupation with mental and/or physical erotic activities. This is a warning. This symbol may also refer to a quiet endurance of one's personal pain.
Raccoon shows an industrious personality; self-sufficient.
Shrew connotes an individual who is never satisfied; a complainer.
Skunk connotes a strong desire for justice to prevail in life. Depending on surrounding dreamscape elements, it may also refer to one's self-preservation methods.
Snowshoe hare is representative of unique defense methods; adaptability.
Tapir pertains to the presence of a personal abnormality one should overcome.
Weasel alludes to a cowardly act. May illustrate evasiveness.

Livestock

Bighorn sheep denotes adaptability; awareness of options.
Black sheep characterizes a personalized or unique path; one who dares to be different.
Bull characterizes a tendency toward narrow-mindedness; self-possessed.
Calf (bovine) characterizes the beginning of an end; a fatalistic aspect; something that will not manifest as planned.
Cattle means a lack of individuality and self-confidence.
Cow alludes to compassion and the expression of same.
Free range See open range.
Open range (cattle grazing) reveals unrestricted possibilities; opportunities everywhere.
Persian lamb emphasizes an enduring bond.
Ram refers to an argumentative nature, or it may be advising one to stop beating one's head against the wall, stop trying to force results.
Sheep is representative of a lack of individuality and/or assertiveness.
Steer See cattle.
Stock See cattle.

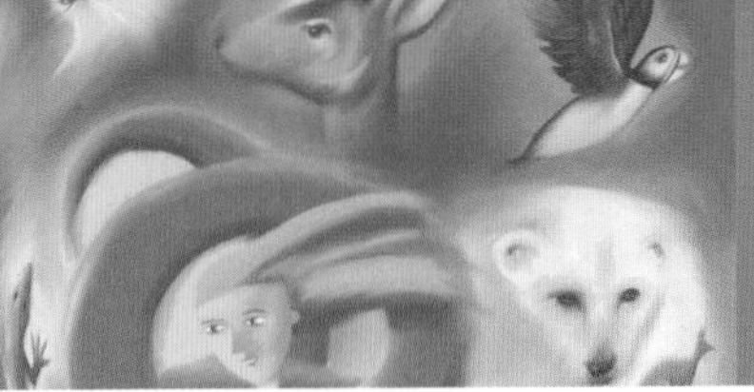

Pachyderms

Elephant stands for a generous and gregarious nature.
Hippopotamus typifies spiritual generosity. A continual giving nature.
Pachyderm See specific type.
Rhinoceros denotes controlled emotions; the utilization of intellect instead of one's emotionally instinctual reactions. May denote thick-skinned personality.

Endangered & Extinct

Dinosaur exemplifies outdated concepts; primitive thought.
Dodo connotes ignorance; a fear of knowledge and the responsibility that attends it.
Endangered species won't refer to an actual animal, instead, it will equate to the word "endangered" and relate to a relationship, situation, or even one's integrity that's heading for serious trouble, perhaps because of an intended decision or planned behavior.
Mammoth (animal) corresponds with an overbearing and/or manipulating individual.
Mastodon signifies an overwhelming situation or idea.
Pterodactyl denotes antiquated thoughts; extinct attitudes.
Tyrannosaur corresponds to an overwhelming situation or demanding individual.

Primates

Ape cautions against loss of individuality.
Baboon represents a tendency to imitate others; lacking individuality.
Bush baby symbolizes heightened awareness.
Gibbon See ape.
Gorilla may indicate mental or emotional dysfunctions, but this symbol usually refers to gregariousness. Surrounding dreamscape details will clarify this dual meaning.
Lemur illustrates enigmatic aspects; difficult to understand situations or concepts; ghostly, indistinct facets in one's life.
Mandrill See baboon.
Orangutan See ape.

Monkeys

Capuchin See monkey.
Chimpanzee See monkey.
Howler monkey denotes egotism.
Marmoset See monkey.
Monkey indicates intelligence hiding behind immaturity or a lack of individuality.
Rhesus monkey vicariously indicates inhumane behavior; arrogance and a lack of compassion.
Snow monkey denotes a strong sense of self.
Spider monkey denotes mental acuity, nimbleness.
Tarsier signifies sharp perceptual skills.

Rodents

Rat may indicate that something is fundamentally wrong in one's life.

Agouti connotes an introverted personality.
Beaver is an ability to recognize spiritual aspects while balancing and using opportunities; an ability to integrate all aspects of life.
Chickadee signifies acceptance from a heightened level of fortitude.
Chinchilla defines egotism; apathy toward others; a dangerous focus on self.
Chipmunk portrays hoarding; emotional reserves.
Field mouse portrays observers one seldom becomes aware of.
Flying squirrel connotes the hidden aspects of self.
Gerbil depicts life aspects that serve as small comforts.
Gopher represents multiple tentative starts.
Groundhog reflects a fear of responsibility; hiding from reality or problems.
Ground squirrel See prairie dog.
Guinea pig reveals lack of self-confidence; fear of experience.
Hamster See gerbil.
Jumping mouse denotes mental agility; efficiency; cleverness.
Kangaroo rat means endurance.
Lemming warns of tendency to be a follower; lack of thought and/or individuality.
Marmot signifies insecurities; a lack of self-confidence.
Mole indicates a lack of communication; fear of reality.
Mouse connotes a negative aspect that has infiltrated life.
Muskrat signifies a repulsive attitude; an aversion.
Pack rat warns of a tendency to collect insignificant or superficial aspects.
Pocket gopher points to lack of trust; insecurity.
Prairie dog portrays communal watchfulness and awareness.
Rat pertains to a "diseased" element in one's life. May reveal a betrayer.
Squirrel refers to the act of hoarding. May indicate a need to reserve something or warn against retaining too much.
Vermin relates to severe negatives in one's life.
Wood rat signifies difficulty recognizing one's priorities. Also see pack rat.
Woodchuck See groundhog.

see also
• Geography & Landscape *pp. 64–71*
• Science & Natural History *p. 234*

Marsupials

Bandicoot implies small blessings.
Kangaroo cautions against overprotectiveness.
Opossum denotes backward or inverted views; a caution to stop turning things around to suit oneself.
Possum See opossum.
Sugar glider (possum) denotes resourcefulness.
Tasmanian devil symbolizes vindictiveness; maliciously aggressive behavior.
Wallaby signifies defensive attitude toward another.
Wombat signifies familial associations.

Wild Cats

Bobcat See lion.
Catamount See lion.
Cheetah signifies swiftness. It is used to indicate a quick action.
Civet is representative of a quick wit.
Cougar characterizes the strength of quiet wisdom.
Jaguar is representative of changeability. It may refer to an altering personality.
Leopard symbolizes a resistance to change.
Lion is representative of a braggart. On the other hand, it may also imply strength of character.
Lynx denotes cleverness; an acute observational skill.
Mountain lion See cougar.
Ocelot denotes patience.
Panther suggests caution; a careful approach to something in the dreamer's life.
Puma See cougar.
Tiger implies an aggressive nature; emotionally volatile.

Cats

Tabby cat denotes friendliness.

Abyssinian cat represents honesty and individuality.
Alley cat signifies a degenerate lifestyle or hard times.
Burmese cat denotes an expressive individuality; outgoing.
Calico cat stands for quiet independence while maintaining a strong loyalty to friends.
Cat (domestic/wild) pertains to one's type of independence. See specific type.
Cheshire cat is representative of the quality of cleverness. It may also indicate a sly watchfulness in someone.
Feline See cat.
Kitten suggests innocence. May indicate helplessness.
Manx cat denotes simplicity of character; unpretentiousness.
Mouser portrays a deterrent to a negative influence.
Siamese cat represents sharp perception.
Tabby cat signifies a gregarious personality.
Tomcat corresponds with indiscriminate behavior.

Wild Dogs

Coyote signifies a preference for solitude. May indicate the trait of slyness.
Hyena implies a lack of seriousness or a vicious nature.
Jackal means predatory nature.
Red fox usually refers to a highly dangerous individual, one to avoid.
Vixen implies a playful cleverness.
Wild dog exposes an unpredictable friend or close associate.
Wolf signifies cleverness and evasiveness. This symbol will sometimes imply a dangerous association.

Dog Types

Puppy represents the beginning of an affinity with someone new.

Bird dog warns of a hounding being done.
Bomb-sniffing dog signifies a friend devoted to keeping others on the right track.
Cadaver dog will usually point to a friend who cares about the dreamer's welfare.
Guard dog will indicate a friend who has your best interests in mind.
Guide dog emphasizes a knowledgeable friend who is capable of assisting another; one who will never steer you wrong; one willing to help people attain personal goals.
Junkyard dog indicates a friend one doesn't fully appreciate.
Lapdog is a friend who is overly eager to give assistance. May also indicate a sympathetic friend.
Mouser portrays a deterrent to a negative influence.
Mutt (dog) represents a friend who will remain loyal.
Police dog indicates a watchful and guiding friend.
Puppy will denote a new friendship.
Seeing Eye dog characterizes a friend who has the ability to clarify confusing matters.
Sled dog represents a friend who encourages an easy life path; one willing to pull another along.
Sleeping dog may indicate a friend who doesn't see her or his own potential.
Watchdog defines a friend's alertness; acute awareness.
Yellow dog refers to a friend who lacks the courage to express an opposing opinion.

Dog Breeds

Dog always refers to one's friends and close associates. See specific breed.

Afghan implies an interfering or smothering friend or associate.

Airedale Terrier denotes a frivolous nature. This suggests that one needs to get focused and be more serious.

Alaskan Malamute See Malamute.

Australian Shepherd represents a friend who can help you keep it all together.

Australian Silky Terrier signifies a dependable friend who will be there for support in any situation.

Basenji denotes a sensitive nature; strength through emotional sensitivity.

Basset Hound symbolizes melancholy; sadness related to a friend.

Beagle refers to a sympathy-seeking friend.

Bearded Collie signifies a friend having unusual or eccentric characteristics, yet who can always be depended on to be there for you.

Bichon Frise represents a supportive friend.

Bloodhound suggests a friend with acute deductive and perceptual abilities.

Border Collie signifies a friend who can help you keep it together.

Borzoi represents acute perception.

Boston Terrier denotes a friend with aggressive defenses; distrust; suspicious nature.

Boxer denotes protectiveness of a friend. May indicate a watchful or hesitant personality.

Brittany Spaniel denotes a compassionate friend; a sympathetic and particularly sensitive nature.

Bulldog denotes a bullish associate or friend.

Chihuahua advises to never underestimate the abilities or power of another.

Chow Chow stands for a friend's inner strength; perseverance; drive.

Cocker Spaniel characterizes companionship; gentle associations. May have communication troubles.

Collie characterizes a faithful friend.

Dachshund implies a caution against the tendency to make the physical aspects a priority; a high interest in materialism.

Dalmatian signifies a traveling companion; a friend having a protective nature.

Doberman Pinscher connotes a friend or associate who represents a law-abiding factor in one's life.

English Foxhound denotes fortitude; focus on a goal.

English Setter symbolizes a friend's loyalty.

English Sheepdog See Old English Sheepdog.

Eskimo Dog stands for a friend's endurance. This suggests a friend who can handle sharing your burdens.

Foxhound signifies a tendency to gravitate to shrewd and cunning personalities rather than thinking for self.

German Shepherd characterizes a helpful friend or close associate.

Golden Retriever denotes loyal companionship.

Great Dane points to a noble friend, one having solid integrity.

Great Pyrenees denotes a friend having great courage.

Greyhound refers to a fast friend or associate.

Griffon refers to a friend who will always listen without judgment.

Husky characterizes a strong friend or associate on whom one can always depend.

Irish Setter denotes a friend capable of providing guidance, pointing people in the right direction.

Irish Wolfhound stands for a friend possessing strong character.

Jack Russell Terrier represents a devoted friend.

Keeshond denotes a protective friend.

Poodle denotes a companion one will always be able to depend on.

Komondor denotes a friend having great inner strength.

Labrador Retriever signifies a determined friend, one who will always return to offer aid after rebuffs.

Lhasa Apso denotes a friend who can give support.

Malamute alludes to a friend or associate who has the capability to ease one's burden or quicken progression along a life path.

Maltese represents close companionship.

Manchester Terrier constitutes a friend or associate who protects one from negative personalities.

Mastiff refers to a friend's gentleness; an even-keeled personality.

Mexican Hairless points to the strong determination or fortitude of a meek-appearing friend.

Newfoundland refers to a staunch friend.

Norfolk Terrier signifies a sympathetic friend, one eager to listen and offer comfort.

Norwegian Elkhound denotes a friend's loyalty.

Old English Sheepdog signifies a loyal, faithful friend, one who can be counted on.

Papillon signifies the tenacity of a friend.

Pekinese portrays a self-serving friend, yet one who will never leave you in the cold or out of the loop.

Pharaoh Hound signifies a dignified, yet faithful, friend.

Pit Bull Terrier suggests aggressiveness.

Pointer stands for a friend who can be counted on to always point you in the right

see also
• Equestrianism & Horse Racing *p. 212*
• Legendary Creatures *p. 363*

Dog Breeds (continued)

direction. A friend who has the mental clarity to give good advice.
Pomeranian signifies heightened awareness in a friend. This symbol may also indicate a friend's feeling of companionable affection.
Poodle is a dependable friend.
Pug alludes to a friend who usually guards his/her opinion and rarely shares thoughts.
Retriever characterizes an analytical friend, one who possesses the skill and wisdom to bring back or show people the true psychological motivations for their unproductive behavior.
Rottweiler denotes a friend's social selectiveness.
Saint Bernard represents a helpful friend.
Samoyed denotes a friend's gregariousness; generosity and outgoing personality.
Schnauzer portrays a friend who watches out for you.
Scottish Terrier characterizes a loyal friend who is prepared to defend your honor.
Sheepdog See Old English Sheepdog.
Shetland Sheepdog depicts protectiveness; watchfulness.
Shih Tzu suggests a nonjudgmental friend.
Siberian Husky See Husky.
Skye Terrier is a faithful friend.
Spitz signifies a companionable friend.
Weimaraner signifies a friend's loyalty.
Welsh Corgi symbolizes a companionable friend.
Welsh Terrier refers to a friend who can be tenacious in helping people stick to goals.
Whippet signifies impetuosity, usually related to a friend.
Yorkshire Terrier stands for a friend's faithful loyalty.

Hogs & Oxen

Boar is a representation of an arrogant, tiresome person.

Bison See buffalo.
Boar indicates a haughty personality; a bore to others.
Buffalo (bison) symbolizes gullibility. May also indicate perseverance.
Hog cautions against tendency to take on too much at once.
Oxen is representative of overwork. It suggests a psychological cause.
Peccary See boar.
Pig See hog.
Sow See hog.
Swine pertains to excesses indulged in.
Water buffalo indicates a spiritual arrogance.
Yak is representative of a wild strength. It may also suggest a lack of discernment regarding the use of inner strength.

Man's Best Friend

Chew (dog treat) refers to a friend's deep thought. May show need to consult a friend.
Choke chain See choke collar.
Choke collar warns of life factors that we allow to control us; manipulation.
Dog bed signifies closest friend(s).
Dog biscuit refers to the many small joys of a friendship.
Dog bone usually signifies a conflict with a friend.
Dog brush reveals a tendency to alter the course of a friend's opinion or perspective.
Dog chew exemplifies a trusting friend.
Dog collar warns against forced friendships or relationships.
Dogfight portrays a serious conflict between friends.
Doghouse represents personal trouble with a friend.
Dog leash warns against an overbearing attitude.
Dog tag (animal's) represents one's strong ties to one's friends. It may point to a cautionary message revealing a necessity to check the loyalty of friends.
Obedience training implies manipulation either of a friend or from a friend.
Pooper-scooper means picking up after a friend's mistakes.
Radio collar points to one's attempt to keep track of another.

Deer Family

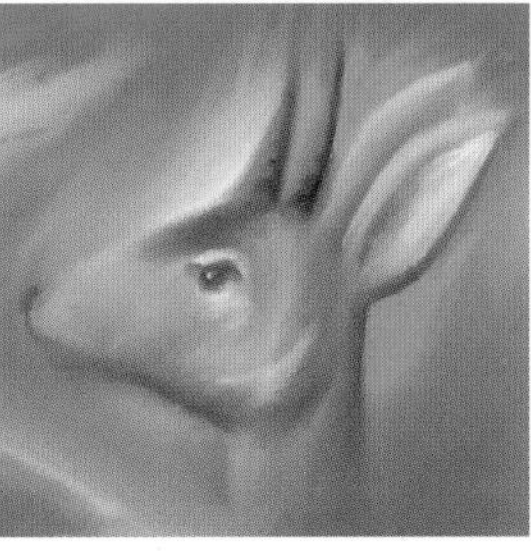

Gazelle denotes artlessness.

Antelope connotes a free-spirited personality.
Buck (male deer) See deer.
Caribou See reindeer.
Deer applies to a tendency to be cautious; watchful; aware.
Doe stands for a source for perpetuating innocence.
Eland represents innocence and gentleness associated with strength.
Elk denotes integrity.
Fawn characterizes an emotionally sensitive nature; innocence.
Gazelle refers to an innocent characteristic; naïveté.
Gnu See antelope.
Impala See antelope.
Moose is a spiritual burden.
Mule deer See deer.
Reindeer connotes a tendency to be easily led or controlled.
Stag is a self-reliant loner. Implies a personal choice to accomplish something by oneself.
Wildebeest denotes a lack of individuality.

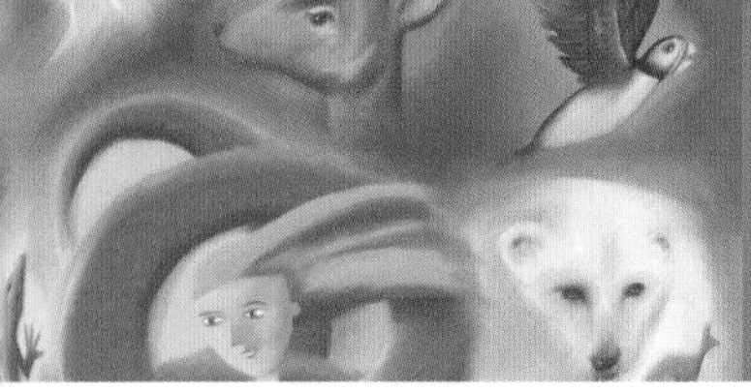

Equines

Bronco represents individuality and the freedom to express it.
Burro See donkey.
Colt stands for the freedoms of youth that maturity usually suppresses.
Dead horse stands for an advisement to accept an issue, leave it, and go forward.
Donkey emphasizes independence, perhaps stubbornness.
Equine See horse.
Foal characterizes new beginnings.
Gelding signifies a need to control the expression of emotional extremes.
Horse emphasizes a wild nature one must continually keep reined in.
Mule may symbolize stubbornness, yet it usually indicates independence; a reluctance to be influenced; a combination of differing elements.
Mustang reveals a wild type of individual freedom verging on recklessness.
Nag (horse) pertains to weariness.
Pack horse suggests an opportunity to have our loads lightened; an aspect that can shoulder some of the weight.
Pinto marks the exercising of multiple experiential freedoms while following one's personal life path.
Pony See horse.
Quarter horse alludes to a preferred choice.
Racehorse illustrates competitiveness; a desire to be better and faster than one's peers; getting ahead of the rest.
Shetland pony pertains to concealed personal power.
Stallion warns of an uncontrolled strength; a need to contain and direct one's energies.
Swayback (of a horse) is representative of a burdensome phase of life.
Unbridled horse constitutes an uncontrolled state, but could imply a freedom to express one's individuality.
Yearling connotes immaturity; a need to grow and learn.
Zebra represents the good/evil, right/wrong polarity of various elements; fulfillment; reaching a goal.

Donkey denotes singlemindedness and a sense of individuality.

Horse Breeds

Appaloosa is inner strength.
Arabian signifies a noble character; integrity.
Morgan denotes dependability; trustworthiness.
Palomino illustrates a gentle freedom; a quiet appreciation for unique individuality.
Percheron is representative of great personal efforts that one has applied to one's chosen path.
Thoroughbred connotes a singular element unaffected by outside influences; a pure aspect.

Amphibians

Amphibian denotes one who is spiritually grounded.
Box turtle is representative of endurance.
Bullfrog connotes a need to give serious attention to spiritual matters.
Frog represents some kind of impaired mental or physical condition.
Mud puppy See salamander.
Newt See salamander.
Polliwog See tadpole.
Salamander suggests the blending of spirituality through daily life.
Tadpole correlates to spiritual immaturity. It represents a novitiate seeker.
Toad See frog.
Tree frog represents an awareness and appreciation of one's bond with nature—the sense of interrelatedness; holding onto one's bond with personal spirituality.

Reptiles

Adder (snake) refers to a venomous nature.
Anaconda reveals an uptight personality; rigidness.
Asp (snake) denotes a threatening relationship.
Boa constrictor means a smothering or constricting situation or relationship.
Bushmaster (snake) denotes a dangerously manipulative personality.
Chameleon may refer to indecision; vacillation; aspects that keep reversing direction.
Cobra illustrates a threatened or dismayed individual. See snake.
Copperhead See viper.
Coral snake See snake.
Corn snake denotes misplaced fears; fearing what one doesn't understand.
Cottonmouth See water moccasin.
Diamondback rattlesnake See snake.
Garter snake denotes harmless qualities or aspects many fear.
Gila monster symbolizes cherished ideals.
Gecko See lizard.
Iguana See lizard.
King cobra warns of a major negative existing in one's life; an individual or situation that could be venomous.
Lizard connotes a lack of scruples.
Mamba (snake) denotes a swift retaliation.

see also
• Marine Mammals *p. 38*
• Horse-Drawn Vehicles *p. 290*

Reptiles (continued)

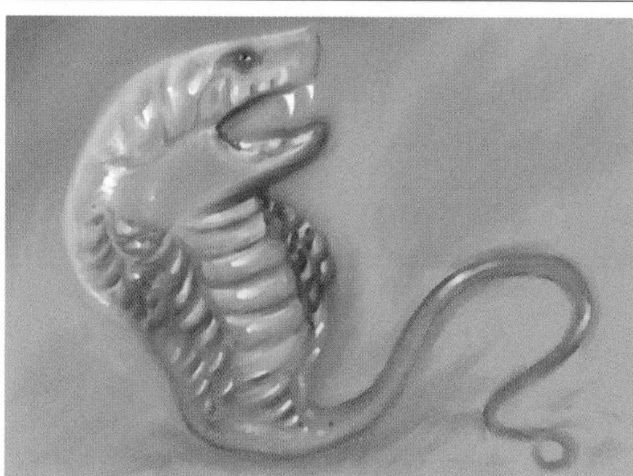

Cobra represents a person who feels endangered and who will lash out.

Mouser portrays a deterrent to a negative influence.
Mud turtle reveals a state of near-constant confusion that is usually self-generated.
Painted turtle is representative of the small joys in life; the little blessings.
Pit viper See snake.
Python warns of a suffocating personality or situation.
Rattlesnake comes as a warning; sign of extreme caution.
Reptile See specific type.
Serpent See snake.
Sidewinder (snake) represents plans that are secretly held until the actual moment for action. This won't always refer to underhandedness or dirty dealings. Whether this is a positive or negative symbol will depend on the surrounding related elements.
Skink See lizard.
Snake (nonpoisonous) exemplifies cleverness; proceeding with discernment.
Snake (venomous) pertains to swift retaliations or attacks.
Snapping turtle refers to retaliations. May also indicate impatience and a lack of tolerance.
Viper signifies vindictiveness.
Water moccasin stands for the presence of a serious negative lying along one's path; the need for acute awareness to step carefully to avoid the encounter or conflict.

Aquatic Reptiles

Alligator connotes spiritual aspects that are self-serving.
Caiman See alligator.
Crocodile connotes underlying negative spiritual aspects.
Gator See alligator.
Nile crocodile signifies a potentially destructive spiritual force.
Water snake represents spiritual elements that may or may not need avoiding. Recall if the snake was poisonous or otherwise dangerous.

Songbirds

Blackbird signifies an omen.
Bluebird refers to spiritual joy and contentedness.
Blue jay See bluebird.
Bobolink is representative of joy.
Cactus wren denotes acting on one's awareness; responding to insights and feelings.
Camp robber See gray jay.
Canary exemplifies singing and may refer to a joyful emotion or possibly a gossip situation.
Cardinal portrays an aspect of high importance; a need to give one's attention to something.
Cedar waxwing suggests the importance of being a good listener. This dreamscape element points to a possible current habit of not truly listening to others.
Finch denotes emotional maturity.
Grackle signifies an important message forthcoming; a need to pay particular attention to upcoming communications.
Gray jay stands for recognizing every opportunity and making the most of each one.
Grosbeak denotes camaraderie; a deep appreciation of one's friendships.
Jay See bluebird; gray jay.
Junco denotes friendship.
Lark bunting stands for joy; heightened optimism.
Lyrebird emphasizes one's state of inner harmony; being at peace.
Meadowlark stands for inner joy; a deep appreciation of blessings; optimism.
Mockingbird denotes a lack of individualized expression.
Mountain bluebird typifies encouragement as one struggles to overcome life's burdens or obstacles.
Nightingale relates to one's outward expression of spiritual joy.
Pine siskin points to fortitude; a heightened sense of self-reliance; enduring drive.
Redbird stands for awareness; heightened observational skills.
Robin emphasizes a rebirth of some type.
Skylark stands for happiness; joy; an optimistic perspective.
Songbird reflects inner joy; personal happiness.
Tanager stands for cheerfulness; optimism.
Thrasher signifies good communication skills; a sharpened range of language.
Thrush stands for spiritual joy; optimism and cheerfulness.
Titmouse represents ingeniousness; a raised level of analytical skills; increased perception when it comes to spotting opportunities.
Towhee stands for common sense.
Warbler stands for communication simplicity; the conveyance of thoughts with clarity and without complexity.
Waxwing signifies a gentle wisdom; subtle intelligence.
Weaver stands for the ability to simplify complex concepts or issues.
Wren symbolizes congeniality; hospitality; a consideration of others.
Yellow warbler indicates a habit of claiming innocence; rarely accepting responsibility.

Owls

Owl signifies acute perception and self-awareness.

Barn owl means intuitiveness.
Barred owl means multifaceted aspects. It usually points to a need to clarify a complexity in one's life.
Burrowing owl characterizes an ability to see through others; acute perception into others' psychological maneuvers.
Elf owl denotes cleverness; inventive and analytical thought.
Great horned owl is wisdom.
Ground owl stands for ground-level watchfulness. This means not advancing further or higher until all current issues or aspects are well developed.
Owl characterizes heightened observational skills and awareness coupled with sharpened perceptive abilities; wisdom resulting from high spiritual enlightenment.
Owlet will signify one on the correct spiritual path.
Saw-whet owl means original thought; inventiveness; increased creative inspiration.
Screech owl will point to a strong warning; a need to raise one's intuitive sense for the purpose of acute watchfulness.
Snowy owl stands for hidden knowledge; an expanded intellectual horizon.
Spotted owl stands for inspiration; growing incidences of insightful thought.
Woodsy Owl reminds us of our responsibility to be earth's caregivers.

Flightless Birds

Emu indicates multiple benefits from an unexpected source.
Kiwi means protectiveness; raised observational skill.
Ostrich connotes subconscious denials. It represents an inability or refusal to face responsibilities and/or reality.
Penguin suggests spiritual duality. May also indicate a successful effort generated from strong determination.

Doves & Pigeons

Dove defines a peaceful nature or condition.
Homing pigeon pertains to a tendency to continually return to a specific belief or opinion.
Mourning dove calls for greater expression of compassion.
Passenger pigeon connotes beauty destroyed by greed.
Pigeon connotes gullibility.

Domestic Fowl

Chicken and egg(s) points to confusion; a need to get priorities in line.
Cock See rooster.
Cockscomb warns of egotism.
Hen characterizes efficiency.
Rooster constitutes an awakening of some type.

Crow Family

Carrion crow typifies the feeding on remains. This is not necessarily a negative aspect. It could imply a cleaning up or utilization of what remains. May even come as an advisement to clean up after oneself, to tie up loose ends.
Crow represents clear messages; straight talk; a messenger of the higher consciousness.
Magpie alludes to the absorption of insignificant concepts.
Raven symbolizes watchfulness for and recognition of spiritual falsehoods. Could indicate a spiritual messenger.

Game Birds

Bobwhite is representative of secretiveness.
Grouse connotes a troublesome factor in one's life; a cause for complaint.
Partridge See quail.
Pheasant connotes a spiritual seeking.
Ptarmigan stands for adaptability; a widened scope of one's potential and resources.
Quail stands for anxiety; fearful thoughts; lacking self-reliance. These feelings raise the sense of having to strengthen one's psychological defenses.

Seabirds

Albatross denotes burdens, sometimes self-created.
Booby signifies misconceptions; illogical reasoning.
Cormorant denotes spiritual nourishment after sorting out truths. It generally indicates a tendency to accept concepts without discrimination.
Frigate bird denotes egotism; a need to impress others. May indicate greediness.
Gull See seagull.
Petrel stands for simplicity; maintaining the essence of one's true character.
Puffin represents spiritual arrogance.

Puffin stands for haughtiness.

Seagull pertains to spiritual thoughts and ideals that are utilized in a person's daily behavior.
Tern signifies analytical thought; increased applied reason and logic.

see also
• Shooting *p. 213*
• Angling *p. 215*

Birds of Prey

Eagle characterizes the liberty to explore unorthodox beliefs.

Buzzard characterizes a gloating nature; one who stands in wait to pick over what's left.
Condor See vulture.
Eagle defines the self-confidence and intellectual freedom to pursue unconventional concepts.
Egret typifies a spiritual sign; a spiritually related message.
Falcon defines our personal relationship with the higher spiritual forces.
Harrier See hawk.
Goshawk points to a predatory nature; a cutthroat way of reaching goals.
Hawk characterizes acute perceptions. It may refer to an ability for quick discernment.
Kestrel See falcon.
Killdeer is representative of protectiveness.
Merlin See falcon.
Osprey See hawk.
Peregrine falcon See falcon.
Shrike stands for a predatory nature; lacking moral/ethical integrity; vindictiveness.
Vulture warns of greedy and aggressive individuals; a user; benefiting from the shortfalls of others.

Fishers & Flycatchers

Flycatcher denotes a positive element in one's life.
Kingbird denotes aggressiveness.
Kingfisher denotes a spiritual curiosity.
Nighthawk connotes extreme high awareness.
Phoebe stands for warm companionship; an enhanced relationship; intensified bond of friendship.
Whip-poor-will stands for melancholia.

Waterfowl

Canada goose is inspiration.
Dead duck pertains to certain failure; death.
Duck pertains to spiritual vulnerability; questionable inner strength.
Duckling suggests a spiritual novice; one who is just setting foot on a new spiritual path.
Geese defines instincts; inherent characteristics. Geese may also warn of one's personal desire to escape problematic issues.
Gosling implies fledgling instincts; the beginnings of newly formed responses.
Grebe denotes spiritual goodness.
Harlequin duck denotes individuality; a solid sense of self without affectations.
Heron defines the beauty of spiritual wisdom.
Mallard applies to strong spiritual beginnings.
Mandarin duck represents brilliant spiritual insights.
Merganser See duck.
Pelican pertains to a spiritual gluttony; possessiveness.
Sandhill crane suggests desire to be more decisive.
Swan exemplifies beautiful and grace-filled spiritual nature; inherent spiritual essence.
Trumpeter swan stands for a refined inner joy generated by the love and appreciation for one's spiritual belief system.
Waterfowl stands for spiritual thoughts.
Wood duck signifies spiritual serenity.

Tropical & Exotic Birds

Bird of paradise illustrates extravagant and elaborate thoughts.
Budgerigar See parakeet.
Cockatiel See parrot.
Cockatoo See parrot.
Hornbill denotes analytical thought.
Hummingbird warns of frequent indecision; mental vacillation.
Kea See parrot.
Lovebird stands for companionship; an appreciation of others.
Macaw See parrot.
Marabou relates to personality affectations displayed for the benefit of others.
Parakeet represents a lack of analytical spiritual thinking.
Parrot typifies verbosity.
Peacock emphasizes arrogance; priority placed on appearance.
Peafowl stands for self-confidence and individuality.
Toucan is beautiful thoughts.

Common Birds

Chimney swift suggests a recognition of home-life priorities; recognizing what's important and what's not in respect to home-life relationships.
Crossbill denotes ingenuity.
Martin See swallow.
Myna depicts congeniality.
Oriole relates to helpful element that has potential to generate a negative effect if used incorrectly.
Sand martin stands for congeniality; gregariousness.
Sparrow corresponds to a gentle intellectual.
Starling stands for innocence; enhanced serenity generated by an appreciation of one's individuality.
Swallow (bird) depicts shyness.
Swift stands for efficiency; a recognition of inconsequential elements.

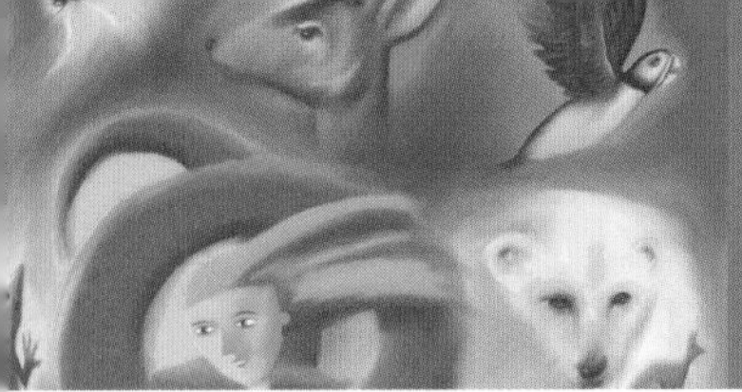

Wood & Marsh Birds

Woodpecker portrays an attempt to eliminate bad things in one's life.

Bittern suggests spiritual serenity; deep solace generated from one's spirituality.
Cuckoo is representative of manipulation.
Flicker See woodpecker.
Lapwing stands for a spiritual cautiousness.
Nuthatch portrays an ability to discover solutions.
Piñon jay suggests the feeling of inner joy regarding one's acts of goodness.
Sapsucker See woodpecker.
Woodpecker refers to efforts to rid oneself of negative aspects.
Yellow-bellied sapsucker indicates a reticence to speak up; a hesitancy to express individuality.

Worms

Angleworm refers to bait; incentives; lures.
Earthworm indicates life aspects that enrich one's foundations. May also mean interference.
Glowworm indicates a light in the darkness.
Heartworm warns of an emotionally destructive force in one's life. This may even indicate a self-generated source.
Hookworm warns of a potentially damaging factor that could easily attach itself to one's life.
Inchworm denotes a slow and steady advancement that is progressing in a natural way.
Mealworm warns of a dangerously negative factor that has infiltrated that from which one is taking nourishment.
Night crawler typifies personal incentive to actively delve into enriching spiritual concepts.
Ringworm advises one to be more aware of going headlong into things without giving adequate attention.
Silkworm connotes the source of great inner strength.
Tapeworm warns of the existence of an internal negative consuming self; this will indicate a psychological aberration.
Worm See earthworm.

Wading Birds

Curlew is representative of one's complex thought system.
Flamingo is an advisement that one should try to keep both feet on the ground. This may indicate a perspective that lacks reality and needs grounding.
Plover is representative of discernment; sharp observational skills.
Sandpiper connotes spiritual ideas; spiritual aspects to one's thought process.
Spoonbill stands for an opportunistic personality; an awareness of options.

Bugs

Aphid is representative of a mentally or emotionally draining personality.
Bedbug tends to come as a warning of a negative aspect related to sleeping arrangements or sleep patterns. May be a life irritant causing excessive stress whereby sleep is disturbed.
Bug See specific type. It will generally portray irritations in life. May have positive meaning when specific insects are shown.
Cicada is representative of a significant obsession with oneself; always wanting to attract attention. May also indicate excessive verbiage; meaningless chatter.
Leafhopper comes as a warning of the presence of one's own attitude or other individual who behaves in a manner that destroys one's efforts; eating away the beneficial results of one's work or good intentions; self-defeating attitudes.

Parasites

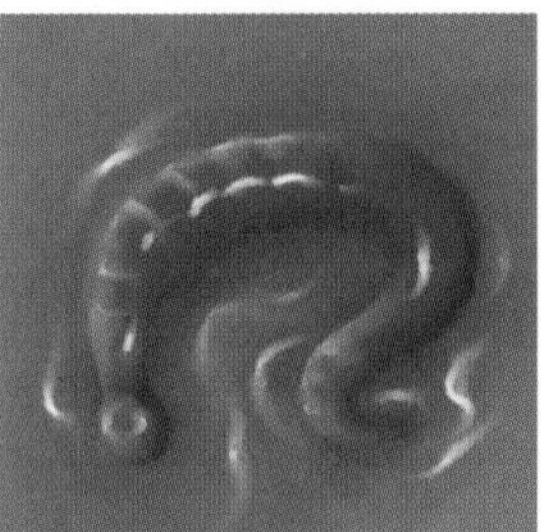

Leech is an irresponsible person.

Bloodsucker characterizes one who diminishes another's motivation; discouragement; negative attitudes; cynicism.
Cootie See louse.
Giardia stands for the negative effects of an intake of contaminated ideas.
Leech is representative of a freeloader; one who lacks self-respect and personal responsibility.
Louse reveals an unhealthy state of being.
Mosquito refers to mild setbacks or temporary irritations that can be disruptive forces.
Parasite alludes to a draining aspect in one's life. This could refer to a physical, mental, emotional, or spiritual element.
Tick is representative of a negative life element that has the potential to fester beneath one's skin.

see also
• Marshes, Bogs & Swamps *p. 68*
• Garden & Exterior *p. 397*

Insects

Ant denotes cooperation; goal-oriented; mental focus.

Army ant exposes strong opposition or force from a source thought to be too insignificant to pay attention.

Beach flea See sand flea.

Beetle signifies negative interferences in one's life.

Carpenter ant indicates a destructive personality, one who tears down that which is being created or which is being built upon.

Carpet beetle warns of destructive elements that are present on one's path; the existence of negative aspects that impair progress. This symbol may point to self-defeating action or thoughts.

Chigger typifies aspects in life that are irritating.

Cockroach refers to major disruptions in one's emotional or physical life.

Cocoon connotes a stage of respite where one absorbs what has been learned before advancing to the next spiritual stage of gaining wisdom from that knowledge; a time of planning; pause before action.

Cricket indicates certain emotionally soothing aspects in life; good fortune.

Daddy longlegs refers to fears that are overcome; unwarranted fears and anxieties.

Deathwatch symbolizes an irreversible situation that is heading toward devastation.

Deerfly refers to the biting aspects in life that can cause temporary irritations if one isn't watchful and aware.

Dragonfly denotes a strong, positive spiritual force or aspect.

Dung beetle reminds us that everything in life has meaning and purpose.

Fire ant cautions of a relationship, situation, or personal attitude that could end up stinging you.

Firefly defines times of intensely emotional spiritual illumination.

Flea refers to an interference of some type.

Fly illustrates a life aspect that has the capability of becoming a harmful interference.

Fruit fly pertains to destructive aspects affecting personal talents.

Gadfly alludes to a life irritation.

Gnat relates to mental or emotional irritations.

Grasshopper signifies a destructive force related to spiritual foundations.

Grubs characterize a destructive force present in an early stage of development.

Hornet indicates the "stinging" events in life.

Horsefly refers to biting remarks.

Housefly reveals a negative aspect that has invaded one's home life.

Insect See specific type.

Katydid See grasshopper.

Lacewing symbolizes a method of getting rid of one's life irritations.

Ladybug connotes a positive aspect that negates the negative and irritating facets of one's life.

Larva reveals the beginning stage (gestation) of a negative aspect in one's life, possibly within oneself.

Locust warns against something that has the potential to destroy spiritual belief systems.

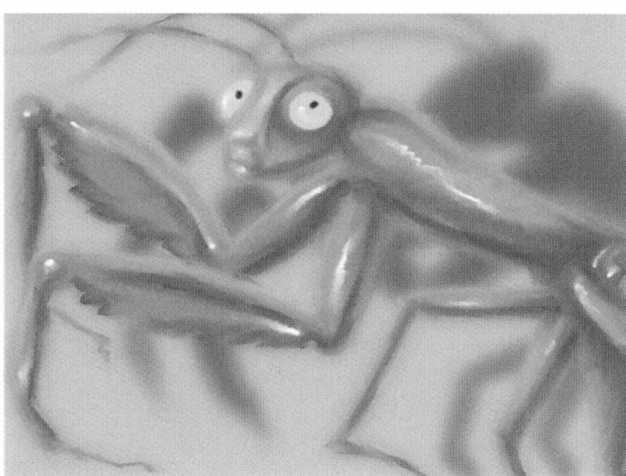

Praying mantis indicates that one is falsely professing certain beliefs.

Maggot reveals a self-serving personality who gains from the efforts of others.

Mantis See praying mantis.

Mite infers small irritations in life.

Praying mantis is representative of spiritual hypocrisy; lip service.

Pupa is representative of a state of transformation.

Roach See cockroach.

Sand flea typifies irritations in life, most often one's juvenile or immature relationships.

Scarab relates to one's inner self; the soul.

Silverfish reveals a damaging element in one's life.

Stinger pertains to a negative rebound response.

Stinkbug stands for talents used in a negative manner.

Termite stands for underhandedness; undermining.

Tsetse fly warns of the presence of an undetected element in one's life that has a great potential to harm one's motivation.

Weevil pertains to particularly negative elements that have the potential to destroy one's natural and inherent abilities.

Insect Infestation

Insect infestation connotes a destructive force that has invaded an aspect of one's life.

Insects in air depict a destructive element connected to one's mental or emotional state.

Insects in attic refer to a destructive factor in one's subconscious.

Insects in basement are representative of a faulty and harmful foundational belief or attitude.

Insects in garden pertain to a destructive use of one's gifts or skills.

Insects in house indicate a destructive element in one's home life.

Insects in kitchen denote the ingestion of a harmful attitude or perspective.

Insects in water apply to a destructive aspect to one's spiritual life.

Moths & Butterflies

Moth represents a negative viewpoint that will end in damage.

Budworm is an extremely negative aspect that damages new beginnings.

Butterfly exemplifies renewal and rejuvenation. May refer to an ability to bounce back after specific setbacks or disappointments; an enlightened change in perspective or attitude.

Cankerworm refers to a destructive force in one's life which damages perspective and attitudes. This force causes such negativity as cynicism, apathy, intolerance, etc.

Caterpillar characterizes the transitional phases in life. May point to a neophyte stage of development; a time for learning and absorbing before experiencing the bloom of awareness or enlightenment.

Chrysalis stands for developing spirituality.

Gypsy moth reveals the presence of a possible destructive force.

Luna moth alludes to spiritual insights.

Monarch (butterfly) connotes perseverance; going the distance.

Moth constitutes a destructive belief, one that will appear to lead into the light yet will result in eventual harm.

Arachnids

Arachnid See spider.

Black widow symbolizes an extremely dangerous individual or relationship.

Brown recluse spider denotes hidden dangers in one's life. Advises increased awareness.

Cobweb indicates sticky situations or relationships; the trap one walks into.

Scorpion will stand for retaliation.

Spider may reveal a conniving individual or a unique type of defensive measure.

Tarantula applies to a fearful perception.

Web (spider) stands for the complexities that one weaves in life.

Arthropods & Mollusks

Centipede suggests an ability or need to overcome life's little irritations.

Millipede relates to acceptance; an ability to overcome small setbacks.

Periwinkle (snail) is representative of an individual's spiritual fortitude.

Slug See snail.

Snail stands for a cautious attitude.

Bees & Wasps

Africanized bee See killer bee.

Bee characterizes industrious and cooperative teamwork.

Bee (caught in hair) points to elements that serve as motivators and facilitators which act as an impetus to respond instantly and get going.

Beehive means the center or focus of activity.

Beeswax refers to an industrious nature.

Bumblebee characterizes a focused mind; industriousness.

Drone (bee) alludes to work done without thought rather than things done on instinct.

Hive see beehive.

Hornet indicates the "stinging" events in life.

Killer bee is representative of a new danger from a foreign source.

Mud dauber pertains to an individual in one's life who has a tendency to interfere and confuse issues.

Paper wasp See hornet.

Queen bee stands for the individual that much activity revolves around. This may or may not be a negative symbol. The surrounding dreamscape factors will clarify its intent.

Swarm suggests an overwhelming element in one's life.

Wasp See hornet.

Yellow jacket See hornet.

Wasp indicates the elements in life that require an immediate response.

see also
• Mollusks *p. 39*
• Plants Poisonous to Animals *p. 44*

Equipment

Bird feeder implies deeper understandings; a thought process that relates to the interconnectedness of all life.

Feedbag illustrates a need for motivation.

Feeder (any type) applies to a supportive life factor.

Flea collar implies one's personal immunity to slight setbacks; strength of character.

Halter suggests forwardness of character.

Hitching post symbolizes the needed pauses taken during our path progression.

Hummingbird feeder indicates a hidden source (psychological) for one's continuing difficulty making decisions.

Lead (tether) See leash.

Leash stands for self-imposed limitations.

Muzzle connotes a restraint on communication or insights.

Rawhide (whip or rope) may allude to one's inner strength, or it may infer a lack of emotional sensitivity.

Snare portrays some type of setup; a trap.

Styptic pencil signifies an attempt to resolve a problematic element.

Tack (stable gear) refers to essential elements required for specific purposes.

Animal Ailments

Canker sore is representative of speech that is infected with a slant toward personal attitudes. May indicate cynicism, intolerance, and so on.

Dander (pet) refers to a friend's irritations that bring about mental or physical reactions.

Distemper refers to excessive irritability; impatience; lack of acceptance.

Feline distemper See distemper.

Foot-and-mouth disease signifies the negative tendency to say hurtful things to (or about) others.

Hoof-and-mouth disease See foot-and-mouth disease.

Kennel cough advises of a negative aspect picked up from a friend.

Mange alludes to the harmful irritations affecting a friend or associate. If the dreamer has the mange condition in the dream, the disease will have been caused by a friend or an associate.

Collective Terms

Brood (many offspring) characterizes the fact that many new opportunities are in the offing.

Flock comes as a caution against a tendency to lack individualized thought.

Herd almost always indicates a warning to follow one's own path in the journey of life.

Pack portrays a multiple of whatever animal is presented in the pack. This will indicate an increase or abundance. See specific animal for further clarification of this symbol.

Animal-Related Phrases

Bear hug indicates someone showing one overwhelming affection.

Bear hug connotes the potential for a smothering or manipulative type of affection.

Beeline denotes an industrious nature; the shortest and most direct route; one who can spot the bottom line and cut through the extraneous elements; an individual who gets right to the point.

Bird's-eye characterizes a broad scope of understanding; a comprehensive overview or perspective.

Catnap advises one to take a break, pause, or short rest.

Cattle call illustrates a desire to alter oneself according to how others wish one to be.

Chicken feed means an aspect of little value.

Counting sheep stands for efforts put into gaining or forcing a relief from daily stress.

Den mother characterizes a woman in one's life who is nurturing of many others.

Doggie bag is representative of the nourishing benefits of friends.

Dog-eared (page) relates to information that one should note.

Fish story alludes to spiritual elaborations; exaggerations.

Gooseneck cautions against excessive curiosity taken to the extent of becoming intrusive.

Moth-eaten represents the results of a destructive negative in one's life.

Mother hen suggests interference; overprotectiveness; a doting personality. It may also indicate pessimism.

Mothproof applies to the individualized protective measures one uses to safeguard against misdirection.

Night owl is representative of a natural knowing of the most effectively powerful timing for one to engage in self-discovery or intellectual contemplation.

Puppy mill warns of insincere friendships; a tendency to form friendships for the purpose of personal gain, then discarding them.

Miscellaneous

Amoeba refers to the beginning formations of an idea, plan, or solution.

Animal will be associated with personality/character qualities. See the specific type of animal for more information.

Animal shelter refers to quality of respect and care given to friends and close associates. Recall the condition of the dreamscape. Was it clean?

Ant farm symbolizes an attempt to understand various cooperative or joint efforts and what can be accomplished from them.

Beast corresponds to crude or unacceptable behavior.

Bestiary denotes a high interest in animals and what can be learned from them.

Bird band represents a unique characteristic (usually perspective) that separates an individual from the crowd.

Birdseed refers to research; the feeding of thoughts. It may refer to a thought process that is nourished.

Broken wing represents a hampered ability to think clearly; a phase of delay in ability to lay plans.

Bug juice signifies a fairly useless element in respect to expecting any benefits.

Carcass represents lack of life; a death. The carcass of a dog means the death of a friendship.

Carnivore implies a predatory nature.

Carrion is representative of the remains of a situation or relationship.

Cold-blooded signifies a lack of emotional response; an individual having absolutely no sensitivity; apathy.

Color phase (pelt/plumage) is associated with a particular phase one is in regarding attitudes affecting behavior.

Crossbreed See hybrid.

Den (animal) refers to our natural instincts; gut feelings; intuitiveness.

Dewclaw connotes an extraneous aspect. This may refer to an attitude, belief, or emotion that is unnecessary for one to hold onto.

Eggshell warns of a fragile or precarious belief, attitude, or situation. This may not be a negative symbol but rather one that necessitates close attention and care in the way of management.

Egg tooth alludes to one's level of developed preparedness to begin a new path in life.

Feedlot (cattle) indicates a situation or relationship that is being deceptively nurtured; congeniality for the sake of self-motivations.

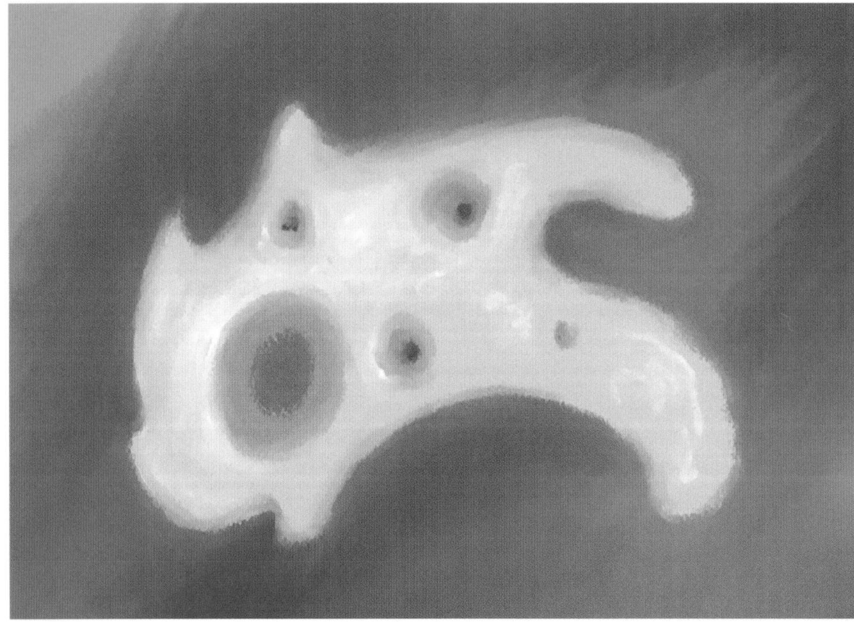

Amoeba represents the germ of an idea or the beginnings of a plan.

Fledgling stands for a beginner; a novice.

Flyblown signifies corruption; a contaminated element.

Fodder typifies useless information; lacking substance or quality.

Fur ball is representative of an unpleasant issue one needs to resolve.

Goose egg represents some type of mistake made; an unfruitful result.

Hair ball connotes a misconception that must be gotten rid of (regurgitated).

Hatch points to the birth of an idea or solution.

Hatchery connotes multiple ideas or theories; one who is full of new ideas.

Hatchling denotes a new beginning; a fresh start or brand-new plan for one's personal direction.

Herbivore will emphasize a more natural lifestyle; a return to the rejuvenating benefits of nature.

Hibernating indicates escapism; a desire to avoid facing reality for a specific amount of time. This points to a desire to avoid having to deal with a certain situation.

Housebreaking (pet) symbolizes the training of a new friend. This constitutes an attempt to inform the friend how you want the relationship to go and also is symbolic of manipulation.

Humane society See animal shelter.

Hybrid portrays a blending of dissimilar aspects to create a new, fresh quality or effect.

Insecticide reveals a need to get rid of negative attitudes or

see also
• Farming *p. 379*
• Skins & Pelts *p. 421*

Miscellaneous (continued)

irritations, through acceptance or greater tolerance.

Lambing ground suggests attempts to connect with personal spirituality.

Litter (offspring) portrays multiple new ideas.

Livestock See specific type.

Manger (feed trough) symbolizes life aspects that serve to preserve the benefits of personal efforts.

Manure represents a fertile situation; an aspect ready for development.

Menagerie is representative of a great assortment of something. Usually this will refer to benefits that have been gained from a wide search, using multiple sources.

Migration (animals) may suggest an actual, physical relocation, or it may caution against conceptual or perceptual vacillation.

Migration (birds) stands for a vacillating spiritual belief; indecision as to what one actually believes.

Milking pertains to taking fullest advantage of something. This may or may not be a positive symbol if one is taking advantage of others.

Mink oil emphasizes a softening aspect in one's life; a factor that is capable of easing experiences that are tough to get through.

Missing link illustrates a hidden factor that brings sense to a puzzling issue.

Molehill pertains to a lack of acceptance; a tendency to exaggerate a situation.

Molting signifies the shedding of negatives or excesses; letting go of the past.

Missing link represents something hidden that emerges to clarify a situation.

Mongrel (mix-breed) defines a compound aspect of a situation, meaning that something has manifested through diverse means and factors.

Mousetrap defines an attempt to rid one's life of destructive aspects.

Natural selection alludes to the power of inner strength; perseverance.

Nesting refers to foresight; insights that hint at needed preparations.

Nestling See fledgling.

Omnivore characterizes a need to take in all elements available regarding an issue.

Overbred means elements that have been used so often that they've lost their effectiveness; an idea or aspect that has so many diluted elements to it that it's not viable.

Pedigree (certificate) refers to a certification of purity. It can also mean unadulterated. Try to recall the surrounding dreamscape aspects for extra clarity in this dream. Usually this symbol will be recognized by the dreamer.

Pest will be different for every dreamer. It's usually a call to stop being annoyed and take action to resolve a situation or deal with it in a better way.

Pet See the specific type of pet for more information.

Picador warns against an action that will serve to hamper or disable a situation, relationship, or another individual.

Plumage corresponds to the quality or health of an idea. Recall the condition of the bird's plumage. What kind of bird was it? Refer to the specific type in this book.

Poison See venom.

Predator most often reveals a harmful individual in one's life.

Prey reveals a situation whereby an individual is the subject of another's negative intent or otherwise a victim. Recall who or what the prey was. More importantly, who was the predator?

Quarry (animal) See prey.

Rattrap See mousetrap.

Reserve (animal) symbolizes the preservation of natural inherent talents.

Rutting (season) is representative of a time to plan; start thinking about making new beginnings.

Shedding (loose hair) refers to the natural course of old ideas falling away.

Shell (egg) See eggshell.

Sheltie See Shetland sheepdog.

Silo connotes that which is stored and may refer to an individual's emotional, mental, or intellectual aspects.

Snowbird is a representation of encouragement; a strong sense of support.

Spoor alludes to evidence; proof of one's passing.

Tallow refers to a necessary element needed to attain an enlightened perspective on an issue.

Trophy (animal) exposes a lack of courage; false power.

Trough (container) usually represents a receptacle-like connotation. This symbol is associated with the need to keep issues separate or elements of an issue together in one place. This suggests that one is mixing issues.

Venom will warn of an element in one's life that has the potential to cause great harm or a fatal effect if one doesn't proceed with acute awareness and be extremely careful.

Chapter 2

Marine Life

This is an enormously important category, for it always relates to an individual's spiritual life. Marine life and its twin category, water, will always be associated with the spiritual.

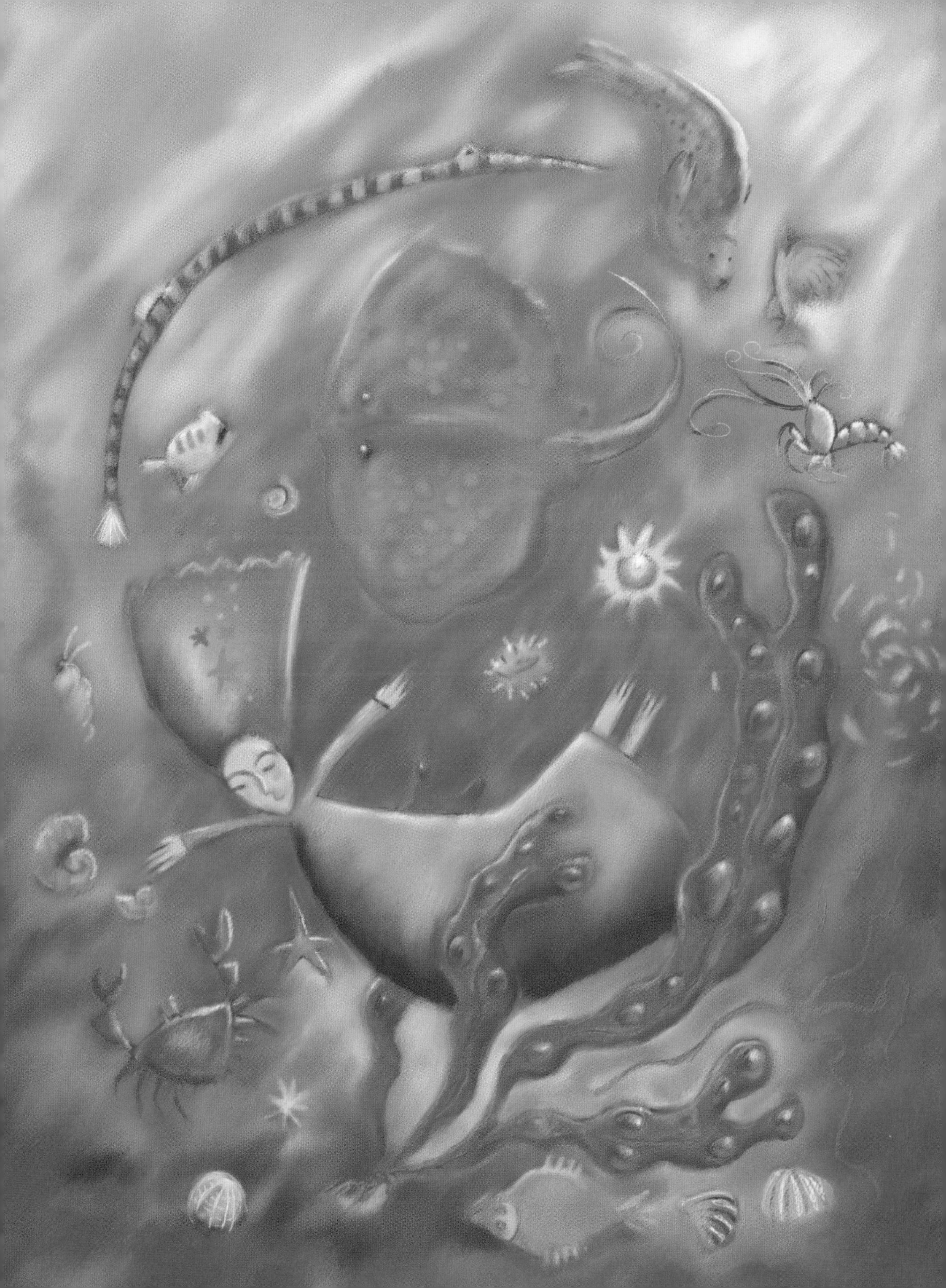

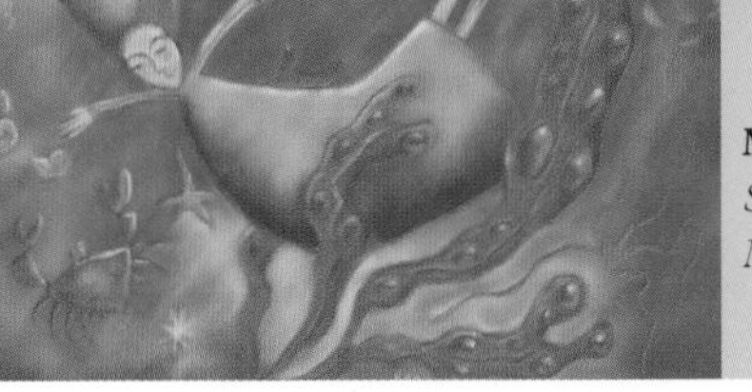

Starfish & Sea Urchins

Brittle star characterizes spiritual reaching; one's research that extends as far as it can be taken.
Sand dollar portrays spiritual riches.
Sea cucumber denotes societal spiritual beliefs; traditional dogma. It signals a need to distinguish commonly held tenets from actual truth.
Sea star See starfish.
Sea urchin denotes spiritual immaturity.
Starfish signifies spiritual truths.
Urchin (sea) See sea urchin.

The Sea

Current portrays the rate of speed one travels along the spiritual path. This will clarify if it is too fast and dangerous or if there is a drag factor.
Deep sea portrays higher spiritual philosophy.
Deep water implies an in-depth spiritual search or path.
Ocean alludes to spiritual facets in one's life.
Saltwater represents elemental spiritual truths.
Sea correlates to life's spiritual aspects.
Seafloor refers to spiritual foundations.
Sea foam stands for spiritual confusion, a stirring of one's beliefs.
Sea level pertains to basic spiritual truths.
Sea salt stands for fortified spiritual aspects and beliefs.
Seascape will reveal the quality of one's personal spiritual search or transition. Was the scene a rough cliff? A tropical and sandy shore? Was it rocky?
Sea spray applies to spiritual gifts and the opportunity to accept them.
Seawater suggests the quenching of a spiritual thirst.
Wake (water) implies the effects left behind after one has performed a spiritual deed.
Water always reflects spiritual aspects.
Wave (water) represents the continually renewing effects of spirituality in one's life.

Wave is indicative of the constant renewal of one's spirituality.

Marine Miscellany

Algae-eater stands for spiritual discernment.
Aquarium means spiritual arrogance.
Bathysphere alludes to a journey into the deeper aspects of spiritual concepts.
Bell buoy serves as a spiritual marker that guides one through a safe passing.
Bottom-feeder means one who tends to have poor spiritual ideals or belief systems.
Buoyancy means spiritual resiliency.
Cod-liver oil advises of a deficiency in one's life.
Cuttlebone advises of a need to sharpen one's speech for the purpose of bringing clarity.
Davy Jones's locker warns of a spiritual fatality; a spiritual path that is leading into dangerous ground.
Dragnet warns against spiritual gullibility; arbitrarily collecting and absorbing every aspect found in the spiritual pool.
Driftwood suggests acceptance brought on by the continual washing of a spiritual faith.
Fin (any type) represents a life factor that serves as a directional or motivational force.
Fish symbolizes spiritual aspects in life. See specific types of marine life.
Fishbowl stands for transparencies of character; a lack of privacy or confidentiality.
Fish-eye means spiritual perceptiveness.
Fishpond illustrates spiritual opportunities.
Fishtail refers to a backlash reaction to some spiritual facet in the dreamer's life.
Fish tank See aquarium.
Flipper See fin.
Gill stands for spiritual breathing.
Goldfish bowl See fishbowl.
Guano is a reminder to reassess things assumed to be useless.
Marina relates to spiritual associates or friends.
Marine life See specific types.
Milt (fish semen) means something that can join with another to create a new idea.
Planarian correlates to an ability to rebound.
Plankton alludes to the basics of something.
Red tide warns of a dangerous spiritual situation or concept.
Saltwater aquarium denotes grasp of spiritual truths.
Scale means spiritual caution.
Sea monster represents a spiritual danger.
Sea serpent See sea monster.
Sea sponge stands for spiritual overabsorption.
Sea world suggests a sampling of spiritual concepts.
Seaworthy shows preparedness to begin a spiritual quest.
Shoal is spiritual shallowness.
Sponge relates to absorption and indicates a need to listen.
Tentacle warns of grasping or flailing for support. Indicates a need to ground oneself.

Seaweed

Algae denotes basic life aspects that are spiritually nourishing.
Kelp corresponds to spiritual health. Recall the kelp's condition as it appeared in the dream.
Seaweed pertains to spiritual indecision; spiritual vacillation.

see also
• Waterscapes *p. 71*
• Gemstones *p. 74*

Coast & Shore

Seawall portrays spiritual constraints that are self-imposed.

Bay reveals a sheltered sense of spirituality.
Beach refers to the transition stage of how well spiritual beliefs are applied to the physical (the living of them). Was the dreamscape beach rocky? Eroded? Covered with red tide? Smooth, fine sand? Was the sand white or black?
Beachhead points to one's first priority for addressing issues needed to confront.
Breakwater stands for a major spiritual barrier. This may be a temporary necessity.
Cape (shoreline) signifies a projection of the way one delves into spiritual aspects; living a spiritual life.
Coast See shore (land).
Coastline represents a position approaching spiritual involvement; the precursor stage to spiritual searching. What was the coastline's condition? Rocky and rough? Sandy and beachlike?
Continental shelf pertains to underlying facets of something that creates supporting extensions; something backed by additional facts that have not yet surfaced.
Cove portrays spiritual security; the sense of one's spiritual beliefs' protective qualities.
Delta relates to the discarded elements of one's spiritual search.
Dune comes as a warning to stop shifting thoughts or attitudes.
Estuary pertains to the point in time where several spiritual concepts converge; the stage when the dreamer relates several spiritual ideas in an interconnected manner.
Gulf advises of a spiritual gap.
Oceanfront See lakefront.
Offshore directs one toward a spiritual aspect.
Point (land) represents an extension into spiritual aspects.
Promontory applies to a testing probe into spiritual concepts.
Quay suggests either the reaping or gifting of benefits or blessings.
Sandbank/bar represents a spiritual concept that requires contemplation.
Seawall refers to self-generated spiritual bounds.
Shore (land) will allude to the boundaries of one's spiritual search or direction.

Turtles

Leatherback symbolizes eternal spiritual truths.
Loggerhead turtle denotes spiritual narrow-mindedness.
Sea turtle typifies a cautious spiritual search or path; an enduring path.
Turtle pertains to a fear of facing up to responsibility or coming to terms with reality. This symbol may also indicate a tendency to know when to keep one's nose out of another's business.

Reefs & Islands

Archipelago signifies resting points along one's spiritual path.
Atoll signifies spiritual serenity through protection.
Barrier reef stands for a time of rest during one's spiritual quest.
Coral reef represents the fragileness of maintaining a spiritual balance within a physical existence.
Great Barrier Reef signifies spiritual concepts that are highly cherished and that are perceived as fragile treasures.
Island represents a time to pause during one's spiritual search.
Key (land) See reef.
Reef illustrates spiritual opportunities that will help one to attain inner balance.

Crustaceans

Barnacle pertains to extraneous aspects that one allows to weigh down or impede progress.
Crab denotes a negative personality or situation.
Crayfish applies to a voluntary withdrawal from an agreed-upon event or responsibility.
Fiddler crab cautions against spiritual gullibility.
Hermit crab denotes spiritual reclusiveness.
Horseshoe crab suggests endurance; perseverance through time.
Lobster advises of a tendency to grab at any new idea or concept. This symbol is a call for discernment.
Sand crab represents the hidden dangers of indecision.

Pearls

Black pearl stands for fortitude from a negative-based drive.
Cultured pearl See pearl (cultured).
Mother-of-pearl symbolizes the best aspect.
Pearl applies to perseverance; spiritually based fortitude.
Pearl (cultured) denotes strength derived from a great expenditure of energy.
Pearl oyster indicates a life aspect that will contain valuable spiritual or motivational elements.
Seed pearl symbolizes small imperfections.

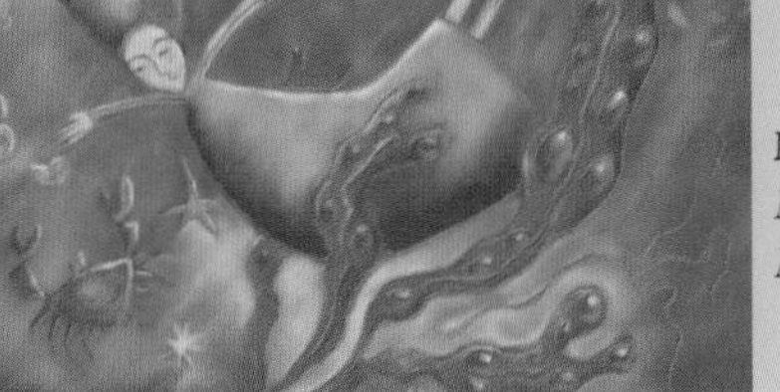

Marine Fish

Albacore See tuna.
Anchovy is representative of a spiritual aspect that is not readily accepted; one that is initially distasteful and rejected.
Angelfish is suggestive of the finer aspects of spiritual truths.
Barracuda characterizes a lack of moral or ethical value; a vicious personality.
Blowfish refers to a tendency to be preachy.
Catfish denotes a cattiness to one's spiritual belief; a pretentious spiritual attitude.
Codfish stands for spiritual arrogance; a sense of spiritual superiority.
Coral fish stands for spiritual protectiveness; guarding beliefs from outside influences.
Eel typifies spiritual vacillation.
Flying fish symbolizes spiritual application; an expanded potentiality for the expression of one's spiritual gifts.

Flying fish means spiritual potential.

Goatfish stands for spiritual independence; making one's unique spiritual journey.
Goby signifies unique spiritual beliefs.
Great white shark will reveal the presence of a possible threat existing in one's life.
Grouper denotes independence.
Grunion signifies a lack of independent spiritual thought.
Haddock represents traditional spiritual beliefs.
Halibut pertains to spiritual nourishment.
Herring refers to spiritual bounty.
Lionfish denotes spiritual arrogance; self-righteousness.
Mackerel infers an unexpected event or development.
Marlin corresponds with spiritual focus; centered spiritual attention.
Moray eel warns against spiritual overexuberance; spiritual aggressiveness.
Pilot fish warns against a spiritual path that imitates another's.
Puffer warns of a dangerous spiritual element that one should defend oneself against.
Red snapper stands for spiritual intolerance.
Sailfish typifies a symbol relating to spiritual destiny.
Salmon warns of going against a spiritual current; a spiritual search that's in error.
Sardine advises one to remove oneself from a suffocating situation or belief system.
Scorpion fish portrays a deadly spiritual element or path.
Sea horse relates to an illogical spiritual search or belief and may indicate beliefs that are more fantasy than reality.
Sea snake See eel.
Shad denotes spiritual insignificance; superfluous facets.
Shark corresponds to religious fanatics.
Smelt depicts small spiritual insights.
Sole stands for independent spiritual thought.
Sturgeon portrays strong spiritual faith generated from a high level of reason and analytical thought.
Sucker reveals a state of spiritual gullibility; a lack of spiritual discernment.
Sunfish refers to the joy taken in personal spirituality.
Swordfish applies to spiritual defensiveness.
Tuna refers to spiritual generosity.
Viperfish applies to a spiritual skepticism.

Tropical Fish

Clown fish portrays foolish factors connected to one's spiritual beliefs.
Cowfish stands for spiritual generosity; spiritual largesse.
Damselfish suggests a deeply seated protective nature toward one's spirituality.
Manta ray characterizes attractive spiritual aspects that may prove to be dangerous.
Platy symbolizes traditional spiritual beliefs; a need for spiritual expansion.
Porcupine fish pertains to spiritual defensiveness.
Psychedelic fish stands for spiritual confusion. It also represents a lack of conceptual discernment.
Sawfish stands for spiritual discernment; a strengthened ability to cut through superfluous spiritual aspects to grasp the heart of the matter.
Stingray exposes a false prophet.
Stonefish denotes spiritual fanaticism. It points out a need for tolerance.
Tarpon symbolizes spiritual narrow-mindedness.
Tetra denotes spiritual fragility. It advises of a need to strengthen delicate spiritual beliefs or the faith in them.

Marine Mammals

Ambergris stands for infusing one's behavior with elements meant to divert or cover up true characteristics or attitude.
Baleen See whalebone.
Blowhole denotes breathing room; aspects in life that give us a breather.
Blubber (fat) signifies excesses.
Blue whale signifies spiritual generosity; magnanimity.
Dolphin reflects spiritual companionship.
Harp seal defines innocence; spiritual vulnerability.
Manatee connotes spiritual largesse; being generous with one's talents.
Killer whale stands for spiritual generosity; magnanimity.
Orca See killer whale.
Pilot whale See dolphin.
Porpoise stands for spiritual guidance; humanitarianism.
Seal portrays the use of spirituality in one's daily life.
Sea lion See seal.
Walrus suggests spiritual righteousness.
Whale corresponds to spiritual generosity or magnanimity.
Whalebone alludes to spiritual strength.
Whale oil defines spiritual and humanitarian qualities that are used for the benefit of others.

see also
• Arthropods & Mollusks *p. 30*
• Angling *p. 215*

Freshwater Fish

Archerfish stands for spiritual focus; a sharpened and defined spiritual direction.

Bass applies to spiritual talents and the generous sharing of them with others.

Bluegill symbolizes spiritual joy; a heightened inner sense of spiritual warmth.

Carp represents the act of nagging; nit-picking; belittling.

Cichlid stands for spiritual companionship; an enhanced depth of spiritual camaraderie and support.

Char denotes a person's emotional sensitivity.

Goldfish warns of a spiritually confining situation, belief, or condition.

Gourami represents camaraderie; an intensified sense of spiritual friendship and companionship.

Grayling stands for spiritual commonality; generalized traditional dogma.

Guppy represents a spiritual neophyte.

Jewelfish denotes spirituality being one's most valued priority in life.

Lyretail denotes spiritual verbosity; superfluous spiritual facets; spiritual fluff.

Minnow reveals spiritual insecurity.

Molly denotes traditional spiritual beliefs.

Moor stands for esoteric aspects of spiritual concepts and their demystification.

Neon will pertain to a spiritual light that one needs to pay attention to.

Perch denotes spiritual neutrality; a lack of spiritual direction.

Pickerel represents spiritual greed or arrogance.

Pike represents spiritual nourishment.

Piranha reveals a spiritual narrow-mindedness; a vicious possessiveness of one's specific beliefs to the point of striking out at those who believe otherwise.

Rainbow trout represents a beautiful element of one's spiritual path.

Siamese fighting fish stand for spiritual argumentativeness. Indicates a tendency to debate concepts and/or the spiritual beliefs of others.

Stickleback stands for spiritual intolerance. Advises of a need to relax rigid thought and increase acceptance of other spiritual possibilities.

Trout denotes spiritual contentedness; satisfaction with one's spirituality.

Coelenterates

Brain coral connotes spiritual intelligence or knowledge.

Coral symbolizes spiritual attributes and/or talents.

Jellyfish warns of a lack of firm convictions; using one's stinging defense mechanisms to maintain irresponsibility.

Man-of-war (jellyfish) stands for spiritual intolerance.

Polyp See coral.

Portuguese man-of-war See jellyfish.

Sea anemone stands for spiritual diversity.

Sea fan is spiritual vacillation.

Shells

Cockleshell signifies the remains of one's emotional feelings; leftover feelings following an emotionally charged event.

Conch represents spiritual aspects that are cherished.

Half shell represents concealed elements; not a whole presentation shown.

Nautilus defines the multidimensional interconnectedness of spiritual aspects and true reality.

Periwinkle marks the presence of a spiritually significant element in one's life.

Seashell defines spiritual gifts and talents. Recall the quality and quantity of the shells as they appeared in your dream. Were they whole? Beautiful? Or full of barnacles?

Shell (sea) See seashell.

Mollusks

Octopus is a warning against lashing out in all directions for spiritual help.

Abalone symbolizes inherent beauty and value of spiritual gifts, talents, or knowledge.

Cockle symbolizes one's innermost feelings.

Giant squid stands for the hidden elements (possible dangers) lurking behind certain motivations related to alleged spiritual behavior.

Limpet refers to one who receives inner strength and nourishment from spiritual aspects.

Mollusk warns against hiding from problems; withdrawal.

Mussel refers to spiritual protectiveness, perhaps bordering on reclusiveness.

Octopus warns of spiritual flailing; a situation where one is randomly reaching out in all directions for whatever spiritual idea one can grab hold of.

Oyster is a representation of inner fears of anything new or of having to interact with others; social anxiety. This symbol can also indicate wisdom gained from deep introspection.

Scallop portrays the ingestion of harmful spiritual elements.

Sea slug warns of spiritual laziness, or entrapment.

Sea snail denotes a slow and methodical spiritual pace based on one's level of comprehension.

Squid represents a haphazard spiritual search.

Chapter 3

Botanicals

The growing plants in dreams will always point to one's attitudes and/or natural talents. The key here is to identify the meaning of the specific botanical and then note its condition.

Horticulture

Bedding plants refer to a good and/or well-developed beginning of something.

Bonemeal signifies a strengthening factor.

Companion planting denotes a mutually beneficial relationship.

Compost See mulch.

Fertilizer exemplifies a need to rejuvenate or nourish a life aspect that could refer to one's mental, emotional, physical, or spiritual facet.

Fungicide refers to a need to attend to a situation, plan, idea, relationship, etc., that has elements that are becoming a growing problem.

Germinating applies to a life aspect that has taken hold within. This could relate to an attitude, belief, or emotion.

Grow light signifies any aspect that is capable of providing light upon one's path.

Hardy (plants) will equate to strong character qualities related to endurance.

Herbicide warns of a destructive force that may hamper the utilization and growth of one's natural abilities.

Hotbed connotes a highly controversial issue; a source eliciting emotional responses.

Hydroponics signifies nurturing by way of spiritual aspects.

Mulch defines a fertile atmosphere; the right timing.

Perennial (plant) will define a lasting element in one's life.

Plant food See fertilizer.

Preemergent treatment (gardening product) stands for actions taken to prevent something from developing.

Root feeder refers to nurturing care given to budding talents or humanitarian aspects.

Rooting material See vermiculite.

Rooting vases represent an effort to perpetuate a good thing. This may refer to any positive element in the dreamer's life.

Seed plant refers to a source for new beginnings or ideas.

Soil conditioner stands for an attempt to create a more favorable medium in which a new idea can take root.

Vermiculite illustrates an uplifting and nurturing life factor.

Weed killer See herbicide.

Plant Anatomy

Berry relates to those life aspects that are fruitful.

Blossom represents the beautiful effect of right living; the bloom of achievement, unconditional goodness, and/or right choices.

Bud (flower) indicates new beginnings.

Bulb (flower) refers to an upcoming budding of talent or other aspect in one's life; first efforts applied toward the actualization of future plans.

Corm refers to storage. It may also refer to preservation.

Flower pertains to one's natural talents that should beautifully blossom as they're utilized. See specific flower type.

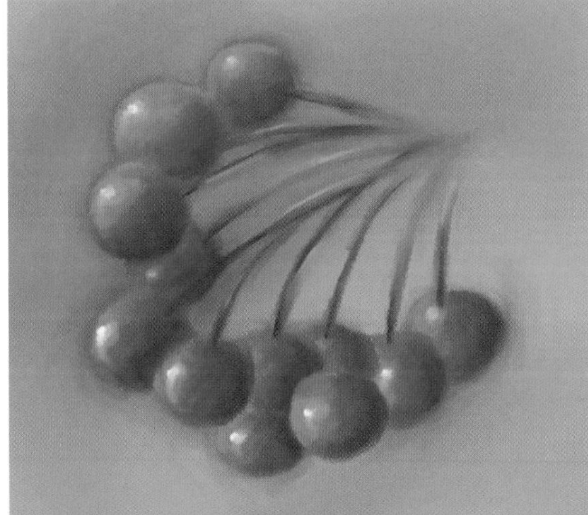

Berry signifies the flourishing of specific parts of life.

Foliage shows natural abilities.

Hip (rose) See rose hip.

Leaf symbolizes natural abilities; natural talents.

Nutshell relates to self-devised shells one uses for self-protection. It may also indicate a need to consolidate one's beliefs or perspectives into a basic, simple form. Recall dreamscape details to determine which interpretation your dream intended.

Petal (of blossom) will denote a magnified emphasis of the presented flower. Refer to the specific botanical type for greater clarification.

Pod (seed) refers to sources of knowledge or opportunities for same.

Pollen indicates elements in one's life that enhance positive aspects.

Rhizome stands for deeply rooted attitudes that affect perspectives.

Root signifies the existence of a hidden personal talent.

Root stalk See rhizome.

Rootstock refers to beginnings. This symbol may be pointing to the past origination or source of something.

Rose hip signifies the healing elements of love.

Seed See kernel.

Seedling stands for the birthing of new understandings. Recall what type of botanical the seedling was. What was its condition?

Shoot (plant) See sprout.

Sprout relates to the birthing of new ideas, especially spiritual concepts or the talents associated with them.

Stem (stalk) represents the supporting factor of an element or issue.

Taproot represents a foundational element through which offshoots develop.

Tendril stands for attachments; twining ramifications of certain behavior.

Tuber stands for an opportunity for a new life or beginning.

see also
• Working with the Land *p. 263*
• Garden & Exterior *p. 397*

Gardens

Topiary cautions against being too self-reliant.

Arboretum suggests the dreamer surround self with higher spiritual aspects.
Botanical gardens represents an ideal spiritual life; a life of applying beliefs in all aspects.
English garden signifies an abundance of blessings.
Garden constitutes spiritual blessings and talents. What condition was the dream garden in?
Herb garden connotes a cultivation of one's inherent talents or abilities.
Kitchen garden signifies fresh ideas; a tendency toward homegrown (innovative) thought.
Orchard almost always symbolizes an individual's inherent talents. For further clarification, recall what condition the orchard was in. Was it fruitful? Diseased? Infested with insects or drought? Flooded?
Rock garden corresponds to the acceptance of life's difficulties and the blossoming of personal talents.
Roof garden is representative of beautiful, bountiful thoughts. Recall the garden's condition to illuminate the dream symbol's meaning.
Shrubbery implies natural talents and the opportunities to use them.
Sunken garden signifies efforts to maintain one's inner integrity and remain grounded.
Topiary warns against attempting to personally shape one's reality.

Herbaceous Plants

Baby's breath (flower) connotes the breath of new life breathed into an aspect of life.
Begonia stands for balance.
Blue flax suggests tolerance.
Flax signifies a life aspect that offers multiple benefits.
Geranium alludes to optimism.
Golden flax means cheerfulness.
Jacob's ladder (botanical/flower) stands for a need to heighten perceptual skills. Points to a sensitive situation.
Peony denotes sensitivity.

Border Plants

Ageratum signifies a fragile personality. It refers to an emotional sensitivity.
Alyssum (flower) typifies inner balance and peace.
Aster stands for one's memories and the importance of certain past events.
Blanketflower suggests an advisement to protect one's sensitivities.
Butter-and-eggs represents a sunny disposition; optimism.
Candytuft (flower) represents life's joyous, brighter moments.
Carnation applies to one who is socially correct; an individual who is overly concerned about social mores.
Cornflower portrays the beauty of one's inner strength that results from self-reliance.
Delphinium See larkspur.
English lavender suggests a quiet dignity.
Forget-me-not advises of a very specific need to remember someone or something important. Surrounding details should clarify this.
Gayfeather reminds us to gain a greater sense of humor.
Goldenrod illustrates a natural talent.
Heliotrope (flower) signifies inherent spiritual talents.
Hellebore exemplifies a state of duality.
Hollyhock (flower) implies cheerfulness; a bright outlook; old standby ethics and common sense.
Larkspur implies spiritual talents that are generously shared.
Lupine (botanical/flower) stands for longevity brought on by maintaining inner balance.
Penstemon (flower) is representative of a sensitivity toward and understanding of life's interconnectedness.
Phlox denotes cheerfulness and how quickly it can spread to others.
Snapdragon illustrates secretiveness; an ability to hold one's tongue; integrity.
Solomon's seal correlates to the strengthening of an individual's inner forces (energies). Also stands for an analytical ability for rationale.
Sweet pea refers to a clinging idea; a solid grasp. Depending on related elements, this symbol may also signify fragile relationships or situations.
Tickseed refers to a need to be more aware, watchful.
Wallflower reveals a lack of self-confidence. Points to a need to identify and appreciate one's admirable characteristics.

Diseased Plants

Blight refers to negative aspects that eat away at one's morals and ethics.
Root rot signifies a bad basic premise; a destructive basic attitude.
Wilted See withered.
Winterkill reveals the loss of an emotion or attitude due to a devastating event.
Withered (plant) signifies a lack of attention or interest.

Conservation

Reforestation portrays a renewal of one's natural talents.

Rotation planting applies to wise planning. It may also refer to the prevention of a very depleted condition.

Soil conservation typifies a desire to maintain firm and fertile foundations.

Soil sample is a check of one's basic character traits, whether they comprise elements that nourish or drain others.

Xeriscape symbolizes giving consideration to the mood or characteristics of a situation and making attempts to work within those limitations.

Cultivation

Air layering means to intermix the application of various thoughts; a blend of ideas or concepts to create a new one.

Graft (botany) connotes an attempt to join forces.

Hardiness chart See zone chart.

Hothouse reveals an oppressive condition or personality.

Hydroponics signifies nurturing by way of spiritual aspects.

Nursery (botanical) represents the concentrated nurturing of one's talents and spiritual gifts.

Planter (container) relates to a specific quality or personal characteristic of the individual associated with it. What was its color? Was there a special design on it?

Planting chart See zone chart.

Weed cutter connotes the routine monitoring of one's beliefs and the clearing out of unrelated concepts.

Zone chart refers to a gauge of behavior, which type is right for a particular situation.

Agriculture

Agricide represents an intentionally destructive nature.

Agriculture symbolizes one's interest in seeing things come to fruition.

Agricultural districting stands for a long-term interest or life goal geared toward nurturing an ideal and seeing it successfully manifest.

Crop dusting connotes wrong beginnings; applying preventive measures before a determination has been made to see if an issue or idea can strongly develop on its own.

Crop rotation indicates a concern for another's welfare; keeping ideas fresh.

Drip irrigation represents slow feeding; nourishment in the form of new information taken at a measured pace.

Dry farming points to a conservative perspective.

Haystack signifies the completion of specific work.

Irrigation suggests a need to use more spiritual aspects in one's life.

Muck signifies a confused mind or situation.

Muckraker characterizes an individual who is focused on the negatives in another's life.

Winnowing stands for efforts expended on sorting out the facts from associated extraneous elements.

Crops

Corn signifies a nurturing power created from within.

Canola indicates proper and well-prepared plans; the right atmosphere for advancement.

Corn typifies a nourishing aspect that comes from within self; a self-generating power source.

Cornfield signifies an abundance of inner strength.

Corn husk refers to additional sources one can enhance their talents and efforts through.

Cornstalk refers to strengthening effects of hard work.

Cottonseed stands for foundational ideals that generate a positive self-image later in life.

Cottonseed oil typifies the richness of a wholesome life coupled with an accepting self-image.

Cover crop represents an aspect that preserves another. It may refer to any kind of protection measure.

Hay implies active efforts; work time.

Mustard signifies a desire to enhance life events. In this way it may refer to exaggerations in general.

Mustard seed will most often indicate a new idea and the planting of same.

Plants Poisonous to Animals

Dogbane represents the value of special relationships; friendship.

Locoweed exemplifies a life factor that generates mental or emotional confusion brought on by experiencing aspects in life having the duality of positive and negative elements.

Ragwort is representative of the need one has for contemplation or introspection in one's life.

see also
• Farming *p. 262*
• Grains & Cereals *p. 429*

Succulents

Agave signifies diversity.
Cactus applies to spiritual beliefs that are protected.
Hen and chickens applies to a fruitful life factor; bountiful.
Prickly pear See cactus.
Saxifrage symbolizes an appreciation of life's more meaningful or memorable moments.
Succulent (plant) connotes a desirable aspect or plan that will be successful; an aspect loaded with benefits.
Yucca relates to a cleansing element in one's life.

Shrubs

Althea See hibiscus.
Azalea signifies hidden talents.
Bayberry pertains to the reminiscing of times past.
Camellia stands for affected beauty and feigned innocence. This warns against a tendency toward pretense.
Crape myrtle denotes an even balance between mental and emotional elements; synergy.
Datura illustrates a life aspect that alters perspectives, reactions, or comprehension.
Dogwood typifies beautiful friendship beginnings.
Firethorn stands for a need to fortify inner strength to deal with forthcoming difficulties.
Forsythia signifies confidence in one's new beginning; a bright outlook for the immediate future or one's newly chosen direction.
Fuchsia represents love, compassion, and humanistic expressions.
Gardenia implies purity.
Heather represents a bountiful stage in life.
Hibiscus denotes spirituality.
Holly corresponds with a fresh spiritual idea or concept.
Hydrangea connotes the utilization of one's spiritual talents in a generous and unconditional manner.
Kinnikinnick denotes bountiful and prolific gifts and talents.
Lilac represents spiritual purity.
Magnolia represents a fragile or delicate aspect in one's life.
Mallow stands for a broad scope of natural talents.
Mangrove illustrates spiritual bounties.
Manzanita denotes a life factor that is capable of cleansing. This signifies the need for some type of cleansing to be done in the dreamer's life.
Marsh elder alludes to gifts of the spirit; spiritual talents.
Mock orange connotes contentedness.
Myrtle refers to gentleness.
Rabbitbrush indicates the inner strength that comes from having strong personal defenses in place.
Red raspberry suggests a cleansing aspect in one's life; a need to rid oneself of a negative element.
Snowberry stands for sharpened awareness.
Thimbleberry indicates one's attention to details.
Witch hazel denotes a healing life aspect.
Wormwood illustrates obstructed creativity; an inability to apply oneself due to distractions.

Ferns

Asparagus fern suggests a fragile-appearing nature.
Bracken stands for a tangled and prickly path due to one's lack of spiritual application.
Bramble See bracken.
Briar See bracken.
Christmas fern is for spiritual growth. Recall its condition.
Dagger fern See Christmas fern.
Fern is representative of fruitful corporal acts. Check condition of the dreamscape fern to determine the quality of these acts.
Maidenhair fern denotes delicate natural talents.

Climbing & Trailing Plants

Betel nut implies a mesmerized state of mind and that which causes it.
Bittersweet reminds us that beauty frequently follows our pains in life.
Bougainvillea portrays a bright spiritual life.
Clematis exemplifies the beautiful and prolific effects of spiritual acts that endure or "cling" to others.
Gourd exemplifies a spiritual opportunity.
Grapevine typifies a life of rumor; the sequential and progressive alteration of facts.
Honeysuckle is representative of earned graces.
Jasmine alludes to a mysterious quality of one's personality.
Kudzu symbolizes a suffocating aspect in one's life.
Moonflower vine refers to the moon opening up the vine blossoms and exemplifies the bountiful spreading of a spiritual deed. It may stand for the blossoming of wisdom.
Morning glory calls for spiritual expression.
Poison ivy denotes semihidden hazards present on one's path.
Trumpet vine refers to many new ideas that may have been generated through spiritual sources.
Twinberry See honeysuckle.
Twinflower stands for duality.
Vine relates to far-reaching effects.
Wisteria reflects spiritual beauty and grace.

Grapevine signifies the distortion of the truth.

Herbs

Angelica corresponds to insights.
Anise corresponds to a strong personality trait that affects one's behavior.
Bay leaf applies to a life aspect that enhances one's life.
Chamomile stands for an easy-going, calm, or difficult-to-rile personality.
Comfrey defines self-healing capabilities; acceptance; tolerance.
Coriander signifies aspects unique to one's personality.
Dill implies an added aspect to something.
Elder pertains to one who has experience and wisdom.
Herbs pertain to a variety of meanings. Nonspecific herbs relate to natural talents. See specific type for information.
Horseradish denotes sharp lessons learned; lessons well remembered.
Juniper signifies the refreshing aspects of spirituality and the living of same.
Lavender portrays a gentle, comforting spiritual belief; spiritual wisdom and the peace it bestows.
Lemon verbena signifies a natural talent or skill that attracts others.
Marigold comes as a sign of encouragement.
Marshmallow relates to an abundance of spiritual gifts.
Nasturtium refers to natural talents that, when utilized for the benefit of others, nourish the self.
Oregano alludes to an added emphasis placed on an issue; an enhancement.
Pennyroyal will symbolize an element in one's life that eases the effects of irritations; acceptance.
Purslane depicts an opportunity to gain inner nourishment; a source of emotional strength.
Rosemary is a sign of remembrance. Advises one not to forget whatever it was related to in the dream.
Sage constitutes renewing elements in one's life.
Salvia (flower) represents hearty sensitivities; strong emotional control.
Snow-on-the-mountain is one's developing talents and the awareness of the many ways to put them to use.
Thyme connotes home life.
Valerian suggests a calming, soothing aspect in one's life and the need for it.
Verbena signifies a need to recognize life's blessings.
Yarrow alludes to a sign of independence.

Wildflowers & Plants

Alpine wildflowers represents choices or decisions made from a spiritual/moral/ethical foundation instead of from what the ego wants.
Beardtongue points to one's sense of humor. This symbol indicates a need to uplift one's outlook on life.
Bleeding heart is representative of a particularly sympathetic personality.
Bluebonnet stands for an aspect-aligned element.
Cowslip denotes steady emotions; serenity.
Edelweiss represents courage. It also refers to tenacity.
Gentian denotes simplicity; innocence.
Golden banner (flower; also wild pea) is representative of joy. It may also advise of a need to raise or uplift emotional outlook.
Indian blanket stands for inner defenses; strong confidence.
Indian paintbrush relates to vibrant spiritual energy.
Indian pipe suggests an openness to ideas. It also refers to communication.
Meadowsweet is representative of the serenity brought on by tolerance and acceptance.
Monkey flower illustrates a carefree attitude.
Nettle suggests some form of major annoyance in one's life.
Poppy pertains to a natural talent having the duality of positive and negative elements, depending on use.
Primrose depicts an idea of perfection.
Pussytoes are representative of gentleness; a need to soften one's harsher personality elements.
Queen Anne's lace represents an element possessing positive and negative aspects. May indicate a potentially harmful situation that, initially, looks inviting and attractive.
Redroot symbolizes perceptual clarity that comes from clearing emotional negatives that block rationale.

Poppy means good and bad abilities.

Sea pink refers to the little blessings that tend to give us an unexpected uplift.
Spring beauty signifies optimistic perspectives; renewal.
Sticker (thorn) See thorn.
Stonecrop stands for destiny and its acceptance.
Tansy denotes strengthened insight; a need to boost one's defensive methods.
Wildflower generally pertains to the beauty of making free choices in life.

Orchids

Coralroot denotes the expression of spiritual behavior and manifestation of compassionate qualities.
Lady's slipper portrays a possession of fragile natural talents; those to be nurtured.
Orchid signifies a fragile talent or benefit that must be carefully maintained. This dream symbol will in addition be associated with feminine traits and perspectives.

see also
• Soils *p. 78*
• Herbs *p. 431*

Mints

Betony cautions one to take care of some type of wound. This may be an emotional injury.
Catnip signifies a mesmerized state. Warns of a need to awaken to reality.
Horehound is representative of that which is capable of clearing and sharpening one's general communication skills.
Lamb's ears symbolizes prayers being heard through personal spirituality.
Mint See specific type such as catnip, horehound, and so on.
Obedient plant suggests a need to stop ignoring one's conscience.
Spearmint signifies a refreshing idea or aspect to an element; insights.

Bellflowers

Balloon flower usually refers to inner joy. Depending on surrounding dreamscape aspects, this symbol may advise one to lessen the tendency to exaggerate.
Bellflower suggests a need to listen to one's inner voice.
Bells of Ireland signifies a reminder to utilize natural talents for acts of goodness.
Canterbury bell is representative of nostalgia.
Cardinal flower signifies intense emotions.
Coralbell points to one's blessings.
Harebell is usually representative of hope, signs of renewal.
Lobelia stands for an emotionally calming aspect.

Pansies & Violets

Pansy refers to a need to boost one's sense of inner power. This symbol advises one to have more confidence in oneself.
Viola suggests practiced spirituality in the way of behavior.
Violet alludes to a healing spiritual element.

Rose Family

Cabbage rose underscores deep affection or admiration.
Cinquefoil represents a bright viewpoint of life; living with a good sense of humor and general happiness.
Climbing rose stands for an enduring admiration or love.
Damask rose suggests a dignified, genteel nature.
Moss rose symbolizes optimism, energetic motivation.
Rose portrays strong admiration.
Rosebud pertains to a beginning or budding attraction.
Tea rose signifies a dignified, genteel admiration.
Tuberose suggests pure intentions.

Lily Family

Water lily echoes the fairest aspects of one's inner life force.

Bluebell is representative of spiritual joy.
Daylily denotes emotional sensitivity.
Easter lily See lily.
Grape hyacinth comes to reveal the presence of one's hidden natural abilities; a need to recognize one's own potential.
Iris is usually representative of hope.
Jack-in-the-pulpit (plant) generally connotes spiritual expressiveness.
Lily stands for innocence and purity; a new birth.
Lily of the valley (botanical/scent) is representative of a delicate innocence or naïveté. In this sense it may refer to one's lack of worldly experience.
Lily pad indicates the fruits of spiritual work and expression, especially if they've bloomed.
Lotus pertains to spiritual sacredness.
Mariposa lily represents hope.
Peace lily usually represents a peace offering, a sign of an apology, or a reconciliatory gesture.
Sand lily stands for an appreciation of small blessings.
Tiger lily See lily.
Water lily reflects spiritual beauty.
Wood lily signifies rejuvenation caused by an energized sense of determination.
Yellow water lily refers to a vacillating opinion of one's spiritual beliefs; tending to agree with whomever one is with at the time.

Daisy Family

Daisy depicts joy and happiness.

Bachelor's button is representative of self-sufficiency.
Blazing star points to sudden insights; inspiration.
Chrysanthemum pertains to the golden time of life; a restful time of introspection; a time of respite and reflection.
Cocklebur is emotional pain.
Coltsfoot suggests carefree footing and comes to advise one to pay closer attention to where one is going or how one is behaving.
Cosmos suggests the use of more of one's goodness in a selfless manner.
Dahlia refers to opportunity.
Daisy illustrates happiness; a joyous attitude toward life.
Daisy chain is exuberance.
Dusty miller suggests need for more unconditional behavior.
Groundsel represents joy.
Maltese cross symbolizes the practice of general spirituality rather than one based in a currently recognized religion.
Marsh marigold brings spiritual encouragement.
Mum See chrysanthemum.
Salsify points to a need to reorganize one's sense of priority; mental focus.
Shasta daisy suggests inner joy from sharing natural talents.
Strawflower suggests a need for greater openness.
Zinnia symbolizes multiple benefits or gifts in one's life that have not been recognized.

Tropical Plants & Flowers

Air plant typifies an intellectual; learning is a priority in life.
Amaranth indicates perseverance and inner strength.
Black-eyed Susan connotes favorable results forthcoming.
Coleus refers to an acceptance of varied personalities of those with whom one is associated.
Four-o'clock (flower) stands for a need to strengthen one's self-confidence.
Frangipani (flower) signifies a sensitive nature.
Gloxinia (plant) exemplifies deep joy; bright happiness.
Henna pertains to repressed emotions.
Love-lies-bleeding designates a state of being heartbroken.
Maranta illustrates nourishing provisions that exist for the dreamer to currently take advantage of.
Raffia palm means a life aspect having the potential to bring multiple uses or solutions.
Rattan depicts a multipurpose talent or ability.
Telegraph plant points to the interrelationship between all living things. It refers to the psychic bond connecting all life forms.
Ylang-ylang (flower) stands for fragile, yet enduring, sensitivities; empathy.

Poisonous Plants

Ivy is a representation of abundant wisdom and imaginative output.

Belladonna (plant) implies an emotional settling is required; a calming.
Black nightshade (plant) illustrates the duality of nature. This may apply to human nature as well.
Buttercup (flower) means life's real joys; inner happiness; laughter.
Columbine (flower) relates to inner peacefulness.
Cowbane signifies warm social interactions; congeniality; a personable individual.
Deadly nightshade See belladonna.
Digitalis refers to an aspect that will ease heart trouble. Usually implies emotional pain.
Foxglove (flower) exemplifies the powerful healing abilities of natural talents.
Hemlock advises of a dangerous factor in one's life.
Henbane alludes to something in one's life that possesses duality.
Indian tobacco emphasizes respect and honor.
Ivy is representative of bountiful knowledge. It also refers to prolific creativity.
Jimsonweed emphasizes the duality or polarity of something in one's life; possessing positive and negative aspects, depending on how it's used.
Mandrake indicates a negative aspect in one's life.
Mistletoe represents good intentions.
Monkshood See wolfsbane.
Oleander reminds us that appearances can be deceiving; an appearance of something in one's life that seems to be good or be a blessing may ultimately prove harmful.
Petunia exemplifies a talent or other personal ability that will proliferate if cared for.
Wolfsbane reflects a dangerous association.

see also
• Seasons *p. 62*
• Remedies & Unguents *p. 115*

Medicinal Plants

Aloe vera warns one to soothe a burning situation or desire.
Arnica points out priorities and the need to get them straight.
Bee balm refers to an ability to ignore small irritations in life.
Bitterroot relates to continual blessings in life that may, initially, appear as negatives.
Black cohosh usually represents an element that brings about a balanced state in one's life.
Bloodroot connotes negative motivations.
Bugbane See black cohosh.
Cascara sagrada warns of a serious need to get rid of wasteful aspects in one's life. These may refer to attitudes, beliefs, or certain situations.
Echinacea (flower) represents intense healing forces geared to reinforce one's fortitude.
Elecampane stands for a healing life aspect.
Eucalyptus illustrates a life aspect that has the capability of nourishing through healing.
Eyebright stands for a life aspect that can bring perceptual clarity.
Feverfew indicates a means to overcome one's psychological negatives and bring about an inner balance; open chi channels.
Figwort suggests priorities; a recognition of what's really important.
Fleabane pertains to a defense or counter aspect to interfering life elements.
Gentian applies to the healing benefits of inner spiritual convictions.
Ginseng corresponds with one's overall health; an aspect that has the capability to bring general wellness.
Goldenseal refers to a healing aspect in one's life.
Hepatica connotes inner strength.
Impatiens signifies the frequent moments of joy that come into our lives.
Ipecac is a severe warning that a highly destructive aspect has entered one's life and there's a need to expel it.
Lady's mantle refers to refined dignity.
Lousewort reveals self-created problems. Suggests greater acceptance and perseverance.
Lungwort is representative of perseverance.
Meadow rue refers to a freedom to let one's individuality show.
Motherwort stands for a solution (cure) for problems associated with a new path or direction.
Mouse-ear is indicative of a need to listen better. Be quiet as a mouse and you are certain to hear the things that you've been missing.
Mullein symbolizes a healing aspect in one's life.
Orrisroot will be suggestive of a particularly stabilizing element in one's life.
Periwinkle represents a fragile talent or inherent ability.
Pipsissewa refers to naturally occurring opportunities that need to be noted.
Pleurisy root relates to a life aspect that has the potential to negate negative ideas or attitudes. This will refer to something that causes a turnaround in respect to a harmful idea.
Purple coneflower See echinacea.
Sandwort signifies an attitude of acceptance, a "whatever" attitude.
Skullcap signifies widening perceptual views to see what's outside the box; new thought and inspiration.
Soapwort signifies a need to cleanse away negative attitudes.
Spiderwort suggests efforts applied to keeping life elements from becoming confusing or entangled.
Starwort points to an appreciation of life's blessings and more valuable aspects.
Sunflower specifically symbolizes spiritual joy.
Wintergreen stands for renewal; a wider perspective toward possibilities.
Wood betony See lousewort.
Woundwort equates to a healing element in one's life.
Yampa is representative of the wisdom of using diplomacy to manage a delicate situation or relationship.

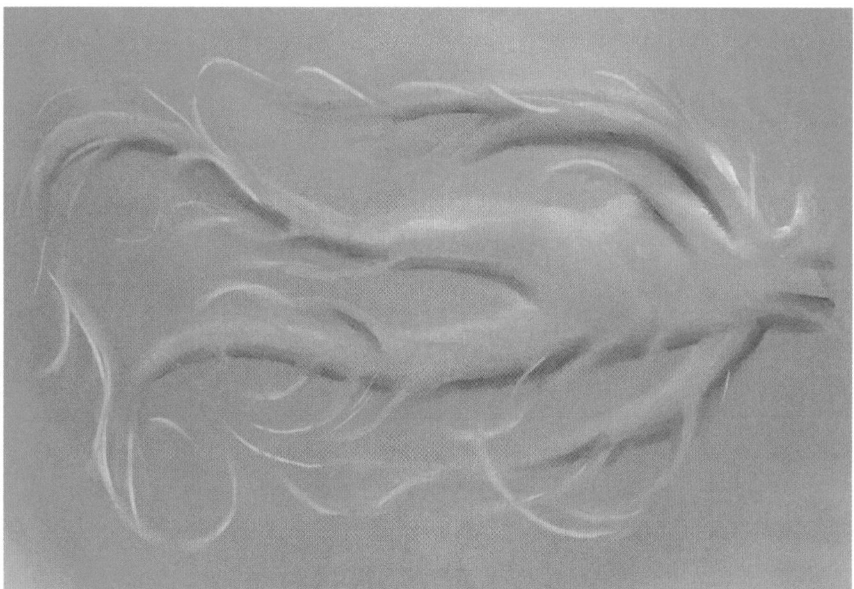

Ginseng reflects and may engender mental and physical well-being.

Dried Flowers

Potpourri indicates a good balance of life forces.

Dried flowers exemplify a need to preserve one's natural talents through continual utilization.
Dried flowers (decoration) represent one's appreciation of natural gifts and the comfort they give when one surrounds oneself with their beauty.
Dried flowers (herbal use) are representative of the extended utilization of one's natural talents.
Dried flowers (in field/garden) come as a warning of one's natural talents going to waste on the vine.
Dried flowers (memento) come to reinforce the importance of remembering the personal significance of another's natural talents.
Flower (dried) See dried flowers.
Potpourri defines a harmonious blend of elements.

Bulb Plants

Amaryllis constitutes a focused, well-grounded personality.
Anemone represents mental awareness and acuity.
Caladium suggests a rich or bountiful natural talent.
Clove (multisectioned bulb) suggests beginnings with more than one generating aspect.
Crocus marks a change in one's direction or situation.
Daffodil portrays the bright prospects of new beginnings.
Freesia refers to an opportunity that won't remain fresh (available) for long.
Gladiolus represents an upcoming span of peacefulness in one's life. It comes to remind us to be grateful for our daily blessings.
Hyacinth (flower) symbolizes the blossoming of a new spiritual gift or talent.
Jonquil refers to peacefulness.
Narcissus illustrates the dangers of egotism. It has narcotic properties.
Tulip stands for self-confidence; encouragement; motivational factors. May also point to a beautiful beginning.

Floral Presentations

Bouquet (flower) illustrates a commendation from higher spiritual sources.
Boutonniere marks distinction. It refers to someone who has been singled out for a specific reason.
Bridal wreath is indicative of a celebration of a new path or perhaps a journey that is just beginning.
Cut flower See bouquet (flower).
Garland symbolizes bountiful spiritual acts. It could refer to the continual utilization of one's humanitarian and/or spiritual gifts.
Nosegay (small bouquet) connotes a small yet extremely meaningful act that serves to encourage or comfort another.
Pompon (flower) See boutonniere.
Posy See flower.

Houseplants

African violet denotes purity of manner and thought.
Christmas cactus is representative of a spiritual blooming; perhaps an epiphany of some kind.
Cyclamen suggests a gentle, yet loyal personality trait; a stand-up quality.
Houseplant corresponds with one's openly displayed personality traits. See specific types for additional clarity.
Jade indicates perseverance.
Peyote connotes the sacred aspects of personal spiritual attainment.
Poinsettia is representative of spiritual celebration. It may in addition refer to an externalized spiritual expression of oneself.
Purple passion (vine) represents intense emotions related to motivation; drive.
Saguaro is a protected spiritual aspect of an individual.
Velvet plant See purple passion.

Plant Products

Alum (root) warns of a need to stop something in one's life. It comes to advise one of a need to staunch some type of behavior.
Coconut oil signifies those factors in one's life that serve to soothe and soften the hurtful or difficult aspects of one's path.
Hemp refers to a strong or powerful factor in one's life.
Linseed oil is representative of protective characteristics one uses.
Nectar corresponds with that which is sweetest in life; attained goals; fruitful relationships or concluding situations.
Resin constitutes a beneficial result.
Rose water indicates an altered element.
Rosin warns against slipping off one's course. A preventative against backsliding.
Sap represents the life force of nature; inner strength.

see also
• Grasslands *p. 70*
• Garden Accoutrements *p. 397*

Grasses & Reeds

Bamboo is developing talents.
Beach grass means strong spiritual roots.
Citronella pertains to the act of conflict resolution by way of positive means; the avoidance of harmful solutions.
Couch grass See quack grass.
Crabgrass means a negative aspect that has spread through life and is difficult to excise. May point to a bad habit.
Grass corresponds to spiritual foundations.
Grass seed pertains to a life aspect that may develop into a spiritual foundation or view.
Lawn See grass.
Pampas grass implies a fragile situation or personality.
Paper plant See papyrus.
Papyrus corresponds with delicate information that requires careful discernment.
Quack grass refers to uncharacteristic attitudes; undesirable qualities.
Reed symbolizes resiliency.
Saw grass illustrates a very troublesome life phase.
Straw means an insulating quality.
Sweetgrass denotes a cherished thing.
Sword grass warns of hazards on one's current path.

Clover

Clover represents spiritual abundance.
Clover leaf (three leaves) See shamrock.
Four-leaf clover represents an attitude of particularly high expectation without factoring in any probabilities or possibilities for failure or disappointment as a result of an action or activity.
Red clover represents a cleansing element in one's life that brings about inner strength and fortitude.
Shamrock is representative of the three aspects of one's personal spirituality.

Molds, Moss & Fungus

Amanita is a dangerous situation or relationship.
Fungus warns against inactivity. The dreamer needs to act regarding a specific life aspect.
Leaf mold represents the creation of a fertile or fruitful condition.
Lichen refers to a fertile atmosphere. It may refer to a bountiful condition.
Mildew illustrates inattention; a lack of awareness; letting something go for too long without giving it proper attention.
Mold (growth) See fungus.
Moss denotes vitality.
Mushroom represents a benefit resulting from a seemingly negative factor.
Peat moss portrays a protective element; a supportive aspect serving to prolong the effects of multiple nourishing factors.
Puffball symbolizes a healing aspect in one's life.
Spanish moss corresponds to a frequently feared concept that one should delve into.
Sphagnum See peat moss.
Toadstool See mushroom.

Weeds & Thistles

Bindweed is representative of tenacity.
Blessed thistle relates to female assistance or support.
Chickweed reminds that there is value in something one has perceived as being valueless.
Dandelion means benefits that are not readily seen.
Fireweed stands for a need to improve perception of negatives. Points to the need for caution.
Goatsbeard suggests a need for discretion.
Knapweed suggests emotional balance.
Lamb's quarter represents food for thought.
Milkweed See silkweed.
Pokeweed refers to a plan possessing a negative premise.
Ragweed typifies an element that has the potential to cause a strong reaction.
Shepherd's purse corresponds to beneficial elements that encourage thoughtfulness.
Silkweed will reveal a beneficial element in one's life.
Snakeweed points to mental sharpness.
Sneezeweed represents an irritation in one's life.
Sorrel suggests a life element that has the capability of providing inner nourishment.
Speedwell suggests something that needs to be overcome.
Sweet clover represents emotional sensitivity.
Thistle See thorn.
Thistledown pertains to a dual nature; the soft side that frequently accompanies a problematical situation.
Thistle seed (niger) refers to research; feeding thoughts.
Thorn relates to the thorny elements in life.
Tumbleweed portrays shallow aspects of oneself; no roots or firm perspective or opinion.
Weed depicts falsehoods. May apply to spiritual ideas that are extraneous and devised for the purpose of control.
Wood sorrel represents a rekindled sense of resolve; encouragement.

Dandelion stands for advantages that take time to reach fruition.

Tree Species

Acacia stands for the complexity of an issue; a multifaceted element.

Banyan symbolizes strong roots or foundations.

Bergamot refers to the healing life aspect in regard to recognizing the duality of one's personality. That which is sour can also be fragrant. This symbol points to a recognition of the upside of difficult situations.

Bitternut pertains to the unavoidable, naturally occurring events in life that are irritating, yet not lasting. It symbolizes life's more difficult lessons, which have to be worked through.

Black haw connotes the rewards resulting from acts of goodness or generosity.

Black locust represents self-confidence; self-assuredness.

Black oak denotes a strong negative aspect in one's life.

Box elder stands for fortitude; courage.

Boxwood stands for a particularly strong natural skill/talent.

Buckthorn signifies a focus on goals; nearing achievement.

Butternut one's receptivity to others; congeniality.

Cajeput stands for motivation; encouragement to keep going.

Catalpa indicates a need to recognize or set better priorities.

Chinaberry indicates sensitivity to delicate situations.

Chokecherry exemplifies life aspects that bring sorrow. May point out spoken words that the speaker wants to retract.

Sugar maple symbolizes inner calm achieved through self-knowledge.

Coral bean indicates the many elements to a complex aspect.

Cottonwood exemplifies the beauty of combining wholesome living with spirituality.

Elm warns of escapism and comes to advise one to face life with greater inner strength.

Giant sequoia relates to ancient truths comprising reality that remain immutable.

Hackberry stands for a need to sharpen analytical thought; heighten discernment.

Hawthorn exemplifies unrecognized benefits.

Honey locust represents resolutions; getting results.

Horse chestnut stands for resolve; determination.

Joshua tree stands for a heightened appreciation of blessings.

Kapok denotes that which one uses to soften life's difficulties.

Larch stands for the fragile state of balance one has caused inherent talents to be in.

Laurel exemplifies honor and praise; having the emotional sensitivity to recognize another's good works.

Mesquite defines the possession of extremely potent spiritual power; exceptional strength of spiritual knowledge and wisdom.

Mimosa denotes a delicate innocence of character; a fragile yet strong nature.

Palm tree will usually have a spiritual connotation, referring to the freedom to feel empowered by convictions. Recall surrounding dreamscape environment and elements for further clarification.

Poplar relates to a personal talent that has blossomed in an accelerated manner.

Prickly ash stands for acceptance and tolerance.

Pussy willow corresponds to bountiful personal talents or gifts.

Redbud stands for a need to bolster one's emotional sensitivity level.

Rubber tree indicates tolerance and acceptance.

Sassafras implies well-being.

Saw palmetto stands for personal philosophical concepts; spiritual freedom.

Serviceberry points to opportunity and the awareness of it.

Silk tree indicates sensitivity toward a delicate situation or relationship.

Slippery elm represents self-healing or correction.

Smoke tree is representative of deepened wisdom of spiritual philosophy.

Soapberry points to a cleansing element; eliminating negatives.

Sourwood indicates an increasing level of acceptance.

Sugar maple symbolizes tranquility generated from spiritual wisdom.

Sumac represents a ready recognition of opportunities.

Sweet gum symbolizes an enriching element in one's life and the appreciation of it.

Sycamore stands for deep emotional responses; admiration.

Tamarack points to spiritual fragility or sensitivity.

Weeping willow symbolizes the beauty and sensitivity of nature.

Willow pertains to spiritual tenacity.

see also
• Construction Materials *p. 310*
• Fruits *p. 428*

Fruit & Nut Trees

Cherry tree connotes life's more pleasurable moments.

Apricot stands for a healing force that comes from within oneself.
Cherry typifies a sweet situation; prime aspects of something.
Chestnut stands for heartfelt feelings; warm emotions.
Fruit tree generally stands for spiritual talents and humanitarian expressions. See specific entries in this section if the type of fruit tree is known.
Hickory highlights the strength and enduring characteristics of one's natural abilities as they are used and developed.
Mulberry represents joy.
Pawpaw stands for an awareness of an aspect's subtleties.
Pecan points to fulfillment after an achievement.
Persimmon indicates an ongoing puzzlement; the need to clarify resolutions.

Forests

After-growth See second growth.
Forest is representative of one's individualized attitudes in relation to natural talents. May also refer to how one utilizes corporal deeds. Recall the condition of this forest.
Old growth indicates perspectives or ideas that have endured and passed the test of time.
Redwood forest stands for inner strength; fortitude.
Second growth (forest) points to rejuvenation.
Sequoia See redwood forest.
Sylvan See forest.
Trillium represents those delicate, yet strong, emotional (empathetic) qualities one has; the seemingly fragile attributes that prove to be enduring.

Tree Types

Bonsai stands for forced attitudes; thoughts or ideas that are not naturally come by; mental manipulation; in this sense, coercion.
Deciduous defines an atmosphere of change, the inevitability of such; a changeable situation.
Shade tree applies to respite.

Timber Trees

Bentwood implies a natural inclination.
Clear-cutting comes in dreams as a symbol having the duality of two possible meanings pointing to either an advisement or a warning. The advisement would be to rid oneself of every aspect of a certain negative in one's life. The warning would be to stop eliminating every shred of a particular element. The dreamer will know what these elements are.
Cordwood is preparedness.
Firewood See cordwood.
Gnarled wood warns of a strongly held negative attitude; a twisted idea.
Green lumber points to an attempt to build on a plan before the tools themselves are well developed or seasoned.
Growth ring stands for a specific age. References time that is meaningful to each dreamer.
Kindling relates to aspects that exacerbate a condition or situation; something that will make matters more intense.
Knothole constitutes a natural aspect; one that isn't covered or made perfect; the beauty of certain unique imperfections.
Log (wood) suggests potential opportunity.
Lumber means driving force for one's advancement.
Plank See lumber.
Twig See kindling.
Undergrowth connotes developing aspects to an issue; yet undetected activity.

Forest represents an appreciation of one's own innate abilities.

Timber Trees

Ash stands for a de-emphasis on materialistic aspects.
Aspen points to a need to strengthen one's sensitivity; compassion.
Alder denotes a need to appreciate life's happier moments.
Balsa applies to our innate personal talents. May refer to thoughts that make light of our burdens.
Basswood refers to fortified strength; determination.
Beech signifies lessons experienced; a need to increase one's level of acceptance/tolerance.
Birch is representative of an open and honest situation or atmosphere.
Black walnut signifies the fulfillment coming from extensive efforts expended; the fruits of one's labors.
Cedar illustrates a need for spiritual cleansing or energized protection of one's spiritual beliefs.

Wood chips keep spirituality safe.

Douglas fir indicates one's cherished convictions or philosophy.
Ebony implies an enduring, ongoing puzzlement.
Engelmann spruce signifies fortitude; perseverance.
Fruitwood signifies the remaining benefit from an element that provided a multitude of them.
Ironwood points to complexity; intricate elements of an aspect.
Knotty pine connotes the attractiveness of natural simplicity.
Lemonwood represents an element with multipurpose aspects.
Mahogany is representative of an inner warmth of character.
Maple portrays current benefits or gifts that one hasn't yet recognized or acknowledged in one's life. It points to a need to recognize or appreciate the benefits (fruits) of one's labors.
Oak denotes an unyielding personality; a lack of sensitivity; rigidness.
Primavera See white mahogany.
Pulp (wood) alludes to leftover elements that still have some value.
Rosewood symbolizes enduring natural talent or ability.
Teakwood stands for an enduring perspective or belief that will withstand spiritual negatives.
Walnut refers to a utilitarian life element.
White mahogany is representative of a rare strength of character.
Wood carries a general meaning related to one's natural talents and inherent characteristics.
Wood chips suggest the common use for mulch. Therefore, this symbol refers to an aspect in one's life that preserves spirituality (moisture) and prevents negative aspects (weeds) from infiltrating one's attitude or behavior.
Wood shavings denote the residual effects left over after one has used a special talent or skill to accomplish something. If the shavings are cedar wood, then they represent additional benefits—aromatic purposes.

Pine Trees & Conifers

Arborvitae is representative of the tree of life. It comes as a symbol of motivational strength.
Blue spruce connotes one's connectedness to spirituality through nature.
Bristlecone pine reflects lessons in life. Reminds us to learn from past mistakes.
Conifer denotes everlasting beauty and benefits of spiritual behavior.
Cypress stands for grief. It may refer specifically to a mourning time.
Evergreens See conifer.
Jack pine See pine.
Lodgepole pine connotes that which one can build on or with; aspects that serve as building blocks or forces; tenacity generated from spiritual convictions.
Norfolk Island pine stands for a heightened sensitivity to others.
Pine pertains to natural abilities; one's bonded relationship to nature; inherent talents.
Pinecone refers to the seeds of one's natural talents.
Yew represents spreading (growing) natural talents; inherent abilities.

Pinecone represents the origins of one's inherent abilities.

see also
• Scenery *p. 66*
• Woodwork *p. 215*

Miscellaneous

Acorn is representative of the source of one's strength. May also point to the beginning traits of an unyielding personality.

Anabiosis advises greater awareness.

Apple blossom symbolizes mental health; rationale.

Arbor applies to the perceptible aura of highly spiritual individuals; surrounding self with spiritual ideals.

Autumn leaf indicates a time to slow down; an acceptance of a natural lull in advancements; a time for introspection before moving on.

Beanpole refers to unrecognized strength. This dreamscape symbol points to something very near the dreamer that has the potential of providing great inner strength but is overlooked because of its simplicity or commonness.

Beanstalk refers to the unique aspects of individuality, strength, and potential that touch our lives.

Blowdown (trees) signifies devastation left in the wake of an emotional conflict.

Botanical symbolizes the quality and quantity of how well one applies spirituality to daily life.

Bower See arbor.

Bur/burr will indicate a troublesome irritation in one's life, a slight or temporary problem that can be easily removed if given a close enough look.

Bush denotes fullness of spiritual or humanitarian acts. Was the dreamscape bush full or scrawny?

Catkin denotes proof that one's idea is about to take hold.

Cherry blossom signifies the sweetness of one's strong faith in oneself.

Chlorophyll stands for the quality and level of one's personal healing ability.

Crazyweed stands for a life factor that causes emotional or mental confusion.

Deadwood warns of a tendency to hold onto the negative emotional effects of past events; a need for closure.

Deep-rooted refers to an attitude or perspective that has been held for a long while.

Essential oil will point to that which is a priority in one's life; that which is essential.

Fig leaf pertains to a concern over trivialities. May point to a tendency to hide certain aspects of one's life.

Fox fire portrays an aspect of true reality.

Fruitless warns of unexercised spirituality.

Graft (botany) connotes an attempt to join forces.

Grassroots defines people power; activism generated by common folk.

Hedgerow implies a guiding facet in one's life.

Herbarium represents a study of the many productive uses for botanicals. This dreamscape symbol would indicate a call for one to utilize personal talents more extensively.

Husk denotes the stripping away the extraneous aspects of an issue; getting down to basics.

Hybrid portrays a blending of dissimilar aspects to create a new and fresh quality or effect. This symbol touches on the theory behind true reality.

Fig leaf suggests a tendency to focus on the unimportant things in life.

Jumping bean typifies restlessness; anxiety.

Outgrowth alludes to a resulting effect or manifestation.

Pasqueflower stands for spiritual inspirations.

Passionflower alludes to the beauty of possessing a positive passion such as empathy, compassion, and so on.

Peat suggests a life factor that has the potential for enriching something.

Photosynthesis portrays an inherent attraction and personal need for knowledge.

Plant connotes a natural talent. Refer to various specific plants listed.

Pinwheel relates to personal tenacity and flexibility to go with the flow and accept whatever comes; a plan that will work no matter which way the wind blows.

Pomander is a tendency to surround oneself with positive elements and personally uplifting or beneficial aspects. If the dream pomander was being gifted to another, this then represents a desire for others to be surrounded by same.

Primrose path portrays a life of ease where all desires and goals are successfully attained; an overidealistic goal and course that has a high potential for ending in failure.

Privet hedge See hedgerow.

Sapling pertains to the tenuous but persevering nature of newly attained beliefs.

Self-pollination stands for one's ability to generate one's own motivating factors.

Shell (husk) suggests a need to break through or get at the core of something in one's life.

Shuck See husk.

Spore constitutes a small element capable of becoming a major aspect in one's life.

Statice stands for tenacity; endurance.

Stele signifies a marker; an impression of something important to the dreamer. This will be different for everyone.

Stinkweed refers to a concealed negative element in one's life. Things look fine on the surface, yet something smells.

Sugarcane field suggests a source producing a desirable aspect.

Thicket See bush.

Tree farm indicates the cultivation of natural talents and gifts; the propagation of same.

Underbrush stands for hidden problems.

Undergrowth connotes developing aspects to an issue. It may refer to some yet undetected activity.

Chapter 4

Natural Phenomena & Weather

These dream elements are directly associated with the quality and condition of one's current mental or spiritual state of being. Events related to earth are associated with ethics. Symbols related to air concern the mind. And symbols involving water, such as torrential rain, carry spiritual connotations.

Wind

Balmy reflects an enjoyable atmosphere free of difficulty; pleasant and uplifting.
Breeze implies low mental activity.
Chill factor cautions one to be aware of additional cooling factors that may affect a situation or relationship.
Chilly refers to cool or unfriendly attitudes.
Crosswind signifies life's unexpected aspects that can blow us off balance.
Cyclone See tornado.
Doldrums warn of a lack of motivation; a slump period; a call to draw on reserves.
Fujita scale See wind force scale.
Gale cautions against over-exerting one's faculties.
Gust pertains to a sudden emotional outburst. Advises a need for greater control.
Hurricane warns of an emotional dysfunction caused by spiritual inundation. This means one has attempted to learn too many spiritual concepts without taking adequate time to properly absorb and comprehend each idea individually.
Northeaster refers to a temporary emotional upset; a phase of emotional distress that can't be avoided.
Prevailing warns against indecision; emotional or mental vacillation depending on the opinion of others.
Sea breeze represents a spiritual sense to something; a hint of spiritual elements.
Tornado symbolizes great inner turmoil. The tornado connotes emotional or mental problems, while the hurricane correlates to spiritual aspects.
Twister See hurricane; tornado.
Typhoon See hurricane.
Upslope (wind current) advises of a blustery emotional situation in the offing.
Upwind stands for exposure; going against the flow.
Wind corresponds to mental activity; the thought process; psychological functioning.
Windchill factor warns of ideas that are more dangerous than they appear.
Wind force scale (Beaufort) suggests one keep an eye on the rate of one's thoughts. Some thinking is done at lightning speed, and important elements are left out.
Wind shear reveals a thought or idea that could cut one down if close awareness or monitoring is not maintained.
Windy signifies a change by way of clearing away negative elements.

Wind Names

Chinook wind is a factor that heartens, encourages, and uplifts one.
Trade wind implies thoughts and ideas that follow a common route; a lack of individual thought.
Whirlwind reveals twisted thought; conclusions or assumptions that have been reached too quickly.
Zephyr (light breeze) symbolizes gentle thoughts and/or insights.

Air & Atmosphere

Smoke means something is wrong.

Air is always representative of one's mental and/or emotional state.
Airflow signifies free-flowing thought patterns. Recall what the air was flowing through. Was it clear or blocked?
Air gauge comes in dreams to recommend one check the atmosphere (mood) of a situation or relationship for building or deflating pressure.
Air hole refers to taking a breather in regard to hard thinking; leaving room to accommodate new ideas.
Airless represents a thoughtless personality; no creativity; no ingenuity; a rigid mind; stale ideas and/or perspectives.
Air pocket symbolizes a temporary loss of ideas or new thoughts on an issue.
Air pollution is representative of a dangerous atmosphere. The dreamer will be able to recognize this situation and relate it to a specific element, such as the dreamer's working environment, social life, or home life.
Air quality (rating) won't necessarily point to physical health but rather to the tone of the atmosphere surrounding a particular issue, situation, or relationship.
Airwaves connote various levels of thought. Also may refer to how the general public is thinking on a specific issue; that is, public opinion.
Downdraft applies to a decline in one's mental or emotional state.
Downslope (wind current) denotes little energies expended on thought. May reveal a situation where heavy thought isn't required.
Draft (air) represents an interference in one's life. May signify a specific thought that keeps returning.
Geothermal (activity) usually comes as a warning of inner turmoil.
Haze (atmospheric) alludes to an unclear aspect, usually a lack of clear thought or understanding.
Hot air refers to bluster; a tendency to exaggeration or pretentiousness.
Mist constitutes a spiritual atmosphere. May reveal a highly spiritual aura around someone. Recall if there was a color to the mist.
Muggy See humid.
Pouring (rain) signifies an inundation of fresh spiritual ideas or insights.
Smog relates to distortion; an unclear perception.
Smoke is representative of a sign that something is amiss and could be close to combustion.
Steam portrays spiritual activity.
Sultry portrays a tough or sticky situation.
Vortex exposes an opening of some type. It may refer to an unconventional course.

see also
• The Sea *p. 36*
• Weather *p. 293*

Water

Cold water represents a diminishing value of spiritual elements; also spiritual disagreements.
Condensation is representative of life aspects that naturally generate spiritual effects or benefits.
Damp indicates the presence of an additional aspect to something in the dreamer's life.
Deluge See flood.
Dew symbolizes a light spiritual touch.
Dew point refers to the stage in one's life where spiritual factors begin to be integrated into daily living.
Drought comes as a warning to the dreamer of self-generated spiritual starvation.
Dry spell stands for a phase of little activity regarding a certain aspect of one's life. This may be perceived as a bad thing, but it usually represents the necessity for further progression.
Evaporation is representative of the absorption of spiritual ideals.
Flash flood warns of an overload of spiritual intake. May indicate a fanatic.
Flood warns of spiritual inundation; drowning in unprocessed spiritual information.
Foam (sea) symbolizes spiritual confusion.
Fog warns of spiritual obscurity; unclear spiritual perception.
Freshet pertains to a sudden influx of fresh spiritual ideas.
Ground fog reveals a situation of being too close to an issue to see it clearly.
Ground water See spring.
Hard water signifies the elements of reality that are difficult to soften (make easier to accept).
High waterline points out a state of full spiritual behavior in the dreamer's life.
Humid is representative of an atmosphere heavy with spiritual aspects.
Lake effect corresponds with the effect spiritual aspects have on one's life.
Puddle represents something that has been left unfinished. This symbol won't necessarily refer to rainwater (spiritual). What type of liquid formed the puddle?
Relative humidity alludes to the depth and quality of spiritual aspects each of us absorbs individually.
Soft water constitutes ground-work having high potential.
Spray is representative of an exposure to new spiritual concepts.
Spring is representative of a well of spirituality within oneself.
Stagnant connotes a lack of vitality; something that has been allowed to go stale.
Stream applies to the changing course one's spiritual search takes.
Streambed connotes the opportunity to discover spiritual riches.
Vapor See fumes.
Water gauge See rain gauge.
Waterlogged comes as a warning of spiritual drowning, an indication of a forced progression whereby spiritual aspects have not been absorbed (comprehended).

Tides & Waves

Ebb tide denotes a time of lessening spiritual involvement or interest.
Eddy warns of an off-course spiritual situation where one is caught in a distracting current.
Ground swell stands for a growing perspective or movement. In this sense it means something or someone who is quickly gaining in popularity or support.
High tide portrays a time of intense spiritual influx in life.
Low tide stands for a time for spiritual discoveries to be made.
Ripple stands for a continuing spiritual effect.
Riptide warns of a dangerous spiritual belief or path.
Rough (waters) stands for a turbulent spiritual path.
Seaquake warns of spiritually shaky ground; the shaking of one's beliefs.
Spindrift See spray.
Surf illustrates spiritual movement; the living essence of spirit.
Tidal wave forewarns of a spiritually overwhelming state if the current course is not altered.
Tide is representative of spiritual vacillation.
Tide pool suggests major new opportunities to experience and appreciate the ever-changing aspects of spiritual beauty.
Tide table stands for a look at possible or predictable future outcomes.
Tidewater represents fluctuating spiritual behavior; inconsistency.
Tsunami is indicative of spiritual overkill or a state of the dreamer being spiritually overwhelmed.
Undercurrent stands for the sense of a different attitude.
Undertone See undercurrent.
Undertow warns of negative spiritual beliefs that will eventually pull one under.
Whitecaps represent the positive effects of a highly active spiritual life.

Tsunami is suggestive of being overwhelmed by one's spiritual needs.

Rain & Storm

Acid rain warns of dangerous spiritual concepts.
Ball lightning illustrates a concentrated effort to gain one's attention. This is directed toward the dreamer and comes as a warning signal.
Downburst See microburst.
Downpour suggests an influx of incoming information, usually relating to spiritual or ethical aspects.
Drizzle signifies a state of gentle spirituality; a peaceful and accepting manner of spiritual intake.
Electrical storm suggests an impending conflict, possibly within oneself.
Geomagnetic storm See magnetic storm.
Heat lightning exemplifies a sudden depletion of one's energy.
Lightning signifies a connection with spiritual forces. May indicate a forthcoming moment of inspiration or an epiphany.
Magnetic storm reveals a disruptive force or aspect in one's thought process; great mental and emotional confusion.
Microburst warns of an unexpected surge of knowledge or incoming information; an inundation. May also refer to a sudden emotional outburst.
Monsoon reveals an inundation of spiritual information. One is attempting to seek out and assimilate a wide diversity of spiritual concepts too quickly.
Rain symbolizes a methodical and consistent search for spiritual truth; refreshing insights.
Raindrop reflects a singular spiritual element.
Rain gauge will reveal one's level of spirituality. May specifically refer to depth of wisdom or application rather than knowledge.
Sheet lightning represents a reflection of one's spiritual essence within oneself; a reminder of such a presence.
Shower implies a gentle touch of spiritual elements.
Soupy (atmosphere) illustrates an unclear or confusing situation.
Squall represents a temporary state of emotional or mental confusion.
Storm pertains to a troublesome time; emotional upheavals.
Storm warning sends an alarm related to a high probability for imminent turmoil in one's life.
Storm watch provides a hint that possible trouble lies in one's path. This comes as a wonderful forewarning that should perk the dreamer's awake-state awareness into proceeding more cautiously.
Tempest symbolizes a violent emotional outburst or confrontation.
Thunder emphasizes an attention-getting warning related to a specific issue the dreamer will recognize in life.
Thundercloud reveals an approaching conflict or difficult situation.
Thunderhead represents forthcoming trouble; a problem or altercation brewing.
Tropical storm warns of temporary spiritual confusion or upheaval.

Clouds

Cloud connotes thought patterns; ability to analyze and reason.
Cloudburst pertains to sudden realizations; a pouring out of new and fresh ideas.
Cloud seeding represents forced or planted ideas; coercive thought; manipulative statements.
Cloudy (atmosphere) suggests a phase of unclear issues.
Funnel cloud See hurricane; tornado.
Mackerel sky suggests distinctive thoughts. It may also refer to the recognition of issues being separate; awareness of the possibility of something altering.
Overcast (sky) suggests mental or emotional cloudiness; a lack of perceptual clarity.

Phenomena

Aura portrays one's spiritual condition.
Aurora borealis comes as a spiritual comfort or acknowledgment.
Cataclysm usually symbolizes the result of a particular event, relationship, behavior, or situation in one's awake-state life.
Corona See aura.
Geyser symbolizes one's active outpouring of spiritual and humanitarian talents.
Global warming suggests an alteration of one's general surroundings. This symbol indicates a change in one's atmosphere.
Gravity defines imagined limitations.
Greenhouse effect will indicate ramifications of one's negative behavior returning to oneself.
Midnight sun reveals the brilliance of spiritual forces or influences that are not always evident during one's darker times.
Northern lights See aurora borealis.
Total eclipse characterizes the darkness (ignorance) before the light (illumination).

Total eclipse represents the enlightenment of the individual.

see also
• Solar Concepts *p. 83*
• Snow Travel *p. 292*

Ice & Snow

Avalanche denotes spiritual smothering; an overload of conceptual data intake.
Black frost warns of a destructive freezing of one's spiritual beliefs or the cessation of spiritual application in life.
Black ice warns against spiritual concepts that are dangerous and difficult to see.
Blizzard warns of a spiritual suffocation; intake of too many spiritual concepts too quickly.
Exposure (weather hazard) warns against becoming too involved in a situation, issue, or relationship. The timing isn't right for such involvement.
Floe See ice floe.
Frost points to a temporarily chilled attitude.
Frost-free suggests open communication or emotions.
Frost line relates to an individual's point of abiding acceptance; the point where one gives up or stops being responsive.
Frosty See hoarfrost.
Hail warns of an inundation of hard spiritual issues.
Hoarfrost means spiritual beauty.
Ice signifies frozen spiritual truths, frequently voluntarily frozen by oneself.
Ice storm represents an inundation of spiritual concepts that one is not yet ready to comprehend.
Icicle relates to a state of growing spiritual frigidity that could become so heavy it falls with devastating effects. It can also indicate an intermittent thawing of a particular spiritual belief—a vacillation.
Killing frost represents an attitude, behavior, or perspective that kills one's spirituality.
Rime (coating) exemplifies a cold or hidden veneer.
Sleet refers to unrecognized spiritual elements that come one's way.
Snow connotes a strong comprehension and grasp of spiritual truths. May also indicate the serenity that can come from one's personally held spiritual beliefs.
Snowball implies a major spiritual concept. Recall who was throwing the snowball at whom.
Snowbound signifies a situation in which one's progression or advancement has been temporarily held up by a problematic spiritual issue.
Snowdrift relates to an accumulation of spiritual issues, usually refering to a confusing buildup regarding a specific aspect.
Snow fence warns of an attempt to keep spiritual elements contained and out of one's way.
Snowflake stands for the multiple shimmering aspects of spiritual truths.
Snowmelt represents a thawing of one's frozen spiritual beliefs or behavior; spiritual regeneration or refreshment.
Snowslide See avalanche.
Snowstorm warns of a condition of spiritual confusion; an inundation of spiritual issues, usually self-generated. Also see blizzard.
Thaw indicates a softening attitude, beginning to express more emotions.
Whiteout See blizzard.

Light

Rainbow stands for recognition.

Ball of light exemplifies high spiritual illumination.
Flash is an attention-getting message and may accompany powerful words of wisdom.
Iridescent comes as an attention-getting message.
Light refers to good perception; added information; understanding.
Luminescence will come in dreamscapes as an attention-getting element. Recall what was luminescent.
Phosphorescence connotes an illuminating (enlightening) element in one's life.
Predawn represents beginning insights that are yet to be clearly defined or wholly solidified; the recognition of a yet obscure theory or concept.
Rainbow comes as an acknowledgment of one's personal accomplishments or efforts.
Ray (of light) comes as a commendation or marks a moment of inspiration.
Saint Elmo's fire denotes inspiration.

Temperature

Cold means a lack of warmth. Specific surrounding dreamscape symbols will clarify this reference.
Cold front means the approach of an unresponsive attitude.
Cold wave typifies a time period of unemotional responses.
Cool signifies self-control. May indicate nonchalance.
Hot most often refers to an intense condition or emotion.
Indian summer denotes a time of peaceful respite. May also mean extra time given to get something accomplished; a reprieve.
Mild (weather) connotes amiability; easy acceptance; lacking extremes.
Sweltering represents an inability to deal well with pressure; a hot situation.
Unseasonable denotes an out-of-the-ordinary element. May indicate that one has been in expectation as to how or when something would manifest.
Warm relates to a comfortable perspective of oneself through humanitarian and spiritual acts.
Warm front applies to a forthcoming time of personal peace; a phase consisting of less stress and fewer problematic situations; a time of open and congenial responsiveness.
Zero (and all subzero temperatures) indicates a cold, frigid state of affairs. This may relate to one's attitude or a frozen situation that isn't going anywhere any time soon.

Climatic Factors & Instruments

Weather vane acts as a warning.

Atmospheric pressure reveals the amount of stress present within one's immediate surroundings; the amount of pressure one is under.
Barometer portrays the amount of pressure one is under.
Climate gives clues to the general attitude or feeling of a dream, one of the overall elements. See specific type.
Climate control means a conscious effort or desire to control one's surroundings.
Doppler radar (weather) will on rare occasions be associated with climate changes but most often refers to the mood of a situation or relationship.
Echo stands for a repeated message for the dreamer.
Extended forecast will usually be an advisement to look ahead, keep one's eyes on the greater picture for more effective planning.
Fair weather alludes to a time without any problems; a span of time when one's life appears to be going well.
Forecast (weather) applies to the utilization of one's senses to perceive developing aspects to a relationship, event, or condition.
High pressure (barometric) refers to better times ahead; clear sailing.
Horizon signifies one's individual perspective.
Ozone layer portrays rarely perceived protective elements in one's life and the ignorant unawareness of same. Corresponds with the protective manifestations created by divine elements, such as our own spirit essence of the higher self or guiding angels.
Polarity pertains to a personality that exhibits extremes.
Skyline See horizon.
Sonic barrier connotes the point at which a person surpasses goals or expectations.
Spectrum will symbolize the full extent of something; the gamut or far reaches.
Vanishing point exemplifies a perceived end or finalization, yet the horizon is endless. This reveals the fact that what is seen may not necessarily be fact but it could be simply illusion.
Weather will bring a multitude of meanings into the overall dreamscape interpretation. Refer to specific type.
Weather balloon emphasizes one's cautionary tendency to test the air of a situation or relationship.
Weathercast denotes a sense for what the mood will be regarding a particular issue or situation; foreknowledge.
Weather map comes as a forecasting of upcoming situational conditions.
Weather radar See Doppler radar.
Weather vane cautions against changing opinions or attitudes depending on whichever way the wind blows.

Times of Day

Afternoon designates a more relaxed time to accomplish something.
Cockcrow (dawn) connotes beginnings; a new day; a dawning aspect.
Current (present time) indicates the present and most often is an advisory message given for the purpose of bringing the dreamer back to the here-and-now.
Date (point in time) comes in dreams to pinpoint an important time frame for the dreamer.
Dawn indicates the light of new beginnings.
Day (time) is representative of the time of light, activity, or progression.
Daybreak See dawn.
Dusk represents a calming period; a time of inner ease.
Evening denotes a rest period; a call from one's labors.
Gloaming See twilight.
High noon emphasizes a specified time when a critical decision or situation will culminate.
Midday (time) See noon.
Midnight refers to intense spiritual energy.
Morning illustrates a new beginning; a fresh start.
Night corresponds to the preferred time to explore hidden aspects of oneself or spiritual matters.
Noon will pinpoint a preferred time designation associated with something one is planning. Each dreamer will associate various events with this time-related symbol. It may also point to a midway point of something.
Sunrise pertains to an inner welling of spiritual joy.
Twilight corresponds to the magic time, the window, when one is most receptive to higher insights.

Seasons

Autumn means a time for reflection; a time to slow one's pace.
Midwinter See winter solstice.
Season See specific type.
Spring defines a time for new beginnings and renewal.
Summer illustrates the fruitful time to give heightened attention and nurturing effort to life goals and spiritual journeys.
Summer solstice See summer.
Vernal equinox See spring.
Winter is representative of a time to contemplate spiritual beliefs.
Winter solstice reflects a time to celebrate the comfort of inner spiritual peace.

Forecasting Agencies

National Weather Service signifies those who watch over us. This symbol can even refer to one's own intuitiveness.
Weather bureau represents a personal effort to monitor one's own awareness of impending situational changes.

see also
• Charting the Earth *p. 67*
• Phobias of Weather & the Elements *p. 157*

Dust

Acid dust warns of a current atmosphere contaminated with harmful attitudes or ideas.
Dust symbolizes unnecessary aspects of one's life that intrude.
Dust devil (whirlwind) comes as a caution to the dreamer to guard against mental vacillations and confusion in one's life.
Dust speck defines an existing distraction.
Dust storm warns of an inundation of distracting elements that confuse an issue.

Fire

Brush fire refers to damaged skills.

Back burn (fire fighting) means using the identical elements of a problem to solve it. A back burn is the intentional lighting of a fire to burn back toward an approaching forest or grass fire. It meets fire with fire. As a dream symbol, it suggests that the dreamer should take a head-on approach.
Back draft symbolizes a combustible situation nearing flash point that can come back at you.
Ball of fire suggests a highly efficient and energetic individual.
Blaze See fire.
Brush fire stands for a willful neglect or destruction of one's talents; a voluntary cessation of spiritual acts.
Combustion See flash point.
Eruption forewarns of a serious confrontation or exposure of something.
Fire means extreme emotional intensity.
Fireball represents an uncontrollable, unstoppable ramification to one's explosive emotional expressions.
Firelight symbolizes emotionalism that has the ability to affect many others.
Firestorm warns of an extended state or time of intensive emotional outbursts or displays.
Flame signifies great intensity, usually connected to the emotions.
Flash point forewarns of the approaching stage where a situation or relationship will come into serious trouble.
Forest fire cautions one against the popular belief that one's inherent talents can be exhausted through overuse.
Heat connotes one's energy.
Heat wave defines a span of time during one's path walk when extra efforts are required for advancement.
Wildfire emphasizes a loss of control; something has gotten out of one's hands.

Earth

Arid is representative of a low level of spirituality in the dreamer's life.
Dirt will generally indicate hard work, or it might refer to an unclean or marred aspect. Surrounding details will clarify this intent.
Earthquake is suggestive of dangerously shaky foundations or beliefs in the dreamer's life. Could forewarn of an earth-shattering situation on the horizon.
Earthquake scale See Richter scale.
Earth-shattering (event) See earthquake.
Epicenter is representative of the source of great pressure. This will normally refer to an issue, relationship, or situation in the dreamer's life but may also reference an idea, plan, or individual.
Quake See earthquake.
Richter scale (earthquake) will usually illustrate the resulting quantitative effect of an action or event and its level or intensity.
Sandstorm stands for mental confusion.
Temblor See earthquake.
World-shaking (event) See earthquake.

Miscellaneous

Corrosion stands for the deterioration of something in one's life.
Ember emphasizes the present existence of some life left in something in the dreamer's life. This could be an attitude, perception, relationship tie, and so on.
Fairy stone represents the natural oddities of true reality that tend to continually prick at our curiosity. See also Stonehenge.
Marsh gas connotes heavy spiritual contemplation; fermenting ideas.
Methane See marsh gas.
Ring (residue) pertains to a need for routine or consistent cleansing through self-analysis.
Rust will advise of a condition of spiritual atrophy.
Slush applies to spiritual fallacies and extraneous, frivolous aspects of same.
Sunbaked suggests a natural way to finalize or develop an idea.
Timberline represents the demarcation point between being surrounded by opportunities and having to rely on one's own resources.
Virga are representative of a spiritual thirst or lack of fulfillment in the dreamer's life.
Weathered correlates with extensive experiential difficulties and the inner strength and power that has been gained.
Windblown alludes to an inundation of ideas; overwhelming concepts.
Windbreak indicates a personally devised method of protecting oneself from being overwhelmed or inundated by useless information or gossip-type talk.

Chapter 5

Geography & Landscapes

These landscapes come in all forms to depict an overall condition of a current life phase. They reveal a real-time state of affairs.

Geographical Terms

Bank (built up) implies a situation, concept, or relationship that requires that additional supportive aspects be applied.
Continental divide advises of a major division in one's life. This may be a serious disagreement in a relationship, or it may relate to a divisive element within oneself.
Continental drift suggests the possibility of a firm decision, perspective, or attitude shifting position.
Copse stands for one's personally inherent attributes that serve to benefit others.
Countryside stands for the beautiful aspects of innocence and simplicity; unsophisticated attitudes; an honest and down-home personality and perspective.
Ecohazard stands for an attitude, idea, perception that presents a potentially disruptive element for one's basic foundational beliefs or qualities.
Fallow (field) symbolizes an unproductive condition or state.
Farmland represents the nourishment of one's natural talents and inherent goodness. Recall if the farmland was fallow or fertile. What was growing on it?
Field suggests openness; opportunities.
Frontier characterizes a new and exciting path that holds the promise of multiple discovery opportunities.
Furrow See groove; trench.
Greenbelt pertains to preservation; realizing something's worth.

Landslide denotes a caution against a moral lapse.

Groove is representative of an old routine; old tendencies or methods.
Ground denotes a generally defined beginning point, yet it's really what is underneath (unseen) that must be discovered.
Ground cover defines prolific spiritual or humanitarian qualities that are fruitfully used.
Grove pertains to the need to pause and contemplate.
Impassable reveals a need to retrace one's steps. This will refer to a specific situation in the dreamer's life that she or he will readily identify with.
Isthmus See land bridge.
Jungle warns of a confused spiritual state. Could indicate schizophrenia.
Land bridge signifies a path traveled with spirituality being to one's right and left; one who wants one's spiritual beliefs to guide the way.
Landlocked denotes a self-generated condition preventing access to higher concepts or advanced knowledge.
Landslide advises of a backsliding condition.
Lowland denotes a relatively level path or phase of one's development.
Lushness denotes fertile ground to work from; multiple opportunities.
Mainland will usually represent a grounded state; one's home base.
Plantation signifies the quality and quantity of one's talents. Recall who was working the plantation. What was planted? What was the condition of the growing vegetation?
Pollution characterizes the negative elements that adversely affect one's quality of life or advancement. The key here is to recall if there was a specific individual causing such affectations. Was it someone you know? Was it yourself? Do you need to change some of your ways? Pollution can also be verbally disseminated.
Rugged (terrain) represents a life path that contains difficulties to either accept or overcome.
Rural refers to a more open perspective; less affected.
Trench denotes perseverance and personal faith in oneself.
Tropics suggest stifling spiritual beliefs.
Verdant (setting) reflects an abundance of natural talents and bounties that surround one.

Scenery

Easement (scenic) points to a need to have a place of calming respite in one's life; a place or time reserved for rest and rejuvenation.
Landscape in dreams is a major symbol in itself. It sets the scene and often the mood as well. Always recall what the landscape was.
Panorama (view) implies a need to obtain a wider perspective of something in one's life.
Scenery plays a major roll in dream interpretation, for the scene of the dreamscape will always reveal important elements that are essential. Refer to specific scenic types and mood settings.
Vista is representative of a wide view; a panoramic perspective.

see also
• On the Road *p. 294*
• World Heritage Sites *p. 374*

Charting the Earth

Acre symbolizes the extent of one's spiritual aspects.
Atlas indicates expanded world knowledge is required. More information is needed. May also reveal that a situation in the dreamer's life carries the potential to have far-reaching ramifications.
Cardinal point (one of the four directions) indicates one's directional priority. See specific direction.
Compass connotes direction. This usually points to a path different from the one the dreamer is walking or believes is right for her or him.
Contour map reveals the ups and downs of an intended path. Takes the lay of the land into consideration.
Coordinates (map) will represent a goal. Often points out that a substitute will not suffice in this case.
Dateline pertains to time or place of origination; the source of something.
East marks beginnings.
Equator denotes a central point; basic premise.
Latitude represents some form of freedom; no limitations.
Longitude denotes a measure of acceptance or patience.
Magnetic north emphasizes the greatest intensity of something; strongest draw, force, or quality.
North denotes a direction that may need to be taken. North indicates a higher position.
North Pole comes as a directional advisement to obtain balance. North indicates higher conceptual aspects to focus on.
Prime meridian symbolizes a starting point or point of reference.
Relief map connotes a need to gain a sharper perspective of one's position in relation to purpose.
South connotes a lower level or a going back-to-basics message.
South Pole pertains to basic elements of an issue or concept that are difficult to discover.
Topographical map stands for a good idea of how the land lays to do with an intended path.
West connotes a near-completed goal.

Manmade Landscapes

Cairn illustrates markers along life's path. This serves as a guiding aspect.
Labyrinth calls for patience and acceptance while one walks a complex path for a time.
Maze may illustrate a type of mental or emotional confusion, but it most often corresponds with the unnecessarily complex manner one is going about in a life path.
Reservoir is representative of the quality of one's spiritual aspects, specifically one's natural talents. What condition was the reservoir in? Was the water polluted or clean? Did it have a color to it?

Outstanding Landscapes

Ayers Rock may point to a spiritually exceptional person.

Adirondack Mountains mean a call back to nature, to the simple, basic things.
Amazon (jungle) symbolizes a confused or convoluted path.
Amazon (river) warns of a spiritual path fraught with dangers.
Appalachian trail refers to a concerted effort to follow the natural way; simplicity.
Ayers Rock alludes to the spiritually obvious; an aspect or even an individual who spiritually "stands out" in respect to her or his moral or ethical behavior.
Black Forest symbolizes an attitude of mystery behind spiritual gifts.
Chaco Canyon portrays ancient wisdom; hidden human heritage.
Denali (mountain) represents strength and power of the spirit.
Easter Island typifies those solid, worldly aspects that stand to point the way to reality.
Everglades are representative of spiritual sluggishness; mired or tangled spiritual aspects in one's life.
Galapagos Islands portray perseverance. They may also refer to a long-lasting condition or situation.
Great Lakes emphasizes a surround of multiple spiritual reserves.
Great Salt Lake exemplifies an unexpected event.
Landmark comes as a personal message for each dreamer. Recall what the landmark was. What state? Did it represent a specific historical site or time period? Did it pertain to a specific historical individual? In what condition was it?
Mount Everest represents the presence of a challenge in one's life.
Nile (river) pertains to one's spiritual life.
Rain forest constitutes spiritual bounties.

Hills & Mountains

Mountain range indicates a major, often self-imposed, hurdle to surmount.

Alpine See mountain.
Bluff (promontory) connotes a front associated with a bluffing situation or aspect.
Cliff signifies a situation that is on the edge in life; living on the edge.
Crest See ridge.
Drop-off (clifflike) advises of an abrupt decline or decrease in something. Warns one to move slowly and watch footing.
Foothill points out a life aspect that presents a slight upward climb; a time when more energies are needed for advancement.
Hill stands for a time when extra efforts are needed.
Hillside represents continued efforts.
Hilltop corresponds with reaching a goal; a place of accomplishment.
Hogback indicates a need to do some backtracking to capture missed lessons or incomplete aspects that were overlooked or left behind.
Knoll indicates high ground and would suggest an upcoming need for more personal efforts to be expended in one's life.
Mesa is a representation of high spiritual truths.
Montane (zone) See mountain.
Mound (earth) exemplifies hidden aspects that one hasn't perceived.
Mountain refers to a major obstacle to overcome in life.
Mountain range relates to a major block one needs to overcome and conquer, this oftentimes being a self-generated restriction.
Mountainside pertains to an insight into what one must encounter and overcome in the immediate future.
Mountaintop See summit.
Pass (mountain) relates to a way through a difficulty.
Saw-toothed mountains denote a difficult phase of travel. May refer directly to one's intended journey.
Scree refers to a difficult path.
Sierra See saw-toothed mountains.
Talus constitutes fragmentation; a breakup into multiple elements.
Uphill indicates a phase when extra energy will be needed in order to make advancements.

Highs & Lows

Acme See summit.
Apex See summit.
Chasm illustrates perceived difficulties; differences of opinion.
Depression (low point in path) indicates a low point or an aspect that has sunk below the normal level.
Escarpment signifies a resulting condition or situation caused by a lack of foresight or planning.
High country illustrates a path that presents deeper conceptual ideas for one to learn from.
High ground is representative of a perception or feeling of superiority.
Hump (in road) indicates a point in one's path where difficulties may arise and extra efforts will be required.
Incline See slope.
Plateau will generally mark a time to pause and level off during one's journey through life.
Ridge relates to a major decision; a potential turning point.
Sheer (steep) emphasizes caution in respect to there being no room for error. Also see steep (vertical).
Slippery slope warns of a worsening situation or type of behavior.
Slope may represent a slightly more difficult path forthcoming or it may stand for a slanted perspective or path, depending on the related details of the dream.
Steep (vertical) will most often stand for a great depth, rich in meaning or philosophical content. This symbol may also represent a difficult or exacting aspect.
Summit stands for high points in one's life or spiritual journey.
Sunken represents a lowering direction that usually applies to an attempt to reach basic elements or get in touch with oneself by being grounded.
Tableland See plateau.
Underground symbolizes the need for an individual to keep certain elements private. This may also advise the dreamer to get out in the open and contribute one's talents. The surrounding dreamscape details will clarify this.

Marshes, Bogs & Swamps

Bog illustrates something that bogs one down, keeps one from going forward in an unfettered manner.
Dismal swamp comes to the dreamer as an important warning of a mental or emotional state of self-generated hopelessness.
Marsh constitutes spiritually saturated ground one is walking on.
Morass refers to an overwhelming aspect in one's life.
Muskeg See bog.
Peat bog See bog.
Quagmire symbolizes a dilemma; a mired situation.
Swamp constitutes a weak or confused spiritual foundation.
Wetland stands for the richness of spiritual bounties or inherent natural gifts; a wealth of both.

see also
• Camping *p. 207*
• Outerwear *p. 402*

Mud

Mud may represent perceptual distortion, or it may indicate a healing factor in one's life. Recall the surrounding dream details for further clarity.
Mudflow is representative of an inundation of confusing aspects that have somehow found their way into one's everyday life.
Mud slide See mudflow.

Cracks to Canyons

Abyss warns of a path to nowhere. May refer to a loss of will or purpose.
Canyon symbolizes the more troublesome times of one's life walk; the deeper, more shadowed paths one needs to move through.
Channel (trench) pertains to a directed flow or worn path; a direction traveled by many in the past.
Crack (fissure) is representative of an aspect in one's life that has an imperfection. It may in fact refer to one's belief system, personal perspectives, or even one's outward presentation.
Crevice applies to unexpected situations that make one's life path more difficult.
Fissure warns of a crack or deep separation beginning to form within a specific aspect in one's life. Surrounding details will serve to clarify this symbol.
Fjord defines the narrow and often dangerous rites of passage one experiences through one's spiritual life.
Gap may indicate an opening opportunity, or it may refer to a missing aspect in one's life.
Gorge (ravine) denotes the narrow and oftentimes rocky stretches of one's unique path.
Grand Canyon exemplifies solid evidence; time-tested, visible effects.
Hollow (shallow ravine) See valley.
Vale See valley.
Valley won't indicate a low point in life, rather it symbolizes a place (or time) of respite.

Gorge represents the difficult confines of life's journey.

Ice & Snow

Berg See iceberg.
Glacier is representative of frozen spirituality. It acts as a call to thaw and to use one's talents.
Iceberg applies to spiritual aspects looming on the horizon of the dreamer's life. This is an attention-getting message.
Ice cap relates to a hard spiritual shell one has created to surround oneself; a spiritual hardness that prevents the open giving of one's gifts or talents.
Ice floe represents intermittent periods of spiritual frigidity; selective spiritual expressiveness.
Permafrost is indicative of a frigid personality; one with a cold and unsupportive exterior.
Polar cap alludes to spiritual frigidity; lack of interest in spiritual matters.
Polar regions portray a cold and frozen spiritual attitude; one that isn't exercised or shared.
Snowcap portrays a spiritual priority.
Snow line illustrates a person's attempt to separate spiritual aspects from daily secular elements. This may indicate the hiding of one's beliefs.
Snowscape signifies the beauty of spiritual serenity.

Rocks

Outcropping is an attention-getting dream symbol. This attempts to draw the dreamer's attention to something important in his or her waking life.
Precipice comes to the dreamer to reveal a decision-making moment.
River rocks signify a spiritual roundedness to one's life.
Rock bottom emphasizes a time to pick oneself up and go forward by looking to the sun; nowhere to go but up.
Rock slide applies to an inundation of temporary difficulties.

Caves & Holes

Cave is representative of natural defenses. It refers to inherent knowledge.
Cavern alludes to nature's hidden aspects of the extended realities.
Chuckhole See pothole.
Grotto reveals a need to take spiritual respite time.
Hole usually refers to an opening; an opportunity. Rarely will it represent a defect. Surrounding dreamscape details will clarify which interpretation was meant for the dreamer.
Pit (deep hole) constitutes a deeply troubling or difficult situation.
Pothole is representative of a negative element in one's life course that usually can be avoided; a temporary irritation.
Tar pit comes to the dreamer as a warning of a pitfall situation about to enter his or her life.

Wastelands & Wilderness

Desert alludes to falling back on one's inner resources.

Backcountry alludes to simplicity. May also come as a sign pointing out the importance of something relevant in one's life that isn't readily visible or obvious.
Badland pertains to places one should not be. This may refer to geography, life situations, belief systems, or personal relationships.
Boondocks represent spiritual remoteness; spiritual apathy.
Chaparral refers to an aspect that's capable of bringing about an emotional healing.
Desert (hot, sandy region) connotes a life stage or condition whereby one needs a reserve of strength and perseverance.
Deserted (devoid of human habitation) stands for a call for self-reliance and ingenuity.
Dust bowl warns of an extremely unproductive stage in one's life, lacking any nutrient quality.
Hinterland See backcountry.
Leach field stands for disbursement of residual elements.
Moor (landscape) means a stage in one's life where one allows oneself to become bogged down by spiritual concepts that are too heavy or deep to currently comprehend.
Scrub (terrain) alludes to an inactive stage of one's life path.
Tundra typifies spiritual aspects yet to be discovered.
Wasteland signifies a barren or unproductive phase in one's life.
Wilderness connotes an unaffected element, untouched and undisturbed, thereby existing in its original and pure state.
Wildwood See wilderness.

Volcanoes

Caldera represents a formerly hot issue or situation and the possibility of it reactivating in the future.
Crater See caldera.
Volcanic explosivity index stands for a gauge of one's withheld emotional pressure and suggests a need to seek harmless methods of releasing it.
Volcano may forewarn of an actual event, yet this symbol most often indicates a serious confrontation or emotional explosions.

Meadows, Plains & Flatlands

Alkali flats See salt flats.
Bottomland represents a fertile element.
Flat (level ground) is representative of a span of obstacle-free pathway.
Flatland See flat (level ground).
Floodplain warns of potentially dangerous ground. This usually refers to one's thought process or a specific situation.
Great Plains allude to a span of time when one journeys through an unproductive period; a time of neutrality lacking advancement.
Lea See meadow.
Level (ground) corresponds with a time frame when one's life path is relatively smooth.
Meadow represents inner tranquility.

Salt marsh is spiritual domination.

Salt flats signify a phase in one's life when situations, relationships, or issues leave one parched for refreshing elements.
Salt marsh emphasizes an inundation of spiritual elements. In this sense, it may infer a frequency of overwhelming spiritual aspects.

Grasslands

Grassland See prairie; savannah.
Pasture represents one's voluntary usefulness in life. Was someone out in the pasture? Who was in the dream pasture? What were they doing? What condition was the pasture in? Was it full of flowers or weeds? Was it completely barren?
Plains See prairie.
Prairie reflects a clear path ahead.
Range See prairie.
Savannah represents an exposure to personally sensitive concepts or ideas. In addition, it may refer to one having a clear view of the state of one's life or what lies ahead.

see also
• Grasses & Reeds *p. 51*
• Water *p. 59*

Waterscapes

Arroyo denotes dangerous probabilities that are currently present along one's path; the dips and low points that carry a high probability for trouble or difficulties.

Artesian well signifies free-flowing spirituality; spiritual behavior that is routinely given or expressed.

Babbling (brook) reveals incoherent or convoluted spiritual beliefs.

Bank (land) See riverbank.

Bayou portrays a spiritual situation where one has become complacent or sluggish in advancing or has willingly allowed aspects to stagnate.

Brook See stream.

Cascade See waterfall.

Cataract See waterfall.

Confluence stands for the act of joining or coming together. This usually indicates a need for an agreement to take place.

Creek See stream.

Culvert denotes the direction and manner in which one utilizes personal spiritual gifts.

Drop-off (lake/river bottom) pertains to a spiritual pitfall.

Dry bed (creek/lake) indicates a spiritual belief that has lost its viability. May reveal one's loss of spiritual interest.

Fountainhead points to something's source. This can be very revealing for the dreamer.

Freshwater will usually symbolize a viable spiritual element.

Frozen lake warns of spiritual aspects not being used.

Gulch stands for a temporary situation when extra efforts are required.

Gully See gulch.

Headwaters stand for a spiritual source.

Hot spring warns of an underlying anger in respect of a spiritual issue.

Lagoon represents spiritual tranquility.

Lake suggests spiritual aspects in one's life.

Lake bed indicates spiritual foundations; basic concepts.

Lakefront (land) emphasizes a need to be close to one's spiritual beliefs, taking daily comfort in them.

Levee connotes the purposeful directing of one's spiritual path.

Maelstrom warns of confusion; an inability to focus thoughts or single out ideas.

Meander (stream) means an aimless spiritual path.

Midstream cautions not to stop efforts before something has been accomplished.

Millpond defines spiritual benefits; an abundance of spiritual gifts.

Millstream represents a motivating factor; a source of energy.

Oasis pertains to rejuvenating respite phases.

Old Faithful (geyser) denotes trust and dependability.

Oxbow (stream configuration) indicates a meandering spiritual path that is destined to bring enlightenment.

Pond symbolizes a spiritual source in the midst of daily life. Recall the pond's condition and health to determine if this source is a positive or negative one.

River corresponds with the spiritual elements running through one's life. Recall its rate of flow, quality, and color.

Riverbank symbolizes a close proximity to a spiritual search, aspect, or awakening.

Riverbed See lake bed.

Riverfront See lakefront.

Rivulet refers to a new spiritual idea or insight.

Seasonal creek/stream points to a part-time spirituality; a tendency to use spiritual behavior discriminately.

Spring stands for a well of spirituality within oneself.

Thermal spring See hot spring.

Upriver reveals a more difficult path; progression that goes against the natural flow.

Waterfall represents a flow of spiritual energy.

Waterfront See lakefront.

Water hole infers a source of spiritual nourishment.

Watershed exemplifies a diverted spiritual course; the source of one's spiritual belief system.

Water table implies a spiritual grounding.

Whirlpool exposes a spiritual entanglement that could ultimately pull one down.

White water warns of highly dangerous spiritual paths that could harm those not well prepared to travel on them.

Waterfall symbolizes the outpouring of spiritual strength.

Chapter 6

Gems & Geology

These natural beauties are associated with an individual's personality characteristics and behavioral responses. They frequently present themselves for the purpose of uncovering traits one is in denial of or needs to put into practice.

Crystalline & Translucent Stones

Alexandrite stands for mood fluctuations. This symbol will advise of a need to stabilize emotions.
Calcite stands for misunderstandings. Calls for situational clarity.
Celestite points to fragility. It may indicate a need for one to reinforce one's emotional sensitivity.
Cerussite stands for one who is easily manipulated.
Chrysoberyl points to intellectual clarity.
Fluorite provides protective forces against external negativity; defenses against life irritations.
Idocrase symbolizes mental confusion. It may refer specifically to indistinct thoughts.
Moonstone empowers spiritual talents. Strengthens abilities.
Morganite points to indecision and calls for a need for clarity of thought and quicker decision making.
Quartz correlates to spiritual purity of truths. Recall if the dream quartz had color, then incorporate that symbol into the complete meaning.
Rose quartz represents recognized and cherished spiritual gifts. May refer to new inspirations or deep affections.
Smoky quartz indicates a clouded perception.
Wulfenite (mineral) represents an emotionally calming element in one's life that serves to soothe erratic aura activity.

Fossils

Ammonite reflects an ability for intricate thought; high intelligence and great wisdom.
Fairy stone represents the natural oddities of true reality that spark one's curiosity. See also Stonehenge.
Fossil relates to preserved, immutable truths; validations.
Living fossil represents an enduring element.
Petrified forest will correspond with one's inherent natural talents that have enduring qualities yet are not used.

Ammonite represents great acumen.

Gemstone Shapes

Baguette depicts a supporting aspect in one's life—a belief, individual, or situation.
Facet stands for one of the many concurrently existing aspects of self.
Intaglio validates humankind's kinship with intelligent life.
Triangle refers to the divine essence—often considered to have three aspects.
Trilliant See triangle.

Gem Terminology

Birthstone depicts a vibrationally aligned set of aspects that will best serve an individual.
Crystals (natural) relate to the clarity and depth of one's personal spiritual attunement.
Gemstone alludes to personality characteristics and behavioral responses. See specific gem type.
Geode emphasizes the inherent beauty of the living spirit within everyone.
Jewel See gemstone, specific type.
Precious stone See gemstone, specific type.

Gemstones

Black diamond stands for ill-use of material wealth.
Diamond exemplifies perfection. Was the dream diamond truly perfect? Did it have color instead of being perfectly white and clear?
Emerald (gemstone/color) signifies the presence and quality of one's specialized talent to heal others.
Ruby (gemstone/color) refers to life force; motivational energy and fortitude.
Sapphire depicts a fragile spiritual nature.
Star sapphire symbolizes spiritual truths.

Semiprecious Stones

Amethyst means spiritual inner beauty that shines forth.
Aquamarine pertains to healing benefits of spiritual truths.
Beryl alludes to pure intentions; true life offerings that come our way.
Black opal is associated with the more mysterious elements of reality; the unknowns awaiting discovery.
Cubic zirconia denotes a lack of genuineness; an attempt at grandeur through imitation; misrepresentation.
Garnet (gemstone/color) refers to intense emotions. (Garnet can be a variety of colors; this interpretation corresponds to the more commonly known color of deep, dark red).
Marcasite refers to multiple spiritual elements and comes in dreamscapes to enhance recognition of the many spiritual opportunities one has to utilize goodness.
Opal (gemstone/color) is representative of truths from many sources.
Peridot (gemstone/color) denotes a sunny disposition that serves as an uplifting and healing force for others.
Rhinestone reflects an effective alternative to a more costly method or course.
Tanzanite represents deep spiritual wisdom and insight.
Topaz is representative of optimism.
Turquoise defines spiritual health and well-being.
Zircon (natural) constitutes a grounded and centered individual.

see also
• Metals *p. 283*
• Jewelry *p. 411*

Metals

Aluminum signifies the need for reflection.
Antimony stands for a multifaceted aspect.
Bismuth symbolizes a multifaceted element.
Black Hills gold stands for sacred spiritual wealth.
Black Hills gold (mined) refers to a defilement of sacred spiritual wealth.
Cadmium reflects an additional aspect to something, possibly an external facade of some type.
Cobalt (blue) signifies behavior based on a rich spiritual base.
Cobalt (green) suggests materialism; fiscal wealth.
Copper (metal) denotes a choice aspect for one to utilize for the purpose of communicating something.
Fool's gold warns against jumping to conclusions; not thinking things out; lacking appropriate knowledge; needing discernment.
Gold means financial aspects; facets of one's physical life.

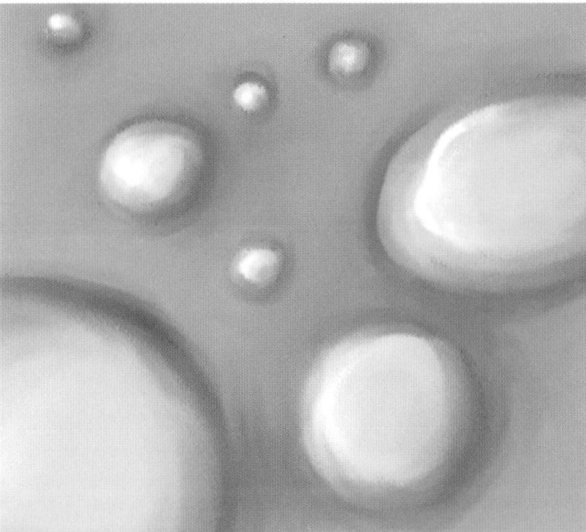

Mercury reflects an unstable state of affairs in one's life.

Gold dust usually refers to material benefits gained from one's giving behavior.
Iron (metal) signifies strength.
Lead (metal) illustrates a potential negative aspect in one's life that could cause harmful effects.
Magnesium denotes a clarified perspective. It may also refer to enlightenment.
Mercury (element) implies a fluctuating situation; vacillation.
Nickel (metal) implies a replacement method or means to use in place of a formerly planned approach.
Pewter signifies a simple form of basic spiritual value; a warm and personal embracing quality.
Placer (gold) represents a life aspect that has a trace amount of value.
Platinum (metal) represents a life aspect that possesses multiple opportunities.
Plutonium refers to a life element with a highly dangerous potential.
Pyrite (iron) See fool's gold.
Quicksilver See mercury (element).
Silver (color/metal) stands for the spiritual elements that exist for everyone. The key is to recall what form the dream silver took and what was being done with it by whom.
Sulfur means a disagreeable element in one's life.
Tin most often connotes an inferior element.
Titanium symbolizes strength and resistance to corruption.
Uranium warns of a contaminating aspect in one's life.
Zinc portrays a galvanized issue; a protective or defensive measure.

Opaque Stones

Amazonite comes to represent a healing element in one's life.
Amber connotes resiliency and loyalty. May also denote preservation, which would mean that something in one's life needs to be treasured or always remembered.
Andalusite means depression. It stands for a healing aspect that improves perspectives and raises one's general outlook.
Aventurine stands for stubbornness. This symbol is calling for a better attitude of acceptance.
Azurite denotes high spiritual capabilities.
Barite represents longevity. This symbol denotes intensified attitudes.
Carnelian refers to false expressions; personality affectations.
Feldspar stands for communications; a need to transmit ideas better.
Fire agate stands for confusion.
Goldstone See aventurine.
Hematite is representative of the power and strength of one's life force.
Jade alludes to healing qualities or talents; protective aspects.
Jet (gemstone/color) alludes to a deep mystery; high concepts; pessimism.
Lapis lazuli connotes deep interest or research into high spiritual concepts.
Lazulite stands for spiritual awareness.
Nephrite refers to a healing aspect in life that sustains self-healing capabilities.
Obsidian is representative of the beauty of the more esoteric spiritual concepts and gifts and the protection of them. Denotes strengthened empowerment.
Sinhalite refers to depression and calls for one to strive for a brighter outlook.
Sodalite denotes spiritual wisdom and comprehension.
Staurolite represents intellectual complexity.
Tourmaline infers a healing element in one's life.
Watermelon tourmaline points to optimism and its healing benefits.

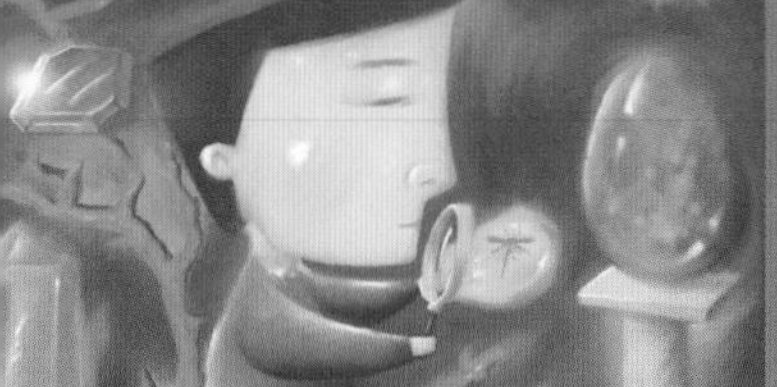

Rocks & Landscape

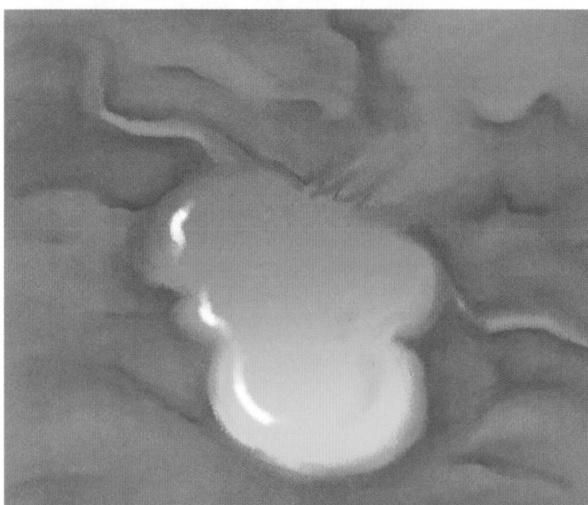

Lava implies the need to release pent-up emotions to improve self-assurance.

Basalt applies to an individual who has become hardened after a highly emotional life stage; verging on apathetic. Also may refer to the need to avoid diversionary side roads while traveling one's path.
Batholith applies to wisdom of the ancients.
Bedrock stands for strong and enduring foundations.
Black Hills means sacred aspects that need protection and reverence.
Boulder represents major problematic aspects in one's life.
Brimstone relates to a passionately demonstrative attitude connected to a specific cause or issue.
Carlsbad Caverns depict the inherent beauty of natural talents and abilities when freely shared with others.
Clay portrays a necessity to be resilient as one walks life's path.
Dry hole indicates a situation or personal attempt that came up empty. May refer to an idea that's not viable.
Erosion comes as a caution of a need to give more supportive efforts to some aspect in one's life; something being worn away. This could point to trust, perseverance, love, and so on.
Fault line advises of negatives generated by self; one's own faults.
Firestone denotes a life aspect that can emotionally motivate one.
Flint signifies a quick response or reaction.
Granite depicts a solid foundation.
Granule illustrates a fragment of a whole; a part of something greater.
Lava warns of a personal state of inner turmoil before self-confidence is gained. This symbol calls for a release of these withheld emotions or attitudes so that they can be replaced with inner strength.
Limestone corresponds with a foundation type of belief or attitude.
Lode symbolizes a bountiful aspect or supply.
Lodestone indicates a strong attraction; a compelling force or drive.
Magma comes to the dreamer as a warning of internalized negative attitudes or emotions. These need to be released.
Marble (stone) refers to an enduring or lasting effort or aspect.
Mica relates to the shiny bits and pieces of joyful moments people experience while making their life journey.
Molten implies an embroiled emotion or situation; one needing cooling.
Monolith signifies a particular facet of one's life that is perceived as being a great goal or burden.
Moraine relates to a stage in one's life when a seeming excess of burdens is presented.
Moss rock portrays determination and fortitude.
Pebble implies an element of diversity.
Pipestone emphasizes the sacred manner in which a spiritual aspect is held within oneself or performed.
Plate tectonics emphasize the fact that an action will cause a reaction; the importance of routinely attending to one's stress level.
Pumice stone suggests that something in one's life needs to be smoothed out.
Quarry (pit) is representative of a mother lode of knowledge or information; a rich source.
Rock refers to the hard elements or phases in life. May signify loyalty or steadfastness, depending on the surrounding dreamscape elements.
Sandstone corresponds with a weak foundation; lacking strong basics.
Shake (shingle) is representative of flammable thoughts; ideas capable of inciting others.
Shale pertains to loose footing; a current state of instability.
Sinkhole indicates the pitfalls and dangerous regions of one's life path.
Slate (rock) is representative of a defensive or protective hardness to one's personality.
Stone usually refers to life's smaller irritations.
Touchstone connotes excellence.

Water

Hot spring warns of an underlying anger in respect to a spiritual issue.
Spring (water) stands for a well of spirituality within oneself.
Washout See erosion.
Well relates directly to a spiritual source. May refer to spiritual resources. Recall if the well was full or empty. Was it contaminated? What grew around it?
Wellhead refers to a marker for a spiritual source.
Wellspring signifies an unending source. It may refer to a fountainhead.

see also
• Gas Power p. 281
• Fuel & Emissions p. 294

Nonmetallic Substances

Anthracite stands for a motivational aspect; an inner drive not readily perceived by others; encouragement.

Asbestos connotes the duality of one's personal choice of insulating method. This particular one, of course, can be self-destructive.

Ash signifies a de-emphasis of the physical aspects in deference to the higher spiritual ones. May also indicate a complete riddance of something from one's life.

Borax denotes a lack of quality.

Carbon denotes the harmful effects of negative actions.

Charcoal represents positive outcomes from negative aspects; the event of good effects generated from bad happenings.

Cinder See ash.

Gypsum represents a gentle faith; security with one's beliefs.

Hydrogen peroxide is a symbol that contains duality, yet it most frequently refers to a healing aspect in one's life.

Iodine indicates that which will soothe and heal. Surrounding dreamscape details will clarify this.

Lead (graphite) See pencil.

Nitroglycerin emphasizes the existence of a highly explosive personality, situation, relationship, or belief system.

Plaster of paris represents a method of imitation or the re-creation of something.

Plastic illustrates changeability; lack of high quality.

Polyurethane (varnish) illustrates an attempt or desire to preserve a successful conclusion or finish to an accomplishment.

Quicklime refers to a highly destructive element in one's life.

Rock salt implies a personal effort to break through certain spiritual concepts or searches.

Silicone represents a multifaceted and versatile tool or opportunity.

Gaseous Substances

Carbon monoxide comes as a warning of a dangerous situation, or relationship that appears innocent; danger from an unexpected and unsuspected source.

Chlorine advises of a need to clean or purify specific aspects in one's life.

Cyanide stands for the dangerous ramifications of making financial gain a priority.

Fluoride relates to misconceptions; a tight-fisted grip on old false ideas.

Natural gas alludes to potentially explosive factors in one's life. This is a symbol pointing to something that carries the potential for great negatives in spite of its useful benefits.

Propane exemplifies a life aspect containing the positive/negative duality aspect.

Radon correlates with forces or elements in daily life that are hidden destroyers.

Swamp gas refers to spiritual gas signifying conceptual waste.

Oil & Oily Substances

Black gold See oil field.

Coal oil See kerosene.

Coal tar illustrates that which one utilizes for the purpose of insulating oneself from hurtful elements.

Crude oil is representative of an unrefined and often rude personality.

Fluorocarbons are primarily representative of life aspects that are dangerous.

Kerosene denotes one's ability to energize or motivate others in certain areas of life. What other factors are in the dream that might explain the areas of influence indicated?

Mineral oil connotes a soothing aspect; a factor that eases rough phases in life.

Naphtha connotes a versatile factor.

Offshore drilling relates to efforts given in search of deeper spiritual meaning.

Oil means a lack of abrasiveness or friction. It also means that which soothes and eases; an element essential to keeping things going smoothly.

Oil field indicates a poor choice of opportunities, one that carries multiple negative side effects.

Oil slick warns of a need to proceed cautiously, with high awareness.

Oil spill points to dangerous behavior that suffocates one's spirituality.

Oil well is a great opportunity that must be carefully planned out in order to optimize its potential for good.

Paraffin signifies a need to preserve or seal something. The dreamer will make the associative connection.

Petroleum relates to an element in one's life that has multiple aspects and diverse uses. The dreamer will usually make this association.

Petroleum jelly signifies a life element that has the potential for soothing or easing a rough or difficult situation in one's life.

Oil spill signifies acting in a manner that smothers one's life force.

Soils

Acid soil represents a hardness to one's basic, foundational attitudes and behavior.
Alluvial soil stands for an unstable foundation brought by skewed spiritual concepts.
Gravel is representative of loose footing. It is suggestive of a need to pay attention to one's path walk.
Humus stands for a fertile condition or situation.
Quicksand signifies a declining situation from which one needs to extract oneself as soon as possible.
Sand suggests a shifting perspective or attitude.
Sediment represents that which remains or is leftover; nonessential elements.
Silt relates to spiritual elements that are not germane to one's personal advancement or development.
Sludge refers to waste in one's life. May depict elements that are extraneous or useless.
Sod typifies an attempt to recover lost ground.
Soil corresponds with a person's foundation; ground to build on or progress along.
Topsoil is representative of surface issues, emotions, or appearances.

Veined or Banded Stones

Agate means multiple talents.
Alabaster refers to a hard coldness in attitude. May refer to a perspective generated from an aloof attitude. Can indicate a stubborn and unyielding attitude.
Cat's-eye symbolizes a watcher in one's midst.
Jasper denotes a life aspect that has the capability of drawing negativity from the body.
Malachite typifies healing qualities or forces.
Marble (stone) refers to a lasting effort or aspect; enduring.
Onyx defines an attraction to high wisdom. Often signifies compassion and emotional sensitivity.
Rhyolite is representative of protective qualities. It may refer to enduring traits.
Serpentine stands for one's duality of character and suggests a need for greater balance to be maintained between the extremes.
Soapstone connotes the creativity that comes after acceptance has been gained.
Tigereye connotes awareness. It may signify acute perception.

Minerals

Calcium symbolizes those aspects in life that serve to strengthen us. A caution is indicated for dream symbols that portray an excess of calcium.
Lime See quicklime.
Mineral See specific type.
Quicklime is a destructive element in one's life.
Vein reveals the presence of a beneficial aspect in one's life.

Mining

Mine denotes truths that one can find out for oneself.

Borehole alludes to a testing aspect in one's life that should be followed through with.
Coal portrays deep-seated negativity; undesirable attitudes; behavior covering the beauty of one's spirit within.
Coal mine advises one to dig down and bring out negative attitudes for the purpose of neutralizing them.
Core signifies a center point; beginnings; a most emotionally sensitive or vulnerable aspect; one's most inner feelings. May also point to the bottom line cause or source.
Core sample refers to an attempt to discover the cause of something.
Diamond mine depicts a source of wealth, usually not in reference to monetary aspects.
Glory hole (mining) represents a source of wealth. See mother lode.
Goldfield indicates an opportunity.
Gold mine denotes a great material benefit; a highly beneficial source.
Mine (earth) represents truths and natural talents that exist for one's self-discovery.
Mine shaft represents in-depth research; digging down further and further for the more hidden aspects of something.
Mother lode stands for the most bountiful source of something.
Natural resources represent inherent characteristics and talents; personal natural gifts.
Nugget applies to a small treasure found in one's life; a valuable piece of information.
Salt mine represents a source for gaining fortitude and grounded thought.
Shaft See mine shaft.
Sill (geologic) suggests an out-of-character response, or it may indicate a need to diverge from one's normal course.
Stamp mill represents intellectual deduction; extracting all informational elements from a singular aspect.
Strip mine implies a negative aspect that distorts the quality or inherent integrity of something.

Chapter 7

Space & Time

The often vivid elements of space and time represent unlimited potential. They indicate the need to recognize possibilities that have yet to be considered.

Space Travel

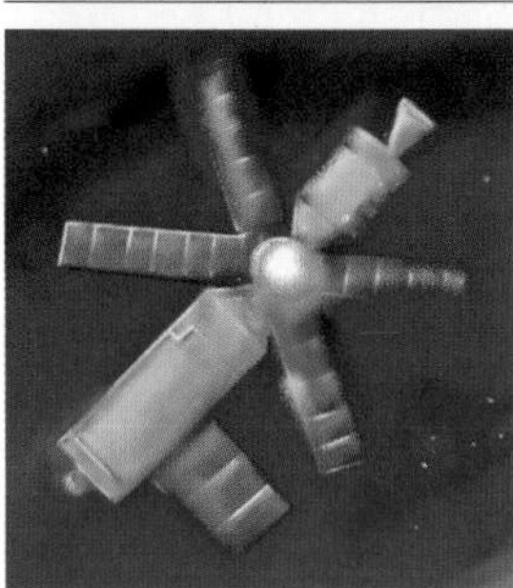

Space station shows options in life.

Blue streak is representative of one's spiritual swiftness; some spiritual aspect that has come to you as a bolt of lightning. It can also mean a quick spiritual awakening and response; a possible epiphany.
Capsule (space) represents an exploration of the unknown with the intention of not being touched by it; a reserved interest.
Downlink symbolizes inspiration; insights received from one's higher self or from a universal consciousness.
Launchpad connotes a need to get something off the ground; put something into action.
Launch window stands for a critical span of time or phase when a particular behavior or beginning moves can be made.
Mission control represents one's higher self, one's conscience.
Nose cone pertains to a planned path that is efficiently austere; a direct methodology.
Orbit advises of an unproductive course, one that's going around and around without advancing to a concluding goal.
Outer space is representative of a deeper knowledge; a reach for greater understanding of true reality.
Retro-rocket stands for a need to slow one's rate of advancement. Too much is being missed.
Rocket means high motivation.
Rocket engine symbolizes a personal impetus.
Satellite (man-made) reflects an orbiting of the truth instead of reaching and stretching oneself beyond the safe and charted confines of tradition.
Satellite (planet) denotes peripheral elements on which one places importance.
Spacecraft is representative of a means or opportunity to intellectually reach toward a beginning comprehension of the true reality.
Space Needle (Seattle) signifies a sign or reminder of a former achievement.
Space probe represents an individual's choice or opportunity to extend a spiritual search to the farthest reaches.
Spaceship See spacecraft.
Space shuttle reflects the existing freedom to self-discover the reaches of true reality.
Space sickness stands for an inability to comprehend unconventional concepts or think outside the box.
Space station comes in dreams to reveal the existence of other semiparallel realities existing within the scope of true reality.
Space suit portrays a fear of venturing into the farthest reaches of true reality; a sense that one needs protection from discovering the truth.
Space walk represents the uttermost tip of humankind's potential.
Tracking station represents heightened awareness, particularly in respect to spiritual insights.
Warp speed suggests an immediate need to hasten a closure or conclusion.
Weightlessness usually reveals an individual's freed spirit experience.
Zero gravity comes in dreams to advise of the need to get oneself grounded.

Planetary & Other Celestial Bodies

Asteroid signifies minor events in one's life.
Celestial object symbolizes pure spiritual aspects. See specific terms.
Comet defines enlightening insights; spiritual awakenings.
Earth symbolizes humankind's physical side; the three-dimensional touchable aspects of our world.
Halley's comet relates to the continual fluctuations of true reality.
Jupiter (planet) refers to the provider in us; caring for oneself and those around us.
Mars (planet) refers to the warrior within; inner strength; fortitude.
Martian brings a subconscious subject or fear to the forefront.
Mercury (planet) depicts an impossibility.
Meteor represents an influx of enlightenment or inner awareness.

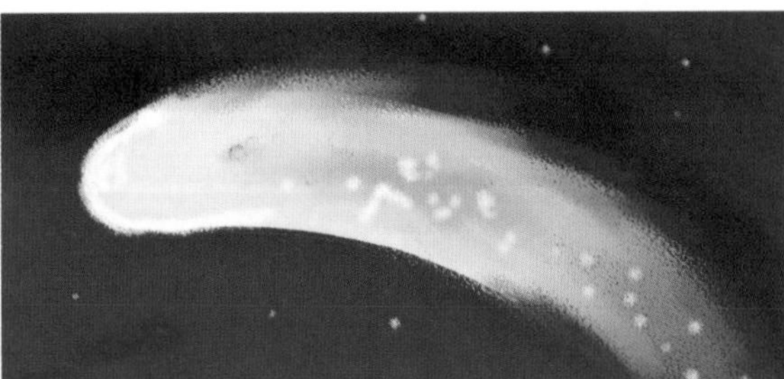

Comet symbolizes sudden spiritual discoveries.

Moon See Lunar Concepts.
Nebula pertains to an obscure idea.
Neptune (planet) refers to one's inherent natural abilities; spiritual gifts.
Planet refers to an influential element in one's life. See specific planet.
Planetarium denotes a need to expand one's perceptual scope.
Pluto (planet) indicates a healing element in one's life.
Saturn (planet) is representative of wisdom and the attainment of same.
Sun See Solar Concepts.
Uranus (planet) suggests one attends to philosophical issues.
Venus (planet) alludes to dreams and their associated symbology. May refer to an individual's personal dream or desire.

see also
• Solar Power *p. 283*
• The Flight *p. 300*

Lunar Concepts

Blue moon implies rare and valuable spiritual wisdom.
Crescent moon points to a sliver of one's glimpse at high wisdom regarding a spiritual epiphany or an understanding of reality. This refers to having nothing more than a fleeting thought of inspiration.
Eclipsed moon stands for forgotten wisdom.
First quarter moon denotes a turning point; a change is on the way.
Full moon refers to a period of strong magnetic pull; a time of heightened interest in something; a time when an individual's efforts could be most effective.
Half-moon exemplifies partial illumination of one's path. Underscores enough light to be guided by. This refers to someone having difficulty finding their way, who believes no guidance is at hand.
Harvest moon denotes the time to benefit from one's spiritual works; a time to reap the bounties that return to one through selfless giving.
Hunter's moon relates to the time to be on the watch for new spiritual issues to enter one's life. This symbol calls for increased awareness lest an important aspect pass unnoticed.
Last quarter moon signifies a winding down period.
Luminaria represents spiritual celebration.
Lunar rainbow refers to inner knowings one is subtly aware of yet cannot reach.
Moon corresponds with spiritual wisdom or gifts and their application.
Moonbeam comes to shed a revealing or awakening light on one's spiritual talent. This will usually be a call for more active use of one's spiritual wisdom and talent.
Moonbow See lunar rainbow.
Moonlight signifies the light of spiritual knowledge and talent use.

Moonrise suggests the emergence of a particular talent.

Moonquake refers to an attention-getting attempt to help one recognize a need to reconnect with one's inner knowledge; an advisement to remember an important issue.
Moonrise reveals an individual's rising spiritual talent or wisdom; a developing gift or insight.
Moon rock points to a denied or forgotten spiritual concept.
Moonscape suggests that an individual has entered new spiritual territory where discoveries and perhaps inspirational epiphanies will be experienced.
New moon alludes to hidden spiritual concepts or wisdom that will be revealed.
Waxing moon signifies growing inner strength.

Solar Concepts

Afterglow signifies inner light. May refer to residual good feelings or a knowing of something's rightness.
Alpenglow indicates one's gentle nature.
Solar See sun.
Solar eclipse advises of a need to reaffirm spiritual beliefs.
Solar flare implies a disruption or intensification of personal strength and/or energy level.
Solar system pertains to a fragment of true reality.
Solar wind is a call to give heightened awareness to one's subtle insights.
Sun stands for personal spirituality.
Sunbeam pertains to spiritual illumination.
Sunset constitutes the most spiritually powerful or intense time.
Sunspot connotes heightened spiritual activity.

Astronomical Measurement

Astronomical clock comes in dreams to advise people to remember that they should let nature take its course. Suggests greater acceptance for the passing of the natural phases of time.
Light-year defines a great distance removed from something; a time in the far distant future.
Pulsar connotes inspiration.
Quasar stands for a revelation; spiritual insight.

Astrological Concepts

Astrological planting timetable represents an aspect in an individual's life that has the capability of providing the highest probability for a successful outcome.
Zodiac comes in dreams as commendations from the highest source.
Zodiacal light symbolizes the beginning formulation of an inspirational idea.

Stellar Concepts

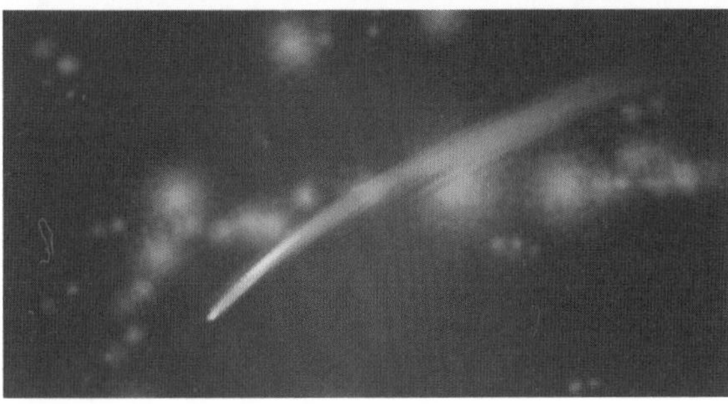

Shooting star indicates a loss of faith or belief.

Binary star means wisdom shining forth from knowledge and reason.
Daystar See morning star.
Double star See binary star.
Evening star signifies a guiding aspect in life; light in the dark.
Falling star applies to personal disappointments.
Lodestar defines a guiding force or light.
Morning star defines encouragement. Mornings can be extremely difficult emotional times of day, and the star shines to give support.
Shooting star indicates the loss or failing of an important spiritual element. Suggests that one has ignored, forgotten, or allowed major spiritual truths to die out. May point to a loss of faith. Depending on related dreamscape elements, it may also point to an appreciation of one's uniqueness.
Star exemplifies truth and the ultimate search for it.
Star being corresponds with the reality of all humankind. It may in addition refer to the totality of existing intelligence in all forms.
Stardust stands for moments of inspiration or illumined insights.
Stargazing represents spiritual speculation; intellectual reaching toward a grasp of the true reality.
Starlight connotes a spiritual opportunity to accept truth.
Starship signifies the relatedness, the connective bond, between all intelligent species.
Variable star comes as a warning against depending too much on the fluctuating opinions of others to control one's unique individuality and brightness.

Cosmology

Astral plane indicates a call for the dreamer to stay in the here and now.
Big bang theory denotes explosive beginnings.
Black hole pertains to depression; a feeling of futility. It may also refer to a place of no return.
Cluster (stars) reveal that there's more than one opportunity or solution.
Cosmic dust represents the constant presence of spiritual forces in our lives, forces we're rarely aware of.
Cosmic noise pertains to the sounds within the silence; eternal vibratory frequency activity; subliminal suggestions our consciousness picks up.
Cosmic ray signifies the intellectual dawning of a profound spiritual truth; epiphany.
Cosmos means the higher spiritual realm.
Deep space stands for great extensions of thought; contemplation of the philosophical possibilities; the serious consideration of the far reaches of physics; thinking outside the box.
Ether stands for the higher dimensional aspects to reality; possibilities yet undreamed.
Firmament represents the unimagined expanse of true reality.
Galaxy See cosmos.
Intergalactic implies a beginning phase of understanding reality.
Macrocosm implies the entirety of something. This will be associated with a specific facet of each dreamer's awake state consciousness.
Microcosm signifies a small example or replica of a larger comparable.
Outer space is representative of deeper knowledge; a reach for greater understanding of true reality.

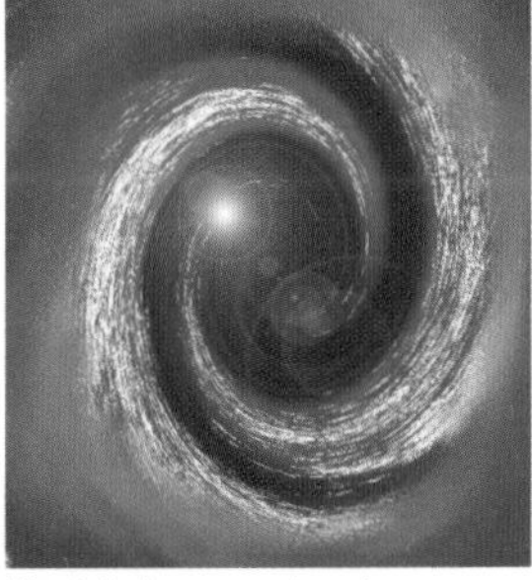

Black hole means despair.

Sky reflects the venue for one's thoughts. Different types of sky will represent specific thought patterns and tendencies on the part of the dreamer. Recall the color of the sky. Did it appear to be calm or angry? What type of clouds were in it?
Space See cosmos.
Universe See cosmos.
Vacuum (space) relates to an emptiness, usually a lack of emotion. It can refer specifically to apathy.

Constellations

Big Dipper reminds us that, although we might well strive to routinely perform small spiritual acts in our lives, they should be starred by a few larger ones in addition. See also Little Dipper.
Constellation appearing in dreams is representative of the need to give recognition for spiritual behavior.
Little Dipper comes to us in our dreams to help us to remember that small spiritual works should be a continual aspect in our lives as well as the occasional large spiritual works that we may be involved with. See Big Dipper.

see also
• Seasons *p. 62*
• Ghosts & Spirits *p. 479*

Days

Monday suggests the time to review one's motivations and strengthen them for the purpose of actively going forward.

Tuesday suggests a need to sharpen one's awareness. Now is a time for one to attend to sharper perceptions and discernment.

Wednesday correlates to a suggested time for reenergizing oneself.

Thursday is the time when one should attempt to analyze situations and events. It is indicative of a time to give deep thought to one's recent behavior.

Friday is the day on which to address closures. It is a time to attend to loose ends in one's life.

Saturday suggests a time to give one's personal attention to oneself. This symbol may refer to a wide variety of aspects such as physical, mental, or emotional rest and attention.

Sunday is representative of a time of reflection on one's behavior, perceptions, and life course.

Weekend usually refers to a time for leisure; to a time when one should be away from stressors.

Alien Encounters

Abductee (alien) denotes the dreamer is experiencing a feeling of helplessness in his or her life; a situation that one has no control over. It may specifically refer to a particular situation in which one is in over one's head, meaning one doesn't have the knowledge base or experience to deal with the particular situation.

Alien (earthly being) is representative of that which is perceived as being foreign or unfamiliar.

Alien (other world being) represents the existence of a wider reality. The dream symbol comes as an advisement to the dreamer to expand perspectives to those possibilities outside the box.

Changeling illustrates a state of evolution; a metamorphosis; transition.

Close encounter points to a personal experience that nearly happened.

Contactee (alien) is representative of an individual who is attuned to her or his higher self, is aware of insights and gut feelings.

Extraterrestrial See alien (other world being).

Flying saucer See Unidentified Flying Object.

Fourth dimension alludes to higher knowledge or level of experience.

SETI (Extraterrestrial project) represents a method of searching based on an assumption.

UFO See Unidentified Flying Object.

Unidentified Flying Object (UFO) represents the totality of intelligent life; an aspect of true reality most are still skeptical of and afraid to believe in.

Months

October represents a time to enjoy life with one's loved ones.

Month denotes a time frame and has a specific meaning for each dreamer.

January pertains to a time of contemplating one's past path and of casting an eye to the future road.

February is a time to begin the formulation of new plans.

March is a time to activate steps toward desired goals.

April is a time to expand renewal efforts on one's path.

May relates to the time to experience spiritual joy; rejoice in one's beliefs.

June denotes a time to review one's relationships.

July denotes a time for self-examination; meditation.

August denotes a time to repair relationships. It is a time to address closures.

September represents a waning period; a winding down.

October represents a uniting time; sealing relationships; reaffirming personal bonds. This also stands for a time to reap (appreciate) the blessings of home and family.

November is a time to count one's blessings; appreciate the positive elements in one's life.

December stands for a time of renewal and reflection.

Celestial Events

Eclipse (lunar) pertains to an awareness of true existential reality.

Eclipse (solar) comes as an advisement to the dreamer of a need to reaffirm his or her spiritual beliefs.

Meteor shower comes to the dreamer as a warning of an inundation of spiritual ideas or concepts in his or her everyday life. This dream symbol is a caution for the individual to be discerning in his or her selection of spiritual beliefs.

Supernova marks the recognition of a major spiritual insight in the dreamer's everyday life.

Time Miscellaneous

Access time points to a designated or proper time to do something.

After hours represent the need for additional work applied to a life aspect.

Around the clock typifies a necessary span of time to fulfill an activity that one is planning in one's life.

Belated is representative of inefficiency; lacking attention to one's awareness level. Or it may also appear to remind dreamers of something important that they forgot.

Borrowed time warns against overdoing things. One should avoid trying to accomplish too much too fast.

Busy season points to a phase of greatest activity.

Cuckoo clock characterizes an extremely regimented personality, efficiently attentive to details.

Date (time reservation) marks a need to give attention to an activity or meeting.

Daylight saving time denotes an attempt to alter reality.

Doomsday clock will usually be directly associated with the dreamer rather than an overall worldly intent. It refers to the amount of time until a major event happens in one's life. Something is on a fatal course. What time was shown on the clock?

Downtime usually is a call to rest. This is a cautionary message for one who is working or searching too intently.

Eleventh hour comes as a message of fair warning that one's time is running out to take advantage of the last chance of accomplishing something.

Epoch symbolizes a specific span of time. The meaning of this epoch will be unique to each dreamer.

Expiration date will usually be a personal indicator for the dreamer that reminds her or him of how much time is left to accomplish a certain thing.

Fortnight comes as a unique time message for the dreamer.

Happy hour typifies a short period of time when troubles can be set aside.

Hereafter connotes the future.

Hourglass reveals how much time is left to accomplish something.

Last minute denotes a state of urgency.

Late implies a time expectation that is not met or was originally unrealistic.

Leap second advises one to accept the timing of events unfolding along one's path. Don't attempt to speed things up or hold them back.

Leap year indicates that an adjustment to one's personal timing needs to be made. This suggests that one is going too fast or too slow.

Minute represents a small measure of time. Recall surrounding dream aspects for further clarification and associative factors.

Minute hand signifies the passing of time. Will advise of the importance of mere minutes.

Off-peak See off-season.

Off-season signifies a time when an activity is not generally carried out, yet this symbol may suggest that the off-season is the preferred time to accomplish something the dreamer is contemplating. Surrounding details will clarify the message intended.

Post time is representative of a phase in one's life when chances are about to be taken.

Renaissance (setting) illustrates a fertile atmosphere for renewal and opportunities for enlightenment.

Eleventh hour comes to urge the dreamer to complete a particular task.

Rush hour symbolizes a time to act.

Shelf life connotes a specified span of time for an element in one's life to be viable.

Short run signifies a plan that reaps early benefits.

Short-term defines a qualified span of time. Recall what this time was related to.

Space-age pertains to a minuscule step toward discovering the aspects of true reality.

Stopwatch cautions one to pace life according to acceptance rather than attempting to force matters, thereby making life more complex and difficult.

Time card refers to a regimented personality that gives oneself no leeway and makes no alternate plans for other probabilities.

Time clock comes as an advisement to stop watching the clock.

Time line comes to reveal a history of events regarding a particular issue.

Time lock reminds one of the unalterable amount of time in which something can either be accomplished or can happen in one's life.

Timer denotes a stressful situation that has been self-generated through one's obsession with deadlines.

Timetable pertains to schedules.

Timeworn most often stands for an outdated aspect.

Time zone portrays the fact that time is perceived differently among people; time is relative, nonlinear.

Chapter 8

The Body, Disease & Medicine

These symbols reveal the condition of one's life. They generally depict the mental, physical, and spiritual aspects of one's life and the appropriate actions that need to be taken to improve them.

Stature & Physique

Barrel-chested denotes a giving personality.
Bent refers to an aspect in life that isn't straight (true/honest).
Bowlegged illustrates perseverance throughout one's life.
Bullnecked reveals a stubborn personality; one who can be obnoxiously assertive due to a false self-image of superior strength.
Double-jointed advises against being impulsive or hasty.
Dwarf denotes the existence of power regardless of size.
Formless (shape) constitutes a lack of definition to one's opinions, attitudes, and perspectives; an unclear or vacillating viewpoint.
Full-bodied means intensity.
Gargantuan (size) illustrates an overwhelming aspect to life.
Giant pertains to one who is idolized or looked up to.
Half-pint defines a smaller aspect that may be as important as a larger one; something that is not to be overlooked or viewed as insignificant.
Knock-kneed pertains to a specific difficulty walking one's path. This unique problem will be recognized by the dreamer.
Lanky defines efficiency; sticking to basics without adding anything extraneous.
Light-footed indicates a cautious progression; a reluctance to interfere in another's life; awareness.
Midget emphasizes a caution to never correlate power or knowledge with size. Larger never means more or greater.
Muscle-bound warns against arrogance; self-love.
Petite (size) reminds us that size cannot be used for comparison when evaluating potential or power.
Physique (of people) stands for a multitude of symbolic characteristics and personality traits. Refer to a specific trait.
Pygmy constitutes unrecognized strength.
Small merely connotes size and, depending on the associated dreamscape details, this may indicate a positive or negative message.
Statuesque (appearance) pertains to a dignified personality.
Stoop See bent.
Tall (stature) usually has a psychological symbology rather than a physical one. It will refer to one's attitude of superiority, that of looking down on others.
Underdeveloped relates to a lack of full preparedness; something needing further growth; immaturity.

Body Art

Body art symbolizes one's attitude or character traits. This can be an extremely revealing symbol.
Body piercing is a suggestion of contrariness; boldness.
Piercings See body piercing.
Tattoo signifies how one perceives oneself. Recall what the tattoo was. What was the color and size?

Appearance

Albino represents a lack of individuality; a fear of showing one's true colors. Can mean a tendency for noncommittal attitudes.
Barefoot characterizes an individual who walks a path with full knowledge of what each step means.
Bareheaded signifies an expressive individual who is honest or forthright.
Chic means an overemphasis placed on appearance.
Dandy (appearance) warns against a preoccupation with one's appearance.
Debonair suggests an exterior presentation of classiness that may not be a true representation of oneself.
Decrepit alludes to timeworn and will most often refer to the mental state of defeat or lost motivation.
Delicate (appearance or behavior) usually stands for a frivolous personality but can also refer to a highly optimistic individual.
Frat member suggests rigid opinions and right-wing perspectives. May represent an individual who needs to blend in with the accepted crowd, fearful to allow one's individuality to show (and shine).
Geek generally points to assumptions regarding another.
Greaser suggests a liberal, left-wing attitude. May also point to a personality who doesn't let the attitudes of others interfere with the freedom to express oneself.
Greek god suggests desirable attributes.
Half blood constitutes a rightful identity or authority.
Half-breed See half blood.
Headless warns of a thoughtless person; one who has no intellectual pursuits or interests; a lack of opinion.
Homebred portrays an individual who was raised with family values.
Homely reminds us that beauty is subjective to one's personal perspective.
Hominoid represents any being that resembles the human form, a humanoid. Many times, this will have an extraterrestrial connotation.
Mangy (appearance) indicates a rough life that has been endured.
Mousy pertains to a timid or introverted personality.
Posture represents a multitude of interpretations. Recall if one was slouching, standing straight (too straight?), bent over, etc. These will depict obvious states of mind, character, or attitude.
Preppy implies a specific characteristic, usually studious and efficient and, perhaps, needing to be popular.
Rough may indicate a difficult life or a coarse personality.
Rumpled is representative of a persevering individual who is a little worse for wear but maintains motivation and continued effort.
Scrubby may signify a weary soul, or it may stand for apathy depending on the dream's related details.
Self-portrait shows how one sees oneself and is a very important and revealing dream symbol.
Shabby will usually denote weariness.

see also
• Weights & Measures *p. 281*
• Beauty Aids *p. 410*

Characteristics

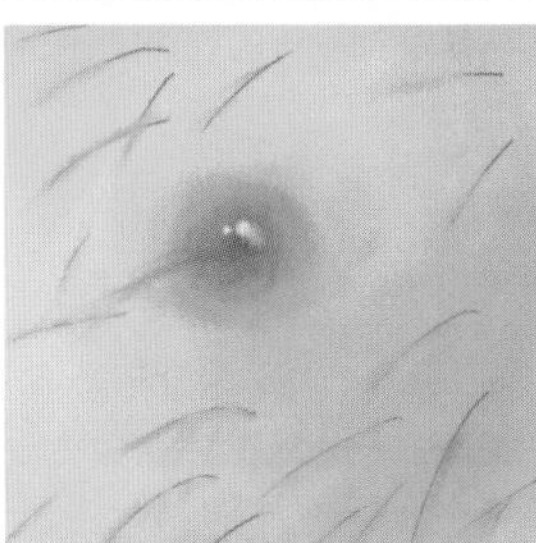

Mole reveals a distinctive trait.

Agility signifies an individual's talent to persevere.
Awkward (gait) suggests a path one is uncomfortable with.
Beautiful is, as always, in the discriminating eye of the beholder. Recall what was given this specific characteristic. Was it truly beautiful?
Classy is often associated with a quiet dignity or wisdom.
Egg-shaped (skull) stands for an intellectual, someone who is a deep thinker.
Faculty (natural ability) defines those talents or intellectual factors that are available for one's constant use in life.
Foot-dragging warns against a reluctance to continue along one's life path; a possible inner fear causing procrastination.
Footless suggests the need for an alternate way of achieving one's goals. This symbol isn't a negative one, it comes to reveal the presence of an alternative direction or method.
Foxy symbolizes a draw or attraction that may, in reality, be a cover for less desirable traits. This symbol may also come to actually reveal an individual who is clever to the point of being conniving.
Frail pertains to a weakened state of something.
Handsome (appearance) suggests an attractive aspect. Recall surrounding details to see if this is true or the opposite is meant. Outward appearance can be deceptive.
Hot (appearance) See foxy.
Invalid (person) calls for courage to continue on one's path regardless of adversities.
Jaded connotes weariness; cynicism.
Listless may denote a lack of motivation, or it may indicate a state of apathy.
Lumbering (gait) won't necessarily refer to laziness or a lack of motivation. This symbol usually commends perseverance and tenacity.
Mole (blemish) reflects a distinguishing characteristic; individuality; uniqueness.
Suppleness suggests tenacity; an ability to cope with and manage almost any situation.

Deformities & Disabilities

Amputee points to the wholeness of one's being comprised of heart and soul, emotions and thought.
Cleft lip stands for impaired speech relating to errors in perception or attitude.
Cleft palate stands for untruths; unbalanced statements; the addition of personal input into alleged statements of fact.
Clubfoot connotes difficulties traversing one's path, meant for the dreamer to overcome.
Conjoined twin usually exposes a compatible individual. May reveal someone who is totally dependent upon another; a lack of individuality.
Crippled defines an impairment that will not halt advancement and may be an advisement to stop believing one is impaired.
Deformity (physical) denotes an opportunity for growth.
Disfigured pertains to a specialized life purpose.
Dowager's hump portrays a life that is filled with extensive intellectual pursuits and efforts applied to obtaining wisdom.
Handicapped indicates subconscious fears holding one back.
Humpback stands for perseverance in spite of a hard life.
Lame defines ineffectiveness.
Peg leg denotes the existence of an alternative.
Pigeon-toed defines an introverted manner of walking one's path; additional difficulties due to personalizing external elements or events.
Polydactyl (extra toes/fingers) stands for a heightened ability to efficiently accomplish goals.
Round shoulder means weight one carries; perseverance in spite of ongoing stressors.
Siamese twin See conjoined twin.

Weight

Beer belly indicates overindulgence. It refers to a lack of self-control.
Bloated (appearance/feeling) warns against excesses.
Cellulite comes to the dreamer as a caution against the acceptance of extraneous aspects in life; excesses.
Cholesterol stands for life's positive/negative duality.
Fat (people) See obesity.
Fat farm reveals a need to shed extraneous attitudes or perspectives that one is carrying around.
Limber emphasizes tenacity; resourcefulness; acceptance.
Lithe connotes tenacity; endurance and perseverance.
Obesity portrays an overindulgence of some type; an inability to deny oneself; lack of self-control. This symbol may also point to a love/hate conflict within oneself.
Overweight (not obese) will not imply obesity, yet it means that one is carrying excessive burdens and responsibilities; a need to rid oneself of superficial or hampering aspects. This is most often in reference to emotional psychological self-generated mechanisms.
Paunch connotes waning awareness and motivation.
Potbelly (stomach) alludes to an absence of motivation and/or energy.
Pudgy infers a need to shed some type of excess.
Skinny constitutes a frail and timid personality. Denotes a lack of motivation and energized determination.
Starvation implies a serious lack of a nourishing element in an individual's life; the absence of mental or emotional nourishment.
Svelte is representative of a tendency to keep to the essentials, basics.
Underfed represents a lack of information; withheld knowledge or nourishment.
Underweight symbolizes a lack of recognizing one's own potential or worth.

Face

Ashen (complexion) warns of ill health or discovery of one's negative action.
Beauty mark portrays the distinctive qualities one has; personal uniqueness.
Birthmark advises one to accept imperfections.
Blemish illustrates an imperfection connected to an aspect of the dreamer's life.
Bloodless warns against a lack of motivation; apathy; denial.
Closed mouth relates to trustworthiness; integrity; loyalty.
Countenance relates to facial expressions and what can be read from them. See specific expressions.
Deadpan (expression/response) portrays an individual who is expressionless; one who does not show emotion.
Dead ringer suggests a need to remember whatever has been presented as a double. May represent a déjà vu incidence.
Dimple (skin) is an indication of individuality.
Distorted face indicates the presence of some mental aberrations.
Doll face indicates a presentation of innocence but is rarely a truism.
Double chin signifies melancholia; self-pity.
Face (characteristics) reveals one's true personality.
Faceless points to someone who's unreadable; a tendency to withhold a show of expression or any clue to what one is thinking or feeling. It may also indicate a desire to keep one's distance from others. It could also stand for no sense of individuality; a conformist.

Double chin is a representation of dwelling on one's misfortunes.

Flushed (complexion) implies embarrassment or guilt. May indicate repressed emotions.
Flushed face warns of an explosive personality, or it may point to withheld emotions.
Freckles denote a congenial nature; sunny disposition.
Heavy makeup denotes hypocrisy or a false front.
Jowls relate to many difficulties overcome throughout life.
Long face signifies either sadness or disappointment.
Look-alike portrays one who imitates you. May reveal an individual's alter ego.
Moon-faced connotes an emotional openness.
Oversized face means egotism and arrogance.
Pale complexion characterizes an introvert. May also mean someone in a dispirited state.
Plain Jane comes in dreams to remind us that appearances can be deceiving.
Poker face indicates a strong business sense; an ability to keep plans or secrets confidential; closed-mouthed.
Pretty corresponds with a pleasing element.
Profile See silhouette.
Red cheeks depict a shy personality.
Red-faced reflects embarrassment; possible guilt.
Round face suggests avarice or greed.
Ruddy (complexion) reveals an individual who routinely expends efforts toward a goal or assisting others.
Sanguine See ruddy.
Scarred face is perseverance.
Silhouette cautions one against accepting an outline as the whole.
Square face denotes an adamantly opinionated nature.
Strawberry mark See birthmark.
Suntan refers to a routine exposure to spiritual elements.
Tan See suntan.
Thin/gaunt face implies a reserved personality.
Two faces allude to a hypocritical nature.
Ugly denotes a disagreeable aspect.
Undersized face means an introvert who thinks small.
Unremarkable face applies to a conformist.
Weather-beaten constitutes a difficult life and the fortitude that exists to continue on.
Weatherworn See weather-beaten.
Wrinkled (skin) exemplifies fortitude gained through great personal effort.

Skin

Chapped skin implies an inability to accept differing ideas or attitudes of others.
Collagen stands for the revitalizing and binding aspects in one's life.
Dermabrasion See exfoliant (skin).
Exfoliant suggests one shed all remnants of former affectations. It comes to the dreamer as an advisement to keep one or one's face (presentation) free of old attitudes.
Flesh pertains to one's overall character. Recall its condition.
Graft (skin) See skin graft.
Keratin depicts inner strength; that which generates strength.
Pore alludes to the existence of an opening, exit point, or opportunity.
Scalp (head) exemplifies an individual's sensitivity. Recall its condition.
Skin (human) relates to one's inner strength and general stamina. The condition, texture, and color are important elements to notice.
Skin graft means an attempt to improve one's stamina. It also refers to renewal and efforts expended to accomplish it.

see also
• Phobias Related to Conditions *p. 154*
• Cosmetics *p. 409*

Skin Problems

Abrasion (skin) means aspects causing friction in life. Could refer to an element causing surface irritations and may signify a caution not to make a bigger issue of them.
Abscess connotes aspects leading to negative conditions. Elements carrying the ability to exacerbate a situation.
Acne signifies the need to remove negative aspects from one's life.
Bedsore warns against not being motivated to work; lingering for too long in a rest period.
Blackhead indicates bad aspects that clog understandings; obstructions to clarity.
Blister stands for the burning effects of one's actions.
Boil (skin) warns of suppressed emotions; an irritation remaining under the skin.
Bruise characterizes minor emotional or psychological injuries sustained.
Callus characterizes a hardened attitude or nature. May also indicate a need to protect oneself behind a barrier.
Carbuncle denotes a currently festering negative aspect that can cause personal harm.
Cold sore See herpes simplex.
Contact dermatitis advises one to avoid a life aspect that causes extreme irritation, stress, or anxiety.
Cyst denotes the presence of a destructive negative aspect that has taken hold. This may be a negative spiritual concept, a negative idea or attitude, or a harmful emotion.
Dermatitis stands for life's irritating aspects; annoyances that get under the skin.

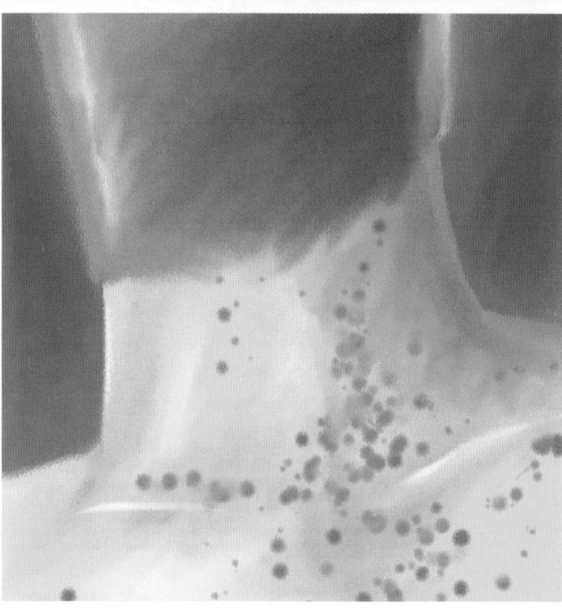
Rash characterizes problems caused by social detachment.

Eczema connotes an attitude that needs to be overcome.
Fever blister See herpes simplex.
First-degree burn indicates a lesson learned through a lack of awareness.
Flesh wound marks a temporary setback.
Gall (growth) represents a negative element that's growing from within.
Gash denotes a temporary setback; a hurtful incident from which an individual quickly recovers.
Graze portrays nonchalance; a skimming of the surface.
Heat rash relates to the use of energy for self-defeating purposes; an unproductive effort that has been made.
Herpes simplex signifies dormant inherent negative qualities of one's personality that can be activated through a lack of control.
Hives characterize a lack of acceptance; a continued state of active irritation over something.
Impetigo emphasizes the need for balancing, most often a physical condition.
Keratosis advises one to be more sensitive to others.
Laceration signifies a temporary setback; a slight injury to one's ego.
Prickly heat See heat rash.
Rash (skin) indicates emotional irritations or psychological difficulties generated by a lack of acceptance.
Rope burn (on palms) suggests hard efforts expended to accomplish a goal.
Scald most often identifies a spiritual burn of some type that results from accepting false concepts.
Shingles (on skin) reveal an emotional disruption within oneself; internal conflict.
Skin disease will suggest a weakened state.
Sliver means an element that has the potential to irritate.
Splinter exemplifies the entry of a foreign element or belief; an aspect that doesn't belong; an invasion or defilement. Also see sliver.
Spot may indicate a defect or marred element in one's life, or it can pertain to an attention-getting mark.
Sunburn forewarns of a state of being spiritually burned by a false concept or perception.
Wart pertains to a negative aspect (perhaps emotion or attitude) that one has allowed to grow under one's skin.
Water blister stands for a spiritual burn.
Welt (skin) exposes an injury other than a physical one, such as a business event, an emotional hurt, and so on.
Windburn reveals the dangerous condition of being burned by allowing oneself to be exposed to negative or harmful ideas.
Wound See welt.

Scabs & Scars

Pockmark (skin) typifies a life fraught with difficulties or negative aspects; a hard life.
Scab (wound) indicates a healing process.
Scar is representative of a former wound that an individual has previously sustained.
Scar tissue See scar.

Hair

Afro (hairstyle) alludes to confused thought.
Bald (head) characterizes a thoughtless individual; one who rarely thinks for oneself or has original ideas.
Big hair See bouffant (hairstyle).
Blond (hair) refers to a sunny disposition; an optimist.
Bouffant (hairstyle) characterizes an egotistical personality; one whose ideas are blown up and inflated for the purpose of impressing others.
Braid (hair) pertains to twisted thought patterns; confusion; a convoluted thinking process; twisted perspectives.
Brunet (hair) implies level-headedness; a down-to-earth attitude and generally optimistic perspective.
Chignon implies that thoughts are knotted; a need to sort things out.
Comb-over (hair over baldness) refers to baseless opinions; thoughts brought in to hide that one has no real opinions on an issue.
Conditioner (hair) denotes a desire to keep one's perspectives and thoughts well aligned with logic and reason.
Corn braid See cornrow.
Cornrow (hairstyle) portrays the beauty of mental efforts applied to organized planning.
Cowlick portrays a perspective out of line with others.
Crew cut (hairstyle) represents short-sighted thinking or perspectives.
Crimped (hairstyle) refers to uptight perspectives. Can indicate a type A personality.
Cropped (hairstyle) usually points to individuality of thoughts or perspectives.
Dandruff implies a need to shed misconceptions.
Dreadlock indicates intellectual analysis. The quality and accuracy depends on the condition of the locks.
Ducktail (hairstyle) symbolizes a middle-of-the-road attitude.
Extension (hair) See hair extensions.
Fair-haired indicates an even temper.
Fake hair See wig.
Flattop (hairstyle) alludes to surface thinking; having no interest in deeper thought.
French twist (hairstyle) suggests knotted or twisted ideas; plans or situations needing straightening out.
Frizzy (hair) See fuzzy (hair).
Fuzzy (hair) points to unclear thoughts; confusion.
Hair symbolizes thoughts. Refer to specific hair types, conditions, and colors for specific interpretations.
Hair coloring shows thoughts colored by personal attitudes. This refers to an attempt to alter one's perspectives.
Haircut symbolizes an attempt to cut away extraneous elements; a desire to stay focused on the main issue.
Hair extensions are an attempt to appear as a deep thinker.
Hair-growth products indicate efforts to think deeper.
Hair implants mean new ideas from alternative thought.
Hair loss implies a shift to more shallow thinking. Perhaps one has grown less thoughtful.
Hair transplant See transplant (hair).
Layered (hairstyle) implies one who keeps thoughts trimmed; sticking to the basics.
Lock (hair) stands for treasured aspects of another.
Long hair illustrates analytical thought; mental exploration; complex contemplation.
Lovelock (hair) points to love's mementos; the remembrance of a cherished relationship.
Mohawk (hairstyle) reveals one with a single train of thought; an inability to refocus an attitude or perspective.
Pageboy (hairstyle) suggests shyness.
Pigtail See braid.
Pin curl shows restricted ideas; an unyielding thought process.
Plait See braid.
Platinum blonde pertains to a shallow thought process.
Plug (hair) stands for new ideas or solutions that have come from a different issue.
Pompadour (hairstyle) indicates an opinionated personality.
Ponytail reflects an accepting attitude; an ability to rebound.
Receding (hairline) indicates a superficial and apathetic thought process; resting on false assumptions.
Redheaded alludes to a temperamental nature; easily incited.
Ringlet (hair) refers to an idea or thought process that turns back on itself or is complex.
Roach (hairstyle) represents one-mindedness; rigidly focused ideas.
Salt-and-pepper (hair color) suggests gaining wisdom while still learning from experiences.
Scalp lock (hairstyle) represents narrow-mindedness.
Shaggy (fabric/hair) represents a disorderly thought process.
Slick (hair) usually points to slippery behavior. May point to slippery thoughts, those which aren't based on solid foundations.
Spit curl stands for an attempt to gain attention.
Split-ends (hair) stands for quibbling; splitting hairs.
Streaked hair warns of false ideas or perspectives mixed in with natural ones.
Stringy hair warns of ideas that have coalesced into multiple separate issues; a loss of an ability to intellectually perceive the whole picture.
Tangled signifies confused thoughts.
Topknot (hairstyle) represents attitudes tied to a strong basic premise. Usually points to being opinionated.
Toupee reflects false thinking.
Tousled (hair) stands for a need to get one's thoughts in order.
Transplant (hair) signifies new ideas taking root.
Untangled means straightening out the facts or elements of an issue; applying efforts to finally understand something.
Upsweep (hairstyle) shows a tendency for lofty ideas or perspectives; perhaps an overblown self-image.
Widow's peak (hair) reveals a strong characteristic to one's personality, most often a type of singular ideal.
Wig may reveal false thoughts as in deception, or it could mean an attempt to alter thoughts or correct them.

see also
• Beauty & Fashion *p. 248*
• Hats *p. 404*

Facial Hair

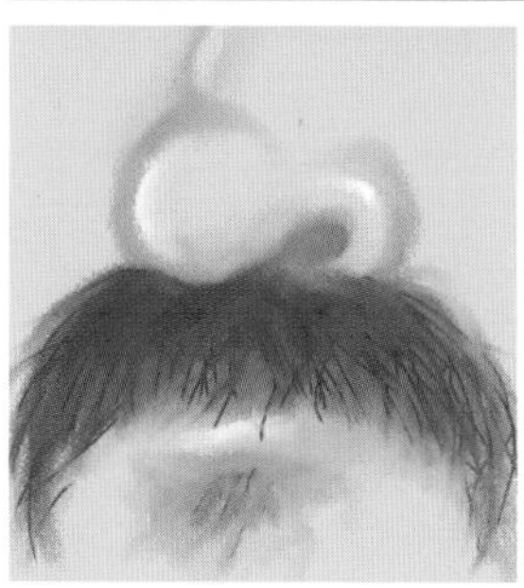
Mustache is poor communication.

Beard symbolizes hidden physical aspects in one's life. In addition, it may point to one's tendency toward duplicity by holding opposing philosophies—one that is shown in the public arena, one that is hidden from others.
Clean-shaven illustrates a desire to keep things out in the open; honesty. It may refer specifically to an aversion to hidden aspects.
Five-o'clock shadow (beard) represents overwork; time to take a break.
Goatee indicates a pretentious personality.
Gray beard equates to an experienced, conservative personality, usually an elder individual.
Handlebar mustache reveals pretentiousness.
Moustache See mustache.
Mustache illustrates a tendency to ineffectively express one's thoughts.
Muttonchops (sideburns) imply spiritual verbosity.
Peach fuzz suggests immaturity.
Sideburns connote a desire to appear intellectual or more mature. May also indicate attitudes or ideas that are held off to the side (not openly expressed).
Stubble (bristly) represents roughness; incompleteness.

Eye Disease

Black eye (bruise) implies interfering actions. May point to a retribution.
Bleeding eye indicates an empathetic nature.
Cataract (of eye) denotes impaired perception; a clouded viewpoint.
Conjunctivitis warns of a major error in perception. Strongly advises to clear up one's way of seeing things.
Eye bath See eyecup.
Eyecup indicates a negative aspect has infiltrated one's perception.
Eyedropper (for eye medicine) connotes a need to add another factor to one's perceptual viewpoint to gain greater clarity.
Eyedropper (general use) refers to an aid for using a small amount of something. This could be associated with just about anything, so recall other dreamscape elements associated with the dropper.
Eyestrain shows a habit of straining one's perceptions. This indicates a tendency to make more of something than there is.
Eye surgery (elective corrective) stands for a personal effort made to perceive more clearly.
Eyewash exemplifies a life aspect that clarifies one's perceptual ability by washing negative attitudes from it.
Floaters (eyesight) suggest impaired perspective; reading extraneous elements into something; assumptions.
Glaucoma represents a deteriorating perspective; losing one's perspective.
Pinkeye represents a perspective that is infected with some type of negative or distortion.
Sty (eye) applies to a negatively affected perception.

Eyesight

Astigmatism symbolizes the lack of clear understanding; perception is skewed.
Blind (awareness) points to an insular type of perception. One's view is designed for self-preservation.
Blind (sightless) connotes self-induced lack of understanding; purposeful ignorance; denial.
Blind spot advises of an obstructed view or perception; a specific angle of perception that isn't a clear view.
Double vision usually defines heightened perception.
Eye chart suggests a need to check personal perceptions for clarity and accuracy. This implies one isn't perceiving something accurately.
Eye patch stands for a willful slant to perspective of reality.
Eye test indicates a need to see something clearer. May point to a problem with perspective.
Farsighted reveals a perception that sees the forest but not the individual trees; a need to understand the elements making up the whole.
Fuzzy (vision) See unfocused eyes.
Lazy eye is an inability to focus on a particular issue. May refer to ability to see both sides of an issue simultaneously.

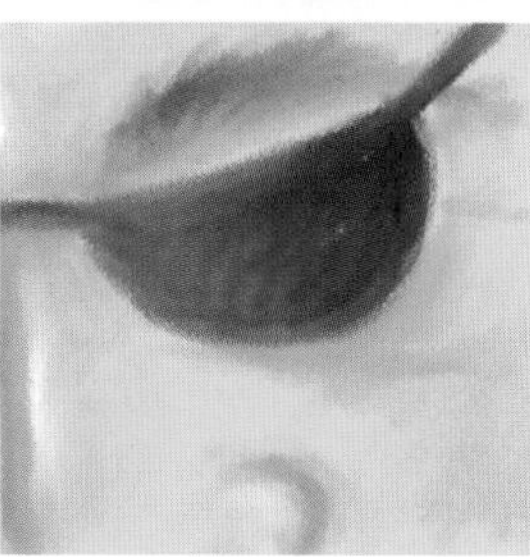
Eye patch is a determined outlook.

Mosaic vision is representative of an ability to immediately perceive all elements of an aspect.
Myopia (nearsightedness) emphasizes a lack of long-range perspective.
Nearsighted See myopia.
Night blindness warns of a self-induced ignorance.
Patch (eye) See eye patch.
Shortsighted refers to inability to perceive the full scope or long range aspects of an issue or plan. Also see myopia.
Sightless. See blind (sightless).
Snow blindness exposes spiritual blindness, usually self-imposed.
Trifocals emphasize multiple perspectives as utilized to gain a complete comprehension.
Tunnel vision advises of the wisdom of widening one's perceptual scope.
Unfocused eyes are disinterest; undefined perceptions.

Eyes

Artificial eye See glass eyes.

Beady-eyed suggests a suspicious, envious, or malicious personality.

Bedroom eyes exemplify a magnetic personality.

Black eyes (iris color) suggest dark perceptions; a pessimistic point of view.

Blank eyes characterize apathy.

Bleary-eyed connotes a need to pace one's intake of information; a call to rest; overworked.

Blinking eyes refer to a lack of seriousness.

Bloodshot eyes represent one who is confused regarding motivational factors.

Bug-eyed connotes ignorance; amazement due to a lack of knowledge or understanding.

Clear-eyed symbolizes one who sees clearly; a lack of distortion.

Cloudy eyes denote a lack of clarity.

Cockeyed alludes to foolishness; absurdity.

Cold-eyed characterizes a lack of personal opinion or involvement.

Colored eyes have unique meanings. Refer to specific color.

Cross-eyed infers a distorted perception.

Darting eyes signify a vacillating perspective.

Dilated (pupils) suggests a need to see more clearly.

Dull eyes characterize a lack of interest or ability to comprehend.

Eye bank comes as an advisement of a need for one to view something through the eyes of another and suggests a current state of misinterpretation going on.

Teardrop represents a sentimental reaction to an event.

Eyebrow reveals the manner in which one's personal perceptions are shielded from others.

Eyelash is representative of protection of one's opinions or perceptions.

Eyelid relates to aspects utilized during the perceptual process. What condition were the dream eyelids? Were they infected? Clean? Closed?

Eye socket See socket (eye).

Eye view will represent an individual's unique perception of a situation or issue.

Feline eyes portray an acute awareness; watchfulness.

Glass eyes are representative of an individual's greatly heightened ability to perceive vibrational images through an extended awareness of true reality.

Goggle-eyed is indicative of astonishment; stunned.

Green eyes (depending on brilliance versus dullness and depth of color intensity) can refer to healing abilities or jealousy.

Hawk-eyed stands for heightened awareness.

Hazel eyes mean a cheery, down-to-earth personality or attitude.

Hooded eyes represent a calculating approach to perceptions.

Large eyes pertain to a broad-scoped perceptual skill.

Misty-eyed connotes an effort to control one's emotions; sensitivity.

Eye Anatomy

Cornea stands for an individual's inherent or genetically inspired perceptions.

Iris (eye) will reveal one's quality of perception. What color was it? Was it cloudy or clear?

Pupil (eye) portrays one's perceptual qualities. Recall this symbol's associative details. What color was the iris surrounding the pupil?

Moon-eyed reveals a sense of wonder or amazement.

Owl eyes are related to an individual's ability to perceive what others overlook.

Pop-eyed symbolizes an astonishment; a fear.

Protruding eyes point to gullibility; an amazement at everything.

Red-eye comes as a strong warning that the dreamer will understand. This symbol may point to overwork or an overindulgence.

Shiner See black eye (bruise).

Slanted eyes warn of perceptions affected by personal opinions/skepticism.

Small eyes come to define a small perceptual scope; short-ranged perception.

Socket (eye) would imply that the socket is empty and therefore denotes a total lack of physical sight yet does not exclude perceptual sight or insights. A single empty eye socket would point to a condition of perceiving only half an issue.

Squinty eyes represent self-imposed perceptual selectiveness or suspicion.

Staring eyes indicate judgmental perceptions.

Starry eyes symbolize an individual's unrealistic, overly optimistic perceptions.

Teardrop (literal or shape) indicates an emotional response that, depending on the dream's surrounding details, may connote sorrow, joy, or empathy for the individual dreamer.

Wild-eyed most often represents fear or great confusion.

see also
• Thought Processes & Intelligence *p. 130*
• Feelings *p. 136*

Brain & Head

Amnesia indicates forgetfulness, perhaps intentional; denial or escapism.
Blackout (consciousness) exemplifies selective memory.
Brain pertains to one's thought process and quality of same.
Brain damage applies to thought patterns or perspectives that are not correct; an inability to correctly reason or perceive logically.
Brain disease points to a certain dysfunction in an individual's thinking or perspective.
Brain fever denotes a condition that inflames one's thoughts.
Brain tumor points to an inability to apply logic and reason to thought.
Brain wave connotes mental impulses; inspiration; sudden ideas or epiphanies.
Cerebral palsy illustrates intellectual clarity accompanied by aspects that hamper physical action; an understanding of one's direction and path with some trouble with carrying it out.
Cerebrum See brain.
Coma means an unresponsive state. This does not imply a lack of awareness.
Concussion defines a personally, mentally, or emotionally shocking event.
Dizzy stands for confusion; lack of balance or comprehension. This may refer to a hectic (dizzying) pace taken through something.
Drowsy is a call to awareness; a wake-up call to be attentive.
Encephalitis warns of an individual's distorted thoughts due to unchecked anger.
Epilepsy typifies dream symbols that represent one's involuntary perceptions and the experience and response to the same.
Fainting denotes a lack of inner strength. This may also reveal an individual's reaction to an unexpected shock.
Giddiness won't normally indicate juvenile traits but will usually reveal nervousness or a lack of self-confidence.
Head pertains to the thought process.
Headache exemplifies difficulty in processing one's thoughts; a problematical situation needing resolution.
Hydrocephalus pertains to an obsessive fascination with spiritual matters, especially the esoteric qualities.
Left brain pertains to a control or dominance over the establishment; a convincing power.
Migraine indicates a state of intense pressure; great stress usually caused by oneself through a lack of acceptance or tolerance.
Mind connotes one's thought process.
Mind's eye defines mental visual insights; mental images.
Passed out usually comes to indicate overindulgence or overstress.
Pate denotes personal energy, possibly inner strength.
Semiconscious exposes a state of half awareness. Advises one to be more aware and focused.
Stroke (brain) warns of a harmful idea or emotion existing within oneself.
Twilight sleep denotes a willful state of numbness regarding emotional pain.

Neck

Neck reveals a person's inquisitiveness; curiosity.
Neck, broken indicates the result of sticking one's neck out where it didn't belong.
Neck, long refers to high curiosity and imagination.
Neck, no suggests an absence of curiosity to the extent of having no imagination or interest in creative thinking.
Neck, short is representative of a mild amount of interest in something.
Neck, stiff reflects set ways and attitudes. May warn of an individual's inability to easily view all angles. In this sense, it refers specifically to an individual's limited perceptual range.
Stiff-necked See neck, stiff.

Circulation

Aneurysm warns one to cease dwelling on emotional pain.
Angioplasty warns of a need to open up (unclog) an attitude or emotion that's preventing free flow. This free flow can be related to emotions, communication with another, a negative perspective, or nearly any other form of negativity one is harboring.
Aorta refers to aspects closest to the heart; highly emotional aspects.
Artery refers to aspects in life that emotionally affect us.
Capillary is a finely defined aspect to one's life.
Hemostat connotes a stanching factor of one's energy outflow. This may be required or warned against depending on other dream details.
Jugular (vein) is representative of a vital aspect in one's life; that to which one is most vulnerable.
Pulse (heart) applies to emotional stability. Recall if the dream revealed an actual heart rate.
Spider vein connotes fortitude. It refers to progression despite burdens.
Varicose vein reflects a difficult path that has been traversed.
Vascular disease warns of a harmful condition caused by allowing stressors or frustrations to build up. A call to release (let go of) grudges and those life aspects that one has no control over.
Vein (blood) relates to a life force element; an essential factor in life.

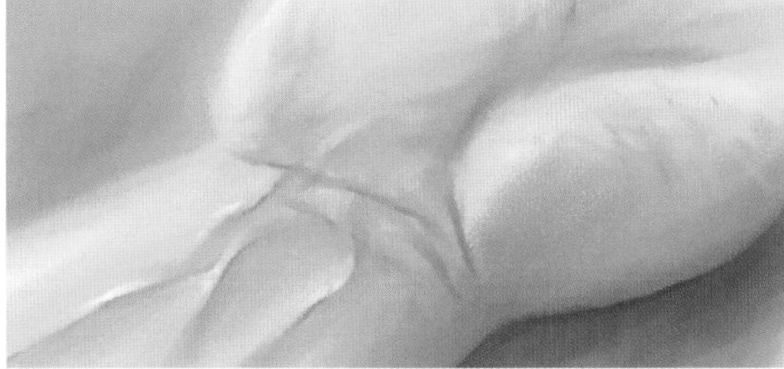

Vein (blood) characterizes a vital part of one's existence.

Heart

Angina warns of overdoing and voluntarily placing oneself in stressful situations.
Arrhythmia denotes an irregularity of one's emotions; emotional vacillation.
Athlete's heart stands for compassion, generosity, tolerance; a big heart.
Cardiac arrest warns of over-exertion or overstressing oneself. May precede an unexpected event or news.
Cardiac massage illustrates a need to externalize emotions and attitudes.
Cardiopulmonary resuscitation (CPR) advises to reactivate an aspect in one's life that has been left behind or abandoned; an element representing a new lease on life.
Defibrillator warns against stress and refers to a positive life aspect that will help one to accomplish this.
Heart applies to the emotions and their health.
Heart attack portrays an emotional setback.
Heartbeat signifies emotional stability. Recall if the beats were steady or irregular. Were they fast or slow?
Heart disease usually refers to a lack of empathy, but may also indicate emotional stress or damage due to a lack of acceptance.
Heart failure signifies apathy. It refers to a lack of emotional sensitivity.
Heart transplant See open-heart surgery.
Open-heart surgery comes as a strong advisement to correct damaging emotions generated by psychological dysfunctions.
Pacemaker pertains to a need to regulate one's emotional displays and signifies a need to calm routine excitability.

Blood

Blood represents the spur to achieve.

Anemia indicates a lack of basic facts. May also be literal; a lack of basic nutrients.
Bleeder See hemophilia.
Bleeding indicates a loss of essential life elements; waning energy and motivation; a lessening of one's inner strength and power.
Blood pertains to those aspects that equate to one's life force or driving motivation.
Blood bank applies to a reserve of perseverance.
Blood count alludes to the need to review those aspects that motivate the dreamer. Perhaps some of these are not all positive ones.
Blood donor See donor (blood).
Bloodletting characterizes misconceptions that lessen one's motivation; a draining of one's strength, perseverance, and/or determination.
Blood meal signifies a revitalizing element.
Bloodmobile will represent an opportunity to express/utilize one's goodness by helping others. In some dreamscapes, depending on the related elements, this symbol may indicate an aspect in one's life that has the potential to drain one's resources or energy.
Blood poisoning means dangerously negative motivations.
Blood pressure alludes to one's motivational energy level and interest.
Bloodstain pertains to the effects of one's motivation; what one's actions leave behind due to their specific type of motivation.
Bloodstream portrays the motivating current that flows through one's life.
Blood test suggests one's motivation is in question.
Blood transfusion See transfusion (blood).
Blood typing relates to a desire to stay true to one's motivational aspects.
Donor (blood) typifies a compassionate individual who freely gives of self.
Embolism is representative of a self-induced path obstruction.
Fibrillation (heart) pertains to instinctual responses.
Hematoma warns of a need to release a blockage of one's continuously circulating energy flow within the body. This means that some type of clearing is needed.
Hemophilia warns of a dangerously low energy level; some aspect in an individual's life that is draining energy.
Hemorrhage is a sudden outpouring of one's energy. It may indicate a needed course of action for the dreamer.
High blood pressure warns of a need to slow down and be more accepting.
Lifeblood refers to one's driving force.
New blood (people) indicates a need for new and fresh ideas and perspectives.
Plasma will represent an essential element to one's existence. This may not refer to a physical aspect but usually indicates an emotional or mental factor.
Transfusion (blood) connotes bad blood is present within; a need to repair bad relations.

Blood Clotting

Blood clot depicts a negative aspect that is blocking one's motivation. May also point to something that has the potential of blocking an individual's way or his or her advancement or progression in life.
Clotting factor may come to the dreamer as a revelation of his or her ability to heal after he or she has experienced a hurtful or destructive event.
Coagulate See blood clot.

see also
• Heart & Hand Phrases *p. 142*
• Eating *p. 426*

Ears, Nose & Throat

Adam's apple symbolizes difficulty in swallowing foreign ideas; an inability to think outside the box.

Adenoid implies difficulty in speaking or expressing oneself.

Cauliflower ear suggests the habit of listening to gossip.

Deaf usually refers to self-denial or a willful avoidance of the truth.

Ear symbolizes the quality of auditory reception; how well one listens and, consequently, processes and responds.

Earache represents the result of listening to too much verbiage that is extraneous.

Eardrops advise of measures needed to repair some damage caused by what one has heard or listened to.

Eardrum shows how well one listens in respect to comprehending with the application of logic and reason.

Earlobe shows the quality and quantity of one's receptiveness to verbal communication.

Ear piercings refer to behavior that obstructs hearing (perceptual) clarity.

Earwax warns of self-generated misconceptions due to personal selectiveness.

Hard of hearing denotes difficulty understanding concepts. May point to willful denial.

Hearing aid indicates a lack of attention and awareness. Implies one only hears what one wants to hear.

Hoarseness implies unclear communications. May mean a failure to make one's repetitive communications understood.

Goiter warns of a current state of perceptual aberration.

Laryngitis denotes inability to express oneself adequately, perhaps self-induced for psychological reasons.

Larynx portrays expressiveness. Recall the condition of the larynx if a view was provided in the dream.

Nose corresponds to a person's sense of direction; instincts; ability to recognize insights.

Nose, broken points to a wrong direction taken or an error in judgment.

Nose, large corresponds with an inability to differentiate important elements from the insignificant ones.

Nose, none reveals no sense of direction or lack of instinct.

Nose, small shows mild ability for accurate discernment.

Nose spray stands for a need for breathing room. Suggests a suffocating situation.

Otoscope represents a need to analyze the cause of one's unbalanced perspectives.

Protruding nose refers to an interfering nature.

Pug nose is a lack of acceptance; a disagreeable nature.

Strep throat exposes a state of negative communication. Indicates a current stage of negativity toward another.

Swimmer's ear warns of receiving negative effects after listening to or accepting questionable spiritual matters.

Throat portrays the inflections in speech; how one often doesn't realize how one's tone of voice sounds to others.

Throat culture reveals a need to listen to oneself and realize the need to alter the tone in which one speaks.

Tone-deaf stands for one's unique talent of hearing (perceiving) things in a way that others don't.

Velum signifies a wispy veil separating the known from the unknown; a state of near-understanding.

Digestion

Acid reflux refers to a need to slow the rate of ingestion. Points to a tendency toward taking things in too fast; gulping; a rushed intake. This may apply to food ingestion or may be indicating a habit of mentally taking in information at too quick a pace.

Alimentary canal implies a need to focus on one's priorities.

Bellyache See stomachache.

Bile portrays aspects in one's life that are considered bitter.

Burp infers some irregularity with an aspect in one's life. A life element causing irritation.

Colic signifies life aspects that are not well accepted.

Colitis warns of intolerance.

Colon (anatomy) stands for preparations or a time frame preceding the act of shedding some excesses in one's life.

Colostomy denotes the use of alternate means of shedding one's excesses or extraneous aspects; bypassing the normal means.

Constipation is an inability to express oneself; a repressive personality; a possibly manipulative relationship.

Diarrhea defines an aspect in one's life that is difficult to control.

Esophagus denotes level of gullibility. Recall surrounding dreamscape facets and health or condition of the esophagus.

Excrement alludes to extraneous life aspects that one has successfully shed.

Flatulence relates to a pretentious nature; tedious verbosity.

Food intolerance refers to an idea that one can't accept.

Food poisoning warns of nourishment obtained from contaminated sources, showing a situation where one is absorbing false concepts, misconceptions, delusions, etc.

Gullet See esophagus.

Heartburn connotes emotional pain that can easily be alleviated if one so desires.

Indigestion indicates a situation or other aspect that one finds hard to stomach and points to a lack of acceptance.

Pancreas connotes a vital aspect in life that maintains a balanced perspective.

Pancreatitis warns of a perception that is in error.

Regurgitate corresponds to something one needs to bring up or get out of one's system.

Stomach alludes to fortitude.

Stomachache reveals a lack of inner strength or may indicate heightened sensitivity. May be a complainer or something one lacks stomach for.

Ulcer warns of stress that has been internalized and the need to alleviate it.

Vomiting See regurgitate.

Teeth

Baby tooth See milk tooth.
Bitewing (dental X-ray) suggests a need to check one's language for negativity or harmful words.
Braces (dental) indicate that one's verbal tendencies require strengthening. This may be pointing to stronger words needed, or it may imply a need for better aligned verbal expression (straight talk).
Bridge (dental) implies half-truths spoken. This may also indicate the need for more information regarding an issue.
Buck teeth show an outspoken individual, often one who speaks before thinking.
Cavity (tooth) warns against speaking infected words. This would indicate gossip, slander, false accusations, or a crass manner of speech.
Clenched teeth indicate controlled anger or the rising of same.
Dental exam advises a closer look at one's manner of speech; that perhaps a less harsh manner is indicated.
Denture denotes a new manner of beautiful speech. This would include the voicing of new, enlightening perspectives.
Dry socket indicates a negative effect resulting from one's verbiage.
False teeth See denture.
Filling (tooth) refers to an active effort to remove negative aspects from one's speech. This does not single out obscenities but is most often meant to relate to an individual's expression of overopinionated attitudes or hurtful expressions.

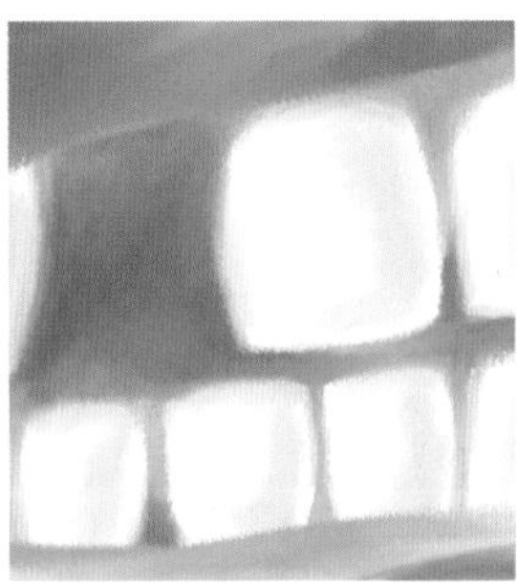

Gap-toothed means secretive.

Gap-toothed stands for holding back information or the whole story. Indicates an individual who doesn't reveal everything, preferring to keep some elements close to the vest.
Gold tooth signifies a brazen, pompous attitude regarding one's intellect—the verbal delivery of it.
Impacted (tooth) signifies a serious need to extract some negative type of speech. This could refer to the verbalization of a specific attitude that is causing harm to oneself and others.
Incisor alludes to cutting remarks.
Milk tooth symbolizes one's first experiences; beginning lessons in life.
Molar (tooth) represents an ability to process ideas. Recall the condition of the molar for further clarification of this intended meaning.
Overbite represents the withholding of select thoughts.
Plaque (dental) represents a careless attitude regarding the manner of one's speech; unguarded communications.
Primary tooth See milk tooth.
Retainer (dental) points to an attempt to maintain one's quality of speech or manner of communication.
Root canal symbolizes an urgency to clean out and medicate an infectiously harmful manner of speaking.
Sweet tooth correlates to an individual's strong desire for life to contain only desirable aspects; an inability to deal with reality without the urge to sweeten it.
Tartar (dental) points to a buildup of misspoken words or falsehoods.
Teeth are representative of the manner of an individual's speech that reflects their inner personality.
Teething ring constitutes an attempt to ease one's pain.
Tooth See teeth.
Toothache stands for emotional pain from something said or from withholding something that needs to be voiced. The dreamer will understand which was intended.
Toothless suggests an inability to express thoughts, opinions.
Wisdom tooth won't be associated with intellect but rather common sense required in the dreamer's life.

Mouth

Bad breath See halitosis.
Bleeding gums See gum disease.
Chapped lip refers to a need to soften one's language or manner of speaking.
Gag (reflex) refers to the inability to swallow something; a lack of acceptance; having to deal with a distasteful issue.
Gingivitis See gum disease.
Gum disease implies infected (negative) speech. This symbol could imply a tendency to gossip, or it could stand for half-truths or exaggerations.
Halitosis applies to offending language. This is usually associated with crude or insensitive comments that hurt others; thoughtlessness.
Lip See mouth.
Mouth represents the manner in which one speaks or communicates.
Mucus implies a protective agent in one's life. An excessive amount may point to a complex situation.
Palate corresponds to one's sense of taste in reference to behavior, choices, interaction, perception, and so on.
Pyorrhea reveals falsehoods. It may specifically refer to a faulty premise.
Saliva is a reference to softened speech; thoughtful communication.
Spittle See saliva.
Stammering is a representation of an inability to express oneself clearly.
Taste buds connote personal opinions and perspectives; a fact bearing on relativity and subjectivity.
Thirst signifies inner need or void. Exposes a drive or desire.
Tongue relates to the quality of an individual's manner of communication.
Tongue depressor advises silence. Indicates gossip.

see also
• Language *p. 131*
• Dentistry *p. 245*

Dental Care Products

Dental floss warns against making innuendos or voicing assumptions.
Dentifrice See toothpaste.
Electric toothbrush See toothbrush.
Floss See dental floss.
Teeth whitener stands for efforts expended toward improving one's manner of speech.
Toothbrush suggests a need to clean up one's speech. This may indicate hurtful or thoughtless words.
Toothpaste is representative of the attitude, belief, or perspective that will clean up one's manner of speech.
Toothpick connotes the presence of a negative aspect lodged in one's routine communication style that may need to be changed.

Abdomen & Urinary System

Abdomen means to take heed of one's inner prompting.
Adrenal glands signify aspects affecting one's emotions.
Adrenaline/epinephrine refers to situations or individuals who bring about high emotion; a passionate response or causal factor in one's life.
Belly See abdomen.
Bladder stands for an aspect in one's life that holds negatives within. Warns of a need to release negative elements.
Cirrhosis warns of a situation filled with negatives; a negatively congested aspect.
Gallbladder relates to accumulation of life trials. Recall condition.
Gallstone characterizes accepted tribulations; life stressors that have taken their toll on one.
Jaundice warns of an individual's waning strength.
Kidney represents a cleansing factor, usually refers to mental or emotional aspects.
Kidney stone advises of a blocking factor in one's life.
Kidney transplant See operation.
Liver illustrates fortitude.
Liver disease warns against giving up; losing motivation.
Liver spots represent hard work and hardships one has endured through life.
Liver transplant See operation.
Spleen means hidden emotion.
Urine is representative of necessary waste. More specifically, it refers to the idea that some elements in one's life are harmful if they are retained.
Urine sample advises of the wisdom of testing ourselves for any negative attitudes.

Hepatitis

Hepatitis A is an advisement of a harmful effect caused by something to which one has innocently exposed oneself.
Hepatitis B is representative of a harmful effect caused by bad blood and/or by bad relationships.
Hepatitis C reveals a harmful effect caused by something to which one has willfully exposed oneself.

Respiration & Lungs

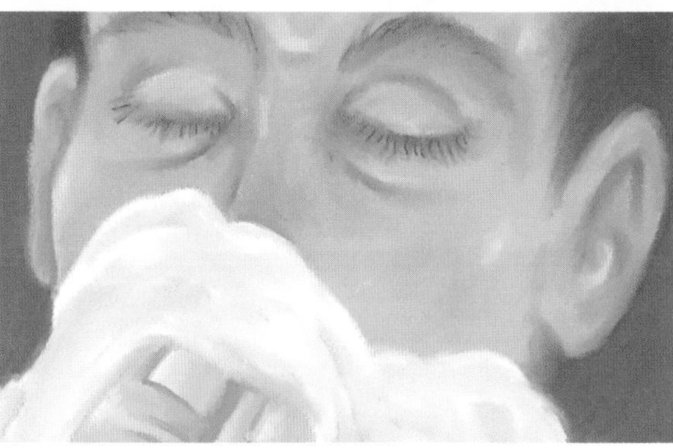

Sneeze represents an attempt to expel something that is annoying one.

Airway most often refers to inspiration. New life breathed into an idea or old thought. Was the dreamscape airway open or blocked?
Asphyxia means something is smothering the dreamer.
Asthma connotes more breathing room is required.
Breath exemplifies one's inner life force.
Breathless cautions the dreamer to slow down.
Bronchitis alludes to inability to clearly process thoughts and ideas. May reflect a congestion involving emotions.
Chest refers to our protected emotional center.
Congestion (lung) See pneumonia.
Congestion (sinus) refers to a suffocating situation requiring clearing so one can breathe freely. Suggests a need to clear the air.
Cough portrays a fear of disclosure; fear of the truth.
Dyspnea cautions of a need to slow one's pace for the purpose of breathing more deeply and more freely; a need for breathing room.
Emphysema cautions of dishonesty.
Inhalator See respirator.
Inhaler corresponds with an aspect in an individual's life that has the capability of easing tension or stress.
Lung connotes one's ability to take in and sort out the positive from the negative.
Lung transplant See operation.
Phlegm indicates a congested condition, usually within one's mind; confusion.
Pleurisy results from an intake of a negative idea or concept.
Pneumonia means a lack of breathing room.
Respirator denotes something that helps one breathe easier by filtering out impurities. This symbol implies that there are negative attitudes affecting one from outside sources.
Short-winded usually points to something said in a concise manner; the main issue packed in a nutshell.
Sinus congestion See congestion (sinus).
Sneeze usually stands for an effort to rid oneself of an irritation. May point to the presence of an irritating element in one's life.
Spitball refers to unethical practices.

Reproduction, Sexual Health & Diseases

Breast relates to emotions, usually unexpressed sensitivity.
Change of life See menopause.
Crabs See sexual disease.
Erectile dysfunction will sometimes equate to the body itself but will most often indicate an ineffective attitude or course of action.
Eunuch alludes to an individual uninterested in the physical aspects of life. May point to some type of inadequacy or ineffectiveness.
Flaccid means a loss of resilience; lack of motivation or energy.
Genitalia may suggest a need to be more productive in life, or it may warn of some type of negative aspect specific to a physical condition.
Impotency won't normally have a sexual association. Usually this refers to generalized ineffectiveness.
Infertility doesn't usually refer to the physical reproductive system. Rather it indicates a lack of spiritual fruitfulness; an absence of spiritual giving.
Jock itch alludes to problems of a sexual nature. Usually these are not physical but rather tend to indicate a psychological source.
Libido usually denotes personal motivation; one's mental and emotional strength.
Menopause defines a life or path change. This dream symbol could well reveal that a key element in one's life has stopped being effective and advises of a total acceptance of that loss rather than trying to replace it or keep it active.
Menstruation can have a variety of meanings depending on the surrounding related elements. It could point to a phase of fertileness. It may indicate an unfruitful situation, relationship, or path. This symbol might indicate a time when one is in one's power. And, for some, it spells relief.
Neuter denotes a cause or source barring effectiveness.
Night sweats usually stand for the fears and anxieties that one keeps hidden during the daytime hours. Also see menopause.
Penile augmentation refers to an individual's belief that one is not effective; an attempt to improve one's self-image. May point to misplaced priorities and is rarely associated with an actual physical augmentation but relates to a sense of needing a greater type of power, such as being perceived as being influential or close to an A-list personality.
Penile dysfunction suggests an inability to carry out one's intent or see things through to their conclusion. Usually this symbol will not be literal but rather refers to plans, goals, resolutions, and the like.
Period See menstruation.
Premenstrual syndrome (PMS) crosses the gender line to reflect a life element that personally affects someone and causes stress.
Sexual disease exposes the result of indiscriminate behavior; lack of responsible discernment and restraint.
Venereal disease See sexual disease.

Pregnancy

Abortion symbolizes a voluntary separation from something; a conscious choice to distance oneself. This dreamscape symbol is rarely literal.
Amniocentesis represents an inner knowing or precognition. It may point specifically to an ability to see though superficial presentations. A skill that allows one to get to the core of an issue.
Amniotic fluid refers to the safeguards in place to protect a new endeavor.
Artificial insemination is an allusion to a way around barriers to produce the same goal or result in an aspect of the dreamer's life.
Barren implies a lack of new life or lack of new emotional, intellectual, or spiritual growth. May warn of an apathetic perspective.
Eclampsia warns of a hazardous path chosen.
Ectopic pregnancy comes to the dreamer as a warning of the danger of forcing new beginnings before one has reached the appropriate time and place along one's path. Groundwork needs to be done before one can put plans into action.
Embryo illustrates the beginning stage of a new direction or belief.
Fallopian tube indicates the initial aspect that could lead to a new beginning.
False pregnancy naturally stands for a false start after trying for a new beginning or path in one's life.
Fetal position means a severe lack of self-confidence; fear of facing reality or responsibilities. It may specifically indicate how one's new path is lining up.
Fetus characterizes a new life; new beginning.
Gestation period represents the phase of preparation and development of a new idea or venture.
Miscarriage denotes the shedding of an erroneous spiritual belief.
Morning sickness implies an inner anxiety to make a new beginning; doubts.
Placenta corresponds to an essential element in one's life; a nourishing aspect.
Pregnancy signifies an embryonic stage of a specific type of awareness or enlightenment. May point to the beginning formulation of a plan or idea.
Pregnancy test refers to a question as to whether or not this is a good time to start a new venture or beginning.
Prenatal typifies the phase or time before the actual beginning of a new course.
Stretch mark is a reminder that one has stretched his or her potential or perceptions in the past and can do it again.
Umbilical cord signifies vital connections; a strong bond.

see also
• Love & Sex *p. 126*
• Children *p. 127*

Birth

Afterbirth refers to aspects leading up to the birth of an idea. May also be pointing to hindsight.

Baby blues See postpartum depression.

Birth always points to some type of new life; renewal; new beginnings.

Birth canal means the path to some type of rebirth, perhaps the way to a revelation.

Birth certificate may be suggestive of a past-life identity that represents one's spiritual heritage, or it may come as a validation of new thought.

Birth defect cautions one to watch out for some type of defect presenting itself along a new path taken.

Birthing center reveals the atmosphere or surroundings that will provide opportunities for new beginnings.

Birth pang signifies adjustments required along one's new path. No path is without obstacles or patches of rough road.

Blue baby connotes a new beginning that is struggling for air; a difficult start.

Breech delivery warns of a backward or upside-down outcome to a developing relationship or situation.

Cesarean section reveals an immediate action needed to save a new beginning.

Colostrum defines an aspect that nourishes and protects.

Crib death (SIDS) represents an individual's voluntary withdrawal from reality.

Delivery room See birthing center.

Difficult labor (maternity) signifies great personal efforts being applied to changing one's life.

Labor pains represent the difficulties one faces when starting afresh.

Emergency childbirth (unplanned birth) signifies a premature manifestation of a goal or new life.

Fetal distress warns of dangerous aspects related to new beginnings.

Forceps warns against forcing a spiritual rebirth.

Freeborn comes to encourage one to cherish uniqueness and express independent behavior and thought.

Full-term is an indication of completeness; the achievement or development of something that won't succeed unless it's given its full measure of time to manifest according to plan.

Incubator denotes special nurturing care one gives to newborn concepts or paths.

Labor (birth) See difficult labor (maternity).

Labor pain stands for the tribulations encountered while making a new start or beginning a new journey.

Lamaze (training/method of natural childbirth) symbolizes good intentions.

Newborn corresponds with a new life, path, belief, or other type of personal discovery.

Postpartum depression means anxiety and self-doubts after beginning a new direction.

Postpartum pains are suggestive of the need to let go of a hurtful aspect.

Preemie See premature.

Premature is a representation of something that is not developed enough to attempt or give greater attention to. The timing isn't right yet.

Receiving blanket corresponds to an individual's quality of preparedness for accepting a new direction. The key here is to recall the blanket's condition and color.

Shaken-baby syndrome connotes the willful destruction of a new idea or opportunity.

Stillbirth portrays an unproductive beginning; a bad start.

Test-tube baby connotes a personally engineered plan for a new life or direction.

Babies

Breast-feeding usually refers to a nurturing nature. May also indicate immaturity and/or a fear of being independent.

Breast pump suggests a need to give nourishment to another.

Children connote a stage of acceptance and innocence; a belief in possibilities and one's dreams.

Crack baby reveals a new plan or path having negative aspects right from the start.

Diaper rash refers to a life element causing irritation. May also point to a need to get moving, get motivated.

First-born characterizes one's initial achievement of a new beginning that leads to additional ones.

Offspring signifies aspects of ourselves or those qualitative elements one leaves behind.

Pacifier indicates an easier path chosen.

Progeny See offspring; children.

Triplets constitute three new beginnings or starts. This doesn't mean a choice between them needs to be made. These three new aspects will usually be very different from each other and will exist simultaneously in one's life.

Twins are representative of the duality or polarity of life.

Weaned is representative of inner growth.

Sexuality & Nakedness

Castration is suggestive of efforts expended to control an individual's wanderlust.

Nakedness connotes an open heart. It suggests that one has nothing to hide; no agendas or ulterior motives.

Nude See nakedness.

Nudist colony portrays honesty among one's associates.

Sex change is representative of an inability to accept and relate to the specific elements one's spirit has chosen to utilize for one's current path progression. This symbol may also reveal a strong recognition with one's prime spirit identity that cannot be overcome by the current life status.

Contraception

Birth control (methods) warn of a reluctance to change one's life or make new beginnings; a reluctance to start over.

Condom connotes the level of one's protective concerns.

Contraceptive See birth control (methods).

Family planning pertains to personal responsibility for one's future.

Intrauterine device (IUD) See birth control (methods).

Rhythm method See birth control (methods).

Vasectomy represents a behavior that results in ineffectiveness; an inability to generate new beginnings.

Skeletal Anatomy

Forehead is a representation of one's outlook on life.

Back (anatomy) refers to unseen or unanticipated events; surprises. May also point to a need to watch one's back, meaning either physical or situational aspects.

Backbone pertains to strength of character. Recall the condition and alignment.

Bare bones apply to essentials; bottom-line facts.

Bone represents aspects in one's life that signify foundations. This could be attitudes, relationships, or belief systems.

Bone marrow pertains to the life of an individual's foundational beliefs.

Brow See forehead.

Cartilage implies tenacity; a resilient personality.

Cast (bone) comes as a cautionary message. Warns against going too fast; a headlong pace without looking where one is going.

Coccyx signifies one's base or foundational attitudes.

Forearm alludes to defense attitudes or preparations.

Forehead indicates a clue to how one perceives life aspects.

Forehead, broad applies to an open mind.

Forehead, narrow denotes narrow thinking.

Forehead, pitted relates to ingrained opinions; single-mindedness.

Forehead, scarred stands for lessons learned through previous misconceptions.

Forehead, slanted depicts biased or prejudiced perceptual handicap.

Forehead, wrinkled would mean one who worries or is overly skeptical.

Funny bone corresponds to the funny feelings one gets; perceptual sensations that accompany sudden insights.

Hip may refer to relationships, or it may be indicating an actual physical aspect.

Ingrown (nail) warns of self-imposed grief, stress, or pain.

Jaw pertains to the level of one's inner strength. Was the jaw strong? Thin?

Ligament defines an essential bond or connection in one's life.

Marrow See bone marrow.

Muscle signifies effort applied. This symbol will reveal the quality of effort by displaying the condition of the muscle.

Pelvis (anatomy) relates to the center or beginning point of one's inner strength.

Rib (all types) stands for one's aspects supporting the heart (emotions).

Rib cage implies an emotionally protective element in an individual's life.

Rubberneck points to a nosy individual, one loving gossip.

Sacrum correlates to the root of emotion.

Shoulder (anatomy) denotes the quality and quantity of one's inner strength. Recall if the shoulder was slouched, rounded, padded, thick, etc.

Sinew symbolizes a staunch character; having stamina.

Skeleton may signify the bare bones of an issue, or it may allude to personal hidden elements.

Skull represents the encasement of one's thoughts; the embodiment of a person's overall thought patterns.

Solar plexus is the center of one's sensitivity and power.

Spinal cord signifies the strength of an individual's inner life force.

Spine See backbone.

Tailbone See coccyx.

Whiplash warns against allowing others to push or force progression.

see also
• Hand & Arm Movements *p. 175*
• Footwear *p. 408*

Hands & Arms

Age spots (on hands) suggest knowledge gained through experience.

Ambidextrous denotes one's ability to see all facets or perspectives of a situation.

Arm signifies personal work or efforts applied to one's purpose.

Artificial nails See false nails.

Digit See toe or specific finger.

Dishpan hands indicate concerned efforts to communicate well or one who is almost obsessive about tying up loose ends.

Elbow signifies personal space affording comfortable distance from others.

Fake nails See false nails.

False nails represent a false sense of security.

Finger usually represents various types of behavior.

Fingernail connotes the quality of one's personal efforts. The condition it is in will clarify.

Fingers (crossed) are an indication of hope.

Fist comes to the dreamer as a caution about building internal emotions.

Forefinger See index finger.

Hand connotes service done for others. Recall condition of same.

Handless suggests a feeling of helplessness.

Hangnail denotes a lack of acceptance; worries or anxieties one tends to pick over; fretting.

Index finger usually implies an accusation of some type. Also can indicate something to which the dreamer needs to give attention or notice—a pointing finger.

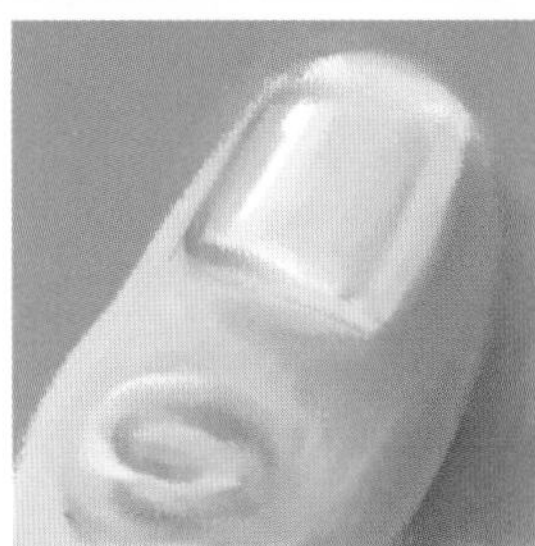

Thumbnail is incomplete knowledge.

Knuckle may refer to a conflict, frequently within self, or it may be relating to a need to apply oneself in a more serious manner.

Left-handed means ambiguous; perplexing statements or situations; tactless or cryptic.

Little finger refers to the smaller aspects of the self that help to create the whole character.

Middle finger indicates centeredness; a balancing element in one's life.

Nail (finger/toe) See fingernail.

Nail biting stands for a lack of acceptance; anxiety and worry; lack of faith.

Palm (hand) emphasizes revealing qualities of one's character. Recall if the dream palm was soft or calloused. Did it hold something? Was it in a giving or taking position?

Pinkie See little finger.

Right hand suggests trust and reliability.

Ring finger alludes to how an individual chooses to present oneself to others; affectations of character.

Southpaw See left-handed.

Thumb implies a grasp (understanding) or guide.

Thumbnail will usually indicate a sketchy plan or level of understanding.

Legs & Feet

Ankle denotes support of one's burdens in life.

Feet indicate how one travels one's path. Recall condition.

Flat-footed illustrates an uncompromising nature.

Foot signifies one's journey along one's path and the type of behavior used to progress.

Footsore is a warning. Your walk along your life path has been too full of attempts to force goals. There is a need to ease up and allow events to unfold naturally.

Heel symbolizes exhaustion.

Knee corresponds with adaptability; resiliency.

Kneecap See patella.

Lap refers to a closeness.

Leg denotes a supportive aspect in one's life. In what condition was this symbol? Was it strong or weak?

Little toe pertains to an aspect that adds to stability or the creation of balance in life.

Metastasis means something has spread, widened in scope.

Patella is a vulnerable aspect.

Toe refers to an aspect in one's life that contributes to a balanced course.

Weak-kneed relates to an individual's lack of courage or self-confidence.

Diagnosis & Testing

Biotelemetry portrays self-awareness. It may refer specifically to a heightened awareness of all aspects of the self.

Clinical (explanation or description) means the basic facts of something, of a particular issue.

Contraindications are the possible negatives one may encounter by a certain behavior or chosen path.

False negative (test result) stands for a wrongly accused innocent individual.

False positive (test result) is representative of a negative element mistaken for being positive.

Inkblot test See Rorschach test.

Mammogram advises of a need to examine one's recent expressions of compassion or emotional sensitivity. This also may refer to a physiological condition.

Misdiagnosis advises of a wrong cause or source attributed to a life event.

Personality test calls for self-analysis; introspection into the root causes behind one's behavior and attitudes. It may reveal one's trouble areas in getting along with others.

Petri dish calls to the dreamer for a need to develop or expand a particular aspect in one's life.

Rorschach test points to a different valid way to view something.

Scratch test (for allergy) is an attempt to define the source of one's life irritations.

Skin test See scratch test (for allergy).

Terminal (diagnosis) most often refers to a dead-end situation, one that has no chance for revitalization.

Tissue-typing is representative of a need to keep life elements compatible.

Mental Disorders & Behavior

Aeroneurosis warns of excessive thought given to an issue.

Alzheimer's disease is a suggestion to be more focused.

Autism indicates the willful suppression of an individual's inner light and/or spiritual knowledge.

Bipolar denotes duality or the center between two extremes. May point to indecision.

Bipolar (disease) See manic-depressive.

Bulimarexia (bulimia and anorexia) comes to illustrate a lack of self-control; a love/hate attitude.

Bulimia connotes an inability to voice or stand up for personal opinions. It means that one publicly agrees with popular opinion but secretly rejects them.

Catatonia characterizes an autistic-type of perception; extreme apathy.

Cold sweat indicates nervousness, fear, or anxiety.

Crack See mental breakdown.

Delirium suggests a loss of all control.

Delusion comes to reveal a false belief, perhaps an instance of fooling oneself or creating a false belief so as not to be forced to face a reality.

Dementia See insanity.

Depression (mental) comes as a warning against a perception of hopelessness or loss of acceptance.

Dip (depression) suggests a temporary diversion from the norm.

Dyslexia stands for impaired perception, usually reversing or transposing the main aspects of an issue or idea.

Malaise indicates an uneasiness or sense of disturbance in one's life; a disquieting sense. Often forewarns of an impending disruption.

Manic-depressive (illness) pertains to a vacillation between extremes.

Mental breakdown denotes a lack of acceptance; an inability to cope with reality.

Monomania indicates a destructive fanaticism.

Multiple personality will reveal inner thoughts or attitudes.

Nerve block usually refers to a self-generated, psychological blocking being done; selective sensitivity.

Nerve-racking indicates an inability to overlook life irritations; a need for acceptance to generate inner tranquility.

Nervous breakdown signifies a need for inner strength and acceptance.

Neurosis defines a lack of acceptance resulting in a loss of inner peace.

Neurotic characterizes multiple inner fears; lack of trust and acceptance.

Oblivion means a state of mind devoid of emotion, purpose, or humanitarian aspects.

Paranoia is an illustration of one's subconscious anxieties and apprehensions.

Panic attack stands for an overwhelming situation.

Paranoia reveals inner fears. Also see fear.

Phantom-limb pain underscores the reality of one's essence.

Posttraumatic stress disorder exemplifies extremely severe effects remaining from a highly stressful or emotionally impressionable experience.

Primal scream warns of being pushed past one's limit or endurance; a phase of ultimate stress.

Problem will relate to just that—a problem in an individual's life, yet a dream problem will frequently define the difficulty more clearly and could offer a solution.

Schizophrenia marks someone who is not (or has a hard time being) true to oneself.

Seasonal affective disorder advises of a need to stay on an even emotional keel and not be affected by external shifts in opinion or attitude.

Senility See Alzheimer's disease.

Sensory deprivation is usually a warning to stop depriving oneself of emotional expression or interaction. Indicates insensitivity; possible apathy.

Shell-shocked exposes traumatic effects from an experience.

Split personality stands for indecision, vacillation.

Stress warns of a mental and emotional state that lacks the quality of acceptance.

Stupor implies a state of mental confusion or unawareness.

Vertigo reflects dizziness or confusion; an inability to think straight.

see also
• Extreme Behaviors *p. 137*
• Psychiatry *p. 245*

Diseases

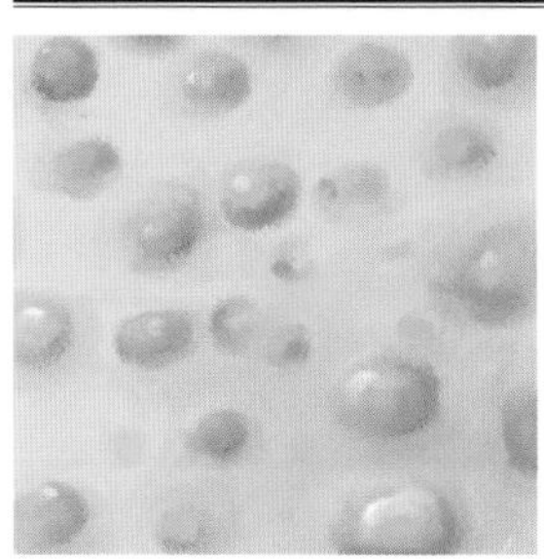

Smallpox represents a bad thing.

Anthrax is representative of the often fatal effects of being a follower rather than an original thinker.

Bacteria denotes infectious situations or relationships; a warning symbol.

Black death means a fatal situation or relationship.

Black lung (disease) corresponds to the acceptance of dark thoughts and ideas.

Botulism comes to the dreamer as a caution against the severely damaging effects of negative thought and action.

Bubonic plague pertains to highly contagious negative attitudes. Demonstrates the speed and destructive force of following the crowd when the crowd is in serious error; a contaminant.

Cancer is a grave warning to watch for an extremely dangerous negative.

Cat scratch disease suggests a negative response to one's expression of independent behavior or thought.

Chicken pox warns of the negative effects caused by a lack of courage or faith.

Cholera means a lack of intestinal fortitude.

Cold (illness) See head cold.

Diabetes alludes to an imbalance in one's life.

Diphtheria symbolizes the potential vulnerability of one's emotional state.

Disease exemplifies a mental, physical, or spiritual state lacking well-being. See specific disease.

Dysentery indicates a mental state that lacks the ability to absorb or retain information.

Flu See virus.

Germs signify negative aspects with which one could contaminate oneself.

Head cold signifies a clogged mind; a need to clear one's thoughts.

Influenza See virus.

Legionnaires' disease indicates the presence of a hidden, potentially harmful negative aspect in one's life.

Lesion pertains to a life irritation that one has allowed to get under the skin; a lack of acceptance.

Lockjaw See tetanus.

Lyme disease warns of internalizing personal irritations; a lack of acceptance.

Lymphoma reveals an inability to defend oneself, usually self-generated by controlling psychological manipulations.

Mad cow disease reveals the danger of ingesting (accepting) negative ideas that were never viable from the outset.

Malaria usually equates to an obsession; fanaticism.

Malignancy is a harmful negative in one's life.

Measles warn of the act of internalizing negative feelings.

Melanoma See malignancy.

Mumps denote an inability to express emotional responses.

Muscular dystrophy refers to an inability to motivate oneself.

Pertussis See whooping cough.

Plague pertains to a serious negative element in one's life that has the potential to be emotionally, mentally, or spiritually fatal.

Pneumonia represents a negative element that is causing a suffocating effect; a lack of breathing room.

Poliomyelitis shows a negative aspect that has hampered an individual's ability to develop or advance as planned. Calls for an alternate plan.

Pox stands for a phase of misfortune; continual bad luck.

Rabies refer to a potentially fatal negative element.

Salmonella applies to seriously negative results from ingesting harmful ideas or influences.

Sleeping sickness suggests little time spent in full awareness. This symbol warns of possible efforts expended toward denial or avoidance of reality.

Smallpox pertains to a negative element that has infiltrated a person's life.

Tetanus reveals a lack of awareness. It may also refer to carelessness.

Tuberculosis comes to the dreamer as an advisement of a need for breathing room. Something in one's life is suffocating the very breath out of one or drowning one with a sense of being overwhelmed.

Tumor warns of the presence of a negative attitude that has the capability of consuming oneself.

Virus will pertain to a dangerous negative element that is contaminating one's life.

Whooping cough reveals an individual's inability to deal with reality, life.

Fevers

Cabin fever signifies an individual's desire to be close to nature without being vibrationally aligned; a forcing action applied to one's wants or goals.

Fever usually refers to fanaticism. This symbol may also indicate a self-generated negative state that one must internally fight to overcome.

Hay fever warns against a reluctance to work; laziness.

Heat stroke connotes overwork; unregulated energy usage.

Scarlet fever represents the harmful results of accepting a negative idea.

Spotted fever typifies the negativity (illness) brought on by allowing life irritations to "get under the skin" and infect one with feelings of resentment or blame.

Swamp fever indicates the effects of becoming immersed in spiritual confusion.

Typhoid fever warns of the harmful effects of spiritual untruths.

Yellow fever exposes a poor self-image. Frequently signifies a huge ego that constantly needs stroking from all those around one.

Skeletal Disorders

Arthritis is representative of a hidden fear or retained life stressors.

Backache is indicative of burdens carried, possibly in a silent manner, which can frequently internalize emotional pain.

Back pressure is representative of a restrained condition in the dreamer's life.

Brittle (bones) suggests weakness in respect to fortitude and perseverance.

Bursitis is representative of a reluctance to act or go forward in one's life.

Carpal tunnel syndrome warns of repetitiveness. Suggests the use of alternatives.

Fracture (bone) implies a defect; a crack in one's personality or plan; something amiss. Surrounding details will clarify this specific meaning for the dreamer.

Growing pains are an advisement to slow down. They indicate a forcing of development or advancement.

Hammer toes indicate difficulty walking one's path.

Immobilized See paralysis.

Maimed denotes a temporary difficulty to overcome. The key here is "overcome."

Monoplegia reveals a self-generated mental or emotional handicap.

Muscle cramp/spasm signifies a hitch with plans or behavior.

Neck ache stands for a self-generated block to one's desire to gain further knowledge on a specific subject; frustration over trying to solve a problem or figure out solutions.

Osteoporosis indicates a failing of an individual's inner strength; waning motivation or sense of purpose.

Paralysis characterizes a psychological state of denial; a tendency to be emotionally numb or remain in an immobilized state.

Paraplegia emphasizes the true essence of an individual. Underscores the "mind" as being one's beingness.

Quadriplegic enters dreams to remind us that mental skills can take priority over physical ability.

Rheumatism See arthritis.

Sciatica exposes a displaced attitude or perspective; a constant wear on one's nerve.

Scoliosis (curved spine) portrays an inability to stand up straight for oneself.

Spinal cord injury points to a weakened sense of fortitude.

Sprain corresponds with a temporary setback caused by a lack of awareness.

Tennis elbow comes to the dreamer as an advisement of the negative effect of routinely attempting to hit the ball back into another's court.

Sleeping Disorders

Insomnia characterizes one who fights acceptance.

Narcolepsy (sleepiness) denotes escapism; denial.

Nightmare emphasizes one's inner fears.

Night terror relates to vulnerability; an individual's deeply subconscious susceptibility to awake-state subliminal suggestive impressions.

Sleep deprivation warns of a severe need to cut back on work and/or stressors.

Sleepwalking may stand for walking through life without awareness, or it may indicate a true other-state awareness during the sleep state.

Somnambulism See sleepwalking.

Minor Ailments

Blue lips show poor communication.

Aches represent life pains one allows oneself to feel.

Airsickness symbolizes a fear of having or expressing one's unique or different ideas.

Athlete's foot cautions against giving priority to physical accomplishments rather than focusing on spiritual aspects.

Blue lips suggest an inability to express opinions, attitudes.

Carsick shows an inner recognition of a wrong path taken.

Chill connotes a cooling-down aspect to a situation or relationship. May advise one to stop being angry and give more thought to something.

Fatigue is a call to reenergize oneself and usually indicates energy ill spent due to a weakened condition.

Hangover denotes the negative results of irresponsibility.

Heat exhaustion warns of a depletion of one's energy; a time to rest and recoup.

Hemorrhoid corresponds with a harmful situation in one's life. Usually it relates to anxiety and stress.

Hiccup is an interruption. Surrounding dream details will relate this to a situation in the dreamer's life.

Motion sickness reveals psychological restrictions placed on oneself to prevent development or path advancement; a fear of advancing; a lack of self-confidence or reliance.

Nosebleed implies an interfering nature.

Pins and needles most often correspond with a high state of anticipation or anxiety. This is synonymous with an expectation that is in direct opposition to acceptance. This is an advisement to gain acceptance in one's life.

Queasy will reveal guilt or a conscience-stricken mood. May also point to a fear.

Restless leg syndrome stands for a need to pace oneself. May indicate anxiety.

Seasickness stands for an individual's state of spiritual confusion; spiritual dizziness or nausea from taking in too much too fast.

Stitch (pain) comes as a caution against going too fast or forcing an issue.

Sunstroke represents a lack in personal spiritual discernment; an inability to control which concepts are accepted.

Swoon portrays an overwhelming response.

see also
• Illness & Physiology Phobias *p. 155*
• Sleeping *p. 179*

Conditions

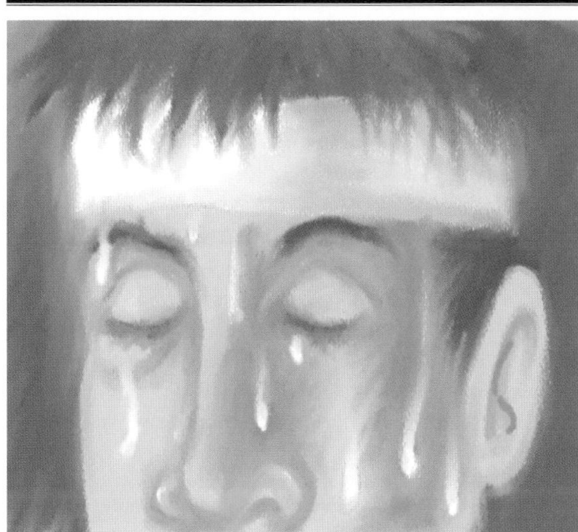

Sweat is a reflection of one's struggle to achieve something.

Aging denotes the passing of time in life; maturity. May refer to a new stage of mellowness, acceptance.
Allergy indicates negative aspects directly associated with relationships or belief systems.
Altitude sickness symbolizes haughtiness or aloofness.
Bedridden is a forewarning against working too hard.
Body odor is offensive behavior.
Clammy cautions of unpleasant aspects in one's life. Indicates an uneasiness; apprehensiveness; nervousness.
Collapse indicates failure; lack of support or strength.
Dead spot characterizes a mental block or lack of communication.
Dehydration (of body) usually points to a spiritual need.
Drug reaction See allergy.
Feebleness warns of a dependency.
Gangrene denotes a self-destructive aspect in one's life.
Goose bumps connote one's immediate reaction to fear.
Grand mal (seizure) indicates that serious repercussions will be forthcoming.
Groggy warns against a lack of awareness.
Hernia reveals a forced action taken in one's life.
Incontinence will not signify a physical condition in one's waking state, but rather it will caution of a need to use more restraint in life.
Infection points to the negative effects of a destructive element in one's life. Something needs to be dealt with before it gets worse.
Lactose intolerance indicates emotional sensitivity.
Lightheaded can refer to a state of being overwhelmed, or it may indicate a frivolous personality who has no handle on reality or responsibility.
Male menopause See midlife crisis.
Midlife crisis indicates a lack of acceptance; an inability to recognize the divine force within oneself.
Mountain sickness See altitude sickness.
Pain is a harmful element in one's life caused by external sources or self-generated.
Palsy suggests a self-generated impairment.
Perspiring alludes to great energy and effort expended. It may also refer to embarrassment or a stressful situation.
Photosensitivity depicts a psychologically based negative response to spiritually related truths or higher knowledge.
Precancerous (condition) warns of a highly dangerous situation that has the potential of developing into a hopeless or fatal conclusion.
Purulent See infection.
Pustule See infection.
Radiation sickness reveals negative ramifications spreading far enough to affect innocent parties.
Rupture denotes a flaw in a plan or one's thinking.
Seizure warns of a serious adverse reaction; negative aspect that causes an instantaneous response. It may also point to denial.
Spasm most often represents an awakening type of reaction.
Stamina will represent perseverance; fortitude.
Stroke (sun) See sunstroke.
Sunstroke represents a lack in personal spiritual discernment; an inability to control which concepts are accepted.
Sweat indicates personal effort expended. May also point to expectation and impatience.
Weakness (physical) represents a lack of courage; fear of responsibility.

Immune & Deficiency Diseases

AIDS represents fear of expressing intimate feelings. May indicate bad intentions.
Beriberi signifies a repulsive or distasteful aspect that one tries to avoid getting close to.
Deficiency disease See specific disease.
Lupus stands for repression.
Malabsorption disease reveals an inability to tolerate ideas one doesn't believe in.
Malnutrition warns of a seriously imbalanced perspective or behavior.
Rickets reveals an individual's lack of positive reinforcement; a poor self-image.
Scabies stand for a parasitic (negative) aspect that one has allowed to invade oneself.
Scurvy defines a lack of inner strength; a weakening of foundational elements.

Swellings

Edema warns of too much focus being done on a specific spiritual aspect.
Swelling See swollen.
Swollen indicates an expanded element. May refer to an excess of something.
Water retention usually stands for a withholding of one's natural talents. It comes as a warning to release one's inherent abilities and share them. Practice more spiritual goodness.

Medical Terms

Affliction represents aspects in one's life that one allows to cause negative effects.

Bends (decompression) warns of the ramifications of trying to advance too quickly.

Bill of health characterizes one's state of health.

Biological clock always denotes physical age and the passing of time. This means one is getting older, so it'd be wise to attend to priorities.

Biorhythm characterizes our vibratory and cyclical connectedness to earth and all life upon it.

Contagion warns of an extremely harmful influence.

Contagious connotes a perception, belief, or attitude that will quickly be accepted by others.

Convulsion portrays a violently uncontrollable response; a strong knee-jerk reaction.

Cure refers to healing or the preservation of something.

Donor (organ) reveals a generous heart; someone willing to freely give of self. See transplant (specific organ).

Donor card (organ) verifies one's generous heart and goodness.

Immunity connotes level and strength of personal methods of protection against negative aspects. This may point to a talent for exceptional perceptiveness. This symbol could also refer to innocence or a lack of guilt regarding something in particular.

Implant (medical, nonspecific) signifies a need to replace a negative in one's life. This may refer to a physical, mental, emotional, or spiritual aspect.

Internal clock See biological clock.

Lymph node represents personal defense mechanisms.

Malignancy reveals a harmful negative existing in one's life or within oneself. This usually won't be associated with a physical cancer.

Medical record refers to one's history of behavior and whether or not it was healthy.

Nerve will correspond with a specific type of emotional sensitivity. Recall dreamscape details for further clarity.

Numbness warns of a self-induced state of emotional or mental selectivity; a willful ignorance or insensitivity.

Off-color points to something that's been compromised by an affecting attitude, perhaps a judgment or opinion that's biased or affected by personal perspective.

Organ (anatomical) See specific type.

Patient (infirm) implies a need for care or healing. Recall the dreamscape details for clarity.

Pressure point (physiological) refers to one's specific area of contention.

Referred pain reflects a refusal to acknowledge the specific source of a harmful element in one's life; the creation of a scapegoat.

Remission signifies an abating or diminishing element.

Sick people illustrate mental dysfunctions or physical diseases. Recall what the illnesses were. See sick-out.

Sick-out refers to people who share a disagreement about an issue and protest silently; a passive expression of protest.

Sickroom won't necessarily refer to a literally sick individual but more often points to the negative elements (bad feelings) in an individual's life that are withheld or carried around and have the potential to ultimately cause harm to oneself or to others.

Sterile symbolizes a condition free of negative elements yet may also point to a tendency to isolate oneself instead of jumping in and getting one's hands dirty.

Syndrome suggests a particular personality aspect generated from various causes. May denote a unique perspective derived from multiple experiential sources.

Transplant relates to new ground in which to develop; a fresh beginning.

Vegetative state warns of an attitude of indifference, apathy, and/or unawareness.

Waiting list illustrates a popular or desirable aspect. What was the waiting list for?

Anesthesia & Pain Management

Analgesic reveals that painless resolutions are possible. Refers to the existence of a life aspect that has the properties of a soothing balm.

Anesthesia warns of apathy.

Anesthetic (general) signifies one's total apathy.

Anesthetic (local) symbolizes one's selective apathy.

Aspirin signifies the need for respite.

Chloroform warns of a dangerous lack of awareness or attention to vitally important elements in one's life.

Codeine represents life factors that we believe help us get through more difficult times.

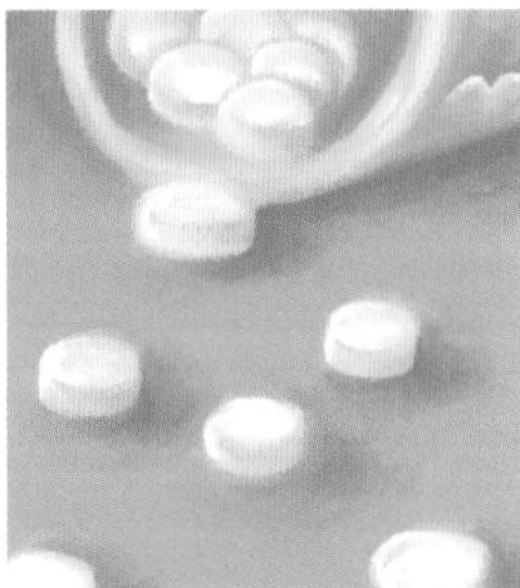

Aspirin warns one to take a break.

Curare warns against continual states of stress; a need to relax.

Ether (anesthetic) warns of total apathy or a stage in one's life where selective awareness is utilized. This comes as a warning message.

Knockout drops are something that takes one by surprise or is completely unexpected.

Laudanum See opium.

Laughing gas See nitrous oxide.

Local anesthetic See anesthetic (local).

Nitrous oxide refers to a psychological mechanism one uses to ease life's pains.

Novocain warns of a state of self-induced apathy; an individual's purposeful avoidance of life aspects.

Opium means that which one allows to dull one's senses, intelligence, reasoning, or perspective.

Painkiller See analgesic.

see also
• Medical & Pharmaclinical *p. 246*
• Health *p. 378*

Medical Equipment

Antiseptic reveals a need to protect against a negative situation, relationship, or belief system.
Artificial limb See prosthesis.
Athletic supporter symbolizes the guarding of one's weak or vulnerable points.
Autoclave See sterile.
Backboard warns against a reluctance to seek emotional support or counsel. May reveal a need for assistance in strengthening perseverance.
Bedpan cautions against an inability to rest well; a tendency to bring work into times designated for rest.
Catheter applies to a need to get rid of what one is retaining; the need for routine self-analysis.
Compress (bandage) advises of an urgent need to attend to an unhealthy situation; needing pressure (energy) put on something to staunch the outflow of information or ramifications; something requiring heat (energy output) or cool (acceptance) attention.
Curette refers to a life aspect that has the capability to remove a negative factor from one's life.
Disinfectant advises of a need to maintain efforts toward countering negative aspects that could contaminate one's mental, emotional, or spiritual well-being.
Feeding tube comes as a warning against an idea being force-fed.
First aid kit comes to the dreamer as an advisement of an urgent need to patch up or heal the harmful effects one's actions have caused. This may refer to a quick-fix healing of oneself.

Prosthesis represents a replacement or other option.

Gastric lavage See stomach pump.
Gauze (bandage) relates to a temporary setback; a minor injury.
Germicide See disinfectant.
Hypodermic needle/ syringe shows a serious need for one to regain inner balance. This may refer to any physical, mental, or emotional negative condition currently present.
Lancet See scalpel.
Lysol See disinfectant.
Neck brace points to efforts to support or bolster one's inquisitiveness; perseverance in regard to pursuing an issue.
Needle (medical) See hypodermic needle.
Pillbox advises one to carry one's personal inner healing abilities with one. It implies one's talents are not always utilized at every opportunity.
Plaster cast (bone) represents a supportive factor that carries one through a healing period.
Poultice will reveal a healing aspect specific to the dreamer. Recall where the poultice was applied. What it was made of?
Prosthesis denotes a substitute or alternative.
Scalpel implies a need to excise a negative element from oneself or another.
Sling pertains to a condition of being temporarily handicapped.
Splint suggests a supportive measure; an attempt to maintain stability during a healing period.
Stethoscope is representative of a check on one's emotional sensitivity.
Stomach pump exposes an attempt to rid oneself of an undesirable life aspect.
Stretcher signifies a forewarning. Who was on the stretcher?
Suture correlates to an initial aspect that serves to promote healing.
Swab pertains to a need to go over something; possibly recheck or review.
Syringe represents a means of interjection or application.
Tourniquet denotes an effort to staunch further progression of something.
Wheelchair pertains to an inability to stand on one's own feet but is not a negative connotation. It usually implies a temporary setback regarding one's path progression.

Cosmetic Surgery

Breast implants symbolizes one who needs to bolster one's self-image; misplaced perception of self-worth; a need to increase nurturing nature.
Cosmetic surgery means altered appearance or self-image.
Cosmetic surgery show refers to a display of the many ways one can alter oneself.
Debridement comes to the dreamer as an advisement of a need to go into something and clean it up.
Eye lift is an advisement to open up one's eyes or of a lazy attitude or perspective.
Face-lift symbolizes a focus on oneself; possible hypocrisy; a dissatisfaction with one's natural beingness.
Liposuction reveals that one requires help in getting rid of extraneous aspects in life.
Nose job See rhinoplasty.
Plastic surgery See cosmetic surgery.
Reconstructive surgery implies the need for one to change an attitude or way of looking at things.
Rhinoplasty stands for an attitude adjustment.
Stapled stomach refers to drastic measures to force self-control.

Therapy

Chelation therapy suggests the presence of poisons (negatives) in one's system and advises of taking steps to eliminate them.
Chemotherapy pertains to the utilization of negatives to attempt positive outcomes.
Chrysotherapy represents an understanding of the healing qualities of natural aspects.
Gold therapy See chrysotherapy.
Group therapy advises of the wisdom of talking through one's problems.
Heliotherapy advises of a dark, depressive condition that needs brightening with a recognition of one's blessings.
Homeopathy stresses solutions contained within the problem.
Hormone replacement therapy warns one against attempting to recapture or replace something that's meant to be left in the past. An advisement to remembering the past; that nature knows best, nature is natural.
Hydrotherapy characterizes the use of spiritual elements as healing tools.
Light therapy designates the power of knowledge, acceptance, and tolerance.
Phototherapy is representative of a personal recognition of and appreciation for the rich healing value of one's knowledge.
Physical therapy corresponds to a need to restore the normal function of some element of oneself. Recall what was being manipulated or exercised, as this will pinpoint one's area of required improvement.
Play therapy (child's) indicates a need to discover current psychological problems that are rooted in one's childhood experience.
Primal therapy is suggestive of a need to rid oneself of withheld and internalized stress and negative emotions such as anger, frustration, and resentment.
Radiation therapy suggests the use of a negative to counter a negative.
Radium therapy pertains to an attempt to correct or heal a condition through potentially destructive methods.
Speech therapy indicates a need for the dreamer to convey thoughts with better clarity in his or her life.

Artificial Respiration

Artificial respiration is representative of an element in one's life that serves as a life-saving factor.
Breathing tube See artificial respiration.
Iron lung is an advisement to be more independent; think for oneself; to make your own decisions.
Life-support system is a dream symbol that emphasizes an essential supporting factor in one's life.
Oxygen mask exemplifies a sense of suffocation. It may refer to an inability to accept new ideas and the psychological panic they cause within oneself.

Surgery

Amputation strongly suggests the need to cut off something. Could point to a relationship, habit, addiction, and so on.
Appendectomy indicates the need to remove an unnecessary element in one's life.
Biopsy indicates a need to look closer or examine something in life.
Bone marrow transplant refers to a need for new life brought into one's foundational beliefs or attitudes.
Brain surgery reveals a serious need for a dramatic change in thought, perspectives, or sense of reasoning.
Circumcision calls for a need to excise an aspect in one's life.
Elective surgery is usually representative of a desire for self-improvement. This rarely has to do with cosmetic surgery but rather relates to wishing to get rid of a negative trait or habit. This would relate to a situation left unattended too long.
Exploratory surgery points to an attempt (or need) to get to the bottom of what's causing a particular negative in one's life. This will usually relate to a negative attitude or a perspective one knows one shouldn't have.
Laser surgery constitutes a step up from primitive thoughts or methods.
Lumpectomy stands for a need to rid oneself of a possible negative in one's life.
Mastectomy reveals a fear of heart pain.
Microsurgery implies a delicate maneuver; a fragile move; great care required in order to avoid a wrong move.

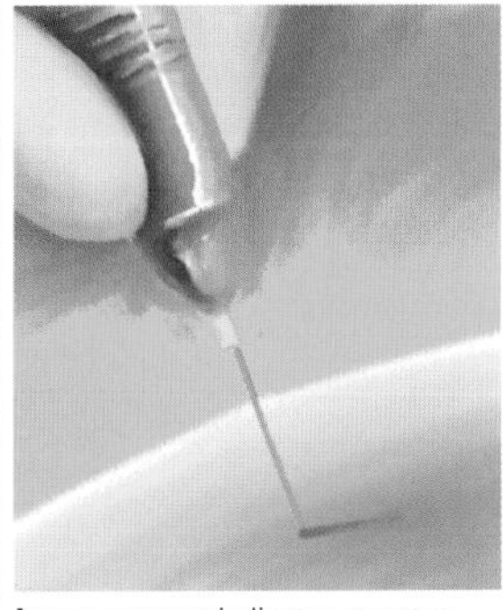

Laser surgery indicates progress.

Operation (medical) advises of a need to correct a dysfunctional element or negative aspect in one's life. Recall what type of operation was displayed. Who was being operated on? Who was the surgeon? In what condition was the operating room? What other factors were important in the dreamscape?
Organ transplant See transplant (specific organ).
Pre-op represents the time or phase immediately preceding the activation of a plan or behavior.
Tonsillectomy relates to the removal of negative elements that have hampered one's ability to communicate or adequately express oneself.
Transplant (heart) stands for a change of heart; greater emotional sensitivity.
Transplant (kidney) denotes a new, clean perspective.
Transplant (liver) pertains to renewed energy and motivation.
Transplant (lung) is usually representative of a new ability to take in (inhale) positive aspects and let go of (exhale) negative elements in one's everyday life.

see also
• Medical *p. 234*
• Nursing & Care *p. 247*

Treatments & Care

Acute care (medical) signifies a need to take care of a temporary unhealthy situation. This could even refer to an attitude, manner of current behavior, or relationship.
Back rub represents the care of one's burdens; an ability to take burdens on while pacing oneself.
Bed rest comes as a caution that one is working too hard and needs to take a break. This symbol may also point to a need to put something to bed and give it a rest.
Botox (injections) cautions against a tendency toward altering one's true self. Indicates a desire to be something you're not; non-acceptance of one's natural beingness; pride. May warn of a poisonous aspect that one willingly invites.
Brain scan advises one to self-examine thought processes and paths of logic; a check of reasoning abilities or processes.
Diagnosis points to the specific cause of something.
Dialysis implies a need for certain aspects of one's life to be separated from others.
Donor (organ) reveals a generous heart; someone willing to freely give of self. See transplant (specific organ).
Electrolysis signifies the destruction of personally rejected ideas.
Enema advises of a situation that requires assistance in helping one shed extraneous life aspects. Usually this refers to erroneous attitudes or perspectives. May indicate some behavioral negatives that aren't productive.
Drip-feed See intravenous feeding.
Footbath denotes an attempt to ease the aches of traveling one's path.
Foot massage like a footbath, is representative of a tiredness regarding traveling one's path and the efforts to accept the tribulations by working to soothe each trouble spot and gain the fortitude to keep going.
Heimlich maneuver advises of a need to get something out of one's system or get an internalized emotion or attitude out in the open.
Home care stands for the need to attend to one's own problems before attempting to give help to others.
Ice pack alludes to efforts applied to gaining spirituality, yet there remains a small measure of doubt.
Injection applies to new aspects entering one's life. Recall what substance was injected to determine if this is a positive or negative message.
Intravenous feeding comes to warn of a serious lack in one's life. Most often the dreamer will automatically understand what this is.
Medevac advises of an immediate need for emotional or psychological help.
Organ donor See donor (organ).
Outpatient illustrates a negative condition within the dreamer that can only be healed by oneself.
Over-the-counter (medication) signifies easily obtained remedies for a negative situation or element in one's life; something not requiring a major remedy.
Pedicure marks an attendance to one's manner of path progression.
Physical examination (health) portrays a need to either have an actual physical exam by a physician or else to seriously engage in introspection.
Placebo exemplifies an aspect that serves as a temporary replacement in one's life. These will be those elements that are phony or false. Frequently these refer to one's mental or psychological excuses for not following one's inner guidance.
Primary care applies to routine maintenance and attention given to one's mental, emotional, and physical condition.
Radiograph can reveal one's hidden character, or it can come in a dream to advise one to be extra watchful.
Shot See injection.
Sick bay exposes a spiritual sickness of some type that may be caused by external sources or that may in fact be self-generated.
Side effect exemplifies multiple ramifications of an action that has been taken.
Steam bath exemplifies being steeped in spiritual endeavors or elements.
Stress test comes to the dreamer as a personal advisement to check oneself for how one is dealing with troublesome situations.
Tanning bed/booth stands for the willful absorption (acceptance) of spiritual concepts one knows are substitutes for the pure truth.
Trauma team will stand for a critical need for the dreamer to take care of the most obvious and harmful negative elements in his or her life.
Triage advises of a need to establish or maintain priorities; quick decision making.
X-ray suggests a need to thoroughly analyze something; look at what lies beneath the surface.

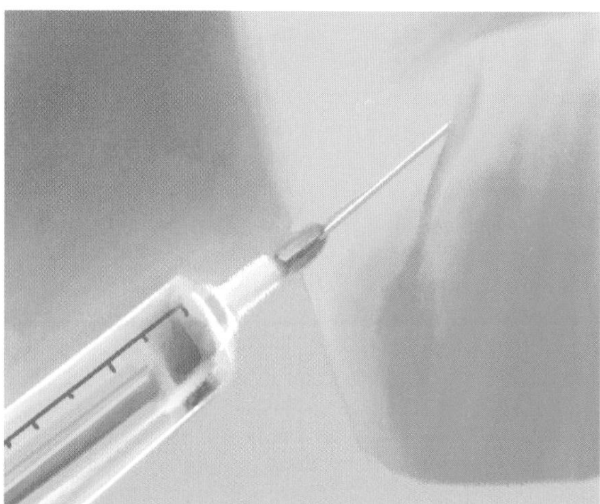
Injection symbolizes the arrival of something new in one's life.

Prescribed Medicines

Antacid warns of stressful situations or relationships.
Antibiotic signifies need for increased defenses, protection.
Anticoagulant warns the dreamer to keep things fluid and moving along.
Antidepressant (drug) points to a need to gain more acceptance and/or recognize one's many blessings.
Antihistamine symbolizes aspects in an individual's life that allow breathing room and times of respite.
Anti-inflammatory portrays a need to reduce stress in one's life. May point to someone who has the potential to keep relationships or situations from flaring up.
Appetite suppressant points to a voluntary control of one's desires; an effort to take one day at a time.
AZT may not mean the presence of AIDS. More likely, it will represent an effort made or some type of aid utilized for the purpose of maintaining a status quo position; a tool for holding one's own; prevention of a decline.

Pill denotes a means of restoring well-being to one's mind, body, or spirit.

Beta blocker stands for a need to be calm; to not show inner nervousness.
Cortisone typifies a person's inherent aspects that have the capability to heal and restore.
Diuretic implies a life aspect that will aid one in ridding oneself of negatives.
Expectorant denotes a life aspect that helps one to release negative emotions, attitudes, or energies.
Growth hormone comes as an advisement to grow up; to stop the immature behavior. Depending on the related dream elements, this symbol may also warn against trying to fit into shoes one isn't ready for. It may also represent more time needed for one to grow into something or more time for something to develop more fully.
Insulin is a substitute for a vital aspect one needs in life. The surrounding dreamscape details will help to clarify this for the dreamer.
Morning-after pill points to reconsiderations; a stop-gap prevention move.
Penicillin calls for protective measures to be applied. The surrounding dreamscape details will usually clarify this; if not, the dreamer will most often make the right association.
Pill represents an agent of personal healing or correction. This may refer to an emotional, mental, spiritual, or physical aspect of oneself. What type of pill was it? Color? Shape?
Relaxant refers to a need for one to relax one's focused mental or emotional energy. This specific dream symbol warns of a current state of overly centered efforts or concentration that is hampering one's big-picture comprehension.
Sedative pertains to a calming element in one's life. May indicate a need to gain greater acceptance.
Sleeping pill exemplifies respite from life's stressors.
Streptomycin See antibiotic.
Strychnine See poison.
Tranquilizer will represent any life aspect on which an individual depends for soothing effects; a means for calming.
Vaccine pertains to the awareness of having the foresight to protect oneself from negative elements in one's life.
Viagra stands for the need of an aid in order to be effective.

Medicine & Drugs

Antidote means a solution; an aspect in one's life that has the capability of countering a negative element.
Capsule See pill.
Dosage points to a proper amount of something.
Drug (prescribed) points to aspects in one's life that serve as aids in keeping one aligned.
Generic drug represents the presence of an alternate; a choice that contains equal value (benefits) yet is less costly in the long run.
Hard hitter (pot) represents frustration; a perceived need to calm anxiety or mellow out; a lack of acceptance.
Hookah refers to an attempt to cool a heated situation.
Medication connotes external solutions rather than working from within.
Megadose signifies an extraordinary amount of something. This symbol can come as a warning regarding too much or it can come as an advisement that more is needed.
Miracle drug will stand for a solid solution.
Overdose pertains to an excess. This will help the dreamer determine the proper amount of something required.
Paregoric suggests a need for greater acceptance.
Prescription (medical) will indicate what one needs to maintain mental, emotional, or physical health. This symbol may also reveal the best course of action.
Stimulant applies to a motivational factor.
Tablet (pill) See pill.
Water pipe See hookah.
Wonder drug represents a powerful healing element or solution.

see also
• Medicinal Plants *p. 49*
• Pharmacy *p. 247*

Remedies & Unguents

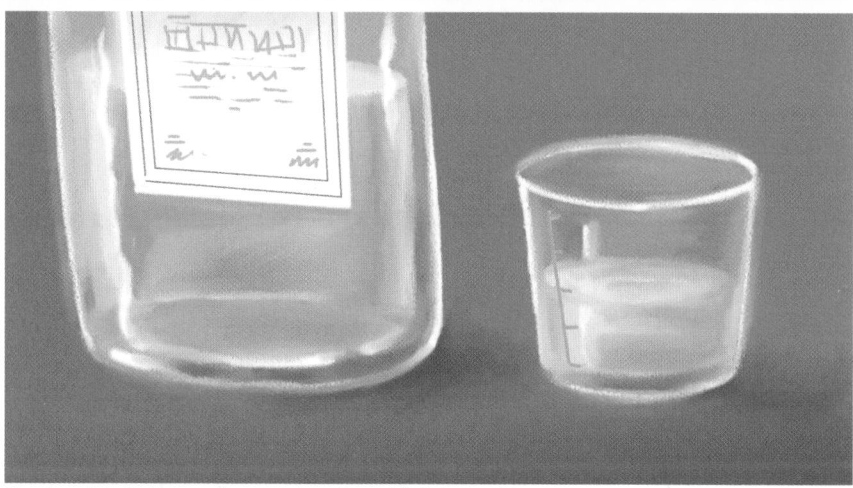

Mouthwash reminds one to choose one's words carefully before speaking.

Balm points to that which soothes in one's life.

Calamine (lotion) represents a solution to a current life irritation.

Camphor oil is representative of a relief of some type. This will usually refer to something that provides breathing room or eases some type of pain.

Castor oil advises of the need for a personal purification; a cleansing. This may refer to emotional, mental, or situational aspects.

Clove oil stands for something that temporarily relieves emotional pain.

Corn silk (diuretic) is representative of the inner healing aspects of personal efforts.

Cure-all comes to the dreamer as a warning of a misplaced belief or faith in something. Equates to a false panacea.

Demulcent will refer to a soothing aspect that may be needed in one's life.

Epsom salts pertains to an aspect in one's life that produces a calming effect. Perhaps the dream symbol is advising of a need to gain a greater measure of calm or serenity in one's life.

Fish oil stands for a highly beneficial element or characteristic.

Laxative advises of a need to rid oneself of some type of negative aspect.

Liniment portrays that which soothes life's more difficult moments.

Lozenge characterizes an individual's need to correct one's manner of speech.

Medicine bundle corresponds to one's personal inner power.

Megavitamin will normally indicate an individual's need for motivation.

Milk of magnesia is indicative of a stressful situation or condition. Advises more acceptance.

Mouthwash comes to warn against using harmful or abusive language.

Mustard plaster denotes a need to address negative factors in life that repress freedoms; a need for breathing room. Fresh air is required.

Ointment signifies a healing or emotionally soothing element in one's life. What type of ointment was shown? Who was offering or using it?

Petroleum jelly signifies a life element that has the potential for soothing or easing a rough or difficult situation.

Psyllium portrays a person's tendency to take the easy path and suggests a more difficult course.

Quinine signifies that which serves as a healing agent in one's life.

Remedy (any type) reflects a corrective or healing source.

Salve See ointment.

Smelling salts illustrate a warning to wake up and get focused.

Suppository suggests that something within oneself is lacking.

Tincture represents a healthful element of which one needs only a small amount. This would indicate something one would benefit from by taking on a routine basis. This may not be referring to medicine but rather an attitude like acceptance.

Tonic stands for a helpful or healing element that could be difficult to accept.

Vaseline See petroleum jelly.

Wart remover stands for that which is capable of removing or dissolving a negative element an individual is carrying around.

Zinc ointment relates to a healing element available in one's life.

Immunization

Booster shot warns against not following through with something; of a need to be mindful of one's continual progress. May also indicate the need to reenergize an idea or plan, perhaps a relationship.

Immunization advises one of a possible negative aspect invading one's life. Extra awareness and protective measures are needed.

Inoculation See immunization.

Tetanus shot stands for a diligent level of awareness. It refers to preventive measures the dreamer should take to avoid accidents.

Holistic Therapies

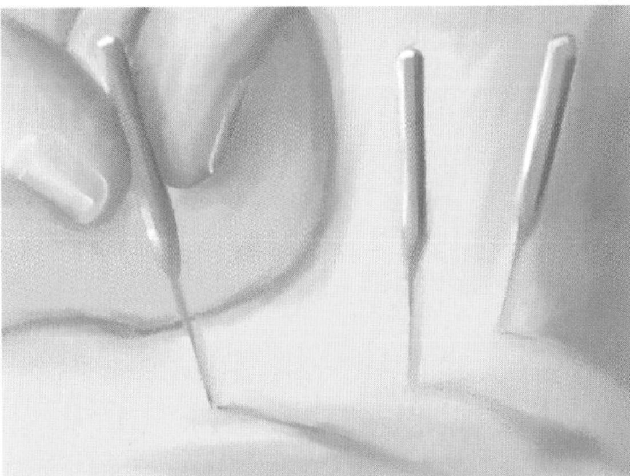

Acupuncture points up the need to examine a certain problem in more detail.

Acupressure See shiatsu.
Acupuncture denotes the need to give closer attention to specific aspects (points) of a situation that need addressing.
Chiropractic adjustment emphasizes desire for inner balance and alignment to current path.
Folk medicine pertains to a natural healing capability.
Holistic may not be relating to health aspects. It usually refers to an advisement to stop fragmenting one's thoughts; a need to think in terms of whole concepts or ideas.
Massage suggests a need to work out an internalized problem or negative.
Rubdown See massage.
Shiatsu (massage technique) portrays a need for clearing mental and emotional blocks.
Sports massage denotes a high interest in staying in the game and a determination behind it.
Sports medicine represents a high interest in healing those who sustain injuries while progressing along their life paths or who are determined to accomplish their goals.

Microbiology

Cell relates to the wholeness of one's life experiences.
Cell division denotes exponential growth of an element, such as one's behavior.
Cell memory refers to a pure element in one's life.
Chromosome advises one to know oneself.
Clone cautions of the tendency toward the imitation of others.
DNA indicates individualism.
Enzyme relates to a motivating catalyst.
Gene is a trait that's unique to the dreamer.
Genetic disorder reveals those aspects one has to overcome.
Hormone is a life factor affecting one's emotional or mental reponses.
Metastasis means something has spread or widened in scope.
Reprogram suggests an attempt to alter something.
Stem cell stands for a neutral element that has a multitude of beneficial uses.

Body Care

Bathing signifies a lack of negatives in the dreamer's life; a cleansing of negatives.
Cleanser connotes some type of cleansing is needed. This symbol will point to the tool one needs to achieve that end.
Cotton swab denotes a cautious attitude.
Deodorant implies a cover-up or an attempt to avoid offending another.
Depilatory alludes to an aspect or agent that has the capability of drastically negating another's thoughts or views.
Dusting powder refers to the utilization of small opportunities that help us personally feel better.
Emollient (lanolin, etc.) refers to any personal element one uses to soften or smooth life's rough aspects.
Fragrance comes with unique interpretations associated with specific scents. Refer to specific scents.
Green soap connotes a healing factor, usually emotionally.
Lanolin advises of a need to smooth out or soften some type of roughness or hardness in one's life. This could be associated with single-mindedness, stubbornness, insincerity, and so on.
Lip balm relates to an attempt or desire to keep communications from being harsh.
Lotion denotes a soothing aspect; a factor that smoothes out a rough situation or relationship.
Nailbrush refers to a need to change one's ways; clean up dirty methods and tactics.
Nail clippers illustrate an advisement to cut down and temper one's aggressive or rough behavioral tendencies.
Nail polish can reveal one's underlying personality or character. Recall depth of color and condition of polish.
Nail scissors See nail clippers.
Perfume refers to an effort to conceal; a cover-up. May also point to an attempt to feel better about oneself. If the specific scent is known, it may be found elsewhere in this dictionary.
Q-tip See cotton swab.
Shaving (hair) stands for a reluctance to reveal thoughts. May also point to an effort to present a veneer of integrity.
Straight razor suggests a serious and focused personality.
Sunblock denotes an attempt to keep a specified distance from spiritual matters.
Sunscreen See sunblock.
Talcum powder represents a personal means of self-control.
Unwashed comes as an advisement to remove the negative elements from some aspect in one's life.

Designer Drugs

Black beauty See designer drug.
Blue velvet signifies a desire to shift away from reality; using a negative to manifest a negative; denial; escapism.
Designer drug warns one against using self-styled crutches in life.

see also
• Alternative Medicine *p. 246*
• Genetics *p. 285*

Recreational Drugs

Acid (drug) denotes a desire to alter one's reality; a dependency on a shifted perspective in order to face reality; a belief in the false premise that one can't face reality without first altering it in some way.

Acid trip indicates a willful desire to alter one's worldview or perspective.

Amphetamine warns of one's lack of energy or awareness.

Angel dust symbolizes dangerous practices.

Benny See amphetamine.

Blue heaven (also blue angel or blue devil) warns of a need to escape responsibility or reality. Possibly an aid to bolster one's desire for denial.

Bong usually symbolizes an element that facilitates level-headedness; a tool that cools down a heated situation or makes something more palatable to accept. This won't necessarily be symbolically associated with drugs.

Cannabis See marijuana.

Chemical abuse See substance abuse.

Cocaine warns of an inability to cope with reality; a lack of responsibility; escapism. May point to an elitist hypocrisy.

Cold turkey stands for immediate and absolute withdrawal of something in one's life; complete abstinence and distance.

Cook (person, drugs) points to one who concocts or manufactures negative elements.

Crack See cocaine.

Crank See cocaine.

Deck (pack of drugs) cautions against the utilization of negative or altering aspects to accomplish something.

Dope See narcotic.

Drugs (illegal abuse) reveals a lack of self-confidence; dependency; escapism.

Fix stands for dependency; lack of responsibility; fear of facing reality.

Freebasing See cocaine.

Glue sniffing denotes an effort or desire to alter one's reality; a form of escapism.

Hashish See marijuana.

Head trip signifies mental exhilaration.

Joint (smoke) signifies a personal manner of calming oneself.

Mainlining won't always imply hard drug use. This symbol will most often refer to a method or practice of absorbing conceptual information via the most efficient means; tendency to recognize and accept the main truths of an issue or subject.

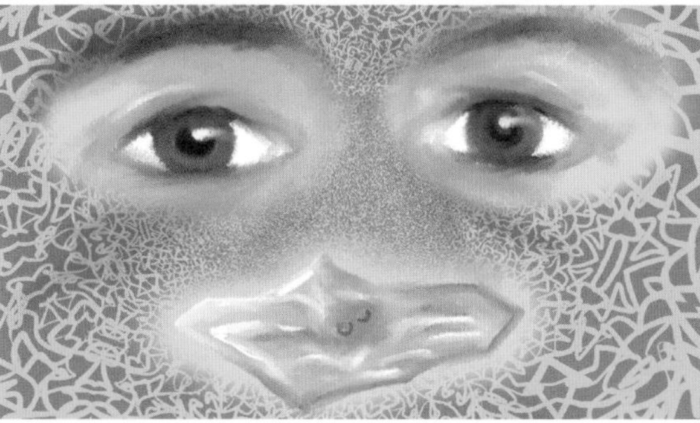

Acid trip represents a determination to change one's outlook on life.

Marijuana is an indication to cut down on stressful situations; of a person's need for emotional balance.

Mary Jane See marijuana.

Methamphetamine connotes a need to either slow down or reenergize oneself.

Mini-whites See amphetamine.

Morphine See narcotic.

Narcosis warns against a self-induced state of apathy.

Narcotic defines an escape from reality associated with a lack of acceptance and personal responsibility. May also refer to an aspect that lessens the pain of a hurtful life situation.

Nose candy See cocaine.

Pep pill See amphetamine.

Popper (uppers) See stimulant.

Pot (botanical) See marijuana.

Recreational drug advises of a need to change one's idea of what constitutes social acceptance. May point to a misplaced motivational method or way of dealing with life.

Reefer See marijuana.

Roach See marijuana.

Score (drugs/points) stands for the obtaining of a goal.

Shooting gallery (drugs) warns of a situation or relationship where potentially dangerous negative elements are present.

Snuff (tobacco) See tobacco.

Substance abuse connotes a lack of self-control; dependency; an inability to face reality or take personal responsibility.

Toke suggests experimentation; a sampling.

Tobacco & Smoking

Chain-smoking is high anxiety; an internalization of problems.

Chew (tobacco) means dwelling on something too long.

Cigar denotes an absorption of specialized ideas or concepts.

Corncob pipe connotes the reaping of benefits generated through one's personal efforts.

Panatella See cigar.

Pipe cleaner is a desire to keep perceptual thought processes clear of distorting elements and impurities.

Smoking indicates denied or suppressed emotions.

Tobacco emphasizes respect and honor.

Poisons

Antitoxin warns one to increase one's personal defenses against a specific danger in the dreamer's life. This dream symbol reveals the presence of a threat.

Lead poisoning pertains to the harmful effects of a negative aspect in one's life.

Poison comes to the dreamer as a warning of an element in one's life that has the potential to cause great harm or a fatal effect if one doesn't proceed with acute awareness and be extremely careful in all that one does.

Toxin See poison.

Death

Autopsy signifies a need to analyze a past action, relationship, or belief system; pick it apart piece by piece. Also denotes a need to for one get to the source of a problem or situation.

Body (unidentified) is representative of outstanding aspects that require attention in one's life.

Body bag depicts a failure to attend to important aspects in one's life.

Body count won't relate to corpses but rather those who have been severely affected by the negative behavior of someone.

Cadaver most often denotes learning opportunities. It also acts as a reminder of our mortality.

Choke hold refers to dangerous situations or individuals in life that threaten advancement. These can be self-generated.

Choking warns against attempting to swallow ideas one knows are wrong or one is not prepared to fully absorb.

Corpse refers to an aspect in one's life that has no more viability; a dead issue.

Cryonics is a strong warning against one's love of oneself and giving priority to one's physical essence.

Dead means lifeless; an absolute conclusion; a final closing.

Death stands for termination; finality. May not specifically point to a physical death.

Deathbed alludes to an approaching end or conclusion to something.

Deathblow signifies a devastating event in one's life.

Death mask may forewarn the dreamer of an actual physical death, but most often it relates to an extremely dangerous situation or relationship that has the strong potential to have devastating ramifications or conclusions if continued.

Death rattle forewarns one of approaching finality; a need to prepare for the worst.

Death wish warns against fatalism; self-destructive perspectives or actions.

Decapitation warns of a situation where one figuratively loses one's head over something. This symbol calls for an immediate return to logic and reason.

Die See death.

Discarnate refers to a hidden life aspect or something the dreamer isn't seeing.

Drowning is a strong advisement to come up for spiritual air instead of oversaturating self with a flood of spiritual research.

Dying forewarns of the death of one's high ideals or an actual physical demise.

Electrocution warns against the desire for power. This can imply many types of power such as knowledge, wealth, leadership, and so on.

Euthanasia signifies deep compassion.

In extremis reveals a short measure of time left to make amends, get affairs in order, or change ways.

Kiss of death connotes a fatal or destructive outcome.

Lethal denotes a highly dangerous aspect in one's everyday life.

Mercy killing See euthanasia.

Postmortem See autopsy.

Rigor mortis symbolizes a dead state; an individual who maintains stiff thinking or conceptual reasoning.

Short-lived points to a fleeting aspect. This aspect could refer to an emotion, a result of something, a positive or negative result, and so on.

Widow(er) may not relate to a physical death but rather symbolizes a solitary state. This may refer to reclusiveness, a need to be alone for a time, an independence, or a remote path that has been chosen.

Wreath symbolizes various sentiments depending on what it's made of, the color, and what occasion it relates to. Refer to the specific flower type, color, and occasion such as autumn, Christmas holiday, or funeral.

Body-Related Phrases

Ankle-deep suggests a considerable involvement in something.

Arm's-length suggests a need to distance oneself from a particular situation or issue.

Arm-twisting characterizes a manipulative individual. It may point to a situation in which coercion is involved.

Beauty sleep won't literally equate to physical beauty but rather the beauty of pacing oneself for the purpose of expending energy on beautiful (selfless) acts.

Belly-up suggests a type of failure, or it could be indicating that now's the time to belly up to the table and take responsibility or action.

Black-and-blue alludes to relationships or situations that will end up harming one.

Brain-picking relates to in-depth analysis. May indicate a need to bounce ideas off of someone trusted to be your sounding board.

Brainstorming is indicative of deep thought applied to problem solving or inventiveness.

Brainwashing stands for a willful destruction of another person's ideals, attitudes, or perspectives. May also point to a need to cleanse one's thought process.

Eyesore comes to the dreamer as a warning of hurtful personal perceptions.

Lip service denotes false intentions.

Pain in the neck will not necessarily be an actual physical indication but rather will refer to a personal irritation usually caused by another individual for whom the dreamer has no tolerance. This suggests a need for greater acceptance.

Red-blooded is representative of a robust and hearty constitution; steadfast determination.

White knuckles may be an indication of fear, anxiety, worry, anger, etc., yet the bottom-line interpretation is perseverance or holding on with all one's strength.

see also
• Death & Decay *p. 172*
• Funereal Occupations *p. 247*

Burial

Burial plot may signify the conclusion of an event.

Bier See coffin.
Burial mound suggests the need to remember a past difficulty; a call to remember lessons learned from past experience.
Burial plot points to ultimate end. May refer to a failure of some type; an irreversible ending or finalization.
Buried alive signifies the smothering or covering up of one's identity, plan, idea, etc.
Cist See coffin.
Coffin may be representative of an emotionally comatose state of being, or it may actually come as a forewarning of a death.
Coffin nail stands for a negative aspect in one's life.
Epitaph comes as a message that summarizes or reveals hidden elements of one's life.
Exhumation comes as a call to reexamine something in one's life; go back and take another look at something that was missed the first time.
Foot in grave indicates a strong advisement to back away from something and stop being involved in a dangerous situation or behavior.
Funeral underscores a state of loss. Relates to an acceptance of losing something.
Grave symbolizes finality.
Gravestone usually reveals one's fatal course. May forewarn of an actual death date.
Headstone See gravestone.
Mausoleum typifies buried memories or thoughts; hurtful memories locked away in the mind's dark vault.
Obituary comes as a warning of a forthcoming death that may be emotional in respect to a relationship rather than an actual physical event. Recall surrounding dreamscape details for clarity. Was there a specific name presented? A date? Cause of death?
Pall See coffin.
Pine tar applies to the healing elements of natural talents and gifts.
Pyre (funeral) reveals the misdeeds and negative emotions that one piles up to create one's ultimate downfall.
Sarcophagus See coffin.
Sepulcher See mausoleum.
Shroud exemplifies concealment of one's darker aspects.
Stone See gravestone.
Wake (death) See funeral.

Recovery

Biofeedback comes to the dreamer as a caution concerning the need to listen to his or her inner promptings more. This symbol emphasizes the strength of one's inherent inner power; the power of thought.
Pick-me-up will relate to any life aspect or condition that provides an additional surge of energy or motivation for the dreamer. This will, of course, be different for every individual dreamer. The surrounding dreamscape elements will help to clarify which particular meaning was intended.
Quarantine comes to the dreamer as an advisement of the need to separate oneself from a negative, harmful situation or relationship.
Recuperation illustrates a span of time that an individual should devote to regaining mental or emotional strength following a draining event or phase.
Rejuvenation will either symbolize a current state of renewal or it will indicate a need for same, depending on the associated aspects.
Withdrawal (symptoms) symbolizes yearning for what one needs to deny.

Accidental Injuries

Bee sting comes as an advisement to get on one's way.
Fleabite alludes to a temporary inconvenience or annoyance.
Frostbite comes when one reacts in a willfully unresponsive manner. Karmic effects of refusing to communicate.
Injury reveals a type of harm done to one. Surrounding dreamscape details will clarify.
Paper cut indicates a careless use of information.
Saddle sore reveals a forced path progression. Advises of a need to ease back on one's efforts that have become overly concentrated.
Shot (wounded) exposes an inability to defend oneself. Refers to an event that emotionally, mentally, or spiritually injured oneself.

Snakebite advises greater alertness.

Snakebite emphasizes a lack of awareness; one is caught off guard.
Writer's cramp advises of the ineffectiveness of trying to force ideas onto others; the need to let things ride.

Miscellaneous

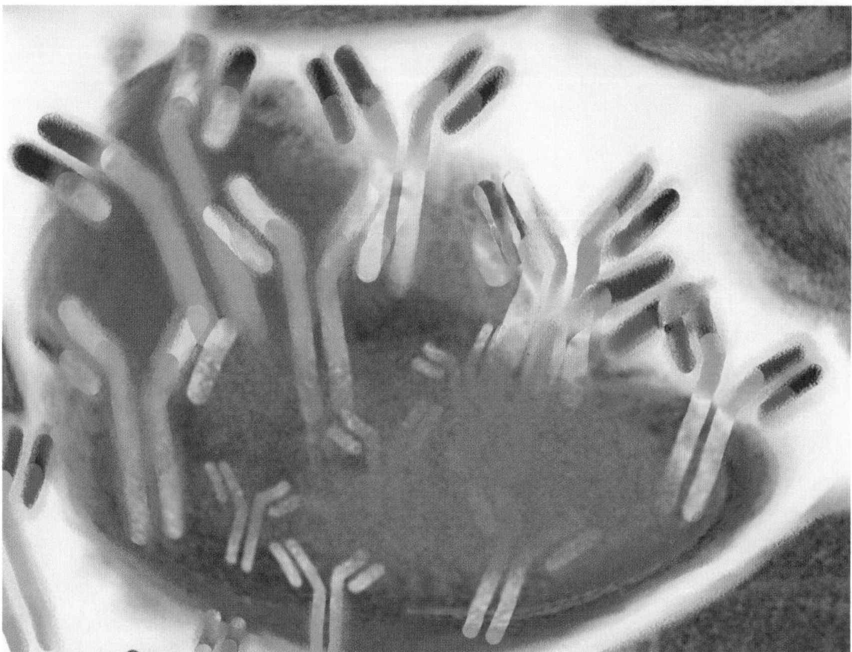

Antibody could signify an individual who might be able to offer the dreamer protection in his or her everyday life.

Ailment signifies aspects in an individual's life that could be detrimental.

Anti-antibody comes as a warning of highly dangerous persons or relationships.

Antibody typifies one's personal defense mechanisms. This dreamscape symbol may point to someone who has the potential of protecting the dreamer.

Antigen denotes destructive aspects in an individual's life.

Bedlam means complete confusion in a person's life. This symbol may refer to a relationship, a situation, or a mental or emotional state.

Cauliflower tumor See polyp (medical).

Contamination warns of the infiltration of an extremely corrupt or deadly facet into one's life. This dreamscape symbol may also refer to a literal contamination of a perspective; a truth that has been compromised.

Dispensary See pharmacy.

Drugstore See pharmacy.

Epidemic cautions of a concept or attitude that is widely held.

Helper T cell portrays an agent that can destroy specific negative aspects in one's life.

Hurt See injury.

Killer T cell means an avenger; something that eradicates a negative facet in one's life.

Leper pertains to strength of character; tenacity in spite of adversities.

Longevity reveals a lasting element in one's life.

Madhouse denotes great confusion or intense activity; pressure and stress.

Nerve damage suggests a self-generated disability caused by not reconciling a past event.

Outbreak suggests a return or exacerbation of an element in one's life, usually a negative aspect that has suddenly increased.

Pandemic suggests a widespread attitude or condition, usually negative.

Pestilence will most often correspond with a negative element that one brings upon oneself.

Pharmacy will suggest some type of medication or healing element is needed.

Polyp (medical) denotes the growth or extension of a specific aspect of oneself. Recall if it was a positive or negative growth.

Psychogenic reveals a mental or emotional source.

Tissue is a life element that can keep negative aspects at bay.

Unwieldy is a representation of a cumbersome or difficult-to-handle issue in one's life.

Vector corresponds to a carrier or possibly even a messenger, depending on the surrounding dreamscape details.

Wrist represents tenacity. It may also refer to a person's ability to maneuver effectively.

Uncontrolled Actions

Bed-wetting is representative of a tendency for self-induced rest interruption. It may refer to one who can't allow time for solid rest.

Belch signifies an individual's need to bring up and air negative attitudes that could eventually be harmful.

Drooling is representative of a lack of control over one's desires.

Itching means a restlessness; calls for acceptance. May point to some type of irritation in one's life.

Scratching implies a personal irritation in one's life.

Teeth clenching/grinding reveals efforts to control frustration, anger, or impatience.

Tic (nervous) exposes a subconscious effect or response.

Twitch See tic.

Unsteady exemplifies a lack of self-confidence; one is on shaky ground.

Wheezing warns of a suffocating situation or relationship; an inability to clearly breathe.

Chapter 9

People, Relationships & Communication

Though often presented as familial, these symbols show themselves to reveal underlying associations between a dream's main characters.

Social Relationships & Activities

Bedroom community denotes a healthy separation between rest and work.
Book club pertains to a wide variety of writings on one subject; shared interests.
Clambake alludes to possible negative aspects to keeping silent about something.
Clique cautions against social arrogance or selectiveness.
Club exemplifies people with a like perspective or interest.
Coffee klatch pertains to the emotional uplift brought by sharing restful energizing times with others.
Good neighbor characterizes a generous, caring, helpful individual.
Hemlock society stands for thought reflecting a realist.
Host suggests a receivership or beneficiary.
Hostess characterizes generosity; congeniality.
Joneses represent who or what one strives to be equal to or better than; one-upmanship.
Key club implies separatism; a specific chosen group.
Ladies' night out comes in a dream to remind us of the importance of friends and making the time to spend together.
Lonely-hearts club signifies a lack of companionship; a reaching out. This symbol may also reveal a bid for sympathy; wanting a "pity-party."
Neighbor will pinpoint someone who exists within close proximity to another, not necessarily an associate or friend of the dreamer.
Quilting bee stands for serenity gained from companionship.
Special interest (group) will reveal an individual's concealed intention or attitude.
Support group signifies supportive opportunities; the existence of support or encouragement if one really needs it.
Tête-à-tête means a private, face-to-face communication.

Neighbor refers to someone who is linked with another in some way.

Classmates & Teammates

Classmate is representative of those who walk the same path as you; those with like interests.
Crew is a reference to those who work together on a common task.
Fraternity emphasizes male camaraderie. In this sense it is a reference to friends sharing a common interest or attitude.
Gang applies to a group of people. Recall surrounding details to determine if this symbol was a positive or negative one.
Reunion (class) indicates a suggestion to reconnect with a former associate.
Sorority stands for female camaraderie. May also refer to a tendency to follow what's popular.

Types of Relationships

Abiding (enduring) connotes a lasting situation. May be advising a greater level of acceptance.
Alliance represents a partner or associate. Depending on surrounding dream details, this symbol may be suggesting an alliance be made or broken.
Audience exemplifies the ever-present watchers in one's life; the eyes on us.
Band (of people) signifies strength in numbers. Depending on the dreamer's specific life circumstances, this dreamscape symbol may point to a need to go it alone.
Blind date exemplifies questionable relationships; a relationship full of unknowns.
Charge (care) refers to an aspect one needs to take special care of; protective wardship; safe-keeping.
Close-knit indicates strong bonds; solid ties with another.
Cohabitation suggests a closeness to another; a bonded relationship.
Collective conscious reminds us of our interrelatedness to all living things.
Common ground refers to a unifying factor.
Dependent pertains to anyone who looks to another for support.
Incompatibility doesn't necessarily refer to a relationship. In fact, it most often will come to the dreamer as an advisement of a person's specific belief in something that is not vibrationally aligned with the individual.
Live-in denotes a surface association with somebody.
Lodger See live-in.
Monogamy may not refer to a marriage or partnership, but most often will correspond with one's belief system or focus of attention.
Platonic (philosophy or relationship) denotes an intellectual focus on spiritual concepts rather than on the physical elements of life.
Plural marriage See polygamy.
Polygamy applies to arrogance and lack of respect for others.
Symbiosis exposes a need for another individual that may or may not be productive or mutually beneficial.

see also
• Employment Status *p. 244*
• Civil Rights *p. 326*

Friendship

Acquaintance refers to people in one's life who have the potential to affect changes.

Allegiance connotes support or loyalty, sometimes misplaced.

Ally refers to friendships that are loyal and true; relationships that can be counted on.

Blood brother portrays a deep-seated, bonded relationship.

Buddy portrays a reluctance to be on one's own; a fear of solitude; a lack of self-confidence or independence.

Buddy system symbolizes a companion needed for security purposes.

Card holder connotes special treatment; a membership; belonging to a specific group. Recall what type of cards were in the holder. Sometimes this symbol can literally point the way for the dreamer by clearly showing who should be contacted.

Chum See friend.

Comrade will be a close associate, one who shares similar ideas, perspectives, and interests.

Crony represents those one is in cahoots with.

Friend usually characterizes loyalty and trust.

Housemate characterizes a close friendship; camaraderie; shared life experiences.

Old-boy network stands for the adage: It's not what you know, it's who you know. This usually reveals a situation in which those outside a circle of individuals are shut out and not afforded the same opportunities as the others. This will have a very specific meaning for each dreamer.

Soul sister characterizes a female with whom one has a great affinity.

Pact signifies a private agreement.

Pen pals are companionable relationships kept at a distance.

Roommate implies companionship. May also allude to suppressed individuality.

Sisterhood is a representation of female camaraderie.

Soul mate usually indicates an individual who one perceives as being the perfect partner or friend.

Soul sister is representative of a woman who shares sympathies, love, and a deep kinship with another woman or a man.

Political Relationships

Race riot means expressing ire.

Apartheid denotes racial prejudice; intolerance; lack of acceptance.

Authority figure mostly refers to someone of greater experience, knowledge, or control. Often this refers to one's conscience or higher self.

Boat people characterize those wanting to be spiritually saved; spiritual freedom.

Chain of command refers to levels of authority. This symbol usually comes when someone is going over another's head.

Citizen implies a group or location with which one is connected.

Integration rarely refers to ethnicity but rather comes as an advisement to combine diverse aspects. This indicates that the dreamer was missing something; not including all possible factors associated with an issue or concept.

Race riot signifies repressed anger and the violent methods of releasing same; a lack of self-responsibility.

Running mate represents a companion; an individual who shares one's views or plans.

Enemies

Adversary is representative of an oppositional aspect in one's life. May reveal the true nature of someone in your life.

Bad blood usually relates to animosities; bad relationships; the holding of grudges.

Betrayal applies to untrustworthy relationships.

Captive usually means unwillingness; a forced situation.

Misogamy points to a hatred of forming close relationships.

Misogyny reveals resentment or prejudice toward women; a male elitist.

Opponent refers to an adversary or competitor.

Rival may not indicate an enemy but rather someone perceived by the dreamer to be an opponent or competitor.

Coworkers & Associates

Accomplice warns of a negative relationship.

Associate characterizes partnerships; a working together.

Client characterizes a person for whom one does a service or duty.

Costar pertains to a second individual in the limelight or in a position of attention.

Mentor usually identifies someone in your life who has the knowledge and wisdom to guide you.

Love & Sex

Love potion signifies a willingness to go to any lengths to be loved.

Affair (love) symbolizes a lack of loyalty; a deceptive nature.
Boyfriend symbolizes male relationships.
Chastity belt implies forced modesty or false humility.
Cherry (condition) stands for something in prime state.
Coitus See intercourse (sexual).
Concubine implies feminine inferiority; chauvinism.
Copulation implies a temporary joint effort.
Courtship stands for a time of persuasion; a period when one tries to impress another.
Cross-dressing implies a desire to share or understand the condition of another.
Dear John (letter) reveals a desire to end a relationship.
Erotica exemplifies life's baser aspects. May warn of being engrossed in pleasing oneself.
Exotic suggests eccentricity.
Harem applies to separatism based on class or position.
Intercourse (sexual) points to a need for an intimate conversation or a heart-to-heart talk.
Intimacy emphasizes a close relationship; a confidante.
John (male client) stands for a source of negativity and the demand that perpetuates it.
Love beads suggest individuality; independent thought.
Love feast/fest signifies a celebration of camaraderie.
Love knot points to a symbol of affection for another.
Love nest stands for a specific place or element of life where a special relationship exists.
Love potion stands for a forced or manipulated attraction.
Lovers denote our loving nature. Recall what they were doing for further clarification of this dream symbol.
Lovers' lane advises of a time and place for affection.
Lovers' leap points to a despair stemming from an unsuccessful close relationship.
Mistress characterizes one who breaks up partnerships.
Necrophilia advises focusing on aspects of one's life rather than dwelling on the past.
Pornography reflects misplaced priority; wasting energy.
Puppy love may refer to a budding affection.
Suitor relates to heightened attention given another.
Sweetheart is one for whom one has special affection.
Valentine implies affection.

Family

Ancestor is a reference to past relationships, which are not necessarily familial.
Aunt relates to a maternal-figure alternative.
Babushka implies a caution against keeping one's thoughts tightly under wraps.
Blood relation refers to individuals who are motivated by the same aspects as the dreamer.
Brother characterizes a close male associate in life; a male who is a close friend.
Brotherhood signifies male camaraderie that has a deeply connecting aspect.
Cousin characterizes a trace association or relationship.
Daddy See father.
Daughter characterizes a younger female individual toward whom one has a nurturing relationship.
Extended family refers to close relationships.
Family connotes associations that should be unified.
Family tree often reveals one's true spiritual heritage, that is, a record of one's past lives.
Father usually represents a fatherly individual to whom the dreamer relates in life.
Forefather See ancestor.
Generation gap stands for differences in attitudes.
Godfather warns us to achieve goals through personal efforts.
Godmother characterizes comforting warmth; a welcoming hearth.
Grandmother stands for a source of women's wisdom; a genteel wise woman.
Grandparent characterizes one who can share great wisdom.
Guardian signifies one who watches out for another.
Hereditary depicts an inherent personal aspect that can be altered through understanding and will. This would refer to a negative characteristic.
Inbreeding won't usually have a sexual or genetic connotation but will refer to an incorrect mixing of ideas.
Incest dramatizes the seriousness of a dangerously negative relationship.
Kin See relative.
Matriarch signifies a woman of wisdom chosen to lead others.
Mother characterizes a nurturing aspect. May represent personal real-time associations.
Nuclear family characterizes those closest to the dreamer.
Parent will represent a person to respect and honor. This symbol may have different meanings for each dreamer, depending on individual personal experiences.
Patriarch connotes a person acting as a figurehead.
Pecking order will attempt to remind one of one's place or position. This symbol usually clarifies the cause of an irritating life situation.
Relative pertains to those in one's awake state who have an elemental association with the dreamer but who may not be a real relation.
Reunion (family) suggests an advisement to reconnect with a family member.
Sister indicates a close female relationship.
Uncle advises one to take personal responsibility and to admit to mistakes one has made in life.

see also
• Affection *p. 168*
• Babies & Children *p. 251*

Children

Adopting connotes a taking in; an act of sheltering something.
Baby relates to false innocence; an immature person or novice.
Baby carriage is unrefined ideas.
Baby steps denote the tentative steps taken when beginning a new direction.
Big brother characterizes a hidden overseer in one's life. Usually reveals the fact that information thought to be private has been uncovered.
Big sister stands for feminine guidance.
Birthright underscores the right to choose new beginnings.
Boy is a representation of beginning or foundational male perspectives.
Boy Scout represents good deeds and the formation of basic life perspectives.
Brownies (young Girl Scouts) denotes development of ethics and feminine perspectives.
Camp Fire Girl advises that young people be taught the value of keeping a balance between work and play.
Child connotes a stage of acceptance and innocence; a belief in possibilities and in one's dreams.
Child care stands for a need to recognize and care for one's inner child.
Child labor is representative of energies expended toward an issue or idea that is still immature.
Childproof reminds one to attend to each advancing stage in life and not attempt things one is not well prepared to take on.

Ragamuffin is suggestive of a cheeky outlook on life.

Child restraint alludes to the importance of having childlike qualities such as trust.
Eagle Scout characterizes one who was presumably trained in ethical standards.
Foster care/home reminds us to take personal responsibility to care for anyone needing it.
Foundling advises one attend to personal responsibilities.
Girl Scout characterizes a female who strives to live according to her beliefs.
Godchild refers to a fundamental spiritual inspiration or insight in one's life.
Grandchild denotes a personal responsibility for nurturing those who follow us.
Identical twin is one's alter ego.
Infant See baby.
Kid See child.
Latchkey kid stands for self-reliance learned early in life.
Love child indicates a new beginning or idea brought on by or shared with another.
Orphan See foundling.
Playmate refers to behavior formulated by those one interacted with at an early age.
Quadruplet constitutes a new life or beginning that has four opportunities or benefits.
Quintuplet constitutes a new life or beginning that has five opportunities or benefits.
Ragamuffin (child) will imply an adventurous or precocious character or attitude.
Sibling will pertain to someone one is meant to interrelate with for a time.
Toddler implies one's beginning steps toward a new endeavor, direction, or belief.
Urchin pertains to a mischievous immaturity.

Partners & Matrimony

Best man characterizes male support in life.
Betrothal refers to intentions toward making a long-term commitment. May suggest the need for a rethink.
Bride portrays a desire or need for a life partner.
Bridegroom is representative of a desire or need in one's life for a companion.
Bride-price means a forced or bribe-generated relationship.
Bridesmaid/best man portrays a need for support in decision making or support while making a life-altering choice.
Cohort See partner.
Companion is one with whom the dreamer closely associates.
Divorce is a clear separation of the self from a formerly associative factor.
Groom See bridegroom.
Maid of honor refers to a secondary placement position.
Mixed marriage refers to nondiscriminatory attitudes.
Mother-in-law depicts added responsibility in life.
Newlywed relates to a new relationship.
Open marriage is a strong warning against deceit.
Partner relates to someone closely associated with you.
Shotgun wedding constitutes a forced relationship.
Significant other is the most important person in one's life.
Spinster is a positive symbol that portrays self-reliance and confidence in oneself.
Spouse will signify a bonded connection to another.
Trial marriage signifies testing one's compatibility with another before making a commitment to that person.
Widow(er) may not relate to a physical death but symbolize a solitary state. It may refer to reclusiveness, a need to be alone, or a remote path.

Organizations, Bodies & Groups

Affinity group denotes a lack of individuality; an inability to stand alone for one's beliefs.

Alternative society refers to a large group of people who share a philosophy that varies from the general public's. This symbol may appear in a dream to underscore the fact that it's okay to think differently from others—you're not alone.

Amnesty International points to energies expended toward the support of another's right to be an individual and have expressive rights.

Captive audience alludes to a mesmerized or enthralled group. It is important with this dreamscape symbol is to recall what or who was the powerful draw.

Chamber of commerce alludes to business associates and the manner of group operation. May indicate a need to find out more about a particular geographical region.

City council can sometimes equate to the limits or boundaries of one's plans or range of effectiveness. However, most often a city council symbolizes one's own inner source of insights, conscience, or vision.

City planning commission See city council.

Civil service alludes to serving others; a selfless nature.

Clan refers to a tightly related group of people bonded by beliefs or perspectives.

Closed shop See labor union.

Colony connotes a group of like-minded individuals who desire to establish a location of camaraderie in relation to ideals.

Commune (group) represents a living arrangement based on the utilization of talents and supplies that are provided by and for all participants; unconditional sharing.

Cooperative (co-op/food) depicts a mutually beneficial relationship or situation.

Encounter group advises of a need to talk something through with others.

Secret police warns one to take more notice of others.

Goodwill (organization) points to a generous helping hand.

Joint (union) alludes to some type of bond or link.

Ku Klux Klan denotes an attitude of superiority, separatism, or intolerance.

Labor union represents justice in the work place; the maintenance of fair play while striving for accomplishment.

League (association) pertains to a specific tie to another; having like interests.

League of Nations advises of an ineffective or meaningless title or representation.

Legion portrays a multitude.

MADD (Mothers Against Drunk Driving) illustrates the powerful effects of working together for a united purpose.

MENSA equates to intellectual brilliance but not necessarily common sense.

Middle class denotes average.

Salvation Army stands for benevolence.

Search party represents the seeking to recoup lost emotions or attitudes.

Secret police comes as a strong advisement to be more aware of those around you.

Secret service signifies a loss of privacy. This symbol may point to someone with ulterior motives who is presenting a false front.

Secret society refers to hidden activities.

United Nations stands for a peaceful relationship or association.

World Health Organization (WHO) equates to those who have the ability and power to affect the health of the masses.

Outsiders

Hermit may advise one to open up more and be communicative, or it might be indicating a need to retreat and contemplate for a time. Surrounding dreamscape details will clarify which meaning this had for the dreamer.

Misfit won't necessarily indicate a negative connotation. This symbol will usually denote individual expressiveness; following one's own drumming.

Mountain folk is a suggestion of down-home attitudes and an appreciation of nature's beneficial, tranquil qualities.

Mountain man is representative of self-sufficiency and fortitude.

Nomad connotes the freedom to follow one's own chosen path in life.

Nonconformist applies to a freethinker. This is someone who is unafraid of expressing his or her individualism.

Outcast pertains to an individual who doesn't follow the crowd; one who thinks for oneself. In rare instances, this symbol may indicate a guilt or persecution complex for being different.

Outlander characterizes a person who stands out as being clearly different from those around her or him. This usually reveals a freethinker, one unafraid to openly express unique and individualistic perspectives or ideas.

Social isolation equates to intolerance of others.

see also
• Unions *p. 244*
• Government *p. 254*

Types of People

Crone See wise woman.
Diner (person) characterizes one in the process of nourishing oneself. Will usually refer to nourishment other than physical.
Elder is experience/wisdom.
Female represents intellect coupled with compassion.
Free agent reminds us we are our own mind; the decisions are ours to be responsible for.
Freeloader denotes a lack of responsibility and self-esteem.
Girl stands for beginning feminine perspectives.
Hominoid represents any being that has a human form.
Homo sapiens See hominoid.
Household goddess refers to spiritual behavior beginning in the home (within oneself).
Human signifies an excuse for mistakes or errors made.
Human being See hominoid.
Lady depicts real femininity and quiet reserve.
Madame (title) See lady.
Masher (man) characterizes a lack of respect for women; selfish ulterior motives.
Middle-aged exemplifies a considerable level of experience but not yet deep wisdom.
Minor (youth) indicates a more immature and inexperienced aspect or perspective.
Mob (of people) signifies a group of people with like attitudes or intentions. May not imply a negative connotation.
Mob mentality warns of losing one's rationale/sense of reason; a loss of ethics and/or morals.
Old folks See elder.
Old-timer will characterize one who knows the history or tales; one who's experienced.
Outdoorsman characterizes a recognition of one's inherent bond with natural forces.
Straggler won't necessarily indicate procrastination but usually symbolizes one who is cautious and discerning when in a group situation.
Trendsetter characterizes an individual whom others follow; one whom others emulate.
Tree hugger characterizes an individual who fully appreciates and respects the living essence of all things; one who deeply cherishes the concept of interrelatedness.
Underdog is an individual perceived as weaker by the dreamer, yet this may come in a dream to advise differently.
Wise woman characterizes attained wisdom carried with quiet dignity.

Mob is representative of a group of individuals who share a common purpose.

Cultures

Aborigine means a back-to-basics simplicity is required. May indicate inconsequential issues that are being given too much time or energy.
American Indian characterizes the inherent human bond with nature.
Amish is representative of simplicity. Solutions may be found through simplifying matters.
Anasazi denotes beginnings and a return to a more spiritual way.
Aztec is a portrayal of ancient belief systems.
Bedouin denotes spiritual separatism; keeping one's beliefs apart from the possibility of other concepts.
Caste (system) pertains to segregation; a separatist; an individual's tendency to classify others.
Caste mark is directly associated with one's self-image.
Highlander denotes someone who has attained an advanced stage of personal development.
Indian (American) See American Indian.
Indian (East) is representative of one who has ritualistic spiritual beliefs.
Mayan warns of the devastating effects of the dark side of spiritual power.
Pueblo relates to a synergistic relationship.
Suttee exposes a negative self-sacrificing act.

Character Traits

Cornball signifies uncommon, often criticized, ideas or behavior.
Dummy is representative of voluntary ignorance. It may also indicate a willful state devoid of personal responsibility or independence.
Lowlife reveals an unethical or immoral character.
Miser is representative of deep insecurities. May indicate selfishness.
Pinhead connotes ignorance; using a minuscule measure of one's intelligence or reason.
Simplicity pertains to a firm understanding of the correct priorities in life.
Sincerity reveals honesty; genuineness.
Single-handed signifies independence; resourcefulness; an ability to perform without the aid of others.
Sleekness is representative of refinement.
Slick See slippery.
Soft touch cautions against being easily manipulated.
Solemnity may indicate high respect, sacredness, or gravity.
Staid portrays a quiet dignity.
Stealthy implies dishonesty or secretiveness.
Stiff upper lip alludes to hidden emotions.
Stuffed shirt reveals a haughty personality.
Suave stands for finesse; diplomacy.
Tinhorn refers to a small-time individual who presents oneself as highly influential, experienced, or skillful.
Unsophisticated most often indicates commonsense wisdom unadulterated by society's mores or elitism.

Identity

Family name calls attention to one's heritage or family core; one's source.
First name usually has a unique meaning for each dreamer. Most often the surrounding dreamscape details will clarify this.
Given name most often comes as an important message that indicates a personal importance for the name. Recall what the name in the dream was and watch for it to show up during your waking state.
Initials are messages that are unique to each dreamer because they'll stand for recognized words or names that appear in the dreamer's awake-state life.
Name(s) will have special meaning for each individual dreamer. The dream name may not correspond directly to an individual's awake-state name but will most frequently be the name of someone the higher self is attempting to draw attention to.
Nameless is representative of a complete lack of ego in the individual.
Nameplate pertains to an identity or a desire for same. It implies a desire to be recognized.
Namesake is indicative of a respected or admired individual.
Name tag not only displays one's identity, it also shows a willingness to do so. This dream symbol refers to mixing and meeting new contacts.
Nickname will usually reveal an important characteristic or hidden aspect of someone.
Pet name will reveal a little-known aspect of a particular individual.
Signature may indicate authority or provide a specialized message for the dreamer.

Negative States

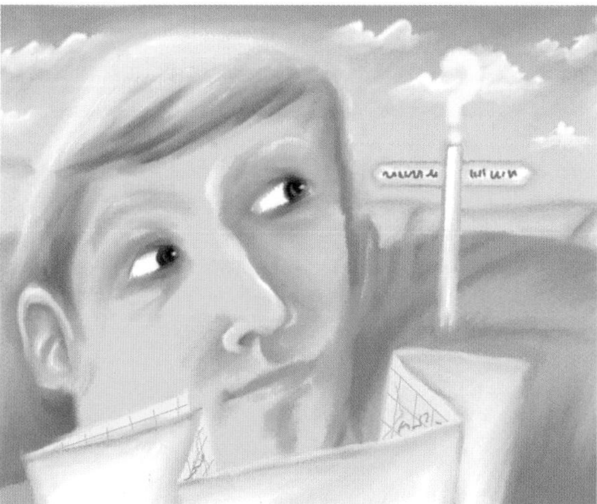

Lost can signify feelings of despondency and insecurity.

Blindsided cautions one to be more perceptive, more aware; the need to look at all angles; a surprise that comes because nobody was aware enough to perceive its first signs.
Burned-out pertains to a state of exhaustion; being worn out. May be an indication of a sense of defeat.
Lost is representative of a state of despondency. It may refer to a time of self-doubt and insecurity.
Unresponsive won't necessarily denote a lack of emotion or communication, but it may suggest deep thought.
Unsociable usually comes to the dreamer to reveal an introvert or shyness.

Thought Processes & Intelligence

Afterthought symbolizes the need to thoroughly discuss something and think it through before leaving it.
Analysis suggests the need to carefully analyze something important.
Assumption cautions one to stick with the facts.
Contemplation advises one to give deeper thought to something.
Flashback represents a need to remember an element of one's past that will be relevant to today.
Mastermind is representative of a highly intelligent person; one capable of complex analysis or planning.
Supposition will not denote an assumption but rather one's deeper thoughts and exploratory reaches into particular theories and concepts.
Total recall naturally refers to the memory of all elements of an event. The key here is why such a memory remains so vivid.

Interaction

Collusion warns of deceitfulness, secretiveness, or betrayal.
Compliment refers to praise from one's higher self.
Confrontation may be giving advice to get something out in the open.
Consultation advises of the need for advice.
Deception is a warning symbol. The word is self-explanatory. There is some type of deceiving going on in your life. The real clue here is: Who is doing it? Oneself?
Interfacing characterizes interaction with others.
Manipulation reveals a desire to control situations or others. Frequently one allows oneself to be manipulated in order to avoid personal responsibility.
Mingling suggests a need to experience diversity. Cautions against being an ideological separatist.
Miscommunication reveals to the dreamer the need to communicate with someone to correct a previous misunderstanding.
Reconciliation denotes an arrangement to settle a disagreement.

see also
• People Phobias *p. 152*
• Fame *p. 186*

Social Extremes

Lunatic fringe warns of an ideology or path that's nearing extremism.
Mad may not refer to craziness or anger, but it often indicates a great difficulty or embroiled situation.
Madcap refers to one who appears recklessly adventurous. In this way, it refers to a more general reluctance to pay attention to warnings or possible dangers.
Wild man stands for a savage personality; violent, erratic behavior.
Wild woman equates to the feminine psyche's connection to the fertile, feral persona of Mother Nature, who can be described as the earth goddess within.

Types of Talk

Baby talk is representative of a voluntary reversion to immature reasoning.
Back talk usually indicates rudeness or impertinence. However, it may also signify a defense of one's opinion or behavior or standing up for oneself.
Flattery comes as a warning of ulterior motives.
Pillow talk is the revealing of secrets; verbal intimacy.
Small talk characterizes an insignificant communication, one geared toward generalities and avoiding the more important issues.
Sweet talk See flattery.
Table talk connotes surface conversation containing no deep or heavy material.

Language

Accent refers to a different way of expressing ideas, feelings, or perspectives.
Ad-lib signifies a call to stop making excuses in life.
Babbling (talk) warns of meaningless dialogue.
Banter infers playful teasing yet usually exposes some type of hidden message.
Buzzword warns against a desire to impress others; a need to bolster self-esteem and worth.
Colloquialism in dreams helps to narrow down meanings in the spoken language of other dream characters presented.
Commentary defines another's opinion or perspective.
Dedicated line represents putting one's energy into a single goal or purpose.
Drawl alludes to a communication hesitancy.
Hearsay implies questionable information.
Intercourse (communication) refers to a need to convey or express opinions more.
Jabbering stands for incoherent communication; confusion.
Jam session (verbal) reveals a need to talk things out.
Jargon indicates concepts or ideas that are beyond one's understanding. This symbol may also point out a tendency to talk above others.
Language in dreams will add another dimension to the overall symbology. Foreign accents, biblical verbiage, obscenity, specialized terms, etc., all reveal clues to correct interpretation along with the mood or tone of voice.
Language barrier warns of ineffective communications.
Last say See last word.
Last word denotes a final opportunity to have one's way.
Lipreading typifies hidden meanings in what others say.
Long-winded stands for redundancy; repetitiveness; a tendency to prolong one's point.
Monologue symbolizes a discussion one needs to have with oneself; something needs to be talked out or analyzed.
Pig Latin refers to a backward way of communicating with others; an inability to clearly express oneself.
Rough (language) indicates a vulgar individual, one who doesn't care about social mores or conventions.

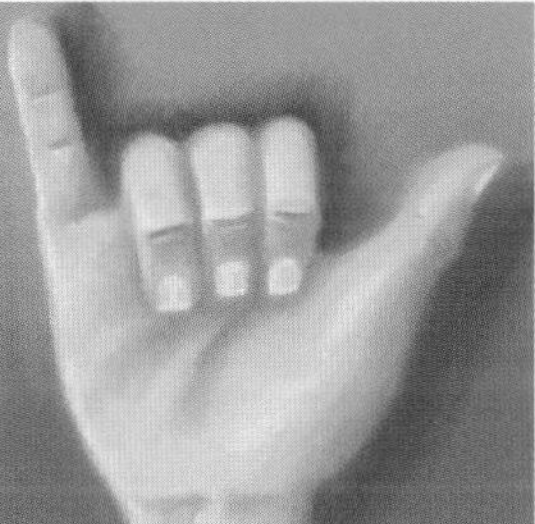

Sign language indicates that there are many methods to communicate.

Sign language reminds us that there are multiple forms of communication that can be effectively used.
Slang will reveal an aspect of an individual's character.
Slurring (words) connotes an inability to communicate accurately.
Sob story pertains to a desire or psychological need to obtain sympathy from others; an absorption with oneself.
Soft-pedal pertains to a willful diminishing of something's value or importance; a rather deceptive maneuver.
Soft soap warns of self-serving methods.
Speechless may indicate a dumbfounded reaction, or it could imply wise discernment, depending on the surrounding dream elements.
Speech-reading See lipreading.
Spiel denotes an effort to persuade.
Spout exposes an inability to contain information.
Sputtering implies incoherent communication; an inability to clearly communicate.
Stuttering symbolizes inability to communicate thoughts.
Tattletale reveals an informant; an untrustworthy individual.
Tongue-tied refers to a loss for words; an inability to respond.
Whispering represents a quiet communication that may have various sources such as another individual, one's inner guidance, or even the conscience.
Windbag reveals meaningless talk; verbosity. It may refer to the concept of much talk and little substance.
Wisecrack will usually reveal one's true attitude that was heretofore hidden.
Word of mouth signifies information passed verbally but cautions against it being totally accurate.

Means of Communication

Braille advises of opportunities to see clearly. Warns against a tendency to claim ignorance.

Cryptogram defines secret communications; hidden intentions.

Glyph depicts some kind of symbology specific to the dreamer. This glyph will reveal a unique symbolism.

Hieroglyph symbolizes spiritual truths beyond one's current stage of understanding.

Invisible ink stands for hypocrisy; deception.

Pictograph will display a message that is unique to the dreamer. What the pictograph displays will be important.

Pony express typifies a mode of communication that travels from person to person; a word-of-mouth dissemination.

Powwow signifies a need to communicate. A get-together is suggested.

Signal board represents one's instincts; inner knowing or perception; lightning psychic impressions.

Smoke signal connotes a hidden message; a private means of communication.

Sounding board symbolizes an advisement to share thoughts and emotions with others.

Talking stick indicates who has the authority (or whose turn it is) to speak.

Written Communication

Airmail refers to one's general acceptance of another's idea; an open mind.

Bad news will most often come as a revelation about something in one's awake-state life, or it will be shown as a forewarning.

Codex suggests highly valuable information or knowledge.

Hate mail reveals negativity or a lack of acceptance.

Illegible (writing) denotes mental confusion; perceptual dysfunction.

Invitation means a request. Recall what the invitation was for. Who was it from?

Message brings a revelation or some type of epiphany.

Mirror writing signifies backward communications. It expresses a need to be straightforward.

No-call list exemplifies those who don't want to waste their time on insignificant or undesirable aspects.

Omega (Greek letter) will emphasize the end element of something in the dreamer's experience.

Poison-pen letter See hate mail.

Thank-you note usually points out a blessing that has been overlooked.

Unlisted phone number stands for an attempt on the part of the dreamer to maintain privacy in his or her life.

Miscellaneous

Ability See talent.

Accompaniment refers to need for symmetry in life or for more balance in relationships.

Ancient connotes old and wise.

Announcement connotes one's need to reveal something.

Apology symbolizes an admission of guilt.

Bigotry means intolerance.

Cartel signifies a controlling group in one's life.

Cartouche connotes an important individual in life.

Common denominator pertains to an aspect that is shared by others. May mean the simplest aspect; bottom line.

Concert (synergy) advises of the benefits of a collaboration.

Conglomerate is representative of the joining of several factors. The dreamer will understand what this means by including surrounding elements.

Gender gap is representative of sex-based disagreements.

Congregation connotes a large group, but this does not specifically imply a spiritual connection.

Customer denotes one who has a right to receive service.

Ensemble will symbolize all the elements of an aspect, perhaps all the members of a group involved in an issue or plan.

Entourage See ensemble.

Gender gap stands for opposing opinions due to difference in gender perspectives generated from sociopolitical situations.

Great divide indicates solid strength. May point to a division in one's life.

Knuckle sandwich typifies forthcoming repercussions.

Peer may relate to personal associates, acquaintances, or friends and their associated characteristics; the quality and type of one's circle.

Pod (group) symbolizes spiritual life.

Predecessor characterizes a person who attempted to present the same attitude, idea, or plan before you did.

Solidarity constitutes mutual interest or camaraderie.

Stereotype is a typecast personality or situation. May warn against profiling people.

Street smarts symbolize personal survival skills and pertain to how well one is prepared to handle difficulties.

Talent corresponds to inherent abilities unique to each person.

Ten-Four represents expressed agreement; confirmation.

Unanimous suggests total agreement; no dissension.

Chapter 10

Emotions & Behavior

Symbols of emotion and behavior represent one's underlying state of mind and manner of thought. Fears, for example, are an exceptionally revealing category of symbols related to one's thought processes.

Feelings

Agony signifies the need to stop dwelling on the past. A greater level of acceptance is needed.

Aimlessness warns against having no ambition or direction in life. This could also be warning against having no opinion or perspective on an issue.

Amazement refers to a revelation in one's life.

Ambition represents the level of one's energy applied to goals.

Anticipation reveals anxiety over future events.

Anxiety represents worry. This is a caution to be more within the attitude of acceptance.

Apathy warns of being emotionally neutral and without compassion.

Ashamed calls for a personal examination of one's actions.

Aversion signifies distaste for one or more aspects entering or interfering with life.

Commitment emphasizes a promise; a responsibility to carry something through.

Desensitized warns of apathy or emotional indifference; insensitivity; a hardened heart.

Disappointment warns against having expectations.

Embarrassment typifies an ill-at-ease state. This can be a telling symbol when combined with surrounding dreamscape facets.

Empathy usually is an advisement to better understand another's situation or response.

Exasperation advises one to be more accepting instead of getting annoyed; one requires more patience.

Flat (bland) represents a lack of emotional expression.

Frustration is a message of acceptance as well as of perseverance.

Guilt comes to reveal culpability, and many times it's the dreamer's.

Humiliation illustrates a feeling of dishonor or discredit. This may also indicate an inferiority complex.

Humility usually advises one to give credit for accomplishments, even to oneself.

Impatience calls for one to accept the proper timing of events in life.

Inconsolable defines a great need to feel loved. Regardless of why someone is consumed with deep grief, being held by another becomes the greatest healing comfort one can get.

Rapture is representative of an enthralled sensation or attitude; being overcome with captivation.

Regretfulness usually implies personal guilt.

Remorse implies personal guilt that one refuses to acknowledge.

Sad See melancholia.

Scared exposes a person's inner fears.

Serenity is an indication of inner harmony.

Extreme Feelings

Anguish warns of immersing oneself in painful memories.
Despair illustrates a lack of faith or acceptance.
Fear signifies one's personal insecurities; a lack of self-confidence (see Phobias).
Grief depicts a needed release of emotions.
Horror reveals one's fears.
Passion will not explicitly infer a sexual implication but rather a nearly consuming emotion.

Attitudes

About-face represents a sudden change in perspective, behavior, or attitude.

Affectations represent a false sense of self or the need to impress others.

Ambiguity symbolizes doubts.

Ambivalence signifies a contrary personality; indecisiveness.

Antsy (excited) typifies a restlessness; perhaps lacking acceptance.

Bias means a slanted perspective; a preferential attitude.

Complacent defines a lack of motivation yet may also indicate acceptance. Surrounding dreamscape symbols will clarify this intent.

Concealment warns of a cover-up or the hiding of something.

Condemnation signifies absolute rejection of something. Who was doing the condemning? About what?

Conservatism marks a tendency to avoid change; fear of something new or innovative.

Coward won't necessarily be a demeaning characteristic but rather will reveal the necessity for gaining greater self-confidence and being less self-deprecating.

Cranky reveals bad-temperedness; unpredictability.

Craven See coward.

Crocodile tears characterize the expression of false emotions for the sake of obtaining sympathy or attention; insecurity.

Egalitarian reflects a perspective of equality; a generally nonracist or nonsexist attitude.

Elitism/ist reflects snobbery; a habit of class separation.

Gall stands for audacity; a provocation.

Guile reveals deceit.

Halfhearted represents a lack of interest.

Ignorance is most often a warning to stop refusing to learn new things; a self-induced fear of knowledge.

Menace reveals a harmful aspect in one's life. Recall who or what the menace was. Was it you?

Ribald pertains to uncouth behavior that reveals a lack of spiritual attainment.

Scrupulous will reveal a conscionable individual.

Self-doubt implies one's personal lack of confidence in oneself.

Sentimentality denotes an open heart; compassion and understanding; emotional receptiveness.

Sophist characterizes a person with a tendency to come up with elaborate arguments.

Sophisticate typifies worldly experience.

Starstruck warns against allowing oneself to become fascinated with others.

Survivalist emphasizes self-reliance; resourcefulness.

Wannabe is representative of a tendency to emulate or imitate others.

see also
• Dangerous Situations *p. 167*
• Communication & Relationships *p. 468*

Behavior

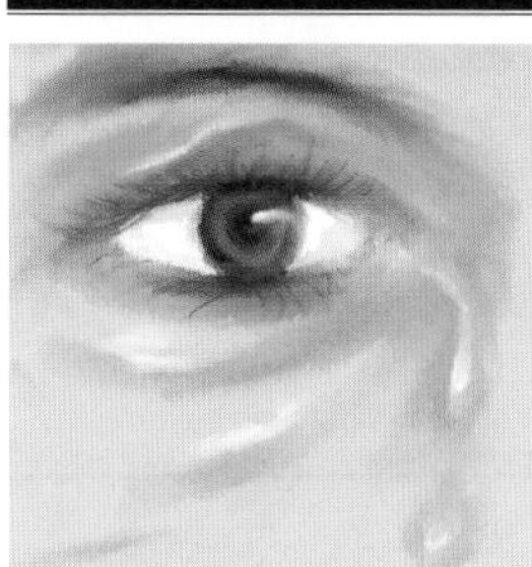
Crying is a sign of self-reproach.

Absentminded reflects a lack of awareness and/or focus.
Affectations represent a false sense of self or the need to impress others.
Asceticism symbolizes a life of self-denial, deferring to others.
Bedside manner illustrates one's level of sensitivity to others.
Bipartisan alludes to having two separate opinions or perspectives on the same issue. May indicate indecision.
Black humor reveals poor taste or an intent to shock.
Candid (behavior/speech) points to honesty or the need for it.
Coddle warns of overindulgence; a lack of discipline.
Copycat cautions against imitating others. We can aspire to acquire virtuous qualities, but we are each uniquely different and distinctly defined.
Crying pertains to the grief of regret or remorse.
Cutesy may simply equate to lighthearted playfulness, or indicate a serious personality affectation.
Flattery comes to warn of ulterior motives.
Fortitude applies to perseverance. Perhaps the dreamer needs this, or the word may denote a commendation.
Friskiness characterizes lightheartedness; joyful acts.
Gall stands for audacity; a provocation.
Hedonism warns against excessive self-indulgence; a preoccupation with self.
Hell-raising usually refers to the act of stirring things up in order to expose wrongdoings or misconceptions.
High-spirited usually equates to energetic enthusiasm and courage. May indicate a mettlesome personality.
Homesick emphasizes emotional sensitivity. May indicate a need to return to one's basic values.
Hoodwink reveals a deception.
Illogical (aspects) indicate confusion or illogical thought present in the waking state.
Imitating cautions one to be true to oneself. Advises against emulating others or following in their footsteps.
Impulse buying denotes a lack of self-control.
Incompetency cautions against attempting to understand or take on higher concepts for which one isn't ready.
Inference implies forthcoming innuendos; possible new insight into something.
Inhumane (treatment) will reveal harsh underlying emotional disturbances.
Late bloomer signifies eventual realizations.
Latecomer characterizes one who is slow to make realizations or decisions.
Lighthearted reveals a state of acceptance in one's heart.
Lightweight (person) characterizes one who is ineffective or of lesser importance.
Lionhearted exemplifies a courageous individual or action.
Litterbug refers to one who broadcasts meaningless ideas.
Morbidity relates to a loss of inner strength; cynicism.
Needy is representative of available opportunities. Some neediness is perceived rather than being actual. In this case, the symbol stands for a bid for sympathy.
Negativism signifies a pessimistic outlook; a cynic.
Repentant corresponds to self-reproach.
Restlessness warns of a lack of acceptance; anxiety and/or impatience.
Rudeness portrays a disrespect for others and implies a lack of advancement.
Self-control reflects a focused individual who has mastered emotional responses and has the inner strength to resist distractions.
Self-inflicted exposes that one's troubles were caused by oneself; self-defeating behavior.
Self-regulating signifies behavior guided by one's conscience.
Self-restraint means willpower.
Social climber signifies a psychological need to be better or more successful than one's peers.
Socialite stands for arrogance; a misplaced self-perspective.
Suicide reveals a loss of inner strength and the perception of being a spiritual facet of the divine essence. May also reveal a self-defeating plan or move.

Extreme Behaviors

Amuck warns of a violent personality, perspective, or relationship.
Compulsion cautions one to gain better control over impulsiveness.
Extravagance comes as a warning against same.
Fit (child's) See tantrum.
Headstrong warns against being obstinate.
Histrionics stands for a tendency to gain attention or sympathy through overexaggerated emotions.
Incorrigibility illustrates a strong character; a refusal to be confined or controlled by another.
Rage comes to the dreamer as a warning of an inability to direct one's energies in a productive manner; emotional immaturity.
Rambunctiousness reveals a lack of acceptance; anxiety and impatience.
Rampage See rage.
Reckless is a representation of immaturity; a lack of responsibility.
Road rage reveals those under pressure who explode at the first opportunity.
Ruthlessness signifies a void of sensitivity; lacking moral fiber; ulterior motives.
Sanctimonious (attitude) reveals false piety.
Shopaholic signifies one who continually seeks self-gratification. May point to a tendency toward conflict or resolution avoidance; tries to replace a void in one's life with gifts to oneself.
Tantrum illustrates a lack of self-control.

Characteristics

Absent is a reference to a void in one's life.
Adept denotes a proficiency.
Adventurous suggests that there is a need for caution.
Cheeky implies audacity; impudence. May also denote strength.
Disheveled stands for priorities placed on higher aspects, such as intellectual pursuit or spirituality; an attitude that doesn't focus on appearances.
Exaggeration warns against embellishments or advises of a situation in one's life where this is present.
Fastidiousness will usually indicate a tendency toward painstaking attention to detail.
Feral will most often refer to an expression of deep passion or fervor. This is not a sexual reference but rather one that reaches to the core of one's being. An example would be a feral love of nature.
Flawless symbolizes a sound aspect or element.
Flimsy indicates superficiality.
Floppy means indecision; a lack of firm attitudes or strong ideals. May also point to an attitude of acceptance, a "whatever" attitude.
Full-blooded will not necessarily refer to heritage, as it usually implies "purity" as in a belief system or an individual's intentions.
Highbrow indicates intelligence.
Inarticulate corresponds to difficulty expressing oneself.
Inconsistency marks some type of discrepancy in one's life. Surrounding dreamscape details will help clarify what this happens to be.
Inconspicuous refers to those subtle aspects in life that one often misses taking note of due to lack of awareness of ones' surroundings.
Indispensable will define that which a person believes is essential in life.
Infallible usually comes as a "don't kid yourself" message but can also point to a trustworthy individual.
Jumbled denotes mental or emotional confusion.
Laid-back usually will indicate a state of acceptance.
Mindless signifies an inability to think for oneself or comprehend information.
Quick wit connotes swift responses; a lightning intellect.
Resilient defines acceptance. This points to the management of problematic events with less difficulty and more grace than others.
Reticence denotes a desire to avoid communication with others; diffidence.
Rigid implies an opinionated thought process; not open to alternative ideas.
Self-taught signifies an individual motivated to seek his or her own answers.
Sharp-witted means astuteness.

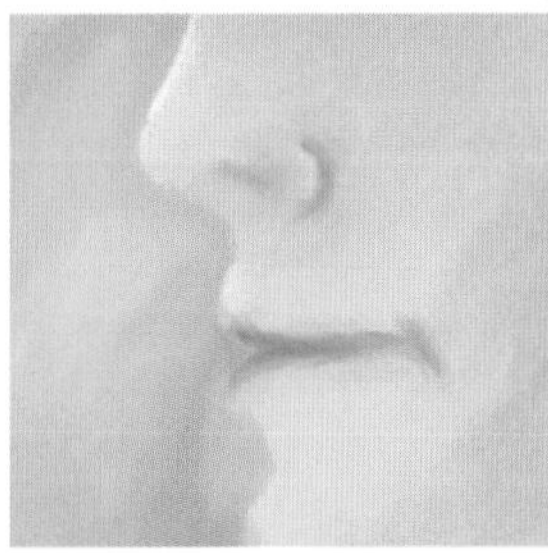
Tight-lipped may indicate shyness.

Skeptic characterizes an individual with a narrow perspective and a mind closed to new, expanded concepts; one having no view to probabilities or possibilities.
Snob connotes arrogance.
Softheaded denotes a compliant and commiserative personality.
Tightfisted warns of selfishness; being ego-centered.
Tight-lipped most often reflects a reserved personality rather than being standoffish.
Uncivilized suggests an absolute disregard for others.
Unconventional frequently comes as personal advice to follow one's own path or ideas. This symbol may also indicate something outside the box, meaning unusual yet workable.
Uncouth implies rudeness.
Worldly signifies a socially or culturally savvy individual; worldly-wise.
World-weariness equates to a mood of depression or despair; a disgust; tiredness related to the materialistic, pleasure-seeking, elitist attitudes and dog-eat-dog state of the world. This symbol is a call to shift perspectives to focus on the beauty of the natural world and the simplicity of one's many current blessings.
Zany usually characterizes an individual who behaves in an outrageously unconventional, yet amusing, manner; who acts on the spur of the moment. This symbol won't normally be a negative element but rather illustrates the freedom that spontaneity brings.

Negative Attitudes

Arrogance signifies egotism.
Exclusionist characterizes a separatist; bigot.
Greed warns against a tendency toward self-interest and self-centeredness.
Hard-boiled defines an insensitive personality.
Hardfisted may indicate determination or fortitude, or it could point to ruthlessness.
Hardhanded reveals a tyrannical personality.
Hardheaded applies to shrewdness; a realistic perspective.
Hard-hearted reveals an aloof personality; someone who is unemotional and insensitive or apathetic.
Hard-nosed refers to a firm position; a difficult-to-change attitude.
Heartless is representative of apathy, sternness, or insensitivity.
Me generation will warn against arrogance, selfishness, and apathy.
Prideful means arrogance; a self-absorbed individual.

Gentle Characteristics

Benevolence is generosity. May be an ulterior motive.
Benign alludes to innocence. It means harmless, neutral.
Softhearted is representative of an individual with a highly responsive and compassionate nature.

see also
• Mental Disorders & Behavior *p. 106*
• Negative Actions *p. 178*

Psychological Conditions

Adult denotes a mature aspect.
Alone signifies a situation that may be needed. A suggestion that solitude or quiet time may bring about emotional healing or mental clarity.
Anonymous represents hidden intentions or a wish to avoid recognition.
Attention Deficit Disorder (ADD) symbolizes inattention and cautions one to begin focusing and concentrating more on an issue in one's life.
Breakdown implies a falling-apart situation or condition; stressed beyond endurance.
Breaking point connotes a critical point where one either breaks away or is overstressed by conditions.
Catalepsy is deep-seated fears.
Confusion usually indicates mental turmoil.
Defense mechanism stands for psychological methods utilized to protect oneself from guilt, low self-esteem, conflict, shame, or other personally injurious feelings.
Dysphoria reveals a lack of acceptance; high anxiety or expectation; restlessness.
Fixation warns against an obsessive nature.
Flashback always reveals an important event or fact for the dreamer to remember.
Free will comes to remind us of our right to make our own choices in life.
Habit signifies repetitiveness; action without thought.
Hyperactivity cautions one to slow down, conserve energy, or comprehend more.
Hysteria comes as a warning against losing control of logic and reason.

Confusion denotes inner turbulence and conflict.

Identity crisis may correspond with past-life personalities that are beginning to break through the consciousness.
Inferiority complex represents a serious lack of acceptance in one's life; a failure to feel the loving essence of the divine within oneself.
Inhibition corresponds with one's fears.
Insanity implies a total loss of reality.
Intuition corresponds with one's insights or feelings. This symbol comes as a message of validation for the dreamer.
Lunacy may not indicate craziness. Instead it may well reveal a mental state of reality comprehension.
Maniac denotes a loss of reason and logic; a psychologically dysfunctional individual.
Megalomania warns of misplaced priorities; a lack of enlightenment; a focus on oneself.
Midlife crisis indicates a lack of acceptance; an inability to recognize the force of the divine within oneself.
Psychopath characterizes an imbalanced perspective.
Self-absorbed warns against placing oneself as one's priority in life; being devoted to satisfying oneself.
Self-centeredness warns against thinking only of oneself; a love of one's ego.
Self-consciousness signifies a tendency to feel inferior to one's peers.
Self-contained stands for having all the necessary elements of something. It may reveal one's sense of self-reliance.
Self-defeating reveals unproductive choices regarding sticking to goals.
Self-deprecating behaviour means one isn't giving oneself enough credit.
Self-destructive warns against continuing behavior that harms oneself.
Self-limiting stands for inner fear that prevents one from reaching for further discovery.
Separation anxiety stands for a need for support; an inability to be independent; a fear of independence.
Teenager relates to a transitional phase.

Emotional States

Accident prone represents a careless individual. Advises the need for greater awareness and to remain focused.
Accursed denotes tendency toward suggestibility; gullibility; a false reason attributed to a situation or condition for the purpose of avoiding personal responsibility.
Altruism corresponds with empathy; selflessness.
Autonomy stands for one's independence and the freedom to express one's uniqueness.
Fussy defines impatience or anxiety.
Gaiety suggests a lighthearted atmosphere or situation.
Garbled (speech) denotes perplexity; talking about issues one has no understanding of.
Immaturity portrays an individual who is not yet ready for the next level of advancement. This could caution one against attempting to gain knowledge one is not properly prepared to absorb.
Isolation usually connotes a self-induced condition.
Mourning See grief.
Self-sufficiency refers to a self-reliant personality; creativity and resourcefulness.

Pranks

Gag See practical joke.
Monkeyshines are mischievous behaviors. They may be negative depending on dream details.
Practical joke applies to a stress-releasing event. Recall whether or not this joke was harmful. Who was the instigator of the practical joke? Who was the victim? What was the response?
Prank See practical joke.

Emotional Challenges

Bereavement reveals a personal sorrow.
Dilemma illustrates the presence of a problematic situation that is difficult to resolve; an extremely difficult decision.
Disagreement connotes conflict. This may even be within oneself.

Communication

Caustic usually refers to behavior or speech that has the potential to burn oneself or another. This symbol might indicate a plan, relationship, or situation that could end up burning the participant.
Disinformation connotes the act of willfully misleading others.
Ebonics (African American slang) refers to speaking one's own type of language. Implies that someone is in their own little world and isn't communicating well.
Excuse cautions against not taking personal responsibility.
Gibberish signifies communications or ideas others can't understand. May even refer to one's own confused thoughts.
Guttural (voice) denotes a surprised or stunned reaction.
Sarcasm may be a positive or negative dreamscape element depending on who said what to whom. Recall the detail for clarity. Just like in the awake state, revelations often come through sarcasm or side remarks.
Satire See sarcasm.
Sharp-tongued denotes an inability to temper one's words.
Silver-tongued characterizes an influential and persuasive personality.
Soft-spoken will usually denote gentleness yet may imply manipulation or deception.

Moods

Addled See confusion.
Amenable designates an agreeable personality.
Amiable defines an agreeable personality.
Confusion usually indicates mental turmoil.
Euphoria typifies a state of absolute joy and serenity. Depending on surrounding dreamscape facets, this may or may not be a positive sign. May indicate overoptimism on the part of the dreamer.
Fatalism is a direct call to use one's free will and assume the responsibilities resulting from the same.
Fervor See passion.
Flippant relates to disrespect; arrogance.
Funk usually refers to a disappointment; an expectation not fulfilled as anticipated.
Hell-bent stands for a level of determination verging on obsession.
Hilarity typifies the importance of humor in one's life.
Hot-blooded signifies a lack of self-control.
Hotheaded applies to a quick temper.
Melancholia denotes a lack of acceptance; self-pity.
Moodiness cautions one to accept more in life; against an inability to reconcile events.
Mood swings signify indecision.
Morose See melancholia.
Self-indulgent advises one to start considering others.

Appearance

Bashful can mean feelings of inferiority, but often it's linked with a desire to remain out of the limelight, or one not wanting acknowledgment or recognition for one's actions.
Brittle reveals dryness. This portrays something that's unyielding; a lack of nourishment that may be mental, emotional, or spiritual.
Clumsiness represents inattention to details; a suggestion to sharpen one's awareness.
Drunk warns the dreamer of overindulgence.
Glow (inner) implies inspiration or emotional warmth.
Gruesome connotes a repulsive reaction; an unacceptable aspect in one's life.
Haggard portrays a long struggle; exhaustion; being tired of continually making an effort without seeing results.
Intoxicated See drunk.
Lifeless portrays a lack of spirit; motivation; loss of energy or will.
Quaint will not mean old-fashioned but rather a refreshing type of element.

Body Language & Gestures

Askance (look) means disapproval or questioned behavior.
Cat-eyed (human) shows a talent for seeing through another's personality or agenda; an ability to see what lies in the shadows and darker places of life.
Deportment will usually reveal one's inner emotional or psychological state.
Eye contact shows personal perceptual connection with another.
Fast-talk warns against making excuses.
Femme fatale pertains to alluring life aspects.
Finger-pointing suggests a tendency to identify a guilty party, or may point to an effort to shift responsibility.
Fistfight comes as a warning against the utilization of negative resolutions.
Flip off equates to rudeness; an inability to control knee-jerk reactions.
Grimace connotes displeasure.
Head-scratching indicates puzzlement; a lack of understanding; confusion.
High sign corresponds with good relationships.

see also
• Face *p. 92*
• Metaphors *p. 481*

Figures of Speech

Animal magnetism denotes one who inherently possesses a powerful personality that attracts the attention of others.
Basket case is an emotionally confused individual.
Blockhead characterizes a narrow-minded individual; an inability or unwillingness to think outside the box.
Brown bagging portrays a frugal nature.
Castle in the sky characterizes unrealistic ideas or goals; impracticality.
Cat and mouse implies games being played in one's life; trifling with one another.
Catfight means vicious disputes; uncontrolled disagreement.
Cold feet portray a lack of faith or courage; giving in to one's fears.
Diamond in the rough alludes to hidden quality and value.
Down-home equates to honest character; simple, straightforward expressiveness without any trace of ulterior motives.
Egg on face stands for embarrassment over being wrong or misjudging.
Excess baggage naturally symbolizes a need to get rid of unnecessary elements in one's life. This most often points out harmful attitudes such as grudges.
Eye candy refers to a sweet deal or idea as perceived by the dreamer's eye.
Fall guy characterizes a person who is falsely blamed; a scapegoat.
Fat cat characterizes one who has abundant resources. This may not have the negative connotations that the term generally implies.
Finger (in pie) is a depiction of meddling or having to be involved in multiple issues or affairs.
Fly-on-the-wall reveals the presence of a (or a need to) spy; a desire to know what's happening or how another is reacting.
Foot stamping signifies an inability to compromise; a tendency to always need to get one's way.
Forked tongue characterizes double-talk.
Free lunch connotes an unexpected benefit that presents itself in one's life; a positive aspect that comes without any thought or personal effort applied to its manifestation.
Free rein relates to a boundless opportunity; a limitless aspect.
Free ride cautions one against depending on others to carry one along the path.
Geek-speak won't necessarily refer solely to techno-talk but will usually be associated with someone who has a tendency to use one-hundred-dollar words in conversation.
Gender bender will rarely have a sexual association but rather will refer to a healthy blending of a person's yin and yang traits.
Girl talk signifies freedom to share female confidentialities.
Golden rule signifies ethical and moral behavior.
Gold fever represents unrealistic expectations.
Gold rush alludes to material or financial desires.
Green power equates to an attitude that money is power.
Gung ho denotes high enthusiasm and a readiness to act on it; being stoked.
Head-on symbolizes a strong will and determination to face reality and/or deal with conflicts that arise.
High horse reveals indignation; a continual complaining. Advises acceptance.
Horseplay denotes lighthearted pranks; a practical joke.
Hot air refers to bluster; tending to exaggerate or lean toward pretentiousness.
Humble pie advises one to admit mistakes and take responsibility.

Forked tongue characterizes someone who deliberately speaks to mislead.

Jawbreaker represents that which depletes one's strength in reference to expending too much energy on whole concepts. This suggests a need to break down these concepts into their various aspects so they can be understood one at a time.
Juicehead See alcoholic.
Jumper (suicide) See suicide.
Label maker cautions against a need to label everything and everyone. Some concepts cannot be defined by a single term or be cubbyholed.
Mound builder characterizes one who cherishes truth and strives to protect or preserve it.
Runaround represents an inability to attain a focused or centered perspective or position.
Savvy is representative of an individual who is well informed; knowledgeable.
Teacher's pet warns against favoritism displayed in life.
Tenderfoot pertains to a lack of experiential knowledge; a beginner aiming to hit a goal.
Top dog indicates one recognized as having the highest authority, skill, or knowledge; the one in charge.
Whistle-blowing points to an informer; betrayal.
Will-o'-the-wisp, as opposed to a dictionary definition, will mean quite the contrary in dream symbology. This little dreamscape fragment stands for subliminal insights or enlightened ideas.
Wye (Y) pertains to a place or phase where paths may cross; possible choices.

Heart & Hand Phrases

Free hand is an indication of independence and the following of one's own ideals and perceptions.
Green thumb corresponds with a nurturing nature.
Hand in cookie jar suggests misbehavior and nosiness.
Hand in glove cautions against forming relationships that are too close, too revealing of oneself, or too interdependent.
Hand in hand signifies cooperation; close association.
Hand over fist suggests a fast pace in life.
Hand over heart usually implies sincerity.
Hands in pockets is reluctance.
Hands over ears point to a lack of acceptance; not wanting to hear certain things.
Hands over eyes warn against voluntary ignorance.
Heart of hearts implies confidentiality; open expression of sincerity; what one cherishes most.
Heart-to-heart implies confidentiality; open expression of deep sincerity.
Heavy-handed is representative of a harsh and tyrannical personality.
Heavyhearted characterizes melancholia.
Iron hand depicts an unyielding personality; possibly indicates manipulation.

Love & Sex

Endearments make one aware of another's personal perception of a relationship.
Free love applies to indiscriminate behavior; irresponsibility.
Frolic See friskiness.
Hard-core signifies a strong opinion or perspective; one that cannot be changed.
Heartache naturally equates to sorrow, emotional distress.
Inexperience underscores one's current level of advancement or personal development.
Intertwined describes a thorough involvement or a convoluted issue.
Love corresponds to feelings of great fondness; being cherished.
Lovelorn symbolizes the empty feeling that comes from a sense or perception of not being loved or appreciated.
Lovesick warns of a lack of emotional control; loss of awareness and focus.
Jilted refers to sudden termination of something in life.
Sex correlates with one's way of communicating; quality of relationships and type of behavior toward them. Recall what the type of sexual presentation was. Gentle? Violent? Possessive? Deviant?
Star-crossed pertains to ill fortune; multiple difficulties.
True love stands for enduring devotion and loyalty.

Movers & Shakers

Activist signifies one who fights for one's beliefs.
Big gun suggests the most influential or powerful element or individual.
Big shot characterizes someone of importance; influential. May be a misplaced attribute.
Challenger alludes to one-upmanship; one who strives to outdo others; one driven to prove his or her worth.
Fiery usually connotes an emotionally impetuous personality; one who often experiences emotional outbursts.
Firebrand characterizes an individual who has tendencies toward stirring emotions that are directed toward revolt; one who riles others.
Flamboyant refers to an elaborate personality; one who must outdo others; a need to stand out in a crowd. This symbol may also reflect one who is very optimistic and can't control overwhelming feelings of joy.

Activist represents a militant person.

High-powered signifies an ability to make things happen.
Hotshot characterizes an adept individual; an expert. In some cases, this may be an aggressive show-off.
Live wire reveals erratic, uncontrolled energies.
Maverick characterizes a nonconformist; one who enjoys living life her or his own way.
Pacesetter See trendsetter.
Pathfinder characterizes an individual who leads others to his or her life path. This is a direct warning, for nobody should tell another which path to take in life: this must be a personal decision.
Pioneer characterizes an individual who fearlessly forges ahead through unknown territory. This usually pertains to one's life path. May indicate perseverance and determination.
Player refers to someone who is actively participating in something, usually involved in a specific situation; one with like sympathies or attitudes.
Prime mover indicates a motivational force; an element seen as one's source of motivation.
Protagonist stands for the central figure; an advocate; a leader.
Self-appointed cautions against making oneself an authority.
Self-made will stand for an individual who reached goals through his or her own efforts and intellect.
Self-proclaimed correlates to how one wishes to be known.
Self-propelled indicates great stores of inner power (energy and motivation).
Self-starter stands for a well-motivated individual.
Trailblazer connotes the courage of one who endeavors to discover a new course.
Whiz kid characterizes intellectual attainment yet may not indicate that this intelligence is accompanied by the wisdom that should go hand in hand with it.
Wunderkind signifies early achievement; reaching goals far earlier than normally done.

see also
• Social Position *p. 187*
• The Oldest Profession *p. 252*

Sexuality

Aberration See abnormality.

Abnormality represents a diversion from the norm. Not necessarily a negative symbol.

Accosted symbolizes a bold confrontation; forwardness.

Alias indicates identification with more than one personality of oneself. The negative side to this symbol is a caution against trying to be someone you're not or presenting a false public persona.

Asexual applies to physical and emotional independence.

Bisexual (activity) signifies an individual who perceives all sides to an issue; indicates a total lack of prejudice.

Bisexual (gender) See hermaphrodite.

Celibacy calls for some type of abstinence that's required. This symbol is not exclusively associated with sex.

Chaste refers to a modest personality. May be an indication of humility.

Child abuse won't normally equate to literal mistreatment but will be associated with abusive behavior being done to destroy innocence, perhaps even to one's child within.

Gay See homosexuality.

Hermaphrodite symbolizes balance; a wholeness of being and thought.

Heterosexism warns against discriminating against those who are different.

Homophile signifies a sympathetic attitude for those who are persecuted by prejudice.

Homosexuality usually signifies a carryover spiritual memory. When attraction or a sense of love is expressed on the spirit plane, there are no genders to differentiate one spirit from another—love is love.

Indecency connotes a rebellion; a psychological need to shock other people.

Insatiability advises of an inner void that needs to be filled.

Lesbian may not have a sexual connotation but reveals a close camaraderie between women friends. May also reveal a feminist perspective.

Masochism reveals a self-abusive individual.

Masturbation reveals a desire to rid oneself of repressed emotions, attitudes, or other types of psychologically damaging factors.

Orgy warns of an inability to control oneself, not necessarily sexually, but in a way associated with impulsiveness or self-indulgence.

Pedophile warns of someone with a tendency to take advantage of innocence.

Peeping Tom See voyeur.

Perversion applies to misdirection or misplaced priorities; an advisement to seek professional guidance or direction.

Pimp denotes a user type of personality; manipulation; ulterior motives.

Sadism exposes an underlying obsession with oneself; apathy toward others; feeling pleasure over another's misfortune.

Shame typifies guilt or humiliation.

Voyeur exposes poor self-image. This usually has little to do with sexual implications but comes to reveal personalities who are incompetent and dependent upon others to feel fulfilled.

Personality Types

Adolescent is representative of a juvenile outlook, belief, or perception.

Alarmist is one who exaggerates in the negative; one who incites worry or fear, envisioning only the worst.

Antisocial refers to an introverted personality.

Aspirant applies to one seeking the highest level; actively reaching higher.

Austere is representative of a disassociating type of personality; one who voluntarily withdraws from society and its trappings. May also refer to an individual who maintains an uncluttered perspective or spiritual belief.

Cold fish characterizes one in the habit of not showing emotions.

Coldhearted refers to a lack of warm emotional expression; apathy; insensitivity.

Comedian characterizes an unrealistic perspective; one who makes a joke out of everything.

Confidante characterizes someone to whom one can openly talk without holding back; one who can be trusted with personal information.

Conformist warns of a lack of individuality or thought.

Doomsayer won't normally equate to pessimism or fearful perceptions; rather, this symbol will appear as a messenger for the dreamer advising of a destructive course.

Egocentric marks a self-absorbed individual or situation.

Exhibitionist warns against the tendency or need to focus attention on oneself.

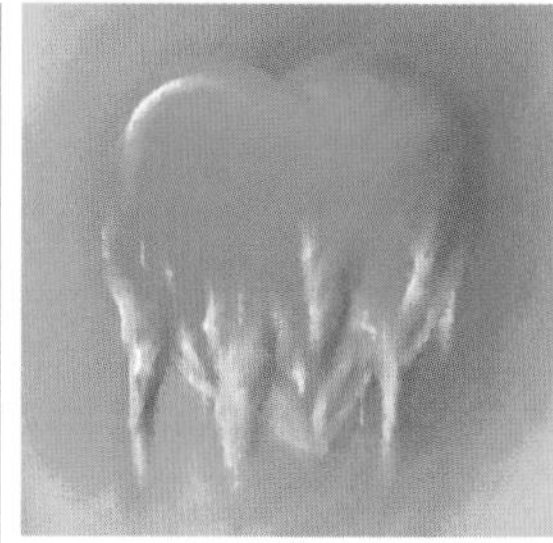

Coldhearted is a lack of sympathy.

Expert characterizes an adept person; one who has specific knowledge and the corresponding experience to go with it.

Extremist will indicate an overreaction; a person who jumps to conclusions and acts on them.

Fickle is a representation of an undisciplined personality; unpredictability.

Footloose signifies acceptance.

Forthright pertains to open honesty.

Huckster See peddler.

Liberal characterizes a freethinker; one not confined by limitation or tradition.

Machiavellian exemplifies an attitude of using whatever means available to reach a goal or gain control; unethical and immoral methods of advancement.

Maximalist symbolizes one who advocates taking an issue to its full extension; a tendency to maximize opportunities or talents.

Wet blanket suggests a lack of enthusiasm; one who is emotionless.

Workaholic comes as a warning to slow down and take time out for oneself or leisure. This is a serious symbol revealing an overworked mental or physical condition.

Aristocrats & Autocrats

Autocrat comes to the dreamer as a warning against manipulating the lives of others.
Blue blood is generally representative of nobility, coming from a long line of socially prominent family members, but in dreamscapes, this symbol will be mostly be associated with an individual's personal, singular quality of having a quiet, dignified wisdom.
Bluenose is representative of moral arrogance. It may refer to prudish attitudes.
Connoisseur is representative of one who has spent a great deal of time gaining full knowledge of something; an expert.
Cosmopolitan (appearance or character) signifies intellectual sophistication pertaining to worldwide cultures. It also refers to an extensive intellectual base.

Bad Guys

Archfiend reveals a person who has great potential to cause harm or negativity.
Blackguard alludes to an unprincipled individual; one who exhibits a vile, abusive manner.
Blackheart will be a malicious, vengeful individual.
Bully characterizes bullish behavior; being outwardly demeaning to others; having a sense of self-importance derived through intimidation.
Deal breaker means asking too much in a negotiation; needing a more equitable compromise.
Hatchet man characterizes an individual who rarely accepts another's opinion.
Insider trading refers to ill-gotten gain or benefits.
Intruder connotes an individual who disrupts specific aspects of one's life.
Larceny See burglar.
Mischief maker spells trouble. Reveals a problematic individual in one's life.
Mole (informant) See informant.
Ne'er-do-well implies unrecognized direction and associated lack of motivation.
Renegade characterizes individual thought and behavior; a break from the crowd.
Shyster portrays an unscrupulous or unethical individual.
Slum lord characterizes a person who takes unconscionable advantage of others or another's misfortune.
Squatter stands for one who moves in on another's territory; an interloper.
Swindler exposes an individual intent on deception and ulterior motives.
Tyrant stands for an arrogance of one's perceived power or authority and using it ruthlessly.
Vandal reveals a lack of respect for others; behavior that negatively affects others.
Villain reveals a wrongdoer yet may only represent whomever the dreamer perceives as being in the wrong.

Good Guys

Miracle worker is a problem solver.

Chivalrous means high respect for others and life; selflessness; unconditional goodness.
Miracle worker portrays a person who provides solutions to difficult problems; one who is capable of making things happen.
Patriot represents loyalty.
Protector portrays a guarding or method of self-protection one has in place. This could refer to the distance one maintains from others, the tendency to keep private matters close to the vest, or any other behavior that is used to semi-insulate oneself.
Soldier of fortune pertains to a self-serving and nondiscriminatory individual.
Superhuman (qualities) relate to inner strengths. Depending on the dream's related elements, this symbol can also come to the dreamer to remind that one shouldn't have such off-the-scale (unrealistic) expectations.
Superman See superhuman.
Swashbuckler is representative of an individual's tendency to dramatize or flaunt in his or her everyday life.

Adventurers

Adventurer characterizes an individual who has a tendency to throw caution to the wind; someone who is often a thrill-seeker.
Daredevil portrays an attitude of overconfidence; a disregard for obvious high risks; a tempting of the fates.
Smoke jumper characterizes an individual who is capable of diverting or halting dangerous aspects in the lives of others; one ready and willing to jump into the fray and fight for a resolution.
Speed freak characterizes an individual who continually attempts to get the most out of life through overexpending energies.
Storm chaser points to an individual who is highly curious and pushes the envelope to get answers.

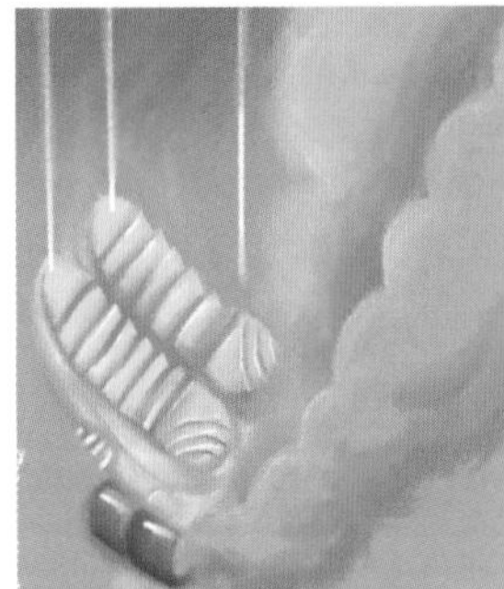
Smoke jumper indicates bravery.

Thrill seeker characterizes an individual who has lost an appreciation of life; a desensitized perspective.
Voyager characterizes an individual who is free to follow her or his own spiritual course.

see also
• Aggression *p. 168*
• Warriors & Fighters *p. 357*

Aggressors

Acerbic warns of a bitterness in one's life; a cynical nature.

Aggressor designates those individuals who may turn on one.

Army brat represents experience in unpredictability; one who can make quick adjustments to routine changes.

Avenger symbolizes an activist on the side of spiritual, ethical, or humanitarian justice.

Barbarian characterizes a severely unmannered individual; crude thought patterns; primitive behavior.

Battle-axe signifies a stern and consistently angry personality.

Big head stands for arrogance, egotism.

Bigmouth reveals a gossiper; one who tells more than is necessary; boastfulness. May even indicate a betrayer.

Cannibal is a fatally destructive individual; one who has no ethics, morals, or spiritual behaviors.

Cloak-and-dagger signifies the act of leading on or may indicate intriguing aspects to a situation or relationship; sequential surprises.

Conspirator reveals one with ulterior motives and agendas.

Dark horse alludes to an individual or situation that surprisingly overcame low expectations.

Desperado specifically refers to one reacting to a desperate condition or situation.

Flasher (exposing) characterizes someone who has negative motivations and uses negative-impact attention-getting methods.

Fly-by-night constitutes something in the dreamer's life that is unscrupulous and deceptive.

Loan shark reveals self-gain through negative methods.

Lone wolf characterizes one who works best alone; one who walks a uniquely individualized path.

Loose cannon illustrates unpredictability; irresponsibility; untrustworthiness.

Loudmouth indicates one who must be the center of attention in order to feel any measure of self-worth.

Mercenary portrays one who would do anything for personal gain or the pure adventure of it. This may reveal someone who will take care of a problem for a price.

Pirate represents someone who benefits at the expense of others.

Militant won't necessarily denote aggression. It may indicate activism related to righteousness; standing up for one's rights or beliefs.

Pirate characterizes unethical personalities who gain by stealing valuable aspects from others; spiritual greed.

Rabble-rouser characterizes a person who incites high emotional responses. This is usually a negative element, yet it can indicate a motivating force in one's life.

Rascal characterizes a mischievous nature.

Rebel characterizes an individual who follows her or his own path. May also denote a continually disagreeable personality. Surrounding dreamscape details will clarify which intent was meant.

Ringleader points out the instigator of a plan.

Road hog characterizes an individual who isn't focused on her or his path.

Roughneck represents a crude or coarse manner of behavior.

Ruffian See hoodlum.

Saboteur characterizes a two-faced personality.

Sharpshooter suggests a need for discernment and accurate judgments.

Skinhead suggests intolerance; a lack of acceptance of others' individualities.

Slave driver characterizes a person who demands hard work from others or perhaps only from oneself, depending on the surrounding dreamscape details.

Sniper characterizes a person who has a tendency to conceal true intentions. May also indicate underhandedness or a skill for undercutting (as in an eBay sniper). This symbol also may indicate a tendency to withhold one's true intentions until the very last minute.

Sniper (eBay auction) characterizes a winner who comes from behind; a player who reveals herself at the very last minute.

Vigilante characterizes one set on personal vengeance.

War hawk means an aggressive personality who favors the resolution of conflicts through warring means.

Warmonger See war hawk.

Psychological Terms

Anger management naturally is a strong advisement to get one's anger under control.

Anima pertains to feminine aspects, the gentle elements of one's inner being; the positive aspects of character and behavior.

Animus infers the male aspects' harsher elements to one's character, the more aggressive elements.

Behavioral therapy suggests an attitude adjustment is needed; a change in how one behaves because of incorrect thought or perception.

Introvert pertains to quiet acceptance.

Criminal Classes

Arsonist is one who enjoys causing destruction.
Assailant is one who can do harm in some way.
Assassin pertains to an individual who could ruin one's life or reputation.
Bandit characterizes one who possesses that which has been ill-gotten; ulterior motives.
Burglar characterizes an untrustworthy individual; underhandedness; ulterior motives; someone who will end up taking something.
Car bomber signifies one who is destructively vindictive.
Carjacker characterizes one who has no personal direction or motivation; one who solely depends on the efforts of others in order to move along one's path.
Cat burglar portrays a devious or sneaky personality; activity done behind another's back; clandestine activities.
Convict relates to an individual who has done wrong in the past. This does not imply that this person is still doing so.

Arsonist destroys for pleasure.

Criminal characterizes a lawbreaker. This will usually refer to someone the dreamer knows in life.
Cutthroat warns of a vicious personality; a person who has no scruples.
Felon will stand for bad past behavior, not necessarily a current negative factor.
Firebug See arsonist.
Hoodlum characterizes an immature perspective; a self-centered nature; an inability to advance past primal instincts.
Juvenile delinquent characterizes one who rebukes philosophical and spiritual concepts during a beginning stage of discovery.
Killer (of anything) warns of a fatally negative facet in one's life. The dreamer will usually already know what this is associated with.
Kleptomaniac characterizes uncontrolled impulses.
Looter indicates a lack of positive, individual resourcefulness. It is also indicative of gaining from the efforts of others.
Mugger signifies one who gains through the efforts of others.
Parolee characterizes a person who needs to carefully watch his or her behavior. This parolee will not necessarily indicate a bad individual, but the associative concept that's vital for the dreamer is the extreme necessity of watching your Ps and Qs for a time.
Pickpocket pertains to a lack of positive resourcefulness or motivation; an individual having no personal responsibility or self-respect; having ulterior motives for getting close to someone.
Poacher corresponds to stealth and dishonesty.
Prowler is representative of stealth. Recall who the prowler was in the dreamscape.
Pyromaniac characterizes an individual who enjoys making trouble for others. May indicate a person who likes digging up skeletons in the closets of others and exposing them; one who enjoys an explosive and fiery event.
Repeat offender will come as a strong advisement to learn from past mistakes instead of repeating them. Warns against behavior that precludes advancement.
Rogue characterizes an unprincipled individual.
Suicide bomber signifies one who is obsessed with destroying another; a willingness to die for one's cause.
Terrorist stands for one who is lacking the most basic respect for life.
Thug characterizes someone with no conscience.

Opportunists

Ambulance chaser means one who takes advantage of another's ill-fortune. A self-serving personality, one with ulterior motives.
Bad boy will reveal one who ignores convention or traditional behavior.
Bad egg is associated with a negative individual; one who isn't the least interested in reforming.
Bargain hunter is one who seeks the best course of action; identifies a solution having the least resistance or fewest number of problematic elements.
Bounty hunter symbolizes misplaced priorities; wrong motives; expectation of rewards for good deeds done.
Cardsharp/shark characterizes one with ulterior motives; having a hidden agenda; deviousness.
Carpetbagger signifies one who takes advantage of another's misfortune. Depending on the surrounding dream elements, a carpetbagger may also indicate an individual who has his or her priorities straight.
Charlatan means pretenses.
City slicker indicates someone who expertly utilizes societal aspects but may be lacking in managing the more basic elements of life.
Claim jumper warns against forming friendships for ulterior motives.
Confidence game See swindler.
Domain squatter will reveal an individual who collects and hoards what others want or need, then sells it on at exorbitant prices.
Impersonator reveals one who is dissatisfied with oneself.
Imposter characterizes a deceiver.
Lookout is representative of watchfulness; a personal awareness.
Profiteer characterizes an individual who takes advantage of others or seeks self-serving opportunities through negative means.

see also
• Social Relationships & Activities *p. 124*
• Law Enforcement *p. 253*

Betrayers

Double-faced (two-faced) is representative of a betrayer or hypocrite appearing in the dreamer's life.
Pretender usually denotes a hidden activity or behavior. Recall who the dream presented as the pretender. It also could be oneself and, in that case, the symbol is coming as a message from one's subconscious for the purpose of telling you to look at what you're doing.
Turncoat is representative of a reversed attitude or perspective.
Two-faced See double-faced.
Whistle-blower exposes a betrayer. May portray an aspect of oneself that would then signify one's own conscience being the source of this symbol.

Control Freaks

Backseat driver is one who gives orders and opinions without a right to them.
Bullheaded characterizes a stubborn nature; one rarely given to compromise. May indicate narrow-mindedness.
Busybody stands for an interfering personality.
Chauvinist denotes an attitude of superiority.
Codger portrays a disinterested or irascible elder.
Dyed-in-the-wool advises of an unyielding personality or attitude.
Fanatic warns of a lack of applying wisdom to one's perceptions.
High-strung indicates a need for personal restraint. This symbol implies a person who flies off the handle without giving logic and reason to reactions.
Iconoclast characterizes a spiritually destructive individual.
Kingpin corresponds to a major or central player in a relationship or specific situation; the one in absolute control.
Moralist may be positive or negative, depending on the dream moralist's behavior.

Codger is an angry old person.

Motormouth points to an individual who talks a lot yet has little of value to convey.
Pooh-bah signifies an ineffective person who believes he or she carries great authority.
Purist comes as an advisement to attain greater acceptance. Portrays one who is overly critical.
Puritan characterizes a rigid personality; a suspicious nature.
Zealot correlates with fanaticism.

Passive Personalities

Absentee will be an individual who chooses not to participate in something. This symbol may represent of denial or unwillingness to face an element of reality.
Adrift means spiritual drifting.
Amicable represents a good-natured individual. This may have a negative meaning in that one could be easily taken advantage of.
Bland alludes to neutrality or uninteresting aspects.
Blimp illustrates cumbersome thoughts and ideas; overblown concepts; a cluttered thought process.
Bore (dull) cautions against a lack of motivation. Suggests the need to expand interests or be more expressive.
Bystander usually refers to apathy; one who watches yet does not act. In some dreamscapes, it may indicate a witness to something; a guiltless party; innocence. Or it may point to knowledge gained through observation.
Chickenhearted refers to a lack of courage.
Church mouse characterizes a quiet spirituality; cherished spiritual beliefs.
Devotee characterizes an unrealistic and fanatical attraction to something. This is a warning message.
Dewy-eyed suggests sentimentality. May indicate naiveté.
Flatlander characterizes an individual who is fearful of taking risks or encountering difficulties in life.
Gutless comes as an advisement to gain more courage, self-confidence, and the ability to stand up for oneself.
Head in the sand naturally points to denial; a refusal to face reality; escapism.
Martyr characterizes one's psychological belief of being persecuted; paranoia.
Party pooper won't necessarily point to an unsocial individual but rather one who doesn't take life frivolously.
Peacekeeper portrays an individual who attempts to find a peaceful way of resolving conflict. A dream peacekeeper may symbolize one's own higher self.
Pilgrim indicates a searching or the need to discover something important.
Pushover signifies a weak personality; one who is easily manipulated or controlled.
Scapegoat means an innocent individual. Warns of a tendency to place blame on others; a lack of personal responsibility.
Sissy signifies a possible lack of courage, but it may also be hiding independence; a determination against being coerced.
Sitting duck pertains to the act of going out on a limb and placing oneself in a position of exposure.
Spineless emphasizes a lack of courage or personal responsibility. May also indicate a lack of individuality.
Supplicant implies a lack of self-confidence and reliance. May also point to an overscrupulous conscience, possibly false guilt.
Underachiever indicates one's performance or energy output is less than one's capability or potential.

Persnickety Personalities

Bean counter characterizes someone who looks at all aspects of a relationship, situation, or problem.

Biddy (old) points to a particularly fussy, nit-picking, crabby individual.

Bureaucrat is a reference to narrow-mindedness; focused on self-serving issues, or being centered on one's own agendas.

Cheapskate warns of a tendency to hoard abilities, knowledge, or one's personal humanitarian assets.

Clock-watcher connotes the wasting of time; one who ill-uses time. Suggests impatience, anxiety.

Close-fisted warns against being greedy or stingy. May also allude to a need for anger management.

Company person will be associated with watching one's own back; taking care of Number One by prioritizing a mutually beneficial loyalty rather than sacrificing that same faithfulness in lieu of loyalty to a friend.

Paper pusher signifies one who is overly concerned about everything being by the book; one who can't bring oneself to bend the rules.

Penny-pinching indicates a frugal mindset. Recall surrounding dream details to determine if this was a caution or advisement.

Perfectionist characterizes a type-A personality; one who is easily frustrated and full of angst. May also indicate intolerance and/or impatience.

Tightwad will reveal stinginess related to a multitude of elements depending on the symbol's related aspects. This stinginess can refer to emotional support or sensitivity, finances, general helpfulness, and so on.

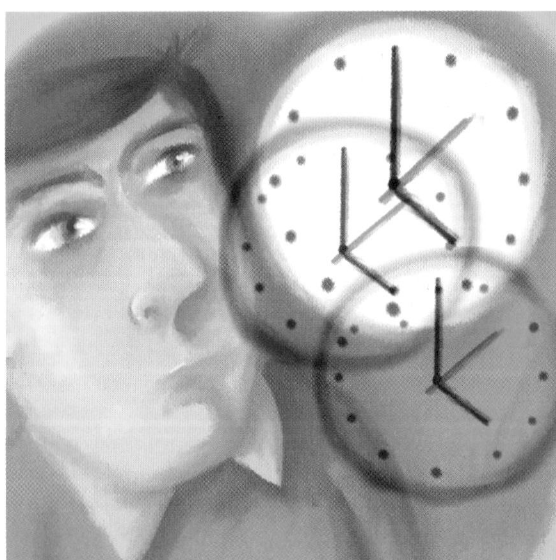

Clock-watcher characterizes someone who does not make the most of time.

Faces of the Feminine

Alluring connotes temptations; distracting characteristics; something that diminishes focus on a goal or issue.

Barbie doll refers to an unrealistic image to emulate.

Bawdry exposes crudeness.

Bimbo portrays misplaced priorities; one who has little interest in intellectual aspects or is generally inept.

Bluestocking refers to a woman with spiritual wisdom.

Cheerleader characterizes those who encourage us in life.

Cheesecake (photo) connotes misplaced priorities; enticement; the use of wrong methods for obtaining goals.

Countrywoman characterizes a genteel individual with quiet dignity.

Debutante warns against the need for attention or to be recognized; making one's class or social position in life a priority.

Domestic diva/goddess will indicate an individual who is skilled at efficiently keeping the foundational aspects of one's life in order.

Drama queen See histrionics.

Earth mother signifies the warm and flowing essence of love within all living things; absolute compassion and innocence.

Enchantress characterizes an individual who has the talent to communicate the beauty of multifrequency perceptions to others.

Feminist characterizes equality regardless of separatist characteristics or attitudes.

Flapper is a representation of a frivolous nature.

Girlish (qualities) signifies a touch of innocence to one's character.

Homebody connotes contentedness; one who has few needs and even fewer wants.

Home builder will normally indicate an individual who is capable or skilled in providing a home base for others.

Homegirl refers to a provincial personality; one who is unsophisticated yet genteel.

Jezebel refers to one who tempts another into wrongdoing; manipulator.

Modesty stands for awareness; a considerate, respectful, and refined personality.

Paragon characterizes one who has made an ultimate achievement at something; a person who has attained a prime position or status in respect to personal accomplishment.

Sob sister characterizes a woman who has great empathy for others; a woman who has deep compassion and can be counted on as being a sympathetic sounding board.

Teenybopper stands for immaturity; an inability to face reality or a denial of certain elements of it.

Tomboy defines the expression of one's individuality; personal freedom.

Valley girl suggests immaturity; an inappropriate sense of priority.

Waif characterizes a victim of circumstance; those less fortunate.

War bride refers to an action taken before its time.

see also
• Thought Processes & Intelligence *p. 130*
• Deprivation *p. 200*

Subservient Types

Brownnoser points to a desire to impress people.
Henchman portrays one who is content as an underling; one who gains self-esteem by pleasing another.
Slave denotes servitude. The key here is to recall who was the slave and what he or she was doing for whom? One could be a slave to one's own desires or habits.
Stooge characterizes one who is particularly easily manipulated.
Yea-sayer indicates a tendency to be agreeable to the point of fearing to express an opposing opinion.
Yes-man warns against agreeing with others for the purpose of wanting to be liked or accepted.

Dreamers

Birdbrain connotes a lack of intelligence, reason, or logic. May refer to silliness or flightiness. It is suggestive of one who has a tendency to make light of serious matters.
Dreamer may appear in a dreamscape for one of two reasons. Depending on the surrounding related elements, this symbol may equate to one's unique independent thought that stretches into the realm of being visionary, or it can imply the opposite—that one is thinking in an unrealistic manner, perhaps being overly optimistic.
Muddle corresponds to mental confusion; an inability to do things right.
Scatterbrained is representative of a loss of emotional or mental focus.

Losers

Buffoon See clown.
Butterfingers caution against letting things slip through your fingers. Denotes a need to get a grasp on oneself, one's life, or some important aspect.
Chump means a foolish person or one with a habit of being disinterested in things; someone never having an opinion.
Couch potato cautions against laziness, physical and mental.
Deadbeat warns against personal apathy; being emotionally unaffected.
Klutz points to awkwardness but not necessarily coupled with being inept. May refer to a characteristic comparable to the absent-minded professor who is just too intellectually distracted to pay attention to the small stuff.
Lame duck is representative of inconsequential actions; ineffectiveness.
Loon is representative of mental or emotional confusion or a convoluted thought process.
Loser alludes to a temporary setback. May refer to a lack of foresight or insight.
Shiftless implies a lack of motivation or energy.

Intellectual Personalities

Airhead denotes one who cannot discern incoming information; an individual who fails to recognize the varying values of thoughts and ideas; fragmented thought; inability to focus.
Book lover reveals one's particular type of interest. This symbol won't necessarily equate to a love of knowledge, because what if the book lover's books were erotica? Recall if any titles or subject matter were displayed.
Bookworm warns against a tendency to accumulate knowledge without applying it; a habit of voraciously consuming information yet doing nothing with it.
Brain-dead portrays total apathy. May also come as a premonition of someone's physical demise.
Brainless characterizes irrationality; unreasonableness; illogical thought.
Chatterbox characterizes an individual who does little in-depth thinking; a gossip or someone who incessantly speaks of issues that are unimportant. May indicate one who rarely listens.
Clear-headed represents an individual who reasons calmly without letting personal perspectives or extraneous factors interfere.
Close-minded warns against being opinionated or lacking the desire to intellectually seek an understanding of new theories.
Cynic defines a distrustful personality; skepticism. May indicate a hopeless attitude.

Feeble-minded shirks obligations.

Doubting Thomas signifies skepticism. May imply a lack of faith; needing proof of everything.
Feeble-minded advises of a self-generated condition of psychological escapism for the purpose of avoiding personal responsibility.
Fool warns against willfully avoiding knowledge and also against the intellectual processing of same.
Humanitarian characterizes a compassionate and giving nature.
Idealist stands for one who has high hopes yet lacks a clear perspective of reality.
Idiot usually comes as a message that advises how one is responding to a specific given issue or situation.
Intellectual characterizes one who has knowledge yet may not have the wisdom to go along with it.
Know-it-all displays a lack of wisdom.
Know-nothing may know more than the know-it-all. Those who admit they know nothing usually know more than we think.
Light-minded stands for a lack of seriousness; one who focuses on frivolous issues.
Simpleton See fool.

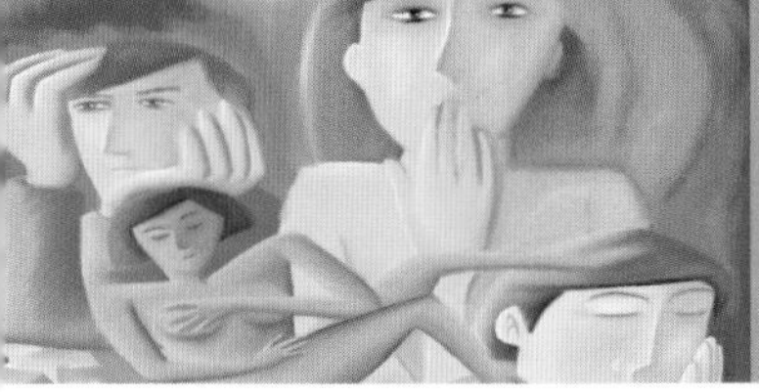

Eccentrics

Avant-garde stands for the expression of one's character by way of attitudes, perception, or behavior that is unorthodox by the general public's standards.
Bag lady characterizes priorities; giving attention to only those life aspects that are necessary basics; the needful things in life.
Bagman portrays debts or underhanded dealings.
Beatnik See hippie.
Bohemian refers to a freethinking personality; one who is not afraid to live an unconventional lifestyle or have differing attitudes and/or perspectives.
Bum See tramp/hobo.
Cave dweller stands for one who lives by one's instincts.
Cliff dweller denotes one who finds security by living on the edge; self-confidence; reliance on a carved-out position in life.
Derelict (person) characterizes a need to be motivated, usually through a new perspective of self-worth.
Dirty old man warns against growth that never makes a priority of spirituality; a life that is immersed in physical gratifications.
Disorganized calls for a need to get one's life in order; set priorities; take one thing at a time. May be a reference to one's thoughts.
Eccentric alludes to the freedom that stems from separating the "I" from the self, whereby one exercises intellectual pursuits and special interests without regard to public opinion.
Flower child See hippie.
Hippie characterizes a diversion from established traditions or ideas; the freedom to express one's individuality and attitudes that differ from the general populace.
Punk rocker is an implication of immaturity.
Recluse characterizes a remote and/or distant personality. May be an indication of a need to withdraw for a time in order to focus on one's purpose or path.
Tramp/hobo characterizes a freethinker; a nonconformist.
Transvestite exposes an identity crisis; an identification with a past life that still retains strong and overwhelming elements.
Vagabond characterizes a person who follows her or his own course.
Vagrant will reveal self-reliance; an independent person.
Veteran will characterize an experienced individual.

Rural Personalities

Country-bred characterizes down-home common sense; a more pointed sense of real priorities.
Country cousin advises of the many benefits and strengths that come from being honest and unsophisticated.
Country folk signifies those who have a down-to-earth sense of priorities; knowledge of solid basics.

Negative Personalities

Stubborn signifies determination.

Cold shoulder comes as a warning against judging others. Calls for forgiveness and a resulting response of at least neutrality.
Frigid indicates a stiff and unemotional personality; a rigid and straitlaced nature.
Frivolous means lacking any importance or relevance; inconsequential.
Gauche implies a lack of tact or sensitivity.
Grandeur represents arrogance; a tendency to be showy.
Narrow-mindedness cautions one to expand intellectual explorations and perceptions.
Naysayer reveals a pessimistic or cynical attitude. May also imply contrariness.
Pessimism connotes a lack of acceptance and may indicate one who uses this attitude as an escape mechanism to avoid personal responsibility.
Pushy represents a nagging or demanding nature.
Single-minded suggests one should stop being so focused that one is blind to all others.
Stubborn implies a strong sense of direction; determination.
Superficial reveals a fear of becoming involved; a hesitancy to delve into the deeper aspects of true reality.
Unconcern speaks of apathy.
Uppity equates to an intractable personality or an inflated sense of self.

Positive Personalities

Freehearted links to compassion and emotional generosity.
Free spirit characterizes an unconcern for conventional aspects; the ability to wholly express one's unique individuality.
Good egg will refer to an easy-going, agreeable personality.
Gutsy symbolizes confidence in one's belief; being unafraid to speak out or act in an unexpected or unconventional manner.
Lenient exemplifies forgiveness; making allowances.
Mellow relates to a state of acceptance.
Openhanded means generosity; willingness to give aid.
Open-minded suggests an intellectual perception, one primed for gaining wisdom through attained knowledge.
Optimist characterizes one who has a tendency to look on the bright side of things; having a great measure of hope. This may or may not be a positive symbol. Recall surrounding dreamscape details for clarity.
Patience usually comes as an advisory message.
Sure-footed relates to high confidence; self-reliance.
Wanderlust corresponds with one's inner promptings to get going and be on one's way.

see also
• Mental Disorders & Behavior *p. 106*
• Outsiders *p. 128*

Stereotypes

Chowhound denotes an insatiable appetite. This is usually associated with a seeker of knowledge who takes in things in a voracious manner, possibly without absorbing any of it.

Conehead portrays unrealistic perspectives. May point to an out-of-touch personality.

Cracker-barrel (rustic character) connotes informal discussions and the need for these to be continued.

Flimflam man is a depiction of fraudulence; deception; delusions. Who was this symbolic person? You? A business associate?

Grave robber is an individual who enjoys gaining from the downfall of others.

Greenhorn is a reference to inexperience.

Groupie is a caution against following others instead of listening to the inner voice that leads the self.

Gun-shy refers to reluctance; hesitancy to take control or make a big step forward.

Gunslinger points to an overconfident individual, one who gets pushy/manipulative.

Johnny Appleseed portrays an individual who spreads ideas; plants the seeds of specific concepts or ideas.

Junk collector is a reference to hidden values.

Redneck implies a bigoted personality; being highly opinionated and narrow-minded.

Shock jock is someone who blurts out whatever she or he is thinking without consideration for the sensitivities of others. Depending on the related dreamscape elements, this symbol may have a positive connotation: someone who tells it like it is (bottom-line honesty)—and usually this honesty is directed toward someone needing to hear it.

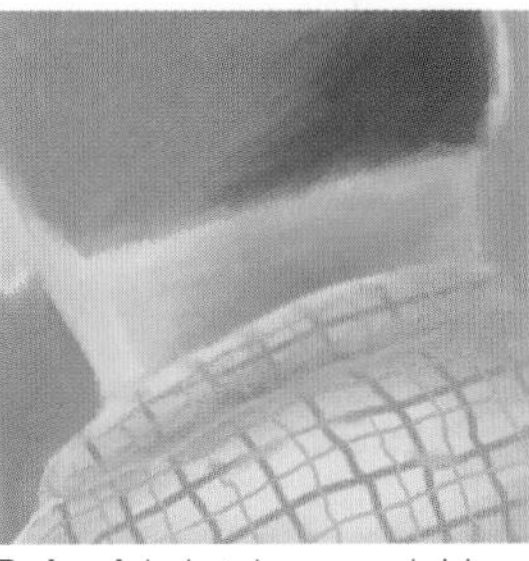
Redneck lacks tolerance and vision.

Space cadet reveals a lack of mental focus.

Stage-door Johnny will usually indicate one who finds self-esteem by rubbing shoulders with public figures or famous people.

Techno-geek in dreams actually reveals someone more interested in intellectual matters than in societal issues. Contrary to popular assumption, this is not a negative dream symbol.

Youngblood indicates a need for fresh ideas.

Yuppie warns against being overly materialistic and self-centered.

Introversion & Extroversion

Alienation designates a separateness imposed. May be self-induced.

Lonely usually indicates a lack of companionship and, in some cases, may point to having a perspective few others share or are willing to accept.

Mute may call for silence from the dreamer.

Pussyfoot portrays a timid personality. May also denote a cautious manner of advancement.

Show-off is representative of the dreamer's personal need for attention.

Shyness may reveal innocence or a lack of self-esteem.

Social anxiety reveals feelings of inferiority. It may refer to a need to view oneself in a brighter light.

Solitude advises of a need to contemplate; a need for mental or emotional rest.

Solo emphasizes the fact that an individual has acted alone or must proceed along his or her path alone.

Spaced-out signifies a willful escape from reality and responsibility; an inability to keep one's mind focused; being easily distracted.

Stagestruck portrays a fascination and great desire to perform before others; a need to be seen and heard by many.

Confrontational Types

Abolitionist signifies one who is compassionate; empathy; one who abhors mistreatment of others and expends energy to prevent or stop it.

Advocate designates an action one should take.

Bloodthirsty stands for vengeful motivation; being out for blood.

Blowhard characterizes a gossip; a braggart.

Champ See champion.

Champion refers to one's proven abilities or talents.

Conscientious objector pertains to one who stands up for personal beliefs; one willing to perform civil disobedience.

Devil's advocate illustrates self-examination. This means that there is a reason to examine motives or attitudes.

Headbanger characterizes one who has a tendency to easily release stress.

Personas

Adamant See stubborn.

Aloof connotes an arrogant personality.

Amorous suggests a desire for a greater measure of closeness.

Bachelor/bachelorette portrays a reluctance to make relationship commitments.

Bourgeois exemplifies middle-class conventions and attitudes.

Brat signifies an ill-mannered, juvenile attitude.

Caricature warns of one's tendency to perceive others in a distorted manner; an exaggerated view of others; failing to look beyond the obvious surface features.

Chutzpah portrays one who displays great nerve; gutsy.

Class act alludes to high quality; distinction.

Jester characterizes a lackadaisical attitude; rarely attending to anything serious.

People Phobias

Beggars suggest powerlessness.

Bad men/burglars (Sclerophobia) relates to a sense of vulnerability.

Beggars (Hobophobia) indicates a disquieting feeling when faced with another's desperation; wanting to avoid feeling helpless to improve another's situation.

Bogeyman (Bogyphobia) indicates a desire to avoid everyone who causes any type of uneasiness or trepidation.

Children (Pedophobia) stands for an inability to relate to youth; a fear of releasing the child within.

Clowns (Coulrophobia) represents distress for those who are socially reserved and fear the exposure of their lighter side.

Crowds (Demophobia) shows a retiring or introverted personality. This shows trepidation over situations where a possibility exists for one to be judged or criticized.

Dentists (Dentophobia) connotes an anxiety over being criticized for one's expressed attitudes or perspectives. This means a fear of someone trying to alter or change one's mind.

Doctors (Iatrophobia) alludes to an aversion to anyone who may offer suggestions. This denotes an arrogant personality or individual who believes he or she knows the best way to do everything. May also point to a fear of learning that something is wrong.

Gays/lesbians (Homophobia) signifies a general aversion to human diversity or traits opposite from those of oneself.

Human beings (Anthropophobia) signifies a distrust of worldly aspects. It may also indicate an introvert or pertain to an aversion to germs.

Mother-in-law (Pentheraphobia) shows a complete lack of self-confidence. This fear is associated with anything that may represent a powerful and overbearing individual.

Old people (Gerontophobia) signifies dread over being faced with one's mortality or the idea of aging.

Opposite sex (Sexophobia) relates to a yin-yang imbalance; a condition of being out of touch with the characteristics of one's opposite gender.

People See human beings.

Photographers/photographs (no specific term has been coined) connotes a personal fear or intolerance of knowledge or aspects of enlightenment. May point to an inferiority complex.

Politicians (Politicophobia) denotes distrust.

Pope (Papaphobia) is representative of a fear of spiritual domination.

Relatives (Syngenesophobia) denotes an aversion to others knowing everything about oneself.

Strangers (Xenophobia) stands for distrust.

Law-Related Phobias

Lawsuits (Liticaphobia) depicts angst over a possible demand of retribution.

Stealing (Kleptophobia) indicates a fear of wanting to achieve goals without expending energy to that end; a sense of undeserving.

Wrongdoing (Peccatiphobia) denotes a fear of reprisals.

Vision-Related Phobias

Blindness (Scotomaphobia) refers to a dread of losing one's sharp perceptive skills.

Double vision (Diplophobia) applies to a fear of losing one's own ability to see things clearly.

Eyes (Ommatophobia) relates to an introvert with severe insecurities.

Phobias Related to Feelings

Aloneness (Autophobia) refers to a dissatisfaction of one's beingness. It may require the presence of others to give oneself validation.

Dependency on others (Soteriophobia) suggests not only a fear of losing one's independence but also one's high impression of one's self-sufficiency. This borders on the idea that the dreamer doesn't need anyone.

Failure/defeat (Kakorrhaphiophobia) comes from a goal-oriented person who is an overachiever and can't face the humiliation of an unsuccessful outcome.

Fear (Phobophobia) signifies a self-assured individual who panics at the thought of showing distress, anxiety, or apprehension over anything. This is someone who believes her or his feathers can't be ruffled.

Gaiety (Cherophobia) pertains to the belief that something bad will happen to detract from joy felt.

Laughter (Gelophobia) applies to a reluctance to express joy due to the possibility that it will be balanced by grief or hardship.

Love, falling in or being in (Philophobia) signifies one who panics at the thought of a broken relationship or being abandoned; therefore, one fears being in love.

Pleasure (Hedonophobia) suggests that one believes she isn't deserving of the more enjoyable elements of life.

Ridicule (Katagelophobia) reflects feelings of inferiority; a fear of being criticized.

Social inferiority (Social phobia) refers to belief that everyone's better than you. This indicates an inferiority complex.

Solitude (See aloneness).

see also
• Insects *p. 29*
• Eyes *p. 96*

Living Creature Phobias

Animals (Zoophobia) shows a misunderstanding regarding the interrelatedness of all living things.
Ants (Myrmecophobia) refers to an inability or reluctance to cooperate with others.
Bacteria (Bacillophobia) characterizes an individual's dread of being affected by others in some way.
Bees (Apiphobia) signifies insecurities toward teamwork.
Birds (Ornithophobia) reveals an inability to deal with the various personalities of others.
Bulls (Taurophobia) refers to anxiety over losing one's open-mindedness; a fear of becoming opinionated.
Cats (Ailurophobia) denotes a near panic in regard to the possibilities of losing one's independence.
Chickens (Alektorophobia) alludes to anxiety; fear of being near anything that may elicit anxiety or stressful moments.
Dogs (Cynophobia) will reflect a tendency to distrust people, especially friends.
Fish (Ichthyophobia) usually stems from a revulsion of anything associated with religious or spiritual aspects.
Frogs/toads See toads/frogs.
Fur/animal skin (Doraphobia) exemplifies a fear of exposing one's self-centeredness and hesitancy to go it alone.
Horses (Hippophobia) refers to one's wild nature and the fear of letting others see it.
Insects (Entomophobia) relates to an inability to deal with life's little irritations.
Mice (Musophobia) refers to worry over something

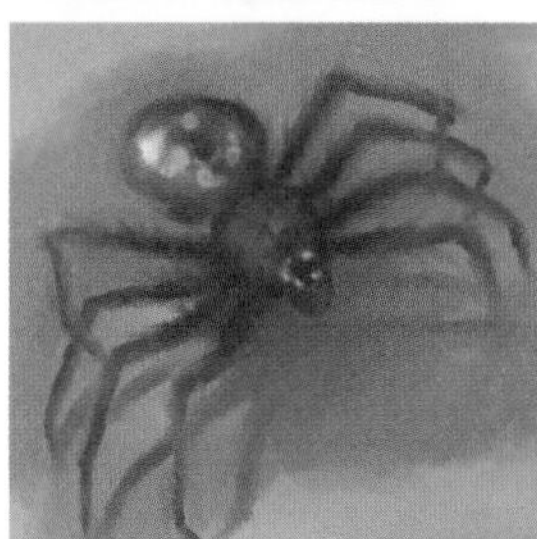

Spiders reveal fear of being used.

invading and upsetting one's set and secure routine.
Moths (Mottephobia) is representative of a fear of being drawn into spiritual beliefs that could ultimately cause one harm.
Reptiles (Herpetophobia) indicates an abhorrence for all things one doesn't understand.
Shellfish (Ostraconophobia) denotes a fear of spiritual overload.
Snakes (Ophidiophobia) pertains to an aversion for facing things that one doesn't understand.
Spiders (Arachnophobia) stands for a fear of being caught in sticky situations or being manipulated by someone's ulterior motive.
Toads/frogs (Bufonophobia) signifies panic over the possibility of becoming mentally impaired.
Wasps (Spheksophobia) alludes to a fear of being stung by someone; an ongoing suspicion that friendships or plans will backfire.
Worms (Scoleciphobia) signifies a fear that one's orderly and comfortable life will be interfered with. This is a tendency to look at everything with suspicion.

Substance-Related Phobias

Alcohol (Methyphobia) denotes doubts regarding one's grip on self-control.
Blood (Hemophobia) relates to apprehension over losing one's motivation, inner strength, or perserverance.
Chemicals (Chemophobia) denotes a fear of confusion, a mixing of various negative elements that may pose difficulties or great problems.
Drugs (Pharmacophobia) symbolizes a reluctance to accept help from outside sources. May indicate an unrealistic attitude of being able to handle things oneself.
Flavors/taste (Geumophobia) applies to someone who is most comfortable with mundane and bland elements of life. This would also be someone who prefers not to experience new things.
Food (Cibophobia) typifies one who is fearful of nourishing a particular aspect of oneself or one's life.
Hair (Chaetophobia) illustrates a concern over another's thoughts.
Meat (Carnophobia) implies an aversion to accepting basic premises, opting instead for convoluted ideas that are interwoven with personal perspectives.
Medicine (Pharmacophobia) refers to a lack of trust.
Poisons (Iophobia) suggests angst over being close to a certain element in life that could cause serious harm.
Rust (See poisons)
Sourness (Acerophobia) represents a tendency to avoid anything in life that has the possibility of causing a bitterness; a desire to evade hard-to-take situations.

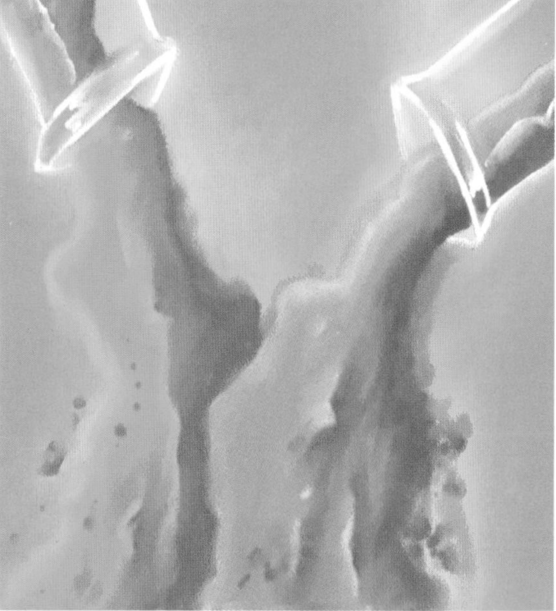

Chemicals illustrate a combination of factors that may cause great hardship.

Phobias Related to Conditions

Baldness (Peladophobia) implies trepidation of losing the ability to think clearly.
Beards (Pogonophobia) points to suspicion over what someone may be hiding.
Blushing (Erythrophobia) links to a lack of self-confidence; fear of embarrassment.
Body odor (Bromidrosiphobia) suggests a dread of offending others and diminishing their opinion of self.
Death/corpses (Necrophobia) refers to an attempt to deny reality. Depicts a fear of having to accept one's mortality; a misunderstanding of true reality and the essence of oneself.
Deformity (Dysmorphophobia) alludes to an inability to see potential in everyone. Signifies a skewed perspective in regard to another's value as a productive individual. May indicate a fear of a situation where one is forced to face another's strength of character.
Fat, becoming (Obesophobia) reveals a fear of losing control.
Fatigue (Kopophobia) suggests a belief that one's endurance is unsurpassed.
Hypnotized, being (Hypnophobia) implies distress caused by the possibility of being made to do something foolish or being humiliated.
Ignored, being (Athazagoraphobia) comes to underscore one's sense of self and avoiding situations where that sense could be eroded.
Imperfection (Atelophobia) implies unrealistic expectations and the fear of them not materializing. This converts to a denial of reality.
Overworking (Ponophobia) suggests a fear of becoming a type-A personality.
Poverty (Peniaphobia) applies to a fear of recognizing some element of one's beingness that's severely lacking.
Single, staying (Anuptaphobia) reflects a low self-esteem; a lack of self-confidence.
Ugliness (Cacophobia) applies to a strong desire to perceive everything as though viewed through rose-colored glasses. This is an inability to face reality as it is.
Untidiness (Ataxiophobia) points to one who detests disorder. Life must be orderly, efficient, and well-structured.
Wealth (Plutophobia) points to the perspective that wealth causes the world's ills.

Activity-Related Phobias

Bathing (Ablutophobia) implies concern over exposing oneself to life's negatives.
Bed, going to (Clinophobia) reflects an individual's fear of dying before certain goals are accomplished.
Changes, making (Tropophobia) indicates unadaptability.
Coitus (Coitophobia) won't necessarily refer exclusively to a sexual meaning. It will most often point to the issue of getting close to another. Indicates a fear of having a close relationship that could grow into the kind of intimacy where confidentialities are shared.
Cooking (Mageirocophobia) stands for an aversion to having to plan things. This relates to a follower rather than a leader.
Dancing (Chorophobia) refers to a dislike of showing emotion.
Decisions, making (Decidophobia) points to a lack of self-confidence; fear of taking a responsible position.
Dining (Deipnophobia) displays self-consciousness.
Dreams (Oneirophobia) characterizes apprehension over revealed truths.
Jumping (Catapedaphobia) pertains to a fear of becoming impatient.
Learning (Sophophobia) stands for a fear of discovering if one is advancing or falling behind.
Performing/being on stage (Topophobia) implies panic over being watched and then judged. This reflects a deep-seated feeling of inferiority.
Sitting still (Cathisophobia) usually points to a type-A personality but may be associated with someone who fears being someone's target.
Sleep (Somniphobia) illustrates a dread of dying. This may also portray angst over being surprised or caught unawares.
Speaking aloud (Phonophobia) alludes to an individual's fear of saying something wrong or being criticized for speaking one's mind.
Stuttering (Psellismophobia) depicts trepidation over the possibility of being humiliated while expressing one's opinion.
Test-taking (Testophobia) connotes anxiety regarding possible failure; trepidation regarding one's ability or competence.
Thinking (Phronemophobia) reveals a lack of faith in one's thought process.
Touching/being touched (Aphephobia) indicates an aversion to the possibility of being contaminated in some way from another.
Writing (Graphophobia) reveals an inhibition to express oneself outwardly.

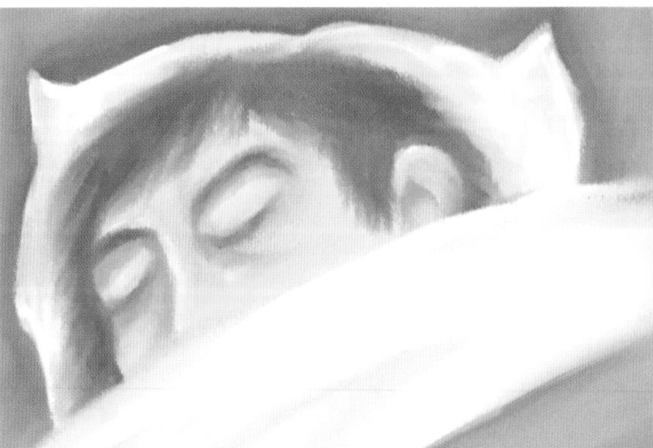

Sleep represents a fear of being caught or even of death itself.

see also
• Deformities & Disabilities *p. 91*
• Diseases *p. 107*

Illness & Physiology Phobias

Amnesia (Amnesiphobia) relates to an insecurity of one's identity; being fearful of losing one's sense of self.

Brain disease (Meningitophobia) illustrates a terror of losing one's sense of reason and logic.

Cancer (Carcinomaphobia) relates to a fear of a great negative aspect coming into one's life. May also signify a lack of acceptance; an inability to deal with problems.

Choking (Pnigophobia) suggests a fear one will misspeak or have to eat one's words at some point. Denotes a verbally cautious tendency.

Constipation (Coprastasophobia) applies to the alarming sense of being unable to express oneself.

Contagious, being (Tapinophobia) is associated with the ego; wanting to be liked. This is a fear of being separated or isolated by others.

Disease/illness (Pathophobia) indicates a mind-set of perfection; a fear of negatives or problems in one's life.

Dizziness (Dinophobia) refers to a fear of being confused or involved in a complex situation or relationship.

Fever (Pyrexiophobia) characterizes an individual who dreads showing emotionalism; someone taking pride in routine displays of inner strength.

Heart attack (Angionophobia) represents an attempt to escape emotional shock.

Heart disease (Cardiophobia) alludes to a fear of being emotionally hurt.

Infection (Molysomophobia) refers to an effort to avoid negative elements in one's life that are believed to bring harmful ramifications.

Injections (Trypanophobia) signifies a fear of anything new or different invading one's personal space.

Injury (Traumatophobia) alludes to concern over some type of harm breaking through one's sense of strong protection.

Insanity (Lyssophobia) signifies a fear of losing grip on reality.

Menstruation (Menophobia) can be generated from a religious source because various religions believe a menstruating woman is unclean and others believe that the menstrual blood holds great, fearsome power. A dream displaying this type of fear will point to someone who holds antiquated and false beliefs.

Nosebleeds (Epistaxiophobia) relates to a fear of routine being interrupted.

Pain (Algophobia) indicates a dread of being hurt in life. This doesn't solely relate to physical pain but is usually associated with heartache.

Skin infested with mites (Acarophobia) reveals an illusion of persecution; a false belief that one is always being attacked; paranoia; a person's suspicious nature.

Surgery (Tomophobia) shows anxiety over losing control. May also be associated with a fear of dying.

Swallowing (Phagophobia) stands for a fear of becoming gullible.

Vaccination/vaccines (Vaccinophobia) signifies distrust; a conscious choice to avoid protective measures because of suspicion.

Venereal disease (Cypridophobia) relates to a fear of close relationships.

Vertigo See phobias: dizziness.

Vomiting (Emetophobia) pertains to a fear of accepting or ingesting harmful ideas.

Weakness (Asthenophobia) will reveal an egotistical individual who is fearful of displays of frailty.

Weight gain See phobias: fat, becoming.

Wrinkles, getting (Rhytiphobia) reflects a fear of appearing old. This characterizes jumbled priorities.

X-rays See phobias: radiation.

Events-Related Phobias

Accidents (Dystychiphobia) is representative of one's inability to focus on the moment during everyday life.

Aging (Gerascophobia) represents a subconscious demeaning perspective of the elderly; a lack of appreciation for life stages. It may indicate that the dreamer places too much emphasis on having a youthful appearance.

Atomic explosions (Nucleomituphobia) denotes strong empathetic sensitivity toward all living things. This symbol may display an uneasiness about others having such destructive control.

Attack (Scelerophobia) relates to an insecurity regarding one's personal defenses.

Buried alive, being (Taphephobia) signifies a fear that a pending plan or situation will be buried before it has a chance to prove itself.

Changes (Metathesiophobia) indicates rigidity.

Childbirth/pregnancy (Tocophobia) means trepidation over starting anything new, especially brand-new beginnings. This may also relate to new ideas.

Good news (Euphobia) means a pessimist. Suggests a belief that all good news has a down side.

Long waits (Macrophobia) refers to an evasion of experiencing impatience, anxiety, or stressful situations.

Marriage (Gamophobia) denotes a fear of close relationships.

Memories (Mnemophobia) denotes a hesitancy to delve into the past. Perhaps there have been traumatic events the dreamer is fearful of revisiting. A fear of memories points to someone who lives for the present and only faces forward to the future.

Moving (Tropophobia) portrays a severe insecurity over leaving one's comfortable and familiar surroundings. This indicates a fear of new places, experiences, and starting over.

War See phobias: injury.

Phobias of Inanimate Objects

Asymmetrical things (Asymmetriphobia) indicates an inability to accept anything veering from the norm.
Books (Bibliophobia) connotes an attempt to shield oneself against any information that may invalidate one's perception, belief, or attitude.
Bullets (Ballistophobia) signifies a fear of losing one's grip on self-control; angst over possible emotional explosions or situations that could bring them on.
Clocks (Chronomentrophobia) reveals a time-stressed individual who is almost anal about keeping to scheduled appointments. Usually signifies a type-A personality.
Clothes (Vestiophobia) relates to someone who puts a priority on external appearances. This is associated to one who fears his or her clothing may not present the best possible first impression.
Crystals/glass (Crystallophobia) implies a reluctance to look at one's overall spirituality or spiritual behavior.
Dolls (Pediophobia) denote a disquietude regarding the motives of others. This may pertain to a tendency to look at another's motives with a suspicious eye.
Fabrics, specific (Textophobia) reveals a fear of a specific type of personality.
Firearms (Hoplophobia) alludes to a tendency to avoid conflict, even if it will harmlessly come to resolution.
Gold (Aurophobia) refers to a lack of trust regarding wealth. This lack of trust may be associated with oneself—an inability to handle finances.
Metal (Metallophobia) signifies an attempt to avoid any negative life elements that one could feel threatened or contaminated by.
Mirrors (Catoptrophobia) signifies apprehension over facing (knowing) oneself.
Money, touching (Chrematophobia) implies an attempt to avoid responsibility. The thinking behind this is that if one doesn't touch something, one isn't responsible for it.

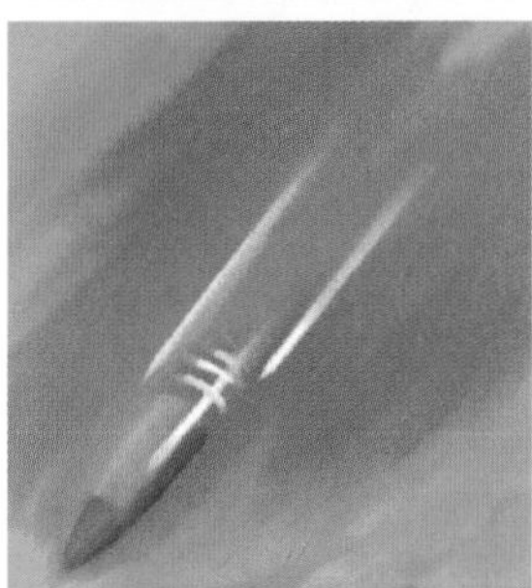

Bullets are fear of emotional conflict.

Needles/pins (Belonephobia) points to a pessimist. This is because the focus is a fear based on the negative aspect (being pricked) of the object instead of the positive (a tool used for repair) side of it.
New things (Cenophobia) alludes to an aversion to putting the familiar aside.
Noise (Acoustiphobia) pertains to a low stress tolerance. This signifies someone who is easily irritated by simple distractions.
Paper (Papyrophobia) is usually connected to the printed word and pertains to a fear of reading something one doesn't understand or is reluctant to know.
Pointed objects (Aichmophobia) implies a fear of having to get to the point. This reveals a tendency to avoid issues. It also refers to a reluctance to get near anything that has the possibility of having duality, meaning possibly negative or harmful aspects to it. This would usually point to a pessimist who only perceives the negative side of things.
Sharp instruments See pointed objects.
String (Linonophobia) signifies great anxiety over having to start something new; being fearful of entanglements.
Symbols (Symbolophobia) applies to a great dislike for anything that isn't spelled out; a tendency to shy away from obscure ideas.
Symmetry (Symmetrophobia) refers to a suspicion over anything that appears to be precisely balanced. Seeming perfection is suspect.
Tombstones (Placophobia) reveals a fear of facing one's mortality; of the possibility of the date of one's death being revealed.
Ventriloquist's dummies/wax likeness (Automatonophobia) stands for a disquietude regarding unnatural or artificial sources.

Concept-Related Phobias

Everything, fear of (Panophobia) denotes severe insecurity.
Freedom (Eleutherophobia) signifies insecurities; a hesitancy to go it alone.
Ideas (Ideophobia) is representative of an inability to process new information. This may also point to a disinterest in doing so.
Infinity (Apeirophobia) reflects an insistence on closure for everything. This implies an individual's tendency to fear anything that could remain in an ongoing state.
Knowledge (Epistemophobia) denotes a reluctance to shoulder the responsibility that knowledge brings.
Music (Musicophobia) signifies a desire to shield oneself from being emotionally affected.
Philosophy (Philosophobia) stands for a fear of learning the root causes of one's own behaviors.
Poetry (Metrophobia) represents an anxiety over the possibility of unexpectedly hearing or reading hidden messages that hit home. This relates to an overscrupulous conscience.
Progress (Prosophobia) portrays trepidation over the possibility of failure or an inability to keep up.
Punishment (Poinephobia) pertains to a fear of doing something wrong. This suggests particular anxiety over the possibility of future failure.
Responsibility (Hypengyophobia) suggests anxiety about failure in any aspect of one's life.

see also
• Weather *pp. 56–63*
• Objects & Attributes *pp. 442–474*

Environment Phobias

Clouds (Nephophobia) imply an inclination to feel anxiety over anything one perceives as being a threat to attitudes, perception, or beliefs.
Comets (Cometophobia) portray having qualms about experiencing epiphanies or spiritual awakening.
Dark (Nyctophobia) stands for an abhorrence of anything one can't see. This relates to suspiciousness of another's intentions or ulterior motives.
Dawn (Eosophobia) connotes a fear of starting new things.
Daylight (Phengophobia) signifies a dread of exposure or of light illuminating an issue.
Dirt (Mysophobia) portrays angst over anything that isn't straightforward or black and white. This means an attempt to avoid anything not cut and dried or perfectly clean.
Drafts (Aerophobia) signifies a fear of one's perspective, attitude, or conclusion being disturbed by the entrance of new angles or aspects.
Dryness (Xerophobia) implies a need to keep hitches out of one's life; a desire to avoid any form of slow or declining phases; a need to keep things well oiled.
Dust (Amathophobia) typifies one who must remain active and on top of things.
Electricity (Electrophobia) represents a dislike and distrust for any type of control from a source other than one's own.
Filth (Rhypophobia) symbolizes a loathing for anything having negatives associated with it; a fear of being contaminated by another's characteristics or attitudes that the dreamer perceives as being negative traits.
Germs (Spermophobia) applies to a dread of contaminating oneself. This usually pertains to personal perspectives defining social status.
Light (Photophobia) reveals anxiety over having clear perception without the shadows of one's many attitudes.
Radiation (Radiophobia) portrays a fear of the possibility of being the recipient of harming effects caused by outside sources.
Slime (Blennophobia) is representative of a fear of being involved with a difficult situation that has to be dealt with.
Smells (Olfactophobia) stands for a dislike of being affected by external sources.
Stars (Siderophobia) depicts an individual's aversion to any reminders that one needs to keep vigilant in respect to one's spiritual behavior.

Phobias of Weather & the Elements

Aerophobia (fear of drafts or airborne matter) signifies one's fear of expressing one's own opinions or thoughts. This dream element may also indicate a reluctance to be open to new ideas.
Cold (Frigophobia) equates to a worry about losing one's sensitivities.
Cold, extreme, including frost and ice (Cryophobia) applies to a fear of becoming apathetic.
Dampness/moisture (Hygrophobia) implies a distasteful attitude toward the slightest indication of anything spiritual.
Fire (Pyrophobia) exemplifies an abhorrence of emotional outbursts or a situation that looks like it may develop into a heated confrontation.
Floods (Antlophobia) relates to a fear of being spiritually inundated.

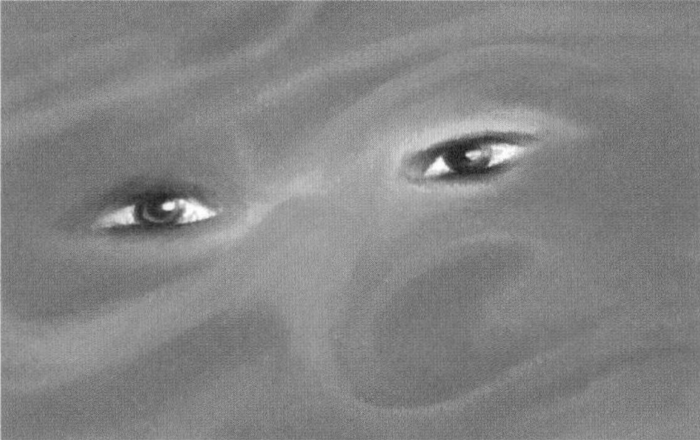

Fog represents concern about not being in possession of all the facts.

Fog (Nebulaphobia) reveals anxiety over obscure or undefined ideas, relationships, or other situations.
Heat (Thermophobia) refers to an evasive move to avoid being faced with motivational elements. This points to procrastination.
Hurricanes/tornadoes (Lilapsophobia) relates to an aversion to fanaticism and the chance one may be drawn into it.
Lightning/thunder (Astraphobia) alludes to a reluctance to experience spiritual aspects, such as epiphanies, visions, or insights.
Northern/southern lights (Auroraphobia) denotes trepidation over experiencing or being touched by uncommon spiritual events in one's life.
Rain (Ombrophobia) could be tied into the fear of getting wet. This typifies anxiety over the possibility of new or enlightening aspects affecting one's solid belief system.
Snow (Chionophobia) signifies an attempt to avoid being touched by spiritual elements.
Sunshine (Heliophobia) may reveal a suspicious nature; fear of something that causes shadows (questionable aspects).
Thunderstorms (Astraphobia) applies to a fear that one's spiritual or ethical misbehavior will be discovered.
Water (Hydrophobia) reveals someone who has great trepidation regarding all things religious or spiritual.
Wind (Ancraophobia) suggests trepidation over showing or revealing emotions, especially strong ones.

Travel Phobias

Automobiles (Motorphobia) signifies some type of uneasiness regarding one's physical self-characteristics, attributes, or how one presents oneself to the world.

Bridges, crossing (Gephyrophobia) denotes trepidation over being cut off from those one is connected to in life.

Flying (Aviophobia) equates to a fear of having and/or expressing unique thoughts in public.

Railways (Siderodromophobia) implies an aversion to paths, decisions, or situations that have no alternative course in the dreamer's everyday life.

Speed (Tachophobia) will generally reveal someone who has to take things extremely slowly in order to remain focused on the current issue.

Trains See phobias: railways.

Travel (Hodophobia) relates to a deep anxiety over being away from one's secure ground. Indicates to a fear of being in unfamiliar territory.

Vehicles, riding in (Amaxophobia) is representative of a particular distrust of another's judgment.

Walking (Basiphobia) alludes to a dread of having to go it alone. It refers to a fear of being independent.

Phobia of Places

Empty rooms suggest a dearth of imagination and foresight.

Buildings, high (Batophobia) refers to an apprehension over having one's feet far off the ground; a fear of being forced into a situation where one doesn't feel grounded.

Cemeteries (Coimetrophobia) usually means a fear of having secrets exposed.

Churches (Ecclesiophobia) pertains to a tendency to avoid anything connected to religion or spiritual issues.

Claustrophobia warns of being in a closed-in situation or relationship. This may also be self-generated.

Confined places (Claustrophobia) refers to a fear of being closed in or getting into situations where one is put in "tight" circumstances.

Depths See phobias: bathing.

Empty rooms (Kenophobia) suggest a lack of creativity. Reflects an individual's lack of vision.

England/anything English (Anglophobia) will be a dream symbol revealing a basic attitude of ethnic intolerance.

Forests (Hylophobia) connote a strong reluctance to acknowledge one's abilities or natural skills.

Heights (Acrophobia) indicates a lack of self-confidence; reluctance to advance due to fear of failure. May imply being intimidated by lofty plans or new challenges.

Hospitals (Nosocomephobia) denotes rejuvenation and the fear of not being the same afterward.

Houses (Domatophobia) applies to an apprehension over losing one's safe and secure refuge. This apprehension turns into an actual fear of what is most prized.

Narrowness (Anginophobia) depicts an individual's need for personal space.

Open spaces (Agoraphobia) represents insecurities; being greatly stressed by the feeling of being exposed, "out there."

Outer space (Spacephobia) relates to trepidation over feeling helpless, weightless.

Precipices (Cremnophobia) denotes anxiety over the possibility of being pulled into making wrong decisions. It also refers to an individual's fear of being coerced or manipulated.

Ruins (Atephobia) indicates a sense of dread over witnessing evidence of a social or cultural decline. This is associated with a fear of impermanence.

Safe place, leaving See phobias: open spaces.

School, going to (Didaskaleinophobia) portrays a lack of understanding one's own potential.

Sea (Thalassophobia) implies a fear of being overwhelmed by spiritual aspects.

Stairs (Climacophobia) signifies a fear of moving in a direction that's vertical to one's comfortable course; being afraid of advancing or backsliding.

Streets, crossing (Agiophobia) refers to a fear of having to get to the other side of something; a reluctance to alter a course.

Theaters (Theatrophobia) stands for a fear of any situation that could distract one from focused attention.

Woods See phobias: forests.

see also
• Travel & Transportation *pp. 286–305*
• Places *pp. 370–382.*

Metaphysical Phobias

Crucifixes/crosses (Staurophobia) denote an aversion to "looking back" or being reminded of the sacrifices made in life.

Demons/goblins (Demonophobia) imply an inability to deal with life's negatives. This could point to a fear of having to engage in a conflict with one's demons in order to overcome them.

Doctrine deviation (Hereiophobia) suggests a fear of discovering flaws in one's perception of belief.

Ghosts (Phasmophobia) indicate a fear of certain elements of one's past returning for the purpose of demanding closure.

Gods/religion (Theophobia) reveals an aversion to the idea of divinity and all its elements.

Halloween (Samhainophobia) signifies dread of discovering the hidden aspects of another person's character.

Heaven (Uranophobia) portrays spiritual denial.

Hell (Hadephobia) usually represents a fear of depression.

Magic (Rhabdophobia) indicates an aversion to things one doesn't understand or can't logically figure out.

Monsters (Teratophobia) illustrate anxiety around whatever one perceives as having power over oneself.

Myths (Mythophobia) exemplify an avoidance of hearing stories that hit home. This applies to a fear of suddenly hearing the truth about something.

Religious ceremonies (Teleophobia) reveal a loathing for anything related to structured spirituality.

Sacred objects (Hierophobia) allude to a sense of awe and its corresponding feeling of being unworthy.

Saints (Hagiophobia) relate to feelings of inadequacy.

Satan (Satanophobia) indicates a fear of being touched by evil or negative influences.

Sermons (Homilophobia) relate to a dislike for being lectured to.

Sin (Hamartophobia) means an overscrupulous conscience.

Witches/witchcraft (Wiccaphobia) indicates a fear of those of whom one has little knowledge.

Demons/goblins indicate a reluctance to deal with and resolve problems.

Natural World Phobias

Shadows reveal a mistrust of anything that isn't straightforward.

Flowers (Anthophobia) refer to a denial of inherent talents.

Garlic (Alliumphobia) points out a belief that life's negative elements must be acknowledged if one needs to use protective measures against them. Therefore, one fears the idea of protective measures.

Gravity (Barophobia) applies to a very specific fear of reaching one's personal limitations.

Moon (Selenophobia) refers to an individual's trepidation over spiritual or psychic aspects that have esoteric elements. It may also symbolize a fear of female power.

Night (Nyctophobia) pertains to an overactive imagination. This usually indicates to one who envisions things going bump in the night.

Plants (Botanophobia) reveal a fear of utilizing one's natural talents and not measuring up.

Shadows (Sciophobia) may indicate paranoia or a suspiciousness of anything that isn't black and white.

Time (Chronophobia) exemplifies an individual's anxiety over meeting deadlines.

Trees (Dendrophobia) denote apprehension over the effectiveness or quality of one's natural talents.

Technology Phobias

Computers (Cyberphobia) indicate one's comfortable position with what they know and point to a fear of having to learn new things or expand one's current base of knowledge.

Machinery (Mechanophobia) implies a desire to avoid help. This means a tendency to rely on one's own ingenuity or energy to accomplish goals.

Technology (Technophobia) characterizes a distrust of advancements.

Telephones (Telephonophobia) imply an aversion for communicating with a faceless person; avoidance of situations where one can't read another's body language.

Philanthropists

Benefactress is representative of the source or impetus that serves to provide ways for an individual to advance or succeed.
Patron characterizes a supportive individual.
Philanthropist means a generous nature. It may also show opportunities to be selfless.
Provider is representative of a patron, caregiver, or contributor.
Visionary characterizes one who has attained deep wisdom through experiential knowledge.

Color & Number Phobias

Black (Melanophobia) denotes a shrinking from problems and everything that one can't immediately understand.
Colors (Chromophobia) reflects an introvert who has a fear of expressing individuality; a fear of standing out.
Figure 8 (Octophobia) indicates a fear of having irrational or distorted thoughts; one who boasts of always being rational.
Friday the 13th (Paraskavedekatriaphobia) characterizes a deeply superstitious nature.
Purple (Porphyrophobia) indicates a deep anxiety over gaining spiritual enlightenment or wisdom in one's life.
Red See phobias related to conditions: blushing.
White (Leukophobia) is representative of a fear that one's imperfections might show.
Yellow (Xanthophobia) denotes a fear of being perceived as extremely cowardly and having no inner strength.

Mouthing Off

Foulmouthed denotes a person's arrogance and a lack of respect for others.
Name-calling can portray an individual's true attitude toward another.
Nuisance may exemplify one's conscience. It may refer to one's higher self.
Obscenity won't necessarily denote a negative sign. It may present itself as a means of emphasis or revelation of an individual's hidden personal attitudes.
Outburst (vocal) stands for an emotional expression of feelings, which may have a positive or negative connotation depending on the related dream details. It is important here to recall who said what.
Outspoken marks a candid, uninhibited communication; basic honesty.
Potty mouth See obscenity.
Pout depicts selfishness. It may refer to an absence of acceptance.
Profanity See obscenity.
Slobbering exemplifies an inability to communicate one's ideas.

Intellectual Ability

Depth perception denotes analytic ability; being capable of extensive reasoning and logical thought (unless the depth perception was shallow).
Genius symbolizes high intelligence. This dream detail may be a warning to use wisdom in connection with intellectual brilliance.
Precociousness advises one of a need to control one's mental energies; too much information or too many elements being missed due to a racetrack mind.
Proficiency represents applied efficiency coupled with skill.
Prolific correlates with continual productivity.

Laziness

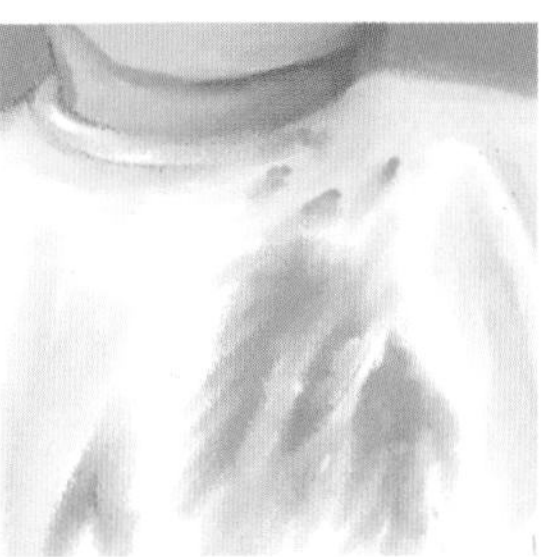

Sloppy has a variety of meanings.

Lethargy most often reveals a depressive state; lack of motivation or faith.
Plodding usually denotes perseverance; slow but steady.
Poky (slow) may not imply procrastination, but rather this symbol usually alludes to an extremely careful and cautious manner of approach or progression.
Sloppy can be one of those relative symbols that will signify different meanings for each dreamer. The surrounding details will be the clarifying factor.
Sloth warns against procrastination.
Slowpoke may not be laziness but careful progression.

Disagreement

Agitation symbolizes aspects that cause mental or emotional disturbances.
Bickering comes to point out inconsequential disagreements or nit-picking.
Last laugh signifies one's opinion had been proven; a verification.
Monday-morning quarterback cautions against claiming false foreknowledge or wisdom; seeing through the lens of hindsight.
Nit-picking frequently comes from one's own conscience to reveal a criticizing tendency.
Objections will reveal an individual's true opinion. An objection in a dream can also be a message from one's higher self.
Outrage comes as a message to gain a greater measure of acceptance and intellectual reasoning.
Passive resistance will advise a peaceful way to resist or express opposition.
Short fuse comes to advise one to be more patient or tolerant.
Slow burn signifies growing frustration or anger.
Standoff See stalemate.

see also
• Colors *pp. 416–17*
• Eating *p. 426*

Weakness

Dependent pertains to one who looks to another for support.
Leaning (dependency) represents a need for some type of support system.
Passivism suggests a peaceful personality yet may advise to start expending efforts toward a goal; passive resistance.
Programmed refers to conditioned responses; being brainwashed or manipulated.
Put-on typifies an exaggeration; a teasing. May reveal phony affectations.
Soft spot exposes a specific sentimentality.
Submissiveness refers to a tendency to be easily manipulated. May point to a feeling of inferiority.
Subservience denotes a tendency to defer to others instead of standing up for oneself. May point to an underlying desire to please others for the purpose of being well liked.
Tagalong portrays a lack of purpose or life course.

Greed

Glutton characterizes a greedy personality. It may refer to insatiability.
Gold fever represents unrealistic expectations.
Gourmand characterizes a gluttonous nature.
Splurging suggests self-indulgence; an attempt to comfort or satisfy oneself.

Immaturity

Beginner is representative of a lack of experience or knowledge; perhaps immaturity as well, depending on surrounding dreamscape elements.
Buck fever exposes that which destroys innocence; a passion to prove oneself; a destructive predatory nature.
Panty raid comes as a warning of immaturity; juvenile perspectives.
Virgin is an unadulterated idea or perspective.
Wild oats means immaturity, recklessness, and promiscuity one needs to get out of one's system before real maturity and progression can begin.

Sorrow

Breast-beating is sorrow. It may represent a desire to elicit sympathy from others.
Misery implies a lack of acceptance. Could reveal a self-induced state.
Pining alludes to a refusal to accept something in one's life; a great personal loss.
Pity usually refers to self-generated feelings; a way of eliciting sympathy; a self-defeating attitude.
Sorrowful is representative of regret, empathy, or melancholia.
Wallowing relates directly to self-pity or self-indulgence.

Escapists

Addict symbolizes one who is not in control of his or her life.
Alcoholic is an individual who attempts to escape his or her current life's problems or past.
Backstage Johnny characterizes an intrusive personality; one who disrespects another's privacy.
Barfly characterizes a tendency to shrug responsibility. This dream symbol may point to apathy or despair as a main emotion in one's life.
Beach bum characterizes an individual who lives one's spiritual beliefs at all times; someone who literally walks his or her spiritual talk.
Beachcomber is representative of someone who is looking for spiritual rarities that he or she can treasure.
Boozehound See alcoholic.
Castaway is indicative of dependency on another's spiritual direction instead of being the captain of one's own ship. It may also refer to being lost without the spiritual direction or leadership of another individual in one's spiritual life.
Cokehead is representative of total irresponsibility and a lack of interest in dealing with reality.
Junkie will not equate to only a drug addiction but any strong habit that one should overcome.
Runaway stands for an element in one's life that has escaped one's grasp.

Devious Behavior

Alter ego is a need to know the completeness of oneself.
Malevolence reveals the existence of multiple negative qualities or forces.
Malice stands for a desire for revenge; an intent to harm.
Meddlesome applies to an interference by another, perhaps by the dreamer.
Name-dropping is a suggestion for the dreamer, and this will indicate someone or something to connect with or avoid. Recall surrounding dream details for further clarification.
Nonchalance may not necessarily mean apathy or indifference. It may indicate an attitude or opinion that's reserved until further knowledge has been obtained.
Pander advises one to stop giving in to weaknesses.
Side-glance symbolizes personal observations; a surreptitious awareness.
Stone-faced signifies a desire to conceal responses.
Straight face See stone-faced.
Strong-arm (tactics) warns of the harmful effects of attempting to force issues or results.
Subterfuge indicates some type of deception.
Surreptitious refers to an action performed without announcement. May also indicate deception.
Two-faced is representative of duplicity.
Underhand applies to unethical practices.

Fear & Anxiety

Fright (sudden) advises one to maintain awareness; realize that the unexpected is part of reality.

Overprotective is representative of a fear of letting go. It also refers to anxiety over spreading one's wings and becoming more independent in one's life.

Petrified (fear) See scared.

Preoccupied (mental state) connotes an inability to focus attention on the issue at hand.

Qualms characterize doubts; apprehension; perhaps indecision.

Stage fright reveals a fear of expressing oneself.

Strung out warns of an inability to cope or deal with one life aspect at a time.

Suspense warns against the wisdom of maintaining acceptance.

Terror See fear.

Wringing (hands) stands for fretting; worry; anxiety.

Comfort & Support

Allowance refers to the need to make allowances in life; be more tolerant.

Benefit of the doubt is a representation of trust.

Buffalo heart represents great inner strength. It also refers to endurance through intense adversity.

Open arms naturally express acceptance; an invitation. They can also be a sign of receptivity or support.

Solace reflects some type of comfort that may come from others or that may even be self-generated.

Soothing will represent a stress-relieving element.

Sympathy may reveal a need to give compassion to another, or it may warn against drawing it for self-gratification.

Tough love suggests a need to stand one's ground in a relationship.

Honorable Types

Etiquette is representative of a particular concern for social attitudes. In this sense, it may refer to a focus on politeness. Etiquette could also advise against an overconcern regarding what others think.

Frugal may commend thrift or advise against it. Thrift in this context usually refers to the utilization of one's talents or perhaps to expressions of emotions. The surrounding dream details will help to clarify this intent.

Genteel doesn't necessarily refer to a prudish attitude. It may be an indication of simple refinement.

Prim is representative of a rigidly formal or puritanical personality.

Propriety is representative of respectability; appropriate behavior.

Square shooter exemplifies honesty; integrity.

Straitlaced usually refers to an individual with an opinionated, unyielding, and overly conservative nature.

Happiness

Belly laugh means great joy; hearty amusement.

Laughter applies to a humorous situation or happiness. Recall who was doing the laughing. What was the quality of it? Sarcastic or genuine? What was being laughed at?

Revelry directs the dreamer to the cause of the revelry, which will reveal an important element that was missed in the awake state.

Silliness doesn't necessarily imply immaturity, but it may indicate a need for an individual to be less serious for a time. This symbol says, "Hey, loosen up! Chill out!"

Smile may well suggest friendliness, yet the precise interpretation will depend on the surrounding dreamscape details. This smile may turn out to be a disguised or sarcastic one.

Spring fever portrays inner joy and anticipation for the start of new beginnings.

Zest illustrates high interest and motivation. It may specifically be a reference to excitement.

Zinger may reveal a hidden attitude exposed through a remark, or it may turn out to be a revelation of some type.

Shock

Aftershock signifies negative effects remaining after an event. It may also mean ramifications.

Open-mouthed implies a mental state of expectation or narrow perspectives.

Startled is representative of an unexpected event in one's life.

Thunderstruck relates to a stunned response to an unexpected event in the dreamer's life.

Insanity

Apoplexy is a warning of a self-induced inability or affliction, usually to avoid responsibility or gain sympathy.

Crazy See insanity.

Frantic usually warns of a lack of acceptance; lack of faith.

Haywire means the final work to be done before completing something. This may also imply that something has gone completely wrong.

Insanity implies a total loss of reality in one's life.

Lampoon comes to suggest ridiculousness; a sarcastic or humorous attitude toward an issue or individual's behavior.

Pandemonium emphasizes a state of confusion in one's emotional or mental state.

Unbalanced warns of a lack of alignment or an unstable factor that's present in life.

Unconscious usually denotes ignorance or unawareness yet may indicate complete insensitivity.

Uncontrolled signifies a lack of direction or planning. May indicate an aspect that has gotten out of hand.

see also
• Mental Disorders & Behavior *p. 106*
• Love & Sex *p. 126*

Attraction & Repulsion

Admiration cautions against excesses in this area. Recall who was giving or receiving the admiration.
Adoration is a warning symbol. Only the divine is deserving enough to be adored.
Avoidance comes as a warning against running away from situations or relationships. This symbol could also point to denial or apathy.
Flirting connotes an attempt to approach in a testing manner.
Foreplay alludes to preparations that are being made for something; getting into the right frame of mind.
Lechery reveals an individual who is not spiritually aware or advanced.
Leery means distrust.
Lewdness reveals a lack of spiritual development; an individual's preoccupation with the physical world.
Loathing defines a personal aversion. This may reveal another's inner attitude that is not externalized in a public manner.
Lust constitutes a severe craving for something but does not necessarily have a sexual connotation.
Obsession will stress an overemphasis applied to a specific issue. This is a warning symbol.
Ogle applies to a lack of respect and acceptable behavior.
One-night stand signifies a one-time event or experience that carries no commitment.
Penchant See predilection.
Picky indicates a firm sense of self. This may not connote any type of negative attitude but will usually be associated with "knowing one's mind."
Predilection will reveal one's preference or tendency. Recall what this referred to. Was it a positive or negative element in the dream?
Promiscuity warns against apathy in regard to oneself. It may refer to a loss of self-respect.
Repulsive corresponds with a life aspect that is personally offensive. This may refer to a situation, event, statement, idea, and so on.
Risqué is representative of an impropriety; offensive behavior. Reveals an unenlightened individual.
Seduction warns of a situation that may lure an individual astray. Though this dream symbol may be visually presented as a sexual image in the dream, it will most often have a real-life relation to something in one's awake state that is acting as a deterrent from central focus. It may generally refer to a distraction of some type.
Sex appeal will not necessarily relate to a temptress, for this symbol most often refers to an individual's personal magnetism; a type of personality that attracts others.
Sleazy portrays extremely poor taste. May indicate a contemptible element.
Spellbound connotes a personal fascination of some type and warns against being in a state lacking logic and reason.
Squeamishness alludes to an individual's lack of courage or self-confidence.

Miscellaneous

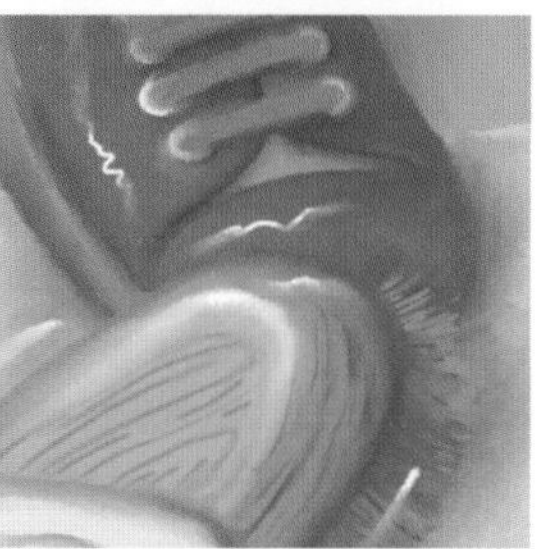

Shoe shine represents a show-off.

Advertiser is one who attempts to get people's attention.
Gypsy characterizes a free spirit.
Pauper reveals a person who doesn't recognize the value of personal abilities or worth.
Peasant connotes simplicity and the value of same.
Peddler can reveal unexpected opportunities.
Phobia corresponds with fears and elements of great anxiety.
Plebeian will refer to commonality; the general public in regard to an attitude or segment of people.
Prima donna stands for an egotistical individual; someone expecting to be admired.
Prodigy (child) means inherent talents, memories, or knowledge from accumulative experiential existences.
Protégé is an individual who has a personal mentor or special teacher.
Reductionist characterizes an individual who has the ability to simplify and clarify matters.
Runner-up represents acknowledgment for efforts expended toward a goal. This will come as a positive symbol, which gives encouragement indicating that one only need to put a bit more effort into reaching one's goal.
Savant exposes past-life knowledge or talents.
Scab (worker) warns of a wrong substitution or replacement; a wrong alternative.
Scalper (ticket) refers to personal gain made through unethical means; taking advantage of others.
Scavenger usually exemplifies resourcefulness, yet whether this symbol is meant to imply a positive or negative message will depend on the related surrounding dreamscape details.
Separatist will not necessarily depict a negative meaning. It may caution one to keep diverse concepts separate instead of combining them erroneously, or this symbol could also come as a personal advisement to stay out of other people's business.
Shoe shine refers to a desire to impress others with one's method or manner of moving through life. This might identify someone who hints at or boasts that life is easier for him or her.
Sidekick reveals a close companion; an individual who can be counted on.
Straight shooter signifies honesty.
Strikebreaker represents a negative element that temporarily prevents one from changing her or his life course.
Taskmistress will usually refer to the feminine conscience.
Teetotaler characterizes an individual who claims or believes he or she needs no support in life.
Wrangler characterizes a confining thought process.

Chapter 11

Actions, Activities & Situations

Activities and positions of people in dreams offer invaluable insights into one's overall intentions and can frequently reveal hidden agendas. In this case, actions truly do speak louder than words.

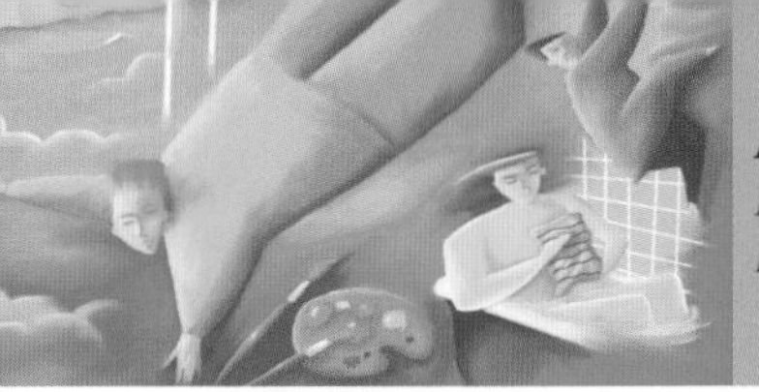

Liquid Actions

Drip depicts information overload.

Congeal characterizes a coming together or nearing solidification.
Dilute means a softened or lessened situation.
Drench indicates a saturation point, implying an issue that has no more new information.
Dribble (trickle) indicates a state of consistency; a slow-paced advancement allowing full absorption of lessons.
Drip represents a saturation point; overflow. It may also refer to a need for some type of containment.
Melting may refer to a need for some type of softening or it may indicate a loss of definition (uniqueness or purity). The surrounding dream facets will clarify the intended meaning for the individual dreamer.
Pouring (liquid) typifies an act of disseminating information. Recall what the liquid was. Who was pouring it?
Sloshing pertains to carelessness; a lack of control; efficient behavior.
Trickle (water flow) is actually a positive sign because it shows that there's enough of one's spirituality left to save and increase.

Vision

Display applies to visual communication; showing something to others. What was displayed? Was it old or new?
Expose forewarns of some type of public exposure in one's future. May hint of a betrayer in one's midst.
Preview defines a sampling of something before a decision is made.
Show-and-tell comes as a private message for each individual dreamer. Recall what was shown and told about. Who was doing the showing?
Sightseeing warns of superficiality; cursory knowledge.
Unveiling correlates to a discovery of some type.

Preparation

Appointment signifies a need to communicate with another.
Booking See appointment.
Drill (practice) illustrates the importance of routine use of one's talents.
Outline signifies a need for planning; suggests deep thought be applied before taking action.
Plan denotes an intention or method of proceedings.
Plot (plan out) pertains to thought given or required.
Practicing advises of a need to gain more experience.

Reduction & Fading

Depressurize advises of a need to reduce stress levels.
Downgrade means a lowering of value or condition.
Downshift advises of a need to slow one's pace.
Downsize cautions one to lessen the scope of something, such as goals and expectations.
Downtrend equates to waning interest in something.
Drain (empty) warns of an energy-depleting aspect.
Fade illustrates a lessening of something. This could be a positive or negative sign depending on the surrounding dreamscape elements.
Fade in forewarns of a specific event or personal attitude beginning to enter one's life.
Fade out pertains to something in one's life that is losing strength or interest.
Phaseout connotes a waning situation or condition; some element in one's life that should be let go of. May advise greater acceptance.
Shrinking pertains to a waning effect; a diminishing factor in an individual's life.

Enclosure & Limiting

Check (stop) cautions one to get something under control; put a stop to something.
Curb advises of a need to curb some aspect in the dreamer's life; a caution against excesses. This usually points to some type of negative behavior.
Cutback advises an individual to ease up on something; lessening the amount of energy spent on an issue.
Cutoff (limit) denotes the need to detach self from a harmful element.
Encapsulate portrays a self-devised enclosure of self; emotional distancing.
Gift wrap denotes joy taken when helping others or from expressing acts of kindness.
Pigeonhole implies a tendency to classify others rather than viewing them as unique individuals.
Seal (closure) refers to a need to conclude an aspect in life.
Shut-in comes as an advisement to go within for the purpose of self-discovery.
Tether indicates a constraint from which one needs to break free.
Trap (catch) illustrates the pitfalls that entrap one in life such as arrogance, the ego, materialism, and so on.

Deception

Cover-up is representative of an attempt to hide something.
Double-dipping denotes the questionable act of receiving two benefits generated by the same source.
Eavesdrop is a representation of information of which others are cognizant.
Sleight of hand reveals deception.
Whitewashing exposes a cover-up; deception.

see also
• Sailing Craft *p. 303*
• Defenses & Refuges *p. 353*

Leading

Following warns of a person's lack of self-confidence or individual thought.
Lead (guide) refers to someone who is capable of showing the way; guidance.
Lead (lure) warns of being deceived, manipulated.
Lead (precede) usually signifies a messenger or someone communicating with one.
Lead-in is representative of broaching an issue or the beginning moves to reveal a specific attitude toward something.

Examination

Bed check indicates a need to make sure one is where one needs to be as far as one's own life progression toward goals. Doing what one knows one is supposed to be doing; a continual monitoring.
Check (examine) connotes a need to substantiate something in life.
Checkup stands for some aspect in the dreamer's life that requires examining.
Dissect signifies the act of or need to thoroughly analyze or examine something in one's life. On the other hand, this symbol can also point to a need to stop dissecting everything in one's life.
Experiment stands for personal attempts; trials; first starts.
Extricate signifies an overreaction; one who jumps to conclusions and acts on them.
Fact-finding suggests a need to do some in-depth research or gather more information. This indicates lack of complete facts.
Field test suggests the need for a dry run of something the dreamer is planning. This could indicate a need for further planning or a switch to an alternate plan.
Fieldwork denotes knowledge gained through experience.
Filter denotes a need for personal discernment; keeping the main issues uncluttered.
Follow-up advises of a need to recheck something or make a second communication with another individual.
Pore (study) depicts intensive research or analysis.
Pretest suggests attention given to one's qualifications or knowledge.
Probe means exploration; investigation; research.
Review is an advisement to become more familiar with a situation, idea, or individual.

Making Noises

Chime denotes a call to listen; a calling to something in one's life.
Clap See applause.
Clatter represents a great disturbance. Usually this will refer to one's vibrational field or personal aura.
Click means that something has finally been understood. It accompanies certain psychic experiences, therefore, it may relate to this factor.
Honking (horn) defines a warning; a call to attention.
Hum denotes vibrational shift.

Ship Actions

Bail (water) cautions one to empty one's mind of damaging spiritual concepts.
Billow implies expansion of something related to the dreamer's life.
Capsize means a spiritual reversal; an overturn.
Cast off (boat) means beginning a spiritual journey.
Furl suggests a need to open or uncover something.
Scudding connotes a forced progression.

Purposeless Actions

Ambling means nonchalance or loss of clear direction or purpose. This symbol may also refer to a defeatist attitude.
Drifting comes as an advisement to let one know that one is veering off course. This may apply to one's life path, an attitude, or leaning in the wrong direction.
Fiddle See fidget.
Fidget denotes restlessness; impatience; anxiety; lack of acceptance.
Loitering implies a lack of purpose; apathy.

Dangerous Situations

Accident alert means minor altercations that cause minimal damage to something.
Air alert warns of an attack on one's attitudes, perspectives, plans, or beliefs.
Close call implies a need to give closer attention to one's own actions.
Close shave See close call.
Disaster (area) implies a devastating event or great emotional distress.
Endanger cautions of the current time frame that is approaching, some type of hazardous or personally compromising situation.
Evacuation warns of a situation or relationship from which the dreamer should withdraw.
Explosion forewarns of an emotional event.
False alarm alludes to one's false fears; imagined fears.
Marooned reveals a self-imposed state of remoteness; willful distancing from others.
Rescue mission will point to a last resort in regard to saving something. This symbol may reveal a need to put greater effort into acceptance or perseverance.
Threat exposes an opposing or interfering element.
Wake-up call will symbolize the opening of one's eyes; sudden realization.
Warning will always denote just that, a warning. Recall the dream's surrounding details for specific information.

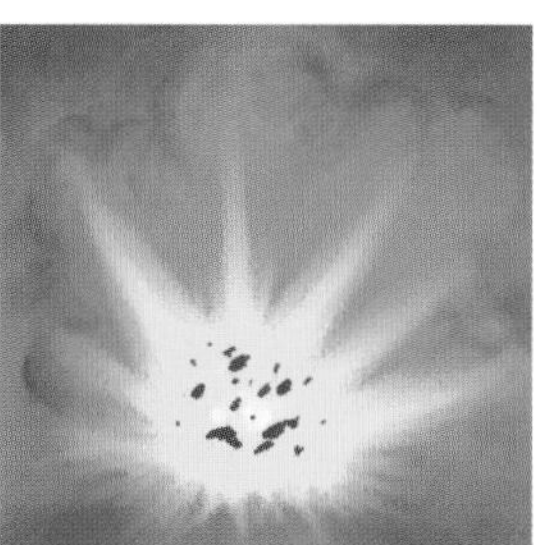

Explosion warns of fervent outburst.

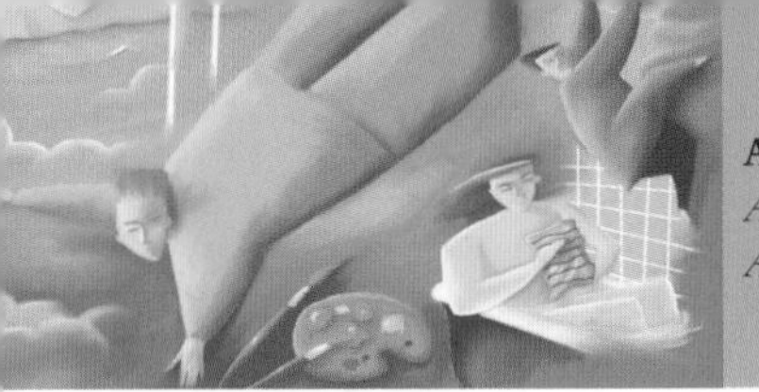

Affection

Caress is a manifestation of feelings of affection.
Embrace implies a closeness; a special connection.
Hug connotes a desire to touch others; a desire to be close and convey same.
Kiss demonstrates intention.
Nestle means a comfortable situation; a feeling of security.
Nuzzle corresponds to emotional expressions of love and companionship.
Snuggling (with another) suggests warm companionship.
Stroke (soothe) reflects sympathy; an effort to comfort oneself or another.
Suckle depicts a dependence on another.

Annoyance

Aggravate warns of a life aspect that is capable of making situations worse. May refer to an attitude, plan, perspective, or an individual in the dreamer's life.
Annoy See irritate.
Irritate denotes a lack of acceptance; inability to release negative attitudes.
Rankle implies irritation. May be an intended aggravated act.

Acting

Acting out stands for a desire to force the manifestations of desires or outcomes.
Audition cautions against trying to always be what others want you to be.
Mime represents honesty; visible attitudes and character.
Role-playing shows an attempt to understand another's view.
Upstage points to a tendency to outdo others.

Avoidance

Bypass pertains to the avoidance of unnecessary aspects; going around something.
Duck (evade) is a sign of awareness or watchfulness.
Hedge exemplifies a habit of circumventing; evading issues or responsibility.
Shun represents a voluntary disregard for something. Depending on the related elements of the dream, this may be a positive symbol for the dreamer.
Sidestep correlates to a diversionary tactic; an avoidance of something.

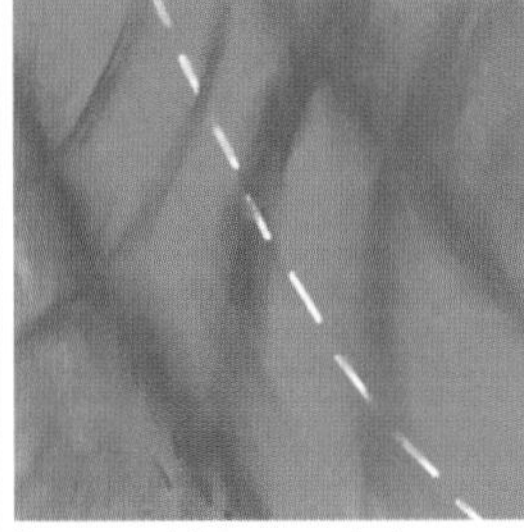

Swerve advises one to look out.

Swerve comes as warning to heighten awareness. Use perceptual awareness to accomplish avoidance.
Veer may be an attempt to avoid something or a diversion from one's life course.

Agreement

Acquiesce refers to a giving-in situation; warning of the need for more tolerance.
Agreement represents an aspect that must be resolved.
Assent See agreement.
Hands down stands for complete agreement; a reinforcing sign.
Nod (of head) suggests recognition; agreement.
Thumb (pointing down) obviously indicates disapproval or some form of rejection.
Thumb (pointing up) stands for approval, acceptance; a sign of acknowledgment.

Aggression

Abuse means the serious misuse of something in one's life. This may refer to a type of addiction, or to the treatment of others.
Ambush connotes a deceitful situation or relationship; an act of betrayal.
Annihilate represents a need to eliminate a particular aspect in one's life.
Attack refers to a specific conflict in one's life.
Battle indicates a tough time ahead; a real struggle to reach a goal.
Behead implies the need to bring one's thinking back in line because of losing one's head over something; that one is in serious trouble and is getting closer to the chopping block.
Brawl cautions against loss of temper; of inability to settle differences in an intelligent and reasonable manner.
Browbeat points to forced beliefs or perspectives. May indicate a manipulative personality; coercion.
Buck (kick) pertains to attempts to reject or refuse something; reluctance.
Feud indicates a state of altercation; an ongoing conflict.
Fight warns of aggressive opposition.
Hit (strike at) exposes unrestrained emotions; impulsiveness.
Lynching signifies guilt, usually self-guilt.
Maul (attack) defines an overwhelming aspect in one's life.
Rape reflects a low self-image; a need to continually manipulate others to raise self up to a position of power and dominance; the vicious taking of another's inherent right. Regarding land, this symbol points to a wanton clear-cutting, taking everything of value.
Scrimmage corresponds to a type of struggle.
Scuffle refers to an altercation of some type, possibly within oneself.
Slam portrays emphasis; force.
Stalking warns of a silent pursuit, usually of another. Recall who was stalking whom for what purpose.
Stamp (foot) relates to emphasis. May denote impatience or anger.
Stomp typifies an adverse reaction; an inability to contain emotions.

see also
• Love & Sex p. 126
• Aggressors p. 145

Trade

Auction warns one to always attempt to get the most out of relationships and situations. Giving the nod to the highest bidder; self-serving agendas.
Barter is representative of give-and-take; a sharing of talents.
Borrow implies a temporary solution or situation.
Charter (rent) See lease.
Closeout reveals the last of something; the final remnants.
Deal (distribute) means active sharing of something.
Discount (reduce) represents an opportunity to choose a different path leading to the same end.
Hazing signifies a price paid for certain advancements; desire to be accepted. This symbol also points to a meanness lying just below the surface that comes to the fore at every available opportunity.
Hock See pawn.
Lease represents an extension of time. Recall what the specific time was.
Market (sell) refers to an attempt to convince others of something's benefit or value.
Overspend represents an over-extension of oneself.
Pawn (hock) connotes a problematic solution or possible outlet.
Scrimp indicates extreme frugality. Recall surrounding dreamscape details to determine if this is a positive or negative message.
Shoptalk represents a need to attend to one's business at hand; a return to one's life goal or plan.
Survey (measure) cautions one to exercise precise planning. May also advise of a need to stay within one's own realm of business.
Swap meet represents the opportunities to share talents and abilities.

Change

Bend (shape) See bent.
Bent refers to an aspect in life that isn't straight (true/honest).
Changeover means a change of thought or attitude.
Convert denotes a change in one's belief or attitude.
Disguise warns of hypocrisy. May reveal one's true nature or intention.
Exchange (merchandise return) refers to an individual's need to replace an inappropriate or wrong attitude or idea with a correct one.
Lengthen connotes an extension of some type being done or required.
Modernize implies an updated aspect in one's life; making something current.
Overhaul portrays an interest in caring for and maintaining optimum condition of an element in one's life. This could refer to an individual's physical, mental, emotional, or spiritual aspects.
Reshuffle suggests a rearrangement of priorities or elements of a goal-reaching plan.
Shuffle (cards) connotes an altering of probabilities; changing possible outcomes.

Betrayal

Abandon means that which has been left unattended or shed.
Backbite means vindictiveness.
Backstab points to a vindictive personality; betrayal.
Bad-mouth points to a critical, disparaging personality.
Catcall means disrespect; uncouth expressions.
Desert (forsake) See abandon.
Double-cross warns of a betrayal; ulterior motives; personal agenda.
Ensnare comes to suggest underhandedness.
Forswear connotes denials.
Plot (scheme) corresponds to a devious nature.
Snarl warns of unfriendliness. May indicate entanglement.

Assistance

Advising is indicative of action or counsel that one should heed.
Aid is representative of assistance.
Alleviate constitutes a life element that serves to lessen intensity or severity.
Backup (offer) refers to a contingency plan. May also indicate a slim chance taken.
Brace means support. What is being braced? This answer will clearly define what needs support in the dreamer's life.
Favor represents generosity of spirit.
Handout is representative of sharing.
Lend is indicative of helpfulness or assistance given to another.
Rescue will come to emphasize the saving effect of one's efforts. Recall who was rescued. Who was the rescuer?
Shore (support) pertains to a temporary supportive move.

Agricultural Activities

Cornhusking denotes the actual work of one's personal efforts.
Cotton-picking applies to the wholesomeness of honest, hard work.
Cultivate defines a nurturing personality or life aspect.
Harrow implies a greatly disturbing incident.
Harvest portrays the fruits of one's shared gifts.
Haymow refers to efforts expended toward the completion of a specific project.
Leach implies a dilution or breaking down. Suggests that one is too fanatical or zealous and needs tempering.
Mowing warns against cutting one's abilities or talents.
Plant (sow) illustrates an attempt to establish or begin some element in one's life; an act of promoting or fostering.
Plow stands for a determination and perseverance to plow through difficulties encountered in life.
Reap See harvest.
Sow See plant.
Till (earth) stands for a freshening of one's natural talents or gifts; the turning over of abilities through use.
Winterize applies to spiritual preparations.

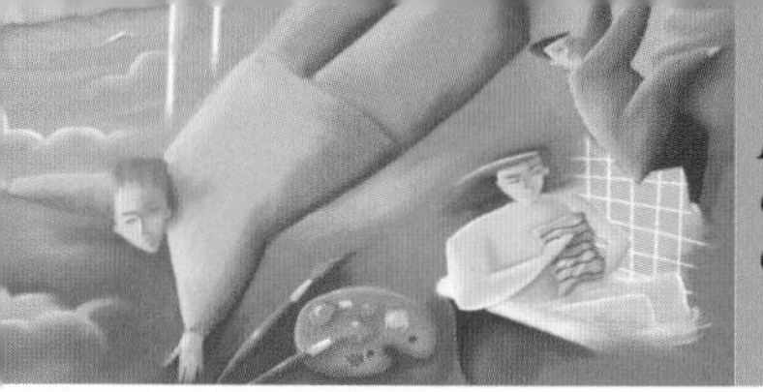

Cleaning

Bleach cautions against a tendency to whitewash things so their negativity can't be seen; a habit of being overly optimistic; a desire to sterilize negative elements so they can be ignored or overlooked.
Buff (polish) represents the act of finishing something to the best of one's ability.
Cleaning (act of) points to an attempt to clean up one's act; efforts to improve a situation.
Degrease exemplifies an action that caused friction.
Detoxify advises of a great need to get rid of damaging or harmful aspects that are associated with one's life.
Dredge applies to the act of scraping the bottom of some issue. This usually is a warning to leave well enough alone. Depending on surrounding dreamscape facets, this dream symbol may actually be doing the reverse and advising the dreamer to scrape the bottom.
Gargle indicates an effort to clarify an individual's communication skills.
Hand wash signifies the giving of special care to something.
Preening may not imply an arrogant or self-absorbing nature. It usually refers to a cleansing or attention to personal aspects.
Rinse (water) advises of a need to clarify something. Indicates a misunderstanding or misconception.
Sanitize is an effort to remove negative aspects from an element in one's life. May also point to a cover-up.
Scour depicts deep cleaning. Recall what was being scoured. Who was doing the cleaning?
Shower (bathing) indicates that some type of inner cleansing is needed.
Soak denotes a permeated condition of something.
Washing portrays one's desire to be surrounded by positive aspects in life.

Delay

Adjourn means a needed time-out or a required respite. A pause is required to step back from an issue.
Bay (hold off) represents procrastination; an effort to extend the time when one must deal with something. May be pointing to denial, laziness, or irresponsibility.
Fumble relates to a temporary setback; a small glitch.
Hold (stop order) refers to a temporary pause in action on an issue or situation.
Hold up (keep from advancing) defines a delay of some type.
Linger may refer to a delay. It may indicate a person's persistent nature.
Postpone may advise the dreamer to temporarily set something aside or the symbol may indicate a need to stop procrastinating.
Stall (put off) indicates a temporary postponement of forward progression.
Waver implies a hesitation, perhaps indecision.

Cooking

Boil depicts a situation where the emotional temperature is rising.

Bake relates to something finished; bringing to fruition.
Baste (cook) cautions against allowing spiritual beliefs to dry up.
Boil (hot liquid) stands for an agitated or heated situation or attitude.
Boil over signifies an element gone past tolerance.
Brew (concoct) symbolizes a mix of various thoughts or ideas; long contemplation on innovative concepts; inventiveness.
Broil refers to heat from above; pressure from one's boss or higher self.
Churn (butter) applies to the personal efforts applied to enrich one's path.
Cook (food preparation) connotes the act of planning; the process of completing something.
Curdle implies changes that may go bad.
Defrost advises of a call to be less rigid; more understanding, compassion, or tolerance.
Dice (cut into small cubes) denotes a need to break down ideas to easily digest or understand components.
Fermentation usually refers to a state of in-depth analysis; contemplation. It can refer to extensive research that has been done.
Fillet signifies a way of getting to the meat of an issue.
Fry implies quick conclusions.
Marinate symbolizes a need to let something rest for a time; a need to absorb all details or aspects of something.
Pare connotes the need to pare down something in one's life. Associative dream aspects will pinpoint this issue.
Peel See pare.
Presoak stands for a need to give added attention to an issue before it can be cleansed of negatives.
Roast (cook) represents a developing plan or idea.
Simmer exemplifies thoughtfulness. It can also mean contemplation, time expended on logic and rationale. It can warn against stewing over something, clear the air, and quit fuming.
Sizzling stands for intense withheld anger.
Stir implies that something in one's life is being stirred up and suggests watchfulness.

see also
• Cleaning *p. 389*
• Cook's Ingredients *p. 427*

Communication (Verbal)

Allude See infer.
Appeal refers to an effort to convince others to see things your way.
Apprise See inform.
Articulate cautions one to fully express oneself.
Bargain will emphasize a good plan or course of action.
Blurt (outburst) points to unauthorized announcement or revelation; possible betrayal.
Boast See brag.
Brag exemplifies a lack of peace within oneself.
Call points to communication with others.
Canvass See survey (poll).
Chat suggests passing conversation; surface communication.
Command is an authoritative directive. The clue here will be whether or not the authority figure is a positive or negative one as perceived by the dreamer.
Counter (response) usually refers to a compromise.
Croak typifies a fear to speak. This usually refers to the voicing of truths that are preferably kept to oneself.
Cross-examine indicates a need to double-check something; a need to look at something from a different angle.
Cuss See swear (cuss).
Debate advises listening to the perspectives of others, not for the purpose of changing your mind, but to come to a greater understanding of another's point of view.
Defame warns against gossip or maliciousness. Advises forgiveness and closure.
Denounce corresponds to an open condemnation, denial, or accusation.
Double-talk warns against making excuses. May indicate a tendency to talk in circles, or go around the main issue.
Grouch implies a need to talk to someone.
Growl warns of adversity; a potentially threatening situation or relationship.
Grumble advises one to accept those life aspects that cannot be altered.
Haggle See bargain.
Hang-up (phone call) represents a missed communication or message. May indicate a change of mind, a reluctance to make a contact.
Harangue cautions against sermonizing to others.
Harp (nag) indicates a lack of acceptance; a tendency to interfere in others' affairs.
Haze (harass) stands for a ridiculing personality or situation; amusement at another's expense.
Heckle warns against a tendency to irritate another person; taunting.
Horselaugh indicates a disdainful reaction; a jeering or mocking response.
Howl relates to desolation; despair; loneliness.
Infer implies forthcoming innuendos; possible new insight.
Inform comes as a guiding message and suggests that the dreamer communicate with a particular individual.
Lisp reveals an inability to verbalize thoughts accurately.
Lobby (persuade) is an attempt to sway one's opinion.
Misquote warns of a lack of concern for accuracy.
Mumble denotes a fear of expressing one's opinion or emotion.
Mutter indicates insecurity; a lack of acceptance.
Nag (bother) may correspond with one's conscience. Recall surrounding dream details for further clarification.
Prattle reveals mental confusion or an obsession with superficial or insubstantial life aspects.
Protest signifies an energetic objection to something.
Quarrel means a disagreement with someone. Sometimes the dreamer will be shown to have an internal conflict (quarreling with oneself).
Quibble portrays a nit-picking attitude; splitting hairs.
Quip usually comes as a smart remark that reveals an important element that one has overlooked or voluntarily refused to acknowledge.
Rant portrays an individual's lack of self-control.
Rave constitutes a state of extremely high emotion. Recall dream details to determine if this was a positive or negative symbol.
Renounce constitutes a denial; a strong rejection.
Reprimand usually comes from one's own subconscious level of conscience to reflect a misdeed or other negative act.
Ridicule indicates a serious lack of understanding. Reveals an unenlightened personality.
Roast (friendly sarcasm) portrays companionable respect; an ability and freedom to speak one's mind and be honest without ill feelings or repercussions.
Scoff represents the expression of an opposing opinion.
Scold illustrates a reprimand.
Slander pertains to vindictiveness; falsehoods.
Swear (cuss) implies an intent to express emphasis.
Swear (vow) signifies personal validation.
Taunt See nag (bother).
Tease often symbolizes one's hidden attitude.
Telegram signifies a personal message for the dreamer.
Vent represents an opportunity to get rid of negative factors in one's life that will ultimately cause harm if retained. This usually refers to negative emotions or attitudes.
Veto comes as a decision-making advisement or suggestion to someone.
Vow stands for a promise; strong intention; a pledge, often to oneself.
Wager See bet.
Whine signifies self-pity.
Wire (send) See telegram.

Encouragement

Backslap usually refers to a congratulatory or friendly gesture.
Cheer connotes encouragement; that which spurs an individual on.
Exalt is a message to remember that all people are equal and nobody should be exalted above another.
Pat (on back) denotes a sign of encouragement.

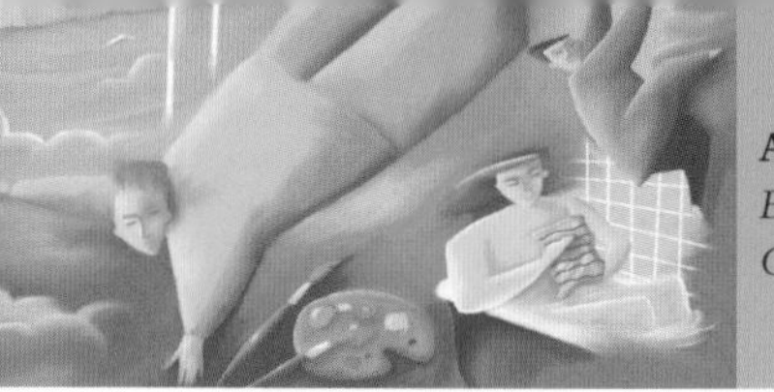

Emotions

Abhor is representative of a hidden aversion or a need to face a fear.
Blanch denotes shocking information.
Blubber (cry and mutter) refers to grief. Could also point to self-pity.
Blush represents embarrassment.
Cringe denotes a personal reaction that may indicate revulsion, fear, disappointment, or dismay.
Flinch relates to a failure to control responses or reactions.
Gasp advises against being caught unaware or off guard.
Giggle stands for inner joy. It may be more revealing to recall what one was giggling over.
Quiver See tremble.
Scream (silent) denotes repressed emotions or unvoiced calls for help.
Seethe warns of a need to release pent-up emotions; need for a cooling-off period; a need for tolerance and acceptance.

Blush illustrates discomfit.

Shiver (tremble) signifies effort to counter a negative element.
Shudder suggests an inner fear and the recognition of it.
Shrug points to indecision or nonchalance.
Sigh typifies disappointment or weariness.
Snicker suggests concealed amusement.
Tremble reveals a loss of control; instability.
Weep reflects sorrow. Recall dream details to find out what this sorrow is associated with.

Death & Decay

Atrophy warns of letting talents go unused.
Cull warns against a tendency to choose only the best of something.
Decay representts a decomposing situation, relationship, or perspective; a rotten element that is long past having positive or productive capabilities.
Die off reminds us of the wisdom of accepting the natural order of life.
Embalm advises of a need to preserve something.
Fester advises one to release pent-up emotions.
Flatline reveals a dead issue; no reason to keep putting energy into it because there's no chance of it being revived.
Putrefy See decay.
Resurrect stands for a renewed interest in something.
Smother See suffocate.
Suffocate reflects a state of perceived smothering. Usually reveals a self-generated condition.
Suicide watch characterizes a recognition and attentive monitoring given to those who have lost their course in life and the strength to persevere.

Creation

Airbrush warns against touching up, changing one's basic ideas to please others.
Carve (wood) suggests the need to make one's own way; express greater individuality.
Crop (trim) means shortened prematurely or an aspect that should not have been altered.
Cutout (paper) represents an element in life that needs to be cut out or stopped.
Decorate (act of) relates to special preparations. What is being decorated? How? With what type of items?
Draw See sketch.
Dye signifies misrepresentations; alterations.
Engrave denotes something that's unalterable.
Etch suggests firm opinions and attitudes.
Festoon defines a joyous state of being.
Forge (mold) connotes a standard that may not be right for everyone.
Gild warns against a personal need to enhance oneself.
Layout will reveal a specific plan to the dreamer.
Makeover pertains to an attempt to change self. This may be a positive or negative message, depending on the dream's surrounding details.
Meld See merger.
Merger is a blending; a bringing together; a compromise.
Paint represents a cover-up of some type being done.
Pasteup See layout.
Photofinishing is a growth through understanding.
Quillwork portrays an attitude of openness in reference to one's inner power or strength.
Scribble symbolizes a lack of mental focus.
Scrimshaw See carve.
Sketch is a trial and error formulation of a new idea.
Trace (draw) cautions against attempting to copy another.
Trim refers to final touches.

Cutting

Bisect suggests an importance to a middle position or path.
Clip (cut off) pertains to a separation; severing; shortening or trimming.
Cut refers to the act of severing something.
Hew refers to personal efforts put forth.
Pierce is differentiated from perforate in that pierce implies a breaking-through event, an advancement, or discovery.
Rip reflects a dysfunction or some form of negative element associated with a life issue. Recall the entire surrounding dreamscape details for clarity. This is usually a quickly recognized symbol for the dreamer to understand.
Sever refers to a cutting off or cutting out of some type of aspect in one's life.
Shear (shave) relates to a desire to clearly comprehend the basics of an idea or concept.
Slash See clear-cutting.
Stab is a symbol containing duality. This could refer to an unexpected retaliation or injury from another, or it might signify an attempt at something.
Tear (rip) See rip.

see also
• Death *p. 118*
• Eating *p. 426*

Eating & Drinking

Binge signifies an excessive personality; overindulgence. People can binge on things other than alcohol. A tirade or bouts of rage could be symbolized as bingeing; an obsession could be implied.
Bottle-feed means forced ideas; thoughts; concepts.
Chew (masticate) suggests a need to give some deep thought to something.
Eating portrays the consumption or absorption of something, usually perceptions or ideas.
Engorged See gorge (eating).
Force-feed warns against forcing opinions or concepts on others. Who was being fed? Who was doing the feeding?
Gnaw is an advisement message to get focused and get to the bottom of something in one's life.
Gobble characterizes a ravenous appetite, usually for information.

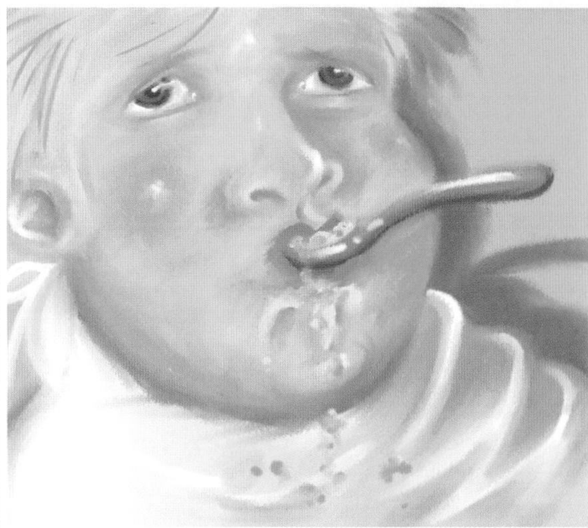

Force-feed cautions of views that are imposed upon others.

Gorge (eating) warns against periods of excessive ingestion. Usually refers to intake of specific information.
Guzzle warns against impatience; inhaling information instead of digesting it with comprehension.
Hand-feed can indicate ideas that are force-fed or it can mean caring enough to ensure another is nourished by certain healing ideas. The related elements to the symbol will clarify which interpretation was intended for the individual dreamer.
Lap (lick up) pertains to an eagerness to obtain or gain something.
Nibble is representative of a manner of taking in new information through discretion (nibbling).
Overfeed signifies the ingestion of too much information. It may also refer to a pushy personality.
Pig-out emphasizes avarice; gluttony; greed. This will rarely refer to the physical act of eating.
Quench relates to information obtained or a goal attained.
Swallow (consume) implies the ingestion of a specific aspect of something.
Swig suggests an ability to accept and deal with disagreeable elements.
Toast (honor) comes as a personal message for each dreamer. Recall who was toasted by whom and what was said.

Destruction

Cast off (discard) refers to that which one disregards; shedding one's relationships, attitudes, or beliefs.
Cave in symbolizes a loss of instinctual reactions or knowledge; some aspect in life that won't turn out as planned.
Deep-six exemplifies a total rejection of something due to spiritual beliefs.
Deface warns against vindictiveness; uncontrolled anger or retaliation.
Delete (computer command) reveals one's capability or option to rid oneself of something. Usually the surrounding dreamscape elements will clarify what this is pointing to.
Dent connotes a life aspect or action that has made a small difference or effect.
Detonate comes as an extreme warning that some aspect in one's life has reached an explosive stage.
Disassemble usually signifies a need to look at the parts of an issue, idea, or situation. It may also refer to a confused state of mind that's scattered.
Discard connotes the act of getting rid of an unusable aspect; a rejection.
Dismantle may indicate a need to take something apart and give it a closer look or it may warn of behavior that will ultimately tear a situation or relationship apart.
Dissolve denotes a changed or terminated life aspect.
Fieldstrip (disassemble) implies preparedness.
Fieldstrip (leaving no trace) advises to be thorough. Leave no trace or loose ends.
Grinder advises of a need to apply greater effort.
Liquidate suggests a need to unload superficial aspects in one's life. This may refer to emotional, mental, spiritual, or materialistic factors.
Mangled See mutilated.
Mutilated refers to the destruction of integrity.
Nick (dent/mark) alludes to a setback or disappointment. May refer to marks of experience gained along the way.
Pulverize See grinder.
Rend (tear) may imply that something has been split apart or denote a defective element such as a belief system.
Shatter refers to a totally destroyed element.
Tear down points out willful destructive behavior.

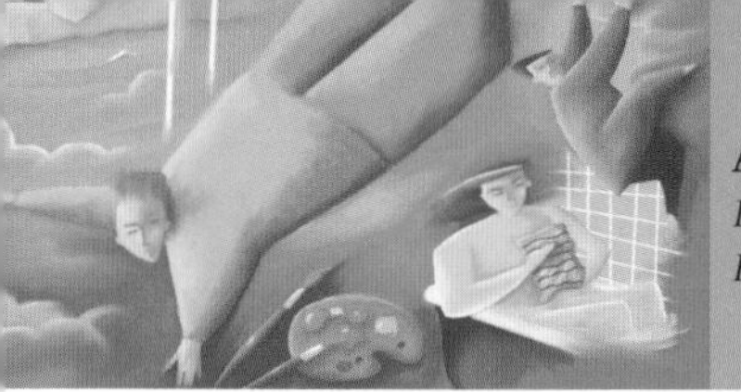

Flying

Airlift is representative of a renewed spark applied to old thoughts and ideas in one's life.
Flying (in plane) pertains to beginning awareness. May indicate spiritual aspects.
Flying (without plane) points to an attained high level of awareness.
Nosedive depicts a headlong immersion into something. This may be a positive or negative symbol, depending on surrounding dreamscape aspects that will clarify the intended meaning.
Tailspin implies total confusion; chasing one's tail.

Exclusion

Annex signifies the need to join something. Could be thoughts, relationships, and so on.
Banish symbolizes an exile type of situation or attitude. What does the dreamer want to get rid of for good? Is the dreamer behaving in a manner that banishes self from something?
Bar (exclude) implies denial or exclusionary attitudes. Who was barred from what?
Blackball denotes negative choices or shutting something out.
Boycott means a demonstrative protest; an active coercion.
Disqualify means an aspect eliminated from one's life. May point to an attitude or perception that isn't relevant. Could even refer to one not qualified to participate.
Expel represents a rejection or denial of a formerly held attitude.

Gathering

Collect stresses the need for gathering something of importance for the dreamer. This may refer to information, emotions, or even the collecting of self, indicating scattered emotions, thoughts, or beliefs.
Gathering (collecting or picking) indicates the act of seeking out and obtaining required specialized information or other aspects vital to one's unique path advancement.
Grab comes to the dreamer as a warning against impulsive behavior.
Hoarding comes to the dreamer as a warning against his or her tendency to selfishness. This dream symbol may also indicate a need to save up for something. The surrounding dream details will clarify this.
Roundup advises one to gather up personal beliefs instead of allowing them to stray far afield or lie fallow.
Woolgathering alludes to daydreaming that may or may not be productive thought, depending on the nature of the surrounding dream details.

Facial Expressions

Beam (facial expression) stands for inner joy; happiness.
Blink implies inattention; a temporary loss of awareness. May point to backing down.
Frown indicates displeasure or sorrow.
Gape (stare) means a reaction of awe or astonishment.
Gawk connotes rude attention that has been given.
Grit (teeth) pertains to negative emotions. May denote stress.
Leering reveals an ulterior motive.
Staring is focused intensity and isn't necessarily negative.
Wink illustrates an unspoken message.
Yawning shows lack of interest and suggests getting motivated for learning and progression.

Fixing & Improving

Cure (harden/set) refers to the temporary state of fragility before something is finalized.
Dovetail characterizes a harmonious relationship.
Fence-mending comes in dreams to advise of the wisdom of mending relationships and correcting any misunderstandings.
Fine-tune represents an attempt to make something as good as it can be or the last, final improvements.
Fix (mend/repair) reflects a desire to correct or repair a situation or relationship.
Hone implies a sharpening aspect in one's life; something that brings a factor into finer definition or proficiency.
Inflate emphasizes something blown up, out of proportion; exaggerations and embellishments.
Recondition suggests a repair or renovation of an element in life; a current state of further usefulness or viability.
Reconstitute signifies a rejuvenation or a reimplementation of an element in one's life.
Refinishing exemplifies a desire to improve something; efforts to make something better.
Refurbish See refinishing.
Regenerated See reconstitute.
Repair See fix (mend/repair).
Retouch pertains to final details and the attention given to same. May point to an intent to alter something.
Retrofit suggests a need to revise one's perceptions by including new experiential or evidenced elements.
Rewire is a strong advisement to examine one's psychological processes and make correct connections.
Splice signifies an attempt to join aspects; a bond or linkage.
Tie (fasten) pertains to tying up loose ends.
Touch-up relates to an improvement; an effort to bring completion or wholeness.
Tune-up stands for a need to make internal adjustments and suggests a perception or attitude that's out of alignment or in need of tweaking.
Unclog typifies the act of ridding oneself of a confusing issue or relationship; reaching the solution to a problem.
Welding connotes an attempt to make strong connections.

see also
• Hands & Arms *p. 105*
• The Flight *p. 300*

Falling

Drop (fall from grasp) shows the need to get a handle or grip on something.
Falling exemplifies one's fear of failure or the unknown; a lack of self-confidence.
Falling down means a misstep; a failed attempt that one needs to get up and recover from.
Free-fall represents the loss of one's grounding as aspects. May also indicate a headlong dive into an issue, situation, or relationship.
Stumbling depicts an attempt to find one's way; an unsure course.
Trip (stumble) is representative of a temporary setback that may serve contrarily to provide a beneficial element to one's life.

Fire

Blaze See fire.
Burn (clothing) connotes a ridding of an individual's outward affectations; a change in persona.
Burn (hair) indicates forgetfulness, which is perhaps due to a conscious desire to be rid of certain memories. It can therefore refer to the destruction of thoughts, perspectives, or attitudes.
Burn (incinerate) means a total destruction of something.
Cauterize advises of the need to heal a wound; a closure is required.
Finger (burned) signifies interference into another's affairs.
Fire means emotional intensity.
Fire drill is the importance of emotional control; preparedness to face the unexpected.
Scorch means too much pressure or heat brought to bear upon something.
Sear See burn (incinerate).
Singe See scorch.

Failure

Defeat may apply to a winning situation or a losing one, depending on other aspects of the dream. Either way, it reminds one to act the same way—accepting the outcome without the expression of pride or jealousy.
Failure signifies a call for acceptance and perseverance; a message to make further attempts at something.
Flounder warns of spiritual faltering or vacillation.
Flunk is representative of a failure of some type in the dreamer's life.

Indecision

Fence-sitting is representative of indecision.
Oscillating (motion) comes to denote instability; a continual variation.
Straddle usually applies to indecision. May indicate a desire to remain neutral.
Swaying suggests a tendency to change mind; indecision.

Hand & Arm Movements

Pinch stands for attracting attention.

Beckon almost always applies to a draw or inclination toward something.
Clasp signifies holding onto something; keeping a connection going.
Clench depicts a need to grasp something; act of holding on.
Clutch See clench.
Feeling (tactile motion) connotes a cautious approach.
Finger (raising) symbolizes a cautionary advisement.
Grope alludes to a lack of direction.
Handclasp represents a unifying force.
Handle (touch) means getting the feel for something.
Handshake portrays good intentions.
Handspring relates to a sudden burst of joy or excitement.
Handstand depicts elation; extreme happiness.
Hand-wringing defines worry; lack of acceptance. Many times this will point to one's ploy for gaining sympathy.
High-five represents elation; success.
Kneading indicates time and effort given to something in one's life.
Knocking usually is an attention-getting message. This means one needs to give more notice or serious attention to something in life that has previously been ignored.
Paddling (discipline) See spanking.
Pat (on head) implies a patronizing response.
Pinch usually represents an attention-getting sign.
Point (finger) indicates an accusation or serves as a directional motion to draw one's attention to something. Recall surrounding dream details to determine what was intended.
Poke (jab) either comes as an attention-getting symbol or it signifies a testing type of inquisitiveness.
Pushing warns of a forcing action in life. This indicates a need to gain more acceptance and stop attempting to push things before their time.
Rubbing (skin) has several meanings depending on the dream's related elements. Rubbing the skin may indicate an act of soothing, being bothered by an irritation, or ridding self of a distasteful or negative factor by attempting to debride it.
Salute defines an acknowledgment of another; respect; recognition.
Seize is most often an advisement to grasp an opportunity while one can.
Shove usually represents a type of motivational push.
Spanking most often suggests a wrongdoing for which one should make reparations.
Squeezing signifies pressure.
Thumb-sucking denotes immaturity; being clueless.
Wave (greeting) pertains to an acknowledgment given to another person.

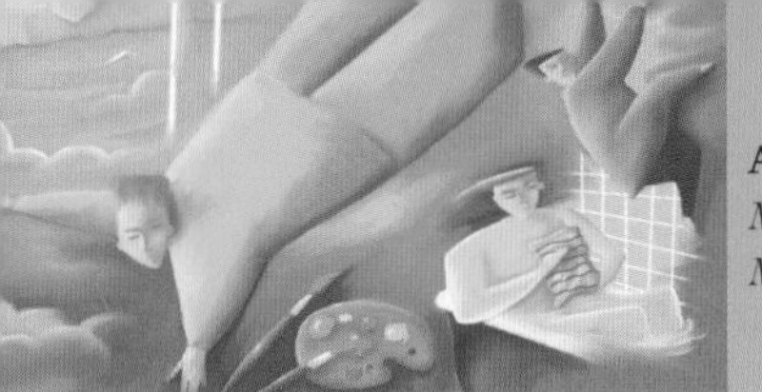

Meeting & Greeting

Bow (greeting) is usually representative of an act of respect. It may also refer to a concession.
Cold call stands for the sudden introduction of a completely new issue into one's life; an issue or situation that came without warning.
Curtsy See bow (greeting).
Drop in characterizes the unexpected in life.
House call pertains to an extension of one's generosity in regard to giving service to others.
Kowtowing may be representative of respect or it may indicate a state of subjugation.

Information Handling

Abridge symbolizes a need to curtail or shorten something. May also be pointing to an individual's habit of cluttering the issue with minor, insignificant details.
Authenticate characterizes verification.
Blue pencil refers to a need to make some type of correction.
Cross fencing represents the act of keeping issues separate from each other; an attempt to keep individual issues from affecting or contaminating one another.
Cross-reference advises of a need to check out some aspects to determine the facts.
Decode(r) means comprehension; clarity of understanding.
Deprogramming is a strong advisement to counteract some negative aspect in an individual's life.
Document (verify) pertains to proof of something; a validation.
Download implies the gaining of information from another.
Extrapolate comes as a caution against attempts to extend one's knowledge for the sake of others.
File (claim) implies an act of exposing or making something public.

Blue pencil points out an error.

Research signifies an individual's need to obtain greater knowledge or information about a specific issue.
Scan represents the need to go over or review something.
Scroll See scan.
Skim (read) See scan.
Tabulate advises an individual to gather up all elements of an aspect and analyze it in a concise manner.
Uninstall points to a dropped belief. May also be associated with a character quality or such elements as lost faith or acceptance.
Upload is representative of one's transmission of thoughts to another. It may also refer to one's expressed attitude or perspective.

Movement in Water

Dive signifies a headlong plunge into something.
Dive (into water) pertains to a plunging into spiritual concepts.
Sidestroke is representative of the fact that one is traveling one's spiritual path and only seeing half of what's there to learn from.
Sinking is a reference to the beginnings of failure or sense of defeat.
Skinny-dipping means an intent to immerse oneself in spiritual concepts; a joyful desire to gain spiritual knowledge.
Swimming symbolizes a submersion in an individual's spiritual search.

Lawbreaking

Bait and switch comes to the dreamer as a warning against being taken in through deceit or false promises; ulterior motives; unethical practices.
Bribe means ill-gotten favors, benefits, or goals.
Clip (swindle) means the act of taking advantage of another; ulterior motives.
Debauchery warns against a tendency to focus on the physical aspects of life, especially sensual pleasures.
Embezzle warns against taking or claiming something that belongs to another.
Frame-up warns of deception. May mean a scapegoat.
Hot-wire typifies an individual's attempt to advance without having the prerequisite learning experience or knowledge (key).
Joyride comes to the dreamer as a warning about carelessness; a lack of personal responsibility. Sometimes this symbol points to an actual joyful time.
Kidnap warns against desire to own another or another's idea.
Misdeal alludes to deceit.
Pillage reveals a lack of overall respect for self or others. This indicates a total disregard for authority and order.
Plunder See pillage.
Shoplift See steal.
Steal reveals an unwillingness to expend efforts toward goals; impatience.

Looking

Gander implies self-imposed ignorance; willful or feigned ignorance.
Look behind reveals insecurity or paranoia. May point to distrust.
Look down implies defeat or embarrassment.
Look in denotes in-depth thought or deeper curiosity.
Look out means awareness.
Look over means discernment.
Look past is representative of an individual with a far-reaching perspective.
Look under symbolizes perceptual depth.
Look up signifies acceptance and progression.
Rubberneck applies to the act of exhibiting unrestrained interest or curiosity.
Squint relates to an effort to see something better.

see also
• Swimming & Water Sports *p. 210*
• Criminality *p. 323*

Mental Activity

Apprehend denotes catching or taking hold of something important.
Brood (deep in thought) cautions against a tendency to dwell on specific aspects without productive results.
Calibrate connotes a striving for perfection.
Contemplation advises one to give deeper thought to something.
Daydream pertains to personal, private thoughts, often expressing unrealistic scenarios or desires. This may point to a veering from reality; escapism. On the other hand, this symbol can also refer to one's mental probing for possibilities existing outside the box.
Dream (hope) implies strong aspirations or optimism.
Dream (imagine) connotes wishful thinking.
Estimate represents approximations, that which cannot be pinpointed or predicted as an absolute.
Fathom connotes puzzlement in one's life. Most often, this is a spiritual type of puzzlement.
Guess reveals a lack of knowledge or information; an assumption.
Learning will validate an individual's inner questioning as to whether or not one is progressing or acquiring additional knowledge. This symbol comes to denote an affirmative answer.
Meditation advises one to be passive. This comes when one has been too active in something, perhaps being too intrusive in another's affairs or diligent to the point of being obsessive.
Memorizing stands for a need to learn or remember something important.
Mull (think something over) See contemplation.
Musing See contemplation.
Perusing See reading.
Quiz centers on questions the dreamer needs to ask self.
Reading correlates to the attainment of information. The key here is to recall what was being read.
Recall usually doesn't imply one's memory but rather it denotes a need to revive a forgotten element in one's life.
Recant points to a denial; changing one's mind.
Reckoning advises of the wisdom to balance one's behavior or character; to appraise one's past deeds and attitudes.
Recollect See remembering.
Remembering illustrates a need to recall a specific event or conversation to gain further clarity.
Reminiscing pertains to a state of nostalgia; the pleasure derived from retrospection.
Romanticizing reveals an inability to perceive reality without attributing overly optimistic or emotionally sensitive qualities to it.
Self-examination stands for a need to analyze one's perspective or behavior.
Speed-reading corresponds with a caution to absorb more of what one attempts to learn. This is suggesting that the dreamer is missing something along the way.
Train (teach) cautions against indoctrination; being formed into a particular mold.

Obscuring

Baffles signify a thwarted aspect in life. It warns that something may not succeed.
Blind (hunting) warns against a tendency to hide one's true intentions. May indicate underhandedness; vindictiveness; a hidden agenda; ulterior motives.
Blindfold represents confusion; being misled.
Blur denotes a need for more clear understanding.
Smudge (to clear) signifies an attempt to maintain clarity and rid oneself or others of negativity.

Retreating

Backpedal means retreat; going backward; a possible retraction required.
Backsliding warns of slipping back; a loss of forward movement or progression.
Backtrack stresses the need for an individual to return to the beginning of a path.
Breakout (escape) signifies a form of retreat or freedom; distancing from something; extraction of oneself from a negative element; perhaps overcoming something.
Capitulate means giving in; a surrender of some type. This dream symbol usually comes as an action advisement when a situation is futile.
Drop out exemplifies the act of withdrawing from something. This symbol may come as an advisement to do so or as a prompting to stay with it and keep going.
Escape advises of a way out of something.
Fall back may be representative of a forced move made to step back to get a better perspective of a particular issue.
Recoil points to a knee-jerk response.
Regression is an indication of a backward direction. Recall the dream's surrounding details for more clarity.
Relapse won't always indicate a negative element in a dream, for it may come to remind an individual that, sometimes, progression is accomplished only by taking a step or two backward.
Retrace advises one to look at something again, closer this time. May imply a need to retrace one's steps.
Rewind (audio/video) applies to going back to the start, but not necessarily replaying the same information. This may advise of a need to retrace steps back to the beginning and go down another trail.
Stand-down applies to a withdrawal; a relaxing of immediate plans.
Surrendering usually comes as an advisement to accept more rather than having expectations or attempting to force results.
Trail (drop back) may not be the negative symbol it initially appears to be, for frequently one needs to drop back to get a better perspective of what's ahead.

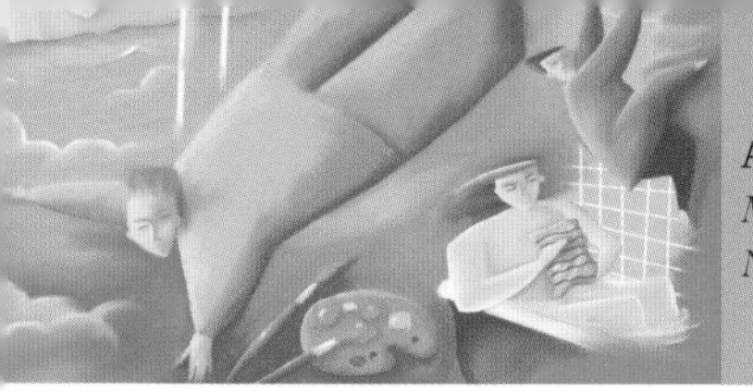

Motion & Exercise

Bounce indicates a suggestion to be more resilient.

Caper refers to those unnecessary aspects that one believes are important; a self-generated need for more interesting and exciting aspects.

Charge (race forward) means a committed intention backed by an urgency to carry it out. May point to impatience or impulsiveness.

Chase symbolizes going after something; pursuit.

Climbing symbolizes an upward or forward striving.

Crawling means a slow pace and may not come to infer a negative intent.

Descending (directional motion) implies a downward or lowering move and could refer to several aspects in one's life, depending on surrounding associative symbols.

Dive (through air) refers to plunging through thoughts; not taking the time to analyze quickly formed opinions; impulsive judgments.

Drag (pull along) may refer to perseverance. It may warn against a tendency to brood or complain about problems.

Flex (muscles) denotes a challenge.

Footwork connotes how one reacts to events and opportunities encountered along life's diverse pathways.

Forward advises one to refrain from stopping one's path walk; of a need to continue going.

Gallop means bounding speed; a fast-paced advancement.

Grand march symbolizes vanity; fatuousness.

Headstand indicates the act of doing everything one can (even standing on one's head) to accomplish something.

High-stepping advises against a tendency to be drawn to the fast life.

Hobble reveals perseverance. See limp.

Hotfoot advises of a need to slow down.

Jumping implies impatience with one's path progression or advancement.

Kicking calls for acceptance. Denotes impatience or lack of self-control.

Knee bends portray an individual's continual efforts applied to staying resilient.

Knee-jerk (reaction) symbolizes a first impression; uncontrolled responses.

Kneeling suggests a state of subjugation.

Leaping implies rapid progression; making great strides in advancement. May also suggest a need to slow down to stop missing important elements that require notice or actual attention.

Limp (hobble) comes to denote perseverance.

Lope characterizes a steady progression or advancement.

Marching alludes to strength of belief. Recall who was marching and the manner of marching. Proud? Weary?

Pacing interprets into anxiety or worry. This symbol comes to underscore the futility of such mental exertion; more acceptance is needed.

Panting symbolizes overexertion or anxiety regarding high expectation. Indicates a need for acceptance.

Prancing illustrates a lighthearted mood; true contentment or acceptance.

Rambling represents a shiftless nature; lack of direction or motivation.

Roaming usually indicates a seeking for what feels right.

Rove See roaming.

Running reveals an attempt to escape or catch up, depending on the dream's related details.

Sashay comes to signify a carefree attitude.

Scale See climbing.

Shuffle (feet) applies to a defeated attitude. May imply weariness.

Sit-ups signify an advisement for one to gain greater tolerance—gut fortitude.

Skidding warns of a loss of control.

Skipping suggests joy, yet may also pertain to indifference.

Streak (run naked) pertains to an unexpected event or something presented for its shock value. May even mean a personal wake-up call.

Stretching suggests reaching farther; expanding one's mind or perception of possibilities.

Strut (stride) exposes arrogance or overconfidence.

Swagger usually refers to an overly confident attitude; overly self-assured.

Tiptoe suggests proceeding with caution.

Waddle signifies a personal burden; great weight carried.

Wading stands for testing spiritual waters and getting one's feet wet with new spiritual issues.

Walking connotes progression.

Walking (on air) symbolizes the qualities of acceptance and centeredness that come with spiritual joy.

Walking (on water) reveals spiritual arrogance.

Walkout applies to defending ethics; standing up for beliefs.

Walk-through stands for an attempt to familiarize oneself with an issue or element.

Negative Actions

Abjure See forswear.

Bad rap denotes the perception of negativity regarding an innocent element or individual.

Blacklist represents prejudice; censure.

Blame reminds us to double-check our thoughts and actions. This may not apply directly to the dreamer but to another person.

Critique stands for personal assessment; judging through one's personal perspectives.

Disavow stands for a disclaimer of responsibility or prior knowledge. It may also refer to repudiation.

Discount (disregard) means a choice to not believe or accept something.

Disinherit warns against the decision to leave nothing behind. We should all make a difference through our life.

Disrobe alludes to a removal of all extraneous aspects of self; honesty; the real self.

Forswear connotes denials.

Hairsplitting indicates faultfinding; pettiness.

Peck (pick at) implies a lack of acceptance; irritable responses.

Revenge shows lack of spiritual enlightenment and attainment of acceptance in life.

see also
• Sleeping Disorders *p. 108*
• Gymnastics & Body building *p. 211*

Relaxing

Leaning (angled stance) reveals a slanted perspective; nonchalance or indifference.
Sitting may indicate a lax attitude. This symbol may come as an advisement to take time out.
Slouching may be an indication of weariness or laziness depending on the dream's surrounding details.
Snuggling (alone under the covers or with a teddy bear) suggests feelings of insecurity or fear.
Watching television reveals the quality and state of one's perspectives. A cartoon represents immaturity; news represents keeping current with daily events, and so on. The key is what one is watching.

Sleeping

Doze illustrates a restful pause, often needed to refresh self. This could come as an advisement to stay more aware.
Nap (sleep) indicates a need for rejuvenating respite. This may sometimes advise one to stop sleeping on the job.
Nodding off either denotes a need for respite from overwork or it points to an inability to remain aware due to disinterest or boredom.
Oversleep indicates unawareness; inattention. This element comes as a serious warning to wake up! Be aware!
Sleeping correlates with unawareness, possibly by one's own choice.
Snooze See nap (sleep).
Snoring advises that one isn't getting solid rest. Indicates a need to improve the quality of respite periods. May warn of an inner restlessness.

Joining & Splitting Up

Abdicate denotes a need to leave something alone, or admit it's time to let another take over the reins.
Affiliate will point to an individual, group, or perspective the dreamer shares an affinity with.
Aggregate defines a need to consider the whole instead of focusing on the separate parts.
Assimilate refers to the need to take in that which is important; to understand. It may also come as a caution to be a better listener.
Bond (fasten) signifies a connection in one's life.
Breakup shows the separation of a specific life aspect. This may be promising, because it could point to a new freedom or independence.
Collate advises one to give detailed attention to the orderly integration of facts.
Combine connotes a blending or mixing of something in the dreamer's life.
Disband means a separation from associates.
Enlist suggests a need to join something, perhaps be an activist for a specific issue or to openly express a belief.
Enroll See register (enroll).
Fall out shows a possible future disassociation from someone in the dreamer's life. May also represent destructive ramifications from a confrontation or a particular behavior.
Falling out underscores the fact that one has had a considerable disagreement with another, but the relationship can recover if both parties aren't stubborn.
Fusion emphasizes a need to incorporate several different aspects into a centrally focused issue. This will be specific to each dreamer.
Matchup represents comparable, nearly equal skills or levels of development.
Merger refers to a blending of elements; a bringing together; a compromise.
Register (enroll) stands for the signing up or voluntary participation in a new venture.
Rematch may advise of a need to recommunicate with someone or attempt a second effort to achieve something.

Search & Selection

Appoint is representative of a chosen position. It may also be indicative of an arrogant attitude.
Browse pertains to selectiveness. It may also refer to looking for specifics.
Draw (select) pertains to choices in life. May point to the fact that some things just happen in life and aren't connected to karma or luck.
Earmark emphasizes to the dreamer a distinctive characteristic or something that has been set aside for a specific purpose; something that is allocated.
Foraging pertains to efforts actively applied to taking advantage of every benefit, trial, and opportunity presented in life.
Handpicking means personal choice or decision.
Pick (choose) corresponds with a specific choice one made or is contemplating.
Pinpoint will define the current existence of something in one's life that may not have been recognized. This is usually a good symbol that gives hope.
Prospecting represents a search of some kind.
Pursuit usually represents a personal quest of some type. If it depicts an actual chasing pursuit, the surrounding details need to be factored in. Who was pursuing whom or what? Were there weapons involved? Was the pursuit public or stealthy?
Ransack corresponds with a thorough search. This may not indicate a negative reference.
Rifle (search through) may not imply a negative connotation but rather this symbol usually comes as an advisement to search through one's own possessions, meaning motives and behavioral responses.
Searching is representative of a desire or need for specific information.
Track (follow) refers to a search.
Unearth corresponds to the exposure of something; a new aspect come to light.
Wild-goose chase signifies an unproductive effort.

Miscellaneous

Abolish denotes a warning to get rid of something in one's life. May refer to an attitude, perspective, or relationship.
Acclimatize indicates the need to accept situations, or take a wait-and-see position.
Adjudicate advises of a need for an individual to make a legal or public statement; a personal type of disclosure.
Admonishment is always a strong warning symbol.
Aggrandize is a serious caution against boastfulness. May be stressing a warning against placing an ideal or individual on a pedestal.
Aim reflects a goal, purpose, or chosen course in life.
Airdrop connotes the dropping of ideas. This symbol could come as an advisement to drop false or damaging perspectives and attitudes.
Allay refers to a need for one to be rid of fears of the problematic aspects to life.
Appease suggests that a compromise is needed.
Ascending always indicates one's advancement; a rise to higher standards.
Autograph relates to someone important to the dreamer. Can also refer to the act of leaving one's mark on another's life.
Backfill signifies a life element capable of filling a void in one's life.
Backfire indicates repercussions; something not working out according to plans.
Backhoe denotes a need to dig back for more information.
Backwash refers to an aftermath in turmoil; spiritual truths coming back at a reluctant individual.
Bail (eject) warns against staying in a situation; it's literally time to bail out.
Barb implies hurting, sharp aspects in life.
Barhopping shows restlessness.
Bask connotes voluntary absorption of something; a pleasurable time of rejoicing in happiness or well-being.
Body slam represents a severe emotional blow or reaction.
Bore (drill) implies perseverance; pushing forward.
Bounce light refers to an effort to soften the harshness of something.
Brand (cattle) denotes possession; the exclusive owner; originator; titleholder.
Break in (tame) refers to a need to become acclimated or tone down a wild idea or behavior.
Break in (wear down) advises one to reach a comfortable point or position; take the stiffness out of something; become more familiar and comfortable with something.
Breakthrough means a great advancement or realization has been accomplished.
Bucking See buck (kick).
Burying (act of) stands for cover-ups; secrets; hiding something. May also indicate intentions to forget and forgive, yet nothing worth burying can really ever be forgotten. Can mean denial.
Cater means the act of waiting on or serving another person; subservience.
Cease-fire obviously means to stop fighting or maintaining an ongoing disagreement.
Charge (energize) illustrates a strong motivation; excitement.
Chugging (stilting steps) shows determination; moving forward despite difficulties.
Clinging warns of a need to let go of something or someone.
Clog (obstruction) warns of a life factor that requires immediate attention (clearing) before further advancement can occur.
Coasting warns of a downward path; sliding downward.
Compromise shows the need to make some concessions in life.
Confiscate implies a need to retrieve or seize something.
Countdown cautions of a need to keep an eye on the time. Warns of a situation where time may be running out.
Counterbalance connotes an action or response that offsets another or one that serves as a balancing factor.
Counting (act of) advises of a need to take stock of something; there is imperative reason to count blessings or opportunities.
Counting to ten refers to an attempt to gain patience.
Crack (attempt) advises one to proceed in spite of doubts or fear of failure.
Crack (to solve) means a resolution is forthcoming.
Crave implies an inner weakness of some type.
Crisis management comes to advise of a need to control one's reaction to stressors.
Cross-matching implies an attempt to seek compatibility. This may not refer to the obvious aspect of one's relationship with another but could indicate the search for belief systems that feel right for oneself.
Crossover pertains to appropriate crossing points along one's life path.
Crouching symbolizes insecurities; poor self-image.
Crowd illustrates wide appeal; an attention-getting aspect.
Curl (hair) pertains to an analytic thought process.
Dabble represents a lack of seriousness. May indicate part-time interest in something.
Damage control refers to the need to counter a negative.
Dare refers to intimidations; challenges.
Debriefing denotes the wisdom of conducting frequent mental self-examinations. We learn from ourselves when we spend time double-checking our motives, responses, perspectives, and actions.
Default stands for a life aspect one has failed to follow through with. Could indicate a falling back to old ways.

Sewing

Backstitch cautions of the need to make amends from the past.
Baste (sew) refers to a temporary pulling together of some aspect in the dreamer's life; a makeshift repair until further attention can be given.
Cross-stitch alludes to precision and the need to give it attention.
Patch (repair) symbolizes a temporary solution.

see also
• Pranks *p. 140*
• Riches *p. 190*

Miscellaneous (continued)

Defuse depicts a need to halt further progression toward an explosive situation, relationship, or belief.

Discarnate refers to a hidden life aspect.

Disembody See discarnate.

Disengage alludes to an act of releasing something; a break from a life aspect.

Dismount refers to a return to congeniality. Warns against arrogance.

Eloping connotes strong individuality.

Ever-bearing points to an element, behavior, or characteristic that will produce ongoing benefits or positive ramifications.

Fizz signifies activity, usually one that is mental.

Flail reflects a tendency for one to blame others, strike out, or retaliate.

Float See meander.

Flutter implies perplexity.

Flyby pertains to a need for close observance of something in the dreamer's life.

Foretell See prediction.

Free-for-all points to a situation in which the participants are getting out of control.

Fumigation symbolizes full-blown measures to take care of a problem.

Glaring (brightness) is an advisement against jumping to conclusions.

Glow (light) suggests some type of radiance; resplendence.

Grovel alludes to a lack of self-respect and inner strength.

Hand delivery points to a desire to be assured a communication has been made.

Handoff applies to an exchange being done; passing of information or benefits.

Hardscrabble characterizes perseverance in the face of adversity; advancing despite little to work with.

Harness represents control and/or containment.

Hit (inhale) indicates a need for additional support; utilizing an assisting aspect.

Holdout characterizes a determined opinion or attitude.

Homecoming applies to a return to one's roots; beginnings.

Horseplay denotes lighthearted pranks; a practical joke.

Hotdogging warns of spiritual irresponsibility.

Hot flash pertains to a sudden flash of inspiration, what people prefer to call a power surge.

Import pertains to new ideas.

Impregnate rarely pertains to sexual intercourse. This symbol alludes to one's success at getting through to another for the purpose of helping in some way.

Jackknife indicates impatience.

Jiggle suggests an unstable condition.

Jolt denotes a call to attention and sharper awareness. The dreamer is missing something important in life.

Knockdown refers to a destructive event or action. May point to a temporary setback.

Lamination implies a need to preserve something important.

Liftoff denotes an activated beginning.

Lurking indicates a stealthy nature; underhandedness.

Meander means an aimless spiritual path.

Milling points to an effort to reshape or redefine something.

Barb refers to life's painful aspects.

Mince signifies a halting manner or progression.

Misdial depicts a situation where one gives information to the wrong party.

Misfire usually advises of a blessing that kept one from making a mistake or serious error in judgment.

Moving See relocation.

Near miss denotes off-center or unfocused direction; a path that will lead off-course.

Nudge symbolizes a push from one's higher self.

Online shopping suggests ultimate convenience for obtaining one's needs. This usually points to a reminder that certain things are more easily attained or accomplished than one realizes.

Ooze (exude) will indicate an element one can no longer contain or hide.

Open (position) denotes a state of affairs. This may indicate an individual's need to close something, such as one's mouth or wallet. It may also refer to information that allows the dreamer to see how open something is.

Overflow emphasizes a state of abundance. Recall what was overflowing. Did it have color? Consistency? From what was it flowing?

Overhang suggests a protective shield, covering.

Overlap suggests full-coverage; making sure there are no loose ends.

Overlay may reveal an ulterior motive or it could represent a protective layer of defensiveness. Recall surrounding dream details for clarification.

Overlook (scenic) indicates a need for a wider view of an issue. Something is literally being overlooked.

Override suggests an idea or plan superseded by another.

Overshadow stands for something or someone not given proper attention because another aspect or person is more prominent or noticeable. May be an implication that one is vying for position, or a suffocating or demanding situation is manifesting.

Overshoot means that one's goal or target was closer than one thought.

Overspend represents an overextension of oneself.

Overstep symbolizes an attempt to step over the line or cross limits. This is a message from an individual's higher self or conscience.

Packing up suggests a forthcoming move. This may not refer to physical relocation but may relate to an employment move or a situational one.

Palpate symbolizes the act of giving deeper inspection or attention to an issue.

Parry relates to a defensive position or action taken.

Pass (move past) may suggest something missed in life or it may indicate an element that doesn't require attention.

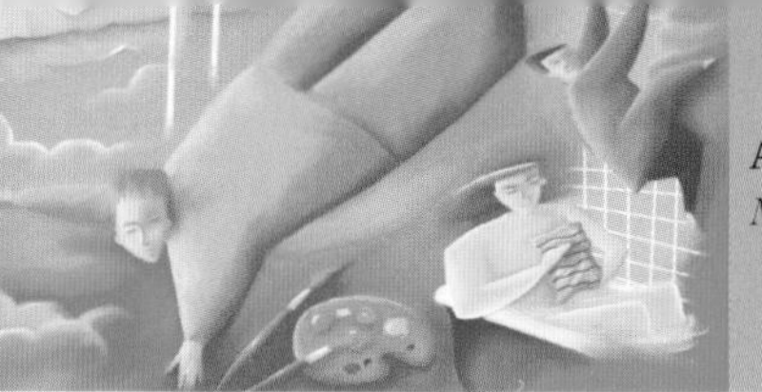

Miscellaneous (continued)

Pass (sanction) will reveal an acceptance or agreement of something one is planning.

Pass (succeed) indicates a stage or goal that has been accomplished.

Patrol pertains to watchfulness; an acute awareness.

Peel (face) signifies a desire to keep one's public persona as honest as possible.

Pep rally stands for an effort to build enthusiasm for a specific event.

Pickup (person) stands for someone who was helped along the way.

Pillory denotes guilt and self-reproach. This symbol suggests that one shouldn't be too hard on oneself.

Placate denotes an effort to soothe or ease a troublesome situation or mood.

Playback connotes something one needs to listen to again, hear what one said, or how it was said.

Pledge indicates a promise. Recall what was promised. To whom was the promise made? To oneself?

Plucking comes to symbolize resourcefulness.

Point (phase) emphasizes attention or focus on a particular phase of one's life or path.

Point (verge) corresponds to an individual's need to make an important decision.

Pool relates to one's quality and quantity of goodness; level of humanitarian interaction with others.

Pounce warns of an unexpected aspect; a surprise revelation.

Prediction may in fact come as an actual event.

Premix is a reference to having all the necessary elements (ingredients) to develop or accomplish a goal.

Press (squeeze) reflects quality rest time; tranquility.

Press (straighten) advises of a need to straighten out a relationship, perception, or situation in one's life.

Pump implies motivation; that which serves as an impetus.

Purring signifies contentedness; satisfaction.

Put-down stands for a taunting attitude that may be generating from oneself.

Put off can pertain to disgust, yet it most often symbolizes the act of putting something off; procrastination.

Qualify indicates a need to prove one's skill or knowledge.

Quest stands for a major goal in one's life.

Question comes in a dream to pose a self-discovery element. Points to an issue or element that one hasn't considered.

Queue implies that one is not alone; there are many others in the same situation.

Quick draw suggests a tendency to jump to conclusions.

Quick fix shows a temporary solution; a stopgap move.

Quick-freeze signifies an immediate halt to something, perhaps a sudden denial or rejection.

Quit may come in dreams as an advisement to quit something or it may reveal one who is behaving like a quitter.

Raid portrays the possibility of being discovered or caught at something.

Rebound denotes a return or backlash effect.

Recycling stands for a life aspect's multiple uses; personal resourcefulness.

Reissue will usually relate to a popular idea or life aspect.

Rekindle exemplifies new life brought into an aspect of an individual's life.

Reload (ammunition) stands for a reluctance to give something up; a doggedness.

Reneging warns against ignoring promises made.

Reorganizing denotes an adjustment in priorities.

Replenishing pertains to a current bountiful state; a desire to maintain full potential or level of energy.

Repression connotes a self-generated state of limiting controls. May point to denial.

Reprisal warns against vindictiveness and vengefulness.

Reschedule advises of a more effective time to execute an effort or attempt an activity.

Resume stands for a need to honestly review one's accomplishments and goals. This may show a gap in an area of experiential knowledge.

Resurface (appear again) exemplifies a spiritual concept or other element that has come back into one's life.

Retch is an attempt to rid self of a disagreeable situation or other life element. May reveal a lack of acceptance or evince psychological escapism.

Retool implies a time to utilize a new set of plans and associated aids. This may refer to one's behavior or perspective.

Retrace advises one to look at something again, closer this time. May indicate a need to retrace one's steps.

Revere cautions an individual against excessive admiration or worship of anyone but the divine essence.

Ricochet denotes an event that will produce multiple effects. Also may point to something that failed to make its target.

Roughhousing typifies an advisement to release pent-up emotions and/or stress.

Run-through suggests a trial effort or a need to review all angles of a plan.

Sacrifice may indicate actual awake-state sacrifices one makes for the attainment of spiritual goals or it may have a negative connotation that warns of a potentially dangerous direction or intent.

Safari (hunting) represents a life path that follows that of another in which innocent victims are harmed along the way; a ruthlessness.

Safekeeping stands for efforts expended toward preserving or cherishing something.

Sagging comes to reveal some type of weakness or weakened condition.

Salvage (operation) connotes an attempt to save and restore something that would otherwise be lost.

Sample pertains to foreknowledge, knowing what one is getting into.

Sanction equates to permission. May indicate a behavior aligned with one's higher self—one's conscience.

Sandblasting pertains to an effort to get down to basics; discover the basic, foundational facts or issues.

Scatter pertains to a loss of essential elements.

see also
• Recreational Drugs *p. 117*
• Weapon Terminology *p. 353*

Miscellaneous (continued)

Score (drugs/points) stands for the obtaining of a goal.
Scrabble (grope) reflects an uncontrolled progression; lack of planning.
Scratch test (for genuineness) represents a watchfulness for imitations.
Scrawl indicates a communication made in haste.
Self-sacrifice stands for placing others before self; an ability to resist life elements that one knows will be self-defeating or a detriment to goals.
Self-service represents a call to help self instead of depending on others.
Send-off reflects an expression of encouragement and support. In some cases, a dreamscape send-off can refer to something the dreamer needs to get rid of.
Sharing portrays selflessness.
Sharpen See hone.
Shell (bombard) constitutes an inundation.
Shift (action) signifies an altered perspective, attitude, or pace. Also may literally refer to transmission.
Shore leave symbolizes a break from one's spiritual search that will provide contemplative time or a required period of respite.
Shunt means an intentional diversion; a setting aside for a time.
Shuttle illustrates intermediate paths and/or directions in life.
Sideways (movement) usually connotes a move to avoid something; an elusive tactic.
Sift means extensive research.
Sight-reading points to acute perception and lightning responses.
Signing in represents one's readiness to actively participate in something; an intent to expend energy.
Signing off/out signifies one's intention to leave something; one has chosen not to expend more energy on an issue.
Signing up denotes joining something. This may or may not be willingly. The key here is to recall what one was signing up for.
Sit-down expresses an active difference of opinion; a protest. May also point to efforts put into resolving a disagreement or conflict.
Skim (remove) indicates the act of selective choosing.
Skipping rocks refers to spiritual inattention; a lack of focus on one's spiritual behavior.
Smell applies to the act of testing; discernment.
Sniff See smell.
Snowmaking connotes the act of bringing one's personal spiritual beliefs into every aspect of life, which may be a negative act depending on this dream's related details.
Snuff (extinguish) portrays a desire to bring something to an end; a closure.
Sounding corresponds to a probing attempt; a method of discovery.
Spot zoning represents favoritism; showing preference. May point to an activity that is out of the ordinary.
Squash (crush) refers to the act of ending something abruptly.
Squirm implies an uncomfortable situation.
Stagger indicates one's need for support; unsteadiness.
Stampede warns against losing self-control and personal direction. Refers to the use of emotionalism rather than one's intellect.
Standby relates to preparedness; readiness. May point to something one is most comfortable with.
Stand-in indicates a capable replacement or alternative.
Standing shows an adherence to one's convictions.
Steep (soak) is thoroughness.
Steer (guide) connotes directional control. Each individual needs to steer oneself along her or his own life path.
Stifling cautions of a repressive element or situation.
Stoke implies a need to rekindle some aspect in one's life. Usually the dreamer will be aware of the individual intent for this symbol.
Straw vote denotes an interest in the opinions of others.
Strikeout denotes unsuccessful attempts.
Strikeover signifies an indifference toward one's mistakes; no attempt made to cover them correctly.
Struggle usually defines an internal conflict; a lack of acceptance.
Subdue is a reference to the act tempering an individual's overemotionalism.
Substantiate signifies some type of verification.
Surge connotes a sudden increase in activity, energy, or interest.
Tail (follow) means a personal interest taken in someone.
Tampering warns of an alteration; intent to change the integrity of something.
Trip (set off) cautions one against expending too much energy or efforts on a specific issue; an overload is about to happen.
Trolling comes as a warning against accepting spiritual debris.
Try on (clothing) See dressing room.
Tryout stands for an attempt to test or gauge one's attained level of development. It may also point to a check on one's path progression.
Twinkling refers to the sparkle that accompanies enlightened insights.
Undercut reflects the act of undermining; attempting to better another.
Undulating (motion) suggests progression; self-motivation.
Unload comes as an advisement for self-analysis. Suggests a need to express oneself.
Unmasking symbolizes a need to accurately perceive others; seeing with clarity and through another's facade; getting rid of that which one hides behind.
Unpacking signifies the act of looking at different aspects. May indicate a need to unload or unburden oneself.
Unscrewing reflects a lessening of stress and pressure in an individual's life.
Wassail implies festive attitudes; goodwill.
Wind up stands for determined motivation; efforts spent on re-energizing oneself.
Wrap-up represents the concluding efforts that have been applied to a project or goal.

Chapter 12

Fame, Fortune & Finance

These elements are associated with blessings and one's means for achieving a life goal or bringing a project to fruition.

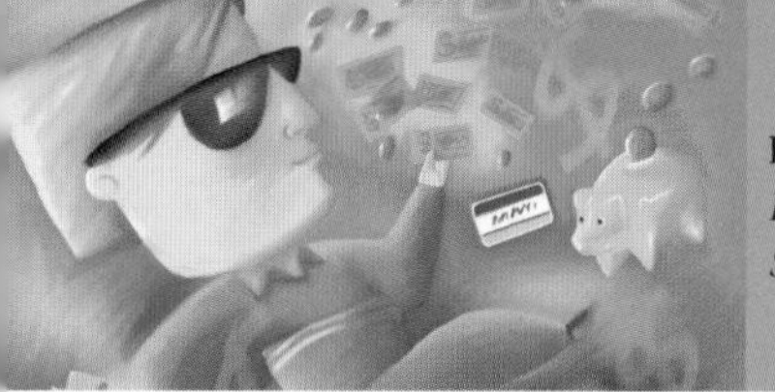

Fame

Ace means an agreeable outcome; a winning situation.
All-star reflects an idea that is composed of the best elements.
Bed of roses signifies a prime, most desirable situation.
Bejeweled means self-aggrandizement; perceiving oneself as brilliant and full of great worth.
Big league pertains to the highest level; aspects holding the power.
Big ticket stands for costly in the way of energy or emotions expended.
Byline denotes an acknowledgment; giving credit where credit is due.
Credit line (of article) See byline.
Destiny exemplifies life aspects that cannot be altered.
Diva points to a woman who excels in her specialty and is usually admired for such attainment.
Eulogy reminds us to focus on another's good points instead of any negative characteristics.
Fame usually comes as a precognitive symbol.
Glory See fame.
Headliner signifies the main event or attraction.
Idol corresponds to whom or what one overly admires or is fascinated. This gives a clear look into one's priorities and level of advancement, for no human or material object should be idolized.
Prestige pertains to personal distinction or stature among one's peers. This symbol may reveal a perceptual level the dreamer was unaware of or it may indicate a caution to stop inflating one's self-image.
Superstar is a representation of great potential. The key here is to discern how this potential is used.
Title role stands for the main person involved in an issue or situation.
Urban legend is a reference to a common belief that a relatively small group of people hold.
World famous symbolizes an individual, concept, or situation that is familiar to people everywhere.

Idol cautions against excessive admiration of people or objects.

Recognition

Limelight may imply self-importance.

Curtain call denotes appreciation for one's shared talents.
Front page reflects priority; a place of importance; something to take note of.
Hero worship warns against an obsessive admiration of another. Advises of a need to follow one's personal path.
Limelight may reveal a superior attitude or it may point out someone to whom one should listen. The surrounding dream details will clarify the meaning of this symbol.
Ovation comes as a sign of recognition or personal commendation from one's higher self.
Praise correlates with recognition of personal efforts applied to one's life path by a person's higher self or spiritual forces.
Public eye refers to open exposure.
Red carpet implies superiority or inferiority, depending on the dream's associated factors.
Spotlight points out and reveals important aspects for the dreamer to give attention to.
Status symbol reveals self-absorption; a desire to possess prime material goods. This dream symbol exposes a person who judges an individual's worth or success by what one owns.
Track record denotes experiential validation.
Tribute denotes an acknowledgment; recognition.

Standards

Gilt-edged (pages) connotes an advisement to note the high quality of value.
Guarantee marks verification; reassurance.
Hallmark exemplifies a sign of approval.
High-end (product) usually indicates higher quality or expense, yet it may also refer to a tendency to go for the most expensive brand name for the purpose of bolstering one's ego.
Hope chest relates to one's dreams and aspirations.
Hope Diamond applies to an individual's high hopes in regard to achieving goals.
Luxury doesn't necessarily refer to physical pleasure or material riches; it frequently relates to the inner feeling of comfort stemming from spiritual or moral fiber.
Public opinion represents the attitude of the majority of the general public. This symbol may be a call to stick to one's own opinion if it differs from many others.
Top dollar denotes something that will demand the greatest cost to obtain. This cost won't be in the form of money but will usually relate to other life elements such as emotional costs.

see also
• Movers & Shakers *p. 142*
• Cinema & Film *p. 221*

Performance Assessment

Accolades come as praise.
Applause sign reveals insincere expressions of appreciation; forced responses.
Encore represents a need to repeat something. The surrounding dreamscape facets should clarify what this is.
Endorsement applies to an individual's personal approval of something.
Evaluation suggests a need for self-examination in respect to one's actions, beliefs, motives, or attitudes.
First class defines optimum quality or mode of operation.
Five-star (rating) defines the highest quality.
Flying colors signifies a sense of achievement; success; an overwhelming triumph.
Four-star (rating) represents excellence.
High-grade is superior quality.
Red ribbon actually represents a second place position, so as a dream symbol it indicates high accomplishment.
Second-rate suggests a slightly inferior element.
Small-time applies to a minor aspect, of little importance.
Third class represents a commonality; less importance.
Third-rate symbolizes an acceptable yet undesirable element or position.
World-class means outstanding performance or skill.

Five-star signifies the best.

Social Position

A-list pertains to those people thought to be a specific field's cream of the crop.
Crème de la crème stands for the best manifestation of something; highest standard. It also refers to the most desired element.
Head table is representative of the fact that one has achieved a position of great importance.
High profile advises of high visibility. This is a cautionary symbol that reminds that one is being observed by others; behavior is rarely private.
Inner circle indicates privileged information and those who perceive themselves as having a right to it.
Jet set characterizes misplaced priorities.
Receiving line reveals those who claim alliance with another. The key word here is *claim* and may not necessarily indicate a true attitude or position.
Retinue infers a belief that an individual requires a support group in attendance.
Top-drawer refers to a rating of excellence.
Upscale characterizes an improvement.

Honors

Honorable mention constitutes a commendation from one's higher self.
Honorarium warns against expecting recompense for gifts voluntarily shared.
Honor roll is recognition for hard work and achievement.
Honor system reminds one to behave in an honest and trustworthy manner even when no one is watching.

Awards

Award most often exemplifies commendations from higher sources. It may refer to a recognition of personal achievements.
Bonus points imply the accumulation of good karma.
Booby prize is indicative of a forthcoming benefit or reward.
Bronze star is representative of a recognition for one's perseverance in life.
Commendation is a portrayal of approval.
Consolation prize shows that benefits are derived from the act of participation alone.
Demerit connotes negative behavior or karmic debt.
Door prize indicates extra benefits gained by taking opportunities.
Emeritus (title) will reveal one who retains the honor and respect of others.
Emmy (award) is a warning message. No one in life should receive an award for acting. This is an advisement to start being yourself.
Gold medal portrays the highest achievement attainable.
Gold record signifies recognition for accomplishment.
Gold star signifies recognition of superior efforts expended.
Grammy (award) relates to receiving recognition.
Hall of Fame is representative of someone's narrowly perceived greatness.
Merit badge refers to the recognition of accomplishments. The refining element with this symbol is if the dream presented it as a commendation or as a caution to not wear one's accomplishments for the purpose of boasting.
Nobel nominee points to recognition for great efforts applied and resulting successes.
Nobel prize pertains to recognition by higher forces for efforts expended toward others. Symbolizes a great achievement.
Pulitzer prize reveals a prime accomplishment and recognition for it.
Purple Heart characterizes recognition for one's service to others; courage and bravery.
Tie (winners) signify equal skill, talent, or knowledge. May apply to a caution against competitiveness.
Triple Crown stands for three main aspects to a goal, issue, or situation that need to be attained or hurdled for success.
Trophy (award) comes as a sign of accomplishment and serves as motivational encouragement to keep striving.

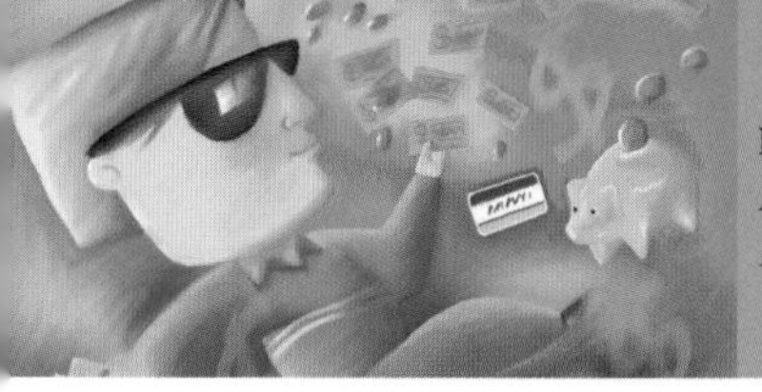

Monetary Terms

Golden handcuffs define bribery; manipulation; an attempt to snag one in a Catch-22 situation.
Golden handshake stands for an incentive to quit something.
Golden parachute represents a measure taken to protect oneself against a loss of beneficial aspects; assurance of being well compensated.
Gravy boat signifies a life aspect that has the capability of providing an easier course.
Gray market refers to a slightly unethical way of accomplishing something; in the same vein as telling a little white lie.
Grubstake denotes ulterior motives behind the assistance one gives another.
Hard cash symbolizes immediately available means to accomplish something.
High life warns against having misplaced priorities or a shift in what one places importance on.
Hot seat pertains to a situation where one is deeply involved in an undesirable position.
Inflation (economic) usually comes in a dream to advise the dreamer that he or she is expending too much energy on something.
Kickback warns against expecting recompense or monetary benefit from service given or efforts expended.
Midas touch alludes to a record of success; an individual's ability to conclude efforts in a positive manner.
Nickel-and-dime denotes an insignificant amount that has the potential of growing into an impressive volume.
Payola connotes misdeeds and misplaced priorities. Indicates one who would do anything for money; bribery.
Plow back means a covering-up act or behavior; an attempt to bury; possibly denial.
Poor farm/house stands for an inability to externalize one's inner wealth; withholding one's humanitarianism.
Pot of gold (at rainbow's end) stands for unrealistic goals; chasing after dreams or targets that will only prove illusory in the end.
Rate of exchange suggests the fact that people perceive differing values of things.

Financial Status

Affluent comes to signify earthly wealth.
Bankrupt denotes one who is wealthy yet remains devoid of spiritual assets; a miser. May also indicate a literally penniless individual; apathy.
Billionaire exemplifies great personal monetary wealth and the spiritual responsibility to help others.
Breadline denotes a lack of necessities or livelihood elements. This may indicate one's basic moral, emotional, or spiritual aspects.
Breadwinner characterizes one who supplies necessities; one who does the work.
Break-even point suggests a time or phase when one's applied energies are about to pay off and show progression.
Deep pockets imply a current status of considerable wealth. This may not mean financial aspects but may refer to a wealth of knowledge, information, blessings, talents, etc.

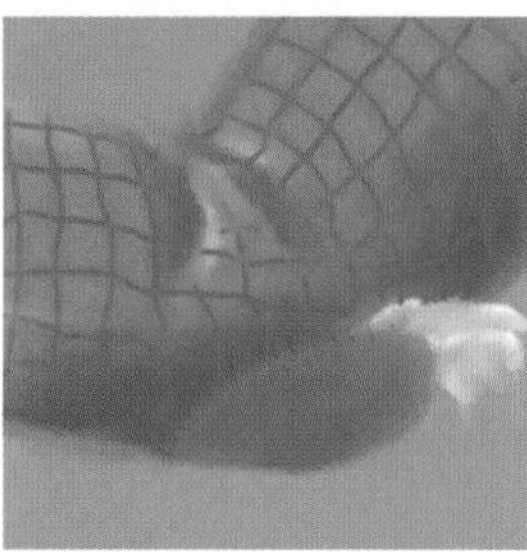

Poverty points to character defects.

Destitution means a complete lack of basic foundations.
Dirt-poor may not refer to a monetary connotation but rather emotional and spiritual riches that are lacking.
Disadvantaged applies to a lack of a basic need or quality.
Easy street defines a desire for an easier life. May point out a phase that is less stressful and things will go right for a time.
Executive privilege denotes one's right to privacy. This may not equate to secrecy but relates more to the idea of one not having to divulge everything to everyone.
Hand-to-mouth connotes a time of great tribulation; desperation; lean times that one must get past. This difficult phase won't always be associated with finances but may refer to a time when one is going through a stage of lean spiritual behavior, such as apathetic feelings.
High roller characterizes an individual who has a tendency to take great risks.
Impoverished usually won't imply a financial meaning but rather will address one's emotional or mental aspects.
Jobless may indicate a push toward being more productive or it may suggest a need to rest a while. The dream's surrounding details will clarify which interpretation is meant.
Lean times mean a phase when things are more difficult.
Nouveau riche warns against an attitude of arrogance regarding one's possessions, material wealth, or talent gifts. Points out a great responsibility in regard to how one's wealth is managed generously.
Penniless will generally not refer to monetary aspects but rather comes to emphasize the value of humanitarian or spiritual riches.
Poor usually is a reference to the condition of a specific element in an individual's life rather than denoting a monetary aspect.
Poverty usually represents some type of character quality that's lacking. Also see poor.
Rich (wealth) See money.
Spendthrift connotes efficiency; foresight.
Super rich identifies those with the greatest amount of assets, thereby revealing those who should have the greatest spiritual responsibility to help others.
Wage earner points to one who puts out personal effort to supply needs.

see also
• Math *p. 234*
• Finance & Insurance *p. 259*

Money

Black money represents hidden assets; secret wealth.
Empty moneybag connotes poverty.
Face value implies initially perceived value of something; value without anything extraneous associated with it.
Found money implies a sudden realization of one's talents or blessings.
Front money stands for an individual's intent; a life aspect that reinforces a greater measure of confidence.
Full moneybag portrays an abundance.
Gold is representative of physical wealth.
Hard money stands for cash-in-hand; assets that are available to work with.
Mad money corresponds with extra assets not designated for necessities. This usually refers to assets available for long-shot possibilities.
Mint (money) denotes a high value on something.
Mint mark refers to an originating source.
Money stands for riches; wealth.
Moneybag symbolizes a quantity of wealth.
Money roll indicates abundance of personal assets. These may refer to monetary, mental, or emotional wealth. It will not signify a spiritual factor.
Money tree pertains to riches gifted to another.
Newly minted money represents new or forthcoming wealth.
Old money signifies inherent talents meant to be freely used to benefit others.
Paper money is representative of opportunities to share wealth.
Petty cash depicts one's current supply of available resources. Usually refers to personal talents or abilities.
Pin money represents the reserve resources that one keeps handy in the event one has need of them.
Play money suggests an unrealistic perception of value. Perhaps a reference to excessive spending habits.
Pocket money indicates a state of readiness; a tendency to maintain provisional elements in one's life.
Rare money signifies an exceptional form of wealth one needs to fully utilize for the benefit of others.
Seed money stands for an abundance of talent reserved for a specific purpose; a readiness to begin a certain objective.
Silver denotes spiritual wealth.
Small change comes to represent insignificance.
Torn moneybag is a situation where an individual is allowing some form of wealth to waste away. It may point to excessive spending or a loss of understanding of the value of one's wealth.
Uncirculated money comes as a warning against being miserly with one's talents.

Currency

Buck (money) See money.
Coin is representative of the rarely recognized opportunities that come one's way or the blessings one rarely counts in everyday life.
Coin counter is a symbol that advises us to count our blessings.
Coin purse denotes a recognition and appreciation of an individual's gifts.
Coin sorter suggests a need to differentiate the various values of multiple benefits and blessings that we're continually being touched by.
Coin wrapper represents saving opportunities. This indicates appreciation of their value.
Currency See money.
Dime represents basic needs; life necessities.
Dollar See money.

Ingot represents a preoccupation with wealth and goods.

Gold coin is representative of a valuable aspect in one's life. This symbol will usually point to the high value of something else to the dreamer; a sign of value.
Half-dollar depicts a starting point; all is not lost.
Ingot is representative of materialism as being one's priority in life.
Nickel (coin) connotes the presence of a means that has the capability of gaining power to accomplish a goal in one's life.
Penny See money.
Quarter (coin) See money.
Silver dollar is representative of honesty.
Two cents implies a worthless aspect; not worth one's time or energy.

Riches

Black bag points to ill-gotten riches. These riches could relate to aspects in life other than money.
Bonanza suggests a great find of some type; coming across something that has been searched for.
Booty illustrates that which has been obtained through stealth or manipulation.
Bounty means a reward for something accomplished.
Bullion See gold or silver.
Buried treasure denotes true value that is rarely identified as such. An example would be spiritual generosity when one helps another without an expectation of payment. Unconditional goodness is a buried treasure few perceive as having great value.
Cash pertains to genuineness; having the resources one claims to have.
Cash box refers to the safety of one's liquid assets. May indicate hoarding.
Cash cow suggests any element that provides ongoing benefits.
Cash crop characterizes an individual's personal efforts to support self; a successful means to an end.
Charmed life indicates an appearance of good fortune.
Chest (treasure) See treasure chest.
Cold cash refers to immediately available assets. These may be in the form of money, emotional support, virtues, means of assisting others, etc.
Community chest symbolizes one's reserves of generosity; one's ability to share or give to others.
Dime bag stands for a cheap form of temporary escapism.
Dollar sign defines some type of beneficial effect. May also indicate a cost or expense for the dreamer. Surrounding dreamscape elements will clarify this.
Dowry designates bought aspects. This could refer to friendships, benefits, favors, employment, loyalty, etc.
High finance doesn't necessarily refer to money. Rather, it usually alludes to a difficult or complex situation in one's life that warrants careful consideration and planning.
Ransom represents the price of attainment for certain desires or goals.
Treasure signifies a personally perceived boon.
Treasure chest represents the expected or awaited-for boon. The key with this symbol is to recall if the chest was full or empty. What was in it?
Treasure hunt characterizes expectation.
Treasure island usually implies a dreamer; not willing to work for one's goals.
Wad represents an amount or measurement implying a considerable quantity.
Wealth usually relates to inherent, natural abilities; will denote monetary connotations if presented as gold.

Assets

Asset represents all that has value in the dreamer's life.
Equity stands for the accumulated value one has earned from efforts expended.
Estate connotes the whole of one's assets. This may be all-inclusive of the four aspects of life: emotional, mental, physical, and spiritual.

Banking

Bank (financial) pertains to that which one saves or values as being highly meaningful; personal riches.
Bankbook characterizes an individual's personal wealth. Is all the money hoarded or withdrawn to help others?
Bank card signifies one's right to aspects in life that would be considered personal assets.
Bank deposit signifies an effort to accumulate reserves. This can relate to any element in an individual's life and related dream details will clarify what was intended.
Bank draft See certified check.
Bankroll (money roll) portrays personal wealth. This symbol may indicate generosity, depending on the surrounding dreamscape details.
Bank statement suggests a reconciliation between how one thinks one is doing in life regarding behavior and how one is actually performing.
Bank transactions indicate how well riches (talents) are managed and utilized.
Blank check stands for unlimited resources or opportunities.
Cancelled check represents verification; proof of what one expended in the form of energy or resources.
Cashier's check alludes to guarantees; a secured aspect.
Certified check means solid facts; guaranteed aspect.
Charge-back signifies a mistaken benefit, one which turns out to be a debit.
Charge card alludes to impatience; lack of priorities.
Checkbook represents one's personal distribution of assets; where one utilizes abilities.
Clearinghouse indicates a need to sort out issues or feelings.
Debit points to a deficiency in some area. The surrounding dreamscape elements will help to clarify what the intent is here.
Debit card refers to an easy access into debt. This may not be indicating finances but be pointing to some other type of indebtedness.
Deposit (money account) portrays asset accumulation. This will refer to finances unless silver was deposited.
Direct deposit signifies the quickest way to receive a return on one's efforts.
Draft (money) refers to solid intentions.
Electronic banking suggests a more efficient method of managing one's talents.
Money order is an assurance that an asset or benefit is positive and valid.
Passbook See bankbook.
Postal order See money order.
Rubber check is a groundless or empty factor in one's life.
Standing order defines a manner of behavior that is practiced until some element alters its effectiveness.
Wire transfer (funds) refers to the passing of benefits to another.

see also
• Information Handling *p. 176*
• Taxation & Finance *p. 328*

Capital

Controlling interest is usually representative of the one with the greatest input and having the most to lose.

Slush fund portrays reserve resources.

Venture capital exemplifies one element in association with preparing for a goal or new course; reserves backing a new beginning.

Working capital stands for the talents and personal qualities one has. This dream symbol will rarely relate to a monetary aspect.

Savings

Honey pot symbolizes the origin of an abundance of gifts.

Hoard warns against selfishness. May also indicate a need to save up something. The surrounding dream details will clarify this.

Honey pot stands for the source of great multiple benefits. Also see mother lode.

Loot refers to a multitude of valuables. Surrounding dream details will show whether or not this symbol was positive.

Lump sum is an abundance of something the dreamer will recognize.

Mother lode means the most bountiful source of something.

Nest egg symbolizes preparedness; efficient planning.

Piggy bank indicates immature goals. May also point to the value of appreciating every benefit or blessing that may be overlooked because it appears too insignificant.

Savings account See bankbook.

Savings bond portrays foresight; an opportunity.

Silver certificate represents a highly valuable aspect in one's life; a rarity.

Stockpile could advise one to stop hoarding and share with others. This depends on what was shown to be stockpiled in the dream. Also see storage.

Storage means preparedness.

Taxation

Audit (tax) denotes suspected transgressions committed; a call to maintain honesty.

Duty-free pertains to life aspects that bring extra benefits.

Estate tax indicates that someone is taking something from you that they've no right to have.

Income tax exemplifies required payments or dues. This usually connotes a karmic aspect.

Inheritance tax denotes strings attached to a benefit, gift, or windfall.

IRS implies benefits that haven't been personally earned.

Luxury tax reminds us that some types of nonessentials can carry hidden costs.

Property tax implies a price attached to ownership; dues for what one has. These dues will not refer to a monetary aspect.

Revenue stamp serves as a verification that one performed an obligation or certain responsibility.

Sales tax pertains to a hidden cost to something obtained.

Tariff represents a cost attached to the exercising of one's skills or talents.

Tax represents an additional responsibility or debt.

Tax credit suggests that a break is being given; an unexpected return on an individual's efforts.

Tax deduction represents a benefit; a counter to the outlay of efforts expended.

Tax-exempt stands for a release of a specific responsibility; something having no strings attached.

Tax-free signifies a full benefit that doesn't carry an additional cost.

Tax haven denotes a way to keep more of one's resources without having to disburse it to others.

Tax refund Because tax refunds have to be claimed on the following year's return, this symbol points to a false benefit, a benefit with a future cost involved.

Tax return represents an individual's finances. May portray one's assets.

Tax shelter indicates an attempt to avoid responsibility and debts owed.

Treasury department exemplifies the source of an individual's assets, meaning inherent talents and qualities.

Duty-free is representative of life's unexpected bonuses.

Credit

Credit implies an assumption of one's good character; a certain level of confidence.
Credit bureau represents a record of one's life activities. Frequently refers to the book of life or one's personal karmic record.
Credit card relates to a life aspect that allows one to obtain something in advance of one's readiness to reciprocate or pay back. This dreamscape symbol may also refer to the good points on one's karmic record—one's good credits.
Credit hour indicates learning or knowledge acquired or needed. May also be associated with the acknowledgment of efforts applied to a goal.
Credit line (monetary) indicates the amount of leeway one has before it's time to answer for one's actions. This dream fragment can also refer to one's life span.
Creditor usually pertains to those to whom one owes a karmic debt.
Credit rating comes to the dreamer to signify an individual's level of trustworthiness and his or her attention to personal responsibility.
Credit report stands for an overview of how well one is managing one's affairs.
Credit risk comes in a dream to reveal the level of one's integrity toward following through with responsibilities.
Credit score refers to opinions based on personal perspectives. Usually refers to opinionated, class distinction.
Credit union refers to an opportunity.
Creditworthiness underscores one's high trust and confidence, or the lack of the same.
Finance company illustrates a life factor that serves to provide a means to a goal.
Letter of credit reveals one's level of responsibility. Was the letter a good or bad report?
Line of credit See credit line (monetary).

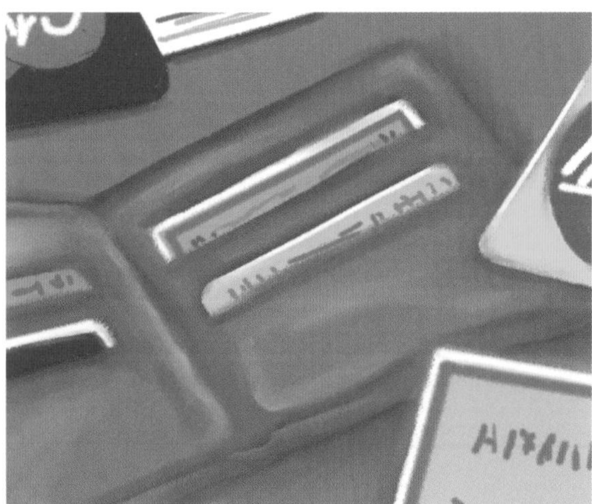

Credit card may relate to the amount of good karma one has accumulated.

Financial Fortunes

Accrual comes to the dreamer as a warning of the need for further knowledge to be gained.
Accumulation usually is an indication of excesses. This may denote an emotional buildup, or reveal one's extraneous elements connected to a specific issue.
Depreciation advises of something that has reached a state of lessening value.
Depression (economic) forewarns of a need to watch finances.
Shortfall suggests something that was overrated or held in expectations that were unrealistic; disappointment.

Security

Alarm system (bank) is representative of one's finances. Depending on surrounding dreamscape elements, this symbol comes as either a warning signal that brings attention to a developing financial problem, or it signifies successful financial safeguards that are in place.
Fort Knox defines a situation, relationship, or opportunity that has the possibility of bringing great rewards or benefits.
Safe alludes to an element in an individual's life that provides personal security of some type.
Safe-deposit box stands for a need to keep something from being lost, damaged, or adversely affected by negatives.
Security deposit represents a promise or a safeguard against the possibility of a negative event happening.
Till (cash drawer) connotes reserves.
Vault (bank/safe) signifies worth; that which one values. Was the dreamscape vault full of something?

Accounts & Accounting

Account represents the balance of payments (karma) in an individual's life.
Accounts receivable/payable reminds us of our personal balance sheet and reveals debts owed and/or repayments received. Debts will be issues one still needs to resolve or rectify. The repayments will be those already taken care of.
Balance sheet refers to one's karmic record.
Bill stands for a debt that comes due. It may also mean something that will end up needing recompense for.
Bottom line signifies the point of something. It may also refer to the bare facts.
Budget cautions against the practice of disproportionate activities. Suggests a need to prioritize; long-term foresight and planning.
Profit and loss (statement) suggests an individual's need to look at his or her life balance sheet as far as behavior goes.

see also
• Sales *p. 257*
• Intelligence & Security *p. 327*

Stocks & Shares

Bear market stands for a financial decline; a drain on (or waning of) one's energies or fortitude.
Blue chip portrays preferred spiritual beliefs or behaviors. This may be a negative element if connected to fads or current popularity.
Blue ribbon pertains to praise; recognition.
Bond (monetary) applies to a need for security; an element of security in one's life.
Bull market implies a solid or improving financial condition.
Dividend pertains to benefits gained from energy expended.
Fortune 500 characterizes those with the greatest measure of wealth and the heaviest burden of responsibility.
Gift certificate characterizes unconditional assistance from another.

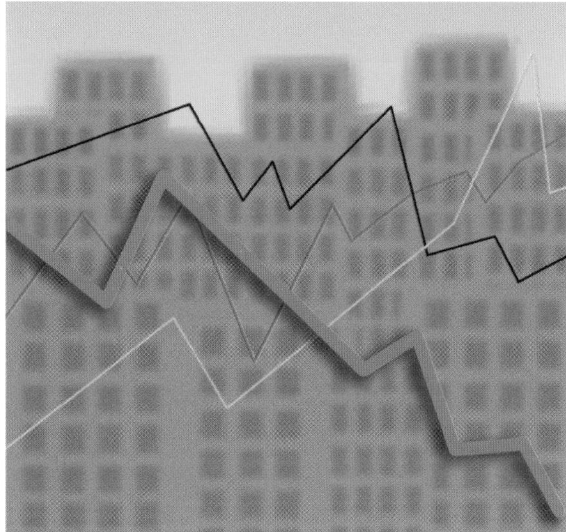

Stock market refers to financial matters that cannot be relied upon.

Investing doesn't usually refer to finances but rather what one is accepting as truth and into which one is placing all one's energy.
Junk bond comes as a warning of a high risk.
Mill bond points to additional funds or energy needed to achieve something.
Preferred stock indicates a priority.
Return on investment identifies a situation whereby an individual's efforts were either beneficial or detrimental (gain, neutral, or loss).
Securities and Exchange Commission stands for the maintaining of integrity.
Shareholder indicates those who have contributed toward something and have invested their resources and confidence.
Stock See stock certificate.
Stock certificate relates to a personal interest (stake) in something.
Stock exchange signifies great stress in one's life.
Stock market See Wall Street.
Wall Street indicates economic elements that may not be solid or dependable.

Insurance & Compensation

Accident insurance See insurance.
Annuity represents good karma returning.
Claim (insurance) See insurance claim.
Compensation depicts a return for something; amends; balance or counterbalance. May refer to an unexpected benefit from having to accept an alternative.
Compensatory damages relate to retribution; payback.
Damage deposit symbolizes the recognition of possibilities.
Death benefit relates to life aspects associated with a finalization of something; aspects that result from a conclusion.
Disability insurance represents preplanning or provisions made regarding the ensuring of one's continuing path progression in the event of a misstep/mishap.
Earthquake insurance stands for foresight; an individual's belief in possibilities.
Flood insurance stands for an individual's spiritual preparedness; an open mind in respect to spiritual possibilities; a guard against spiritual overload or inundation.
Health insurance denotes self-doubt; a lack of faith in one's own healing abilities.
Insurance implies protective measures. If a great amount of insurance was shown, that means a lack of faith.
Insurance claim stands for a benefit reaped from one's protective methods or an injurious event.
Life insurance advises of a state of fear; a lack of faith.
Medicaid stands for a means of assistance that has questionable elements.
Medicare applies to a dependence on others to protect you against future negative aspects.
Mutual fund means speculation.
Recompense means a compensation or reimbursement.
Replacement cost refers to the current value of something and the cost it would entail to replace it if it were lost or damaged. This usually refers to a relationship.
Term insurance refers to a phase of protective coverage that has a time limit.
Title insurance points to a clean history; an element having no negatives associated with it.
Unemployment compensation signifies a benefit gained from a time period when one isn't actively applying oneself. This usually refers to the need for rest and a distancing from stressful elements.
Uninsured correlates to high confidence.
Workers' compensation portrays benefits or alternative aspects that enter an individual's life while temporarily unable to proceed along one's chosen course or path.

Buying

Bulk rate illustrates getting something done more efficiently.

Acquisition signifies something added to one's life. Could point out a new perspective or a new relationship.
Affordable indicates an element that's well within one's reach to obtain or attain without expending much energy.
Bargain will emphasize a good plan or course.
Base price usually signifies the very least amount of cost something will mean for us. This cost won't be monetary but rather an expending of one's emotional involvement or energies.
Bulk rate signifies a more cost-effective way of accomplishing something; a way to achieve a goal through the output of less energy.
Buyback denotes a change of mind; getting something back that one lost or even gave away.
Buy-down signifies unloading a larger aspect in exchange for a smaller one. This is usually a positive dreamscape symbol.
Buyer's market pertains to the best time to take advantage of specific opportunities.
Buyout connotes an acquisition of the whole; obtaining something in its entirety; having it all. Who is doing the buyout in the dream? The dreamer, or someone else?
Cash discount stands for benefits gained by one's resourcefulness.
Layaway plan signifies impatience. It may relate to working for what one wants in life.
Purchasing power reveals the quantity of one's personal assets. These will not be monetary but rather humanitarian elements.

Refund

Rebate signifies benefits that have been gained through efforts applied.
Refund pertains to a return benefit.
Reimbursement See refund.
Resale value characterizes the extended long-term value of an action or communication.

Selling

Asking price stands for a negotiable issue, one having leeway.
Assessed value signifies one's individual perception of worth that may or may not be accurate.
Best seller means that which is most popular; aspects having a great draw. This dreamscape element reveals a common interest held by a large group of people and can be a gauge for determining that group's level of spiritual, philosophical, or ethical advance while on a path's journey.
Book value denotes the true value of something.
Capital gain represents an increase in return for personal efforts expended.
Cash-out refers to a decision to reap immediate benefits from a positive aspect that could be held for a longer period of time.
Closing costs refer to the final efforts or resources that are required to conclude an issue or reach a goal.
Closing date (mortgage loan) signifies a time to shoot for in regard to achieving something.
Commission (sales) points to rewards for energies that have been expended.
Consignment store (charity store/thrift store) refers to a possible source from which to receive benefits.
Cost-cutting stands for an attempt to preserve resources or energies.
Fair market value signifies that one's opinion/attitude is a generally correct one.
For-profit cautions against a tendency toward self-interest as an individual's prime motivational force.
For sale by owner denotes the choice to accomplish a goal without the aid of others.
Off-brand represents a cheaper alternative; a substitute that may work just as well as one demanding more energy output.
Package deal signifies multiple benefits rolled into one.
Premium illustrates a specific type of benefit an individual gains from participating in a specialized activity.
Prime rate stands for the idea that those with the best record of showing they've been responsible with assets get the best opportunities or breaks.
Prime time points to the most productive time or phase to achieve optimum effectiveness.
Proof of purchase stands for verification of an action taken.
Receipt stands for evidence or proof.
Sales slip See receipt.
Secondhand defines a useable element or idea.
Seller's market symbolizes lack of opportunities; few choices.
Selling point connotes a convincing aspect; an attractive element.
Wholesale represents a deal; getting something for less cost to oneself.

see also
• Trade *p. 169*
• Property Law *p. 331*

Payments

Advance (payment) symbolizes responsibility; trust and faith.
Arrears reflects an overdue communication; time to get caught up on something.
Deposit (initial payment) marks firm intentions.
Deposit (security) pertains to some type of assurance given; a promise; an insuring factor.
Down payment denotes proof of intent; good intentions.
Installment (payment) connotes balancing one's karmic debts.
Money order connotes guaranteed payment; an assurance that an asset or benefit is a positive and valid one.
Stop payment (order) means a sudden change in plans.

Debt

Debt is most often representative of a nonfinancial aspect in one's life. However, it can still relate to actual monetary conditions.
Debt consolidation represents an active interest and attempt to repay all debts; a desire to make retribution.
Debt counseling indicates an interest in getting assistance and advice for repaying one's debts. This dream fragment may be pointing to life aspects other than financial.
Deficit indicates an inadequate aspect in one's life. The dreamer will usually know what this aspect is.
Deficit spending indicates overwork; possibly putting the cart before the horse.
Garnishment (monetary) signifies a forced payment or collection of an individual's debt to another.
Grace period refers to a time extension given.
Insolvency won't normally equate to finances but rather refer to a quality in which one has become bankrupt.
NASDAQ relates to a source of specific information that may be valuable to the dreamer.
Sharecropper characterizes the expending of efforts for the good of the whole.
Skid row is a situation or issue in which one is now derelict.
Squalor won't necessarily stand for a physical condition but rather it usually pertains to an individual's state of mind or set of ethics.
Sweat equity stands for a value of something being assessed by the work one put into it.

Skid row shows a situation in which one is no longer able to support oneself.

Mortgages & Loans

Balloon mortgage is usually representative of the ultimate payment of debts coming due. This usually relates to an emotional aspect in an individual's life—relationships. May also reveal an upcoming time when one must pay the piper.
Bridge loan refers to a stopgap plan; an interim move to take up the slack.
Charge (debt) pertains to the realization that payment for something will come due; a deferment of reciprocation for a time.
Collateral signifies insurance against failure when one is taking risks.
Late charge advises that there will be a penalty or cost for not accomplishing something on schedule.
Loan applies to a temporary stopgap solution.
Loan commitment refers to a promise to give aid.
Mortgage pertains to an extended or long-lived debt; a karmic responsibility.

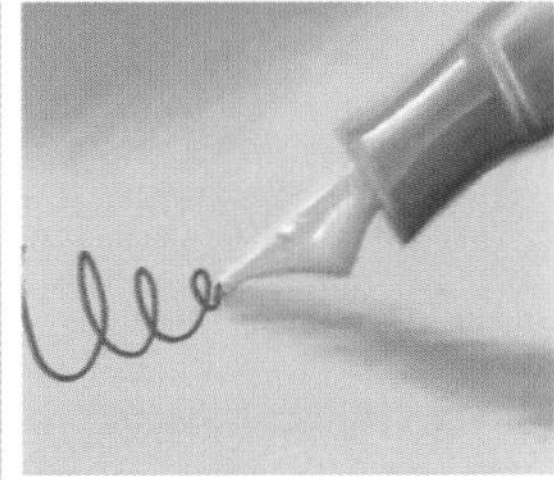

Signature loan is gain without risk.

Promissory note defines one's firm intention of paying a debt back.
Refinance suggests that a move to actively readjust one's life is needed for the purpose of easier management.
Second mortgage may be symbolized by the visual of two mortgage papers on a table. Sometimes the symbol is presented as a house double or shadow. This dream fragment stands for a good prospect or solid plan.
Signature loan represents a risk-free benefit.
Upside-down loan reveals a situation in which one owes more than the value of something.

Charity

Alms See donation.
Charity stands for opportunities that are available.
Donation signifies an offering; thoughtfulness; generosity. Recall what was donated: money would refer to finances; clothing would point to giving goodness; wigs would mean the sharing of one's thoughts, and so on.
Endowment characterizes an unexpected opportunity that has been freely presented or gifted.
Foundation (nonprofit) indicates a selfless cause.
Fund-raising is representative of the act of helping other people; getting others involved.
Giveaway is indicative of generosity; materialistic unconcern.
Poor box suggests being generous with our humanitarian acts.
Tithe relates to spiritual support, never financial support.

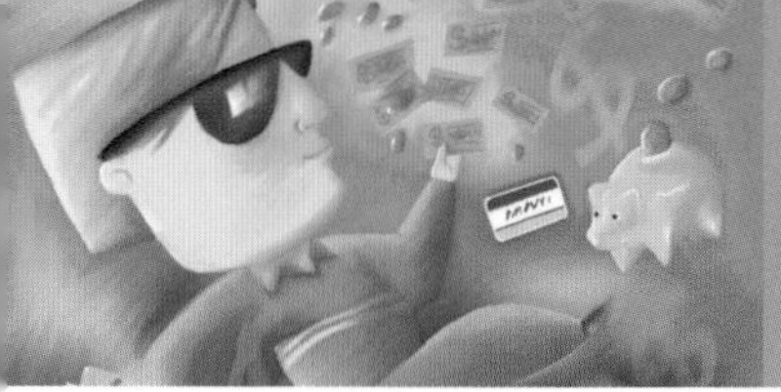

Losses

Brunt denotes one's main burden or responsibility.

Out-of-pocket portrays determined personal effort; using one's own resources to accomplish something.

Overbid means a lost opportunity due to an underestimate of its value.

Over budget reveals bad planning; something costing more than expected.

Overcharged is a symbol that converts a karmic overpayment from a balanced status to an asset position.

Overdraft corresponds to impatience: one is too anxious and jumping ahead of oneself.

Overdrawn doesn't usually refer to finances but rather points to overextending oneself in regard to energy output or possibly promises that can't be kept.

Recession implies a time of losing ground; slipping backward.

Repossessed characterizes the resulting effect of irresponsibility.

Underbid refers to a failure to understand the true value of something.

Underpaid implies a lack of appreciation or recognition of one's experience, skill, or knowledge.

Unprofitable comes in a dream as an advisement for the dreamer to think about his or her idea of value and what is being perceived as profitable.

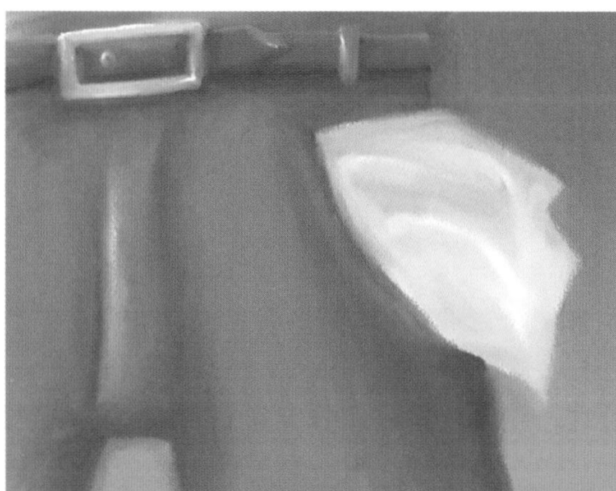

Out-of-pocket means drawing on one's own reserves to achieve something.

Retirement

Individual retirement account (IRA) suggests planning with an eye on the future. In general, it refers to long-term planning.

Keogh plan See retirement.

Pension signifies benefits earned from long-suffering and perseverance.

Retirement is representative of finalization; a life-stage completion.

Pricing

Cheap designates something of low value; obtaining something without putting much effort or personal expense out.

Free (cost) represents blessings; opportunities.

Free delivery stands for something handed to one without expending cost in the way of energy to obtain it.

Hangtag See price tag.

High-priced signifies something that will exact a cost greater than an alternative.

Inexpensive See cheap.

List price usually represents something placed at the highest price according to what the market will bear. This is an advisement that that something, though having value, can be obtained at a far lesser price.

Low-budget signifies an attained goal that was fairly easy to manifest, especially in respect to few resources or little energy involved.

Markdown (price) indicates that something one needs in life is just as valuable but now is more accessible.

Market value in dreams will usually reveal what something is really worth. Will rarely indicate an inflated value.

Markup points to an inflated value of something.

Postpaid indicates a well-planned communication.

Price (of something) usually denotes true value. Sometimes this symbol will reveal an exaggerated inflated value or indicate a worth that isn't fully recognized by presenting it as ridiculously inexpensive.

Markdown (price) is within reach.

Price-cutting suggests too high a value placed on a life aspect; inflated perspective of worth.

Price-fixing shows a misrepresentation of value and worth.

Price tag stands for a cost attached to something one wants or needs. Also see price.

Price war characterizes a state of competition so strong that the participants may actually lose in the end.

Reproduction cost points to the current value of one's skill or talent. This dreamscape symbol usually comes to point out someone's worth.

Rollback (prices) represents overshooting a goal and the attempt to pull back for the purpose of gaining lost ground.

Sticker price depicts an exaggerated worth.

Subsidy exemplifies some type of assistance that has been given or obtained.

Surcharge exposes an overwhelming situation.

Toll-free represents a communication or journey phase having no personal cost associated with it; one of life's little freebies.

Underpriced reveals an element worth more than one perceives it to be; selling oneself short.

see also
• Failure *p. 175*
• Human Resources & Recruitment *pp. 242–43*

Interest

Cut-rate normally equates to a good deal.
Interest (on debts) usually signifies increased indebtedness.
Interest (earned) signifies added benefits gained through the sharing of one's talents.
Interest rate indicates the long-term cost of being in debt. This debt may not relate to actual finances but could be associated with favors that others grant you.
Locked (interest rate) is representative of a guaranteed position.
Variable rate means that sometimes there are situations in which timing plays a key role in determining what our behavior ends up costing us.

Fees

Contingency fee symbolizes a reward or benefit resulting from a successful outcome.
Co-payment is representative of a shared expense and responsibility.
Cover charge implies a price for certain benefits enjoyed.
Fee alludes to some type of cost attached to something. Surrounding aspects will clarify what this specifically refers to.
Finder's fee represents the price for having others uncover or provide opportunities for you.
Retainer represents intention.
Service charge represents an encumbrance connected to a decision or idea; a price associated with something one wants.

Income

Base pay exemplifies required time and work; a tendency to avoid doing more than necessary. This dreamscape symbol means that more effort is required to receive additional benefits.
Bonus pertains to actions or decisions that will lead to the manifestation of greater benefits than first realized.
Exchange rate implies karmic balance.
Expense account pertains to the amount of an individual's personal talents, opportunities, or tools available for a goal's utilization.
Fixed income stands for one being limited to what one can work with.
Income rarely corresponds with finances; rather, it pertains to the return benefits generated from the spiritual talents shared with others.
Job benefits signify the rewards that come with expending energy on advancing and being productive.
Livelihood won't necessarily correspond to one's awake-state career. This symbol usually reveals a hidden aspect of one's character.

Unearned income symbolizes undeserved rewards.

Merit pay portrays the earning of additional karmic assets.
Minimum wage won't necessarily indicate a negative aspect; it most often underscores a benefit (though small) to an effort one expends.
Net income suggests the benefits or assets left after one subtracts the output elements. This symbol is advising one to weigh the pros and cons of a situation or plan.
Paycheck usually represents the value of one's behavior, beliefs, or relationships. Recall what amount the paycheck was for. Was it minimum wage? Was overtime included? Bonus?
Pittance denotes the existence of some aspect in one's life that was thought gone or nonexistent. This dream symbol won't necessarily have any reference to finances or a monetary connotation.
Profit signifies benefits from expending one's efforts.
Profit sharing characterizes a synergistic relationship where everyone benefits from group input.
Salary symbolizes recompense for efforts expended.
Salary cap stands for the maximum benefits one can expect to receive from efforts expended.
Severance pay exemplifies a benefit or reward for efforts expended toward a former life aspect. May indicate a time to move on.
Sick pay is representative of the benefits gained from taking the time off to care for oneself. This symbol usually comes as an advisement to the dreamer.
Stipend is indicative of an individual's allowable limits.
Unearned income signifies benefits received and acknowledgment given for efforts one never applied. This dream symbol also refers to false recognition.
Wage See salary.

Inheritance

Addendum may reveal extenuating aspects are present.
Beneficiary is a recipient. Perhaps good fortune is in the offing; the one who benefits.
Bequest is a representation of the act of giving.
Codicil See addendum.
Estate sale points to a betrayal of self—one's individuality. It indicates a selling of self; loss of self-esteem and integrity.
Heiress characterizes one's right to something. This could be a multifaceted symbol in that it may refer to factors such as knowledge, material goods, an employment position, etc. Surrounding dreamscape details will clarify this specific meaning.
Heirloom signifies something of great personal value.
Recipient will reveal the beneficiary of something that may pertain to an object, benefit, reprimand, praise, or other life aspect. The surrounding dream elements will clarify this.
Trust fund represents one's intentions for others.

Heirloom represents something one holds in high esteem.

Overheads & Outgoings

Cost of living usually refers to the personal cost of actions, thoughts, and motivations.
Overhead is the cost of implementing a plan or proposed move. This is a suggestion to figure out if the output is going to be worth the result.
Payroll usually reveals the value of associates. Recall who was doing the payroll. What were the check amounts?
Rent (payment) is representative of an access to an opportunity to accomplish something.
Rent control refers to a cost cap; a specified amount of energy needed to accomplish or maintain something.

Gambling

Chance characterizes the unexpected; that which comes our way.
Entry form points to the intent to participate in something. This may indicate a bid to take advantage of a possible opportunity.
Heads or tails denotes an opportunity to make a choice.
Jackpot emphasizes benefits and rewards received throughout life.
Keno applies to the taking of slim chances; taking risks.
Lottery connotes a tendency to take chances that have little potential for success.
Lottery ticket is representative of a possibility, but one that is a long shot.
Penny ante suggests a small risk; an element or idea that won't exact a high price if it doesn't succeed.

Lottery means taking a long shot.

Prize represents specific goals or attainments as personally perceived; an individualistic idea of what a benefit or blessing is.
Prizewinner portrays an achievement or an unexpected benefit.
Raffle See lottery.
Reward is representative of personal benefits derived from positive behavior and good deeds.
Sweepstakes See lottery.

Class

League is a stage one is at.
Lowborn denotes humility.
Lowerclass man See underclassmen.
Riffraff may represent those who most need one's help.
Underclassmen are those who are less experienced in life.
Upperclassmen/women are those who have gone before you, and have traveled the same path.
Upper crust characterizes an individual's arrogance; placing oneself or others into a high-class position.

Trade

Balance of trade pertains to our daily give-and-take equilibrium.
Economic plan is representative of thought that is given to how one can best utilize skills and talents.
Trade beads are indicative of the exchange of natural talents. It refers to helping another person in return for her or his former help. It can mean give and take in the more general sense.
Trade-in points to assets (talents) an individual can bring to the table.
Trading card usually depicts a visual of an important message for the dreamer.

see also
• Gambling *p. 204*
• Store Personnel *p. 259*

Shopping

Back order signifies a wait for something one wants.

Bulk purchase typifies a need for security. Expresses a need to be well provisioned.

Comparison shopping advises of a need to research something; not to accept the first presentation or offer.

Prepaid indicates something one has already earned.

Return (merchandise) suggests a change of mind; a rejection.

Shopping emphasizes looking for something; searching.

Sold-out signifies a popular issue. May mean a lost chance; a need to reschedule plans.

Sticker shock comes as a call to perform a reality check: goals have a greater cost (energy) than originally thought.

Stocking stuffer stands for those little blessings we're gifted with throughout life.

Window-shopping implies a search for ideas.

Shops & Businesses

Anchor tenant signifies a main attraction; an element that will be the main draw.

Cottage industry means self-sufficiency.

Counteroffer refers to an active negotiation; a time of give-and-take.

Deal (transaction) refers to a specific condition or event in the dreamer's life.

Deal breaker points to asking too much in a negotiation; needing a more equitable compromise.

Dealership connotes a specialized source; an outlet supplying the individualized needs of others.

Franchise means the right that frees one to pursue a specific endeavor; within one's rights.

Mass-market means something widely known or available.

Open stock represents current availability; something one can still take advantage of.

Pyramid scheme stands for a plan to use others for personal gain; amassing benefits by enticing others to do the work.

Stock represents preparedness; resourcefulness; forethought. Was the stock scanty or plentiful? Recall the type.

Takeover means overwhelmed; a loss of authority or personal responsibility.

Financial Analysis

Market analysis is usually representative of the fact that research should be done in a specific area.

Market research comes to the dreamer as a call for the need to compare something in one area of his or her life; a hard look at priorities.

Risk analysis generally points to a need to very carefully weigh the pros and cons of something.

Risk factor reveals a life factor that has the potential to be a dangerous or harmful aspect in one's life and one needs to pay careful attention.

Success

Marquis almost always brings an important message for the dreamer. Recall what the marquis said, who else was present at the time, and all the reactions to the message, if possible.

Millionaire characterizes an individual possessing great resources yet, with that, comes great responsibility to act on opportunities to perform acts of goodness for others in one's life.

Pay dirt denotes a new element in one's life that has the capability to bring one multiple benefits.

Queen for a day connotes a recognition of one's efforts and perseverance.

Strongbox is suggestive of a recognition of life's valuable aspects.

Talents correspond to inherent abilities or skills that are unique to each individual.

Luck

Auspicious stands for an upcoming situation, decision, or relationship being a favorable or meaningful one; a perfect time for something to happen.

Bet signifies chances taken; a willingness to second-guess outcomes. It also indicates a tendency to dismiss or give weight to facts.

Charm exemplifies a lack of faith. May indicate a superstitious personality.

Fringe benefit connotes an extra benefit to something; additional rewards or unexpected benefits.

Lady Luck stands for the ideology of an imaginary angelic persona who either smiles and brings blessings or frowns and brings misfortune; a scapegoat.

Lucky charm See charm.

Mixed blessing denotes an element having both positive and negative aspects.

Opportunist may not imply a negative connotation. It may well indicate a need to begin taking advantage of opportunities presented along the dreamer's path.

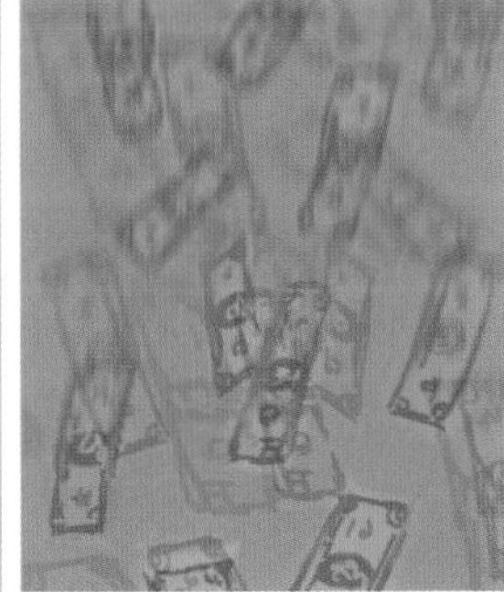

Windfall is a surprise bonus.

Peril comes to the dreamer as a warning of a forthcoming harmful event.

Providential alludes to a fortuitous event or element in one's life.

Silver lining reveals an unseen or unexpected benefit.

Unlucky pertains to a lack of self-confidence.

Windfall pertains to an unexpected benefit or bounty.

Wishbone implies hope.

Wish list applies to one's wants, not necessarily the priority needs.

Miscellaneous

Across-the-board points to all-inclusiveness.
Amortization connotes a need to pace oneself. This could mean the individual tends to lump problematic situations together and be overwhelmed; therefore, clearer thinking is required to take one thing at a time.
Bottom drawer represents one's hopes, future goals.
Central booking points to being caught for doing something negative.
Dutch treat reminds us of individual responsibility.
Earnest money stands for a serious intention; putting one's money where the mouth is.
Grant applies to some type of life aspect or event that serves to clear one's way toward achieving a goal.
Gratuity implies thankfulness; a reciprocal response denoting appreciation.
Group rate suggests a situation, relationship, or course that will benefit from the participation of several people.
Hard sell suggests coercion; a pushy, insistent personality.
Hitch (snag) implies a temporary setback.
Inducement is representative of some type of personal motivation entering into one's life.
Insignia reveals one's privately held attitude or sympathies.
Landgrab usually denotes greediness. May also indicate a desire to take advantage of a good opportunity.
Option presents itself as a dream symbol to reveal opportunities or alternative choices one has in life.
Oversold suggests a promise that can't be kept; exaggerations made for the purpose of personal gain.
Patent signifies recognition or the protection of one's innovative ideas.
Peon indicates a low class. This represents a personal attitude toward oneself or another.
Scarecrow signifies a reinforcement of one's personal protection. May also reveal a stern veneer over a soft heart.
Souvenir symbolizes a reason to remember a specific event in one's life.

Gratuity indicates one's efforts have been acknowledged.

Stinginess comes to the dreamer as a warning against selfishness, greed, and being within a self-absorbed state.
Straw man may refer to one who serves as a front for another who wishes to remain in the background or private. Also see scarecrow.
Thankless naturally equates to unappreciative, often referring to efforts expended without any acknowledgment.
Ticket (admission) validates one's right of entry or preparedness.
Tie-in (merchandising) represents imitating elements that spin off from an original idea.
Want ads are a representation of opportunities.

Postage

Postage due indicates a situation of failed communication because not enough efforts were put into it; a weak or half-hearted attempt at communication.
Postage meter stands for the cost or value of communicating something.
Return receipt (postal) signifies a desire to see something through.
Subscription (magazine/newspaper) exposes an individual's attitude, tendency, or personal interest. May even illustrate hidden perspectives or opinions.

Deprivation

Begging stands for desperation.
Belt-tightening points to severe self-restraint; self-denial. Sacrifices are needed.
Deprivation may indicate a need to live without something or it may refer to something one is willfully leaving out of life.
Displaced homemaker stands for an inability to make new beginnings or adjust to a new situation.
Forfeit pertains to a life aspect that needs to be abandoned or given up.
Have-not characterizes an individual who refuses to recognize her or his own gifts; a lack of acceptance; ignoring one's real riches in deference to materialism.
Panhandle (beg) is usually representative of a state of desperation. Depending on the surrounding elements of the dream, this symbol may also warn of laziness.
Pawn ticket stands for a way out of a problem; a solution.
Tin cup refers to a handout or request for one.

Chapter 13

Pastimes, Sports & Entertainment

These dreamscape aspects not only represent the manner in which an individual's leisure time is spent, they often point to specific behavioral traits.

Board & Table Games

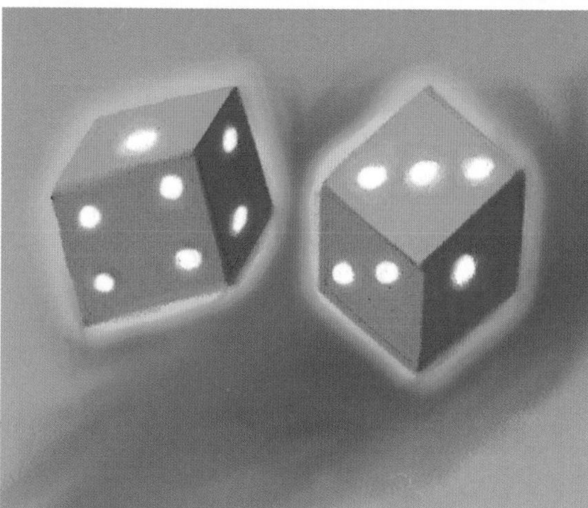

Dice represent the many different opportunities that life has to offer.

Backgammon applies to a noncommittal relationship in one's life.
Board game will be associated with the games one plays in life, usually psychological ploys put into play in interacting with others.
Checker (game piece) represents one aspect of a planned direction.
Checkerboard typifies the many decisions in life; planning; the wisdom of analyzing situations.
Chinese puzzle denotes confusion; difficulty in finding resolutions.
Craps (dice game) warns against taking slim chances.
Dice (game pieces) pertain to changeability; the many probabilities for each outcome.
Domino stands for one aspect of a questionable situation.
Foosball (game) hints at lighthearted competition hinging on one's skill level.
Game board reveals moves made in life.
Jacks (game) pertain to the pressure under which one lives. This usually is a self-generated situation.
Mah-jongg (game) implies a right combination is required. This will be a hint to a problem-solving resolution.
Monopoly (game) alludes to misplaced priorities; a tendency to want it all.
Roulette (table) stands for questionable chances taken.
Scrabble (game) warns against the tendency to play word games and not communicate in a direct and clear manner.
Shuffleboard (game) exemplifies congenial competition; friendly contention.
Snake eyes (dice) points to someone who is easily persuaded.
Tick-tack-toe signifies alignment. Implies a need to work at priorities.
Tiddlywinks refer to a haphazard approach to accomplishing goals.

Gambling

Ante means putting your share of time or energy into something.
Daily double represents a situation that has the capability of bringing multiple rewards or disappointments.
Gambling refers to an attempt to win at something; taking advantage of a slim chance.
Numbers game refers to a slim chance one has taken or is thinking of taking in life; risks.
Odds reveal probabilities for success in relation to something the dreamer is anticipating doing or is concerned about.
Offtrack betting constitutes a chance taken without being aware of all the associative factors involved.
One-armed bandit See slot machine.
Outside chance indicates the existence of a slim probability for something to manifest.
Raffle ticket is representative of a chance that is taken when an opportunity manifests itself. This symbol may also signify a goal having little potential for success.
Roulette (Russian) warns of chances taken that have the potential of causing great harm or having severely adverse effects; risks with stakes that are too high.
Russian roulette See roulette (Russian).
Side bet represents an unofficial risk.
Slot machine represents the chances taken in life; the shortcuts attempted.
Stake (bet) indicates a personal interest in something.
Sweepstakes See lottery.
Syndicate is an affiliation of like-minded individuals with a common goal.
Tote board denotes information at a glance; an overall view of how things are faring.

Crosswords & Puzzles

Anagram signifies solutions available within the problem itself; a need to shift perception and look at something in a different way.
Crossword puzzle denotes miscommunications; trouble communicating.
Jigsaw puzzle indicates a problem in one's life. This dreamscape fragment may actually show the dreamer how to put the pieces together.
Picture puzzle See jigsaw puzzle.
Puzzle See jigsaw puzzle.
Puzzle piece denotes a part of a solution; one facet of the whole.
Tongue twister reflects a difficult idea or concept that one may or may not be able to articulate through understanding.
Word association signifies those triggers that serve as emotional triggers of the subconscious.
Word games come as an advisement to speak clearly instead of beating around the bush, making plays on words or innuendos.

see also
• Gambling *p. 252*
• Carnival *p. 481*

Card Playing

Ace in the hole symbolizes a hidden advantage.
Bargaining chip characterizes an ace in the hole; an inducement.
Blackjack (card game) suggests a tendency toward playing the odds; taking chances in life.
Bridge (game) See card (playing).
Card (playing) refers to insecurities.
Card counter (blackjack) represents someone who achieves goals through negative means.
Cribbage pertains to some aspect in one's life that has been exposed.
Deck (cards) implies game-playing in connection with one's interaction with others.
Deuce (wild card) refers to unexpected options and/or outcomes; the existence of many possibilities.
Down card represents a questionable, unknown element that could be either a benefit or a detriment; a risk.
Face card indicates a personal message revealing how one is currently acting in life.
Fish (card game) connotes intermittent cooperation from others.
Hearts (card game) implies a manipulation of another's emotions.
House of cards symbolizes precarious and insubstantial foundational traits or perspectives.
Long suit corresponds with best quality; greatest talent.
Old Maid (card game) implies an anxiety or fear of age. May refer to a fear of having to care for an elder. This may also stand for a woman's independence. Surrounding dreamscape fragments will clarify which meaning was intended.
Pinochle depicts a method of playing out one's life situations through the manner of maneuverability and also cleverness.
Pit (casino card area) applies to a situation or atmosphere that holds questionable elements; a call to caution when proceeding; a situation where every move is being watched.
Playing card See card (playing).
Poker (live card game) implies ulterior motives; stealthy behavior.
Poker (video card game) suggests an opportunity to make choice moves.
Pontoon suggests a lackadaisical spiritual attitude.
Queen of Spades represents the key element of a goal.
Royal flush (poker) points to a winning hand or idea.
Rummy (card game) connotes a suggestion to gather one's facts.
Solitaire stands for a state of aloneness; a singular element. May also point to the games one is playing with self—the psychological mind games.
Spade (card suit) denotes verification; assurances.
Strong suit reveals an individual's area of strength or talent.
Trump card signifies the key to a goal or successful conclusion.
Wild card pertains to a questionable element of an aspect.

Chess

Checkmate signifies an unavoidable aspect in one's life. May indicate a defeat or a personal conquest, depending on the dreamscape symbols.
Chess illustrates the intricacies of life; many moves are available, yet few right ones.
Chessboard exemplifies the options that life presents to us; a situation with many options.
Chess piece reveals which directional moves are open to us. See specific piece.
Pawn applies to one who is used by another. May also indicate an opinion of oneself.
Rook portrays a deception in one's life.
Stalemate exposes a futile situation; no chance for an altered course or change.

Circus & Fairground

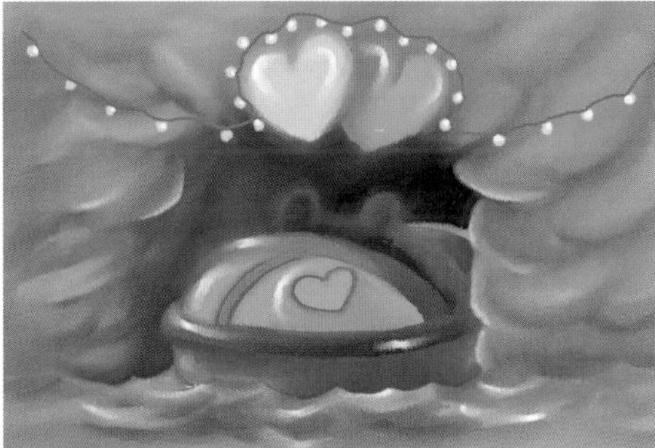

Tunnel of love may signify a secret affair.

Big wheel refers to someone of influence, wealth, or power.
Bumper car refers to a tendency to conflict for the thrill of winning.
Carousel means a path that is going around in circles and will prove to be unproductive.
Disneyland warns against unrealistic perceptions or goals.
Dodgem car See bumper car.
Fairground means a good atmosphere conducive to success.
Ferris wheel emphasizes a circling in place; lack of advancement or development.
Merry-go-round is a lack of progress; intellectual or searching advancement made. Also see carousel.
Sideshow refers to aspects in one's life that are ridiculous or outrageous in respect to one's serious path or purpose.
Tunnel of love can be hidden affections, but also warns of harboring secret resentments.
Whirligig denotes acceptance; a carefree attitude that goes with the flow and takes changes with the perspective of "that's life."

Children's Games

Blindman's bluff reflects grasping in the dark; trying to proceed without adequate information or perception.
Brainteaser signifies a problem in one's life that's difficult to resolve. Calls for deeper analytical thought.
Cap pistol pertains to baseless verbiage; idle threats.
Charades stand for an inability to verbalize thoughts or adequately express self.
Child's play defines an activity that's easy; simplistic. It may be a call to give your inner child more freedom of expression.
Cowboys and Indians signifies an ongoing conflict (perhaps hidden) between two people of varying opinions.
Croquet exemplifies vindictiveness that is hidden behind sophistication.
Daisy chain symbolizes exuberance.
Dress up (playacting) cautions against the attempt or desire to be someone other than self.
Finger painting is an immature way of expressing self.
Finger puppet means an attempt to hide behind excuses.
Four-H club connotes good values instilled early on in life.
Frisbee is one of many symbols that refer to a good intent in communicating.
Game depicts mental stimulation. Certain games may indicate risks taken.
Hide-and-seek typifies the games people play in life; manipulation; ulterior motives; hidden agendas.
Hopscotch warns against jumping only to chosen points along one's path instead of covering all the ground.

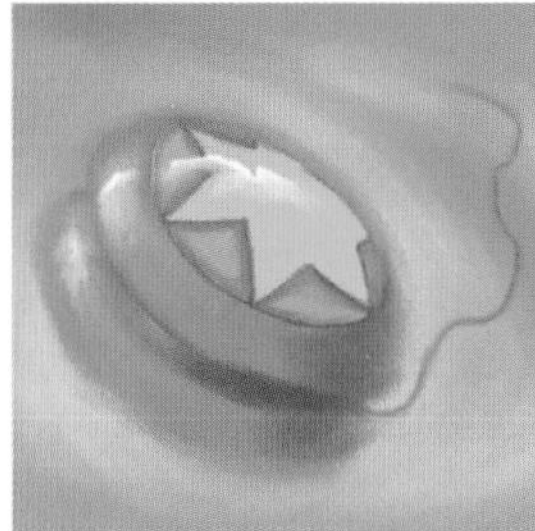

Yo-Yo denotes indecisiveness and lack of emotional stability.

In-line skates See roller skates.
Jack-in-the-box implies insensitivity; an inability to recognize the more serious sides of life.
Jump rope pertains to being directed by others, perhaps to the point of subservience.
Jungle gym warns of a self-generated state of confusion and twisted perspectives.
Kiddie car suggests a childish approach to one's life path.
King-of-the-hill translates to a desire to be in control and have that power recognized by others.
Kite represents the effort one expends on understanding emotional impulses.
Leapfrog usually illustrates competition; continual one-upmanship.
Marbles applies to immature competitiveness.
Model (toys) denote a smaller version of something larger; an imitation on a lesser scale.
Monkey bars relate to contorted maneuvers to emulate others.
Musical chairs defines a stagnant phase of one's path; a lack of forward movement; going in circles.
Nature trail connotes a life path chosen for the value of its multiple lessons.
Paintball characterizes a lighthearted test of skill or survival, yet it may also point to a practice of evasiveness (hunter/prey).
Peekaboo warns of game-playing in life. Sends a message to stop vacillating or creating personal agendas.
Piggyback reveals personal irresponsibility. Recall who was riding piggyback and who was carrying another.
Pinball stands for a striving to better oneself; improving one's success rate through repeated experiences.
Playpen refers to a babyish manner of behavior.
Pogo stick warns against attempting to advance along one's life path in an emotionally detached manner.
Popgun usually symbolizes drawing attention to a situation with the potential to elicit high emotional responses.
Puppet reveals an easily manipulated individual.
Roller skates show a desire to skate through life without taking responsiblity for dealing with distasteful/difficult issues.
Sandpit exposes a stage or place along one's life path where indecision will need to be overcome.
Seesaw may be life's ups and downs. May also be vacillation.
Skateboard exemplifies an attempt to dodge life's burdens and difficult periods.
Skating (roller) suggests a desire to skate through life without encountering the tribulations that are meant to be dealt with and overcome.
Slide (playground) warns against a tendency to slide through life without giving attention to important aspects.
Slot car stands for a false sense of control.
Snowman emphasizes a state of spiritual arrogance; spirituality that is selective and temporary.
Sparkler emphasizes inner joy generated by insights.
Squirt gun is surprising events.
Starquake (computer game) symbolizes the shattering of idolization.
Stink bomb signifies retaliation; a serious rebounding action.
Swing (child's) denotes perceptual innocence; an ability to be open to alternative views or concepts.
Tag warns against avoiding responsibility or a tendency to place same upon another's shoulders.
Teddy bear is a soothing and comforting aspect in one's life.
Teeter-totter See seesaw.
Three-legged race suggests highly coordinated efforts.
Tinkertoys provide an opportunity to experiment.
Top (toy) represents spinning, often out of control.
Toy implies a lack of seriousness, or toying with something. Sometimes a reference to a childlike nature.
Toy box suggests returning to some of one's childlike perceptions or qualities.
Trick-or-treat actually refers to the concept of cause and effect—one reaps what one sows; action bringing reaction.
Water gun See squirt gun.
Yo-Yo denotes an unstable emotional life or a lack of decision-making capabilities; a tendency to vacillate or arbitrarily change course.

Hobbies

Beadwork stands for taking deserved pride in one's work, skill, or accomplishments.
Bingo (game) cautions against expectation.
Bird-watcher stands for watching one's thoughts, analyzing self and how conclusions are reached.
Candle-making represents those activities that bring light and compassion to others.
Casting (ceramic) refers to fragility; a weak idea having temporary qualities and few lasting effects.
Collector connotes a specific interest (often kept hidden) and the strong attraction for all aspects of same. This can be a revealing dream if one recalls what was being collected.
Competition will most often be associated with a goodwill or lighthearted type of rivalry, often oneself taking both challenger roles for the purpose of pushing limits or expectations.
Cook-off refers to competitive planning.
Decoupage exemplifies the addition of specialized aspects to something. May point to an overplay or glossing of facts.
Do-it-yourself (book/project) means self-reliance/sufficiency. Points to something one must accomplish alone.
Game room symbolizes a concerted effort applied to one's mental stimulation. May also stand for a meeting place.
Handblown signifies personal energy put into creative efforts.
Hand-dipped candles represent personal efforts expended toward gaining independence (or attempting to gain more enlightenment on a subject).
Handicrafts denote creativity from personal efforts.
Handmade points to personal efforts; a desire to personally accomplish something.
Handprint denotes that which one leaves behind; a mark of one's identity.
Hand puppet represents expressiveness once removed. This means a tendency to attribute the originality of one's ideas to another.
Hayride reveals an inner joy taken from hard work.
Hobby relates to a manner of relaxation and interest. Each hobby will have its own interpretation. See specific type.
Hobbyhorse connotes an obsession.
Hobby shop represents vast opportunities for constructive mental diversions, in relation to satisfying one's need to rest from intensive work and study. See specific hobby.
Knitting implies planning.
Macramé represents twisted truths or convoluted ideas; complicated issues.
Origami symbolizes a tendency to reconfigure events; a warning against altering facts or rearranging them to suit self. This symbol points to ingenuity; something carrying great potential.
Paper dolls denote choices for the expression of individuality.
Shuttle (weaving) pertains to a facilitating element in life.
Silk flowers exemplify lasting beauty. See specific flower type for deeper meaning.
Silk-screen denotes replication. May bring a personal message for each dreamer.
Spelunker characterizes a person who delves far to broaden understanding.
Spindle denotes an important secondary factor connected to a primary element.
Spinning wheel corresponds with plans. Mental maneuvers.
Spin-off signifies a resulting product; a benefit or problem stemming from a primary source.
Spool See spindle.
Weaving loom See loom.
Yarn pertains to falsehoods; misunderstandings; gossip.
Yoga applies to self discipline; a way to gain inner peace.

Hand puppet represents giving others the credit for one's own opinions.

Camping

Camper (person) characterizes an individual who is on a short break from life's hectic pace.
Campfire denotes an inner tranquility; inner peacefulness with one's current place in life or along the path.
Campground pertains to an understanding of life's frequent temporary conditions and/or situations; the need to balance stressful work with relaxation.
Camping refers to a temporary return to a calmer situational or emotional state. May mean that more acceptance or tolerance would reduce current stress or anxiety.
Camping gear signifies the need to equip oneself with more tools to achieve a less stressful state of mind; gear up to gear down.
Camp stool implies situational ease; one is comfortable in most situations; adaptability.
Camp stove denotes an emergency source of energy (heat/cooking). Refers to an element of preparedness.
Encampment See campground.
Fire pit See campfire.
Ground cloth suggests a protective measure taken.

Golf

Golf course characterizes an inconsequential element of one's life.

Course (golf) See golf course.
Driving range suggests the practicing of one's methods for taking long shots.
Golf applies to the easiest path chosen.
Golf bag refers to the collection of our perceived tools to achieve certain goals.
Golf ball denotes a goal marker; what one aims for as a course marker then follows.
Golf cap warns against lazy thought; a lack of seriousness.
Golf cart denotes haughtiness.
Golf club emphasizes a life aspect that one utilizes to lessen personal efforts needed to achieve a specific goal.
Golf course typifies an area of one's path that is not taken seriously.
Green's fee refers to the price paid for taking the easy path.
Leaderboard reveals one's progress. May also point to a situation of competition.
Miniature golf suggests a trial run; a practice before the real thing is attempted.
Putt depicts a cautious move.
Putter refers to an individual who idles time; expending mental efforts on insignificant elements.
Sand trap exemplifies problems in life; aspects that are intended to test one's inner strength and problem-solving abilities.
Tee (golf) will most often point to an irritating element in one's life, something that gets one teed off.

Racquet Sports

Backhand shows a versatility in handling problems.
Backspin applies to an emotional shock or revelation.
Badminton denotes a back-and-forth situation or relationship. May also refer to one's own thought process; indecision; vacillation.
Baseline symbolizes a point at which to begin gauging progress or decline.
Grand slam defines the best possible outcome.
Match point symbolizes a winning effort.
Squash (game) suggests a competitive situation, possibly even against oneself as efforts at breaking old records or improving oneself are made.
Tennis is representative of a constantly altering element in one's life.

Ice Hockey

Goalie gear applies to preparation taken for the purpose of entering a conflict that blocks one's way toward advancement.
Hockey represents a spiritual game one plays.
Hockey helmet shows one is ready for spiritual conflict, indicating a situation where one has a strong, almost fanatical, spiritual attitude.
Hockey puck is associated with a spiritual concept or belief that is controversial.
Hockey stick indicates a willful batting of a controversial spiritual concept. This could point out an ongoing debate or continual criticism. It may also indicate a desire to keep pushing it away so one doesn't have to look at it more deeply.
Puck (hockey) See hockey puck.
Stanley Cup is representative of the success of a goal in one's life.

Ball Sports

Ball game See specific type.
Basketball (ball or game) suggests an active situation where one needs to keep on one's toes and stay aware of what others are doing.
Bat (sport) relates to the condition and quality of one's progression.
Batter (sports) alludes to the one who scores or a main player.
Batting average reveals the state of one's progress.
Boundary line defines the accepted playing field.
Club (bat) indicates a bullish personality; manipulation; coerciveness.
Free throw offers a clear opportunity to take advantage of a situation.
Halftime advises of a time of respite; a break to reenergize and regroup.
Handball depicts personal efforts expended.
Hardball denotes a tough situation to deal with. May reveal an insensitive person who plays hard to get or manages situations or dealings with a sense of strictly business acumen.

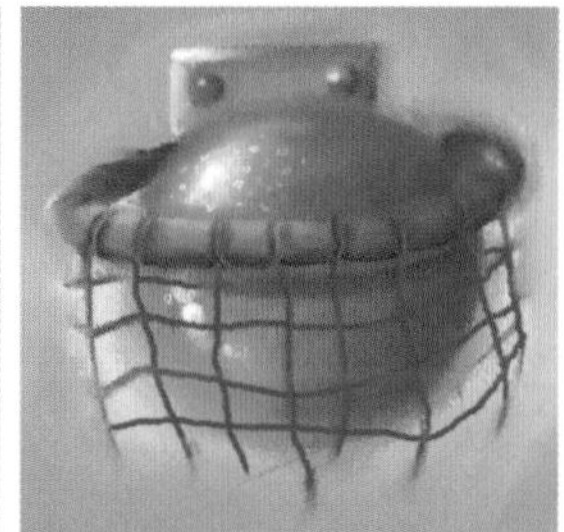
Basketball means staying alert.

Hat trick suggests ulterior motives; intellectual or psychological maneuvering.
Kickball suggests a tendency to bounce ideas around.
Slam-dunk indicates assuredness; confidence.
Triple Crown stands for three main aspects to a goal, issue, or situation that need to be attained or hurdled for success.
Volleyball denotes a reluctance to accept responsibility, always batting the ball back into another's space.

see also
• Sports *p. 263*
• Sports, Pastimes & Leisure *p. 379*

Baseball

Backstop symbolizes safeguards one creates for self.
Ballpark symbolizes one's recognition of limits; bounds.
Baseball relates to winning through skill and speed. Not necessarily a totally commendable symbol depending on what surrounding symbols show.
Baseball diamond denotes one's tendency to follow the same pattern to achieve goals.
Bleacher warns of a tendency to sit back and watch others do the work; complacency.
Bull pen (baseball) represents one's backup resources; a source of reserve energy or support.
Bush league See minor league.
Center field indicates a position where one is able to maintain balance through an awareness of one's placement in life.
Curveball comes to the dreamer as a warning against having expectations; events or happenings that don't turn out as expected.
Fastball advises of a need to sharpen one's personal awareness. This symbol may forewarn of something coming into the dreamer's life that wasn't foreseen.
First base suggests success in accomplishing the first phase of a goal.
Foul line represents the boundaries that encompass the atmosphere of rightness. To cross this warns of misdeeds done.
Home plate represents a specific goal one has.
Home run reveals an attainment of a goal. It may also refer to having come full circle.
Inning reveals one's advancement on one's path. Recall what inning it was.
Left field connotes new ideas; difficult to accept concepts. May also reveal a perspective that's way off-track.
Low ball symbolizes an underestimation.
Major league suggests a higher position acquired through greater experience and knowledge.
Minor league defines a secondary factor, one that isn't perceived as a priority issue.
No-hitter underscores a successful endeavor that carried no setbacks or problems with it.
Pinch hitter pertains to someone who can take over for another at a critical point in time or phase of development.
Pitcher (baseball) portrays an individual in one's life who may attempt to foil another's advancement or success.
Relief pitcher characterizes an individual who has the knowledge and capability to stand in for another; a temporary replacement.
Right field indicates a tendency to follow accepted ideas.
Second base stands for evidence of progression.
Seventh-inning stretch advises of a need to take time out from overexpending efforts.
Shortstop characterizes a versatile individual.
Sidearm (pitching style) represents exceptional inner strength.
Third base refers to progression to the point of almost achieving a goal.

Football

Backfield relates to a secondary position of support.
End zone relates to a point of rest beyond the goal; the place in one's path where personal efforts are rewarded.
Field goal exemplifies achievements that are less than the expected goal.
First down (football) denotes a first chance or opportunity.
Football relates to winning through force and deception. Who were the players?
Huddle (football) stands for a conference for the purpose of scheming, planning.
Kickoff marks a beginning.
Linebacker pertains to one's backup or secondary defenses.
Line of scrimmage marks a conflict demarcation between differing perspectives, attitudes, or opinions.
Lineup connotes those associated with one another.
Punt (football) signifies a lost opportunity; an additional chance to reap benefits from efforts applied.
Quarter (football) See inning.
Quarterback usually represents an individual who calls the plays or shots in one's life. Was this you or someone else?
Super Bowl denotes a final contest to determine a winner or a final hurdle to determine success.
Super Bowl ring signifies the success of a goal.
Triple threat reveals a situation or issue containing three dangerous elements.

Soccer

Dribble (ball) implies marking-time stage in life; an interim.
Goal signifies aspirations.
Goal line is an advisement to keep one's eye on goals.
Goalpost is a symbol for one's aspirations or goals. Recall the condition of the goalpost. Was it upright? Tilting? Falling down? In disrepair? Shiny?
Midfield signifies an advancement position placing one halfway to one's goals.
Penalty box is a payment made for a misdeed. Recall who was in the penalty box.
Sideline illustrates a position of observation. May also indicate an extra activity in association with one's main purpose.
Soccer suggests clever moves.

Archery & Darts

Bow (archery) stands for an aspect that helps to target a problem.
Bowstring (archery) connotes that which connects aspects pointing to a specific problem; surrounding elements that help to identify a problem.
Bull's-eye confirms one's right course; on target.
Dart signifies events that we allow to impede our progress.
Dartboard advises to continually vent negative emotions in a positive and nonharmful manner.

Track & Field (Athletics)

Broad jump See long jump.
Decathlon represents the extent to which one goes to accomplish a goal.
Discus thrower characterizes a competitive nature.
False start suggests a need to go back and begin again, only this time, be less impatient.
Finish line marks the stage when one's goals are attained. What was the dreamscape distance to this line?
Footrace warns against a competing attitude.
High jump means one is attempting to avoid or circumvent an issue or life problem.
Hurdle pertains to an upcoming difficulty the dreamer must experience.
Inside track underscores one's advantageous placement in life; a choice position.
Jogging represents a steadily paced progression.
Lap (track) connotes progression. What was the number of the last lap completed?
Long distance (runner) signifies endurance; determination.
Long jump reveals an advancement; a great progression.
Pole vault warns against leaping over important elements in one's life that need to be fully experienced.
Race (speed/fast pace) refers to a warning to slow down. This may indicate competitiveness that is blinding, self-serving. A race may suggest that one isn't absorbing all one needs in life because one is going too fast to focus on the important issues.
Racewalking is an attempt to cover up the fact that one is rushing through life without absorbing important aspects or focusing on the minor, yet revealing elements.
Relay (race) cautions one to not depend on others for personal progression.
Running track warns of unproductive efforts; going fast and getting nowhere.
Second wind implies a re-energized state of being.
Shot put (sport) pertains to an attempt to make the most out of one's applied efforts.
Sprinting suggests a paced progression.
Starting line reflects the beginning point.
Track (sports) signifies circling; lack of progression.

Bowling

Bowl (sport) refers to obtaining goals through unethical means.
Bowling alley denotes a condition or situation where one might be tempted to act in an unethical manner.
Bowling ball symbolizes the tool that one uses to act in an unethical manner. This would be a specific act or a statement voiced. May point to something that comes as a big surprise that bowls one over.
Pin (bowling) represents a target; something one shoots for; a goal.

Swimming & Water Sports

Diving board is impetus for growth.

America's Cup (yacht race) is indicative of spiritual one-upmanship.
Backstroke warns of a need to review; go back over spiritual concepts. This may also point to a need to turn around and look where one is spiritually headed. May caution against attempting to move forward while looking backward.
Belly flop applies to unexpected or disappointing spiritual results.
Bodysurfing symbolizes a willingness to get close to spiritual issues; an adventuresome spiritual attitude.
Breaststroke suggests spirituality taken to heart.
Diving board relates to a spiritual search that needs a motivational impetus.
Dog paddle (swim style) alludes to a spiritual search accompanied by friends.
Flume denotes a quick way to spiritual resources.
Freestyle symbolizes freedom of personal expression and methodology.
Jet Ski warns against racing over or through new spiritual concepts, thereby skimming the depth of them.
Olympic pool signifies an opportunity to immerse oneself in the whole of a spiritual concept.
Parasailing implies a spiritually disassociative state; being close to spiritual matters yet not wanting to immerse self in them.
Rowing depicts a personal spiritual effort made.
Scuba gear represents aspects that allow one to attain spiritual goals.
Skin diving exemplifies a serious spiritual search.
Snorkeling pertains to a surface spiritual search or interest. May point to a tentative look into a new spiritual concept.
Springboard denotes motivation; an impetus.
Surfboard pertains to the participation in a spiritual movement that can be within oneself.
Swim fins stands for impatience to gain spiritual development.
Swimming denotes submersion in one's spiritual search.
Swimming pool reflects a spiritual search going nowhere; spiritual concepts treated with artificial elements.
Synchronized swimming suggests a mimicked spiritual path.
Waterskiing suggests skimming over spiritual matters.
Water wings portray personal preventive measures taken to ensure against becoming spiritually inundated.
Wet suit portrays a willful distancing from spiritual aspects; an insulating measure.
Windsurfing warns against letting popular opinion direct one's spiritual life path.

see also
• Aggressors *p. 145*
• Movement in Water *p. 176*

Boxing, Wrestling & Fencing

Arm wrestling indicates a challenge-loving individual.
Bare-knuckle implies one who is vulnerable.
Bout signifies a confrontation between rivals; a needed meeting to settle differences.
Box (sport) portrays an argumentative personality.
Boxing glove connotes a combative nature. Also may point to a tendency to box one's way out of something.
Boxing ring indicates the arena (issue) of conflict.
Featherweight signifies the presence of intellect and wisdom regardless of size.
Fencing (sporting art) refers to the act of being evasive or keeping others at bay.
Fighter (sport) See box (sport).
Glass jaw warns of one's state of vulnerability.
Heavyweight characterizes an intellectual; a highly influential individual.
Indian wrestling See arm wrestling.
Inning reveals one's progress on one's path.
Jousting applies to a personal combative state, frequently within oneself.
Knockout means impressive.
Middleweight refers to one's level of effectiveness or influence. This connotes an average amount of both.
Mud wrestling signifies a display of fun-loving competition; exaggerated conflict resolution for the sake of show.
Prizefight warns against engaging in altercations for self-serving purposes.
Prize money can stand for the ultimate satisfaction or benefit of achieving a specific goal or it can refer to the carrot that motivates.
Punching bag advises to release pent-up stress or emotions.
Purse (winning award) refers to the payoff benefit for achievement.
Ringside (seats) denote an onlooker position or perspective; one who prefers watching and waiting instead of participating.
Round (boxing) See inning.
Self-defense class suggests a way to protect oneself. It refers to physical defenses and emotional or spiritual aspects.
Shadowboxing reveals a conflict within self.
Sideswiped stands for a brush with a negative element; a close call.
Slugfest indicates a loss of control. May point to being drawn into conflict spurred by the negative reactions of others; a mob-rule contagion.
Tank fighter (boxing) reveals an individual who acts out prearranged scenarios; preplanned behavior.
Wrestling stands for an attempt to get one's way; trying to sway another.

Gymnastics & Bodybuilding

Aerobic exercise cautions against being overemotional.
Backflip See somersault.
Backstretch is a halfway point.
Balance beam (gymnastic) reminds us to walk a balanced path. Usually points to a current situation of imbalance in the dreamer's life.
Barbell alludes to those life aspects that build strength; endurance-builders.
Bench press refers to aspects in life that serve as strengtheners.
Bodybuilding applies to an attention to weaknesses; building up inner strength.
Calisthenics mean one's level of experience; preparedness.
Drill team stands for flawless learning skills.
Dumbbells apply to self-strengthening aspects.
Exercise equipment suggests a need to literally exercise one's mind or body. It may be pointing to a need to exercise one's right or individuality.
Gymnasium is an atmosphere that provides exercise, usually indicating mental exercise.
Gymnast warns of one who contorts and twists facts.
Jazzercise pertains to willful energy applied to perseverance and/or endurance.
Jumping jack signifies acting on the direction or thoughts of those around you.
Medicine ball denotes efforts that strengthen inner self.
Parallel bars signify an equal grip on something in one's life; a firm and balanced grasp of a situation or concept.
Pumping iron See workout (physical).

Barbell represents character-building occurrences.

Rowing machine means efforts to improve or maintain a current situation.
Somersault means complex maneuvers to achieve an aim.
Training table cautions against being fed concepts by others.
Trampoline relates to a tendency to gain insights then discount them.
Treadmill reveals a lack of advancement.
Tumbling (gymnastics) is representative of an understanding that one may fall down while walking one's path, but having knowledge that softens the fall enables quicker recovery.
Weight lifter characterizes an individual's perceived strength.
Workout (physical) reveals the need to expend great effort toward a specific goal.

Motor Sports

Drag race is a representation of a powerful adversary.

Checker (flag) represents the attainment of a goal.
Demolition derby usually represents congenial, lighthearted competition, yet may also signify a destructive type depending on the related dream elements.
Dirt bike implies an attempt to speed over life's rougher roads.
Drag race connotes dangerous competition; a fearsome competitor.
Drag strip indicates a fast lane or a detrimental path where one lines up with vicious competitors.
Grand Prix (race) refers to a dangerous manner of competition—fast, furious, and possibly deadly.
Hill climb (race) warns against participating in a potentially hazardous competition.
Hot rod is representative of an individualized manner of speeding one's advancement in life. This is not a good symbol because it pertains to a disrespect for the law and carelessness. This symbol may also refer to a show-off type of personality.
Pace car usually guides the dreamer into a proper rate of progression. Depending on the speed of the dream pace car, it will indicate an acceleration or slowing down.
Pit (refueling area) is representative of a need for the dreamer to reenergize him- or herself; a break in one's work is suggested.
Pit stop suggests a time for renewal; respite; time to take a breather.
Stock car See race car.

Billiards & Pool

Billiard ball pertains to an aspect of skill and/or ability to preplan.
Billiard table See pool table.
Billiards See pool (game).
Billiard stick See cue stick.
Cue ball is a reference to a beginning move.
Cue stick alludes to the level of precision; a beginning move made.
Dirty pool exemplifies a lack of scruples; underhandedness.
Eight ball is suggestive of a problematic situation or relationship. This may even refer to one's own thought process.
Pocket (billiards) signifies moves along one's path; advancement increments.
Pool (game) suggests cleverness combined with the skill to accomplish a goal.
Pool table refers to the issue or subject of one's plans.

Equestrianism & Horse Racing

Ascot suggests airs; outward affectations one puts on.
Bareback (riding) exemplifies a free spirit; one going forward unrestrained.
Crop (riding whip) represents impatience.
Currycomb connotes the attention and control given to one's wilder aspects.
Derby (race) denotes a competitive personality or aspect.
Dressage pertains to the ability to manage one's life.
Dude ranch connotes an attempt to soften and round out one's stern and sharp personality elements.
English saddle typifies control of one's path.
Hackamore denotes control.
Horseback (riding) suggests a desire to experience every nuance of one's traveled path.
Horse race alludes to a controlled speed; a fast-paced progression that is well controlled by another.
Horsewoman characterizes one who isn't fearful of blazing her own course; an eagerness to gallop forward into unknown territory.
Photo finish (of race) exemplifies a nearly equal level of ability, knowledge, or development.
Polo constitutes haughtiness; a presumptuous personality.
Starting gate warns against life competition.
Stirrup denotes an advisement to get a firm foothold.

Flying Sports

Barnstorming See stunt flying.
Hang glide corresponds with effortless thought; ideas or concepts that come easily.
Stunt flying represents one who has a tendency toward flaunting his or her ostentatious intellect by using one-hundred dollar words. Usually this individual will have little real wisdom behind the show of verbal pretension.

see also
• Driving *p. 297*
• Aircraft *p. 301*

Winter Sports

Curling stone represents a weighty element that has been slid into an issue.
Downhill racer (skiing) signifies an apathetic approach to spiritual issues.
Figure skating See ice skate.
Giant slalom (skiing) comes to the dreamer as a warning message to slow down to avoid a collision course.
Ice dancing (pairs) suggests a relationship in which spirituality isn't freely expressed or openly shared.
Ice skate connotes skating over one's frozen spiritual aspects. This is a clear message to unthaw these and begin using them.
Mogul (skiing) refers to bumps along one's spiritual path.
Rink (skating) correlates to going around in circles; a lack of advancement.
Rope tow See ski lift.
Skating (ice) See ice skate.
Ski jump pertains to the avoidance of spiritual aspects in one's life.
Ski lift represents material aspects one allows to lift one over spiritual responsibilities.
Ski patrol refers to one's conscience.
Ski pole alludes to personal aids one utilizes for the purpose of avoiding spiritual responsibility.
Ski run corresponds with a means to swiftly avoid spiritual issues.
Skiing (snow) connotes spiritual indifference; ignoring one's spiritual beliefs or responsibilities as if they were frozen or nonexistent.
Slalom relates to a personally devised course set to evade spiritual issues.
Snowboard See slalom.
Speed skating/walking won't normally stand for impatience but rather a tendency toward efficiency; a routine manner of handling situations.

Ice skating implies hiding part of one's character from one's partner.

Blood Sports

Blood sport comes to the dreamer as a revelation of someone with the qualities of vindictiveness and maliciousness. It also refers to someone with a dark draw toward ruthlessness.
Bullfight is representative of hard-headedness. It will refer to someone who has an inability to compromise.
Cockfight warns of a tendency to use others to resolve one's conflicts.

Shooting

Bird shot represents a negative element that is used to destroy another's unique attitude or perspective.
Clay pigeon means a life aspect that sharpens responses and instincts. In some dreams this symbol may point to personal weakness—an inability to stand up for oneself.
Deadeye is an expert level of attainment; one who knows exactly what he or she is doing.
Game (hunting) See prey.
Long shot typifies the taking of a great chance; a small probability of success.
Prey (hunting) reveals a negative situation where one person is another's victim.
Shooting match indicates an out-of-control disagreement.
Skeet (shooting) implies a tendency to shoot down ideas and concepts that are outside one's personal range of perceptual belief.
Target shooting exemplifies practice; an attempt to sharpen one's skills.
Trapshooting typifies a desire to maintain personal skills.
Turkey shoot reveals an unfair advantage.

Unusual & Extreme Sports

Aikido/Judo/Jujitsu/Karate/Kung fu/Tae kwon do See martial arts.
Barrel racing often reveals a confident woman.
Black belt symbolizes self-confidence.
Bungee cord denotes secured defenses; safeguards applied when taking life chances.
Bungee jumping means false bravado; a show of bravery when safeguards are in place.
High wire means a questionable leap in one's advancement; a fragile situation.
Martial arts represent multiple opportunities and methods of defense.
Mountain climbing stresses personal efforts expended toward reaching goals.
Nail bed will reveal one's state of health. May also refer to emotional health.
Tai chi relates to self-control generated from spiritual inner peace.
Tightrope signifies a precarious course one is walking. Also see high wire.
Trapeze is an unproductive means of attempting to progress along a life path.
Tug-of-war is ongoing conflict.
War games depict a desire to maintain optimum strategy.

Miscellaneous

Acceptance speech indicates a need to acknowledge or accept something.
Artificial turf suggests one's affected traits or personality emulates another's.
Blinder warns of apathy; self-generated ignorance.
Contest represents a competitive situation.
Contestant points to a competitive nature; a vying for position.
Cosponsor means an associate supporter or provider.
Doubleheader connotes an event, relationship, or situation that will generate two major benefits.
Fan (person) characterizes common interests and a sense of support for another.
Fight song represents a motivational method. This may refer to a way of maintaining inner strength.
Finalist denotes success.
Foul play warns of serious misdeeds. Who was doing this foul play?
Full-time advises of a need to devote more than part-time attention or energy to a specific aspect.
Game plan is a tactical scheme.
Ground rules allude to moral, ethical, and spiritual guidelines.
Head start represents an opportunity.
Head-to-head denotes an intellectual conflict.
Last (position) denotes an end to something.
Mascot portrays a supporter.
Match (contest) implies competitiveness.
Neck and neck connotes competitiveness.
Obstacle course indicates a life path containing difficult situations to overcome. This could be self-generated.
Olympic games indicate a desire to be recognized as being the ultimate best at something.
Open call denotes an unrestricted opportunity.
Personal foul reminds the dreamer of a willful behavioral misdeed or unfair act against another.
Playbook (sports) correlates to the different moves one has.
Play-off stands for a final chance at something.
Prequalify stands for verification of one's ability to perform.
Preseason depicts a time for preparation; a time to apply energies toward laying groundwork.
Rainout symbolizes a temporary delay.
Running start illustrates a position of advantage.
Runoff represents ramifications or residual elements to something. May also point to an overabundance.
Scoreboard/card connotes an individual's personal balance sheet. Recall what it revealed. What color was it?
Spectator reminds us that someone is always watching, even if it's our conscience.
Sports symbolize "the game" and will be related to a variety of issues connected to the symbolism of the specific sport. See specific sport.
Sports bar represents support for another's efforts. May indicate an attitude of expectation or amusement to see how another fairs.
Sportscast suggests a personal interest and will reveal one's level of involvement in it.
Spring training relates to getting oneself in mental shape to achieve an upcoming goal.
Starter (player) indicates the individual who is meant to begin something. Reveals who should make the first move.
Sunbathing applies to a desire to absorb the spiritual within.
Sunlamp reflects artificial spirituality.
Tail wind relates to an element that serves to increase the pace of one's life progression, or the time it takes to reach a goal.
Tally See scoreboard/card.
Team refers to those working together for a specific goal.
Team player is someone who goes along with the crowd, even if the crowd is wrong.
Time-out expresses a break should be taken.
Tournament See contest.
Trophy (award) is a sign of accomplishment and encouragement to keep striving.
Unbeaten denotes skill; never been defeated.

Trophy represents achievement and inspires one to continue one's efforts.

Sports Venues

Grandstand comes to the dreamer as a warning against always wanting to impress others and to act more subtly.
Olympic training center represents great efforts to prove oneself, not to others but more to self.
Rostrum See podium.
Skybox (arena/stadium) signifies a privileged, yet costly, viewpoint.
Stadium denotes the act of observing. May represent a warning to become more involved. Also pertains to the playing field.

see also
• Marine Fish *p. 38*
• Sewing *p. 180*

Angling

Angling denotes a spiritual nonchalance.
Cast (fishing) is representative of spiritual fishing; a reaching for some type of spiritual information.
Casting (fishing) denotes tentative attempts made; moves to test the waters.
Fishhook warns of a lazy or faulty spiritual search. Do not attempt to snag any spiritual concept that happens by.
Fishing represents an unorganized or undisciplined spiritual search.
Fishing line refers to a length or measure of spiritual search or inquiry.
Fishing lure warns of an arrogantly lazy approach to one's spiritual search. An expectation of spiritual information coming to one without having to put out energy to go in search of it.
Fishing rod signifies a life aspect that has the capability of assisting in one's personal spiritual search, yet the method lacks selectiveness or discrimination.
Fishing trip symbolizes an intent to gain further information regarding a particular issue.
Fishnet cautions of a personal lack of spiritual discernment; a tendency to gather up all spiritual concepts without being discriminating in respect to the truths.
Fly (bait) suggests unfair or unscrupulous methods of achieving ends; using personal knowledge of someone to draw him or her to you.
Fly casting comes as a warning against intermittent spiritual fishing.
Fly-fishing points to teasing or tempting with bait for the purpose of achieving a goal or drawing another to oneself.
Ice fishing stands for a search for or expectation of spiritual insights.
Lure (fishing) See fishing lure.
Open season implies a time of accessibility, not necessarily for positive purposes.
Reel (fishing) connotes a life factor that may provide spiritual discoveries.
Shanty (ice fishing) represents an effort to remain diligent at gaining spiritual insights.
Tackle (fishing) connotes spiritual accessories that are unnecessary for enlightenment or development.

Woodwork

Whittling relates to a calculated plan for one's life.
Wood-burning (craft tool) symbolizes focused creativity. It also refers to a gently expressed nature.
Wood-carving typifies creativity through gentleness; acceptance of life.
Woodcut symbolizes a creative way one's natural talents are manifested. What was the woodcut of? How was it utilized?
Woodworking is representative of utilizing one's inherent talents in creative ways.

Needlework

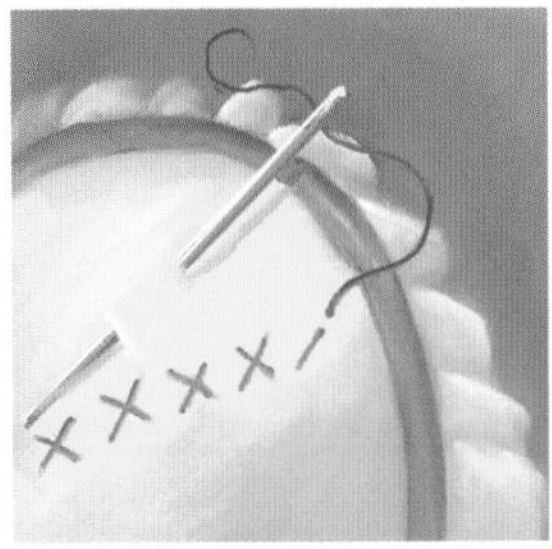
Embroidery amplifies the truth.

Appliqué connotes a tendency to add to or decorate that which can stand on its own.
Blanket stitch reflects an intent to complete a project or goal.
Chain stitch denotes a need to take one step at a time when repairing past mistakes.
Crewelwork (needlework) suggests attention to details.
Crochet (needlework) depicts personal acts done for others.
Embroidery (needlework) depicts exaggerations; a tendency to embellish.
Embroidery floss refers to the choice of embellishments at one's disposal. What's important is to recall the displayed colors.
French knot portrays a socially delicate situation.
Hemstitch applies to the act of finishing something; to a conclusion or closure.
Mending (sewing) typifies an interest in repairing torn or broken relationships. May refer to the repair of one's less-than stellar behavior.
Needle (sewing) pertains to an aspect in life that has the potential to be used for repair or connective purposes.
Needlecraft (hobby) refers to a cleverness for finding solutions; to an attention to details others tend to miss.
Needlepoint illustrates fortitude. Recall what type of needlepoint was presented. Who was doing it? What was the needlepoint image of?
Needle threader represents a desire or attempt to use every aid possible to get to the main issue (eye) of a problem or situation.
Petit point (bead/needlework) represents efforts expended on fine detail; attention to the important little elements.
Pincushion illustrates one's ability to make allowances and/or devise alternatives.
Sampler (stitchery) will imply variety or relay a specific message for the dreamer.
Sewing applies to a bringing together; to a desire to reconnect; to coalesce. This symbol comes when one has been severed from a belief, relationship, or situation that now requires reconnection.
Slipstitch points to a repair or fix done without anyone noticing.
Stitch (sewn) indicates the act of pulling something together; an attempt to connect elements.
Tack (sewing) signifies a temporary repair measure.
Thimble implies a very small amount of something. May also refer to a need to protect oneself.
Thread may refer to a connective element or it may indicate a singular, thin idea or chance.
Treadle applies to the energy applied to keep one's momentum going.
Whipstitch means a quick fix.

Painting, Sculpture & Pottery

Ice sculpture illustrates the futility of trying to keep one's spiritual aspects frozen (hidden) in an unexpressive manner.
Layout (visual arrangement) most often enters a dream as a personal message. It will reveal a specific plan, solution, or condition relating to the dreamer. Was the layout confusing? Was it sharp and vivid? Was it pleasing to the eye?
Matte (frame) portrays individual traits or preferences. Will reveal clues into one's hidden qualities.
Metal sculpture stands for a lasting image. What was the sculpture of?
Motif reveals a dominating ideology, usually the one prevalent in one's life.
Multidimensional (visuals) denotes multilayered factors to whatever is being presented. This is a valuable insight.
Mural will reveal a specialized message for each dreamer. Recall what the mural depicted.

Ice sculpture emphasizes the need to explore one's spirituality.

Objet d'art usually represents a personal message unique to each dreamer. This piece of art symbolizes something important in one's life.
Old Masters (artists) characterize those whose creative achievements of individuality have left valuable contributions in their wake.
Paintbrush pertains to a desire to alter something in life.
Painting (picture) will usually contain an important element to which the dreamer needs to give attention.
Palette (art) indicates multiple opportunities to express one's thoughts and/or show one's unique individuality.
Palette knife applies to an available tool for combining and harmoniously blending ideas and concepts.
Perspective (artistic) denotes either how one currently views something or should view it. Recall dreamscape details for further clarity.
Picture hanger suggests that it's a good idea to place something in full view so it's always in the forefront of one's mind.
Portrait signifies a true revelation of an individual. Recall what type of portrait it was. What was represented? Was it a beautiful representation? Grotesque? A caricature? Dark pigments or soft coloring?
Pose can reflect various meanings depending on the type of posturing that was presented in the dream. An obvious character or attitude revelation will be defined by an exaggerated position.
Position See pose.
Potter's wheel points out a vehicle for one to express creativity and individuality.
Pottery emphasizes the unique character of individuals. Recall who the pottery belonged to, the design, shape, color, and what it was made of.
Sculpting relates to the act of creating and formulating in a personal manner. May reveal one's individualized perception of something.
Sculpture reveals an important element that the dreamer should give attention to. What was the sculpture of?
Statue presents a specific message for each dreamer. The type of statue will have a unique relation to the dreamer.
Superimposed (image) exposes the existence of a dual nature or personality as evidenced by that which one presents to others and that which is kept hidden.
Terra cotta See pottery.
Visual arts symbolize creative expressiveness.

Art Forms & Styles

Cubism (art form) represents a rigid perception.
Drip painting (art form) signifies wild expression of thoughts; uncontrolled emotions; letting the ramifications of one's personal actions land where they may.
Fine art refers to talented skill. This could pertain to any type of skill, such as communication, analysis, and discernment, as well as creative artistic skills.
Folk art suggests an honest, open expression of self.
Junk art denotes an altered perspective.
Kinetic art alludes to the beauty of moving along one's path; making progress.
Montage (art form) indicates a state of thought. Related montage visuals denote a wholeness to one's perspective. Unrelated montage visuals will on the other hand warn of a disconnective or disassociative thought process.
New wave (fashion/music) signifies the expression of innovative, controversial, or unique personal perspectives; a freedom of bold expression without concern of ridicule.
Op art (art form) is usually representative of a simplistic manner of expression.
Pop art depicts a clear visual that's intended as a personal message for the dreamer.
Realism (art form) stands for a perspective free of extraneous aspects.
Romanticism (style) relates to empathy. It also refers to emotional expressiveness.
Still life (painting) generally portrays an important element for the dreamer to give awake-state attention to. This connotation will be different for each dreamer. Recall what the dream still life depicted.

see also
• Designs & Shapes *p. 449*
• Art & Images *p. 463*

Drawing

Annotation constitutes an explanation.

Doodling may represent unconscious thoughts or may indicate a warning against idleness.

Drawing connotes creative expression of inner aspects.

Illustration connotes a visual message specific to each dreamer. Recall what was illustrated.

Lithograph represents a developed ability to keep different aspects separate in life.

Sketch denotes a tentative outline or trial-and-error formulation of a new idea.

Sketchbook represents a wealth of new ideas; mental excursions into possibilities.

Stick figure symbolizes the beginning formation of an idea or theory about another.

Tracing paper stands for attempts to copy or imitate something. This dreamscape element comes to remind one to depend on individual creativity.

Artistic Media

Fresco denotes ingrained attitudes.

Medium (art form) alludes to quality or manner of self-expression. See specific form such as ink, oil paint, etc.

Oil color (art medium) See oil paint.

Oil paint (art medium) signifies an inherent gift of creativity that comes easily to one.

Paint (artist's) denotes personal tools for self-expression.

Pastel (chalk) suggests a person's intent to soften a specific personality trait. Refer to the specific color for further interpretation.

Porcelain applies to an extremely delicate situation, relationship, or other aspect such as mental state.

Watercolor reveals a visual (painting) related to a spiritual aspect in one's life. This dreamscape symbol will be different for each dreamer.

Photography

Double exposure refers to the blurring of ideas together.

Double exposure stands for an unclear picture, the mixing of issues.

Macro lens signifies a need for closer inspection or research.

Photo See photograph.

Photograph reveals a message of importance. Recall what or who was in the photo.

Photo opportunity (photo op) suggests opportunities that shouldn't be missed; a need to maintain constant awareness of unexpected experiences in life that carry valuable lessons or insights with them.

Pictorial portrays a set of corresponding photographs associated with the dreamer in some way. They may send a clear message or convey a story line to which the dreamer will relate.

Picture See photograph; painting.

Picture frame (photo) is a revealing dream element that sheds more clarity on whatever the photograph was of. The frame usually represents one's attitude toward that picture.

Soft focus signifies an attempt to lessen the harshness of an issue. May also indicate a desire to hide the finer details of something.

Trim size stands for the elemental, basic shape of a situation or issue.

Tripod suggests a need to steady oneself; a need to get focused without any distortion.

Vignette denotes a small, pleasing reminder of something. It may specifically refer to a memento.

Newspapers & Magazines

Blurb (review) reflects one person's opinion.

Book review pertains to a message received from one's higher self in respect to to the quality of material and personal relevance of a book title.

Commission (assignment) depicts having the authority to do something; one's right to act or proceed.

Hatchet job stands for an idea or plan that has been ridiculed or picked apart so completely that little remains.

Magazine connotes a different message for each dreamer depending on the type of magazine presented in the dream. Recall if it was illuminated or shadowed. What color was dominant?

Magazine rack indicates multiple opportunities for gaining information.

Newsletter comes as a message specific to each dreamer. Its purpose is to keep one up to date on an aspect in one's life.

Newspaper represents an awareness within oneself.

Newsprint (paper type) implies widespread information.

News release pertains to a special announcement message the dreamer needs to note. This symbol comes as a major personal message and should always be taken seriously.

Newsstand indicates the opportunity for readily available information. This usually refers to someone (possibly the dreamer) who believes he or she has little access to new ideas or information.

Scoop (information) exposes hidden elements to an issue. It may also point to the first person to reveal specific information.

Sidebar corresponds to additional information.

Yellow journalism stands for a pronounced tendency to fixate on the negative; focusing on one's faults, tragedies, or mistakes.

Books & Text

Acknowledgment means some type of response is required. This may also reveal some type of denial is taking place.
Afterword See epilogue.
Blueline (book production proof) comes to advise of a need to read things carefully.
Boldface (type) means emphasis. This is a call to pay attention.
Book burning warns against censorship or an attempt to silence another's right to free speech or expression.
Break (in text) indicates a need to pace the rate of one's informational intake.
Caption defines something; an explanation; further clarity.
Chapter (book) indicates a stage in life; a special period of time.
Chiller (book/film) See thriller.
Endnote refers to a concluding explanation; an afterthought.
Endpaper is the final stage of an issue; a concluding symbol.
Epilogue indicates the final words on something; concluding statement.
Fiction implies an imaginative scenario; perhaps inventiveness.
Font (typestyle) emphasizes one's individual character.
Footnote advises of the need to check informational sources.
Galley proof advises of a need to check for errors that lead to misconceptions.
Glossary advises of a need to correct the usage of one's specific terminology that is in error. This dream fragment may also display a word (or words) that is revealing—disclosing the true character of a situation or of another individual.
Hard copy means a visible, touchable aspect.
Historical novel has a karmic lesson to teach each dreamer.
Literature reveals an important message for each dreamer. Recall what type of literature was represented.
Misprint may indicate unawareness or it might pertain to a message for the dreamer, depending on how the misprint was made.
Mystery (novel/movie) suggests a fascination with suspense and an interest in untangling convoluted situations.
Novel illustrates personal, sometimes hidden, interests one uses as an escape mechanism. Recall what type of novel it was. Mystery? Romance? War story? Gory?
Nursery rhyme can reveal an important message specific to the dreamer.
Old wives' tale reveals a piece of truth that the dreamer will recognize.
Page (book) comes to point out something the dreamer should be aware of. Recall what was on the page. What type of book was it in? Color?
Page proofs signify an opportunity to make changes before the final event.
Parable emphasizes valuable lessons that need to be learned or recalled.
Pen name See pseudonym.
Plot (story line) signifies a synopsis of what is transpiring in one's awake-state life. It gives a vivid look at one's attitudes or lifestyle.
Poem usually serves as a message for the dreamer who will make the necessary association.
Poetic license portrays conceptual development of expansion.
Preface pertains to an introductory communication; an icebreaking element. May be a forewarning.
Prologue reflects an explanatory beginning; an introductory phase of a communication.
Pseudonym may imply a need to protect oneself or it may indicate an alter ego, depending on the surrounding dreamscape factors.
Ream (paper) is a measure of work. Recall if the paper was filled with print or blank.
Redline exemplifies a refusal; rejection; something deleted.
Rhyme may indicate a juvenile perspective, yet this symbol usually comes in dreams to relay a message.
Saga portrays extensive details.
Self-publish relates to personal efforts and determination put into disseminating one's own ideas or perspectives.
Short story typifies a specialized message for the dreamer.
Slipcase (books) suggests a protective attitude toward one's cherished knowledge; a respect for knowledge.
Sonnet See poem.
Storybook reveals a personal message for each dreamer. Recall the storybook's title. What was the message of the story? Was someone reading it or handing it to you?
Table of contents portrays the main issues the dreamer needs to address in life.
Tearjerker usually reveals excessive emotionalism.
Thriller (book/film) suggests a need for suspense in one's life; a love of living on the edge.
Tragedy (drama) reveals a situation with dire consequences, indicating a result one may have been unaware of. This usually refers to one's intentions for near-future behavior or an action one plans on taking. This is usually a forewarning.
Typo pertains to an unintentional error or life mistake.
Underlined illustrates emphasis. Recall what was underlined. This will be what the dreamer needs to give attention to.
Underscore See underlined.

Book burning cautions against removing the right to self-expression.

see also
• Writers & Celebrities *p. 369*
• Text & Books *p. 458*

Writing & Literature

Allegory reflects a parablelike message. It may also refer to a deeper meaning.

Analogy reveals the type of one's relationships, perspectives, and/or behavior.

Antonym signifies opposition.

Cliché has a dual meaning. It may imply that one is too nonchalant or it may indicate that one has acceptance. Surrounding dreamscape factors will clarify this meaning. What did the cliché refer to?

Cliff-hanger exemplifies high anxiety; suspense; left on the edge while waiting for results or conclusions.

Composite character (in story) depicts one possessing a wide variety of qualities and characteristics drawn from other individuals. May stand for a lack of individuality.

Composite story represents a scenario comprised of elements taken from several other situations.

Editing signifies a need to choose appropriate words or phrasing when attempting to define one's thoughts and ideas.

Writer's block refers to a temporary lack of direction in life.

Epigram usually comes as an important message for the dreamer and is unique to her individual life situation.

Free verse expresses the freedom to speak one's mind regardless of unconventionality.

Genre implies a specific category of something. This will generally pinpoint an important factor in one's life and will be unique to each dreamer.

Limerick (verse), although often frivolous, usually brings a personal message.

Magnum opus symbolizes greatness of creativity; a monumental work.

Narrative most often infers a dream as a message. Recall what the narrative was about and who was giving it.

Nom de plume See pseudonym.

Plagiarism portrays an idea that isn't one's own as claimed or presented.

Quatrain See poem.

Quotation most often comes as a message or some type of revelation, perhaps the solution to a problem or pointing out a better perspective.

Synopsis symbolizes a basic idea or elemental facts.

Theme applies to a specific perspective that will shed light on the dreamer's current puzzlement.

Trilogy signifies the existence of three aspects creating a whole. Something in the dreamer's life has three different aspects to it.

Unreadable relates to a personal lack of comprehension and may denote concepts or ideas for which one isn't yet ready.

Writer's block stands for a temporary absence of inspiration. May point to being at a loss as to where to go from here.

Types of Book

Comic book connotes a manner of escape from life; unrealistic perceptions; a hesitancy to face reality.

Field guide points to a need to identify the source of a specific aspect in one's life.

Funny papers See comic book.

Guidebook is a life aspect that serves to keep one on course.

Handbook warns against following a stilted lifestyle; regimentation.

Hardcover (book) relates to an enduring quality; lasting.

Large print (type) usually comes as an attention-getting element that suggests that one has been missing something.

Millboard See hardcover.

Nonfiction most often reveals the truth to a matter in one's life.

Paperback (book) has a personal meaning for each dreamer. Recall what the book's title was. Did the title of the book hold a special meaning for you? What was the book's condition? Where was it found?

Phrase book represents a desire to communicate better and the efforts applied to same.

Picture book signifies a need for a simplified or expanded explanation.

Pocketbook (book) See paperback.

Pop-up (child's book type) points to aspects that are meant to be highlighted or to draw one's attention.

Pulp fiction reflects idle intellect; filling one's mind with useless information.

Sourcebook reveals multiple opportunities to take advantage of. What was the book's subject matter?

Tome reflects an extensive volume of information.

Treatise comes in dreams to advise of a need to gain full information on an issue.

Unabridged pertains to a complete rendition; to leaving no elements out.

Theater & Entertainment

Applause means approval.
Behind the scenes alludes to hidden aspects of what is seen or manifested in the open. May point to hidden agendas.
Bit part (in a play) reveals a small role one is playing or needs to play in a relationship or some type of situation.
Central casting indicates a source of individuals one can choose from for the purpose of selecting a helper or aide who's fit for the project.
Comic relief advises of a need to maintain a sense of humor throughout life.
Cue card defines an individual who rarely speaks for self.
Dramatization is usually a message for the dreamer. Take note of any symbolism acted out in the dreamscape drama.
Dress rehearsal connotes a need to take life seriously.
Entertainment usually comes as a specific message. Perhaps one needs more relaxation time, maybe less. What form of entertainment was shown?
Farce indicates exaggerated perceptions.
Fireworks forewarn of an explosive situation or relationship.
Floor show cautions of misplaced priorities.
Follies (stage) refer to a beginning venue to start using one's talents.
Footlights warn against spotlighting one's individual path for the arrogant purpose of leadership.
Fun house advises one to face one's fears and laugh at them.
Gallery (audience) illustrates those who watch you and listen.

Grease paint suggests a fake persona that one shows to the world.

Grand finale points to a showy conclusion to something.
Grease paint warns of hypocrisy; a false face presented to others.
Grease pencil represents a way to convey a message to a nonreceptive individual.
Greenroom constitutes a waiting period; the pause just before the action begins.
Hand-clap See applause.
Intermission advises of a need for a break from one's work, study, or other type of pursuit.
Little theater connotes experimental methods of manipulation.
Long run (play) simply means extreme popularity. The key is to recall the play's title for the clue to the symbol's intent.
Matinee indicates a suggestion to take time out to alleviate stressful situations.
Melodrama represents gross exaggerations; emotional manipulation.
Mime represents honesty.
Off-Broadway signifies an experimental attempt or move; the testing of an idea.
One-liner reveals sarcasm, how one really feels. It can also reveal a succinct idea or truth.
One-woman show applies to an action one must accomplish alone; a call to be independent in behavior or thought.
Opera connotes a mature perspective.
Opera glasses relate to attentiveness; an interest in understanding events.
Overbooked symbolizes a lack of foresight, planning.
Pantomime See mime.
Peep show warns against wasting time and energy on superficial life elements.
Play (drama) correlates to something going on in one's awake state. This emphasizes or clarifies a situation.
Playbill portrays an attempt to draw attention to something one is missing in life.
Playbook See script.
Pun pertains to innuendos.
Punch line reveals a solution or crux of the matter.
Pyrotechnics See fireworks.
Rehearsal denotes the practicing of one's belief; walking one's talk.
Script suggests a need to play by the rules.
Sellout may be a popular issue or a betrayal.
Shadow play refers to behind-the-scenes behavior.
Show bill refers to exaggerations; making a big production of something.
Showboat warns of spiritual arrogance; spiritual flaunting.
Showstopper reveals an outstanding performance. May also point to an element that cuts off all adversity.
Showtime advises of the time to put an idea into action.
Summer stock stands for phases when one has a tendency to don altered personas.
Tableau illustrates an important message presented as a scene for the dreamer to view.
Theater-in-the-round symbolizes behavior in full view of everyone.
Theatrics means overreaction.
Trapdoor reflects unawareness; possible pitfalls.
Vaudeville alludes to an attempt to try out one's idea or plan.
Voice of America normally represents the truth amid a storm of fabrications, yet sometimes can be the reverse.

see also
• Film, Theater & Dance *p. 249*
• Media & TV *p. 249*

Television

Airtime refers to a tendency to broadcast personal thoughts.

Discovery Channel denotes expanding one's knowledge.

Game show cautions against a boastful intelligence; a desire to be intellectually superior.

Laugh sign (audience) stands for insincerity; manipulated responses.

Laugh track is false happiness; an attempt to hide real feelings.

Miniseries connotes sequential stages of one's experience, search, or path progression.

Outtake (blooper) usually illustrates one's mistakes.

Reality TV reveals behavioral traits of revenge, voyeurism, a sadistic enjoyment from seeing another's fear.

Rerun (program) indicates a need to learn something that was initially missed.

Sequel is a continuation.

Sitcom brings a specific meaning to each dreamer. What was the show's theme?

Sneak preview represents personal insights; foresight.

Soap opera relates to an overdramatized situation.

Talk show publicizes opinions or interests of others.

Television (watching) See watching television.

Test pattern is the sharpness of perspective. Was the pattern well defined or blurred?

Tiebreaker (on a quiz show) constitutes a need to prove excellence or superiority.

Watching television reveals the state of one's perspectives, depending on what one is watching. For example, cartoons indicate immaturity; news means being up-to-date.

Cinema & Film

Animation signifies one's immature outlook on life.

Billboard means a warning or reminder; attention-getting.

Cameo appearance represents a dreamscape's "featured" individual of personal importance to the dreamer.

Cartoon can advise that one should use humor in life, or it may warn of a tendency toward avoiding reality.

Close-up (lens shot) portrays close inspection; analysis.

Colorization (old films) stands for enhancement; enrichment without altering anything.

Cutting room reveals selective perspectives or presentations; lacking objectivity.

Double billing refers to exaggerations of claiming multiple efforts expended that were only done once.

Double feature advises of two important facets of one aspect.

Drive-in (movie) represents an extra effort applied to some aspect in the dreamer's life.

Film clip is a sampling; getting a taste of something.

Final cut (film) signifies the achievement of an acceptable outcome or plan.

Footage (film) denotes solid proof; verification.

Hollywood typifies symbols that relate to superficiality.

Klieg light is an attention-getting message that advises of a need to get light on an issue.

Lip-synching signifies a tendency to imitate the words or perspectives of others.

Movie is a personal message for the dreamer. Recall the subject of the movie.

Movie theater may show an unrealistic perspective and an attempt to clarify it.

Premier (debut) denotes the first time something is presented.

Projector advises of a need to project an idea or attitude to another; a need to externalize and express emotions.

Screenplay represents a proposed plan of action; a speculative idea that envisions the outcome.

Screen test relates to one's desire to perform a specific task or role and the appropriateness of being the right person.

Shooting script represents one's finalized plan or decision.

Slow motion is an attention-getting device; advising you to scrutinize whatever action or event has been slowed.

Subtitle is an explanation or a clue to something.

Movie theater suggests the dreamer does not have a realistic outlook on life.

Chapter 14

Music, Sound & Dance

These important dream elements reveal a state of harmony or discord. Dancing depicts the manner by which one steps to life's rhythms.

Dance Styles

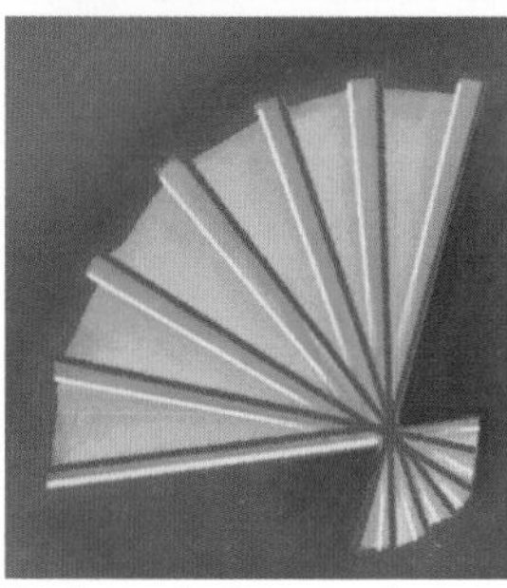

Fan dance signifies temptations.

Belly dance implies a tendency to brag; to show off. May also point to enticements.
Break dancing refers to the efforts made for independence or when expressing your own unique perspectives.
Cancan suggests the presence of unrestrained happiness.
Clogging (type of dance) refers to a difficult path chosen.
Dance refers to a personal way of expressing emotions.
Fan dance means enticements.
Fandango represents a fiery relationship with someone.
Flamenco (dance style) stands for an outward expression of intense emotions.
Go-go (dancing) signifies a frantic bid for attention.
Hat dance represents the joyous feeling of a new love.
Hula signifies body language; communicating your intentions through behavior.
Jitterbug refers to a lack of direction in life.
Kabuki calls for a more frequent expression of one's emotions, especially by men.
Lap dance represents the things in life that one wants but are out of reach, unobtainable, or untouchable.
Limbo suggests a need to go the extra mile, bend over backwards to do this.
Modern dance pertains to the skill to freely express oneself.
Moonwalk (dance move) points out that one only appears to be falling behind, that some backward moves are required to achieve greater (more beneficial) advancement.
Soft-shoe (dancing) represents a routine joy in life; optimism; and an appreciation of one's little blessings.
Sun dance is inner strength.
Sword dance corresponds to the feeling of confidence and self-reliance that one's defensive measures provide.
Tap dance warns against going through life by tapping others' resources instead of your own.

Latin American Dances

Mambo suggests fast moves done with another. May indicate ulterior motives or moving ahead too fast.
Rumba usually represents a troubled relationship, one in which there's routine aggression, then backing down.
Salsa connotes high interest; an exciting and active element in one's life.
Samba signifies a relationship in which partners are at odds.
Tango stands for the synchronized efforts of two people.

Country Dances

Barn dance See hootenanny.
Country dance represents the joys of being completely unaffected by negative worldly aspects.
Folk dance defines a healthy, comfortable sense of self.
Hoedown See square dance.
Hootenanny represents spontaneous joy shared with others.
Jig signifies a moment of elation in your life.
Line dance warns against a tendency toward having to stay in step with everyone else. This advises of the need for independent thought.
Round dance signifies the full interactive participation of all parties involved.
Square dance indicates a formulated interaction with others as opposed to one that is spontaneous and more open.

Mood Music

Background music reveals an underlying mood or attitude.
Elevator music implies soothing elements along one's path.
Mood music is a dreamscape element that serves to set the general tone.
Muzak alludes to subliminal communicative methods.
Soundtrack exposes a personal message for each dreamer. Recall what type of music was played. What were the words? What film was it from?

Ballet

Adagio reflects the need for trusting a partner or associate.
Arabesque is representative of balance.
Ballet represents a situation that has been engineered; dancing through life with prearranged steps instead of letting the moment dictate your movements.
Pas de deux corresponds to a collaboration between two individuals. This may be a revealing event for you.
Pirouette represents inner joy.
Water ballet portrays spiritual inner joy.

Ballroom & Old-Time Dances

Fox-trot indicates tricky maneuvers done regarding a relationship or other situation.
Mazurka connotes the outward expression of great joy.
Minuet pertains to a fragile relationship or situation, one where people need to watch their every move.
Polka portrays a lively and cheerful attitude.
Tarantella represents a passionate relationship. This passion may not always refer to an attraction or love.
Turkey trot See ragtime.
Two-step stands for a relationship in which the partners always have a similar goal.
Waltzing typifies a lack of seriousness; one is waltzing through life.

see also
• Motion & Exercise *p. 178*
• Film, Theater & Dance *p. 249*

Musical Styles

Acid rock is representative of negative influences.
Anthem denotes loyalties and the expression of same.
Ballad relates to lessons learned in life.
Bluegrass signifies a down-home type of spirituality.
Blues cautions against being overwhelmed by spiritual melancholy; a need to balance the lightness of spirituality and the heaviness of living.
Bop (bebop music) suggests a break from the norm.
Canticle denotes inner spiritual joy; a full heart.
Chamber music represents a specialized audio unique to the dreamer; sound that soothes or motivates you.
Classical music applies to aspects in one's lives that one perceives as soothing.
Country music symbolizes one's specific manner of expressing emotions.
Dirge portrays the possibility of a great sorrow on its way. It precedes the end of something.
Disco (dance/music) suggests a personal joy or blessing that is unique to the individual.
Fanfare comes in a dream to denote something important.

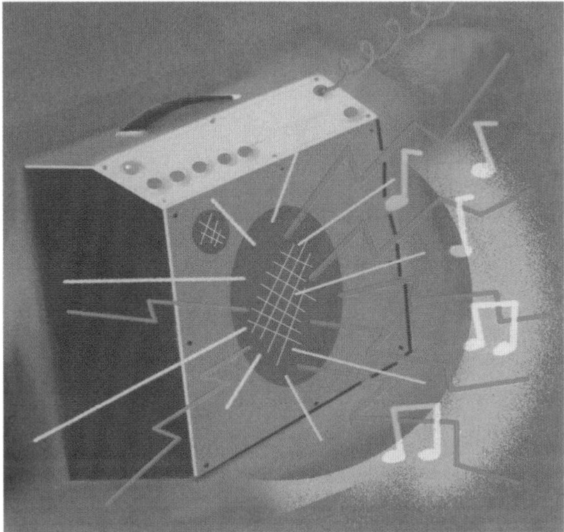

Music may symbolize a happy or unhappy state of mind depending on its type.

Gangsta rap refers to a brutally honest way of telling how things are; a cynical, often degrading, perspective focused on the dark side of life.
Golden oldie represents memories, a spark that sends one back to one's youth.
Gospel music alludes to spiritual joy.
Grand Ole Opry denotes the solidness and enduring nature of tried-and-true ways.
Gregorian chants stand for the practice of prayer.
Hard rock (music) signifies a release of stress, pent-up tension within you.
Heavy metal warns of an extremely negative aspect one needs to either get rid of or accept and move on; a need to expel building stress.
Hip-hop refers to a subculture philosophy or camaraderie.
Honky-tonk signifies an effort to conceal melancholy.
Jam (music) symbolizes a lighthearted mood.
Jazz applies to perseverance.
Love song indicates one's expressed depth of affection.
Lullaby indicates something that tends to lull one into a sense of false security.
Madrigal denotes a shared opinion or idea.
Mariachi connotes carefree joy.
Music indicates a harmonic or discordant state depending on the type of music presented.
Music of the spheres defines spiritual balance and a person's inner peace.
New wave signifies the personal expression of innovative, controversial, or unique personal perspectives; a freedom of bold expression without concern of ridicule.
Psychedelic signifies an altered perspective on something.
Ragtime suggests a phase of perseverance through a sense of humor or gaiety; using one's optimism to get through.
Rap music implies a failed method of getting one's message across by only presenting it to a select group.
Reggae represents an individualistic attitude; the sense of being free to express oneself.
Rhythm and blues (R & B) represents path progression in spite of difficulties.
Rock and roll signifies motivation; a phase of determination to get going and follow one's own unique ideology.
Show tune corresponds with a specific message for the dreamer. Recall what the tune was for more information.
Sing-along relates to shared sentiments in life.
Soft rock suggests a muted or tempered display of one's emotions or opinions.
Song pertains to a specific message according to what was sung.
Staccato defines an abruptness of personality.
Theme song connotes a particular relationship meaning. May represent some type of personal behavior or psychological element.
Vaudeville alludes to an attempt to try out one's idea.
Yodeling defines a braggart.

Musical Ensembles

Band (musical) depicts the beginning of being able to work with others; cooperation; a synergistic association.
Choir signifies shared joys; a group expression; a unified opinion on something.
Chorus (singers) is an idea or perception shared by many.
Glee club typifies short periods of contentedness.
Orchestra refers to group harmony and accord.
Quartet pertains to a harmonic relationship between four individuals.
Quintet depicts five associated individuals/elements creating a harmonic wholeness.

Noise & Silence

Commotion denotes disruption.

Noisemaker represents an issue made of something. This may mean that one needs to bring an issue to another's attention or it may warn to leave something alone instead of making an issue of it. This meaning will be clear after looking at the surrounding dream details.

Noise pollution advises of a need for one to sort through information or communications for the purpose of gleaning the important basic ideas.

Silence is an attention-getting dream element that most often advises us to listen to one's conscience.

Siren defines a strong warning. Recall the associated dreamscape elements for further clarity.

Sonic boom signifies the realization that one has reached a goal.

Musical Tools

Instrument (musical) See specific type.

Metronome calls for a need to pace oneself. Recall if it had been going fast or slow. Was it still?

Pitch pipe represents a life element that will help to keep one on the right track.

Sheet music alludes to the personally composed inner music with which one progresses through life. May bring a special message if the sheet music was titled.

Songbook represents the many choices of perspectives; the many opportunities to view issues/events and react to them.

Tuning fork suggests that something is not ringing true; a call to make an adjustment.

Musical Terminology

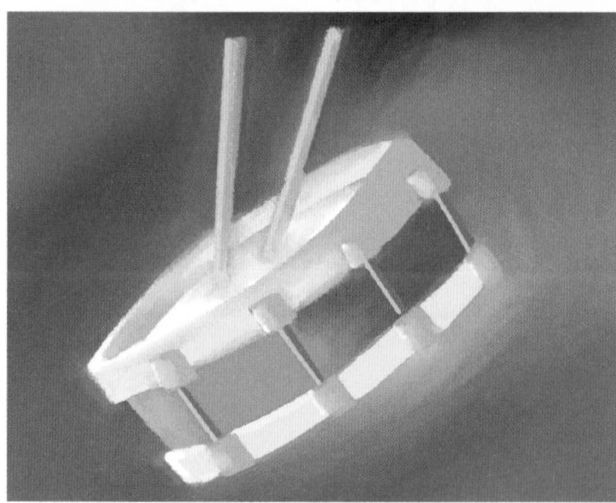

Drumroll heralds a new event in the dreamer's waking life.

Absolute pitch represents something perfectly matched; true alignment.

Bass (tone) refers to depth of meaning or emotion.

Chord (music) refers to an aspect that has a specialized meaning for the dreamer.

Chorus (repeat verse) will come in a dreamscape as a strong emphasis. What message did the chorus convey?

Concert (performance) represents a display of talent or knowledge.

Disharmonious (sound) portrays a vibrationary misalignment.

Drumbeat is a call to the way of nature; natural, heart-moving inner aspects.

Drumroll comes as an attention-getting symbol indicating a precursor to something about to appear in one's life.

Duet typifies a situation that involves two individuals. This in itself may be a very revealing aspect for the dreamer.

Flat (musical notes) shows false, unenthusiastic joy; disinterest.

Fugue denotes a state of unawareness, possibly a self-willed one.

Gamut connotes an entire scope of something; all-encompassing.

Half note implies quicker pace.

Harmonizing pertains to efforts applied to obtaining balance.

High-pitched (tone) is a call to immediately increase awareness; a warning.

Medley (music) signifies a harmonic blend of ideas.

Melody may bring a message via a recognized title of the tune or it could connote a harmonic aspect in one's life. Surrounding dreamscape details will distinguish between the two meanings.

Nocturne alludes to a tranquil state of inner peace.

Off-key illustrates a lack of harmony, perhaps even within self; being off track regarding course or perspective.

Overture stands for an initial move; a tentative testing of the waters; broaching a subject.

Perfect pitch reveals an attitude, plan, solution, or other element that is right on track; alignment; a harmonic aspect.

Philharmonic See symphony.

Rhythm emphasizes the pace at which one is currently progressing. This may also suggest a proper pace.

Serenade stands for an expression of affection. In some cases, this dream symbol may also point to efforts made toward winning over another.

Strumming exemplifies a relaxed attitude; acceptance.

Symphony pertains to coordinated efforts of multiple talents.

Tenor suggests sincerity; a robust integrity.

Tone-deaf won't normally have a negative connotation but rather will stand for one's unique talent of hearing (perceiving) things in a way that others don't.

Tune (music) usually reminds an individual of the lyrics and those words will hold a specific meaning for the individual dreamer.

see also
• Animal Sounds *p. 18*
• Sound & Music *p. 466*

Music Technology

Album (music) reveals the type of inspiration one connects with. What kind of music was the dreamscape album?

Blank tape represents a lack of communication; nothing to hear, nothing to record.

Boom box symbolizes arrogance; a craving for attention.

Broken record denotes repetition.

Demo (music) refers to a sampling of one's perspective, how one's life song is sung; a taste of one's attitude.

Ghetto blaster See boom box.

Gramophone signifies old tunes used as excuses. Cautions against falling back on the same old tunes for reasons behind one's actions.

Jukebox alludes to that which one chooses to listen. This usually comes as a warning to stop being so closed-minded.

Karaoke may represent a desire to be heard or it can refer to unrestrained joy (feeling free to sing as though nobody can hear you).

Mixer (music) represents one who recognizes a multitude of nuances and is capable of blending them to create a new or unique perspective.

Music box means melancholia.

Music video connotes how one applies harmonious inner aspects to life. What type of video was presented? Was it wild or gentle?

Phonograph refers to old information; a need to be updated.

Turntable suggests the need for improved listening skills.

Record (music) comes to the dreamer as a revelation of a message or mood, sometimes even one's character.

Stereo (equipment) stands for the utilization of one's full potential.

Turntable is a reference to a means of listening. If the turntable is broken, it suggests that one isn't listening well enough, perhaps forming assumptions or false impressions because of it.

String Instruments

Banjo characterizes gaiety; lightheartedness.

Bow (fiddle/violin) symbolizes an essential element needed to convey or express something. May mean confidence, courage, and so on.

Cello points to a tendency toward melancholia.

Dulcimer stands for inner contentedness.

Electric guitar cautions of a self-serving need to gain attention.

Fiddle See violin.

Guitar suggests self-expression.

Harp is a suggestion of spiritual peacefulness.

Lute is representative of inner tranquility.

Lyre is a reference to harmony in one's life.

Mandolin See lute.

Moon lute See samisen.

Samisen alludes to a vibratory alignment. It can also refer to the balance within.

Sitar portrays one's expression of inner feelings.

Ukulele exemplifies a carefree personality.

Violin represents emotional range of expression.

Zither illustrates multiple opportunities to express oneself.

Electric guitar symbolizes a warning against attention-seeking.

Musical Sounds

Gong comes to the dreamer as a call to attention. The higher self is attempting to bring the dreamer's attention to something that is important on a variety of levels in the dreamer's everyday life.

Jingling (sound) usually is a call to pay attention to something that's presently being ignored. Surrounding dream details will clarify what this is.

Peal (bells) indicates a call to attention; a need for increased awareness.

Rattle (ceremonial) is representative of an aid to getting in touch with one's inner strength and inherent abilities.

Musicians

Acoustician is representative of one who insists on being accurately heard.
Bandleader portrays an individual who instigates a mood of cooperation among people. Depending on the dreamer's life situation, this symbol could also point to a negative attitude of arrogance or manipulation.
Composer stands for one who creates a harmony or discord.
Conductor connotes an individual who has the ability to bring harmony to a situation.
Disc jockey represents the spreading or acceptance of selected ideas.
Drum majorette relates to boastfulness. This reveals one who advertises everything they feel. May be a call for sympathy.
Drummer characterizes self-confidence and contentedness. May point to one who blazes her own path.
Flutist refers to a balanced and centered individual.
Folk singer characterizes one who keeps tradition alive.
Lyricist characterizes an individual who possesses strong emotions. It refers to an ability to express beautiful feelings.
Maestro characterizes an individual who is capable of leading groups. Recall whether the sounds created in the dream were harmonious or discordant.
Majorette See drum majorette.
Minstrel signifies a person who tends to bring a measure of joy or lightheartedness into another's life.

Conductor signifies a person who helps others join together concordantly.

Musician is an indication of the arrival of spiritual harmony within oneself.
Pianist signifies an individual who desires to have harmony in his or her life.
Piano player stands for an element that requires the least amount of energy output; something that is nearly self-contained and takes care of itself.
Piper See flutist.
Rapper (singer) characterizes one who often conveys feelings or messages in an incoherent or angry manner.
Second fiddle stands for a supportive role.
Singer connotes a communicator. Recall the dream's details to determine whether someone is telling what they know or merely gossiping.
Songwriter characterizes an opportunity to compose and formulate one's own attitude or outlook.
Soprano relates to excitability; an inability to control emotions.
Virtuoso signifies one possessing a masterful talent and skill.

Keyboard Instruments

Accordion means alignment with the truth.
Calliope indicates a whimsical personality; one who fails to take life seriously; optimism taken to the far extreme.
Glockenspiel refers to accuracy. In the dream, were the notes struck right? Were they clear?
Grand piano corresponds with the great potential of one's personal talents. The key here is the condition of the dreamscape piano. Was it highly polished? Were the ivory keys yellowed? Any of them broken or missing altogether?
Harpsichord represents outdated ideas.
Keyboard (musical) pertains to the freedom to play one's own song. Indicates a suggestion to follow one's own path.
Organ (musical) pertains to a complex aspect associated with an issue.
Piano denotes an opportunity to experience or create a harmonic situation or atmosphere, perhaps even within oneself.

Keyboard means individual freedom.

Xylophone is representative of opportunities for an individual to attain balance and personal alignment.

see also
• Radio & Audio *p. 275*
• Parties *p. 349*

Percussion

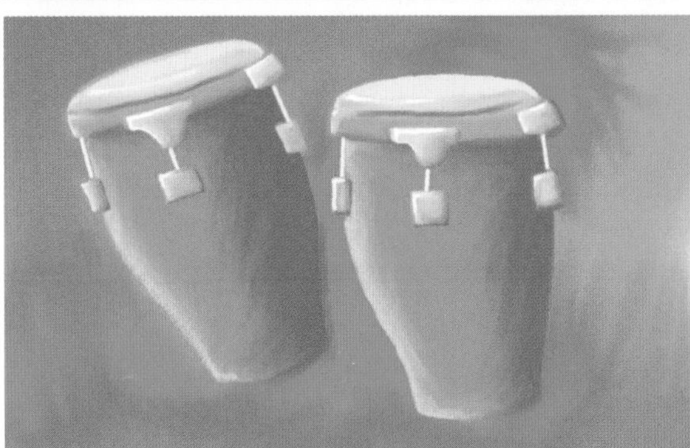

Bongo drums indicate the cooperation of two parties toward one end.

Bass drum is what affects us most deeply emotionally.
Bongo drum stands for dual operations; the working together of two individuals.
Castanet applies to inner delight after proving one right; personal gloating.
Cymbals are attention-getters; a call to listen; an advisement to be watchful and aware.
Drum pertains to the core of one's heart center; deepest emotions.
Drum (steel) refers to lightheartedness.
Drumstick is an aid for soul expression and inner journey.
Kettledrum stands for a call to attention. There is something important in the dreamer's life that isn't being noticed.
Maracas constitute a clearing-out effort; a recognition of negative forces and the resulting act of attempting to repel or dispel them.
Steel drums See drum (steel).
Tambourine relates to a festive or joyful situation.
Tom-tom See drum.

Wind Instruments

Alpenhorn means a call to tranquility. This indicates one is experiencing a particularly hectic lifestyle that requires periods of rejuvenation by way of solitude or respite.
Bagpipe symbolizes an individual who consistently talks about nothing that is important; a gossip; one who talks to gain attention or hold the floor.
Bassoon reflects deep thoughts; high philosophic contemplation.
Bugle is a call to action or attention.
Clarinet symbolizes lyrical verbiage; enhanced statements.
Flute applies to personal power.
French horn implies verbosity; an elaborate way of saying something.
Harmonica corresponds with relaxation; a time for self.
Horn (musical instrument) See specific type.
Kazoo is representative of immaturity.
Mouth organ See harmonica.
Mouthpiece suggests the advisement to speak for oneself.
Panpipe exemplifies lightheartedness. It may refer specifically to a cheerful mood.
Piccolo refers to a higher level; deeper knowledge; more advanced element.
Pipe organ See organ (musical).
Recorder (musical instrument) See flute.
Saxophone alludes to melancholia.
Trombone signifies the deeper elements to an aspect. This indicates the presence of a greater level of complexity to an issue or individual than initially perceived.
Trumpet (horn) reveals a forthcoming message for the dreamer.
Tuba refers to a full-bodied (strong, yet not aggressive) manner of communication.

Musical Venues

Band shell is the chance to experience leisurely fun.
Bandstand refers to a tendency to be the center of attention.
Music hall denotes an interest and appreciation for harmony.
Music shop reveals the state of one's spiritual awareness. What type of music was being perused? Who was doing the looking? What kind of music did the shop specialize in?
Orchestra pit stands for a place for harmony. This symbol suggests that there are some instances in life when disharmony is advised for the purpose of clearing up a misunderstanding or correcting a situation. There are times when we opt for harmony (keeping our mouths shut) in order to not upset the apple cart. This dream symbol is sending the message that harmony shouldn't be pulled out of the orchestra pit to cover up a situation that needs confrontation.
Recording studio symbolizes the opportunity to preserve one's words or history.

Musical Miscellany

Auld Lang Syne is generally representative of an overly reminiscent nature. It will refer to someone who has a tendency for dwelling on the past.
Bandbox is associated with the kind of care that one likes to give to important life aspects.
Dance card usually suggests opportunities for interaction. Recall if the card had only a few names on it or if it was full. Recalling specific names will hold specific meaning for the dreamer.
Recital connotes the act of taking a close look at what one knows and the related application.
Sound system suggests a desire to understand, in a loud and clear manner, what is said.
Stylus is representative of precision.
Swan song stands for an end to a specific life stage of direction.

Chapter 15

Schools & Education

Education symbols indicate that higher learning and deeper knowledge about particular issues are needed.

132 7634
$x^2 = ?$

Types of Education

Alternative school symbolizes free thought; thinking outside the box.

Coeducation symbolizes information that will benefit everyone.

Entry-level denotes a beginning stage. This may point out the real level one is currently at.

Homeschool usually signifies slanted learning; instruction given with a particular perspective slant to it.

Montessori method pertains to a freedom to explore oneself and one's leanings; an expression of abilities.

Private school is a reference to individualized thought processes that are more expanded or limited than those of the general public. The type of private school will clarify whether these thought processes are being more expanded or limiting.

Special education stands for a need to gain additional basics.

Special needs denote just that—they calls attention to an individual or situation needing very special attention, perhaps more tolerance or patience is required.

Specialist Education

Academy (military) refers to unyielding and/or strict indoctrination.

Beauty school See cosmetology.

Charm school See finishing school.

Clinic (instructional) advises of the need to gain further information about something.

Cooking school represents a means of becoming aware of the many ways one can help others in life.

Correspondence school emphasizes learning opportunities.

Driving school indicates a need to review or learn better methods of managing one's way through life.

Educational programming (television) comes in dreamscapes to reveal a subject matter one has a need to be more informed about.

Elective course represents optional information; an opportunity to make a choice about which one wishes to expand a knowledge base.

Extension (school) indicates further learning needed.

Finishing school doesn't normally stand for fine social mores but rather spiritually based attributes such as kindness, compassion, understanding, forgiveness, unconditional love, etc.

Flight school represents a desire to become well educated about a new direction one is planning to take.

Quick study represents intellectual astuteness; absorption of information or knowledge.

Teaching hospital suggests need to learn healing methods. May refer to self-healing.

Trade school refers to specific instruction that will provide skill to progress along one's chosen life path.

Vocational school comes as an advisement to gain greater skill or knowledge in respect to the talents one expects to apply in life.

Young People's Education

Academy (educational) suggests more information or learning is required.

Boarding school is synonymous with the reality of life. We eat, sleep, and learn as we go.

Class (educational) refers to issues/subjects of which one requires better understanding.

Classroom indicates a learning atmosphere or source of information.

Elementary school illustrates the specific developmental stage that one is at in life.

Grammar school See elementary school.

High school typifies a symbol that represents a step up in one's level of learning.

Kindergarten denotes a beginning stage of learning or discovery.

Middle school represents a stage or level of one's current advancement; mediocre experience and/or knowledge.

Nursery school pertains to the learning stages of a novice or beginning seeker.

Outward bound suggests a time or condition that is ripe for self-discovery.

Preparatory school stands for initial research or study.

Preschool applies to basic information; learning essential elements that are needed for working with others.

School may indicate learning or it may refer to the negative aspect of being indoctrinated.

Schoolhouse (one room) emphasizes general information; the basics.

Schoolroom advises of a situation where there's room for learning more, usually about a specific subject. Recall if there were any decorations or book titles in the schoolroom to indicate what subject needs to be studied.

Schoolwork reminds us that we have to continually apply ourselves if we want to learn.

School yard suggests a paced method of study whereby enough breaks are factored in.

Summer camp signifies a recreational, more enjoyable way to spend time learning a particular subject.

Summer school suggests a need for additional information or instruction.

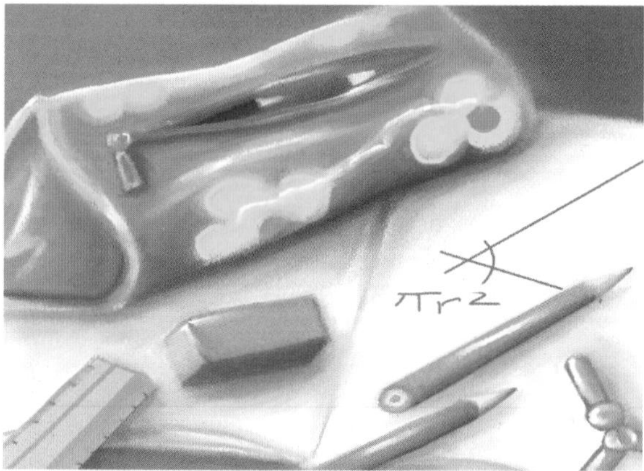

Schoolwork emphasizes the need for constant study to gain knowledge.

see also
• Babies *p. 103*
• Education *p. 251*

Training

Assertiveness training implies the need to be more assertive. This dreamscape symbol usually represents an introverted or retiring personality. It's a call to stand up for oneself. Stop belittling oneself.

Basic training implies having the basics regarding something. This implies further learning is required.

Crash course shows an urgent need to learn or understand something more fully. This points to a situation of misunderstanding, assumption, or lack of information.

Flight simulator represents a sharpening of wit and reaction responses to sudden events; an attempt to be prepared for the unexpected.

Safety film pinpoints a potentially hazardous situation in one's life. Recall what specific type of hazard the film was about.

Seminar connotes expanded education; more in-depth information.

Sensitivity training comes as an advisement for an individual to be more emotionally responsive to others.

Students

Student means needs to learn more.

Exchange student characterizes one who learns from an alternate perspective.

Freshman indicates one beginning a new phase.

Postgraduate stands for advanced research or searching.

Pupil See student.

Scholar characterizes a person who possesses knowledge, usually regarding a specific subject.

Student connotes one who requires further learning experiences.

Trainee is representative of a follower. It may also refer to someone who is beginning a learning phase.

Young Adult Education

Athenaeum refers to further study, specifically through extensive reading.

Campus (university) connotes an attitude of camaraderie toward learning. May also caution against an attraction to learning because of the socializing.

College implies higher learning.

Cow college connotes a learning stage that provides for personal growth.

Free university suggests a need to look into unconventional concepts.

Ivy league denotes intellectual arrogance.

Magnet school is representative of an opportunity to gain from learning from an extensive source of higher knowledge; focus on higher learning.

Reform school warns of a serious need to change one's behavior or alter slanted perspectives.

Seminary pertains to efforts expended for the purpose of gaining deeper spiritual knowledge.

Student union relates to the need for relaxation times interspersed with efforts applied to learning.

University typifies expanded learning.

Varsity is representative of the principal elements or individuals.

Child Care

Crèche comes to the dreamer as a reminder of one's spiritual responsibilities.

Day care alludes to the manner in which one's routine responsibilities are managed in one's everyday life.

Dormitory pertains to an individual's subconscious fear of being alone.

Adult Education

Adult education is representative of the fact that further information is needed regarding a particular issue.

Night school comes to the dreamer as an advisement of a need for immediate learning. There is something in the dreamer's life that must be quickly learned.

Smithsonian Institution represents knowledge and the preservation of it; verification of past events and accomplishments in one's life.

Work–study program refers to learning while doing; putting what one has learned into action while continuing to learn more.

Educational Events

Career day is representative of the wide choices that one has in life. This dream symbol may come to indicate that the dreamer should give consideration to a change in his or her career.

Field trip relates to the possible need for hands-on learning experiences. This may indicate a need for one to personally experience what another is going through in order to be in a position to adequately understand it and react in an appropriate manner.

Graduation implies a completion of learning not yet rounded out by experience.

Graduation cap emphasizes information gained through study rather than through life experiences. It refers to learned perspectives versus those gained through developed wisdom.

Graduation ring comes to the dreamer as a sign of his or her former accomplishment.

Symposium is representative of the convergence of ideas in one's life.

Disciplines & Specialist Subjects

Historical

Archaeology (study of) represents a fascination with the past to the extent of ignoring the present. May also reveal an unhealthy penchant for gossip.

Egyptology (study of) exemplifies a high interest in enigmatic aspects of life; a subconscious yearning to discover human beginnings.

Paleontology (study of) represents an inherent curiosity regarding humankind's beginnings. This will indicate an interest in getting to the bottom of things.

Math

Algebra (study of) signifies one's beginning calculations and process of analysis.

Arithmetic (study of) See mathematics.

Geometry (study of) refers to a high interest in comprehending the interconnectedness of life.

Mathematics (study of) illustrates a high interest in analysis, discovering interconnectedness.

Medical

Anatomy (study of) signifies a need to look at all parts of a problem, relationship, or situation.

Dentistry (study of) indicates a desire to help others express themselves.

Dermatology (study of) characterizes those who are interested in understanding the hows, whys, and cures of other people's reactions to certain life factors. This could also indicate a psychologist, psychiatrist, or a counselor.

Embryology (study of) represents an interest in the many methods of generating new beginnings and the development of same.

Endocrinology (study of) alludes to a deep interest in understanding the powerful functions and applications of our energy centers (*chakras*) and the flow of that energy (*chi*). This, therefore, refers not only to the physical energy flow through the body but also signifies a free-flowing attitude, perspective, or behavior and the possible erroneous attitudes that may be blocking that flow.

Etiology (study of) illustrates a high interest in origins; a desire to understand how things began.

Genetics (study of) indicates an interest in the historical trail of another's behavior or characteristic expression.

Gerontology (study of) represents a high interest in elders. This will be specific for each dreamer in respect to what is focused on. It may also refer to an interest in the future ramifications of a current issue or plan.

Gross anatomy (study of) suggests a high interest in understanding technicalities and/or the many facets that make up a whole. This may apply to issues or situations.

Hematology (study of) illustrates a high interest in understanding esoteric concepts.

Microbiology (study of) pertains to one who is highly analytical and interested in knowing one's enemies.

Neurology (study of) depicts an individual's desire to understand the self-generated restraints used by others.

Ontology (study of) reveals a high interest in gaining an understanding of the connectedness between true reality and self.

Pathology (study of) indicates a need to analyze a negative situation that currently exists in one's life.

Virology (study of) means an interest in learning how to analyze negative elements that affect the well-being of others.

Metaphysical and cosmological

Astrology (study of) denotes an attempt to better understand self and all surrounding elements of one's life, and how they coalesce into one interdependent whole.

Astronomy (study of) signifies one's interest in humankind's ancient ancestry.

Astrophysics (study of) denotes an interest in the composition of certain knowns but has no vision toward what lies beyond.

Cosmology (study of) connotes an individual's emersion from spiritual aspects.

Graphology (study of) denotes an interest in obtaining insights into others.

Metaphysics (study of) represents a desire to understand the underlying principles of causation.

Mythology (study of) stands for an interest in delving through the extraneous to discover the root of a truth.

Numerology (study of) cautions against basing one's overall opinions or perceptions on a singular set of narrow guidelines.

Parapsychology (study of) denotes a high interest in humankind's interconnectedness with true reality.

Phrenology (study of head shape) comes as a warning that one's current research or learning efforts are focused on a false premise.

Reflexology (study of) shows a high interest in understanding the responses of others.

Science and natural history

Anthropology denotes the benefits of learning from past experiences.

Biology (study of) connotes a personal interest in all living aspects of one's world. This indicates a high respect for life.

Botany (study of) portrays an individual who looks for ways to apply spiritual concepts to everyday living situations and relationships.

Chemistry (study of) portrays an interest in many life aspects and how they may or may not interrelate.

Climatology (study of climate) represents an interest in understanding how surroundings affect events or people's reactions in life.

Ecology (study of) calls attention to one's environmental responsibility.

Ethology (study of) alludes to a high personal interest in the interrelatedness of all life.

Etymology (study of) denotes a high interest in language, specifically how a certain communication was passed from one to another.

see also
• The Body, Disease & Medicine *pp. 88–121*
• Technology & Science *pp. 268–285*

Disciplines & Specialist Subjects (continued)

Forestry (study of) represents a concentrated effort to uncover ways of using one's talents for the purpose of aiding others.

Gemology (study of) portrays an interest in understanding natural spiritual talents and the varied methodologies of same.

Geography (study of) connotes an interest in physical characteristics. This may or may not be a positive dream symbol depending on the surrounding elements.

Geology (study of) indicates a high interest in understanding humankind's genetic relationship with earth. Symbolizes one who takes interest in understanding others.

Geophysics (study of) signifies an awareness of the true reality.

Glaciology (study of) indicates an individual's high interest in understanding other people's lack of humanitarian and spiritual responsiveness.

Horticulture (study of) stands for a high interest in cultivating people's natural talents.

Lapidary (study of) represents an individual's desire for precision; exactness.

Metallurgy (study of) represents a high interest in learning the various benefits and faults of using differing tools to accomplish life goals.

Mineralogy (study of) pertains to an interest in natural talents and their practical application in the world.

Natural history (study of) denotes an individual's high interest in the human bond with all living things.

Natural science (study of) denotes a high interest in discovering the extent of true reality; an extended and reaching search.

Oceanography (study of) relates to a high interest in diverse spiritual concepts.

Ornithology (study of) refers to an individual's high interest in learning the various psychological mechanisms one's associates use.

Physical science (study of) See specific science type.

Tectonics (study of) represents a high interest in understanding how certain life aspects are formulated/created and their interaction with other affecting elements; an interest in learning how things come about.

Zoology (study of) indicates a recognition of life's interconnectedness; an interest in further understanding the interrelated facets of life.

Natural science depicts a quest for the meaning of life.

Social, political, and religious

Civics (study of) connotes a desire to understand the workings of surrounding authoritative systems.

Comparative religion (study of) denotes a desire to gain an awareness of all elements of an issue.

Cosmetology (study of) stands for an interest in learning how to make others feel better about themselves, helping to raise their self-esteem.

Criminology (study of) refers to an individual interested in the ways people go wrong and possible reasons why.

Cryptography (study of) indicates an individual's desire to understand esoteric matters and comprehend life's enigmatic aspects.

Economics (study of) usually comes as a personal message to reassess one's current distribution of talents.

Ethnology (study of) indicates a high interest in those different from the dreamer.

Industrial arts (study of) denotes a high interest in learning how to utilize spiritual tools (energy) to help others. Also see trade school.

Law (study of) represents a high interest in societal perimeters. Frequently this symbol refers to spiritual or moral issues.

Social studies (study of) represents an interest in knowing/understanding the life aspects contributing to another's current situation.

Sociology (study of) indicates a personal interest in the behavior of one's peers and their daily conditions.

Educational Status

Bilingual connotes a talent for conceptual interpretation.

Dingbat (symbol) portrays an individual's opportunity for self-expression.

High-level pertains to an elevated level of knowledge.

Illiteracy warns of a condition of self-induced ignorance.

Learning disability advises of a learning capability level. One should stop being frustrated or angry at not being able to understand certain concepts. It is important to operate within one's individual and unique framework.

Literati suggest those who are perceived as intellectuals, yet may not have an ounce of logic or common sense.

Uneducated may either indicate ignorance or it often refers to one progressing through the use of simple logic and common sense.

Unqualified characterizes an immature stage in life; one who needs more experience and knowledge.

Classes

Home economics (class) suggests a need to be more efficient and/or arranging priorities.

Home study illustrates high motivation and an independent search.

Homework advises of more research or information-gathering needed.

Language laboratory constitutes a personal effort to understand and fully comprehend higher knowledge.

Lecture will be an individualized symbol unique to each dreamer. Recall what the lecture was about. This will have personal meaning.

Physical education depicts the need for cleanliness and keeping fit.

Lessons come as a specific message for each dreamer. Take the lesson to heart.

Physical education (PE) comes in dreams to stress the importance of exercise and hygiene. Recall which aspect was emphasized in the dream to gain specifics.

Premed (classes) suggests an attempt to gain the basics of a particular issue or situation; learning/discovering the elements leading up to a certain issue.

Refresher course implies a need to keep abreast of new information. The dreamer will understand this individualized intent.

Remedial (study) depicts a desire to better understand an issue or situation.

Revision represents an advisement to reassess one's life, goals, or path direction.

Study hall suggests serious efforts are required for researching and discovering all facets of a particular issue or concept.

Educational Tools

Finger painting means that one's communication skills are underdeveloped.

Bibliography symbolizes literary works one should peruse; additional research needed.

Cheat sheet indicates advancement through ill-gained means. Depending on the related dream elements, this symbol may also point to a need to remember something.

Conversion chart (measurements) points to options having equal value.

Dictionary illustrates a need to clarify misunderstandings or misconceptions. Was a specific entry word highlighted?

Encyclopedia emphasizes a need to gain a greater depth of knowledge on some aspect in the dreamer's life.

Finger painting indicates an immature manner of expressing self.

Flash card indicates that which must be remembered or utilized on a consistent basis.

Lesson plan represents a tendency toward systematic learning; taking one step at a time.

Phonics signifies a general idea of something; an overall understanding without specific knowledge of the individual associated elements.

Phrase book represents a desire to communicate better and the efforts applied to same.

Primer (text) refers to a need to return to the beginning or foundational aspects of an issue or situation.

Prospectus indicates a need to research an issue thoroughly before accepting it.

Sight-reading points to acute perception and lightning responses.

Thesaurus indicates a need to choose more appropriate words when communicating with others.

Worksheet signifies an individual's need to figure something out; analysis is required.

see also
• Organizations, Bodies & Groups *p. 128*
• Text & Books *p. 458*

Educational Equipment

Binder (notebook) cautions one to retain that which has been learned or recorded.
Blackboard brings messages. What was written?
Blackboard eraser points to a willful denial of information; a refusal to look at facts or messages one doesn't want to hear or face.
Blotter (ink) refers to a need to clean up mistakes; admit to guilt; make amends.
Book signifies knowledge and the need for same; further study needed.
Book bag is associated with the knowledge we carry with us. Suggests a need to not leave our intellect behind.
Chalk portrays subliminal or peripheral knowledge that may or may not be remembered.
Chalk eraser See blackboard eraser.
Clipboard portrays an orderly individual; efficiency; a tool to help one attend to details.
Correction fluid/tape refers to efforts to correct one's mistakes.
Crayon indicates an immaturity; undeveloped ideas.
Dunce cap connotes foolish thinking; a need to reason and apply a greater amount of intelligence and logic.
Eraser shows chances to rub out or reverse something. May indicate indecision.
India ink stands for a need to get something better defined. This refers to some type of gray area existing in one's life.
Lectern implies a need to communicate.
Mortarboard shows advancement; the gaining of greater information that should now be put it into action.
Protractor advises to look at all angles; to have a balanced view.
Schoolbag stands for one's preparedness for expanding learning.
Schoolbook reveals the specific area in which the dreamer is lacking adequate knowledge. Naturally the key here is to recall what type of schoolbook it was.
Textbook indicates a specific type of study needed.
Workbook implies more study is required; a need to work to learn more.

Achievements

Accreditation is representative of an accepted standard of readiness.
Achievement certificate comes as a commendation from one's higher self.
Gold star signifies recognition of superior efforts expended.
Grade point average will come to reveal one's accurate level of understanding, attainment, or general progression.
Letter (varsity) is generally indicative of an individual accomplishment.
Master's degree emphasizes higher learning; greater efforts applied to gaining knowledge or expertise.
Matriculate connotes one who is accepted.
Valedictorian is usually representative of an individual's personal opinion.

Educational Bodies

Board of education refers to those who would confine the gaining of knowledge to specific realms of subject matter.
School board normally indicates those who determine what others are taught and place perimeters on knowledge. This is not usually a positive dream symbol.
School district suggests an environment for learning. The symbol may also relate to immaturity.

Examinations & Assessments

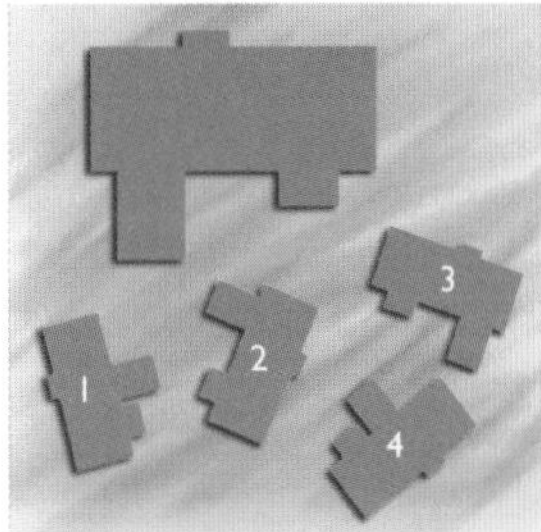

Aptitude test points to one's comprehension of a given subject.

Achievement test means a need to examine one's state of progression toward personal advancement.
Aptitude test refers to one's personal understanding of something.
Diploma alludes to presumed knowledge or an acquired stage of same.
Dissertation See thesis.
Examination usually calls for one to analyze oneself. This could be one's emotions, mental processes, spiritual beliefs, or physical condition. Surrounding dream aspects will clarify which one is intended.
Intelligence test See aptitude test.
Midterms call for a time to stop and analyze oneself; double-checking to make sure that we've retained and learned from lessons that we've experienced along our path so far. Depending on the dreamscape's related elements, midterms may also mark the halfway point of achieving one's goals.
Progress report See report card.
Qualifications reveal the qualities or skills necessary to accomplish a particular task or goal.
Questionnaire corresponds to a need for the dreamer to spend valuable introspective or self-analysis time.
Report card is a revealing symbol that illustrates the quality and rating of the dreamer's current behavior.
Spelling bee exposes specific words for emphasis. These words come as unique messages for each dreamer.
Term paper reveals the extent of one's comprehension of a specific subject.
Test symbolizes a verification of motivation, knowledge, experiential skill, and so on. It frequently refers to self-testing.
Thesis pertains to thought extension; an advisement to the dreamer to carry his or her thoughts further.

Mathematical Terms & Activities

Abacus denotes a need to refigure an old situation or condition. A change in perspective may be indicated.

Abstract number pertains to an unknown or undisclosed amount. A questionable quantity.

Addition (symbol) is generally representative of the fact that one or more aspects need to be included in an issue.

Baker's dozen means personal generosity; giving more than required; going the extra mile for others.

Binary means dual purpose; twofold.

Chart defines specific course perceptions. These may show what the dreamer has planned out or may clarify what should be drawn up.

Cosign signifies an agreement to share responsibility.

Counting (act of) advises of a need to take stock of something; there is imperative reason to count blessings or opportunities.

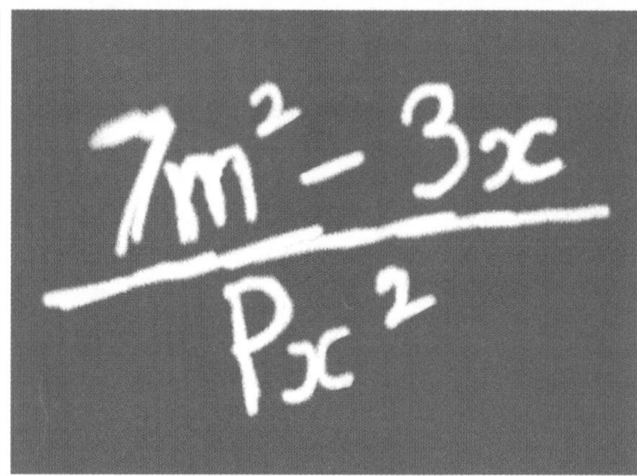

Fraction reminds one to consider other factors.

Decimal point is representative of value.

Diagram advises of the need for clarification before comprehension is obtained.

Division (math sign) indicates a reduction of something into lesser aspects. Surrounding dream symbols will clarify this for the dreamer.

Equation is indicative of a relative balance; a comparable aspect.

Formula (mathematical) comes to offer possible solutions.

Fourscore indicates that the number eighty has some unique meaning specific to the dreamer.

Foursquare See square.

Fraction denotes one part of something greater; one needs to realize that what is seen is not the whole of it.

Long division means something that takes longer to figure out.

Graph See diagram.

Graph paper usually is a call to figure something out on paper before acting on it.

Hexagon refers to mental, emotional, or spiritual protection.

Multiplication sign applies to the possibility of increasing something; opportunity to develop or advance.

Percent (sign) reveals a specialized meaning for each dreamer who will make an individualized association.

Pie chart See chart.

Pocket calculator exemplifies efficiency; preparedness.

Rectangle (configuration) represents firm attitudes.

Ruler (measurement) may advise one to attend to a precise rule or personal belief or to monitor one's use of a specific element.

Short division refers to a quick calculation; something that's easy to figure out.

Slide rule alludes to the need to apply reason and logic.

Sliding scale indicates the consideration of all associated aspects of an issue.

Square denotes rigidness; narrow-mindedness.

Subtraction (symbol) refers to a need to lessen some element in one's life.

Table of measurements stands for a need to understand that differing issues or aspects can have equal value.

Learning

Barrister bookcase symbolizes an appreciation of learning.

Barrister bookcase signifies a respect for knowledge.

Curriculum identifies specific learning areas on which an individual should focus.

Doctrine represents a principle; a belief system.

Faculty See schoolteacher.

Knowledge is a message in itself. It comes to reveal specific information for the dreamer.

Learning validates one's inner questioning as to whether or not one is progressing or acquiring additional knowledge. This dream symbol denotes an affirmative answer.

Recess denotes a period of rest that is being advised.

Sabbatical represents periods of additional learning that are needed. Usually refers to those who consider themselves to be a teacher or leader.

Scholarship stands for an opportunity to attain greater knowledge; a chance to learn something without personal costs being involved.

Schoolteacher is someone who has something specific to teach the dreamer.

Tip sheet represents an aid for lessening risks.

Tuition corresponds to some type of payment due in exchange for the information one desires. Reveals one's unscrupulous behavior if tuition is demanded for spiritual information.

see also
• Writing & Literature *p. 219*
• Chemistry & Physics *p. 284*

Punctuation & Letters

Abbreviation is representative of a need to cut short certain aspects in one's life. This dream symbol may also advise one to focus on the main issue instead of the smaller details that are inconsequential.

Accent mark reveals that more emphasis is needed. Advises that something isn't being given enough attention or importance.

Acronym comes to the dreamer as an advisement that one should give much greater attention and focus to the main elements of one's path or course.

Alphabet suggests a need to return to some basic, foundational elements of an issue. This symbol normally reveals the fact that one has taken ideas too far afield and has lost some elemental ideas.

Ampersand (& sign) reveals the presence of a second (or more) individual or elements involved in an issue. This usually comes when an issue is perceived as standing alone or an individual believes she/he is a singular aspect of something.

Apostrophe indicates an omission in life.

Asterisk is representative of the fact that something has high importance; getting the dreamer's attention. Reveals the fact that there's more to something than meets the eye; extenuating conditions.

Bracket represents an aspect that assists in supporting the personal weight of life problems and adversity.

Capital letter is representative of the fact that there is an emphasis on something.

Colon (punctuation mark) indicates that something will follow, usually an explanation.

Comma (punctuation mark) symbolizes a separation of ideas and cautions the dreamer to avoid running concepts together.

Cross-reference advises of a need to check out some aspects to determine the facts.

Exclamation point indicates a clear message of great importance attached to something in the dreamer's life; an attempt to get the dreamer's focused attention.

Italics are shown for the purpose of drawing attention to something important the dreamer should be aware of. Places emphasis on something.

Parentheses usually contains a word that is intended to further explain something.

Period (punctuation mark) implies an end or conclusion to something. Depending on surrounding elements associated with the period, the symbol could be revealing one's wish rather than an actuality.

Punctuation mark See specific type.

Question mark is generally representative of a doubt or skepticism.

Quotation marks emphasize the words spoken or written in dreams and serve to make them stand out so that the dreamer will recall them when he or she wakes.

Physics

Antigravity refers to personal freedoms and rights.

Butterfly effect reminds us that everything has an effect.

Chaos theory reminds the dreamer that everything in life is interconnected.

Diagram means clarification comes before comprehension.

Magnet reveals a compulsive nature; obsessive behavior.

Magnetic field denotes a strong allure; an enticement or captivation.

Writing

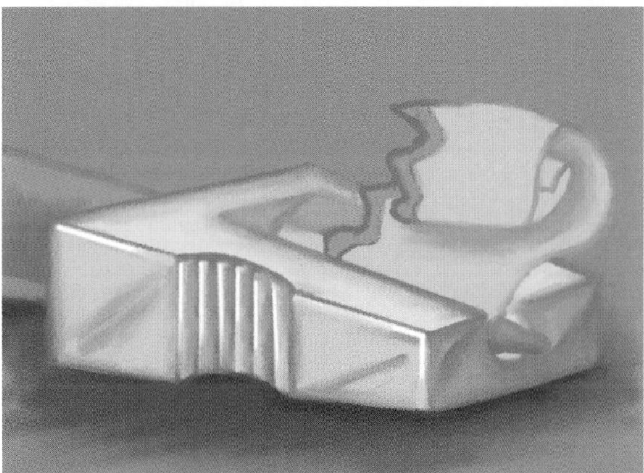

Pencil sharpener indicates a commitment to a plan.

Cliff's notes suggest a lack of details.

Essay alludes to an expression of one's opinion. This usually advises one to be more open about personal attitudes.

Handwriting emphasizes one's inner character. What qualities did it have? Was the writing stilted and stiff-looking? Was it a fancy script? Jagged? Unreadable?

Highlighter (pen or marking) reveals the necessity of noting and remembering certain ideas that are important to the specific dreamer.

Inkblot usually signals that something in one's life is amiss or not balanced.

Marker (pen) denotes a need to note or emphasize something. Recall what was being written or singled out with the marker in the dream. Who was using the marker?

Pen (write) is representative of the need to record something. Surrounding dreamscape details will indicate whether or not something needs to be written down.

Pencil represents an intention that may or may not manifest; tentative plan.

Pencil sharpener denotes diligence or a readiness to follow through with intentions.

Penholder implies a need for recording or noting something important.

Chapter 16

Jobs & Professions

Careers and occupations depict the manner in which one attains goals or goes about the process of daily living.

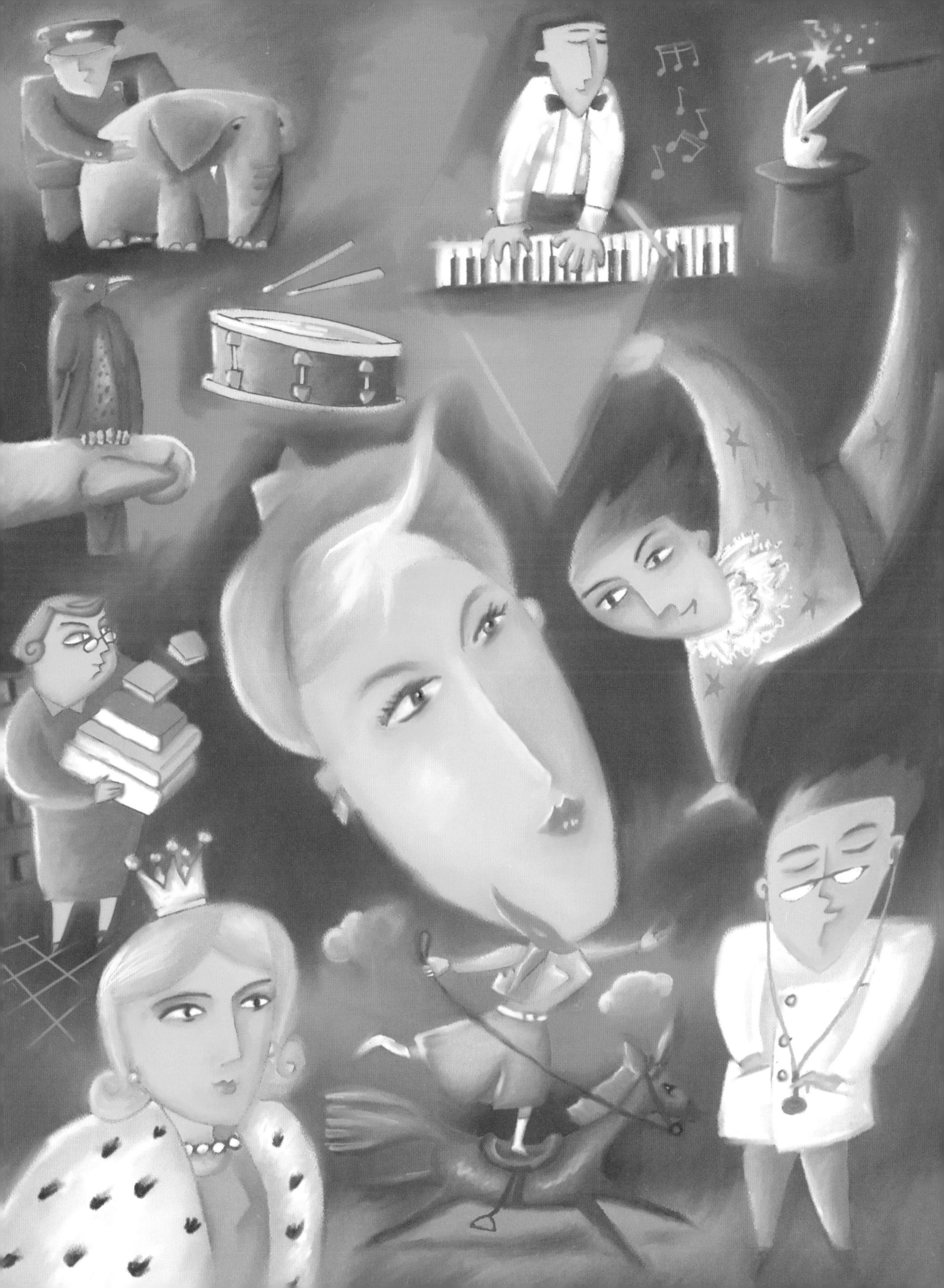

Human Resources & Recruitment

Appointment signifies a need to communicate with another.

Appraisal is representative of an understanding of the true value of someone or something.

Appraiser denotes one who can reveal the true value of something.

Attendance record won't normally refer to one's physical presence but will more likely be associated with mental focus.

Blue flu See sick-out.

Candidate implies a situational position one is headed for.

Competency hearing usually stands for self-doubts, wondering if one is crazy for thinking a particular way or having a particularly uncommon perspective.

Contract labor represents paid help/assistance.

Credentials shows experiential documentation; level of one's knowledge. This is usually a warning dreamscape symbol that comes to advise the dreamer to check someone's qualifications—even those of oneself.

Overworked underlines that one can manage a given situation.

Demotion comes to the dreamer as an advisement of a need to watch out for one's arrogance of heightened perception of self-worth. This dreamscape element will come to cut down an individual's overblown perception.

Efficiency expert characterizes one who defines priorities for others. This is not always a positive dream symbol because people need to define their own priorities.

Employee handbook symbolizes the working perimeters one is expected to adhere to.

Engagement (appointment) See appointment.

Equal opportunity applies to a nondiscriminatory situation or relationship. May advise this attitude.

Facilitator points to one who motivates. This particular dream symbol may in fact be pointing to oneself.

Furlough See vacation.

Grievance committee points to a source for resolving issues of conflict or dispute.

Head-hunting connotes an individual's search for a specific individual or type of personality; a quest for knowledge.

Holiday denotes a rest time. This most often implies that an individual is working or concentrating too hard.

Human resource (office or department) stands for a source for both benefits and opportunity.

Interview advises of an in-depth communication that will reveal more information.

Job (employment) reveals the dreamer's opinion of her/his own work.

Job description refers to knowing everything a specific project or issue will entail.

Job-hopping cautions against instability; undependability.

Job-hunting characterizes motivation; a desire to be productive.

Layoff connotes a forced termination of one's current work or path efforts; involuntary path setback.

Leave of absence alludes to a personal need for rest or diversity.

Occupational hazard refers to a seriously harmful main element associated with one's current or chosen course.

Overqualified denotes one's inflated opinion of oneself. Every type of work supplies valuable learning experiences.

Overstaffed indicates an excessive effort applied to an element in one's life.

Overtime points to extra personal efforts needed to accomplish a goal.

Overworked emphasizes that one can control the level and extent of personal efforts applied to a situation. This symbol attempts to underscore who has the control over this.

Pep talk connotes a motivational impetus; a need to boost morale.

Second in Command

Assistant is one who helps. Does the dreamer need help with something? This dreamscape element may point to stubbornness related to a false sense of independence.

Attendant characterizes a personal helper.

Deputy is representative of one's chosen assistant or associate.

Underboss characterizes an individual having mid-level authority or power.

Understudy refers to an intention of being prepared to take another's place. May also refer to an intention to replace another. Could mean the practice of emulation. Recall who was studying whom. What was being studied in the dream?

see also
• Movers & Shakers *p. 142*
• Performance Assessment *p. 187*

HR & Recruitment (continued)

Personnel (office) may portray a manager of specific records. This could point to a source of benefits or one's personal information. This will be a revealing fragment for the dreamer. See human resource.

Placement test comes in a dream as an advisement to give attention to where one is on one's path; a self-check.

Promotion characterizes advancement; progression along one's life path.

Proving ground pertains to one's life; earthly existence.

Recruit characterizes an individual who recently changed her/his way of thinking; one who has begun a new effort.

Recruiter relates to a person who easily coerces others; a manipulative personality. This may point to empty or misleading promises.

Redundancy reveals ignorance; an attempt to impress with one's knowledge.

Resignation stands for a new direction ahead; leaving a former path or issue behind.

Review appraiser characterizes an individual who is skilled in verifying value.

Shortlist refers to the top-rated, most desirable choices.

Shutdown most often refers to avoidance. May point to outright denial. This symbol could also come as an advisement to stop some type of attitude or behavior that needs to be shut down.

Sick day most often comes in dreams to advise of a need to take a well-deserved break.

Sick leave is a representation of an extended amount of time or phase in a person's life when time is taken for recuperative purposes.

Sick-out refers to people who share an attitude of disagreement over the same issue and join together to exhibit a silent protest; a passive expression of protest.

Sick pay stands for the benefits gained from taking the time off to take care of oneself. This symbol usually comes as an advisement.

Skill emphasizes an individual's unique talents.

Staff (people) characterizes those who are ready and willing to assist another.

Title (position) often discloses one's actual position in life. In some cases, depending on surrounding dream details, this dreamscape symbol reveals how one thinks of oneself.

Turnover (employment) denotes a lack of stability; restlessness.

Underemployed refers to being in a position in which one's full potential can't be utilized.

Understaffed represents a need for additional resources to accomplish a goal.

Unskilled labor refers to work nearly everyone can do. Sometimes this comes to remind us that anyone can volunteer or practice unconditional goodness, as there's always something that we can do to help another.

Vacation signifies the need to get away.

Walking papers come to imply a dismissal; as a sign that indicates the end of a particular issue or the end of the dreamer's involvement in it.

Management

Boss characterizes a higher authority, perhaps even one's higher self.

City manager advises one to handle personal business instead of depending on others to manage it.

Floor manager See floorwalker.

Floorwalker signifies the wisdom of frequently checking one's personal foundational ethics against current actions.

General manager characterizes an overseer. This symbol may reveal someone who has the ability to help manage something for the dreamer in his or her life.

Manager characterizes one who organizes; an overseer.

Master connotes proficiency or one who holds control.

Monitor (person/overseer) relates to observation and usually comes in dreams to advise of a need for closer attention or observation.

Office manager characterizes an individual who has the capability to guide another through a more efficient manner of work or effort.

Overseer usually denotes one's higher self or conscience.

Pit boss characterizes a person who oversees the actions of others. May refer to one's own higher self.

Sponsor characterizes a person responsible for another; the one who enables another to accomplish something.

Supervisor most often connotes oneself or, more specifically, one's conscience.

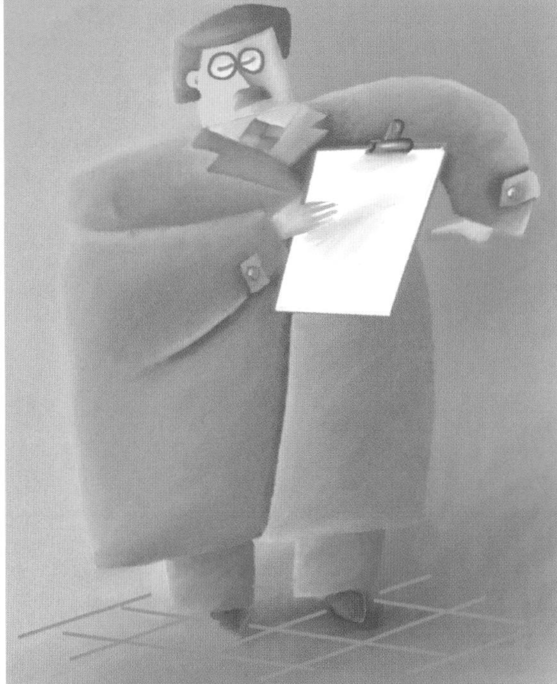

Floor manager means a need to act in accordance with one's principles.

Employment Status

Blue collar signifies one who applies spiritual beliefs to daily life; the actual hands-on work of spiritual behavior.
Contract labor represents paid help/assistance.
Contractor defines an individual who gains by doing others' work. May also point to someone who is capable of materializing others' plans.
Coworker characterizes those associated with one's work. This work may be one's spiritual work or a personal situational relationship.
Freelance portrays the utilization of various opportunities.
Hired hand represents one who is reimbursed for the help they give. This means there are those from whom one elicits assistance and therefore need to be paid in kind.
Househusband characterizes a recognition of a woman's intellect and worth without it feeling threatening.
Menial (work) symbolizes acceptance and humility; an understanding that some advancements can't be accomplished unless the small elements are attended to.
Migrant worker represents resourcefulness; efforts toward advancement.

Unskilled labor is being good.

Self-employed characterizes an individual's self-sufficiency.
Semiretired points to one who keeps his or her hand in things.
Senior citizen characterizes experiential knowledge and wisdom gained.
Seniority denotes a higher position. May refer to attained knowledge, experience, or spiritual advancement. May stand for others who have gone before us.
Silent partner usually stands for one's own conscience; inner guidance.
Subcontractor characterizes an individual capable of assisting another or carrying a specific portion of another's burden.
Subordinate reveals one's position in relation to a specific life aspect or a particular relationship.
Unemployed connotes an unproductive state. This may not necessarily have a negative implication because it could suggest a designated phase when an individual needs to take a break.
Unskilled labor refers to work that nearly everyone is capable of doing. Sometimes this symbol comes to remind us that anyone can volunteer or practice unconditional goodness, and that there's always something we can do to help another.
Volunteer denotes the selfless giving of oneself.
Wage earner points to one who puts out personal effort to supply needs.
White-collar worker signifies confined workspace. May also refer to confined thought.

Unions

Protest means disagreement.

Hiring hall See union hall.
Picket line See protest.
Protest signifies energetic objection.
Shop steward characterizes a person who listens to one's ideas, complaints, and so on, and may have the ability to make changes for the better or bring about a resolution to a difficult situation in the dreamer's everyday life.
Strike (work halt) reveals a personal dissatisfaction with how one's life is progressing; a need for change.
Trade union See union.
Union portrays a sense of security; having a support group.
Union hall corresponds with a desire to utilize one's talents and skills.
Union steward reveals the presence of someone to whom one can turn for help.
Walkout See strike.

Trainees

Apprentice symbolizes a need to learn from the bottom up; a need to gain basic and fundamental information or skill.
Intern signifies one who has knowledge and is gaining applied experience.
Rookie characterizes a beginner. It refers to one who lacks experience and knowledge.
Student teacher signifies a future teacher who still needs more experience.

Executives

Capitalist a dreamscape symbol that portrays someone who does good deeds for the sole purpose of personal gain.
Chairperson characterizes organized leadership of a specialized aspect in life.
Chief defines a prime aspect in one's life.
Dignitary is representative of those individuals specific to the dreamer who are perceived as being highly respected.
Director characterizes the act of controlling. It refers to someone whose behavior is manipulating.
Executive characterizes seniority that is related to a specific area.
Industrialist characterizes one who provides opportunities for others.
Mogul characterizes a powerful and influential individual.
Tycoon is a dreamscape symbol that characterizes an individual who is capable of providing great benefits to others.

see also
• Teeth *p. 100*
• Metaphysical Abilities *p. 479*

Divinatory Professions

Astrologer means one who can pull many aspects together.
Channeler (psychic) shows one who listens for the guidance of others instead of self.
Fortuneteller characterizes someone who lives for the future instead of the moment; a fear of seeking within self.
Medium (psychic) connotes the connective link between the conscious mind and one's higher self.
Psychic corresponds to an individual's inherent natural abilities as they relate to the yet undiscovered elements of true reality.

Fortuneteller avoids the present.

Seeress is representative of an individual who has clear perception of current time situations and sharp instincts for future ramifications of current situations or events.
Soothsayer See seeress.

Work Locations

Agency denotes a controlling center of operation.
Assay office depicts a need to reassess one's priorities.
Assembly line cautions against routine conformity in life. This may be associated with one's way of thinking.
Bindery depicts a need to keep records, thoughts, concepts, or beliefs together. This comes as a warning against letting these aspects become scattered.
Boardroom portrays decision making; the knowing of the higher self.
Boiler room (telemarketing) refers to high-pressured coercion in one's life.
Company store signifies a continual energizing of one's expended efforts; getting a large return on what one puts out.
Conference room points to a need for a face-to-face meeting with someone.
Cubicle (work) suggests a need to keep one's head down and attend to one's own business. This symbol usually appears to dreamers who tend to get into other people's business.
Office always pertains to work or personal efforts applied.
Office supply store implies the wide variety of tools available to accomplish a goal.
Sod farm suggests the transference/implanting of new ideas.
Steel mill is representative of the many forms that strength can take.
Studio (arts) is indicative of one of the arts. Refer to artist, metal sculpture, photographer, and so on, for further clarification.
Sweatshop warns against forcing efforts, especially the manipulation of someone else's efforts.
Tannery applies to a means of preservation.

Office Equipment & Features

Conference table advises that it's time to put it all on the table.
Desk denotes type, quantity, and quality of work being done. This usually applies to individualized efforts given to a life path or advancement.
Desk pad suggests care or attention given to one's work.
File cabinet defines stored information. This is usually within self.
Flowchart details one's best method of progression along one's path.
In-box symbolizes receptivity to new ideas.
Ledger is representative of an individual's life debits and assets; a behavioral balance sheet.
Paper clip suggests a need for attachments. A reminder to keep something secured.
Paper cutter pertains to a need to trim superficial or extraneous elements from a piece of information.
Paper shredder See shredder.
Photocopier stands for repetitiveness. Recall the condition and color of the dreamscape machine to determine whether or not something actually needs repeating or if this is a warning to stop repeating or copying something or someone. Frequently this symbol means that an individual is repeating past mistakes. Who was using the photocopier?
Shredder (paper) represents an attempt to hide or get rid of some type of evidence; concealment. May point to efforts at maintaining one's privacy.
Spreadsheet constitutes an overview, an at-a-glance perspective.
Toner See ink cartridge.
Water cooler is representative of spiritual refreshment in one's life.

Dentistry

Dental hygienist characterizes an individual in one's life who continues to remind or guide others away from making assumptions.
Dental technician is generally representative of one who helps others to express themselves appropriately.
Dentist comes to the dreamer as one who works to help others to articulate their thoughts or express themselves more clearly.
Orthodontist characterizes a person who has the ability and knowledge to help another communicate more effectively.

Psychiatry

Psychiatrist is a dreamscape symbol that characterizes a need for an individual to give deeper thought to his or her behavior, motivations, or belief systems. This symbol comes as an advisement that a deeper look into oneself is required.
Psychoanalyst See psychiatrist.
Psychotherapist See psychiatrist.

Medical & Pharmaclinical

Abortionist denotes a person who instigates some type of separation; one who stops the progression of a new idea, plan, or beginning.

Allergist refers to someone who finds the root cause of people's problems.

Anesthetist points to one who incites apathy in others.

Cardiologist suggests an individual who is capable of helping another through emotional difficulties/strains.

Clinician is one who has specific knowledge; a specialized teacher.

Diagnostician is representative of an individual who has the capability and knowledge to help others pinpoint the source of their problems.

Dietician characterizes a person in one's life who has the knowledge to assist in bringing about a healthful state. This may also include mental health.

Doctor characterizes those in one's life who are capable of bringing about healing aspects. For specific types of healing aspect, see specific ailment or disease.

Emergency medical technician (EMT) characterizes someone in the dreamer's life who has the ability to give the dreamer immediate help or some type of needed assistance.

General practitioner See physician.

Health inspector most often symbolizes one's conscience in respect to watching oneself for unhealthy attitudes or behavior.

House doctor See house physician.

House physician stands for yourself. You have the power to help you to heal negative attitudes and emotions.

Medic characterizes someone in one's life with the knowledge and skill to repair a negative aspect within another.

Midwife characterizes an individual in one's life who has the knowledge and skill to assist in bringing about a new path or rebirth.

Neurologist characterizes one who has a high interest in determining causal psychological factors that prevent others from utilizing full potential.

Nutritionist alludes to one who has the potential to advise others of what their life is lacking; providing what is needed for advancement.

Obstetrician characterizes a person who has the knowledge and ability to bring forth a new life or awakening in others.

Occupational disease indicates a suggestion to alter one's life course or change a harmful situation.

Occupational therapy implies a need to discover, learn, and apply enhanced methods and skills directed toward one's life path and/or manner of communication.

Ophthalmologist characterizes a person who has the insight and ability to straighten out another's altered perspective.

Orthopedist exemplifies an individual who can redirect another's path toward a straight course.

Paramedic defines a person capable of an immediate, knowledgeable response.

Pediatrician characterizes one who has the capability and knowledge to heal or correct beginning problems with one's growth.

Phlebotomist relates to a draining personality; one who uses others.

Physiatrist See physical therapist.

Physical therapist signifies someone in the dreamer's life who has the potential for helping one get back on one's feet.

Physician represents a person who has the knowledge and capability to help another overcome a life disability or illness. This won't necessarily be associated with physical ills. Recall the doctor's specialty, then refer to the specific medical term in this book.

Physician's assistant (PA) points to someone who can provide basic diagnostic information; one who can point another in the right direction.

Proctologist constitutes an individual who has the knowledge and ability to help the dreamer face problems and gain acceptance.

Radiologist is representative of an individual who is capable of acute perception in regard to the hidden aspects of others.

Surgeon relates to precision and skill.

Therapist characterizes an individual who is more than capable of routinely assisting another to a more balanced attainment.

Trauma team generally stands for a critical need to take care of the most obvious and harmful negative elements in one's life.

X-ray technician characterizes an individual who has a tendency to analyze and thoroughly research an issue or concept; having the inherent talent for seeing through people's facades.

Alternative Medicine

Herbalist means simple practices.

Chiropractor characterizes integrity; perseverance; advancement through one's own efforts; one who can help to keep others aligned.

Faith healer comes to the dreamer as a warning to go within for one's strength and to tap into his or her own inner healing.

Healer characterizes an individual who is capable of restoring the well-being of others. Was this dreamscape healer you?

Herbalist denotes natural methods and techniques.

Witch doctor represents the dual aspects of inherent abilities, whether they're used for either negative or positive purposes.

see also
• Death *p. 118*
• Prescribed Medicines *p. 246*

Pharmacy

Alchemist is representative of someone who attempts to force impossible results and improbable goals. It is also a reference to unrealistic ideas or perspectives.

Apothecary See pharmacy.

Detail person (pharmaceutical) warns of an individual who would attempt to convince others of utilizing their specific resource of help. There are many options.

Druggist See pharmacist.

Pharmacist corresponds with an individual in the dreamer's life who has the potential and knowledge to provide a healing element. This element may relate to spiritual, physical, mental, or emotional ills.

Pharmacy generally suggests that some type of medication or healing element is needed by the dreamer.

Funereal Occupations

Coroner See medical examiner.

Funeral director is representative of someone who will help another individual through difficult times.

Gravedigger is generally a reference to someone on a fatal course. It may be indicative of the act of digging one's own grave.

Grief counselor reveals an individual who understands grief and can offer helpful ways of dealing with it. This symbol may not relate to the literal sense of grief, but more to depression, melancholy, disappointment.

Medical examiner (ME) characterizes one who is capable of pinpointing the source or cause of a problem or failure.

Mortician See funeral director.

Pallbearer represents the releasing of personal pain.

Undertaker See funeral director.

Nursing & Care

Candy striper (hospital voluntary worker) alludes to the attainment of inner joy through doing for others.

Caregiver stands for one who cares for another. This may not always indicate a compassionate or loving personality.

Certified nurse assistant (CNA) stands for one who is qualified or has knowledge of basic caregiving.

Chaperon characterizes one's higher self; higher guidance; one's conscience.

Helper refers to one who has the capability to aid another.

Matron is a representation of an experienced female elder.

Nurse portrays a compassionate and selfless personality, one capable of healing others.

Nurse's aide denotes a person who is willing to help another.

Practical nurse relates to a minor personal dysfunction of some type. The surrounding dreamscape elements will clarify what this means for the individual dreamer.

Visiting nurse implies someone who is capable of providing healing assistance or counsel.

Scientists

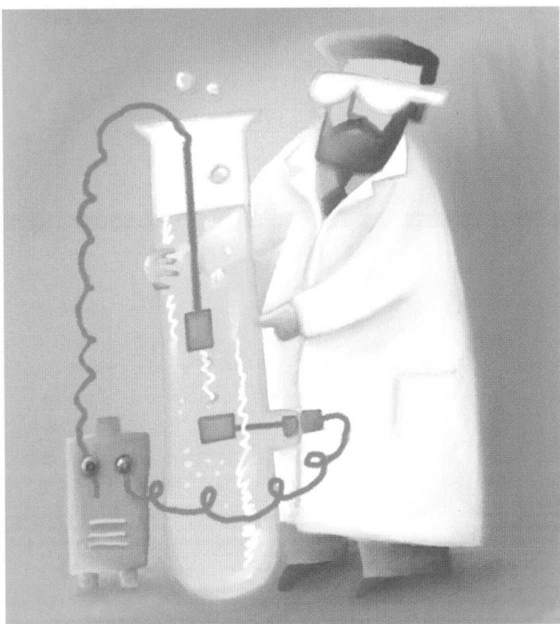

Scientist sets up obstacles against learning despite an eagerness to study.

Amalogist warns against making false relationships.

Anthropologist is one who sparks past-life memories within the dreamer.

Archaeologist is one who ill-uses the past, such as exposing past transgressions of others.

Astronomer is one who intellectually focuses on humankind's ancient heritage as a basis for other life aspects. May refer to the act of delving into possibilities.

Chemist stands for one who utilizes a wide variety of aspects to create desired responses or goals.

Diener (lab assistant) signifies one who has the capability and knowledge to properly clean up the remaining aspects of a concluded situation or condition.

Meteorologist characterizes one who is highly interested in understanding converging factors that can affect conditions or situations.

Naturalist reveals a spiritually enlightened individual.

Physicist characterizes someone who attempts to understand nature and reality; a high interest in the interrelatedness of all things.

Rock hound characterizes a person who recognizes the beauty of opportunities presented by life's difficulties and takes advantage of them.

Scientist signifies one who is highly interested in expanding our knowledge and understanding, yet is caught within self-imposed bounds.

Seismologist emphasizes one's inner sensitivity toward being aware when approaching unstable ground; to be watchful of a questionable issue, situation, or relationship.

Entertainers

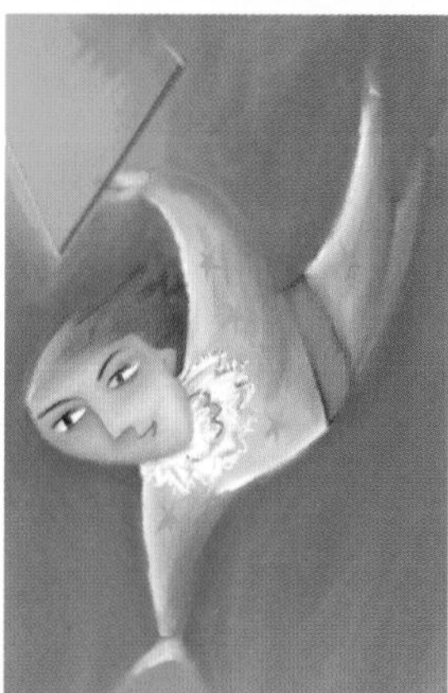

Aerialist may mean arrogance.

Acrobat shows the contortions that one goes through to attain a goal.

Aerialist cautions against compulsiveness in thought or convoluted thought patterns. This symbol may point to haughtiness.

Carny (carnival worker) characterizes one who is out of touch with reality; unrealistic perceptions of life. May also indicate entrapment or a rigged situation.

Celebrity relates to someone in the dreamer's life who stands out for some reason—or should stand out.

Chippendale (dancer) exposes those who entice others toward negative or at least less-than-positive elements; questionable behavior; ulterior motives.

Clown characterizes one's foolish aspects.

Conjurer characterizes an individual who has the capability to make things happen; someone who gets things done.

Contortionist characterizes a manipulative personality. May point to an individual who has a tendency to distort things, make them more complicated than necessary.

Escape artist characterizes one who has a tendency to always cover one's options; never being manipulated or controlled. This may also refer to one who refuses to face or accept personal responsibility; avoidance, maybe even denial.

Fire-eater pertains to one who effectively absorbs intense emotional expressions; being unaffected while dealing with another's emotionalism.

Geisha characterizes servitude; a tendency to react or behave in response to the anticipated desires of others. This is usually a warning symbol.

High-wire (act) connotes a questionable leap in one's advancement; a fragile situation where one must maintain acute awareness and step carefully; high risks involved.

Illusionist characterizes those who manipulate others or attempt to dazzle with trickery.

Impressionist (entertainer) characterizes an individual who has the capability of mirroring others so they can see themselves as they really are. This indicates a need to see oneself clearly.

Leading lady refers to one who is the main player in a situation. May reveal who holds the reins.

Magician characterizes false prophets and manipulative personalities who easily gain the control and confidence of others.

Matador connotes a tempting of fate; seeking admiration through foolhardy means; false bravery.

Movie star may be an indication of hypocrisy or may represent a glamorized or unreal perspective of life.

Puppeteer points to a manipulator. May reveal the one who's really in charge, the one pulling the strings.

Ringmaster signifies one who directs the actions of others; possibly a manipulator. May indicate one who interferes in the lives of others.

Rodeo clown stands for the taking of risks to save others or one who diverts hazardous elements away from others.

Talent agent corresponds with an individual who tries to control where and when another uses her or his natural abilities or inherent skills. This should be an individual choice.

Talent scout characterizes a person who believes he or she can recognize inherent abilities in others and exploit them.

Trapeze artist See aerialist.

Troupe stands for a group of people who travel from place to place for the purpose of displaying a specific idea.

Ventriloquist pertains to a person who tends to speak for another, yet is not necessarily given the authority to do so.

Beauty & Fashion

Aesthetician is representative of someone who has mesmerizing speech, yet may not always speak the truth.

Barber See beautician.

Beautician signifies individuals with a tendency or talent to alter the perspectives of others, easing them into a better sense of self.

Calendar girl See pinup girl.

Cosmetologist See beautician.

Cover girl indicates the tendency to believe one needs dramatic attention-getting aspects to be noticed.

Dressmaker See seamstress.

Fashion designer warns against dictating another's lifestyle or manner of path progression.

Hairdresser represents one who affects the thoughts of others; persuasiveness.

Hairdressing usually signifies controlled thoughts.

Manicurist indicates an individual who has the capability of cleaning up the reputation of others.

Mannequin warns of apathy about whether or not one is being manipulated.

Masseuse depicts one who is capable of easing one's withheld stress.

Model (professional) reveals someone who works to sell something to another.

Pinup girl is generally suggestive of attractive exterior attributes. This usually comes as a reminder to check priorities because exterior appearances are rarely a reflection of inner character.

Seamstress characterizes an individual who is capable of bringing various elements together.

Tailor See seamstress.

see also
• Theater & Entertainment *p. 220*
• Dance Styles *p. 224*

Film, Theater & Dance

Actor/actress warns of the need to stop acting. It could also signify an advisement to drop the false persona.
Ballerina portrays a woman who is a true lady; genteel thoughts, actions, and graceful manner (within and without).
Cameraperson characterizes one who is focused on the truth or facts. May also reveal an interfering personality.
Cast (of play/film) cautions one to take a better look at those involved in relationships or those with whom one is associated; people may not be the same as they present themselves. There may be some role-playing going on.
Casting agency implies the right person for the job. May indicate role-playing; someone who's not what they seem.
Choreographer characterizes an individual who does the planning.
Cinematographer typifies one who is interested in recording life in its reality; one with an eye on recording events.
Dance instructor characterizes those who have the capability to bring out another's emotions or self-expression.
Gaffer (lighting tech) characterizes one who sheds light on an issue or situation.
Movie producer characterizes one who has the capability to bring clarity to a situation through vivid visuals. This, in essence, will show any false perspectives one may have had.
Producer (film) typifies an individual who has the opportunity and ability to enlighten others; one who displays another's ideas to the public.
Scriptwriter represents one who either has control of her/his direction or one who attempts to design a personal reality and expects it to manifest without deviation.
Set designer (film/stage) stands for the perceptive ability to create an atmosphere that is appropriately consistent with the mood of events and their participants.
Show biz signifies a tendency to be in the limelight; a love of an audience.
Stagehand characterizes an individual who is capable of assisting another to express feelings or opinions.
Stage manager points to an individual who has the ability to pull things together.
Stunt double (acting) warns against letting others do your difficult tasks in life. May point to an overblown value of self or even a lack of self-confidence.
Taxi dancer refers to a lack of companionship; a forced temporary partnership.
Wardrobe mistress characterizes an individual who is expert at perceiving another's out-of-character behavior.

Cameraperson may be a representation of a busybody.

Media & TV

Anchorperson points to an individual who is capable of holding things together; one who serves as a grounding element.
Coanchor signifies a dual responsibility.
Referee characterizes life's duality; elements that contain positive and negative aspects, depending on use.
Speech writer is a caution to speak for oneself. This symbol points to someone who puts words in another's mouth.
Spokesperson characterizes a liaison. Also see speech writer.
Voice-over usually comes as an attention-getting symbol that sends a message from one's higher self or conscience.

Publishing

Author(ess) denotes originator; creativity; imagination.
Bindery depicts a need to keep records, thoughts, concepts, or beliefs together. This comes as a warning against letting these aspects become scattered.
Bookbinding See bindery.
Coauthor signifies a tandem idea or plan.
Copyreader See proofreader.
Ghostwriter cautions against doing another's thinking.
Proofreader comes to the dreamer as a clear warning for an individual to discern what is accepted as truth in respect to all relevant incoming information.
Publisher characterizes one who disseminates information. Recall what type of material was being published.
Writer pertains to a desire to express inner thoughts, ideas, or sensitivities.

Journalism

War correspondent means knowing what one's enemy is up to.

Abstracting service is a dream symbol that denotes those who are experienced in perceiving the most important elements of an issue.

City desk comes to the dreamer to reveal a need to be informed of aspects surrounding him- or herself.

City editor characterizes one who is kept abreast of aspects surrounding self.

Clipping service comes in dreams as a representation of one who will search out and collect all known information on a particular subject or for someone to do the research.

Copy editor characterizes one who keeps elements of an issue from contradicting each other; one who keeps things straight, from becoming confusing; a fact-checker.

Copy girl signifies an assistant; one who is capable of transmitting communications.

Copywriter can signify an individual who always knows what to say for any situation, or it can be associated with exaggerations/enticements.

Correspondent refers to an individual who communicates with and for others. May also indicate a source of useful information.

Correspondent (foreign). See foreign correspondent.

Editor characterizes one who gets to the point. This dreamscape symbol may also refer to someone who alters another person's words.

Film critic characterizes one who doesn't hesitate to voice opinions.

Foreign correspondent is representative of a connective line to different ideas. It also refers to one's personal receptivity to such.

Journalist characterizes one who keeps track of events in one's life. Could refer to one's higher self or those who watch us.

Photographer advises of the wisdom of grasping the moment instead of living for the future or what was.

Photojournalism illustrates the act of learning from one's experiential aspects in life.

Press (newspaper) See printing press; reporter.

Press agent is a dreamscape symbol that characterizes an individual who speaks on behalf of another.

Press card is representative of one's right to be somewhere or one's right to be privy to certain information.

Press secretary symbolizes one who speaks for another.

Printing press represents an ability to disseminate information.

Reporter (newsperson) characterizes one who makes the activity of others their priority. Exemplifies sensationalism and exaggerations.

Research and development (R & D) points to the need for thorough planning.

Restaurant critic usually symbolizes critiquing the quality of what one is filling one's life with.

Scribe is a dreamscape symbol that characterizes the recording of communications.

Sportswriter See sportscast.

Stringer (writer) is usually a representation of information that has been collated from differing sources.

War correspondent characterizes an interest in maintaining current information on an opponent.

Home Decor

House painter symbolizes a cover-up for a negative element in one's life. It may point to a freshening of some personal aspect or a change in attitude. Recall the paint color.

Interior decorator is usually representative of someone who continually attempts to change others. This attempt to change could involve the individual's personality, opinions, perceptions, appearance, or beliefs.

Paperhanger characterizes a person who attempts to cover up something; one who conceals or attempts to present a better image. May indicate deception.

Upholsterer relates to one who can provide a new outlook or attitude.

see also
• Babies *p. 103*
• Types of Education *p. 232*

Arts & Crafts

Artisan represents personal expression; sense of freedom and individuality; creativity.
Artist signifies creativity and the expression of same.
Bronze casting exemplifies the resulting product of blending specific life aspects; the touchable goal or creation.
Cabinetmaker See carpenter.
Carpenter means one with the ability to build on knowledge and talents to make constructive life contributions.
Clock maker characterizes an individual who sets limits; one who is highly efficient; one who motivates others.

Potter symbolizes personal abilities.

Cloisonné represents heavily layered and elaborately designed identity presentations; false appearances; a major problem with the acceptance of one's true self.
Commercial art signifies benefits in reaching goals through using one's unique expression of creativity.
Coppersmith characterizes an individual who inherently brings positive influences into the lives of others.
Glassblower characterizes subtle, delicate creativity.
Graphic arts symbolize a talent for communication clarity; a skill for explaining things.
Impressionist (art style) signifies a different way of seeing; an alternative viewpoint.
Mason indicates a person with strong foundational beliefs.
Parquetry (woodcraft) reveals an attention to fine detail and associative thought.
Potter characterizes creativity and talents that express one's individuality.
Silversmith will usually be representative of a spiritually ethical individual.
Tinsmith relates to a specialized skill one has.
Visual arts symbolize creative expressiveness.
Watchmaker constitutes precision.
Woodworking refers to utilizing one's inherent talents in creative ways.

Babies & Children

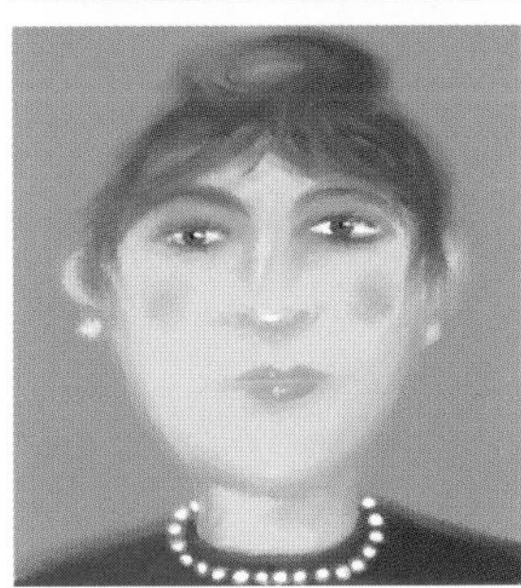

Governess means philanthropy.

Au pair generally characterizes a situation of barter; services that are exchanged for knowledge.
Babysitter characterizes a temporary nurturing and mothering condition.
Crossing guard characterizes protective elements in one's life; someone who cares about the welfare of others.
Governess corresponds to the quality of care given to one's humanitarian aspects.
Housemother characterizes a surrogate mother figure; someone who watches over a group of young adults, offers advice, and acts as their sounding board.
Nanny See babysitter.
Nursemaid is representative of a caregiver. This dream symbol usually reveals an unruly, incompetent, or reckless individual who will require routine watching over.
Obstetrician characterizes a person who has the knowledge and ability to bring forth a new life or awakening in others.
Scout leader is suggestive of a person who can serve as a guide to the dreamer along one's life path.
Wet nurse is indicative of an individual who is capable of providing nourishment to other people, usually of the emotional kind. It is a general reference to someone who provides comfort.

Education

Coach (tutor) warns us to use discernment when being advised or taught by another. May point to manipulation.
Headmistress characterizes an individual who helps to guide another's learning process.
Instructor See teacher.
Principal relates to a main person or element.
Professional refers to a level of experience or skill gained.
Professor See teacher.
Schoolteacher characterizes someone in the dreamer's life who is capable of teaching something important. This will be a specific element unique to the dreamer.
Teacher characterizes specific knowledge and the ability to transfer it.
Tutor points out one capable and willing to assist another.

Teacher represents a particular area of expertise and the facility to pass it on.

Social Work

Caseworker signifies an individual who attempts to assist many others.

Social service is a reflection of humanitarian intentions.

Social work comes in dreams to define a desire to help those less fortunate.

Welfare work See social service.

The Wrong Side of the Law

Drugs indicate dependency.

Drug dealer characterizes an extremely negative individual in the dreamer's life who has the ability and knowledge to manipulate, control, and make the dreamer a dependent.

Gunrunner indicates a person who is capable of privately supplying other people with protective means. This does not not normally carry negative connotations.

Hired gun warns against having other people deal with one's problems.

Hit man See hired gun.

Safecracker characterizes an individual who has the skill to break through the defenses of others. It may point to a skill for problem solving or identifying the core source of a problem.

Smuggler generally refers to deception.

Gambling

Bookmaker (bookie) is indicative of someone who is seen as an instigator or someone who is a negative influence.

Croupier characterizes someone who urges another to take chances, or an individual who will benefit or lose by the chances the dreamer takes.

Dealer (card) is a reference to someone who is a questionable source, someone who may be expert enough to manipulate outcomes.

Oddsmaker characterizes a person who has a knack for sensing probabilities.

Slot tech (casino) characterizes one who is instrumental in

Croupier is a fomenter of risk-taking.

keeping opportunities (or risks) available for another person in the dreamer's life.

Verifier (casino) points to someone capable of providing proof of something.

Safety & Protection

Bodyguard connotes an awareness of one's protective aspects (tools) and the utilization of the same.

Bouncer characterizes one who keeps order and maintains a peaceful atmosphere.

Censor characterizes a manipulative personality; one who would have others view life according to the perspectives and attitudes of self; a fear of thinking outside the box.

Fire chief characterizes an individual who is experienced at helping to get one's emotions under control.

Firefighter represents emotional self-control.

Guard denotes a protective measure or factor.

Night watchperson characterizes one's personal defenses; protective measures.

Search and rescue (team) is indicative of a need to

Bouncer is a peacekeeper.

search one's motives and to rescue oneself from misconceptions and negative attitudes that have been causing bad behavior.

Security guard characterizes an individual who is capable of providing protection and monitoring. May even be one's own conscience.

Sentry See guard.

Ski patrol usually refers to one's conscience.

Watchman See guard.

The Oldest Profession

Call girl represents a lack of self-respect; poor self-image; one who lacks individuality and requires the guidance and/or attention of others.

Harlot See prostitute.

Hooker See prostitute.

Madam (brothel) connotes an individual who gains from the efforts of others.

Prostitute applies to ill-gotten gains; a loss of self-respect; selling oneself short.

Streetwalker See prostitute.

Crime Detection

Detective characterizes one who has a high interest in understanding the facts and the sequential process of development.

House detective advises a person to perform a mental self-examination regarding motives and performance.

Private detective/investigator correlates to a need for each person to do her/his own thinking and searching. This symbol may reveal a need to watch something more closely.

Private eye See private detective/investigator.

Sleuth See detective.

see also
• Gambling *p. 204*
• Criminality *p. 323*

Law Enforcement

Arson investigator implies suspicion of wrongdoing. This usually indicates a situation that sparks questionable elements.
Attorney characterizes a need for complete honesty.
Attorney general relates to a need to reassess major moves that are planned.
Bailiff characterizes one who maintains order.
Bailsman See bondsman.
Barrister See attorney.
Bondsman characterizes a trusted individual. It may refer to someone who provides temporary security.
Chancellor portrays a ranking position; authoritarian aspect.
Constable See sheriff.
Consumer advocate points to someone who watches for negatives associated with a wide variety of life aspects. If the dreamscape consumer advocate was the dreamer, this symbol is pointing to oneself, the conscience.
Court clerk characterizes one who keeps track of schedules and appointments. An orderly and efficient individual.
Court reporter warns against repeating falsehoods; to get the facts right.
Crime scene investigator characterizes one who is proficient and experienced at getting to the bottom of things.
District attorney characterizes one's higher self—in other words, one's conscience.
Executioner may warn against paranoia or it may actually refer to an individual or event in one's life that is capable of bringing personal disaster. Lastly, is the executioner you? This would warn against a tendency toward self-persecution or playing at being the judge of everyone.
FBI agent represents one who has an analytic nature; one who has a tendency to check background details.
Highway patrol signifies protective forces present along one's path. May also point to occasional restraints that keep us from speeding too quickly over that path.
Informant portrays an individual who possesses information or specific knowledge. This symbol may point to an instance of betrayal.
Justice of the peace stands for rash decisions; impulsiveness.
Lawyer See attorney.
Leak (of information) See informant.
Legal aide characterizes a person who is capable of helping another get justice.
Legislator pertains to one who places restrictions on others.
Magistrate denotes an official authority.
Marshal characterizes authority, usually one's higher self; one's conscience.
Paralegal characterizes a person who understands the basics of an issue; someone who may be able to point you in the right direction.
Parole officer indicates someone who is devoted to making sure you won't go off track in life; someone responsible for keeping an eye on you. This someone may even be your own higher self or conscience.
Prison guard equates to one's higher self, the conscience that keeps one in line.
Probation officer characterizes those who serve to guide and advise. Use discretion with this, for someone presented as a probation officer may not be right for the dreamer. Recall the officer's attire and actions. Recall colors that were associated with the dream person. In many cases, this symbol can point out a domineering individual in one's life or it can also be associated with one's own conscience.
Process server reveals an individual who has the potential to bring bad news or drop the proverbial bomb in one's lap.
Profiler characterizes an individual who has a knack for perceiving another's thought processes and behavioral motivations.
Prosecutor (legal) characterizes higher judgments. May point to one's own guilt and come as a berating symbol.
Public defender implies unbiased justice.
Sheriff typifies an authority figure representing the rules or laws.
Solicitor is a reference to someone who acts for or with another.
Summons server is representative of a conscious awareness of one's wrongdoings; an inability to hide from the truth; an instrumental element in an attempt to get at the truth.
Truant officer represents one's own conscience.
Turnkey indicates completeness; entirety; everything is already in place and ready for one to make one's move.
Warden applies to imprisoning elements in life, which are often self-induced.

Prison guard represents one's sense of right and wrong.

Government

Administrative leave advises a need to take a break from planning, even thinking too much.
Aide denotes someone capable of giving assistance.
Alderperson See councilperson.
Ambassador refers to goodwill and helpfulness.
Attaché is the front person for another's mission or purpose.
Campaign manager is associated with one who facilitates action and keeps the momentum going.
CIA agent characterizes one who knows all about something or has access to private information.
City clerk generally represents a record-keeper; an individual who can provide a wide variety of specific information.
Councilperson exemplifies one who researches and decides something.
Counterspy See double agent.
Double agent characterizes hypocrisy or willful deception.
Emissary cautions against having others speak for you or do your work.
First lady characterizes a woman who epitomizes something specific.
Foreign minister characterizes an individual who presents new and innovative concepts to others.
Governor points to the one running the show and reminds that that individual should be oneself.
Intelligence agent denotes an invasion of one's privacy. This advises discernment when opening up to associates or friends.
IRS agent characterizes one who gains from the efforts of others; a leach.
Lieutenant governor usually points to the possibility of tandem power; an individual who has a strong possibility of being in control.
Mayor usually represents one's higher self—in other words, one's conscience.
Monarch (ruler) will not necessarily depict the meaning of ruler; however, it will usually indicate one's inner power and one's inner strength. In some cases, this symbol may carry the negative significance of someone who has a tendency to rule every relationship and situation.

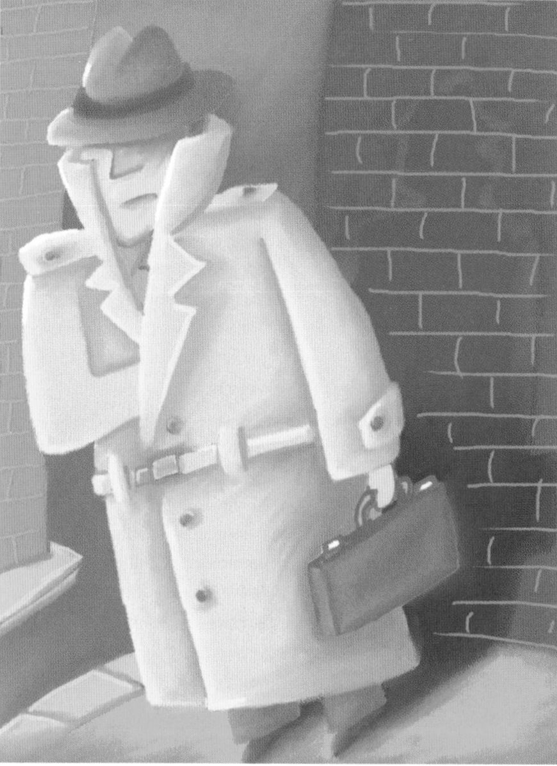

Secret agent reveals someone in one's life who has a hidden agenda.

Politician is a representation of a self-serving and hypocritical personality; a double-talker.
Prefect indicates a person of moderate authority.
Premier (person) generally stands for the prime individual in a situation.
President (of a country) characterizes an individual who has the authority and power to lead many. This dream symbol may not, in actuality, refer to a specific presidential individual and, likewise, may not be a thoroughly positive symbol.
Prime minister characterizes one who carries great responsibility for the welfare of a multitude of people.
Public service alludes to efforts given to help others.
Ruler (person) characterizes an authoritative figure who may imply oneself, that is, one's conscience.
Secret agent exposes an individual who has ulterior motives in a situation.
Senator is representative of an individual who is in a position to listen to the problems, complaints, and wishes of others and expend efforts to change things for the better.
Stateswoman is indicative of a respected person of authority in the dreamer's life.
Tax collector characterizes a freeloader.

Divers

Aquanaut is one who totally immerses self in a spiritual life; a cloistered nun, monk, or reclusive visionary.
Frogman characterizes an unhealthy spiritual attitude or belief system.
Pearl diver typifies one who gleans spiritual pearls from searching efforts.
Scuba diver depicts the attainment of spiritual gifts. Recall what the diver was looking at or collecting? Was the water clear, cloudy, colored?

see also
• The Sea *p. 36*
• Organizations, Bodies & Groups *p. 128*

Marine & Naval

Admiral signifies one who is in command, not necessarily properly so.
Boatbuilder See shipbuilder.
Boat captain is representative of the one who spiritually leads. This should be none other than self following one's inner guidance.
Cabin boy refers to a young individual who is capable of helping one along his/her spiritual journey.
Captain is indicative of someone who leads others. This may advise the dreamer to be captain of self.
Coast Guard characterizes those who work to provide spiritual safety for others; one's advisors or spiritual guardians.
Deck hand characterizes one who assists in bringing about one's spiritually enlightened perceptions.
Harbor master characterizes an individual who has the capability to guide others to a spiritually safe place.
Helmsperson points to one in control. Ideally, this should be the dreamer.
Lifeguard is representative of a savior-type individual in one's life; someone who can rescue a situation or provide a way out of a troublesome problem.
Longshoremen illustrate the utilization of one's spiritual aspects. Were goods being shipped out? Incoming? Busy dock? Empty?
Mariner signifies one who is on a spiritual search or quest.
Petty officer signifies one who possesses a higher than average level of intelligence, experience, and authority.
Purser correlates to one who holds and protects the valuable assets of others.
Sailor means a spiritual seeker.
Shipbuilder characterizes one who expends efforts to carefully and systematically plan out and manifest one's spiritual search.
Shipmate is a reference to a companion on one's spiritual walk. This points to an individual who shares one's beliefs.
Stevedore See longshoremen.

Sailor characterizes one who is looking for inner knowledge.

Military & Air Force

Advance person signifies someone who has the ability to prepare the way.
Aide-de-camp symbolizes one's need to be more regimented and efficient.
Airman represents one who is a concentrated thinker.
Air marshal signifies guarded thought; keeping a diligent watch for negatives or misfit ideologies that may have the potential for adulterating one's philosophy.
Cadet characterizes the beginning stages of developing combative perspectives; one who can be perceived as a fledgling headed for a draw toward the military-machine attitude.
Commander in chief pertains to an authority figure of the highest rank. For the dreamer, this may be in reference to one who is highly respected.
Commando is representative of impulsiveness; knee-jerk reactions; a short-tempered personality. It may also refer to destructive resolutions.
Drill instructor characterizes unavoidable learning experiences in one's life.
Fighter (pilot) characterizes an aggressive personality; one who is used to expertly maneuvering around and through conflict.
Foot soldier characterizes one who walks his or her life path as a warrior.
Joint chiefs of staff symbolize one's personal advisor, together with one's higher self.
Legionnaire connotes an individual who belongs to a large group; someone who has a strong backing.

Soldier is one who fights for others.

Musketeer is indicative of a guarding aspect in one's life. It may refer to a protective characteristic.
Paratrooper usually relates to emotional disturbances.
Private (military) stands for a lesser ranking; less authority, yet prepared for a conflict.
Quartermaster is usually representative of one's personal responsibility.
Reservist (military) characterizes personal preparedness; a reserve of inner strength.
Sentinel characterizes heightened awareness. It may refer to watchfulness.
Sky marshall points to one's own hold/guard on thoughts.
Soldier characterizes a person who upholds the honor and safety of others; fighting for what one believes in. May also indicate a forced participation of a conflict; one who was drawn in.
Storm trooper characterizes a highly aggressive personality.
Warrior usually stands for perseverance; an individual's personal strength.
Yeoman normally indicates a paper-pusher, but in dream symbology it points to one who works behind the scenes.

Engineering

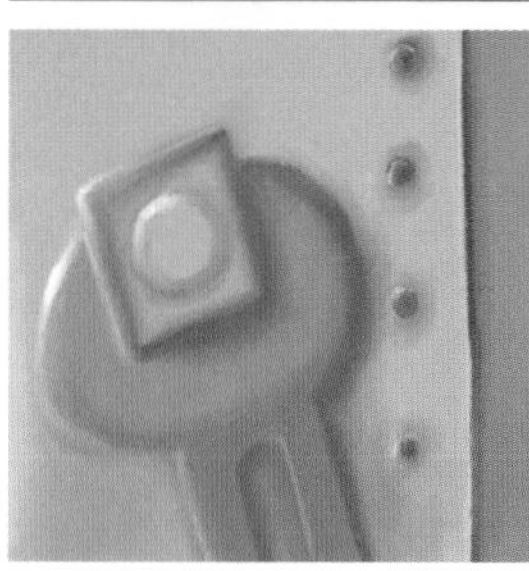

Civil engineer means a facilitator.

Civil engineer denotes an individual who plans and creates amenities for others.
Engineer shows one who is adept at complex planning.
Engineer (architectural) See architect.
Engineer (electrical) portrays one who is proficient at tracing another's thought processes and redirecting them to provide greater clarity and simplicity.
Engineer (train) See train engineer.
Structural engineer characterizes an individual who has the knowledge to gauge whether or not a plan has foundational merit/strength.
Train engineer exemplifies an individual who leads others along the smooth and easy, well-worn path in the course of their lives.

Aviation

Aviator is one who holds to one's own ideals, beliefs, and attitudes.
Bush pilot typifies one who guides others to a spiritually interactive life; one who guides humanitarian causes.
Copilot characterizes confidence; the supportive reserves that one has.
Flight attendant characterizes someone in the dreamer's life who makes one's life journey easier, especially regarding perspectives and attitudes.
Ground crew represents one's emotional support group.
Stewardess See flight attendant.
Test pilot is a representation of self-confidence.
Wingman characterizes guided thoughts.

Computing

Computer programmer generally refers to an individual who believes in the ability to make reality coincide with personal perspectives, desires, or plans.
Data processor connotes the use of information, how one uses what one knows in everyday life.
Programmer characterizes an individual who has the knowledge and ability to manipulate and/or strongly influence others.
Webmistress characterizes a woman who is skilled at setting up another's personal central communication network.
Web retailer signifies the ultimate convenience. It may refer to the concept of minimal effort being expended for the purpose of obtaining a goal.

Manufacturing

Assembly line cautions against routine conformity in life. This may be associated with one's way of thinking.
Cobbler See shoemaker.
Cottage industry means self-sufficiency; an inner contentedness through personal efforts applied.
Ironworker characterizes a strong personality. Depending on surrounding dreamscape details, this may or may not be a positive sign.
Machinist characterizes those who set the example and are looked to for guidance.
Millwright characterizes an ability to put things in motion; having knowledge, skill, and motivation.
Piecework is a representation of the benefits gained after each step of the way.
Production line See assembly line.
Shoemaker characterizes an individual who has the capability to guide the life paths of others.
Smelter signifies an attempt to maintain purity and separation of individual ideas and concepts.
Warehouse worker connotes organizational skills.
Weaver is generally a representation of the totality of true reality and the multidimensional elements that are woven into it.
Wheelwright is a reference to someone who is capable of helping another get back on track.
Winemaker characterizes the quality of an idea; the formulated potential of it.

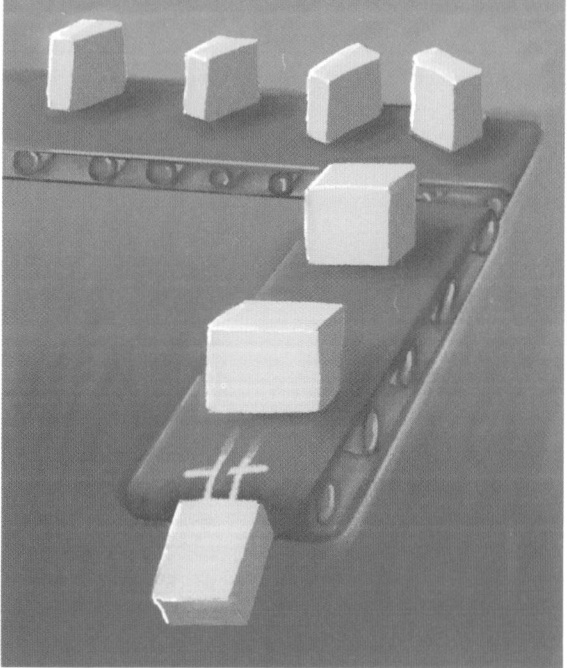

Assembly line warns against becoming stuck in a rut.

see also
• Computing *p. 270*
• Travel & Transportation *pp. 286–305*

Travel & Transportation

Delivery people relate to how one puts oneself across to others and may be a sign of something about to happen.

Air traffic controller indicates the need to keep one's thoughts from crossing or mixing, creating confusion. The need to keep issues separate from one another.
Brakeman characterizes one's immediate support person; an individual who is at the ready to give assistance.
Bus driver (public) exemplifies a caring and giving personality; one who has the potential to help or carry one for a ways.
Bus driver (school) See school bus driver.
Cab driver See taxi driver.
Carriage trade portrays selective relationships; a catering to wealthy, powerful, or influential individuals; elitist attitude.
Chauffeur implies a lack of self-motivation; taking a back seat and letting others do the driving (work).
Conductor (transit) characterizes those who offer helpful guidance along one's path.
Courier characterizes those who serve as messengers; one bringing a message.
Delivery people pertain to one's delivery or presentation to others in life. May also indicate a forthcoming message or event.
Designated driver means a person of responsibility. May refer to an individual who is leading others.
Docent See tour guide.
Gondolier characterizes an individual who carries others along a spiritual path. This is not a good symbol, for it means one is depending on a leader for spiritual guidance rather than following one's own inner promptings.
Guide suggests a person who is capable of showing the way.
Navigator is representative of someone who has planned out a set course in his or her life.
Pilot connotes one who has the capability to control or steer one's path direction. The key here is to recall the dream pilot's condition and ability.
Road grader characterizes a life aspect that has the potential for smoothing one's way.
School bus driver is one who can personally lead another to further enlightenment or attained knowledge.
Signal person stands for an individual who keeps one on the right track. This could even be one's own conscience or inner sense of direction.
Switchman signifies an individual who is capable of altering one's course in life.
Taxi driver characterizes an individual who has the capability of carrying others (for a specified distance) along their path.
Tour guide characterizes an individual who is well informed on a particular issue and is prepared to share that guiding knowledge with others.
Trucker relates to one who is conscientious regarding closures; one who wants to see things through.
Wagon master characterizes one who leads others along a lengthy journey.

Sales

Direct mail/marketing connotes a sales pitch from someone. This dreamscape symbol may not refer to an actual purchase but could pertain to a situation where an attempt to convince will be made.
Entrepreneur characterizes an enterprising individual.
Snake oil salesman reveals a deceiver.
Telemarketing represents fast-talk; an attempt to sell something through impersonal communication.
Trader characterizes one who possesses a give-and-take attitude; open to options.
Traveling salesperson is a representation of a person intent on spreading beliefs far and wide. This may indicate a fanatic.

Service Industries

Agent refers to a middleman who is not necessary; one who represents self as a facilitator. Usually points to one having a personal agenda or ulterior motive.

Antique dealer points to one who seeks out and offers old ideas or ways to others.

Auctioneer is one who exaggerates value.

Booking agent relates to someone who takes care of logistics. In some dreams, this symbol may point to a manipulative individual.

Broker See agent.

Concierge portrays one who serves to make life easier.

Doorkeeper means one who must be communicated with before an opportunity can be taken advantage of.

Doorman characterizes one who is ready to open doors for the dreamer as long as the dreamer is deserving or well prepared.

Dry cleaner comes as a strong advisement to give more care to the removal of negative factors from one's life.

Emcee See master of ceremonies.

Escort characterizes a close associate in one's life.

Escort service points to an individual who provides another with a temporary associate or support aide.

Exterminator (infestation) characterizes an individual who is capable of helping to rid one's life of negative or unwanted aspects.

Floor duty (real estate) stands for providing another with availability and opportunity to be assisted.

Garbage collector represents a deliberate hoarding of bad thoughts.

Front desk See receptionist.

Garbage collector shows willful accumulation of useless aspects such as negative attitudes, erroneous perceptions or beliefs, or materialistic factors.

Gas station attendant represents one who attends to another's needs, especially to conserve and maintain another's energy level.

Gatekeeper characterizes one's higher self; conscience.

Hatcheck connotes holding back from expressing personal opinions or attitudes.

House sitter alludes to someone you completely trust.

Interpreter signifies a need for better understanding; clearer communication.

Lamplighter characterizes one who lights the way; understanding.

Landlady refers to an individual who provides shelter. This may stand for shelter in the way of comfort, a sounding board, or counsel.

Letter carrier refers to an individual who conveys a message; a messenger.

Locksmith characterizes one who can solve problems. This person should be you. Every problem contains its own solution key.

Mail carrier characterizes one who is capable of bringing or sending a message.

Mail people See postal worker.

Master of ceremonies points to the person who directs operations or ensures efficiency. May point to a manipulative individual.

Paperboy symbolizes delivered information. This may advise one to seek information instead of receiving only that which someone else deems you should know.

Party planner characterizes one who is experienced in managing details and pulling them together to create a successful goal.

Postal worker reflects those who tend to be efficient and orderly to a stressful/detrimental extent.

Postmistress characterizes a person who ensures communications are carried out. This may refer to one's conscience.

Promoter characterizes an individual who supports and promotes another individual or idea for gain. Also see agent.

Proprietress emphasizes the rightful owner or originator of something. Surrounding dreamscape details will clarify.

Public relations (PR) constitutes the dissemination of supportive and positive information associated with an individual, group, or situation.

Real estate agent characterizes one who is capable of helping another obtain goals.

Receptionist characterizes an initial contact.

Sanitation worker See garbage collector.

Ticket agent points to the one who can provide access.

Translator signifies one capable of bringing understanding or clarifying misunderstood communication.

Usher characterizes one capable of guiding another. May represent a counselor, friend, or even oneself.

Utility company stands for work and the efforts applied to it.

Wedding planner means one who gives careful attention to the foundation of an impending relationship.

see also
• Money *p. 189*
• Shopping *p. 199*

Finance & Insurance

Accountant symbolizes the need to make a personal accounting. This may indicate a need for retrospection or rethinking.
Assessor refers to an individual who claims to be an expert in determining the worth of another's talents/skills. This symbol may point to an overly critical personality.
Auditor represents someone who checks up on another in some way.
Bank examiner usually comes in dreams to caution one against trying to fool oneself when it comes to one's behavioral balance sheet.
Bookkeeper characterizes the book of life; one's karmic record; an accounting of one's behavior.
Brokerage stands for a precarious aspect in one's life. May refer to pending plans. Also may point to the need to shop something around.
Certified public accountant (CPA) See accountant.
Claims adjuster shows someone who has the talent for assessing situational damage and recommending solutions/recompense.
Economist characterizes one who is skilled in weighing the pros and cons of a situation or plan; one who analyzes the cost of efforts expended against the benefits.
Finance officer characterizes one who can open up opportunities to fulfill one's goal.
Insurance agent characterizes one who has a predatory nature and takes advantage of another's lack of faith.
Loan officer characterizes one who is capable of helping with another's problem; one who can provide another with the resources to attain a goal.
Money changer represents a conversion of one's assets; altering form such as turning it into a gift or shared talent.
Moneylender characterizes a person who shares wealth for self-serving reasons.
Mortgage broker characterizes someone who may be able to realize one's goals—for a price.
Paymaster characterizes those who recognize the value of a person's behavior in respect to output.
Repo man is a representation of an individual who has the capability to take something away from another person. This dream symbol comes to warn the dreamer of a possible loss if responsibilities aren't met.

Moneylender means selfish goals.

Stockbroker characterizes a person who takes risks with another's assets.
Teller (bank) reveals a person's utilization of personal assets such as wealth, natural abilities, or spiritual gifts. Recall if there was a deposit or withdrawal being made. Was someone in the vault?
Underwriter characterizes approval; an endorsement. This may also point to those who weigh risks.

Messengers & Communication

Announcer is someone who has a message. The words are usually for the dreamer alone. Recall what was being announced.
Bard See storyteller.
Barker (fair) characterizes a loudmouth; one who usually has much to say about nothing; someone who has a tendency to love drawing attention to self.
Delivery people pertain to one's delivery or presentation to others in life. May also indicate a forthcoming message or event.
Directory assistance suggests communication made possible through a middle person or intermediary.
Dispatcher characterizes one's higher self.
Envoy See messenger.
Flag person (construction) comes as a warning message. What type of flag was being waved? Was it a traffic caution to slow down? Stop?
General delivery suggests an unsettled situation.
Herald See messenger.
Messenger shows one who will provide a solution, answer, or important clue to something.
Raconteur See storyteller.
Runner See messenger.
Storyteller characterizes one who is interested in preserving the truth.
Telegraph operator symbolizes information or messages generated from one's inner perceptual senses.
Telephone operator signifies a person capable of assisting one to communicate with others.
Town crier enters dreams as a messenger who brings a warning of some type. Recall what was cried out.
Wire service relates to a source for information-gathering and its dissemination.

Store Personnel

Bagger (at register counter) suggests someone who consolidates another's ideas, pulls them together.
Cashier (store) represents the piper who needs to be paid.
Checker See clerk.
Clerk pertains to the selling of something. May apply to the selling of self or one's personal perspectives.
Counterperson See clerk.
Dealer (merchandise) usually characterizes one who is the source of something; one who can supply something to others.
Salesperson See clerk.
Storekeeper characterizes one who is capable of providing various opportunities.
Window dressing is usually representative of dressed perceptions; the perceptions that one may choose to alter according to individual attitudes, qualities, or even the changing seasons.

Tradespeople

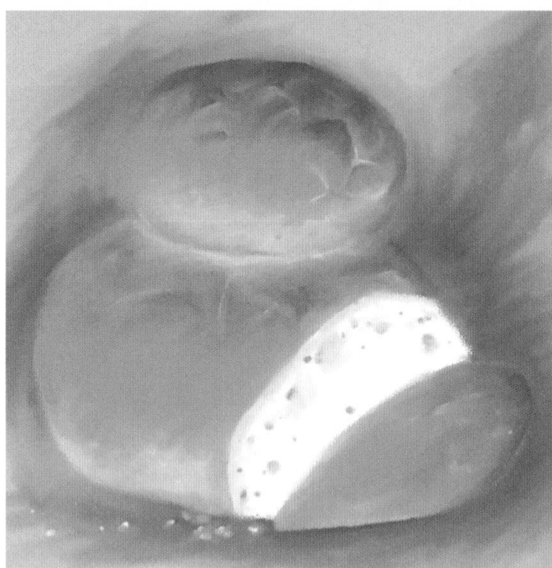

Baker represents someone who can make things happen.

Baker signifies an expanding scope of one's spiritual understanding and personal application. One who has the capacity to bring something to fruition.

Bookseller refers to an individual who can offer a wealth of information or knowledge.

Butcher is representative of a scathing personality. This dream symbol refers to one who focuses on the negative aspects of others; one who cuts apart ideas or plans.

Confectioner points to someone who has a tendency to be an optimist or to brighten another's day.

Florist characterizes one with a multitude of natural talents. What was the condition of the flowers? What type of flowers were featured in the dream?

Flower girl represents the utilization of one's budding natural talents.

Greengrocer characterizes an individual who has bountiful natural talents. These talents are generally related to someone's inner goodness and a giving nature.

Jobber points to someone who has a particular skill to help another.

Merchant denotes one who can offer choices to another.

Milliner is representative of a person who is capable of easily influencing others.

Purveyor points to one who has the knowledge and ability to access what others need. In this sense, this dream symbol refers to a a supplier.

Rag picker characterizes a person who attempts to utilize leftover aspects. This dream symbol may also indicate a resourceful individual who efficiently recycles multiple aspects by recognizing value in things that others no longer perceive as valuable.

Shopkeeper characterizes an individual who provides a service or opportunity for others.

Tinker is representative of an individual who will attempt to perform repairs even though they lack the necessary skill.

Porters

Baggage handler See porter.

Bellboy/hop means personal assistance; possible servitude.

Porter (hotel) characterizes a helper of some type. It is generally a reference to someone who helps carry the burdens of another.

Redcap See porter.

Skycap See porter.

Manual Workers

Auto mechanic is representative of a need for someone to seek a medical evaluation.

Bricklayer characterizes one who works hard and diligently at ensuring the setting up of strong foundational values.

Cotton-picking applies to the wholesomeness of honest, hard work.

Demolition crew means the life aspect (or those associated with it) that brings about a destruction of something in the dreamer's life.

Grease monkey See mechanic.

Hod carrier characterizes one who is willing to do the hard work and who is prepared to put in great efforts in order to help another.

Mechanic is representative of someone who is capable of repairing a dysfunction or negative in another person's life.

Roustabout characterizes a person possessing multiple talents; diversity.

Stonemason See bricklayer.

Bricklayer means someone who is solid and reliable.

see also
• Cleaning *p. 389*
• Food & Drink *pp. 424–441*

Cleaning & Maintenance

Chimney sweep relates to the need to maintain a state of untainted attitudes. The symbol of a chimney sweep points to someone who can expertly clear away tainted ideas.

Cleaning service stands for efforts expended for the purpose of cleaning up after others. This symbol won't usually refer to literally cleaning but rather to fixing or repairing other people's mistakes or handling damage control left in the wake of their actions.

Dry cleaner comes as a strong advisement to give more care to the removal of negative factors from one's life.

Electrician characterizes one's personal thought process and the tendency to get others wired in a like manner. May point to an individual skilled in motivating others.

Gas fitter See pipe fitter.

Handyperson characterizes an individual who is capable of fixing a multitude of problems; one who may have a variety of solutions.

Janitor constitutes a need to clean up one's act.

Lineman characterizes an individual in one's life who has the capability to restore another's strength or to reconnect a line of communication.

Pipe fitter signifies one who has a knack for putting the pieces of a concept or issue together without misinterpretation, error, or misfit parts.

Chimney sweep indicates a person who can clean up one's thoughts.

Plumber usually represents the presence of a negative situation in one's life. May indicate a physical dysfunction or disease.

Repair person is one who can solve another's problems.

Window washer implies one capable of clarifying another's perspective on an issue.

Food & Drink Industry

Barkeeper See bartender.

Bartender is one who frequently serves potential advice to others or provides a sympathetic ear. May not always represent positive communication.

Bottle washer won't ever be a demeaning symbol; rather it indicates someone performing a multitude of tasks.

Brewmaster is normally associated with one who is expert at providing the perfect form of stress-relieving sources unique to each individual. However, depending on the related elements of the dream, a brewmaster may point to a routinely conniving person.

Busboy connotes one who is capable of repairing wrongs done; one who has the ability to clean up what others leave behind.

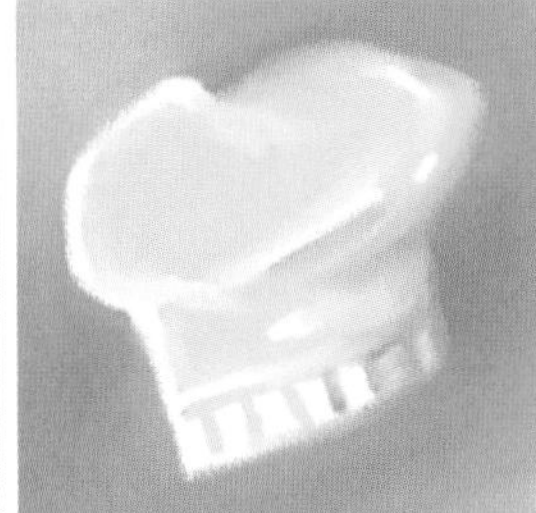
Chef refers to nourishment.

Carhop connotes those who make life a little easier or more convenient.

Chef characterizes the method and quality of food preparation. This may be food for the mind or for emotional fulfillment.

Cocktail waitress characterizes an individual who has the capability of easing one's problems. May also point to someone who aids another in avoiding reality.

Cook (gourmet) See chef.

Cook (person, food) characterizes one who is capable of giving sustenance to others.

Cook (short-order) See short-order cook.

Curb service is a representation of convenience.

Food service cautions against being handed any type of nourishment offered rather then personally choosing for oneself.

Gourmet illustrates high quality nourishment of some type: mental, emotional, or spiritual sustenance.

Hash-slinger See short-order cook.

Head waitperson stands for an experienced coordinator or assistant.

Innkeeper characterizes an individual who is capable of providing rest and comfort to another.

Maître d' is representative of a person in charge; the head person.

Prep cook is suggestive of someone who works behind the scenes.

Short-order cook characterizes multiple capabilities.

Soda jerk is a representation of one who is capable of supplying another with multiple options.

Taste tester usually points to tentative trial sampling of ideas.

Waitperson indicates servitude.

Animals & Wildlife

Animal behaviorist is a symbol that points to a need to better understand a friend.
Animal caretaker refers to an individual's level and quality of compassion.
Animal control (officer) refers to an individual who can be depended on to keep her or his friends out of trouble.
Animal groomer See groomer (animal).
Animal husbandry connotes a nurturing nature.
Animal trainer signifies a manipulation of friends and relationships with others.
Beekeeper characterizes hidden agendas; an individual who wants something in return; one who takes and takes. This may point to one who has ulterior motives for caring.
Breeder (of dogs) is usually representative of an individual who maintains interest in something for the prime purpose of getting something back out of it; an ulterior motive for a quickly made friendship.

Zookeeper indicates someone who is kind and considerate to others.

Broncobusting implies a struggle for individuality. It may also come to the dreamer as a warning of a domineering personality.
Conservationist relates to one who places a high priority on the preservation of positive life aspects.
Cowboy/girl characterizes the sense of freedom in following one's personal path.
Cowhand See cowboy/girl.
Dogcatcher cautions against the manipulations of one's friends. May warn of a situation where one has captured a friend's loyalty. Friends need to be free or they're not really one's friends.
Dog walker suggests giving more attention to friends.
Falconer is one who recognizes, understands, and quietly accepts a connection with higher spiritual forces.
Gamekeeper advises of self-serving motives.
Game warden suggests a need to be aware of how an individual's natural talents are used (or not used).
Gaucho See cowboy/girl.
Groomer (animal) characterizes a compassionate individual.
Herder may not mean one who keeps others in line; it may pertain to a personal need to keep self in line.
Horse-trading implies clever negotiations.
Horse trainer refers to the ability to calm others, help them better handle situations.
Shepherd signifies watchfulness or guardianship.
Taxidermist suggests shallow beliefs or perspectives.
Veterinarian indicates selflessness; compassion.
Zookeeper characterizes someone who has a compassionate personality.

Administrative & Clerical

File clerk means well organized.

Administrator comes as a reference to someone who oversees a situation. May point to an individual who either should or shouldn't be in charge.
File clerk is a characterization of efficiency.
Office boy is representative of someone who makes efforts to help another achieve a purpose or goal.
Secretary (person) characterizes an individual who is capable of providing both support and assistance.
Shipping clerk characterizes an individual who is capable of keeping track of where everything is going, who is getting what. This means the scorekeeper and may even point to oneself and the responsibility to keep one's records balanced.
Stenographer characterizes an individual who remembers another's words; a record of communication.

Farming

Dirt farmer represents perseverance. It refers to great efforts already made or required in the future.
Farmer characterizes one who cultivates spiritual and/or simplistic aspects; one who understands the importance of the basics.
Farmhand points to an individual who is capable of helping one nourish and appreciate another's natural talents.
Plowboy characterizes a down-to-earth personality who clearly perceives the right directions to take.

see also
• Animals, Insects, Birds & Reptiles *pp. 16–33*
• Farming *p. 379*

Working with the Land

Botanist illustrates a person who works hard at applying spirituality to daily life.

Bushman is one who immerses self in a spiritually humanitarian lifestyle; one who places importance on the basics.

Bushwhacker connotes one who is capable of making one's way through life's difficulties. Also can denote one who ambushes others.

Crop dusting connotes wrong beginnings; applying preventive measures before determining whether an issue or idea can strongly develop on its own.

Developer (land) typifies misuse of one's resources.

Environmentalist exemplifies one who possesses inner balance and harmony.

Explorer characterizes a free-thinker; one who follows one's interests or curiosity; a seeker of knowledge.

Forest ranger characterizes one's conscience, specifically related to spiritual aspects.

Fruit grower characterizes one who has a high interest in cultivating talents, abilities, and means of helping others.

Gardener characterizes one who nurtures humanitarian acts and spiritual attitudes.

Groundskeeper See gardener.

Homesteader characterizes independence and confidence.

Hunter may indicate a killing of innocence whereby one obliterates positive attitudes and spiritual truths or it may mean an individual who is searching for something important in life. Surrounding dreamscape details will clarify which meaning is intended.

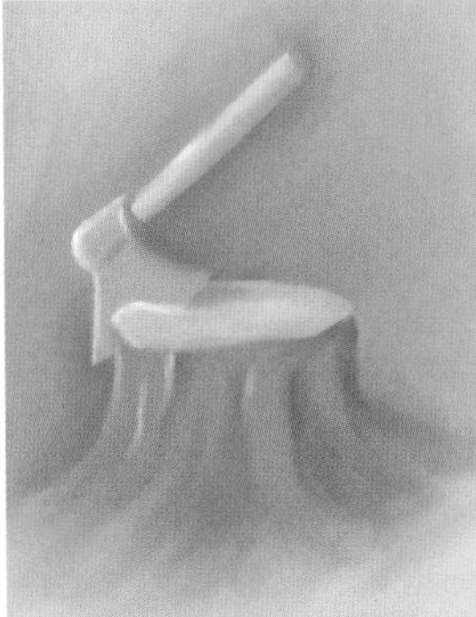

Lumberjack is a cause of inner ruin.

Land developer See developer (land).

Landscape gardener See gardener.

Logger See lumberjack.

Lumberjack emphasizes a spiritually destructive force.

Miner characterizes a spiritual searcher.

Prospector characterizes a person who is searching for something in life. Recall what was being prospected for. Gold denotes financial gain, and silver indicates a spiritual element. A lost treasure points to the expectation of a windfall.

Ranger (forest) characterizes a person who recognizes and respects natural talents.

Topographer characterizes an individual who is capable of charting or directing another's course; one who can point out the pitfalls and areas of smooth-going.

Tracker characterizes a person intent on following another. May denote an intensive search.

Trapper indicates a resourceful, self-sufficient individual, yet may also reveal a conniving personality.

Sports

Archer comes as a messenger.

Athlete signifies physical accomplishments.

Ball boy reminds us of the little, everyday blessings of helpfulness we often overlook or never stop to appreciate.

Batboy/girl is one who can supply another with the tools to further progress.

Caddie represents a follower and implies indecision or an inability to think for self. May also refer to a clinging type of personality.

Commissioner is usually associated with oneself, one's conscience.

Football player alludes to one who uses aggressiveness and complex maneuvers to attain goals.

Goalkeeper characterizes an individual who keeps one motivated.

Jockey (any type) pertains to one who is skilled in maneuvering various aspects into their best position.

Scorekeeper represents oneself; responsibility to maintain a balanced perspective.

Team owner (sports) characterizes one who funds or backs a joint effort.

Umpire characterizes a person's conscience; maintaining behavior that is confined within the bounds or rules.

Wrestler exposes an aggressively manipulative personality. May point to someone who is currently wrestling with an issue; a time of debating.

Jockey indicates someone who is a shrewd operator.

Specialist

Angler connotes an individual who fishes around instead of being direct.

Architect characterizes those who attempt to plan out their lives in great detail; one who attempts to create his own reality; a master manipulator to gain personal goals.

Astronaut characterizes our ability to expand ourselves and traverse finer dimensions.

Bell ringer refers to someone trying to get the attention of others.

Blacksmith illustrates reformations or rejuvenations that will be solid and strong.

Cartographer illustrates farsightedness; an ability to map out one's own path.

Curator defines one who is devoted to the protection and preservation of intellectual pursuits and values.

Custodian pertains to individuals who are designated with the authority to be the keepers, the preservers of spiritual truths.

Demolition expert points to someone who is experienced in ways of eliminating something. This is a dreamscape symbol that has the duality of positive and negative interpretations. Demolishing a negative element would be a positive symbol. Demolishing a positive aspect would be a negative one. Recall what the demolition expert was proficient in destroying.

Distributor (person/outlet) symbolizes a specialized source of something.

Dowser characterizes one who utilizes spiritual gifts.

Farrier applies to someone with a serene personality.

Furrier characterizes a self-serving nature.

Gunsmith characterizes an individual who creates protective aspects for others to use.

Hard rock miner characterizes one who expends great personal efforts to advance along a personal path.

Heraldry signifies extreme self-absorption; arrogance.

Historian characterizes one who is interested in understanding how past experiences relate to the present.

Inventor characterizes intellectual exploration and creativity.

Jeweler characterizes one who places a high priority on material aspects in life. It may symbolize one interested in fine detail. Surrounding dreamscape aspects will clarify this.

Librarian corresponds with an individual who has the capability of guiding one's direction for gaining deeper knowledge.

Linguist characterizes an individual who has exceptional communication skills.

Mapmaker See cartographer.

Master builder characterizes a skilled planner; one who can spot flaws in another's plans or method of operation.

Matchmaker pertains to a person who is capable of organization, bringing things together.

Missionary corresponds to a person with a purpose. We are all missionaries in life. This symbol simply underscores it for the dreamer as a reminder that this is the case.

Muleskinner characterizes someone with an extremely influential personality.

Pawnbroker signifies one who can provide temporary help for another.

Philosopher alludes to one who engages in higher enlightenment through deeper thought and contemplation. May point to a deep thinker.

Poet(ess) relates to the lyrical aspect of oneself that expresses inner thoughts and emotional elements associated with one's life.

Rainmaker signifies one who has a good record of getting results; high rate of success with attempted endeavors. Usually points to spirituality.

Saddler characterizes a person who has the skill to enhance one's journey.

Sign painter generally brings a personal message for each individual dreamer. Recall what was being painted in the dream. What colors were dominant? Who was the painter involved?

Smithy See blacksmith.

Snake charmer is representative of a persuasive personality. It may also indicate someone with a manipulative nature.

Sorcerer warns against the negative utilization of inherent talents or spiritual gifts.

Steeplejack characterizes an individual who is not afraid to approach high concepts or reach for a comprehension to complexities.

Stonecutter See jeweler.

Theologian denotes deeper spiritual study and a need for same.

Astronaut refers to one's capacity for greater personal advancement.

see also
• Angling *p. 215*
• Jewelry *p. 411*

Professional Terminology

Account executive normally refers to one's conscience and reminds the dreamer to keep a check on integrity regarding behavior.
Advisor points to an individual who is capable of giving appropriate counsel.
Agenda cautions one to give more serious attention to responsibility.
Analyst reveals an individual who is skilled at unraveling confusing issues or situations.
Appointment signifies a need to communicate with another.
Arbitrator characterizes the need for some type of mediation in one's life, perhaps from an outside source to resolve one's own inner conflict over an issue.
Assessment stands for taking stock of various life aspects.
Assignment pertains to a message to continue one's work or along one's path. Be more responsible.
Break (time-out) calls for a pause or rest from something.
Briefing reveals a situation where one doesn't have all the facts. Signifies a need to be brought up to speed on an issue.
Business card represents an egotistical personality; a desire to be known and recognized. May serve to reveal someone's identity or purpose.
Calling card (printed) connotes one's intention or outward presentation to the public.
Call sheet symbolizes opportunities to take advantage of.
Case history advises one to look into and know the background information on something important.
Caseload implies an excessive backlog of work or information being processed.
Charter member denotes one who participated in something's beginning stage of development.
Chore denotes something needing to be accomplished.
Colleague See associate.
Commercial signifies an offered aspect; something being shown to the dreamer.
Committee symbolizes a group chosen to perform a function. This would indicate a tone of authority or confirm rightness for the dreamer.
Complaint department usually points to where one can go to get answers or resolutions.
Conditional use permit stands for one's right to temporarily display a variant form of behavior or have a specific type of attitude.
Conference indicates a situation requiring further discussion.
Contract (on life) portrays an agreement about which one must make a choice. Whose life was the contract on? Yours? And who put the contract out?
Corporate image stands for the type of image one desires to project in respect to status, appearances, or behavior.
Corporate reshuffle is a reference to a repositioning of the main players.
Corporation signifies an organized group of individuals who are associated by a common interest.
Day job indicates one's source of sustenance, yet may not point to one's goal or source of satisfying benefits.
Delegate characterizes a representative individual; one who reflects a certain perspective, attitude, or beliefs.
Editorial denotes an expression of personal opinion.
Elbow grease illustrates personal effort applied to something.
Enterprise zone points to choices that benefit others instead of solely self.
Fast track advises that the fastest way is not always the most productive means of achievement.
Feasibility analysis represents the wisdom of taking a cautionary look at the viability of a plan.
File (sort) calls to put one's life or priorities in order.
Fixer-upper points to a deal, as long as one is willing to put some personal effort into improvements.
Form letter signifies a group of people or a situation of considerable size; a situation common to many.
Glass ceiling indicates the hidden barriers that one must break through.
Graveyard shift reveals a darkness surrounding one's life and advises of the wisdom of bringing some light in.
Guard duty represents a call to sharpen one's awareness; an approaching phase when one needs to be particularly watchful.
Guild denotes a group that shares the same interest. This usually advises the dreamer of the existence of such a group.
Highflier characterizes one who has a tendency to go to extremes; extravagance.
Hippocratic oath denotes a determined path; a pure intention.
Impact study points to a need to give a hard look at the possible ramifications of a planned idea or move.
Incentive points to an element serving as a motivational factor.
In-house relates to something that comes from within oneself, usually an attitude, but this dream symbol can also refer to negatives such as self-defeating behavior.
Inside information most often refers to thoughts and insights that come as inspiration.
Joint venture suggests a move to join efforts with another for a specific purpose.
Keynote (speaker) means one who is experienced or has higher knowledge regarding a specific issue.
Lead time suggests a need for more preparation. Denotes a time extension required.
Legwork corresponds with research; a need for gathering more information.
Light duty comes in dreams as an advisement to cut back on the level of efforts expended. This symbol may also refer to stressors and indicate the need for more acceptance.
Logo is a sign that has diverse interpretations for each individual dreamer.
Meeting suggests a need for open communication.
Memorandum (memo) is a call to remember something important. May be a new revelation for the dreamer.
Monopoly (corporate) signals a fear of competition.

Professional Terminology (continued)

Nepotism warns against preferential treatment or behavior.

Networking signifies a chain of information-sharing. Reveals a situation that is no longer private.

Night shift suggests applying oneself during the quiet night hours. This comes as a message for those claiming they have no time for advancing or developing through learning or study. This may even refer to a proper meditative time for the dreamer.

Odd jobs can bring significant learning experiences and usually come in dreams to represent this message.

Outsourcing stands for profit placed before all else.

Paperwork may indicate unnecessary work associated with an element in one's life.

Pink slip connotes an end to one's project or effort. This may be a message from one's higher self that indicates futility if one continues expending efforts on a specific phase or aspect.

Portfolio suggests a need to organize an aspect of one's life, perhaps get thoughts or perspectives organized.

Power play usually stands for taking advantage of opportunity.

Private enterprise defines personal resourcefulness; ingenuity; independence.

Profile (workup) stands for a composite of an individual's characteristics.

Publicity See advertisement.

Rat race is a clear message referring to the act of going nowhere fast.

Red tag indicates a life element that is marked for a particular purpose. May point to a need to remember to return to an issue.

Registrar characterizes one who keeps the records. This refers to the one who knows personal aspects of an individual's life.

Risk analysis points to a need to very carefully weigh the pros and cons of something.

Schedule characterizes regimentation.

Schematic is indicative of a need for careful forethought.

Schematic exemplifies the necessity of detailed and well-thought out planning.

Scutwork reminds us that even menial tasks can have beneficial effects.

Shorthanded points to a situation in one's life in which one is forced to work harder.

Shutdown most often refers to avoidance. It may also point to outright denial. This symbol could also come as an advisement that some type of attitude or behavior needs to be shut down.

Slogan presents a personal message for each dreamer. Recall the exact words of the dream slogan.

Small business administration refers to a source of help for starting a new beginning in one's life.

Soft sell implies subtle enticement; hidden methods of manipulation.

Split shift implies great personal efforts applied to one's purpose.

Spring break corresponds to a need to take time out from one's efforts applied to purpose or life path.

Strategist characterizes an individual who is highly capable of thorough planning or analysis.

Suggestion box is representative of one's ability to make improvements or bring about change.

Swing shift advises one of a need to experience alternate phases and elements of a specific aspect.

Syndicate connotes an affiliation of like-minded individuals who have a common goal.

Target date signifies a time to shoot for regarding achieving a goal or plan.

Teamwork signifies cooperative pooling of talents.

Testimonial underscores or recommends a specific concept or perspective for the dreamer.

Test market connotes an attempt to try something out.

Title company connotes the verification of purity of an element in one's life; proof that an aspect contains no negatives.

Tracking number advises of the wisdom to follow a particular concept through various issues.

Trade signifies one's interest; field of endeavor; where efforts are applied.

Trademark exposes a revelation; true attitudes, beliefs, and intentions of others. Recall the symbols and colors of the trademark.

Trade secret is representative of a unique method or ingredient associated with successful operations or progression.

Troubleshooter characterizes a person capable of discovering the source of a problem and resolving it.

Turnover (employment) denotes a lack of stability. It may also refer to a sense of restlessness in one's life.

Working papers relate to a verification that one is pursuing the right course in one's life.

Yellow-dog contract represents coerced loyalty.

see also
• Flying & Air Travel *p. 301*
• Crime Detection & Arrest *p. 324*

Miscellaneous

American dream refers to basic life goals or rights common to everyone, the good life that is without ties to country, nation, or ethnicity.

Animal rights activist characterizes a devotional concern for the welfare of one's friends.

Auxiliary refers to backup reserves. This symbol may be associated with a variety of personal elements in one's life. It may point to energy resources or knowledge. It may indicate a reserve of faith one falls back on.

Aviator glasses denote a shadowy single vision; only one's personal viewpoint or perspective.

Bookbinding See bindery.

Concessionaire characterizes one who associates with another purely for self-serving purposes.

Conveyor belt signifies a means of communication or delivery.

Counselor stands for one who advises another.

Crack (expert) See expert.

Crackerjack (expert) portrays one who has a talented ability for something specific.

Critic characterizes one who has the habit of looking for another's faults or is in other ways judgmental.

Designer characterizes an individual who creates specific situations or conditions in life. This dream symbol could be a cautionary reminder that one is letting someone else design one's path or perspectives.

Dispatcher characterizes one's higher self.

Dream merchant reveals an individual who encourages beliefs in unrealistic goals.

Flag bearer represents one's outward expression of loyalty.

Foreman characterizes one who has the knowledge and experience to guide another.

Forty-niner connotes that one has high expectations.

Frontierswoman pertains to one who is traveling on a path of self-discovery.

Humorist usually indicates the tendency to look on the bright side; depending on a sense of humor to get one through. It may also reveal a tendency to take this attitude too far when important issues aren't taken seriously.

Inspector stands for one's own higher self who acts as an advisor and guide.

Intermediary See mediator.

Investigator advises doing more in-depth research on an issue.

Jack/Jane-of-all-trades relates to versatility.

Leisure (time) usually exemplifies the importance of taking mental and physical rest from one's work or path advancement in life.

Mathematician indicates a person in one's life who can offer solutions.

Mediator signifies an urgent need for assistance with a personal relationship.

Middleman characterizes someone who is acting as a go-between in one's life. This may be an advisement to communicate directly instead of through another.

Operator (any type) stands for one who has operational capability and knowledge of a specific element or ability. This symbol may point to the one who's in control.

Technician is a problem solver.

Organ grinder suggests a need for contemplation.

Point person represents a forerunner; a messenger; one who checks out conditions before others follow.

Publicist points to one who disseminates information about you.

Quality controller characterizes efficiency and a high standard of behavior or productivity.

Real estate pertains to possibilities; opportunities.

Real estate sign is a marker pointing to an opportunity.

Representative characterizes a person with the authority to speak and act for others. May also point to one who symbolizes a concept, attitude, product, or method.

Reviewer (professional) characterizes an individual in one's life who can provide background information or a general overview.

Scout indicates advanced research and exploration needed in one's life before further progression can be accomplished. May point to hidden aspects that need to be ferreted out.

Shred (any type) signifies a fragment of whatever was depicted; remains.

Speaker (person) usually constitutes a message for the dreamer. Recall what was said and by whom.

Statistician characterizes a person who possesses verifying information.

Superintendent usually signifies who is in charge. Recall the surrounding dreamscape details to determine what this superintendent was in charge of.

Surveyor relates to an individual who is fragmenting his or her life course; someone who draws many lines; a separatist.

Systems analyst characterizes an individual who is capable of discovering the most efficient course of action or means of reaching a goal.

Technician characterizes one who is capable of figuring out specific things.

Ticket scalper See scalper.

Underclassmen/women refers to those in life who have less experience and knowledge.

Underrated signifies an underestimation; lacking an understanding of something's real value or potential.

Union label denotes pride in one's work and appreciation of the work of others.

Unmanned stands for a natural, inherent inner guidance that works without one needing to supply mental input.

Winepress stands for the formulation of good ideas.

Woodswoman symbolizes the inherent connection of feral instinct, fertility, and an inner knowing type of wisdom that women and nature share.

Chapter 17

Technology & Science

Technology is most often associated with ongoing advancements. Depending on the surrounding dreamscape components, this aspect may carry the duality of having both positive and negative characteristics.

0:721
MX7018
97.0 FM

Computing

Accelerator card (computer) represents an increase in the speed of communication or the time it takes to gather information.
Access code refers to the key to something.
Backup (computer) See go-back.
Computer connotes a need for analysis or for better understanding in one's life.
Computer disk symbolizes a great amount of information. Recall the type of disk it was.
Computer graphics symbolize the clarification of communication or an idea through the use of helpful visuals.
Data relates to information the dreamer needs.
Digital enhancement reveals aspects of an individual, issue, or element that have been added for the purpose of making the subject more appealing.
Digital photography sheds a pall of skepticism over what is seen. Things may not be as true as presented.
Disk (computer program) See computer program.
Disk (computer/rewritable) denotes saved information that can be altered or improved; an easy way to work with an ongoing project or situation.
Disk (computer/writable) signifies an easy way to make a permanent record of something.
Error code reveals a misstep or a wrong move. May refer to a recently formed attitude or decision.
Error trapping (software) advises of a need to be more aware or watchful for wrong thinking. Suggests one should behave with care.
Flash drive (computer) refers to the ease of gaining/transferring information; a speedy manner of memory retrieval. May come as a reminder to keep certain information on the front burner.
Go-Back (computer) signifies an ability to change reality by returning to the time preceding a negative event, thereby literally creating a situation clear of the event and its damaging ramifications. In dreams this symbol represents a desire to take back bad behavior or hurtful words—wishing they'd never happened.
Hard disk applies to a wealth of information on a particular subject.
Hard drive refers to the mind; the well of knowledge we've retained. This symbol may also refer to an individual's memory capacity.
High resolution emphasizes clear, vivid dreams that may reveal actual out-of-body experiences.
Home computer stands for the easy availability of information and probably advises the use of it.
Hot-sink (computer) is associated with an immediate transfer of information.
Jump drive (computer) See USB port.
Keyword See password.
Laptop (computer) reveals a desire to have the convenience of information access at all times.
Mainframe emphasizes the brain aspect; the main source of knowledge or information; an intelligent leader or guide.
Media center signifies a source of information.
Motherboard signifies the main source of information.
Password denotes aspects in an individual's life that serve as keys or gateways to prime opportunities.
PDF (portable document format) refers to the convenience and efficiency of receiving, processing, and transferring information.

Motherboard represents the font of knowledge.

Personal computer (PC) See computer.
Port (connector end/receptacle) stands for a correct association made for separate concepts or ideas; a proper sequence of aligned thoughts.
Printout indicates a need for hard copies. This symbolizes proof or verification.
Soft copy refers to an opportunity for change, to make adjustments/alterations.
Sound card (computer) represents one's choice to hear all the elements of an issue. May emphasize one's decision to choose acceptance or denial.
Tech support (computer or programs) characterizes those one can go to for help in utilizing or troubleshooting specific life aids.
Toolbar (computer) represents ease of using available options.
USB port (computer) indicates a source for holding a greater amount of information; additional resources for maintaining one's memory capabilities.
Virtual memory relates to an extension of an individual's surface thought patterns; one's superconscious.
Virtual reality constitutes an individual's overactive imagination; an inability to discern clearly.
Watchword See password.
Word processor relates to the ease of communication that one may be fearing or denying.
Write protection symbolizes a safeguard against losing information.

see also
• Information Handling *p. 176*
• Computing *p. 256*

Programs

Clip art stands for the chance to take advantage of a variety of ways to express oneself.
Computer program means a life aspect that greatly shortens research time and provides extensive information.
Database stands for one's personal scope of attained knowledge or information. This will not refer to the comprehension of same.
Desktop publishing portrays personalized construction of one's precisely delivered communications.
Program (any type/source) signifies an individualized message for each individual dreamer in relation to his or her life. This depicts one's actions or clarifies a situation.
Software is representative of multiple opportunities and information resources.
Spell-checker advises that one gets things right (accurate) during communications.

Hackers, Worms & Viruses

Computer hacker reveals an individual who has an ulterior motive; a person who is unscrupulous and intrusive.
Computer pirate refers to someone who steals; acquisition without ownership right.
Computer virus pertains to disinformation willfully given. Also may point out a new problem with one's formerly accepted perceptions.
Computer worm is generally a reference to a negative element that affects several aspects of one's life.
Hacker (computer) See computer hacker.
Pirate (computer) See computer pirate.
Virus (computer) See computer virus.
Worm (computer) See computer worm.

The Monitor

Blue screen of death (computer) comes as a critical sign alerting one that all his/her efforts are about to be rendered invalid/ineffective.
Cursor reminds one to keep focused; to stay aware and mentally attentive; to remain in the moment.
Monitor (computer screen) reveals a method of viewing or keeping an eye on something. This reveals a means of access one previously thought nonexistent.
Screen (computer) See monitor (computer screen).
Screen saver (computer monitor) is representative of one's efforts expended toward preventing one's perception to be overridden by previous first impressions; an effort to reserve opinion based on a first impression until more information is obtained.
Touch screen characterizes ease of control for making things happen; a method of operation having no intermediary or extraneous steps to perform; one-on-one technique.

Computer Accessories

Blackberry (techno gadget) See PDA.
Cartridge stands for the convenience of easy replacement; the ease by which something is utilized or replaced.
Cartridge (ink) See ink cartridge.
Floppy disk relates to one's stored information; personal knowledge; memory bank.
Head cleaner (CD, printer, etc.) advises one to keep thoughts clear of extraneous elements that compromise or confuse an issue.
Hyperdrive warns against a type-A personality; running on overdrive; obsessing over achievement.
Ink cartridge relates to an ongoing readiness to verify beliefs or solidify agreements.
Laser printer portrays a clear and sharp communication.
Palm pilot See PDA.
PDA (personal digital assistant) stands for efficiency and preparedness; a desire to keep information close at hand.

Ink cartridge is ready to validate.

Pocket PC See PDA.
Printer (machine) suggests finality; one's words imprinted on the fabric of reality.
Surge protector signifies a method of monitoring one's energy levels and guarding against draining elements.
Upgrade points out an improvement; a step-up in quality; an advancement.
Video game denotes unrealistic scenarios, but also points out an enjoyable manner in which one improves skills.

Keyboard & Mouse

Backslash (on keyboard) stands for a break in a message or a separation between messages.
Backspacing suggests the need to go back and discover something that was missed; a need to delete or correct something. Oftentimes, the spaces between events are full of lessons to be learned but not recognized as being such.
Function key (computer keyboard) stands for options at one's fingertips.
Keyboard (computer) is a reference to the ease of communication access. This indicates someone who believes a certain dialog or communication isn't approachable.
Keypad represents options at one's fingertips.
Mouse (computer) corresponds to precise control and the need for same.
Mouse pad (computer) indicates an aid in maintaining a controlled communication or search.
Space bar (keyboard) applies to intentional spacing; a desire for more room; separation of ideas.

Optical

Binoculars imply a need for closer inspection. Pay attention to that which is just beyond the obvious. There's more than what's right in front of you.
Field glasses See binoculars.
Microscope advises one to look at something much closer; more analysis is needed.
Spotting scope stands for taking a closer look at something.
Spyglass See binoculars; telescope.

Microscope calls for a closer look.

Telescope advises one to look beyond surface presentations.

Spyware

Backweb refers to things hidden in the background.
Computer spyware relates to a life aspect that serves as a tool for intrusiveness into one's life.
Snoopware See spyware.
Spyware (computer program) signifies a method of retrieving another's personal information and getting into his or her private affairs.
Spyware detector/blocker (computer program) stands for a way of knowing if another is invading one's privacy and how to protect self against it.

Networking

Ethernet line signifies the communication between associates. May be advising of an urgency to make some type of immediate connection to someone within one's circle. This symbol may also refer to one's intuition or psychic connection to a close relationship.
Modem relates to an opportunity to choose a variety of communication methods for a situation.

E-Mail

Bounced mail signifies a communication that has been rejected or returned unread.
Electronic mail (e-mail) signifies perceptual impressions; readily available information within one's personal surround.
E-mail See electronic mail.
E-mail shorthand denotes a need to convey something quickly and concisely; not be wordy; getting right to the point.
E-signature symbolizes the ease and convenience of giving signed approval.

Photography & Film

Aperture (camera) symbolizes sight or awareness of one's perceptions.
Auto-focus indicates a continually clear perception regardless of one's distance from the subject or issue.
Camera represents that which preserves the truth; the facts. This warns the dreamer to recall things factually.
Camera (hidden) generally refers to a means of security, yet may also indicate a loss of privacy.
Camera cell phone alludes to a chance to capture the moment. Depending on surrounding dreamscape elements, it may point to unethical practices of invading others' privacy.
Darkroom denotes a life aspect that is able to reverse negative factors in one's life.
Developer (chemical) represents a life aspect that brings something to completion or through the sequential stages leading to conclusion; turning a negative into a positive.
Exposure meter denotes one's tendency to monitor self.
Film (photo) advises of a need to be sharply aware of a specific life aspect and to remember it. Surrounding details will clarify what this is.
Filter (camera) See lens.
Flashbulb suggests a need to add more light to something; a need to look closer.
Focal point usually zeros in on the main element of an issue. It advises where to place one's attention and energy.
Freeze-frame emphasizes a scene, object, or individual that is important to the dreamer. The surrounding details will clarify this for the individual dreamer.
F-stop (setting) suggests a need to adjust one's perspective for better clarity.
Halftone suggests subtlety; a need to soften harshness.
Light meter See exposure meter.
Microfiche (machine) portrays a method of consolidating information.
Microfilm illustrates the mind; memory.
Out of focus reveals a blurred perspective.
Photograph reveals a message of importance. Recall what or who was in the photo.
Polaroid (camera/photo) characterizes a need to immediately focus one's attention or memory on something that will be depicted in the photograph.
Shutter (camera) corresponds to one's personal perspective and how well it's used; awareness; insights.
Shutter speed reveals one's level of astuteness.
Snapshot See photograph.
Special effects symbolize emphasis; a need to dramatize for the purpose of greater understanding.
Telephoto lens See zoom lens.
Underexposed (film) signifies an aspect in one's life that requires more time or needs further development.
Video camera See camcorder.
Viewfinder is usually representative of a need for clear perception.
Wide-angle lens advises one to broaden one's perception.
Zoom lens symbolizes an opportunity or need to get a closer look or analyze a specific aspect in one's life.

see also
• Photography *p. 217*
• Glasses *p. 460*

The Internet

Active list symbolizes one's readiness for action.
Adware See pop-ups.
Broadband signifies a wide range of communication skills; an ability to communicate with others on any level; also communications made at a faster rate.
Browser applies to one's personal way to access information.
Chat room reminds that one should communicate responsibly, even though it's done anonymously.
Code word See password.
Cookie represents unrequested information or assistance; being bombarded by things one doesn't want to hear or aren't relevant.
Cookie (tracking) reveals that information is being gathered about oneself; an invasion of privacy; your every move being monitored. The only positive aspect of this dreamscape symbol would be if this came as an advisement for self-examination, to take a good look at your own behavior.
Cybercafé means an information-friendly atmosphere; an opportunity for discovery.
Cybercrime refers to stealthy wrongdoing; negative behavior without witnesses; anonymous underhandedness.
Cyberspace verifies the idea that there is no true emptiness in life, that even the spaces are full. This dreamscape symbol reminds us that undreamed possibilities can, one day, change our entire preconceived concept of what reality consists of.
Cyberspeak points to the appropriate language or communications for specific subjects or issues.
Domain name stands for one's ultimate identity uniqueness; that which separates one from all others.
Dot-com company See web retailer.
E-book refers to a widely known story or block of information that's readily available to everyone.
Firewall (computer) refers to self-protective measures put in place to avoid emotional confrontations.
High-speed denotes ready access to information or a lightning-quick mind.
Home page denotes the life elements that are most basic to one. It signifies one's jumping-off place.
Hyperlink signifies identical conceptual elements or attitudes shared by separate individuals or differing philosophies.
Hyperspace pertains to a doorway to understanding the components of reality.
Information superhighway See Internet.
Instant messaging suggests a need for immediate communication.
Internet denotes information that's easily accessed.
Locked (Web site) is a representation of a protected, safe communication.
Log on signifies an intention to communicate with someone or do research.
Net (Internet) See Internet.
Off-line signifies a break from research, communication, or intellectual expansion either due to a voluntary choice or from one's connection being interrupted.
Pop-ups (Internet) symbolize the unwanted and irritating pushiness we're inundated with by others throughout our daily lives.
Scam-spam (Internet) warns one of the possibility of being drawn into a fraudulent situation or the possibility of being hoodwinked. This comes as an advisement to the dreamer to be on the watch for ideas or opportunities that sound too good to be valid.
Scanner (computer) stands for visual input; a need to mentally retain a visual.
Search engine (computer) stands for a method or source for opening up a wealth of new information.
Spam (Internet) See pop-ups.
Spam blocker is a way to keep out unwanted elements.
System monitors (Internet) stand for a complete infiltration of one's privacy.
Tracking cookies See cookie (tracking).
Trojans (Internet) reveal the presence of malicious programs hiding out on one's hard drive for the purpose of stealing or damaging data. This, then, comes as a strong advisement to sharply attend to one's defensive/protective methods, for there's a high probability that privacy has been (or will soon be) invaded.
User ID (Internet) represents one's personal validation for the right to proceed.
Web See Internet.
Webcam reveals a potential invasion of privacy.
Web site stands for a source of information regarding a particular issue.

Webcam indicates that something may be about to invade one's privacy.

Television & Video

Security camera is a symbol of the fact that one is constantly being scrutinized.

Cable television suggests information obtained through the assistance of others.

Camcorder is a sign to remember some event in one's life. This infers important lessons to be learned.

Channel (TV/radio/scanner) represents choices for receiving incoming information.

Channel blocking (TV) means censorship, usually in relation to protecting someone from emotionally or morally damaging subject matters.

Closed-captioned advises of one's options for further understanding.

Closed circuit connotes one's free-flowing energies; energies that have no blockages; free-flowing current through the chakras.

Dish antenna See satellite dish.

DVD (digital video disk) See movie.

DVD player See video player.

Fast-forward can mean one of two things. It can come as an advisement to give more long-range leeway to plans or it can point to denial, not having acceptance or fortitude to face current issues.

High-definition TV refers to perceptual clarity, intellectual understanding.

Instant replay advises of the wisdom of looking more closely at something a second or third time. This indicates something was overlooked.

Pay-per-view signifies a price paid for the things one wants right now and can't wait for.

Plasma screen (TV/computer monitor) refers to the newest way of looking at things. Note that each new advancement in viewing technology will mean this.

Prompter See teleprompter.

Remote control (device) reveals a state of control, perhaps even manipulation. Recall who had the remote in hand in the dream.

Remote viewing symbolizes a heightened intuitive sense of cognition.

Replay (audio/video) refers to a need to see or hear something over again. Suggests that something was missed the first time around.

Satellite dish suggests a need to be more receptive to others. Implies a personal striving for greater receptivity.

Security camera reminds us that we're always being watched. This symbol may even be pointing to oneself (conscience).

Simulcast depicts a multiple venue of communication.

Split screen (image/visual) advises of a need to look at two issues at once because they may be related.

Station (transmitted) implies a frequency; a vibratory rate. Recall what was being said on the radio or TV station.

Station break refers to a temporary break or to an interruption in one's communication.

Surround sound suggests a need to listen better, yet may also be pointing out that one is hearing a specific idea from many sources.

Tape (video) See videotape.

Teleprompter implies assistance needed to clearly express one's thoughts.

Transmitter portrays a need to send a message to another or express an important communication that at present is being withheld.

Videoconferencing symbolizes convenient communication that enables one to bridge great distances.

Video player (VCR) signifies a method of recalling past events.

Videotape refers to the recording (witnessing) of a particular event and may come as an advisement to remember it.

Wide-screen advises expanding one's perspective.

Surveillance

Acoustical surveillance See listening post.

Bug See listening device.

Hidden camera See camera (hidden).

Listening device signifies an intent to spy; things aren't as private or secret as one originally thought.

Listening post stands for an intent to listen well. May point to being overly nosey.

Silent monitoring See listening device.

see also
• Music Technology *p. 227*
• Media & TV *p. 249*

Radio & Audio

Antenna suggests the need for clarity of thought and ideas; sharper perception.
Audiobook refers to bringing the written word to life; giving fuller and expanded meaning to what is written.
Audiocassette represents other means of receiving messages.
Audiovisuals signify the need to look at differing aspects of a situation or relationship.
Boom box means arrogance; a craving for attention.
Broadcast (airwaves) connotes the spreading of information. May imply gossip.
Bullhorn advises one to voice personal attitudes or opinions; a need to express feelings.
Buzzer advises of a need to make communications in a discreet manner. This will directly refer to a specific aspect in the dreamer's life.
CB (citizen's band radio) advises a person to keep communications open.
Call-in (radio show) See talk radio.
Call sign pertains to one's chosen identity; that which one wants to be known by.
Compact disc (CD) symbolizes condensed information; acquiring a large block of knowledge in a short span of time.
Dead air indicates an interruption in a particular communication or thought.
Earphone characterizes increased perception and/or attention given.
Eight-track tape suggests old messages that are still relevant.
Feedback suggests a need to listen to one's words. Pay more attention to what is said.

Tape helps one get the point.

Feeler See antenna.
Ham operator characterizes one who is able to provide immediate responsive communications; a quickly helpful individual.
Ham radio refers to helpful communications; preparedness; an ability to get through to someone.
Headphones stand for focused thought; the blocking out of unimportant audibles.
Intercom symbolizes communication between one's conscious and higher self.
Loudspeaker emphasizes a message unique to each dreamer. What words came over the dream loudspeaker?
Megaphone can advise that one is not being heard. This symbol can also indicate a message unique to each dreamer depending on who is using the object. It's particularly important to recall what was said through the megaphone.
Microphone suggests a need for one to be heard.
Mike See microphone.
Public-address system See microphone.
Quadraphonic denotes high awareness.
Radio exemplifies a need to tune into oneself for the purpose of understanding motives and responses. This symbol may also advise to remain aware of current events.
Reception (electronic) relates to the quality of an individual's comprehension of a particular situation.
Scanner (radio frequencies) stands for knowing what's going on behind the scenes.
Shortwave (radio) See ham radio.
Sound effects stand for emphasis; accentuating a thought or idea with added emphasis.
Speaker (audio) indicates a need to hear more clearly; a state of inattention, possibly self-generated.
Squelch control represents the act of silencing something or making it clearer for the dreamer to understand.
Synthesizer is generally representative of the means of combining various ideas or concepts.
Talk radio usually reveals an opportunity to express an opinion or other type of previously withheld emotion, problem, and so on.
Tape (audio) See audiocassette.
Tape recorder See recorder (tape).
Transceiver will directly correspond to an individual's open channel within the superconscious mind.
Walkie-talkie is usually indicative of a need for close communication; a situation in which parties need to stay in contact.
Wireless relates to connections to another, mostly emotional. This dream symbol may also point to intuition.

Acoustics

Acoustical (material) stands for an attempt to focus on every related aspect of an issue; blocking out unrelated elements.
Acoustic feedback (through microphone) advises of a need to listen to oneself. This symbol points out bad attitudes or behavior.
Amplifier cautions the dreamer to listen better. Something is being missed.
Depth finder indicates the depth of one's spirituality.
Depth sounder See depth finder.
Listening device signifies an intent to spy; things aren't as private/secret as one thought.
Low frequency indicates easily understood ideas.
Sonar stands for an individual's inner perceptions; insights; heightened awareness.
Sonogram usually portrays a visual impression; an insight; vision.
Sound barrier See sonic barrier.
Supersonic denotes a reach or existence beyond popular, generally accepted concepts; the realm of deeper thought.
Ultrasonic See supersonic.
Ultrasound portrays a need to get inside something. Take a more thorough look at an issue, event, or other element in one's life.
Voiceprint advises of a need to validate oneself. This means that there's a pressing need to know oneself.

Telephonic Communication

Action line (phone) signifies a direct line of communication; keeping a strong pulse in current action/situations in one's life.

Answering machine symbolizes one's preference for indirect communication. May indicate a fear of confrontation.

Break-in (phone operator) stands for an urgent message.

Busy signal denotes a wrong time to communicate with someone. This indicates a communication that wouldn't go well and suggests choosing a later time to attempt the connection.

Call box suggests an immediate need to communicate something or get in touch with someone. The dreamer will know what this is referring to.

Call guide (911 operators) represents immediate availability for responsive advice.

Calling card (telephone) portrays communication preparedness; ensuring ability to be able to reach others.

Conference call advises of a need to communicate with several others on an important matter.

Dial tone advises of nonresponsiveness from another; one's attempts at communication falling on deaf ears.

Disconnected (phone) refers to a severance of communication; a block in communication.

Earpiece stands for hearing what others can't. This doesn't mean hearing voices but rather being in tune with one's higher self, one's inner guidance.

Fax (machine) pertains to a need for a speedy communication. This indicates a situation or relationship that could be saved by immediate communication.

Hold button (phone) implies a temporary pause in a communication; putting an issue, relationship, and so on, off for a short time.

Hotline reveals an unbroken line of communication; the need to keep communication open.

Kill message (phone) signifies an option to stop a communication; a chance to change one's mind.

Landline stands for grounded communications, clear and well understood.

Long distance (call) advises of a need to reconnect with someone with whom the dreamer has been out of touch.

Party line (telephone) reveals the act of listening in on. This suggests someone is privy to another's behavior or private communications.

Pay phone reminds to attend to a communication that's been postponed.

Phone See telephone.

Phone book See telephone book.

Phone booth See telephone booth.

Phone card is an invitation to communicate; a connection that doesn't cost anything.

Phone tag stands for communication that has bad timing.

Redial (phone button) points to continued efforts made to communicate.

Repeater (antenna) stands for clearer communications.

Roaming charges refer to costs involved when one isn't able to communicate with another. These costs aren't financial but are rather emotional due to missed timing.

Speakerphone indicates one's ease in communicating with others or it may allude to a need to share a conversation.

Speed dial suggests an urgency to contact a particular individual. This symbol usually comes as an advisement.

Switchboard signifies an opportunity to make multiple contacts; a means of obtaining expanded information.

Teleconference advises to include several others in a communication or to equally include them in a plan or idea.

Telephone refers to communication. Was the dream phone ringing? Was someone reaching for it as if to call another? Who was using it?

Telephone book pertains to a source of contacts.

Telephone booth exemplifies the availability of opportunities to communicate with others.

Telephone number may reveal a literal phone number that means something to the dreamer, or the individual digits are meant to be added up to total a number carrying significance.

Telephone pole represents a communication element of support.

Telephone tag See phone tag.

Toll call stands for a communication that one is willing to expend extra energy on.

Trunk line relates to the main line of communication an individual uses.

Voice mail See answering machine.

Wiretap reminds one that there is always someone listening, even if it is just one's own conscience.

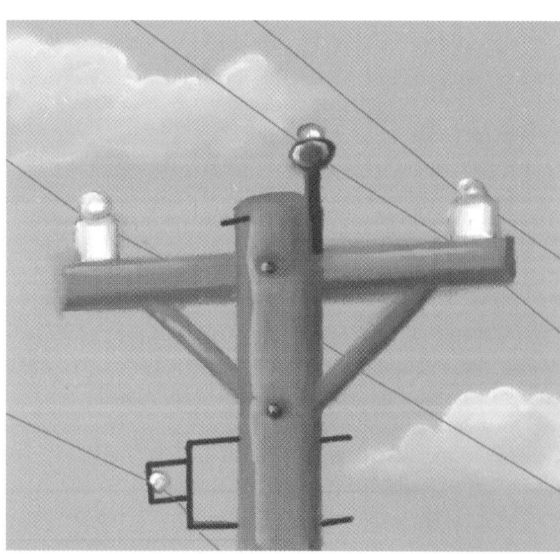

Telephone pole symbolizes a method of using communication for support.

see also
• Means of Communication *p. 132*
• Scientists *p. 247*

Communication

Area code denotes a specific region important to the dreamer.

Bulk mail equates to wide disbursement.

Bulletin draws the dreamer's attention to something that should be known.

Cablegram signifies a spiritual message.

Candy-gram denotes a pleasing message; a sign of a sweet relationship.

Carrier pigeon See messenger.

Certified mail represents a need to make sure something is done or carried out; certain delivery or communication.

Chain letter symbolizes strong possibility of failure; attempting to achieve an end or goal that can only succeed through the actions of others.

Chronicle pertains to developmental stages leading up to the present; a need to research how something came about. This may be an advisement to keep a journal.

Cipher suggests a need to solve or resolve something. Represents a key or solution.

Code stands for specialized communication; hidden messages understood by a select group.

Codebook symbolizes an aspect that serves as the key to understanding something.

Directory advises of a need to contact someone.

Express delivery/mail cautions to instigate a communication as soon as possible.

Font (type style) emphasizes one's individual character.

Morse code suggests communication misunderstanding or a lack of comprehension.

Newsletter comes as a message specific to each dreamer. Its purpose is to keep one up to date on an aspect in one's life.

Newspaper represents an awareness within oneself.

News release pertains to a special announcement message the dreamer needs to note. This symbol comes as a major personal message and should always be taken seriously.

Press kit indicates the dissemination of background information.

Print wheel See font (type style).

Priority mail stands for a high priority communication.

Registered mail denotes a solid communication of some type. Recall who sent the mailed article. To whom was it addressed? What was it? Did it have a specific color?

Scandal sheet correlates to gossip; sensationalism. Comes as an advisement to focus on the important elements in life.

Scientific journal advises of the need to gather further information regarding a specific subject.

Shorthand (note-taking) signifies resourcefulness; efficiency.

Special delivery connotes an important message.

Tabloid See newspaper.

Telegram signifies a personal message for each dreamer. Recall what the telegram said and who it was from.

Typewriter symbolizes preserved ideas.

Zip code reveals a number message or points to a specific locale that holds particular importance for the dreamer.

Meters, Gauges & Testing

Pressure gauge advises one to keep an eye on how one deals with stress.

Flowmeter advises one to regulate energies or emotions.

Gauge depicts quantity. Recall what the dreamscape gauge was measuring.

Hygrometer reveals one's level of spirituality or spiritual comprehension. Recall what the instrument read.

Meter (gauge) denotes the level of one's progress.

Percolation test (soil absorption) refers to a gauge of the amount of spirituality one's foundational aspects contain.

Perk test stands for a question whether or not a concept, idea, or certain behavior will be generally accepted.

Pressure gauge advises one to monitor and stay aware of how to handle stressful situations.

Tachometer indicates speed. Recall if the dreamer was being advised to slow down or increase rate of progression.

Thermometer reflects temperament. Recall what degree was presented.

Water meter reveals a person's use of spiritual talents and overall beliefs.

Well test (water) denotes a check on the quality of one's own spiritual behavior.

Wind tunnel exposes mental aberrations and psychological dysfunctions. It also refers to perceptual inability.

Zymometer denotes attention given to the development of an idea/plan; keeping a close eye on the timing and condition of a specific progression.

Phone Features

Call blocking signifies a desire to avoid talking to a specific individual.

Call forwarding symbolizes heightened attention given to communications; not wishing to miss messages.

Call screening points to the option of choosing whose calls one would like to accept or reject.

Call waiting applies to a desire to accommodate or be available for others.

Caller ID denotes selective communications. May indicate a reluctance to connect with certain people.

Machinery

Wood chipper machine shows a desire to increase one's natural talents.

Backup (generator) connotes a high level of energy reserves.
Chipper (machine) See wood chipper.
Clockwork advises of the proper workings of one's life; things are unfolding as they are meant to in a regular and normally expected manner.
Combine (machine) stands for several tasks being handled by a single aspect or solution.
Compactor advises of a need to diminish the amount of one's wastefulness. May point to a need to make one's life less scattered or realize priorities.
Cotton gin pertains to unadulterated attitudes; pure thought.
Engine denotes aspects of the heart (physical or emotional).
Flywheel reveals a need to stay on an even keel and not fluctuate between overwork/overenthusiasm and underachievement/disinterest.
Gin (machine) represents a personal aid that assists in advancing toward goals.
Grain elevator symbolizes reserve talents; the capacity for great stores of humanitarian deeds. Recall what this grain elevator looked like. Was it in good shape? Full or empty? Any mold around it?
Granary See grain elevator.
Machinery refers to personally devised instrumentations that one uses to hasten or ease a path advancement.
Mainspring relates to that which has the power; the energizing factor.
Stamp mill represents intellectual deduction; extracting all informational elements from a singular aspect.
Wood chipper (machine) suggests an intent to preserve and enrich one's inherent abilities or gifts.

Industry

Blast furnace cautions against internalized negatives such as anger, hate, jealousy, and guilt.
Cast iron shows strength; perseverance; a strong constitution.
Copper tubing denotes a questionable life aspect.
Damper stands for a life factor that can increase or decrease one's understanding, depending on how it is used.
Fiberglass connotes dual aspects to something in the dreamer's life. Surrounding dreamscape facets will clarify by pointing to an aspect that is highly useful but must be handled carefully.
Flux (welding) symbolizes instability; a need for a better flow of communication/information.
Foam (rubber) pertains to exaggerations; something that's being padded for extra importance or weight.
Halftone suggests subtlety; a need to soften harshness.
Heat exchanger pertains to the act of helping to reenergize another or rejuvenate them in some manner.
Heat shield signifies a specific method one uses to conserve personal energy; efficient use of one's time and energy.
High technology refers to advanced knowledge of one's path progression.
Hydraulic (system) constitutes an aspect in an individual's life that is capable of making advancement easier.
Incinerator indicates the complete disposal of selective negatives in one's life.
Industrial strength denotes greater energy or power.
Plexiglas connotes a strong substitute.
Radiant heating signifies an overall warmth of personality one exudes.
Stainless steel stands for durability; resistance to decay or decline.

Cords, Wires & Cables

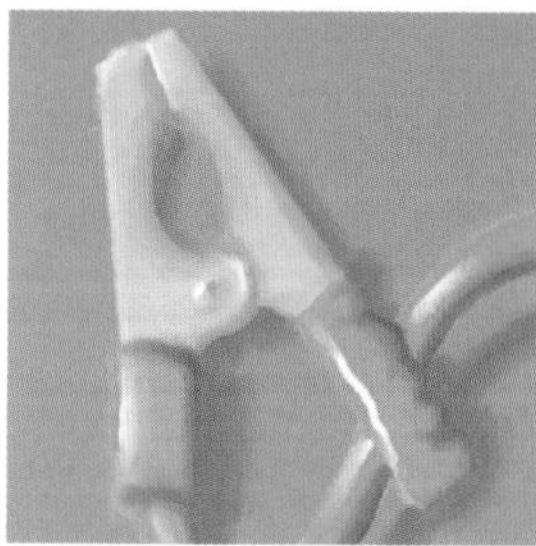

Jumper cable represents alliances.

Booster cable advises that helpful or supportive connections be made in one's life. Refers to an impetus or a need to be reenergized.
Cable portrays an aspect in life that serves as a strong support.
Copper wire is generally representative of clear communications.
Cord (electrical) connotes that which conducts energies; the connection between a source of power and the object of receivership.
High-tension wire corresponds with intense power. This directly relates to a certain aspect that is specific to each dreamer.
Jumper cable See booster cable.
Wire (electric) alludes to the transmission and current of one's inner energy.

see also
• Manufacturing *p. 256*
• Machinery *p. 446*

Cell Phones & Pagers

Mobile telephone shows readiness.

Beeper advises to stay in touch or keep open communication.
Cellular telephone symbolizes preparedness and/or efficiency.
Mobile telephone See cellular telephone.
Pager See beeper.
Roaming (cell phone) is usually representative of a void in the dreamer's life regarding communication.
Text messaging usually shows what the message was and this will be an important specific for each dreamer.

Power Generation

Hydroelectric plant symbolizes spiritual energy and the regeneration of same.
Nuclear power plant stands for a high-risk option.
Nuclear reactor defines a potentially contaminating negative facet in one's life.
Powerhouse correlates with one who has the energy and ability to accomplish goals; one who successfully carries through with plans. This may refer to an overachiever.
Power plant connotes one's inner drive and resulting energy output. Recall the condition of the power plant. Operating at optimum level? Shut down? Just being constructed? Abandoned?
Transfer station (power) signifies channeling of one's energy into specific areas.

Electronic & Electric Equipment

Adding machine represents the need to more accurately analyze one's situations and relationships; closer attention needed.
Addressograph (machine) signifies indiscriminate sharing of information; arbitrary communication; lacking selectiveness in those one chooses to share with; broadcast information.
Automated teller machine (ATM) symbolizes fast cash. A source of solving short-term cash flow situations. A temporary fix to a problem, a fix that usually demands repayment.
Calculator pertains to complex thought patterns; intricate planning; detailed and analytic contemplation.
Cardiac monitor points to a current situation where one needs to monitor emotions or stressful situations.
Cash machine See automated teller machine (ATM).
Cash register symbolizes materialism.
CAT scan advises one to look at all angles. This dream symbol suggests that the dreamer is not seeing something in its totality.
Copy machine denotes an opportunity to emulate another or obtain a personal imitation of something. All opportunities are not meant to equate to positive aspects.
Dynamo See generator.
Electrocardiograph advises of an immediate need for self-analysis in respect to the expression of one's emotions. Implies misdirected attitudes.
Electroencephalograph advises of an immediate need for self-analysis in respect to one's process of thought. Implies the use of disassociative or aberrant thinking.
Electronic fetal monitor advises of a serious need to closely watch the developing aspects leading to one's new path or beginning.
Fan (mechanical) indicates a need for a cooling-off period. This implies a rest period or a need to pull back, ease up.
Fetal monitor indicates a close watch on the progress of one's new path.

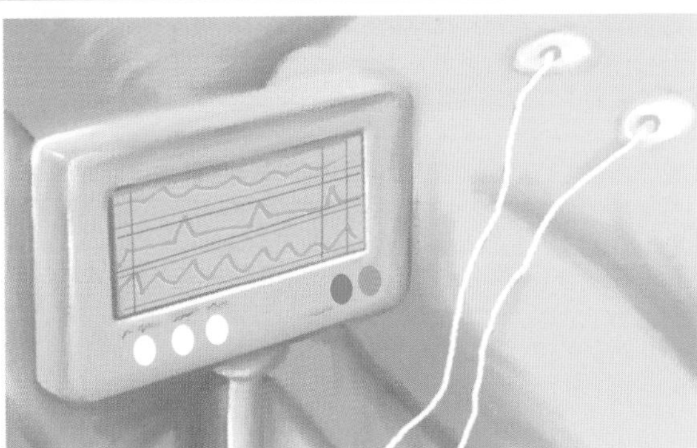

Cardiac monitor indicates that one needs to keep an eye on one's emotions.

Geiger counter pertains to one's intuitive perceptions.
Generator connotes inner sources of energy one falls back on; strength of character.
Lie detector See polygraph.
Microwave tower stands for confidential communications. This refers to a quiet one-on-one transference.
Mimeograph applies to imitation; the utilization of a master image to duplicate its characteristics. This is usually not a positive symbol.
Motion sensor stands for one's awareness level. Recall if the sensor was operating, turned off, or in disrepair.
Polygraph naturally indicates that a question of honesty or integrity is present. The key here is for the dreamer to recall who was hooked up to the machine and who was giving the test.
Register (machine) See cash register.
Scrambler (device) emphasizes a need to be discerning throughout all our communications with others.
Seismograph constitutes watchfulness. Cautions one to be more keenly aware of undercurrents in relationships, business, or personal situations in life.

Electronics & Electrics

Adapter is indicative of an individual's ability to adapt to changing situations. This symbol may be advising one to have more tolerance and acceptance.

Alternating current (AC) is usually representative of indecision or vacillation.

Alternator denotes the source of one's indecision.

Ampere denotes a one-minded personality. This usually indicates narrow-mindedness.

Anode generally denotes one's level of energy, impetus, or drive.

Base load (minimum demand of electricity on a power station) represents one's tolerable stress level.

Blackout (electrical) warns against sporadic or selective perception.

Brownout comes to the dreamer as a warning against overwork; of losing one's former high energy level.

Capacitor See condenser.

Circuit board portrays an individualized thought process; how one perceives life, forms ideas, and deduces and resolves problems.

Circuit breaker warns of a possible situation of mental or emotional overload. Set defensive measures in place to prevent oneself from becoming overly stressed or emotionally drained.

Circuit tester suggests a need for self-analysis; introspection.

Control panel usually comes in dreams to advise of a need to take control of one's life. Displays the fact that the controls are immediately available.

Filament is delicate connections.

Cordless pertains to one's inner reserves of energy.

Current (electrical flow) relates directly to one's personal energy circuitry and may refer to physical, emotional, or mental energy.

Descrambler (electronic device) symbolizes an individual's inherent ability to understand others; a natural capacity for seeing the psychological ploys of others.

Direct current (DC) warns against perceiving only one option or opportunity.

Disconnected (electrical plug) warns of mental aberrations or scattered thought processes.

Electric eye See photoelectric cell.

Electric field represents a surrounding vibrational space that emits perceptual impulses; one's intuitive perception.

Electric meter indicates knowledge. A low reading advises more in-depth study or research is required.

Electric outlet See outlet (electrical).

Electric shock usually represents a need for one to be jolted into awareness. This symbol hints at a tendency to sit on the fence.

Electricity is generally representative of a source of energy/power, usually that which serves as a powerful impetus of motivation.

Electroplating symbolizes a determined effort to ensure the protection or concealment of something.

Filament advises of fragile relationships.

Flex (connector) implies adaptability.

Fluorescent lamp symbolizes one's inner light.

Fuse (electrical) represents energy level. Was it new? Burned out? What type of fuse was it?

Instrument panel portrays the controls one has in life; the opportunities one has to choose from.

Intermittent current is usually indicative of indecision or vacillation.

Junction box (electrical) corresponds with an individual's mental, analytical, and reasoning ability.

Microchip refers to the source of a great amount of information.

Microchip ID (in pets) alludes to a loyal friend who will always come back to one's side.

Outlet (electrical) provides one with an available source of energy or empowerment.

Peak load refers to a phase when life stressors are at their height.

Photoelectric cell (electronic eye) illustrates natural or reflex responses. This may advise one to think before acting.

Plugged in represents attention/awareness, not necessarily participation.

Pylon is representative of a supportive factor in one's life.

Relay (switch) corresponds to one's inner mechanism that maintains behavioral controls; the application of logic and reason instead of emotional outbursts or knee-jerk responses.

Rheostat pertains to the personal control of one's emotional responses.

Safety circuit relates to the personal attention and awareness given to one's thought process; maintaining mental and emotional control; discernment.

Series circuit advises one to deduce in a logical and methodical manner.

Short circuit reveals severe misconceptions and/or mental confusion.

Static (electricity) comes as a warning of a state of mental dysfunction.

Thermostat suggests personal control in being able to regulate the intensity of a relationship or situation.

Three-way bulb suggests a need for more light on an issue.

Toggle switch stands for control one may not realize one has; a personal ability to start or stop something. This may refer to one's own behavior.

Transformer comes as a strong suggestion to switch efforts to a different goal or issue.

Turbine exemplifies a source of power; strong motivation.

Valve portrays control and the regulation of it.

Wattage relates to the quantity and extent of one's inner strength.

see also
• Technology Phobias *p. 159*
• Quantity & Size *p. 448*

Gas Power

Butane represents thoughts that could be damaging depending how they are acted upon.
Compressed air advises one to get more breathing room; move away from some life aspect that feels suffocating.
Compressor represents an individual or situation that brings about better understanding.
Coolant represents an aspect that serves as a settling or calming source for the individual dreamer.
Gas burner is usually indicative of one's personal responsibility regarding how potentially harmful aspects are utilized in a positive way.
Gaslight is suggestive of a perpetual illumination maintained by one's personal awareness.
Gas main exemplifies a potential hazard in one's life that is concealed beneath one's path.
Gas meter alludes to one's energy level.

Gadgetry

Artificial intelligence warns of giving another too much power or control of one's life.
Automation represents a loss of personal input; a shortcut way of doing things.
Bionics refer to the integration of conceptual and technical aspects. May relate to one who can visualize great advances through inventive means.
Digital watch suggests a precise time; no question regarding what time it is in respect to one's path. This time presentation may have a specific meaning for the dreamer.
Gadget represents personal aids utilized to implement goals.
Gizmo See gadget.
Headset signifies an effort to listen well, to thoroughly hear what's being said.
I-pod refers to the ease of changing one's mood through a change in attitude or by focusing on the brighter side or one's blessings.
Robot warns one to begin thinking for self.
User-friendly points to an element that is easy to utilize or compatible with average intellect/skill.

Weights & Measures

Drop (liquid measure) means a minute amount. Surrounding details of the dream will clarify this meaning.
Inch implies a small measurement that is usually related to one's amount of progress.
Jigger (measurement) depicts a small portion. The key here is to recall what was in the jigger. Sometimes a small amount of a volatile substance will be too much.
League (measurement) corresponds with one's level of spiritual attainment: a deeper depth denotes a higher advancement level.
Light (weight) implies simplicity; general knowledge; easily understood or learned.
Magnitude (measurement) indicates intensity or extent of something relevant to the dreamer. This could refer to a personal attribute, quality, knowledge, effectiveness, involvement, and so on.

Scale represents the need to balance an aspect of one's life.

Magnum (measurement) denotes a significant amount.
Mammoth (size) reveals a true proportion of a situation or action in an individual's life. Emphasizes totality.
Medium (amount) is average; middle-of-the-road; neutral.
Micro (size) naturally indicates a very small measurement. The surrounding dreamscape details will clarify what this symbol is associated with for the individual dreamer.
Mite (amount) suggests a very small measure of something. It may also refer to an insignificant aspect.
Narrow (width) denotes a course or aspect with little room for error.
Pinch (measurement) signifies an extremely small amount; negligible.
Pound (weight) generally illustrates a quantity of some quality of character or personal deed. This symbol emphasizes the weight something carries.
Scale (weight) illustrates balance of some type. Recall the kind of scale to determine this symbol's precise meaning. What was being weighed? What type of scale was it? Was anything on it?

Mechanics

Air pump refers to the ability to expand thoughts; take ideas further. Points out a situation, concept, or individual that acts as an impetus.

Axis connotes a central focal point that other aspects revolve around.

Bathometer signifies an aspect that determines the depth of spiritual belief and/or application.

Cogwheel signifies an important aspect of one's life.

Condenser suggests a need to be more concise or look at the basic issue.

Gyroscope stands for steadfastness; remaining true to one's course.

Suction pump represents a withdrawal; a pulling back movement.

Valves & Switches

Limit switch represents the same as a safety valve—it prevents something from exceeding its limits.

Safety valve portrays a personal control over one's emotions.

Shutoff valve represents an opportunity to gain needed control. Reveals the presence of a chance to stop something.

Switch (any type) reminds us that we possess the power to make our own decisions; to take personal responsibility. This symbol says, "You can flip the switch if you want to."

Experiments & Reactions

Boiling point connotes the point at which a condition or relationship in one's life becomes explosive.

Breeder reactor cautions against creating more than can be consumed or assimilated; excesses. May also warn of multiple ramifications associated with a plan or act.

Cathode glow stick denotes a safety measure taken.

Critical mass warns of an attitude/behavior that is currently sustaining the momentum of a negative relationship/situation.

Equation relates to a relative balance; a comparable aspect.

Findings (artisan supplies) stands for options for expressing one's creativity.

Fission portrays the multifaceted individualities of one's soul.

Radiation basically implies a disbursement; far-reaching ramifications. Recall the surrounding dream elements to determine if this symbol indicates a positive or negative meaning.

Radioactivity comes as a warning of a potentially dangerous situational atmosphere.

Scientific experiment will signify a suggestion to move ahead with a particular plan.

Test tube signifies personal experiments.

Toxic waste refers to residual effects of certain behaviors that remain volatile.

Chemicals & Gases

Agrochemical denotes aspects in an individual's life that appear to improve situations yet may prove to be detrimental in the end.

Alkali is indicative of dangerous situations or relationships.

Alkaloid refers to the duality of possessing both positive and negative aspects.

Ammonia warns of dangerous thoughts and points out the existence of a way to neutralize/cleanse them.

Arsenic applies to poisonous aspects a person voluntarily accepts in life.

Benzene symbolizes one's control over highly flammable situations or relationships.

Formaldehyde represents a need to preserve some facet of the dreamer's life.

Gas constitutes duality; the positive and negative aspects of something.

Helium indicates a life aspect that has the capability of uplifting attitudes, emotions, or situations.

Lighter fluid As with any incendiary type of symbol, this equates to a flammable element in one's life which has the potential to spark an emotional or situational explosion. This, naturally, calls for extreme caution in one's life.

Nitrous oxide corresponds with a psychological mechanism one utilizes to ease the pains and disappointments in life.

Salt is generally used to represent an individual who is gregarious and dependable.

Sodium See salt.

Arsenic refers to toxic elements in one's everyday life.

see also
• Gaseous Substances *p. 77*
• Science & Natural History *p. 234*

Metals

Brass points to a harsh, boisterous personality; something unrefined. May also mean something that's changeable. Could indicate a life aspect that mellows over time.
Bronze is suggestive of the beauty that comes from the blending of specific life elements.
Casting (metal) refers to a strong formulation; a strong idea having lasting qualities and/or effects.
Gold digger represents the willful manipulation of others for personal gain; a tendency to use people for selfish purposes.
Gold foil See gild.
Gold leaf See gild.
Gold plate is an indication of unnecessary extravagance; overdone refinement additions.
Ground wire advises one to get grounded. Perhaps one's thoughts or perspectives have begun to run wild.

Spring is indicative of an individual's talent for emerging unscathed following an adverse event.

Metal See specific type.
Plating (metal) constitutes a presentation of higher value that conceals an element of lesser value beneath it.
Rustproof indicates personal efforts applied to protecting and maintaining one's spiritual state.
Sheet metal signifies personal strength that is used in all aspects of life.
Spring (metal) represents a tendency to bounce back after some type of adversity has been encountered; tenacity; resiliency.
Steel relates to strength.
Steel-trap illustrates astute intelligence; a strong and quick mind.
Steel wool symbolizes insensitivity; a strong, yet insensitive nature.
Tin snips signify a life aspect that is capable of making it easier to cut through difficulties.
Verdigris applies to evidence of spiritual affects.
Wire (metal) illustrates a strengthening or supportive factor.
Wrought iron pertains to strong ideas or concepts forged from personal creativity.

Manufacturing

Adhesive represents the need to connect with someone or bring a situation together.
Beveled signifies angles to an issue or situation that should be seen and taken into consideration.
Blueprint signifies spiritual planning.
By-product illustrates that which all thoughts, words, and actions may cause. We don't always see the widespread effects of what we say and do in life.
Hardwired is associated with inherent characteristics.
Latex See rubber.
Made-to-order See custom-built.
Mass production pertains to something produced in a great quantity and without any personal touches.
Solder/soldering gun See adhesive.
Specifications pertain to the details of an issue, situation, or relationship.
Spray gun stands for a convenient and effective method of disbursing information.
Template See die cut.

Solar Power

Alternative energy points to a more natural way of achieving a goal in one's life. See solar power.
Photovoltaic connotes mental and emotional energy.
Solar battery portrays inner strength.
Solar collector is an energizing element in one's life.
Solar panel connotes one's reenergizing capacity. Recall the condition of the panel.
Solar power refers to the fact that one is naturally energized through good works.

Glass

Glass pertains to a state or condition of fragility.
Glass wool is a warning. It advises one to be more aware and stay watchful.
Green glass is generally representative of something of inferior quality that appears in one's life.
Spun glass See fiberglass.

Chemistry & Physics

Acid (chemical) signifies a burning situation or relationship; caustic behavior.

Acid pH (reading) comes in dreams to advise one to soften behavior. Indicates a tendency toward acerbic communications, perhaps cynicism.

Acid test symbolizes ultimate verification.

Aeronautics refer to one's energy applied to thought.

Aerospace symbolizes thought.

Aerospace engineering signifies the manner in which one processes thoughts. May denote a reaching for loftier thinking.

Atom most often refers to the importance of the smallest aspects of one's life; a call to pay attention to details; the little things that are being overlooked.

Atomic clock signifies perfect time. This symbol usually comes as a dream element to remind the dreamer of the timing of things. It's important to not lose sight of the fact that there's a time for everything and, understanding that, one can gain a bit more acceptance/patience with the waiting.

Bunsen burner calls for a need for self-analysis or serious introspection.

Carbon-14 dating implies a need for a generalized verification.

Catalyst alludes to individuals or situations that serve as motivational surges in life.

Centrifuge cautions one against mixing separate life aspects; a need to keep ideas or concepts separate.

Chain reaction exemplifies the vast effects that are caused by the spoken word and by one's actions.

Dry ice represents a stage of spiritual cooling; a decline in interest.

Emulsion portrays the reinforcing message that, although some life aspects cannot completely blend together, they can still coexist in a peaceful and pleasing manner.

Epoxy warns of a need to secure some type of connecting elements in one's life.

Fiber optics characterize the subtle sensory facets of one's perceptive reception.

Fiber optics lights relate to enlightenment, the insights from the light.

Force field means a barrier. This could be a self-created psychological barrier, a barrier caused by fear, or a personal field of one's energy or protection. The surrounding details will clarify this intent.

Laser denotes consolidation or the condensing of multiple aspects into a single form.

Litmus paper refers to a life aspect that has the capability of gauging honesty or the rightness of something.

Litmus test indicates an act of verification; concluding proof.

Low pressure indicates increased emotional tension.

Lubricant indicates an irritated or rough situation or characteristic that requires smoothing to prevent further friction.

Molecule denotes the smallest aspect of something. This refers to the importance of looking at every facet making up an issue or situation as being important.

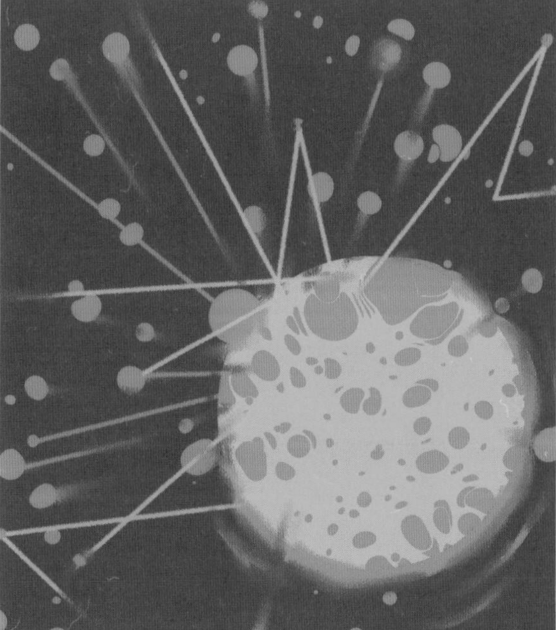

Chain reaction characterizes the effects of words and deeds.

Neoprene defines a willful avoidance of spiritual aspects in one's life.

Nucleus comes as a strong advisement to get to the core of an issue or concept. This indicates a wasteful involvement with superficial facets instead of focusing on the basic premise.

Periodic table usually has a specific chemical element emphasized or highlighted in some manner. This will have a personal indication for the dreamer. Perhaps one needs more iron in one's system. Gold or silver may have specific meaning. Is lead a concern?

Potability test stands for verification as to whether something is viable/workable or not.

Quantum theory represents a beginning peek at and step toward understanding true reality.

Radar portrays an acute awareness; intuition; heightened perception.

Relativity (theory) attempts to emphasize the fact that each individual perceives life elements in a diverse manner.

Science constitutes expanded knowledge regarding a specific subject. Recall what the subject was.

Slide (lab) advises of the wisdom to look deeper into some aspect of one's life; a need for analysis.

Wind load represents an awareness of how much one can tolerate emotional issues.

see also
• Microbiology *p. 116*
• Physics *p. 239*

Hazards & Precautions

Airtight signifies solid ideals or thoughts on an issue; convictions.

Biohazard warns of a high-risk factor connected with an aspect of the dreamer's life.

Blip means a shift from the norm; a call to attention.

Duct tape shows need to make repairs in regard to attitude.

Leakproof connotes a secure condition or status.

Lightproof warns of a self-imposed state of ignorance.

Malfunctions denote faulty functioning. This could refer to an individual's emotional, mental, spiritual, or physical aspects. This might also refer to one's plans.

Regulator (device) represents a specific management setting one attempts to maintain for daily behavior; an intent to establish a balanced synchronization based on spiritual goals.

Shockproof usually indicates a hardened personality, one who expects the worst.

Shock wave applies to future repercussions expected from a deed done.

Vapor lock is representative of an obstructed flow of energy current through one's system. It may also refer to a psychological block that has been causing one multiple dysfunctions.

In the Lab

Cold storage portrays a protection of what one values.

Decompression chamber warns against the tendency to speed through high spiritual concepts without taking the time to thoroughly comprehend them; a fast spiritual retreat.

Fixative See preservative.

Heating pad advises of a need to reenergize oneself.

Hyperbolic chamber stands for a need to adjust how one deals with stress/pressure.

Isometrics imply a conflict within self.

Magnetic resonance imaging (MRI) relates to a need for close analysis.

Pasteurization signifies the intent to discount superficial or extraneous elements from an issue or concept. This is not always a positive symbol.

Preservative clearly indicates a need to maintain an awareness or memory of a specific aspect in one's life. The surrounding dreamscape factors will clarify what this element is.

Pressure chamber See hyperbolic chamber.

Genetics

DNA marker refers to a specific element of one's personality or perception.

DNA test reminds us to keep doing self-exams for defective or harmful attitudes.

Double helix defines the living components of reality. This symbol advises one to attend to priorities.

Evolutionism cautions one to take a closer look at the periodic consistency of a concept, situation, or issue to be aware of subtle changes.

Gene-splicing warns against mixing concepts.

Genetic engineering represents a control over one's behavior; personal responsibility to alter negative behavior generated by psychologically manipulative conduct.

Genetic marker reveals one's susceptibility to something. This could be symbolic or literal, depending on the dreamscape's related elements.

Genetic screening portrays self-examination of one's behavior, especially primary motives.

Miscellaneous

Magnetic card symbolizes access to information or situations.

Ban is representative of an individual's lack of freedom and/or rights. May point out something the dreamer needs to stop doing.

Earth station is indicative of one's inner awareness; intuition. It may also refer to a cognizant link to an individual's higher self.

Keycard illustrates one's right to do something; having authority or permission.

Mag card See magnetic card.

Magnetic card represents access. This access can refer to information or a literal passkey allowing one entry.

Pay-by-touch (fingerprinting) is representative of a price that one has paid for giving up one's privacy.

Smart card signifies memory access. This symbol advises of a need to remember something that one has a tendency to forget or be in denial of.

Uplink stands for one's inner knowing; one's connection to the higher self or universal consciousness.

Voice-activated will generally symbolize a personal, emotional reaction to another individual.

Chapter 18

Travel & Transportation

These constitute a main category, as they directly deal with the physical body and the manner one moves through life. Vehicles and most of their components have counterparts to human physiology.

Automobiles & Leisure Vehicles

All-terrain vehicle (ATV) symbolizes one's versatility; perseverance. May also point out that there are ways to solve a problem that haven't been thought of.
Automobile corresponds to the physical body. Its components are associated with various parts of the physical body.
Beach buggy See dune buggy.
Bumper car suggests a personal enjoyment of the game; a tendency toward conflict for the simple thrill of winning.
Cab See taxi.
Camper (RV) signifies that which is capable of providing one with temporary respite from stress.
Car equates to the quality of one's physical condition. This most often refers to one's personal physiological system.
Caravan denotes a protected life path through a tight association with others of like mind. Depending on surrounding dreamscape elements, this may not be a positive symbol.
Chugalug warns against an impulsive intake of information without adequately understanding it.
Convertible implies a means of exchange; a life aspect that can be utilized in differing ways or forms.
Coupe (car style) implies a questionable situation; a situation with few exit possibilities.
Courtesy car represents benefits that bridge a temporary loss; a suitable temporary alternative.
Dune buggy symbolizes an attempt to override and obtain control over one's shifting thought patterns or attitudes. In some instances, this symbol could point to a manner of traveling through life that doesn't keep one on solid ground.
Four-wheel drive signifies the need for greater strength and extra efforts.
Gas-guzzler (vehicle) warns of using methods of advancement that consume more personal energy than necessary; doing things the hard way.
Go-cart advises of a need to reassess one's direction.
Hatchback pertains to an open-ended situation or relationship.

Bumper car represents someone who gets a kick out of winning.

Hum-vee relates to tenacity; perseverance; determination.
Jalopy indicates a freethinker.
Jeep See four-wheel drive.
Limousine alludes to an obsession with appearances; a preoccupation with self. See four-wheel drive.
People mover symbolizes a helpful element that will speed one's path when it is going in a general direction for a time.
Race car symbolizes a stressful and hectic work environment.
Rattletrap represents a dangerous or unhealthy situation. This is usually associated with one's home life.
Recreational vehicle (RV) usually indicates a time-out from one's work; a needed pause for relaxing activities.
Rental (car) stands for an opportunity to further progression.
Sports car exemplifies a fast-paced lifestyle and manner of behavior.
Taxi pertains to a means of assisting one's progress.
Turbocharged stands for a burst of energy. May refer to a reserve of energy/perseverance one isn't aware of having.
Vehicle correlates to the physiological system. Refer to specific types.

Cable Cars

Aerial railway See cable car.
Cable car connotes advancement generated by a strong supporting aspect in one's life. This symbol can also refer to threatening thoughts.
Gondola (lift) See cable car.
Streetcar See cable car.
Tram See cable car.
Trolley car See cable car.

Motoring Safety

Air bag (vehicle) denotes the need to protect one's thoughts and/or emotions.
Bubble top is representative of one's fear of being injured; lack of confidence in one's protective or defensive abilities. Relates to feelings of vulnerability.
Defogger advises of a need to improve perspectives.
Dual controls stand for tandem control; decision making done in an equitable manner with another. This symbol may also reveal a fight for control.
Roll bar is a specific protective measure; a safeguard.
Seat belt connotes a protective measure in one's life.
Stabilizer bar shows a need to balance some aspect of life.

see also
• Hills & Mountains *p. 68*
• Construction *p. 311*

In the Car

Accelerator symbolizes the rate of one's action taken. Usually indicates a need for one to stop procrastinating.
Accelerator (broken or missing) usually advises of a pause time needed. A time of nonaction is required before further advancing on an issue.
Alarm system (vehicle) directly pertains to an individual's physical body, whether it's a healthful manner of living or a physically destructive one. Was the alarm going off?
Armrest suggests a time to put one's aggression and active conflict aside, let the resentment go, and get on with life; a need for acceptance and forward movement.
Clutch (vehicle) is generally representative of that which causes one to gear up or down; a motivational factor allowing control over the choice of which gear to use.
Cruise control advises one to alter the speed by which one's path is taken. This usually refers to the need to slow down; pace oneself.
Dashboard pertains to protective measures.
Gas pedal See accelerator.
Global positioning system (GPS) advises that one should pay attention to where one is and become focused on the moment. This implies that one is perhaps looking to the future or pining about lost opportunities of the past.
Glove compartment indicates readiness to assist others in a variety of ways.
Hardtop implies thought given to protective methods or aspects.
Headrest indicates intellectual respite; a time to pause from one's pursuit of knowledge.
Head restraint suggests precautions against the possibility of a backlash.
Ignition key pertains to that which is capable of supplying one with proper nutrients that energize.
Moon roof suggests a need to stay open-minded. Points to possible current skepticism.
Odometer displays the amount of progression or advancement one has made in life. High mileage indicates a great deal of ground has been covered. Low mileage suggests a need to get going.
Power steering exemplifies using elements in one's life that make advancement easier; progressing by a less strenuous method. However, this method may not always be the most dependable or the one of choice.
Radar detector represents a perception of another's thoughts, moods, or attitudes; insight.
Rearview mirror typifies symbols that advise one to be aware of what's coming up from behind or what's transpiring behind one's back.
Speedometer indicates the speed at which one is progressing through life. It may advise a suggested pace.
Starter (engine) See ignition key.
Steering wheel stands for control of one's life and destiny. The key to clear interpretation in this instance is to recall what the steering wheel was attached to and whose hands were on it. If no hands were seen, then the symbol is an advisement to place one's own hands on the wheel and stop drifting/wandering.
Sunroof stands for a desire to remain connected to personal spirituality while one is traversing one's life path.
Throttle (control) pertains to a means to closure.

Car Seats

Backseat points to one's rightly designated position. This warns against trying to always be in the driver's seat.
Bucket seat represents self-confidence. It may also refer to individualism or separatism; independence.
Car seat (child's) symbolizes an immature perspective. It may refer to a path taken with juvenile attitudes.
Driver's seat represents the one in control. This can be a revealing dream.
Jump seat warns of gullibility.
Rumble seat suggests a dissatisfaction with oneself for not taking control of one's life.

Heavy Vehicles

Bulldozer illustrates a need for clear understanding; to clear away the rubble that covers the ground-level facts.
Dump truck portrays the act of actually dumping something from one's life.
Earthmover denotes overcoming obstacles.
Eighteen-wheeler See semitrailer.
Forklift connotes life aspects that have the capability to ease one's burdens or paths.
Grader (road) connotes a life aspect that has the capability of smoothing something out in one's life.
Half-track reveals a need to venture into untraveled regions; enter new territory. This refers to knowledge.
Lift truck symbolizes a work/time-saving element in one's life.

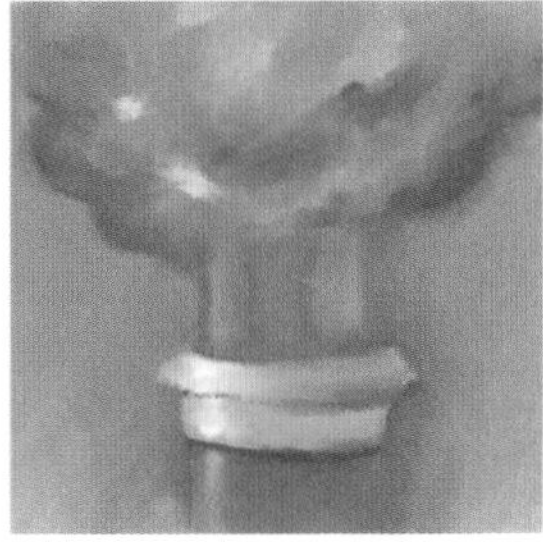

Steam engine is inner driving force.

Payloader suggests a need for major digging to be done; an advisement to do research or background inspection.
Steam engine denotes spiritual motivations.
Steamroller warns of negative control in one's life.
Tanker truck is a warning symbol. Recall what the truck was hauling in the tanker.
Tractor refers to a powerful help; highly effective assistance for the dreamer.

Horse-Drawn Vehicles

Brougham See carriage.
Buckboard signifies a rough ride, yet the rider persists without complaint.
Buggy suggests a simplistic plan for a phase of life journey.
Carriage means antiquated health practices. Also may refer to a physiological system that's low on energy.
Cartwheel refers to feelings of joy.
Chariot cautions one to slow down; a need to utilize reason before taking action.
Coach (conveyance) See carriage.
Conestoga wagon See covered wagon.
Covered wagon stands for a path traveled with courage and self-reliance.
Gurney advises of a serious physical condition.
Hansom See carriage.
Landau See carriage.
Pack train signifies the presence of unnecessary elements.
Phaeton See carriage.
Prairie schooner See covered wagon.
Stagecoach depicts a plodding manner of progression.
Wagon applies to a helpful aid that eases burdens.
Wagon train suggests a lack of direction or inability to gain confidence in a course.

Bicycles & Motorcycles

Bicycle depicts mental, physical, or spiritual balance.
Bicycle path denotes a well-balanced path if smooth and clear of debris, otherwise it means an unbalanced path.
Bike See specific type.
Bike lane See bicycle path.
Biker portrays independence; a freewheeling personality.
Chopper (bike) See motorcycle.
Crash helmet advises of a great need to protect thoughts.
Dirt bike implies an attempt to speed over life's rougher roads.
Handlebar pertains to personal control; a control of direction.
Harley Davidson represents pride in one's independence.
Inner tube applies to one's emotional state as the path walk is made. Recall if the inner tube was patched. Was it full of air? Deflated? Torn?
Kickstand connotes the stopping and pausing points along one's path.
Moped denotes positive thinking.
Motorcycle applies to freedom to follow one's unique path.
Motor scooter signifies a phase of moving away from immature thoughts/attitudes.
Mountain bike represents personal effort expended while taking the rougher road.
Pedicab represents servitude or arrogance, depending on who was pulling the cab and who was riding in it.
Scooter implies an immature method of gaining information or reaching one's goal.
Sedgeway (scooter) stands for traveling over one's path in an attempt to avoid the little bumps in the road.
Sidecar relates to a free ride or attempt to progress without applying personal effort.
Tandem pertains to partnership.
Unicycle denotes self-reliance and resourcefulness.

Trucks & Vans

Cab (of truck) indicates the controlling aspects of one's life.
Cherry picker (truck) signifies high-minded work; high-level work to be done.
Chuck wagon signifies an aspect that serves to nourish us along our path; sustenance while journeying through life.
Clunker implies inefficient or inoperable life factors such as outdated and primitive beliefs that no longer apply in today's world.
Flatbed (truck) pertains to a life factor that constitutes a heavy load for the dreamer to carry.
Milk truck connotes actual dairy products because any vehicle symbol directly stands for one's physical body. This advises of an actual increase or decrease in one's dairy requirement. A truck driving away indicates reduction in dairy foods.
Minivan denotes a moderate amount of personal effort needs to be expended to accomplish something satisfactorily.
Motor home reveals a transitional sense of illness or lack of direction.
Moving van suggests a change of perspective or surrounding.
Panel truck portrays that which is carried over into the workplace, usually personal attitudes or needed tools. Recall associative dream details for deeper meaning.
Pickup See truck.
Propane truck represents a need to eliminate excessive gases from one's system. This doesn't necessarily refer to intestinal gases, but usually indicates other gases within the system. Are you often a braggart? Thinking egotistically? Full of hot air?
Semitrailer exposes a physical overload; physical stress from overburdening oneself.
Telephone truck warns of a hearing impairment; one doesn't listen well.
Tow truck signifies an individual who makes it a habit to help others; one who performs unconditional goodness wherever and whenever the need is evident.
Trailer (semitruck) See semitrailer.
Truck correlates to personal efforts and the energy expended for same.
Van alludes to great personal efforts expended.
Wells Fargo truck illustrates a source of bounties, both material and spiritual. Also may refer to the movement of one's assets from one recipient to another.

Military Vehicles

Armored car/truck signifies one's emotional shield or untouchability.
Armored personnel carrier refers to an expectation of a forthcoming conflict and the defensive/offensive readiness related to it.
Tank (military) warns of uncontrolled aggression; a lack of discernment while progressing through life.

see also
• Equines *p. 24*
• Armor & Injuries *p. 350*

Motoring Services

Car wash implies a need to change.

Body shop suggests repair work needed. This refers directly to some physical aspect in one's life. In some dreams, this symbol points to cosmetic/plastic surgery and one's desire to alter oneself.
Cabstand exemplifies a waiting time. This usually refers to one's inability to advance on one's own.
Car dealership pertains to the physical aspects in one's life. May represent a source for alternate courses in life.
Carfare implies a price for advancement; the need of another to help move one along a course or life path.
Carpool denotes attempts to conserve energy and resources so they are not expended in unproductive ways.
Car rental represents an advancement through the assistance of another.
Carrying charge relates to aspects in life that have a price; an extra price paid for what one wants or does.
Car wash denotes a need to clean up one's act.
Collision shop stands for a source where one can go to repair some type of damage done to a situation.
Crash test refers to a need to reinforce one's defenses. May suggest that one not be so sensitive and stop taking things personally.
Curb service denotes convenience.
Driving school indicates a need to review or learn better methods of managing one's way through life.
Full service stands for the act of giving one's all.
Garage represents a place of rest or stored energy.
Hitch (tow connector) represents a life aspect that helps path progression; that which provides the start-up action from a setback.
Ramp portrays a life aspect that has the capability of easing one's way.
Road test symbolizes an individual's level of current knowledge and preparedness to safely continue his or her life course.
Taximeter symbolizes the personal cost involved in having others transport you along a portion of your journey.
Tow pertains to assistance needed or given.
Weigh station See road signs.

Emergency Vehicles & Public Transport

Ambulance usually warns of a need for medical attention.
Bus pertains to an aspect in one's life that serves to benefit many. May also refer to an overblown situation or even obesity, depending on surrounding dreamscape.
Busing means a forced integration of ideas by another.
Bus station suggests a need to be helpful at a different location. Implies assistance is needed somewhere else.
Bus stop refers to an opportunity. What this opportunity is depends on the surrounding dreamscape elements. This may be an opportunity to make a choice in life.
Crash cart connotes last minute efforts to save some failing aspect in the dreamer's life.
Crash truck pertains to the immediate action taken after an unexpected failure or great disappointment.
Double-decker means twice the amount of something.
Fireboat denotes personal safeguards against spiritual fanaticism.
Fire engine alludes to life aspects that have the capability to control another's emotional explosiveness.
Paddy wagon implies being caught for a misdeed. This reminds one that, in the end, one pays for wrongdoings.
School bus corresponds to the vehicle or way a person can attain additional knowledge.
Squad car symbolizes the mobility (extent) of one's own conscience; an inability to escape one's conscience.
Transfer (ticket) exemplifies a need to alter one's course in life.

Fire engine represents something that restrains another person's outbursts.

Gears

Gear connotes mechanisms used to effect movement; motivational factors, instigators; forceful aspects.
Gearbox See transmission.
Transmission means one should pace oneself.
Transmission fluid pertains to the ease with which an individual can make transitions or accept changes in life. Did the dream insinuate that one needed to add fluid?

Lights

Fog lights (vehicle) symbolize an ability to see through people's pretenses.
Headlight denotes logic and reason; a light on the subject. Usually refers to one's eyes and may be associated with one's clarity of perception.
High beam (light) suggests more light be given to an issue in life that the dreamer is having trouble understanding.
Running light indicates a state of preparedness; someone with an anticipatory attitude.
Stoplight is representative of a temporary halt to one's advancement.
Taillight stands for an aspect (sign) that marks one's presence. It refers to the act of making oneself visible or effective.
Timing light (engine) suggests something amiss or a bit off regarding an individual's timing for things.
Xenon (headlights) signifies a brighter light shed on issues or one's path.

Brakes

Brake warns of a need to halt something, or slow one's actions/movement.
Brake fluid pertains to a life element used to control the pace of one's progression.
Brake light symbolizes one's intention to slow down.
Brake line pertains to the ability to control one's life pace; the essential element that maintains control of one's pace.
Brake pedal refers to aspects in one's life that allows a slower pace; that which brings about a slowing; the personal access to controlling one's pace.
Brake shoes stand for the singular element in one's life that will stop one from progressing into a negative situation. Usually this element is related to self-control, willpower, or other type of self-generated solution.
Disc brake illustrates pressure applied for the purpose of slowing or halting further progression.

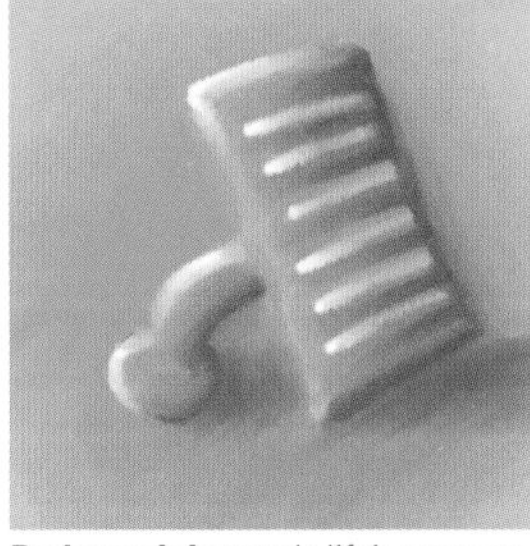

Brake pedal controls life's progress.

Tires

Fifth wheel is an indication of an unnecessary element. May point to feelings of not belonging or not being welcomed. See also spare tire.
Fifth wheel (RV) See recreational vehicle.
Mud flaps See splash guard.
Mudguard See splash guard.
Retread (tire) may denote fortitude or, depending on related dream elements, it might apply to a need to tread over one's former path and backtrack.
Snow tire suggests a desire to comprehend higher spiritual concepts without getting intellectually stuck on them; an attempt to get through the deeper elements.
Spare tire pertains to preparations made for possible eventualities encountered along one's life path. In some dreams, this symbol may literally point to being overweight or carrying a load that's too heavy.
Splash guard connotes defense mechanisms; methods of protecting self from negative elements.
Stud (snow tires) portrays a desire to thoroughly grasp spiritual ideas.
Tire chains/studs represent an attempt to keep a firm hold on one's path.
Tireless (vehicle) points to an inert phase, perhaps due to a lack of motivation or faith that things will work out or get better.
Tires pertain to one's condition progressing through life.
Tire tread indicates a well-prepared and energetic (new treads) outlook toward one's life journey, or a weary and unmotivated (worn) attitude to life.

Snow Travel

Bobsled denotes a spiritual path that's quickly sped over; a rush to a spiritual goal without gaining the riches and depth along the way.
Chairlift connotes a rising on the thoughts of others' unearned advancements through resting on laurels.
Dogsled signifies a spiritual path that follows that of a friend.
Luge relates to "going down a slippery slope." Indicates a situation or relationship or other element such as recent behavior is destructive, sliding downhill fast.
Sled connotes a life aspect that lets one skim through life. This is not a positive symbol.
Sledge may refer to a sled type of symbol or it may indicate a helpful aid in life.
Sleigh indicates a means of traveling along one's path without exerting personal effort.
Snowmobile relates to the ease that an individual moves through her/his utilization of spiritual beliefs.
Snowplow is a dreamscape symbol that denotes paths through spiritual difficulties. This refers to complex spiritual concepts that have been plowed through, thereby clearing the way for unobstructed comprehension.
Toboggan See sled.

see also
• Ice & Snow *p. 61*
• Travel & Transportation *p. 257*

Vehicle Parts & Accessories

Air horn might stand for a sudden thought that grabs one like an epiphany or it can refer to a loud and clear communication.

Air hose signifies a source of fresh ideas.

Antifreeze cautions against allowing spiritual interest to freeze up.

Axle exemplifies a motivating force that helps to support one's actions.

Bumper pertains to one's tenacity; an ability to bounce back from problems or emotional injury; a self-protective measure.

Bumper guard suggests an acknowledgment of the possibility of missteps along one's life journey and precautions taken to allow for them.

Bumper sticker connotes one who is openly opinionated. These are extremely revealing if they can be recalled accurately.

Carburetor represents the mix of elements needed to accomplish a goal or maintain a motivational force.

Caster denotes a desire to protect something.

Coolant represent an aspect that serves as a settling or calming source.

Crankshaft denotes one aspect of several that serve to generate new starts.

Dipstick (oil) advises of impending friction to one's emotional state from stress and the need to reinforce defenses by increasing acceptance and/or tolerance.

Distributor (engine) represents proportionate utilization of one's energies.

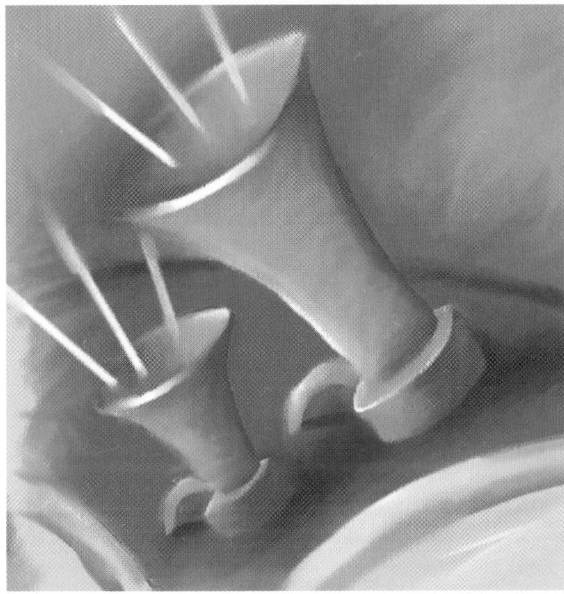

Air horn may be a representation of a striking discovery.

Engine denotes aspects of the heart (physical or emotional).

Fan belt signifies an important life aspect that keeps other life factors going; a motivating element.

Fender portrays one's personal guard; protective factors.

Firewall (vehicle) pertains to one's attention given to preventive measures against certain damaging or explosive life elements.

Footboard (vehicle) See running board.

Front-wheel drive advises of a path traveled half-heartedly.

High gear portrays a phase of intense activity; possibly mental or emotional activity.

Hubcap applies to the center of something to which the dreamer will readily relate.

Lug nut alludes to extra strong protection or assurances.

Motor refers to a life aspect that can provide additional energy or motivation; an impelling force.

Muffler (exhaust) implies a quieting of intended or possible outbursts.

Overdrive advises one to slow the pace. Going too fast and expending too much energy causes a loss of valuable lessons that are not noted.

Radiator (vehicle) represents internal temperature in respect to overheated emotions. Recall the condition of the radiator. Was it overflowing? Needing water?

Running board relates to a convenience; a life aspect that serves to assist one along her/his way.

Shock absorber emphasizes emotional and intellectual stability in one's life.

Spark plug represents an aspect that serves as an impetus toward action or advancement; motivational element.

Sprocket wheel represents a life element capable of maintaining one's forward progression on life's path.

Tailpipe portrays a means or outlet for negative emotions or attitudes.

Trunk (vehicle) corresponds with the hidden aspects carried along one's path.

Turn signal symbolizes one's intention to alter one's present course.

Vanity license plate reveals a personal attitude or idea.

Windshield suggests the eyes through which perspectives are formed. Check on the windshield's condition. Was it tinted? Slanted? Shielded? Cracked? This symbol is very much like that of a window.

Windshield washer fluid suggests one doesn't have a clear perspective.

Weather

Air sock See wind sock.

Headwind constitutes a counterforce to be overcome along one's path.

Turbulence (airplane) denotes disturbing thoughts. This may refer to outside influences that negatively disturb a formerly solid belief or idea.

Wind sock cautions against a tendency to care about the opinions of others by watching which way the wind blows.

Fuel & Emissions

Catalytic converter advises us to make the most out of every situation or opportunity that is given us.
Diesel fuel represents a particular source of energy or motivation that produces negative ramifications.
Exhaust (vehicle) refers to a lack of energy; a run-down condition. This may also indicate some type of finality experienced in one's life.
Exhaust fan represents an attempt to keep attitudes or perspectives refreshed, free of negative or excessively damaging elements.
Exhaust pipe refers to withheld emotions, opinions, or energy. It is an advisement to release pent-up aspects of oneself.
Fuel is associated with one's energy and/or that which nourishes.
Fuel gauge comes as an aid in determining the amount of energy one is running on. Did the gauge read empty? Full?
Fuel tank is associated with our supply of energy and usually pertains to strength of character or perseverance.
Gasoline applies to physical energy.
Gas pump characterizes a source of energy; a source of motivation.
Gas station signifies the source of one's energy or motivational force.
Gas tank (vehicle) connotes an individual's personal energy level. Recall if the tank was empty or full.
High-octane indicates a powerful aspect in one's life. This could refer to a personal characteristic, relationship, or situation.
Lead-free signifies an element in one's life that is free of a particular negative one has been concerned about or trying to avoid coming into contact with.
Refuel naturally indicates waning energy or motivation and the need to reenergize oneself.
Service station See gas station.

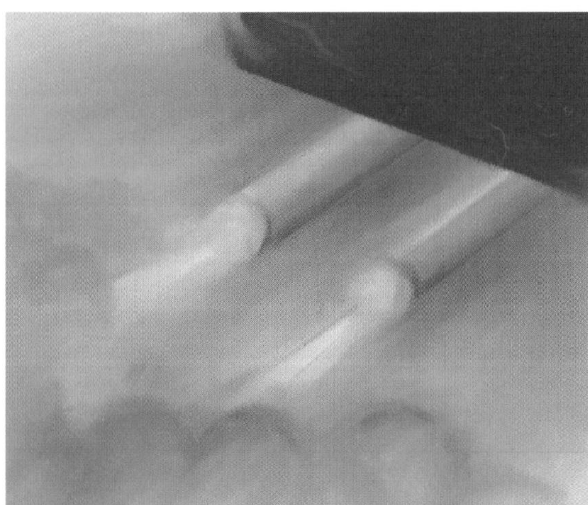

Exhaust signifies that one is worn out or that a situation has ended.

On the Road

Bend (in road) connotes a slight veering away from something; a minor shift in direction.
Blind alley stands for futile efforts.
Bottleneck denotes complications; congested aspects; backed-up thoughts or plans.
Caution (sign) See road signs.
Corner means a turning point in life; a different direction.
Covered bridge represents a connecting path that will be safe to travel upon.
Dead end (sign) See road signs.
Driveway pertains to a region of approach; specific approachability.
Expansion bridge pertains to a way to get to the other side. It comes as encouragement for those believing life's current problems are insurmountable.
Fork (in road) defines a choice in one's direction.
Hitchhiker characterizes laziness; one who advances along the path by way of another's efforts.
Keep left (road sign) See road signs.
Keep right (road sign) See road signs.
Limit (speed) See road signs.
Mile marker/post reveals one's current location along one's life path.
Milestone signifies an event that marks a great accomplishment or turning point.
One-way (sign) See road signs.
Parking (act of) signifies the defining and securing of a stable state or position, usually temporarily for the purpose of gaining needed information.
Parking meter always reveals a specified span of time allotted for an individual to give time or attention to a particular issue.
Right-of-way is self-explanatory. The key here is to recall who had the right-of-way sign. Did you have to yield? Also see road signs.
Road corresponds with one's life path either currently or one that is being advised. Try to recall surrounding dreamscape details for further clarification of this dream symbol.
Roadblock comes as a warning advisement that a person has yet to attain the experiential depth and knowledge to continue progressing along the current course. This symbol may also indicate a self-generated block due to inner fears.
Roadside may indicate a need to pull over and rest while traveling one's path or it may refer to something that should be noticed.
Scenic overlook See road signs.
Sign comes as a personal message for each dreamer. Recall what the sign said. Was it a directional one? Was it a stop or yield?
Speed limit See road signs.
Tollbooth/road applies to a payment required for further advancement along one's chosen course.
Tow-away zone See road signs.
Turnpike See tollbooth.
Twisting road reflects one's fortitude and perseverance while progressing a burdensome and difficult life path that is currently full of twists and turns.
Yield sign See road signs.

see also
• Air & Atmosphere *p. 58*
• Charting the Earth *p. 67*

Types of Road

Back road means thorough research.

Access road points the way. Indicates that one's way or advancement isn't as blocked as previously thought.
Alaska Highway signifies a rugged path with a road that isn't as rough as anticipated.
Autobahn (Austria/Germany) stands for a lightning-fast pace. Depending on the surrounding details, this could be either a positive or negative symbol.
Avenue is generally representative of a wide path ahead; possibly many distractions along the way.
Back road represents in-depth study. The symbol points out valuable information gained or needed by less obvious venues.
Beltway stands for a way around something.
Boulevard pertains to a wide and well-used path. This may not be the best course for the dreamer to travel.
Causeway signifies feeble or uncommitted attempts to delve into spiritual concepts.
Cul-de-sac connotes a need to backtrack or reverse one's path; nowhere to go but back the way one came.
Expressway exemplifies a fast lane; the quickest way to a destination.
Freeway See expressway.
High road portrays optimism. Frequently warns against taking the easier path.
Highway represents a life path taken by many others.
Low road is deceitfulness.
Main drag warns against walking a road traveled by most everyone. This calls for individuality and personal decisions.
Parkway connotes a phase of one's path that produces accelerated, trouble-free advancement.
Private drive/road See road signs.
Service road signifies an alternate, slower and less stressful route that leads to the same goal.
Shelf road represents a precarious path currently being traveled.
Side street represents an off-the-main-track diversion.
Street depicts a byway; a course one has an option of traveling. Did the street have a name? Was it lit or dark? Was it deserted or crowded?
Switchback alludes to retaining past knowledge. Suggests that one isn't retaining what has been learned and isn't applying experiential knowledge gained throughout one's life.
Two-way street alludes to something being available to opposing parties to use or take advantage of.

Road Anatomy

Acceleration lane stands for a time to keep pace with developing issues.
Crossroad pertains to the time for making a major decision in life. This most often has to do with a change in direction or an opportunity for change.
Fast lane is a call to personal responsibility.
Flyover represents an attempt to get an overall picture of an issue or situation before one actually takes action to become involved.
Hairpin curve (in road) indicates a tendency to do a lot of backtracking.
Interchange represents a decision regarding an upcoming change of course option.
Intersection See interchange.
Junction means a joining of forces or it may indicate a new option.
Lane (highway) refers to single-mindedness.
Median strip represents a guideline along one's path; a protective measure that lets one know when one is backsliding.
Merging lane See acceleration lane; road signs.
Overpass reveals a directional solution to a problematical path obstacle.
Shoulder (of road) suggests an emergency contingency.
Soft shoulder See road signs.
Speed bump exposes a need to slow down.
Underpass characterizes a way under something; an alternative course.

Road Construction

Asphalt denotes a serious separation from the grounding aspects in life.
Blacktop See asphalt.
Bump (in road) points to small, temporary difficulties in a person's path.
Bumpy (road) refers to a phase of one's path that presents temporary difficulties.
Cobblestone portrays a bumpy road that one chooses to take.
Dirt road applies to personally chosen paths in life that present a few additional obstacles and take greater energy to traverse than the paved roads.
Roadbed depicts the soundness of one's current path. Of what was the road constructed? Did it have a specific color? Level or bumpy? Straight or curvy?

Cobblestone points to problems.

Rut (in road) pertains to a self-generated state of neutrality; lacking progression or advancement due to one's own inability to perceive opportunities.
Tarmac See asphalt.
Uneven (road) stands for bittersweet experiences; the simultaneous occurrences of the ups and downs of positive and negative elements.

The Journey

Halfway house is an advisement to remove oneself from an undesirable situation or relationship.
Homebound stands for a nearly completed goal or path.
Homestretch advises of a nearly completed goal.
Itinerary implies a planned course. This may not be a positive dream element if there hasn't been time for unexpected events or delays factored in.
Journey forewarns of an upcoming time of discovery or search.
Layover implies a temporary setback; a delay in one's plans; a need to readjust one's timing.
Map comes as a personal directional message that will serve to guide one's path or supply other information pertinent to the dreamer's personal questioning.
Milk run indicates multiple aspects to give attention to.
Odyssey represents a life path full of self-discovery.
Outward bound suggests that a time or condition is ripe for self-discovery.
Progress comes as a message of encouragement if the dream depicts an advancement being made.
Rest area naturally implies a much-needed rest from one's work or a stressful situation.
Rest stop See rest area.
Road map points out the multiple options available to reach a goal. Sometimes the dream road map actually gives a clear visual that literally leads the way.
Round trip implies a return to the beginning or starting point to facilitate a closure or completion.
Route See map.
Sojourn See journey.
Stopover illustrates a need to experience a particular event or communion along one's life path.
Street map suggests that one needs to be sure of one's direction.
Uncharted (course) illustrates an unplanned direction that may, of itself, be specifically planned that way. This indicates someone who desires to let life guide her/him toward self-discoveries.

Traffic Lights

Green light naturally means permission granted; the go-ahead signal.
Red light appears as a strong warning to stop something. The dreamer will make the correct individualized association.
Signal (light) comes as an advisement regarding one's pace through life.
Traffic light marks the rightness of one's path. Did the light show green, yellow (slow down)? Did it indicate a time to turn off onto another road (arrow)?
Yellow light is a sign of caution and comes to the dreamer as an advisement to slow his or her pace.

Dangerous Driving

Chicken (game with vehicle) denotes ultimate irresponsibility and disregard for others, not to mention self.
Lane-switching stands for vacillation; indecision.
Lead foot is an element that reveals recklessness; a need to slow down.
Speeding reveals a cautionary advisement to slow one's pace for the purpose of recognizing realizations that have been formerly missed.
Tailgating represents a lack of individuality. Warns one to stop following another so closely.
Traffic court signifies the costs involved if one loses integrity in respect to one's manner of path progression.
Vehicular homicide comes as a serious warning to halt behavior that is hazardous to self and possibly to others as well. Because the general symbology of a vehicle relates to the physical body, the dreamscape element of vehicular homicide may relate to obesity or another form of destructive habit/addiction one is perpetrating that may indirectly harm friends and loved ones.
Weaving (vehicle) warns of carelessness; a lack of awareness while traveling one's path.

Driving Conditions

Bumper-to-bumper means little movement; a condition or situation in one's life that isn't going anywhere in particular.
Congestion (traffic) See traffic jam.
Detour usually advises that one needs to take a sidetrack off the main path to learn something important. This dream symbol reminds us that one-mindedness can be a detriment if we're not fluidly open enough to recognize when elements along the way are important enough to spend time on.
Dirty vehicle advises of a need for one to cleanse an aspect of oneself.
Diversion cautions one to remain focused.
Gridlock constitutes a deadlocked condition or a Catch-22 situation.

Roadwork implies changing plans.

Roadwork signifies a need to make repairs or adjustments to one's planned course.
Standstill symbolizes a halt to progression or advancement.
Traffic exemplifies traveling activity. Stands for the state of one's chosen path. Was the road crowded? Gridlocked?
Traffic jam characterizes a setback, a temporary one, that appears along an individual's path.

see also
• Travel Phobias *p. 158*
• Motor Sports *p. 212*

Driving

Cone (traffic) signifies a cautionary advisement; cautionary guidelines.

Crash pad exemplifies preparations for the unexpected.

Cross-country symbolizes a long journey traversed along untraveled paths. May indicate a new trail blazed.

Driving time points to the time it will take for getting from one point in one's progression to another.

Downhill may refer to a worsening condition or it may refer to a less stressful or problematical phase where one can coast for a time. Surrounding dreamscape facets will clarify which meaning is intended.

Driver's license denotes one's true identity and comes in dreams to remind us to remain true to that identity. This symbol may also point to one's right to proceed on a particular course.

Emergency brake advises of a critical need to stop something the dreamer is doing.

Fender bender stands for a minor altercation; small conflict, perhaps within oneself.

Four-wheeling suggests a daring attitude when faced with life's rough roads; confidence one will overcome and persevere; the love of a good challenge.

Freewheeling indicates a carefree personality, relationship, or situation. May point to a pride in independence.

Full circle denotes completeness; a return to the start.

Full speed comes as an advisement to slow down.

Green flag characterizes a go-ahead. It's time to begin something.

High speed is most often an advisement to slow down or do things in a more attentive manner.

Low gear refers to a slow pace or progression.

Motorcade denotes emphasis. The surrounding dream details will reveal the precise meaning for each dreamer.

Neutral (gear) typifies a situation that lacks any developmental aspects; a stage of nonmovement; no opinion or desire to express same.

Off-ramp represents a choice or opportunity to get off the fast track for a time.

On-ramp reminds us of the presence of multiple opportunities to begin a new path or direction.

Overdrive comes to the dreamer as an advisement to slow the pace. Going too fast and expending too much energy causes a loss of valuable lessons that are not noted.

Pass (vehicular) comes as an advisement to go around an element in one's way.

Pike See tollbooth.

Reverse (gear/direction) will generally suggest that one needs to go back to learn something or it could connote a retrogressive path or behavior.

Roadkill stands for collateral damage; the unintentional emotional injuries caused by certain behavior or situational events.

Sidetracked depicts a loss of an individual's focus on a life goal or issue.

Traffic cone portrays life's obstacles and reminds one to take care.

Side trip symbolizes efforts put into gaining a more rounded impression or experience of something.

Skid marks are representative of a former loss of footing along one's path.

Shortcut portrays a more efficient method of accomplishing something.

Speed representations greatly vary in dreams and reveal meanings depending on related elements.

Test-drive refers to the testing of a new course or method of traveling that course.

Ticket (traffic) exposes negative methods of progression along one's life path.

Traffic cone comes in dreams to represent guidance around a hazard in one's path. This symbol advises one to proceed with caution.

U-turn advises a person of a need to go back or return to a former issue.

Breakdowns

Blowout illustrates an aspect that will cause temporary delays or setbacks; an overwhelming aspect.

Booster cable comes to the dreamer as an advisement that helpful or supportive connections be made in one's life. Points to a need for an impetus or to be reenergized.

Breakdown (vehicle) refers to a literal physical condition. Directly points to some type of physical illness.

Flat tire stands for a temporary pause in the progression of one's journey; a minor problem needing immediate attention before going any further.

Jump-start stands for a need to be reenergized or motivated. See booster cable.

Puncture comes to the dreamer as an advisement for one to make a breakthrough of some kind or it may denote an inconsistency or defect associated with an element of life.

Stalled engine signifies a waning of one's energy or motivation.

Road Signs

Road signs stand for directional path indicators/advisements, or reveal how a path is being traveled. See below for some of the most common road signs.

Arrows sign (directional) symbolizes those life aspects that literally point the way.

Bike Lane sign marks a more casual approach to one's path, an approach with an eye to appreciating every small blessing along the course.

Bridge Icy When Wet sign advises caution when one's path crosses over ground touched by spiritual elements.

Bump sign comes as a forewarning for a bump ahead or a small glitch.

Business District sign is an attempt to draw one back to matters at hand.

Cattle On Road sign cautions us to heighten our awareness on a particular section of our life path.

Caution sign naturally advises one of the need for increased awareness, watchfulness.

Chains Only sign is a warning of treacherous ground ahead. It advises one to be cautious.

Construction Zone sign indicates a path that's in the process of being developed and to proceed carefully.

Curve sign warns us to be expecting something akin to a curve ball that's in the immediate future.

Dead End sign saves us the time and energy of going down an unfruitful path.

Deer X-ing sign tells us that we should be prepared for unexpected events.

Do Not Enter sign comes in an attempt to keep us from staying off paths that we've no right to enter or aren't aligned with our purpose.

Emergency Vehicles Only sign reveals a section of our path that would be considered an interference or hindrance to others needing immediate help. A path that our presence on would be a detriment to others.

Exit Number signs stand for many opportunities to take different paths.

Falling Rock sign advises us to be prepared for the unexpected.

Forest Service Road sign indicates a path providing additional benefits if one wants to expend extra energy to get to them.

Gas/Food/Lodging sign points to a short detour that provides refreshment, a shot of energy, and respite as one travels one's path.

Handicap Parking sign suggests that we should leave certain benefits to those who need them more than we do.

Historical Site sign advises that there's something in one's personal history (past) that one needs to look at and glean an important element from.

Horse Riders sign cautions us to be aware of and recognize those more vulnerable than ourselves.

Keep Left sign urges us to be a bit more open-minded.

Keep Right sign comes to suggest the dreamer be a little more conservative for a time.

Left Lane Closed sign advises us that, at this point in time, there's absolutely no room for an ultraliberal attitude.

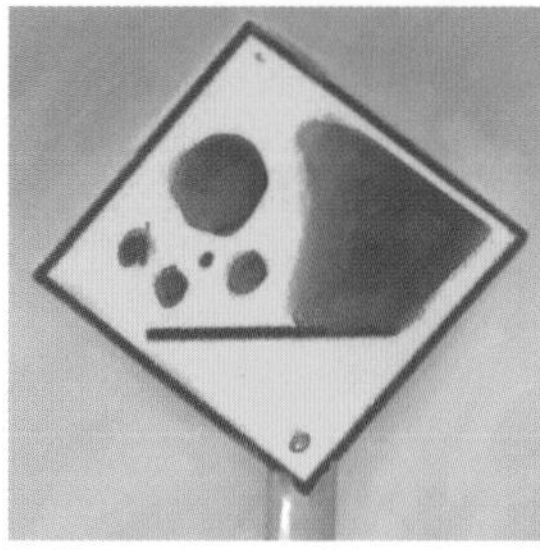

Falling rock warns of the unforetold.

Suggests a time for strictness.

Loading Zone sign points to a place in one's path where many benefits can be gained.

Load Limit sign warns against taking more than one needs. May also indicate a condition of being overloaded or taking on too much.

Local Traffic Only sign refers to territory that is familiar to a select group who have access to it.

Low Clearance sign advises of a phase for keeping one's head down and not craning one's neck out too far. May imply curiosity or nosiness.

Men Working sign advises a slower pace and higher awareness needed.

Merge Left sign suggests a time to be more conservative and keep a handle on our emotions.

Merge Right sign indicates a phase when more compassion and liberal thought would serve us better.

Neighborhood Crime Watch sign reminds us to police ourselves. This is not a good time to attempt a high-risk act.

No Campfires sign hints that a certain place in one's journey is precariously dry (having little nourishment).

No Hunting sign signifies protection. For some, this means a place holding no opportunities.

No Littering sign warns against discarding something that may still have value.

No Loitering comes in dreams as a motivational factor.

No Outlet sign suggests a need to retrace one's steps if one goes down that road.

No Parking sign tells us that we can't stop at this particular point on our path.

No Passing Zone sign suggests an equal pace. This shouldn't be the time to forge ahead or speed up.

No Public Access sign refers to a path that's not generally open to everyone.

No Services sign signifies a path having no aiding elements that may still hold some personal value. This dreamscape element could signify a phase when one must go it alone.

No Stopping In Tunnel sign is a call for perseverance.

No Thru Traffic sign may point to a path leading into a maze or confusion.

No Trespassing sign reveals a path that is not available or open.

No U-Turn sign warns of a point in one's life when there is no turning back; moving forward is the only direction available at this time.

One-Lane Bridge sign signifies a short amount of time when an individual must go through something without the aid of others.

see also
• Livestock *p. 19*
• Flags, Signs & Symbols *p. 469*

Road Signs (continued)

One-Way (sign) is a reminder that there is no turning back/around or reversing direction once begun. This is a call to follow through and keep going forward.
Open Range sign (see Cattle On Road sign; Deer X-ing sign).
Pavement Ends sign marks the beginning of a more rough road.
Pedestrian X-ing sign suggests a time when one may have to give way to others; the possibility of concessions or deference.
Private Drive/Road symbolizes attitudes or elements one desires to keep to oneself, aspects one feels are special or not for public knowledge.
Rest Area sign (see rest area).
Restricted Access sign signals a path that is not open to everyone.
Right Lane Closed sign suggests that, at this time, there's absolutely no room for conservatism or apathy.
Right-Of-Way sign (see right-of-way).
Road Closed sign tells us that a certain path is not open to us, not a viable course.
Road Narrows sign suggests a path's phase that holds little room for error.
Roadwork Ahead sign comes to prepare us for an upcoming situation that is demanding greater efforts to get past it.
Rough Pavement sign indicates a short span of minor difficulty. This could refer to a rash of irritating situations.
RR X-ing sign See train (crossing).
Runaway Lane sign points to the existence of a net in place in case we get ourselves in trouble. It's a symbol that cautions us against going so fast that we can't stop.
Scenic Overlook sign is a call to stop along the way and appreciate the beauty existing along one's path.
School Bus Zone Next 5 Miles sign suggests the possible need to stop and experience our child within.
School Zone sign points to the wisdom of slowing down and having patience for those less advanced or enlightened than we are.
Service Drive/Road sign signifies a slower-paced method of traveling the same course.
Slippery When Wet sign cautions against carelessly treading over spiritual issues. Advises of a time to attend to our footing.
Slow—Children at Play sign comes as a quite literal dreamscape visual. It means the dreamer needs to slow down and have a childlike perspective, take time out for some less serious activities.
Slow-Moving Vehicles sign suggests that one has respect and tolerance for those who, for whatever reason, progress at a slower rate.
Soft Shoulder sign indicates a possible mishap if one veers from one's path.
Speed Limit sign advises of the proper pace one will best advance by. Exceeding that pace implies a lack of understanding will occur.
Standing Only sign refers to a time for idling instead of actually turning off one's engine; a time for staying on the same issue, but giving it some contemplation.
Steep Grade sign forewarns of an unavoidable downhill phase to one's path.
Stop sign represents an advisement to stop one's forward progression for a time. Frequently, this comes as a forewarning.
Stop When Flashing sign (lights) act as a yellow stoplight and tells us to be prepared to stop at any time.
Toll Road sign signals a path that has costs attached to it.
Tourist Info Ahead sign refers to a chance to learn more about where one is headed.
Tow-Away Zone sign refers to possible ramifications if one tries to go back into the wrong issue or situation.
Trucks Entering Highway sign comes as a reminder to acknowledge and respect our hard-working peers.
Trucks Keep Right sign signifies an easier path to bear when surrounded by those working as hard as you are.
Uneven Pavement sign warns of a path that contains a balance of positive and negative elements.
Use Low Gear sign advises us to force ourselves to proceed slower, more cautiously.
Weigh Station sign comes as a reminder to weigh our behavior on the scale of our conscience.
Winding Road sign gives a hint of an upcoming path full of twists and turns. Even though this path takes longer to travel, a snaking path will provide more benefits and present more opportunities for one to learn from than the straight path.
Wrong Way sign is a wonderfully literal message that keeps the dreamer from wasting valuable time.
Yield sign cautions against an effort to oppose an issue or person, perhaps even one's own conscience. Suggests a need to give way to one's better judgment.

Accidents

Collision pertains to a harmful or negative result.
Crash refers to a destructive aspect; serious consequences.
Pileup (vehicular) alludes to a path journey that follows another too closely; inattention to where one is going and the manner of same.
Rollover (vehicle) may foretell of the possibility of an upcoming vehicular accident, but most often this type of dream event indicates a physiological dysfunction or turnaround with one's health.
Wreck (vehicle) is a symbol that correlates to emotional or physiological damage.

The Airport

Air base connotes the mind and its condition in respect to one's thought patterns and process. The basis of one's attitudes and perspectives.
Airfields represent how an individual takes off with new ideas and plans. Could also point out how an attitude or idea was presented (landed).
Airport security refers to a careful watch on one's thoughts. Inspection of motives or attitudes may be required in one's life.
Airport terminal denotes one's ability to sort out thoughts and ideas. This represents choices of thought.
Airstrip represents the manner in which ideas are expressed. Recall the physical condition of the dreamscape airstrip.
Control tower represents a defined source of manipulative behavior.
Heliport corresponds with a grounding aspect in one's life.
Holding pattern constitutes a temporary period of neutrality; a life pause that precludes further advancement for an indeterminate span of time.
Landing strip marks one's intended destination; an immediate goal or next stop along one's life path.
Moving sidewalk symbolizes an effortless phase of one's life journey.
Runway (airport) indicates a pathway leading to (or away from) one's purpose. Surrounding details will clarify what was meant.
Terminal (travel) signifies opportunities for progress in one's life. May indicate a change in direction or goal destination.

Travel Documentation

Passport implies ready to move on.

Boarding pass signifies one's right to make a particular journey or be active in a specific issue/relationship.
Card (green) See green card.
Green card gives reassurance regarding one's current project or course of effort.
Passport illustrates one's rite of passage; a readiness for advancement.
Traveler's checks represent the personal assets (talents) on which one can draw while making life's journey.
Travelogue refers to research into different life courses.
Visa stands for one's right-of-passage; preparedness to proceed, yet only for a specified span of time.

Passenger Craft

Cabin class represents middle-of-the-road; an average rating.
Cabin cruiser alludes to a spiritual cruising along one's spiritual path; a lack of spiritual seriousness.
Cruise (luxury trip) cautions against displaying spiritual affectations.
Cruiser (cabin) characterizes a spiritual journey lacking seriousness.
Liner (ocean) See cruise.
Steerage (class) points to the existence of a less costly way to make a spiritual journey.
Titanic (ship) emphasizes spiritual superiority. Folks claimed it was "the ship even God couldn't sink."

The Flight

Airborne refers to the act of thinking.
Air cargo symbolizes the transporting of one individual's thoughts to another; the burden of communicating something.
Air freight means excessive thought, bulk mental weight.
Air lane symbolizes one's lack of thought diversity and individuality; a thought pattern that remains within a singular, rigid pathway.
Airspace denotes the need to make time to think; contemplation.
Air speed refers to the rate of thought and how ideas are processed.
Collision course warns of a destructive relationship or dangerous perspective, emotional basis, or path.
Crash-landing represents a sudden and unexpected conclusion to something that may or may not end up in total devastation.
Flight (airline) exemplifies a departure from the norm.
Flight bag signifies a planned departure from the norm.
Flight plan stands for a person's intended course or plan of action.
Hard landing is representative of a difficult ending; hard work applied to a conclusion or closure.
International flight represents extended thinking; long-range thought.
Lap belt See safety belt.
Leg room stands for a need for space. Alludes to a pressure or stressed state.
Long haul is a reference to determination.
Midair pertains to an unfinished aspect. It is a reference to something hanging in limbo.
Red-eye (night travel time) refers to taking advantage of less desirable aspects of an opportunity.
Safety belt indicates an opportunity to protect oneself from a possible danger or harmful situation.
Soft landing symbolizes a gentle closure to an issue.
Touchdown alludes to being grounded; grasping a fact; gaining understanding.

see also
• Identity *p. 130*
• Flying Sports *p. 212*

Aircraft Anatomy

Altimeter comes to the dreamer to warn against his or her changing emotions. May indicate a manic-depressive or a self-image that is growing loftier.
Automatic pilot cautions against letting others lead your way or make your decisions.
Black box (flight recorder) indicates a record of events; the recording of one's life; karmic record.
Cargo hold refers to a storage of cherished life aspects. This symbol may point out memories or current elements in one's life.
Cockpit is generally representative of mental or emotional control.
Ejection seat implies the preparedness of planning with precautionary measures in place. May suggest the need to remove oneself from a situation or relationship as quickly as possible.
Flight recorder See black box.
Fuselage most often symbolizes an individual's capacity for understanding new concepts. Recall the size and condition of the fuselage in the dream.
Landing gear signifies a grounding source. Recall if the gear was down or up. Broken? One wheel down and one stuck?
Navigation (instrumentation) is usually a reference to the personal methods or tools we each use to make our way in life. These usually refer to the use of awareness, intellect, inner drive, reflection on lessons gained from hindsight, and so on.
Undercarriage denotes a supportive or foundational element that appears in the dreamer's everyday life.

Aircraft

Aircraft See airplane.
Airliner See airplane.
Airplane is generally representative of the ideals and attitudes that one holds. It may also be a reference to belief systems.
Air taxi (commuter plane) signifies short-term ideas that are quickly exchanged for others.
Biplane implies the tendency to double-check one's thoughts; a habit of caring about the possibility of wrong thinking.
Chopper (aircraft) See helicopter.
Chute See parachute.
Commuter plane See air taxi.
Dirigible (balloon) comes to the dreamer as a revelation of unstable or irrational thinking in his/her life.
Floatplane is generally representative of vacillating thought patterns.
Glider (plane) implies a lack of mental focus.
Glider (swing) suggests a time of contemplation; restful thought times. In a few instances, a glider may warn against self-generated unawareness.
Harrier (plane) See helicopter.
Helicopter reveals a vacillating mental state; indecision.
Jet (high-velocity) applies to a strong force; highly motivated, quick action taken.
Jetliner corresponds with spiritual advancement, the speed of same.
Lightplane represents cursory thoughts applied to an issue.
Monoplane refers to assurance and fortitude.
Parachute reveals psychological rationalizations. Recall the condition and color of the dream parachute. How did it work?
Plane pertains to quality and depth of thoughts. Recall condition, color, speed, etc.
Seaplane symbolizes spiritual thoughts; time spent contemplating spiritual issues.
Twin-engine represents balanced efforts. Recall if both were working properly.
Ultralight (airplane) suggests gentle thoughts. It may also refer to kindness.

Flying & Air Travel

Aerodynamic (shape) is generally representative of streamlined thought.
Afterburner denotes more physical or mental energy is required in order to avoid quitting before something has been accomplished. It signifies the need for an extra boost in a specific area of the dreamer's everyday life.
Air cushion is representative of a time for deep thinking; a time to postpone a decision for the purpose of giving more thought to the issue. It may also refer to the need for the individual to reserve making a conclusion.
Airfare stands for the personal cost of thinking a certain way, following a specific philosophy.
Airworthy means worthy ideas or thoughts.
Altitude sickness is generally symbolic of a high attitude, stance, or position that isn't yet deserved. It may refer to aloofness or haughtiness. It can also refer to concepts one isn't ready to understand or accept.
Chock defines an aspect that prevents one from either backsliding or rushing headlong.
Contrail is representative of a spiritual effect generated by positive perspectives or attitudes.
Flight simulator represents a sharpening of wit and reaction responses to sudden events; an attempt to be prepared for the unexpected.
Frequent flier applies to one who routinely has thoughts that are a departure from the norm; high inquisitiveness.
Ground crew represents one's emotional support group.
Jet lag advises of a need to slow down for the purpose of catching up.
Jet stream defines popular beliefs or ideas; generally accepted and followed beliefs.
Loading zone signifies a point in one's life when extra responsibilities become a priority.
Passenger portrays movement; actively applying efforts to advance along one's path.
Vapor trail See contrail.

Paths & Walkways

Boardwalk cautions against a voluntary separation from one's spiritual aspects.
Bridle path relates to a controlled life path; a path that is traveled at an easy pace.
Crossing (street) indicates an altered direction or course.
Crosswalk defines the safest route to take in life.
Footpath represents one's unique life path that, when walked, presents specialized opportunities for one's particular advancement.
Guidepost marks one's way.
Lane (country) connotes a pleasant phase of one's life journey.
Macadam See pavement.
Pavement implies a separation from one's natural bond with earth and inherent natural ability; a barrier preventing sensitivity.
Path signifies a person's individual road or direction.
Promenade pertains to a stage where a leisure attitude will serve best; a time for acceptance through neutrality.

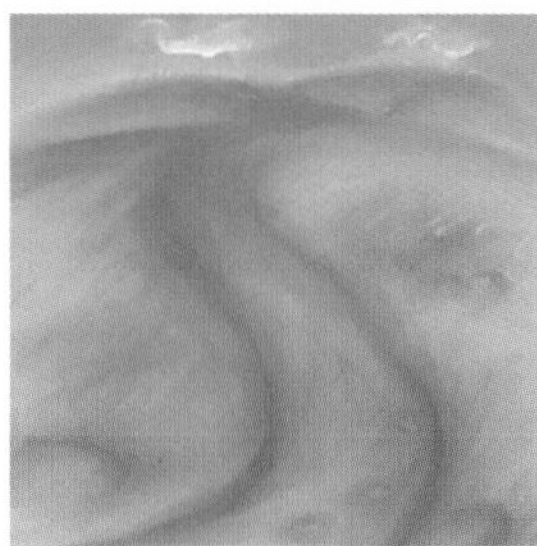
Path refers to the way ahead in life.

Sidewalk relates to directed paths to follow. Implies a need to make one's own course. Recall condition of the dream sidewalk. New? Cracked? Overgrown with weeds?
Slate (walkway) refers to a hard, difficult path.
Stile applies to an aid to advancement; also a way to overcome indecision (sitting on the fence).
Subway stands for an alternate course of action; clever evasiveness; a less obvious manner of getting from point A to point B.
Trail (path) indicates an individual's unique direction or course.

Working Vehicles

Bookmobile connotes the learning of healing methods; physiological research; the reading of medical books.
Front-end loader alludes to a need for intensive clarification. Surrounding dreamscape details will clarify this.
Lightship emphasizes a life aspect that serves to warn one away from destructive or grossly misleading spiritual ideas.
Shrimp boat corresponds with a desire to seek and obtain spiritual understanding.
Snowblower pertains to an effort to rid oneself and one's surroundings of spiritual elements and/or influences.
Snow thrower See snowblower.
Steam shovel pertains to spiritual work.
Threshing machine alludes to getting down to basics.

Trains

Bullet train implies high-speed travel. Advises an individual to slow down to absorb that which is presented along the way.
Coal train See train (coal).
Cog railway denotes that which provides movement for specific aspects in one's life.
Express (travel conveyance) usually indicates an urgent need to get somewhere; to not procrastinate any longer.
Freight train cautions of the negativity and detriment of carrying the excessive beliefs or perspectives of others instead of being more of an independent life traveler.
Locomotive See train.
Monorail is a reference to one-mindedness; an inability or refusal to veer from one's course. This is usually a negative dream symbol, for there are many times one needs to take a sidetracking detour to learn an important life lesson.
Narrow gauge (railway) portrays a straight and very narrow path. This isn't necessarily a positive dreamscape fragment to manifest, for few true paths follow such a set course as a railway because there's no allotment for necessary detours.
Passenger train See train (passenger).
Rail See train.
Train warns against following closely behind another who is following a popular tried-and-true course in regard to being safe and well worn.
Train (coal) refers to pulling a line of negative aspects or issues behind one; being burdened with multiple negatives.
Train (freight) See freight train.
Train (passenger) reveals a journey that is not unique to the individual, one denoting a follower who seeks safety in numbers or is fearful of expressing individuality.
Underground railroad is usually representative of a secretive endeavor and its manner of operation.

Coal train represents the emotional baggage one carries around.

see also
• Swimming & Water Sports *p. 210*
• Seaborne Weapons *p. 354*

Railways & Rail Travel

Boxcar refers to extra aspects one carries around in life that are heavily weighted; negative memories; bad feelings retained.
Caboose means a finalization; the end of something.
Cattle guard connotes the self-created limits and barriers an individual devises to prevent decision-making or exercising individuality.
Chunnel (English Channel tunnel) signifies a diversionary tactic utilized to get around spiritual issues.
Club car pertains to an individual's expectation for preferential treatment.
Cowcatcher illustrates an attempt to clear one's way as one's path is traveled.
Derailment pertains to going offtrack in life. This may point to an attitude or a recent perceptual leaning regarding an issue.
Dining car corresponds with a need to attend to inner nourishment while attending to one's life journey; a reminder to not be so centered on purpose that energizing aspects are ignored.
Flatcar (train) advises of the danger of taking on philosophical perspectives of others that are narrow-minded or one-track.
Handcar cautions against fanaticism related to following another's life or spiritual path.
Pullman (railcar) can have two meanings; the dreamer will recognize which. One advises of a need to rest along one's journey, to take the time to reenergize oneself and absorb new information. The second warns against sleeping while taking a new path and thus missing important elements.
Railroad constitutes a plan or decision that has been forced into an expedited state without time given to adequate thought. This would be a plan or decision without any options for alternate courses factored in.
Railroad crossing See train (crossing).

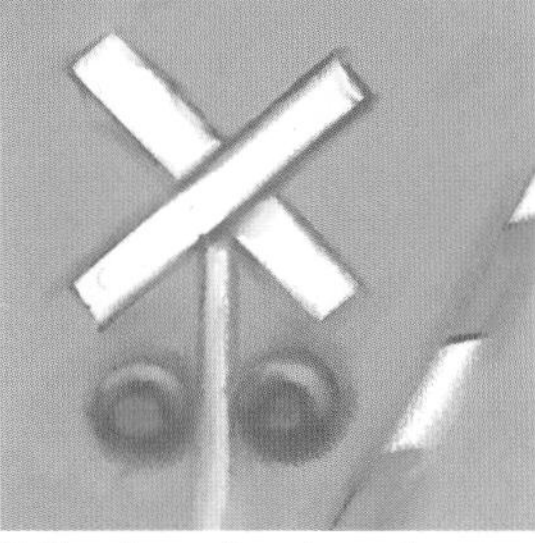
Railroad crossing shows chances.

Railroad lantern refers to markers that light the way along one's chosen path.
Roundhouse suggests a change in one's life course; path options.
Short line reveals a phase of one's path or life that won't be lengthy.
Siding (train track) stands for something that's been set aside for the moment; a temporary postponement.
Sleeper car (train) See pullman (railcar).
Spur track cautions against allowing oneself to get sidetracked.
Standing room may portray a popular concept or attitude, or this element may represent an advisement to pursue another course in life.
Third rail refers to the source of energy/power. This suggests that although certain things in life may appear identical, some carry more hidden weight and power than others.
Track (train) warns against a rigid path with no capability for diversion or alteration.
Train (crossing) suggests opportunities to avoid the well-worn paths in life. Also may come to advise of the wisdom of stopping to let negatives pass by through the use of patience and acceptance.
Train whistle comes as a message that warns against separating oneself from others. Reminds of humanitarian responsibility.
Tunnel connotes an alternative route or a way to discovery.
Way station stands for a stopping point or meaningful situation an individual should experience.

Sailing Craft

Catamaran portrays spiritual freedom; an unencumbered spiritual journey.
Clipper See ship.
Dinghy applies to small spiritual securities; spiritual comforts one falls back on in life.
Galleon connotes an esoteric spiritual journey.
Galley (large rowboat) warns of a spiritual journey propelled by others rather than self.
Mayflower (ship) stands for opportunities and how one takes advantage of them. This symbol is a type of advisement to use opportunities in positive ways. Opportunities can soon turn against one if they're used in any kind of negative manner.
Sailboat relates to a spiritual direction led by destiny.
Ship signifies a method or vehicle that facilitates a spiritual search.
Sloop See sailboat.
Yacht is a sign of spiritual arrogance; a tendency to buy one's spiritual attainment.

Warships

Aircraft carrier symbolizes a caution for the dreamer to cease letting one's thoughts and opinions ride on those of others.
Battle cruiser denotes an ability to easily maneuver through spiritual conflict.
Battleship stands for a well-armed but cumbersome approach to a spiritual conflict.
Frigate (ship) warns of a personal spiritual conflict within self.
Minesweeper stands for heightened awareness; an inner knowing.
Mothership represents a source of spirituality; one's sense of spiritual home.
Troop carrier represents a suggestion to shift one's defensive measures to another target.
U-boat warns of a negative spiritual element in one's life.
Warship signifies a spiritual altercation; readying to defend one's beliefs.

Ships & Boats

Bull boat is a reference to the avoidance of spiritual concepts due to primitive or outdated attitudes.
Coast Guard cutter denotes a life aspect that provides spiritual emergency help.
Flatboat cautions against carrying too heavy a spiritual load; to spread out conceptual spiritual intake over time.
Hovercraft usually represents an out-of-body experience.
Hydroplane See seaplane.
Iceboat suggests a sailing over one's frozen spirituality; ignoring the fact that one should be integrating spirituality in one's daily behavior.
Icebreaker (ship) warns one to break up the spiritual aspects that have been frozen before further path progression can be accomplished.

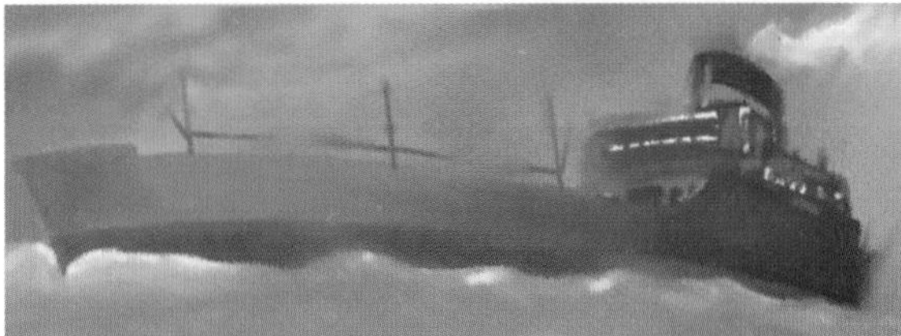

Supertanker advises one to travel light when seeking spiritual knowledge.

Lifeboat means something that spiritually rescues or saves.
Life raft implies a spiritual belief that keeps one afloat.
Mackinaw (boat) pertains to a fresh spiritual search.
Paddleboat (paddle wheel) is an element that serves as a spiritual impetus.
Portage defines a burden of some type, usually effort expended to persevere while taking a spiritual concept over some rough ground to end up in calmer spiritual waters.
Riverboat denotes indecision regarding one's direction or leaning in respect to spirituality versus materialism.
Speedboat warns against speeding in a spiritual search.
Steamboat represents a spiritual search generated by pure spiritual motivations.
Steamship is generally representative of a spiritual journey that is motivated or energized by spiritual elements such as ideals, inspiration, or a desire for enlightenment.
Supertanker warns against carrying excess burdens or elements while traversing one's spiritual course.
Swamp boat defines an effort to overcome spiritual confusion.
Towboat defines spiritual help; an uplifting or comforting concept.
Trawler warns of a belief that drags on one's spirituality.
Tugboat See towboat.
Whaleboat symbolizes that which destroys goodness.
Whaler See whaleboat.

Ship's Anatomy

Berth (sleeping) refers to taking the time to rest while on a path's journey.
Bilge pump refers to watchfulness for skewed spiritual ideas; a readiness to maintain a pureness in spiritual beliefs.
Bow (boat) denotes the leading aspect of one's spiritual search; the forerunner of such a path.
Bulkhead symbolizes an aspect in life that serves as one's main support system.
Deck (boat) connotes deeper spiritual perspectives.
Depth finder indicates the depth of one's spirituality.
Depth sounder See depth finder.
Figurehead represents strength to go forward, regarding a spiritual path or spiritually independent thought.
Helm represents control.
Hold (of ship) See cargo hold.
Hull (ship) refers to our spiritual foundations that keep us afloat.
Keel signifies the foundational and motivational strength of one's personal spiritual search.
Load limit/line usually refers to the amount of stress or work one can take on.
Masthead reveals a name or purpose. This is a personal message for the dreamer.
Porthole correlates to a spiritual perception, usually a narrow view. Recall if the porthole was clear or cloudy.
Promenade deck indicates a time for a spiritual pause; introspection.
Propeller signifies forces that have the ability to propel you along your intended path and bring you into a higher level of advancement.
Prow (of boat) suggests spiritual priorities; where one is spiritually headed.
Rigging typifies supporting elements for a specific aspect in one's life.
Rudder represents the direction and quality of spiritual course.
Sleeping berth See berth (sleeping).
Stateroom cautions against the tendency to compartmentalize spiritual truths.
Sundeck typifies a desire to remain connected with your personal spirituality while on your spiritual journey.
Superstructure refers to any idea, perception, plan, or belief developed far beyond its basic elements.
Waterline signifies one's level of spirituality. Recall if the line was low or at peak level.

Freight Craft

Barge symbolizes a spiritually lethargic rate of progress; spiritual overburden.
Freight denotes mental or psychological baggage that we carry around with us.
Freighter pertains to one's personal spiritual baggage.
Keelboat warns against the carrying of excess spiritual baggage.
Oil tanker represents a method of protecting one's spirituality from being contaminated by dangerously negative elements.

see also
• The Sea *p. 36*
• Marine & Naval *p. 255*

Nautical Travel

Bon voyage stands for embarking on a spiritual journey that many support.
Buoy (channel marker) is a directional marker for one's spiritual path.
Canal denotes spiritual connections; spirituality running through one's life.
Captain's log signifies a recording of events. This may come as a suggestion to keep a daily journal.
Channel locks refer to an aspect that contains several opportunities or useable options.
Channel marker comes as a symbol that keeps one within the bounds of the right spiritual direction or from straying from one's spiritual path.
Circumnavigate advises one of the need to go around something.
Course (route) typifies a visual of one's personal path. This most often refers to that which one is headed for.
Distress signal is always a call for help. The dreamer may be calling for this help or one's higher self may be attempting to awaken the dreamer to this end.
Foghorn is always a spiritual warning. Surrounding details should clarify this.
High seas constitute higher spiritual concepts; a place in one's path where one is ready to spiritually progress.
Landfall represents the end of one's spiritual searching and the beginning of the related practical application.
Lock (water) signifies an adjustment to spiritual level.
Northwest passage signifies guidance for one's spiritual search. Surrounding dreamscape details will clarify.
Sea-lane stands for a well used spiritual path. This is usually a warning against following another's belief system rather than sensing one's own.
Sea legs suggests spiritual comfort; feeling at home with one's personal spiritual beliefs.
Towpath connotes a helpful path or course.
Trade route stands for a method of interacting with others.

Rowboats

Boat represents a spiritual path and its quality.
Canoe symbolizes a well-paced and tranquil method of traveling one's spiritual path.
Gondola (boat) cautions of a lack of spiritual seriousness.
Kayak connotes a highly personal spiritual path.
Pirogue See canoe.
Punt corresponds with a gentle yet cautious spiritual journey.
Raft represents spiritual ingenuity as associated with one's path of enlightenment.
Rowboat is a vehicle for spiritual self-discovery.
Skiff See boat.

Docking

Berth (anchorage) indicates a comfortable spiritual position.
Disembark portrays a grounded condition or state.
Dry dock suggests a temporary rest from one's spiritual search or learning. This symbol indicates an overload or a need to absorb more.
Harbor pertains to a spiritual comfort; a spiritually safe place to be; a secure spiritual belief system.
Harbor lights represent the lights of inspiration, insights.
Hawser represents a life aspect that keeps one spiritually bound to a specific belief system; spiritual constriction.
Port See seaport.
Port of call advises of a need to reexamine one's spiritual beliefs or humanitarian efforts. May exemplify the various advances made while making one's life journey.
Port of entry is a dreamscape symbol that defines a right move while entering a new phase in life. Underscores the right direction.
Safe harbor stands for an unthreatening attitude or situation.
Seaport corresponds to a spiritual transition.

Hawser refers to a spiritual tie.

Nautical Miscellany

Ballast warns of a need to unload. This means one is carrying excessive emotional, mental, or spiritual weight.
Bilge suggests a personal, spiritual transitional stage.
Bilge water means negative or skewed spiritual concepts that need to be pumped out.
Boat lift means spiritual compassion; spiritual rescue.
Cargo suggests aspects one views as personally important.
Convoy indicates strong support; strength in numbers.
Deck chair alludes to acceptance of improved perspectives.
Headroom pertains to time and space to think.
List (ship movement) denotes spiritual imbalance.
Maiden voyage signifies the initial practice of a new spiritual belief.
Mainstay symbolizes a main supporting facet; an anchoring idea or quality.
Outboard motor relates to spiritual motivational factors.
Overboard warns of spiritual impulsiveness.
Paddle wheel represents spiritual motivation.
Rudderless warns of a lack of spiritual direction.
Sail alludes to an attitude of acceptance.
Shipment relates to a forthcoming aspect one is awaiting.
Sluice pertains to the directing of spiritual behavior through one's daily life.
Steamer trunk stands for the spiritual tools and elements we carry with us.
Towline represents assistance.
Wreck (boat) corresponds to spiritual damage.

Chapter 19

Buildings & Architecture

Any building that is a predominant feature in a dreamscape scene carries considerable weight toward a more defined interpretation. Likewise, architectural style serves as a key that fine-tunes a building's representation and points to a key character trait.

Design

Tudor characterizes a solid, well-grounded personality.

A-frame (house design) symbolizes one's lifestyle striving to obtain spiritual alignment.
Art deco (pattern/style) symbolizes a nonconformist or nonconforming attitude, idea, or behavior.
Art nouveau (decor/pattern) represents a flowing expression of individuality; the ease with which one displays one's uniqueness.
Baroque (decor style) usually points to an extravagant personality.
Cape Cod (architecture) represents a settled/comfortable feeling in regard to an individual's spirituality.
Contemporary (architecture/decor) refers to a bland personality with no display of personalized character.
Cotswold (architecture) represents a laid-back personality, one that reflects level-headedness and quiet logic.
Gothic (attitude/style) is one's affinity for the unexplained.
Ranch (house style) relates to efficiency; keeping the aspects of one's life together instead of scattering them.
Rococo (ornate style) illustrates self-aggrandizement; low self-esteem evidenced by giving off an aura of power.
Saltbox (architecture) represents a veneer of simplicity.
Straw bale house stands for a well-insulated home life. This means that an individual desires to keep home a place of soothing respite, separate from the hectic pace and attitudes of the outside workaday world.
Stucco refers to a lasting finish on something.
Tiered (construction/design) signifies various ascending levels to an issue.
Tudor (architecture style) represents strong, well-built foundations/defenses.
Ultramodern (style) is a reference to a lack of cluttering elements; sleek and simple basics.
Victorian (style) most often represents delicate sensitivities. May indicate/advise of a need to toughen up.

Buildings

Abode See house.
Arcade alludes to games people play.
Breezeway denotes thoughts that connect main ideas to form more complex concepts; connective elements.
Building (act of) depicts the act of creating; active efforts.
Buildings See specific type.
Bunker identifies one's lack of faith and/or self-confidence; a fear of one's life path.
Bunkhouse typifies the nature of one's casual relationships; a relationship that will have a short life span.
Cabana symbolizes a need for temporary shelter or to remove oneself from heated situations.
Cabin denotes a life that is aligned with nature; an inner connection or inherent bond with nature.
Castle exemplifies one's perspective that lacks reality or clear vision.
Cell (enclosure) represents one's quantitative quality of experience. Recall how the cell was decorated.
Citadel symbolizes the high point of one's life; the goal or purpose for which one strives.
Closed suggests an attempt to approach a path or obtain knowledge for which one is not yet prepared to absorb.
Depot reflects a directional or course change.
Garrison house (architecture) signifies a top-heavy way of thinking; one's intellect outweighs the emotions.
Gatehouse is usually representative of an individual's right to experience an event.
Grange illustrates an interest in nurturing the talents of others.
High-density stands for a concentrated aspect. This will be different for each dreamer as it relates to individualized associations.
High-rise connotes some multilevel aspects to something in the dreamer's life. The surrounding dreamscape details usually help to clarify this for the individual dreamer.
Keep See tower.
Palace See castle.
Palazzo See castle.
Penthouse is a reference to an attitude of being above others.
Quonset (hut) reflects a temporary situation.
Ruins (archeological) may literally infer a ruination of some type or it may indicate a personal revelation, depending on the surrounding dreamscape elements. Ruins frequently denote deep wisdom or inspiration.
Skyscraper denotes higher thought used throughout one's daily life.
Tower exemplifies the superconscious aspect of the mind where spiritual talents and gifts await to be awakened and utilized.
Turret is generally a reference to hidden psychological elements.
Warehouse exemplifies storage. May refer to one's memory.
Watchtower See lookout.
Windmill comes to the dreamer as a caution against mental laziness. Indicates a lack of original thought.

see also
• Waterscapes *p. 71*
• Types of Home *p. 398*

Housing

Apartment indicates a personal need to be around others.
Bungalow See cottage.
Chalet (architecture) pertains to a gentle personality; homey lifestyle.
Chateau refers to extravagant life goals.
Condominium illustrates self-confidence and independence realized through the support of others.
Cookie-cutter (housing) indicates a desire to surround oneself with like-minded people who share your perspective and attitudes.
Cooperative (housing ownership) signifies a responsibility shared by others.
Cottage signifies acceptance of self; an individual who is comfortable with just meeting basic needs.
Efficiency apartment emphasizes a prioritized personality.
Farmhouse pertains to home and family life. The condition of this dreamscape house will be revealing.
Flat (living quarters) See apartment.
Fleabag (lodging) cautions against misplaced trust.
Flophouse See fleabag.
Fourplex (housing) refers to the three people closest to the dreamer.
Group home is generally suggestive of the advisability of working closely with others; perhaps success is dependent on doing so.
House stands for the mind. See specific types for additional information.
Hovel suggests poor life foundations. It can refer to poor ethical training.
Lodge refers to a safe haven.
Manor/mansion emphasizes a pretentious personality.
Manufactured home See mobile home.
Mobile home represents a temporary position on one's life path; good chance of relocation or moving forward.
Rental (dwelling) reflects a temporary situation.
Rooming house relates to a chance for self-expression.
Row house represents a shoulder-to-shoulder relationship; close associations.
Seasonal dwelling represents a dual nature. May also signify the reaping of benefits from more than one aspect.
Second home See vacation home.
Split-level (house) warns of an internal conflict.
Tenement suggests an unsatisfactory situation.
Tract house refers to one's tendency/preference for blending in with the crowd; a fear or dislike for standing out by expressing one's own uniqueness/individuality. One of numerous houses of similar or complementary design constructed on a tract of land.
Trailer (house type) See mobile home.
Vacation home indicates a desire to maintain one's unique homelike elements in one's ideal getaway vacation/leisure location; cherishing one's homelife and the fact that one takes great comfort in it.
Walk-up represents deeper appreciation for extra efforts expended.

Open Spaces

Concourse alludes to a passing stage or life situation.
Courtyard represents temporary pauses or times of relaxation.
Patio is open-mindedness.
Paving relates to a desire for an easy life.
Piazza See public square; veranda.
Plaza connotes a wide area. This dreamscape symbol informs the dreamer that she/he currently has a lot of room to accomplish something.

Water-Related Buildings

Aqueduct represents a specific spiritual course.
Boathouse corresponds with a spiritual home; the living of spiritual beliefs.
Flood wall portrays personal safeguards that shield one from too much information; an awareness of one's intellectual capabilities.
Houseboat symbolizes a spiritual home atmosphere.
Icehouse corresponds with personality frigidity stemming from the subconscious. These need to be thawed.
Jetty See pier.
Lighthouse connotes spiritual guidance through wisdom.
Pier denotes spiritual interest.
Pilothouse See wheelhouse.
Springhouse pertains to the use of one's spiritual aspects to preserve the secular aspects of life in peak condition.
Tide mill stands for productive behavior flowing from one's spirituality.
Water mill symbolizes the fact that spiritual aspects are the driving force in one's life.
Water tower implies the presence of spiritual reserves.
Water wheel See water mill.
Wharf See pier.
Wheelhouse stands for the singular control one has over spiritual direction.

Water mill represents immaterial factors as the main source of motivation.

Site & Access

Alley offers another way in or out.

Abutment advises the need to touch or get close.

Access connotes the way to or from something.

Address represents an important place. This can signify the pinpointing of a problem or source of answers.

Adjoining properties stand for a connection or association.

Alley means the back way in or out of a situation; another path giving entry or escape.

Beachfront (property) indicates an eye toward spirituality and the desire to live close to one's beliefs. This illustrates a spiritual priority.

Building site symbolizes the groundwork for a new plan.

Built-up signifies development. May be implying one's boastfulness or perhaps egotistical nature.

Construction site signifies a time of building; constructive advancements.

Entranceway represents choices. We all have a choice whether or not to pass through any entrance.

Frontage road See service road.

Residential (setting) depicts a specific background character or atmosphere to one's lifestyle or home life.

Setback (from property line) is usually representative of a limit or boundary line marking the extent one can build on; a point to which one can take plans or action.

Skid row represents a situation or issue in which one has become derelict.

Slum See skid row.

Urban renewal stands for rejuvenation.

Urban sprawl illustrates a loss of control; the ease with which something gets away from the dreamer.

Construction Materials

Anchor bolt (structural) denotes a prevention of foundational movement; surety of foundational premises or beliefs.

Angle iron refers to support required.

Barn wood represents a well-weathered and experienced element.

Baseboard alludes to finished ideas that conclude previous lines of thought and bring them together.

Bear claw (actual or design) stands for a desire to maintain control of one's life.

Board and batten (construction) represents sturdy character foundations.

Brick signifies life's building blocks; one's personal foundational aspects that should be solid and strong.

Brownstone commends one's tendency to give others space; an acceptance of another's totality.

Cement means unresolved or inconclusive aspects in one's life and advises to get these things settled; a need to finalize something.

Cinder block symbolizes lighter foundational elements that are just as effective as heavier ones.

Clapboard implies overlapping of issues in one's life. This could suggest a need to separate out different aspects.

Clear lumber refers to building material without any flaws. This, of course, equates to a plan, idea, or choice of path progression.

Column See pile (post).

Common wall refers to a shared idea/philosophy, yet each person having her/his own unique perspectives of it.

Concrete See cement.

Drywall symbolizes hidden personality aspects.

Face brick suggests a show of strength that may be insincere.

Fiberboard represents the coming together of diverse aspects for the purpose of blending into a new creation; the result of utilizing one's talents and knowledge.

Plaster conceals one's errors.

Fieldstone connotes that which provides building aspects as opportunities are offered and accepted.

Finishing nail is a concealed final touch to something.

Flagstone denotes specific life aspects that serve to pave one's way along one's path.

Glass block (construction material) points to a clouded view of something.

Masonry reflects solid work; strong foundations.

Mortar See cement.

Pane (glass) applies to a separation of self from a life element.

Plaster indicates a life aspect that has the ability to smooth out or cover one's mistakes.

Plasterboard connotes an attempt or chance at renewal.

Plywood connotes an aspect that has multiple uses and resulting benefits.

Premix alludes to having all the necessary elements (ingredients) to develop or achieve a goal.

Ready-mix See premix.

Sheetrock See drywall.

Shim (thin material used to fill in spaces) reflects a temporary solution; a stopgap move.

Stone wall implies delaying tactics.

Stonework See masonry.

Tarpaper is representative of a personal spiritual defensive method.

Tongue and groove stands for ideas or plans that fit well together.

Wire glass refers to perception reinforced by strong opinions.

see also
• World Heritage Sites *p. 374*
• Tools *p. 444*

Construction

Acoustical (material) stands for an attempt to focus on every related aspect of an issue; a blocking out of unrelated elements.
Backfill signifies a life element that can fill a void in life.
Block and tackle stands for aspects that allow us to overcome obstacles in life.
Cement mixer means that an aspect in life needing a resolution or conclusion will manifest in the dreamer's life.
Demolition denotes the total destruction of something. What was being demolished? Who was doing it?
Digging (act of) denotes a search; a deeper search. May also point to the act of trying to hide something depending on whether something was being put into the ground or being taken out.
Dry rot warns of the danger of prolonging a negative period in one's life. Motivation is urged for the purpose of expunging the negative that's spreading.
Fill dirt See backfill.
Groundwork denotes preliminary preparations. This may point to an information-gathering stage.
Jerry-built alludes to a lack of integrity. In some cases it may indicate an attempt to work with whatever resources an individual has.
Land bank refers to an opportunity to obtain the foundational element on which to build.
Ledge signifies a precarious situation or relationship.
Low-density connotes conceptual simplicity.
Overbuilt is an indication of extravagance.
Pile driver indicates a need to express, impress, or make assurances. Something in your life needs reinforcement.
Pre-built suggests partially completed elements; a course of action that already has several aspects in place.
Project (building) is a lack of resources and/or motivation.
Rebuilding See reconstruction.
Reconstruction denotes the analysis of a situation; taking a second look at something and the consideration of redeeming its value.
Scaffold relates to safeguards we create to protect us from hurtful emotional events.
Seismic load (construction) points to the wisdom of making a plan by factoring in safeguards against the possibility of a tremor/shaking future event.
Settling cracks (in building) is the seasoning of an idea.
Soundproofing See acoustical (material).
Stick-built (construction) refers to a commonly accepted way to do something.
Waterproof is spiritual apathy.
Weatherproof See waterproof.
Weather-stripping (draft excluder) symbolizes one's attempt to maintain emotional calm; to avoid difficulties.
Weep holes (construction) stand for tempered sorrow or grief. This is a good symbol indicating one's tendency to release pent-up emotions so that stress or pressure doesn't build up.
Wrecking ball refers to a purposeful destructive force or element used to bring about a new beginning; clearing out the old (perhaps bad attitudes) to make way for a fresh start.

Planning

Bottom-up stands for something begun by the common folk. This equates to a grassroots movement or new attitude.
Building code represents limits/perimeters one sets for an intended plan.
Building permit denotes a final decision/verification to go ahead with a new plan.
Completion date (construction) stands for the time allotted for the attainment of a goal. Also see closing date, deadline.
Conservation easement See easement (conservation).
Construction loan symbolizes the aid of someone who can help another obtain the necessary tools to begin a new path or set an idea in motion.
Construction paper illustrates a need to formulate a plan of agreement to build on.
Inspection objection reveals a flaw in a plan or idea.
Revitalization project refers to the strong possibility of giving new life to an old issue, relationship, or situation.
Shop drawings refer to workable plans.

Church Architecture

Aisle represents a passageway; a way through something thought to be impassable.
Apse connotes the need to make more time for meditation and/or contemplation.
Choir loft depicts spiritual joy.
Church refers to a spiritual connection and its quality.
Cloister is the ability to obtain inner tranquility through one's spiritual beliefs. May also come as suggestion to get out there and make a difference.
Crypt connotes hidden aspects.
Kirk See church.
Spire See steeple.
Steeple suggests a high point to an issue or event.
Vestry denotes a segregation of one's spiritual beliefs from daily life.

International Buildings

Adobe means a down-to-earth attitude or relationship. It may also point to the dreamer's most comfortable position on something.
Hacienda portrays a relaxed lifestyle where individuals are afforded personal space and privacy.
Hogan signifies a natural way of living; simplicity of life.
Igloo constitutes a cold home life; emotionally unexpressive.
Kiva illustrates one's manner of meditating. Recall condition and occupancy to see if this is a good message or not.
Longhouse portrays an accommodating nature; acceptance of others.
Shoji (paper partition) typifies a thin veneer to inner self.

Public & Commercial Buildings

Drive-in See fast food.

Executive (suite/office) denotes place of seniority or expertise.

Extended care (facility) points out the fact that an issue isn't quite concluded yet; a bit more attention is required.

Federal buildings represent major issues in one's life. The symbolic interpretation will hinge on which type of federal building was shown.

Guesthouse represents a personal receptivity to others.

Home center (store) suggests attention to oneself is needed; physical repair (of oneself) is advised.

Motel alludes to some form of transitional phase in one's life.

Motor court See motel.

Outlet (store) stands for possibilities.

Accessory Buildings

Accessory building stands for the important supportive and related elements to an issue. See barn, garage.

Barn connotes life aspects that one shelters from others or keeps protected.

Belvedere See gazebo.

Conservatory represents a recognition of certain life benefits and efforts spent on preserving/nurturing them.

Gazebo is representative of a place or time of respite. It may also indicate that the dreamer should take a needed rest.

Glass house reminds us that we are always being observed.

Greenhouse reveals one's current state of spirituality. Recall what condition the greenhouse was in. Was it full of bountiful and healthy botanicals? Empty? Have wilted plants?

Kiosk reveals important information specific for each dreamer.

Lean-to See shed.

Outbuildings See accessory buildings.

Outhouse illustrates a need to rid self of wasteful or unessential elements in one's life.

Shack (dwelling) exemplifies a personal disinterest in material possessions.

Shanty See shack.

Shed typifies resource reserves; stored energy or inner strength.

Snowshed (built over a road or railway to protect from snow) denotes protective measures along one's path that guard against being overwhelmed or suffocated by unexpected spiritual inundations.

Stable (barn) reveals an individual's attitude toward her/his personal inherent abilities. Recall the stable's condition.

Summerhouse See gazebo.

Sunporch refers to a chance to let the light in; a matter of choice whether or not an individual sees the light.

Tree house relates to living one's spiritual beliefs through the use of inherent talents and gifts.

Veranda represents an opportunity to obtain fresh ideas.

Woodshed applies to thorough planning.

Wraparound deck signifies complete openness.

Construction Features

Air vent is usually a reference to a venting of thoughts and attitudes. It may also be indicative of a reluctance to voice opinions that should be aired. It could come to the dreamer as an advisement for greater assertiveness.

Arch support refers to perseverance, inner strength to keep going forward.

Base refers to foundational elements or a secure position.

Beam (timber) indicates inner strength; a supportive ability.

Bearing wall stands for a main supportive element.

Carvings (fine detail work) stand for fine details to which one needs to give attention.

Clear span (construction) points to something that needs no support; an aspect that can easily and safely stand on its own.

Framework (construction) denotes one's preparations for beginning a new project.

Girder portrays main support; a life aspect that serves as one's main source of strength.

I-beam stands for one's main source of support.

Molding (carpentry) signifies finishing touches.

Paneling signifies an enhancement of some type; an attempt to improve surrounding conditions.

Partition exemplifies a separating or disassociative attitude. May point out a need to keep issues separate from each other.

Pile (post) constitutes a supportive aspect.

Pillar (post) See pile (post).

Rafter (construction) denotes a supporting element in a person's life.

Rebar (a steel bar in reinforced concrete) refers to a strong, supportive reinforcement.

Resurface See paving.

Scrollwork indicates attention given to detail.

Stringer (timber) alludes to a stabilizing factor in one's life.

Strut (brace) connotes a supportive element in an individual's life.

Stud (framing) applies to a supportive factor for an idea or plan.

Stud finder stands for finding the basic or foundational aspects of an issue.

Wainscoting exemplifies a half-truth; an attempt to cover or hide a portion of something.

Girder represents the keystone of one's existence.

see also
• Manual Workers *p. 260*
• Household Substances *p. 396*

Parts of a Building

Alcove represents places of respite. It can also point out an overlooked venue of solace.

Balcony portrays perceptual clarity.

Capstone symbolizes the completion of one's purpose; finalization.

Cornerstone stands for concepts or beliefs that serve as one's foundation.

Corridor indicates a passageway; the way between stages of life; connecting aspects.

Facade (building) represents a false front; phoniness; possible hypocrisy.

False front (building) See facade.

Footings (construction) characterize the foundational basis for an idea's development to build on.

Foundation (building) connotes the moral, ethical, and spiritual tenets by which one lives.

Foyer is usually representative of an entrance to something to which the dreamer will personally relate.

Gallery (balcony) signifies a clarity of perception.

Keystone defines an aspect in an individual's life that pulls things together and brings understanding.

King post (construction) represents the main support of one's thought process. Depending on the condition of this symbol, it will reveal a strong or weak intellectual ability.

Loft denotes high-minded attitudes.

Passageway reveals a way through a difficult situation or confusing concept.

Private entrance represents sole access. This dream symbol may be indicative of unique ideas that one has developed.

Queen post represents the female (yin) that serves as a double support for the male (yang).

Retaining wall is generally representative of a supportive aspect that serves to hold up or hold back something. This dream symbol may also be indicative of the dreamer's denial.

Room divider suggests a separation of space; a demarcation from one issue to the next.

Shell (structure) signifies an incomplete home life or inner aspect of oneself.

Siding (on dwelling) signifies an attempt to alter appearances or efforts expended toward further insulating oneself from something.

Slab floor suggests a firm opinion or foundation, one without any possibility to be open for debate.

Terrace See balcony.

Threshold represents a beginning point; poised at the entrance.

Vestibule See foyer.

Wall may signify various connotations, depending on where the wall was and the surrounding details. In most cases a plain wall symbolizes a type of barrier that needs to be dealt with.

Wine cellar stands for a store of ideas. Was the cellar well stocked? Covered with dust? Full of a wide variety of types of wine?

Structures

Arch portrays a gentle passing through openings in one's life. The ease of taking advantage of opportunities.

Atrium depicts an openness of outwardly displayed attitudes and/or emotions.

Battlement denotes the logic, reason, and foresight given when one is considering a possible forthcoming conflict.

Belfry warns of alarming relationships or situations; a call to take heed or pay attention.

Clock tower portrays a major sign that indicates the right time for major events to happen in one's life. Advises of the wisdom of accepting the concept that there's a right time for everything.

Cornice symbolizes an elaborate concealment.

Crawlspace denotes access to something; room for more research into an issue; the presence of aspects that aren't obvious.

Crossbar/beam illustrates a supporting aspect.

Cupola denotes extensions of thought that typify the activity of an analytic mind.

Divider See partition.

Duplex indicates a double aspect to something.

Geodesic dome represents the interlocking aspects of life.

Minaret depicts a method of gaining another's attention.

Niche symbolizes a designated proper place for something. This may refer to a deed, verbal expression of an emotion or opinion, one's life purpose, or the best possible place or position for alignment or success.

Pyramid represents greater learning.

Pagoda signifies spiritual misconceptions related to one's connectedness to the Divine Essence.

Parapet refers to awareness; the act of being on the lookout and being prepared.

Pinnacle stands for high points in one's life or spiritual journey.

Podium pertains to a life factor that aids in communicating with others.

Portico relates to an elaborate presentation or show of appearances.

Pyramid is a symbol which pertains to higher wisdom and knowledge.

Rotunda is representative of an atmosphere that is rich in opportunity.

Termite shield (foundation) signifies an awareness of the possibility of one's plans being undermined and the defensive steps taken to avert such destruction.

Trilevel (dwelling) is usually suggestive of a mind having the well-integrated perspective or connection between the three mind levels of the conscious, the subconscious, and the superconscious; one who routinely uses intuition.

Types of Rooms

Built-in denotes instinctual behavior; inherent qualities or talents.
Clean room signifies any type of element/idea/situation in one's life that is without negative aspects.
Cranny reminds us of space left in our lives for something; to accommodate.
Room See specific type.
Semiprivate (room) refers to a situation in which other ears and eyes are present. This reveals a need for circumspection even though the dreamer may think he or she is unobserved.
Workroom represents the quality and quantity of effort one puts into achieving goals.

Bathroom & Fittings

Bathroom means a cleansing is needed.
Cistern refers to the spiritual aspects one holds within self.
Dripless (spout) stands for an element that safeguards against wastefulness.
Faucet implies the control one has. Usually this is associated with spiritual aspects and implies control used to turn spiritual behavior on and off.
Hot tub signifies a need to ease tension.
Jacuzzi refers to comforting spiritual beliefs that soothe.
John See bathroom.
Latrine See bathroom.
Lavatory See bathroom.
Restroom See bathroom.
Stopcock See faucet.
Toilet constitutes a need for eliminations. This means any type of negative element present in one's life.
Washroom See bathroom.
Water closet See bathroom.
Water faucet See faucet.

Stairs

Backstairs are usually representative of hidden or secretive movements. This dream symbol may refer to alternative agendas.
Banister See handrail.
Handrail portrays one's personal means of support along the way.
Newel (post) constitutes a main supportive aspect in one's life. This could refer to an emotional, mental, or spiritual issue.
Riser (on stairs) signifies a step above; raising oneself to a higher level.
Spiral stairs will generally point to a circling path toward advancement. This dream symbol may also be a reference to a phase of one's path that involves a return to issues to gain greater understanding.
Stairs pertain to one's ascent or descent in relation to one's life progression or advancement. Recall the type of stairs and the condition of them. Were they a specific color? Lit or darkened? Were there missing steps?
Step See stairs.

Floors

Floor pertains to one's moral, ethical, or spiritual foundations.
Floor joists will usually signify the main basic philosophical concepts our character is based on. These would be ethics, morals, and sense of rightness.
Floor plan constitutes thought planning.
Floor sample/model stands for multiple opportunities.
Ground floor connotes the beginning stage of a project.
Mezzanine stands for a mid-level positioning.
Slanted (floor) illustrates an adulterated aspect; a basic concept/ideal affected by one's opinionated perspective.
Subfloor See plywood.
Upstairs stands for a higher level; upward advancement or greater level of information.

Roof

Slate represents a lack of feeling or emotion.

Butterfly roof signifies a backward way of thinking.
Eaves symbolize protective aspects.
Eaves trough illustrates a directed flow of something away from self.
Gable denotes a differential facet to an individual's thought process; thought affected by a unique quirk.
Gambrel (roof) corresponds with a thought process that is affected by two differing perspectives.
Lightning rod implies a desire to connect with spiritual forces; an active attempt to open communication with the divine.
Mansard (roof style) suggests a tendency to look at things from several angles.
Metal roof indicates an effort to safeguard the home-front aspects in one's life, to protect it from damaging outside influences.
Roof refers to one's priorities; to the highest capping thoughts.
Roofing material See shingle.
Shingle (roof) symbolizes subconscious defense mechanisms and/or the character of one's thoughts.
Slate (roof) stands for apathy; having no sensitivity involved in thought processes.
Snow load suggests a preparedness for being able to carry the weight of heavy spiritual thought.
Thatch pertains to natural defenses.

see also
• Kitchen *p. 388*
• Bathroom *p. 393*

Rooms in Private Homes

Attic pertains to an individual's conscious mind.
Backroom connotes hidden aspects.
Basement stands for the subconscious mind.
Bedroom signifies one's personal atmosphere or surrounding that induces rest periods.
Boudoir See bedroom.
Butler's pantry refers to the comfort and convenience of being well prepared. May point out a storage of methods in which one manifests subservience.
Cellar indicates the deeper aspects of the subconscious where fears, bad memories, etc., are kept hidden.
Closet stands for aspects of self that one keeps hidden. These may even be kept hidden from oneself—an attempt at denial.
Cubbyhole stands for the tendency to segregate people according to personal attitudes and judgments.
Den (room) symbolizes the quality and frequency of one's personal enrichment or restorative time.
Dining room usually typifies a more concentrated and enjoyable manner of being nourished. Surrounding details will clarify which life aspect is being fed.
Dressing room relates to the intentional affectations people display for others. May also refer to the trying-on of new ideas/perspectives or giving a look at new ideas.
Family room symbolizes congeniality.
Galley (narrow kitchen) refers to a narrow assortment of nourishing benefits one chooses to utilize.
Hallway suggests a transition.
Larder See pantry.
Linen closet represents ethical and tolerant behavior. Was the closet full of fresh linen or was it empty?
Living room depicts one's attitudes toward daily life. Recall the color, how it was decorated and furnished. Was it tidy or cluttered?
Lobby (room) refers to neutral ground.
Lounge (room) relates to a designated time to pause or relax.
Kitchen refers to the method of food preparation. May also signify a place of planning, a cooking up of ideas. Recall the kitchen's overall condition, color, style, cleanliness.
Nursery (infant) pertains to the special care given to one's new beginnings.
Pantry stands for a reserve of inner strength. The key here is to recall if the pantry was full or empty. What did it contain?
Parlor alludes to outdated or old-fashioned ideas or characteristics; someone with a stiff personality.
Playroom (child's) suggests opportunities for early interaction with others; opportunities for developing character.
Porch signifies the extent of an individual's personally held distance from other people or life aspects.
Porch (enclosed) suggests a desire to maintain maximum distance.
Porch (open) is representative of a forthright and welcoming attitude.
Porch (screened-in) is usually indicative of a hesitant or cautious attitude.
Reception (room) refers to the phase of waiting just prior to a communication. This may point to the last chance to change one's mind.
Scullery implies a need for cleaning. The dreamer will make the specific correlation.
Sitting room See living room.
Summer kitchen denotes a desire to place oneself in a once-removed position; distancing oneself from the core of a heated situation, issue, or relationship.
Sunroom will be suggestive of a home life permeated with spirituality.

Cellar implies subconscious fears.

Rooms in Public Buildings

Antechamber See foyer.
Anteroom See foyer.
Ballroom represents the place or life arena in which we do our dancing. We shouldn't be doing fancy footwork anywhere in life. May also indicate a reason to celebrate recent decisions. Surrounding details of the ballroom's condition reveals which meaning applies.
Banquet room stands for a place of sharing. The key here is to recall the room's condition, how it was decorated, and if it was full of people or empty.
Bathhouse (pool) points to a serious need to cleanse some aspect in one's life.
Boiler room pertains to one's surroundings that could lead to explosive encounters or outcomes.
Chamber portrays a special room or place unique to the dreamer.
Cloakroom stands for a specific life factor that is not what it seems; full of cover-ups.
Coatroom See cloakroom.
Comfort station signifies the resting points that are necessary along our path.
Dayroom signifies a pause from a person's routine or regimen.
Hall (large room) indicates an important gathering.
Homeroom is representative of one's basic beliefs that are built upon.
Locker room symbolizes an opportunity to alter (change) one's attitude/opinion/ behavior.
Powder room See bathroom.
Suite (rooms) implies a temporary state of comfort.
Utility closet signifies efficient use of one's energy.

Decorating Finishes

Base coat is usually representative of attention to foundational work that finishing work and detailed aspects will be built upon.
Calk See caulk.
Caulk denotes the need to seal something in one's life; a promise; a conclusion.
Chinking (gap filler) applies to aspects that fill in the missing elements in life; factors that make something whole.
Clear coat represents a final finish; implementing a protective element to a finished issue.
Undercoating pertains to a protective/defensive measure; an intent to preserve.

Decoration & Maintenance

Acid-washing refers to a lightening up needed.
Blank wall signifies the sense of having no ideas regarding how to proceed or having no idea what steps to take next; lacking a solution. Usually this phase is temporary.
Dilapidated is a representation of a well-worn aspect that may still be viable.
Maintenance (work) advises of a need to attend to some aspect of one's life, perhaps an emotional or mental facet of oneself.

Ceilings

Ceiling usually means the top of something; one's limitation.
Ceiling (high) signifies an analytical thought process.
Ceiling (low) denotes a need to expand way of thinking.
Clearance (height) denotes the amount of room one has. Surrounding dreamscape elements will clarify this for the individual dreamer.
Drop ceiling suggests hidden thoughts.
Vaulted ceiling stands for high hopes; great expectations; a soaring intellect.

Fireplaces

Chimney usually pertains to emotional control.
Chimney pot portrays an aspect that improves the outward flow of one's emotions; that which draws out feelings and emotional expression.
Firebrick represents an individual or situation that remains unaffected by another's emotional outbursts or tirades.
Fire screen connotes means of emotional protection; methods whereby one guards self from personally displaying emotional outbursts or guards self from the tirades of others.
Furnace connotes emotional intensity. Was the furnace blasting? Was it cold?
Smokestack warns of a dangerous or highly negative aspect in one's life.

Doors

Automatic doors represent current options to the dreamer that are wide open to take advantage of.
Backdoor represents a way out.
Closed door advises against attempting to enter regions through which one is not advanced enough to travel.
Combination door (glass/screen) refers to an open mind.
Door indicates a life factor that one must experience or pass through to achieve advancement or progression along one's path.
Doorbell comes as an attention-getting symbol that calls one to an important experience or opportunity.
Doorknob refers to access to advancement or opportunity.
Doormat may point to a respect for and appreciation of opportunities or may warn against a poor self-image. Surrounding dreamscape details will clarify.
Doorstep points to steps or aspects leading to new opportunities.
Doorstop suggests one keeps doors open.
Dutch door points to the presence of two ways a certain opportunity can be accessed.
Fire door portrays personal efforts utilized to protect self from the intense emotionalism of others.
Folding door stands for an opportunity; ease of entering/exiting a situation.
French door represents a life passageway that offers many opportunities for different perspectives.
Handle (door) relates to comprehension.

Doorknob indicates a chance.

Jamb (door) indicates a situation where one feels closed in.
Kick plate suggests an intent or desire to protect one's record from missteps or mishaps occurring during one's journey through life.
Lintel reveals the strength or rightness of one's new direction. Did the lintel appear sturdy? Was anything decorating it?
Open door signifies accessibility; ease of attainment.
Overhead door signifies a selective perspective; choosing what one wants to see and have an opinion of.
Panic hardware (doors/windows) represent an easy way out. Was the dreamscape symbol already in place? Or making a suggestion to put them in place?
Pocket door represents full availability; a welcoming or totally acceptable attitude.
Portal pertains to an opening or opportunity; a view into another perspective.
Screen (door) exemplifies protected freedom.
Stoop See doorstep.
Storm door relates to one's free will decision to open self to emotional involvement or to remain closed to it.

see also
• Lighting *p. 392*
• Colors, Patterns & Fabric *pp. 414–423*

Windows

Bay (window) denotes a greater view or wider perspective may be required.

Bow window stands for extended perception; a good view.

Circlehead window See fan window.

Dormer signifies an acute conscious awareness.

Double-pane (window) indicates a filtering or insulating process being done in regard to one's perspectives.

Fan window signifies a safe/protective way to let in the light without exposing oneself to possible negatives.

French window signifies an opportunity to have a broader view or perspective.

Lancet window suggests a narrow perspective or view of something.

Louver See shutter (window).

Mullion (window) defines multiple perspectives to an issue.

Oriel See bay (window).

Picture window presents a wider view. This symbol advises the dreamer to look at something with a wider perspective, less conservatively.

Rose window connotes a perspective derived from multiple associated aspects. A rose window made of stained glass represents the mother goddess.

Shutter (window) symbolizes open-mindedness. Recall if the shutters were closed tight or opened wide. What color were they? What was their overall condition?

Sill (window) represents the lower confines of one's overall perspective.

Skylight applies to open-mindedness; a willingness to let the light in. Recall if the skylight was a specific color. Condition of the glass?

Storm window represents insulated (protected) perceptions; a desire to maintain personal distance.

Window shows the quality and quantity of perception.

Window box (curio decor) suggests personal attention given to accurate perception.

Window box (flowers) stand for a deep appreciation for nature's beauty/bounty and the efforts expended on surrounding self with it.

Window ledge may indicate a precarious viewpoint or it may refer to a perception supported by strengthening elements.

Windowpane reveals the accuracy of one's perception. Recall the condition, color, and glass type of the dream windowpane. Was it dirty? Cracked? Shattered? Tinted or rippled?

Insulation

Brick cavity wall denotes one's insular defenses.

Dead-air space exemplifies lack of fresh ideas; stale concepts.

Fiberfill applies to padding being done; exaggerations.

Insulation relates to quality and level of self-protection.

Vermiculite (insulation material) portrays an uplifting and nurturing life factor in an individual's life.

Plumbing & Ancillary Works

Cesspool connotes humanity's most base aspects.

Conduit denotes that which conveys in a supporting, protective manner.

Cooling tower points to a need to temper one's spiritual zealot behavior.

Downspout reminds us to utilize all aspects of spirituality in our daily lives.

Drainpipe symbolizes a need to discard spiritual excesses or unnecessary aspects from an individual's life.

Expansion joint symbolizes possible variations to one's plans and the action taken to accommodate them.

Flue See air vent.

Gutter may indicate the preservation of spiritual aspects or it may warn of a lack of spirituality depending on the surrounding dream details.

Holding tank corresponds with spiritual beliefs an individual is currently deliberating; a time before a spiritual decision is made.

Rainspout is representative of an attempt to channel one's spiritual aspects into a specific issue or method. This is usually an advisement to the dreamer to use his or her spiritual aspects in a broad-scope manner that takes advantage of every opportunity that arises.

Septic tank/system is usually representative of the complete disposal of the extraneous mental/emotional waste of one's life; ridding oneself of the extra burdens one shouldn't be carrying.

Sewer denotes a condition, place, or situation containing highly negative aspects.

Spillway represents spiritual excesses or that which is spiritually unnecessary.

Storm drain is an advisement to release one's emotional or psychological burdens and allow them to flow away from oneself.

Trap (drain) pertains to an opportunity to clean out the negatives in one's life or existing within self.

Water main refers to one's spiritual foundation.

Drainpipe implies a need to ditch the nonessentials in life.

Fencing

Barbed wire connotes an individual's harmful attitude (tendency) to angrily cut oneself off from another; animosity; prickly barriers to a situation yet not impossible to get past.

Cage pertains to an aspect that prevents the exercise of one's freedoms or rights. This may even refer to oneself.

Chain-link fence refers to one's inner need to define ownership; possessiveness; marking personal perimeters.

Fence denotes self-generated barriers; an individual's personal distance.

Fencing (material) denotes that which one utilizes to create personal barriers, perhaps even from self.

Access Services

Chute (utility slide) refers to a quick exit or end to something.

Dehumidifier signifies a life aspect devoid of any spirituality; the act of removing spiritual aspects from a selected portion of one's life.

Dumbwaiter portrays personal resources; self-reliance.

Elevator connotes an easy way up (or down); advancing (or falling behind) with little effort applied.

Escalator cautions against laziness; taking the easy way that uses little energy.

Handicapped access points to a way to alleviate fears of advancing.

Humidifier is an aspect that increases the level of one's spirituality.

Service elevator/entrance denotes maintenance or repairs. It can refer to care that is being done behind the scenes.

Bridges

Bridge (structure) is a symbol that always denotes some type of connective element.

Footbridge is a dreamscape symbol that connotes the connective aspects to one's life path.

Pontoon bridge refers to a bridging or way over spiritual issues that are troubling for the dreamer.

Suspension bridge symbolizes an extended transition period in one's life.

Tents

Bivouac applies to keeping oneself free and unburdened or unencumbered while walking a new path.

Tarpaulin is usually representative of self-devised defense mechanisms.

Tent reflects a temporary situation. May also denote a fragile shelter.

Tepee corresponds to a pyramid configuration that centers and condenses an individual's inner strength.

Safety Features

Exit (sign) points to a way out of something.

Fire tower emphasizes a state of personal awareness regarding one's emotions and their expression.

Firetrap connotes an atmosphere that easily generates emotional explosiveness.

Firewall is a symbol that indicates an emotional barrier.

Grate indicates a protective measure.

Hatch cover means a way out of something.

Shatterproof glass See safety glass.

Tide gate comes to the dreamer as a warning against hoarding spiritual talents; spiritual bounties or gifts that only flow one way, received but rarely given.

Monuments

Air castle means daydreaming; unrealistic ideas.

Castle in sand See sand castle.

Font (receptacle) means abundance.

Fountain (decorative) means spiritual abundance. Recall its dreamscape condition. Was the water colored? Lighted? How was it constructed, decorated?

Mastaba advises one of the wisdom of preserving and protecting truths.

Millstone is a great burden.

Mill wheel represents one's continuing efforts to spiritually advance.

Monument characterizes individual loyalties. A beautiful monument is a correct placement of an individual's loyalty. A decrepit monument reveals misplaced loyalty.

Obelisk denotes an important factor for the dreamer. Dreamscape shapes such as obelisks refer to spiritual conceptual truths.

Sand castle correlates to unrealistic plans; insubstantial ideas; lacking viability.

Decorative fountain is a reference to a healthy spirituality.

Chapter 20

Crime, Law & Government

Crime relates to errors in action and/or thought. The law represents societal parameters and authority. Government is associated with restrictions one lives under.

Crimes

Break-in reveals a dishonest person.

Blackmail is a gross negative use of knowledge; betrayal.
Break-in See burglar.
Breech of contract refers to a wrongdoing; going back on one's word.
Burglary is an untrustworthy individual; ulterior motives; someone who will end up taking something.
Contempt of court stands for willful recklessness; obstinacy.
Defraud reveals ulterior motives; ill-gotten gains or method of achieving a goal.
Driving under the influence (DUI) warns against needing reality-altering elements as a crutch to help get through life.
Driving while intoxicated (DWI) warns of making one's way through life without being in touch with it; lacking courage or belief in oneself.
Extortion is a negative symbol referring to the wrong use of information; betrayal.
False ID represents a false public persona.
Forgery stands for a false representation. May indicate a statement or behavior accredited to the wrong person.
Fraud advises of a relationship, situation, or aspect that is not authentic or what it seems.
Graft (gain) warns against self-gain through unscrupulous methods.
Grand larceny refers to an extremely costly misdeed.
Hate crime signifies behavior borne of intolerance.
Heist See burglary.
Highjack See hijack.
Highway robbery See highwaymen.
Hijack signifies a situation where one is being robbed of benefits personally acquired.
Hoax reveals a deception in one's life. Recall what the hoax was and who generated it for what reason. This will not always be a negative act.
Holdup See burglar.
Identity theft refers to one's power being stolen. This advises you to step forward and take back your life.
Jaywalking implies a tendency to cut corners or not always go by the book.
Larceny (grand) applies to the theft of a major element. This could be associated with the theft of one's identity, livelihood, good name, etc.
Perjury pertains to a falsehood.
Robbery See burglary.
Tax evasion warns against trying to avoid responsibilities.
Terrorist attack denotes unexpected hostilities.
Theft See burglary.
War crimes refer to a time when one's basest attitudes and behaviors are exhibited, usually without prior thought, instinctively, or when rage or revenge are acted upon.
White-collar crime refers to negative behavior from those whom one least expects it.

Murder

Homicide See murder.
Infanticide reveals the willful suppression of an individual's spirituality through loss of belief or lack of use.
Manslaughter warns against being unaware; a devastating effect of being unaware.
Murder usually represents a symbolic death. This may refer to the death of a relationship, plan, or other type of current situation in one's life.
Patricide illustrates a denial of an inherent part of oneself.

Criminals

Accessory (to a crime) warns of an illegal, unethical, or immoral involvement with an instigator or perpetrator.
First offender usually suggests a second chance.
Fugitive advises to stop running from one's problems or fears. This may even refer to an attempt to escape self.
Grave robber is one who enjoys gaining from others' downfall.
Highwaymen characterize individuals who attempt to gain by your life walk; an attempt to take something from your advancement.
Hired gun warns against having others deal with one's problems.
Mafia exemplifies manipulation for self-gain; strong-arm control methods.
Mobster See mafia.
Outlaw indicates one who behaves in an unlawful manner. The lawful aspect can refer to ethical, moral, or spiritual elements.
Racketeer See mafia.
Ring (crime) See chain gang.
Serial killer usually suggests a self-generated condition whereby one routinely performs in a self-defeating manner; the methodical killing of one's opportunities.
Stowaway refers to personal unawareness.
Tomb robber See grave robber.
Trickster typifies cleverness; quick wit.
Underworld (criminal) stands for the hidden negative elements in one's life.

Mafia highlights the use of extreme measures to get what one wants.

see also
• Bad Guys *p. 144*
• Law Enforcement *p. 253*

Criminality

Bent refers to a life aspect that isn't straight (true or honest).
Bill of goods refers to dishonesty; a bad transaction.
Black market applies to underhandedness in obtaining goals; ill-gotten objectives.
Blood money warns of goals gained at the cost of another; ill-gotten gains; the destruction of another.
Bootleg warns against attempting to accomplish or gain something through unethical or immoral means.
Cement shoes indicate something one needs to answer for; an extremely negative deed needs to be repaired or made amends for.
Concealment warns of a cover-up or the hiding of something.
Contraband means the utilization or possession of negative aspects such as selfish motives, apathetic attitudes, and so on.
Counterfeit defines something misrepresented.
Crime (witness) See witness.
Dead drop refers to secrets; extremely private communications.
Double-dealing reveals duplicity.
Funny money See counterfeit.
Gag (over mouth) warns against talking too much; gossip; revealing more than one should.
Gangland (style) represents a harmful, negative method of achieving a goal.
Gunfight portrays negative resolutions.
Gun moll signifies an attraction to power.
Gunpoint (held at) warns of a forced situation; against one's will; coercion.

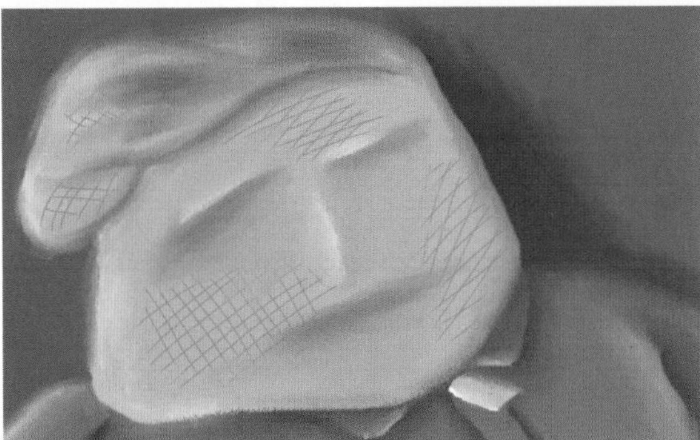

Stocking mask illustrates self-delusion and concealment.

Hate mail reveals a lack of acceptance; intolerance; negativity; insensitivity.
Hit-and-run warns against running from responsibility; a refusal to answer for one's actions.
Hit list usually reveals those who are detrimental in one's life. It can also refer to someone else's list that is extremely informative for the dreamer.
Hostage represents a demand for security; a desire to obtain a goal without working for it.
Hush money See bribe.
Intruder connotes an individual who disrupts specific aspects of one's life.
Lawlessness warns of a disregard for authority.
Letter bomb means a devastating communication or revelation.
Moll See gun moll.
Narc characterizes a person who exposes the secrets of others; one who can't be trusted with confidences; betrayer.
Nightrider warns of underhandedness; hidden aggression.
Off-limits comes as a severe warning that one is trespassing where one shouldn't be.
Off-the-books reveals hidden assets or an attempt to keep something secret.
Out-of-bounds stands for exceeding a limitation or restrictive barrier and may commend one for doing so.
Racket See scam.
Scam reveals insincerity; ulterior motives.
Sexual harassment reveals a lack of respect. More importantly, it reveals a lack of spiritual advancement.
Shakedown refers to a forced method of obtaining something.
Shell game applies to evasion; a possible swindle; unethical methods; an attempt to confuse.
Shortchanged correlates to a debt owed. Recall who was shortchanged.
Skeleton key illustrates a life aspect that serves as a key opening multiple opportunities.
Stash stands for hidden elements in one's life; that which an individual conceals and hoards.
Sting (situational backfire) represents an ulterior motive.
Stocking mask refers to deception; an attempt to hide oneself.
Swiss bank account stands for an attempt to conceal, usually related to one's assets (talents).
Under-the-counter/table represents unethical or secretive dealings.

The Arrest

Arrest refers to being caught for negative behavior.
Busted See arrest.
Citizen's arrest indicates one's responsibility to take action against negative elements. Points to activism.
False arrest refers to a situation indicating false blame. This is a revealing dream fragment.
Fingerprinted (being) suggests an advisement to be true to oneself, one's uniqueness of identity.
Handcuffs reveal restraints. Usually points to a plan that can't be implemented or a situation that can't be interfered with.
House arrest indicates a need to remain in a neutral position; a need to force oneself to stay out of an issue or situation.
Mirandize (reading one's rights) points to knowledge of one's rights. This symbol rarely points to a wrongdoing, but rather the recognition of intent.
Mug shot reveals something important to each dreamer. Who was it of ? What was it in reference to? Oneself ?

Crime Detection & Arrest

Alibi signifies guiltlessness.

Allegation signifies unproven claims made.

Bail (bond) means a temporary reprieve.

Body search indicates a suspicion of concealment; possible dishonesty.

Breath test points to adulterated speech. May mean prevarications, gossip, etc. A self-analysis is advised.

Charge (accuse) implies a placing of blame; to implicate.

Circumstantial evidence means a lack of solid proof.

Clue comes as a hint from one's higher self or inner knowing.

Code name refers to a secret identity.

Cold case (file) means something in one's past that's been left unresolved.

Detainee defines one held against one's will. This may refer to a number of aspects, even self-confinement or denial.

Detention center/home signifies a situational condition that is confining; restrictions or self-denial due to efforts to correct a certain behavior.

Entrapment reveals underhanded behavior. Recall who was entrapping whom.

Evidence denotes validation or proof.

Evidence table (courtroom) points to multiple verifying elements.

Eyewitness indicates verification of one's perception of something; truth to an issue.

Fingerprint (visible) reveals the fact that someone is/was present or involved with an issue.

Forensic medicine emphasizes a need to examine all aspects of a situation, relationship, or event before forming an intelligent conclusion.

Frisk (body search) cautions to be aware of concealments.

Gumshoe signifies a stealthy individual or personality.

Lead (possibility) suggests possible options/openings/chances.

Lead (primary) designates a paramount concept, individual, or event.

Manhunt suggests that one needs to find someone; a need to seek out and locate someone who will be important in one's life.

Passive restraint connotes an automatic, usually concealed, method of restraint that is either self-controlled or manipulative.

Posse suggests one's assumptions and prejudgments.

Rap sheet illustrates one's offenses; a record of misdeeds. This usually comes to give a visual of one's true behavior.

Red-handed stands for being caught at something.

Search warrant portrays an invasion of privacy. Important elements associated with this symbol are the answers to such questions as who was serving the warrant on whom? Why?

Sobriety test is most often a call from one's conscience to maintain awareness.

Speed trap warns of the pitfalls of going too fast along one's life path.

Spot-check connotes a wish to maintain status quo; a monitoring and watchfulness.

Stakeout advises of a need to be acutely watchful of a particular aspect in one's life.

Straitjacket comes as a strong advisement to straighten out one's life, thoughts, emotions, perceptions, or belief systems.

Strip-search verifies that one isn't hiding anything; a call to be more open and forthright.

Surveillance advises of a need to heighten one's awareness or watchfulness.

Surveillance camera See camera (hidden).

Surveillance room refers to eyes on many matters. This could advise the dreamer to pay closer attention to details or it could come to reveal that many eyes are watching you.

Suspect marks a questionable individual, plan, or concept.

Tear gas implies a means of controlling another.

Third degree relates to great intensity.

Truth serum comes as a strong advisement to be forthright.

Undercover represents secretiveness.

Vice squad usually stands for one's own conscience.

Crime Prevention

Alarms (security) represent a severe warning; taking notice. May be pointing to an isolated individual, fearful of sharing perspectives with others.

Alarm system denotes a need for higher awareness of one's environment or immediate surroundings. This symbol can also reveal one's self-devised shield, perhaps a fear of letting anyone get too close or a self-preservation.

Alarm system (business) signifies safeguards one places on life dealings. This symbol isn't exclusively associated with the workaday aspect of one's life but is tied into one's philosophy of daily living and covers such elements as attitudes toward others, tolerance, and unconditional goodness—how others are treated on a daily basis.

Alarms act as an urgent caution.

Burglar alarm stands for an awareness for certain negative eventualities and one's efforts to circumvent them.

Curfew cautions against a prolonged activity. Suggests a time for everything; time management.

Mace (spray) signifies personal defenses against external negative forces or influences.

Restraining order reminds the dreamer to make an effort to keep one's distance from a negative aspect.

Security system See alarm system.

Silent alarm equates to our inner awareness; instinctual warning system and sense of forewarning.

see also
• Criminal Classes *p. 146*
• Aggression *p. 168*

Trial & Court

Defendant means to clarify actions.

Accusation is suggestive of possible wrongdoing. Depending on the situation in the dreamer's real-time life, this could point to a false accusation.

Acquittal generally denotes innocence.

Arraignment is a call to explain one's actions, a time to face up to deeds or responsibilities.

Bench warrant seriously warns against wrongdoing.

Court is a venue or option for receiving a conflict resolution.

Courthouse refers to legal aspects.

Court-martial alludes to an infraction of the set of rules by which one agreed to abide.

Court order symbolizes an imperative aspect in a person's life; a must-comply type of directive.

Courtroom connotes an analytic atmosphere; a situation where an individual attempts to get at the truth.

Defendant most often characterizes an individual who has a need to explain self.

Expert witness refers to someone who has knowledge of a particular issue. This symbol may come as an advisement to consult a knowledgeable individual.

Federal case warns of serious ramifications associated with one's behavior.

Gavel means finality; a message from a higher authority.

Grand jury comes as a severe warning. Surrounding dreamscape details will clarify the precise meaning.

Hung jury relates to indecision, usually within oneself.

Indictment signifies a serious accusation.

Jury pertains to an individual's higher self.

Jury pool applies to those whose opinions count.

Jury-rig suggests improvisation.

Justice department (federal) See court.

Mistrial implies faulty procedure followed or a failure to agree on something. Surrounding dream details will point to the intended dream meaning.

Pardon typifies an exoneration; forgiveness intended to negate personal guilt.

Plaintiff reveals the individual who brings a problem to attention. May also represent someone who has an issue with something or a person who's a chronic complainer, perhaps even a pessimist.

Plea-bargain implies a desire to escape blame or responsibility.

Pretrial hearing exemplifies clarification groundwork aspects.

Probable cause illustrates the existence of a specific motive.

Punitive damages suggest repayment over and above damages/wrong done. May be a karma-balancing event.

Recuse suggests a need to remove oneself from a specific issue, situation, or relationship.

Sentencing stands for a manner of retribution needed; an advisement to balance out or correct a wrongdoing.

Subpoena stands for a need for important information to be communicated.

Summons exposes a serious warning for one to answer for erring ways or participate in a process of justice.

Test case denotes a precedent-setting situation or element.

Trial comes as a suggestion to honestly analyze one's motives and recent behavior.

Verdict pertains to a settled decision.

Witness reminds us that someone is always watching, even one's own subconscious.

Witness stand connotes the exposure of a formerly hidden deed or thought.

Serious Crimes

Abduction denotes the taking of something without the right of ownership; a type of takeover. This could also mean a manipulative or domineering nature.

Acquaintance rape warns of betrayal or dirty dealings performed by someone the dreamer knows fairly well.

Arson stands for willful destruction done in a person's life.

Drive-by shooting warns of collateral damage done by one's explosive reactions.

Genocide won't normally indicate an issue of racism but rather refers to one's adamant refusal to even broach a subject/issue that needs to be excised from one's life.

Sexual assault denotes an irresistible desire for control. This symbol reveals a belief that the only way one can gain control is by forcing it.

Skyjacking exposes the stealing of another's thoughts or ideas.

Strangulation exposes a choking condition; a need to free self from a suffocating relationship or situation. Who was strangling whom?

Types of Court

Appellate court is associated with the people who have the capability of altering your future course.

High court See supreme court.

Juvenile court is indicative of the law as it applies to a searching beginner; basic or novitiate philosophical concepts.

Kangaroo court constitutes one who is too quick to judge.

Night court represents the time for self-analysis.

Probate court pertains to a source for sorting out elements of a problem.

Supreme court alludes to a need to give time to a major decision or plan.

Punishment

Ball and chain refers to a burden one carries; a weight.
Capital punishment refers to excessive retaliation; unjust judgment; vindictiveness.
Cell mate characterizes a person of like mind.
Chain gang stands for individuals who are strongly connected by a shared negativity.
Death house See death row.
Death penalty means no opportunity for a second chance; no way out.
Death row relates to the realization that one cannot hide or run from making retributions.
Death sentence reveals a bad decision or intended behavioral move.
Death warrant applies to a life aspect that will seal one's fate in an extremely negative manner. Who was signing the death warrant? Was it you?
Dungeon pertains to self-induced states of negativity; self-imposed denial or restraint.
Electric chair warns of the finality of one's actions; unavoidable retribution.

Gallows illustrate a need to accomplish something.

False imprisonment warns of a serious error in judgment.
Gallows is indicative of a need to complete or finish something.
Gibbet usually warns against an action or personal course that could result in self-destruction; a path toward hanging oneself.
Guillotine warns against sticking one's neck out; interference.
Hangman characterizes one who is capable of posing a dangerous threat to another; someone who could hang you; a betrayer. But was the dreamer the hangman? That points to behavior that will end up hanging oneself; self-defeat.
Hard labor (penalty) relates to serious ramifications for past or planned behavior.
Juvenile detention (center) advises to halt immature tendencies to ignore what one knows is right; a need to take time out and think about being more mature.
Manacle refers to limitations or restrictions. Most often these are self-generated.
Maximum security signifies a need for heightened guardedness or secrecy. May also refer to a situation or path holding many restrictions or operating limitations.
Minimum security denotes a situation or path that holds few restrictions or operating limitations. Could also indicate little need for secrecy.
Parole represents a time of testing one's integrity; putting learned lessons into action.
Penalty corresponds with a balancing element; a corrective justification.
Probation implies a cautionary phase or time; a time to watch one's behavior.
Punishment correlates to recompense. May imply personal guilt.
Solitary confinement exposes a situation of absolute exclusion. May advise that one's state of aloneness has been self-induced.
Stir crazy denotes a lack of acceptance and/or patience; a need to look at one's current situation in a different, more creative way.
Writ of execution is usually representative of verification from an individual's higher self in regard to an intended plan; an authorization to proceed.

Civil Rights

Civil disobedience symbolizes one's right to disagree with those in authority.
Civilian exemplifies one who is not subject to the demands or wiles of others.
Civil liberties mean the basic rights everyone has. This may be associated with a right the dreamer is being denied or the dreamer may be denying someone else a basic right.
Civil rights reminds us of our personal freedoms or the positive aspects of personal perspectives and private planning.
Freedom march connotes organized protests against injustice or oppression.
Freedom of speech comes as message reminding one that one has a right to speak up.
Freedom of the press reminds us everyone has a right to express an opinion, even in writing, but as others may not agree, they don't have to read it.
Freedom of the seas defines a right to explore all spiritual ideologies; spiritual freedom.
Free enterprise denotes the following of one's dream with little outside interference.
Free speech reminds us not to be fearful of expressing self.
Free trade represents relationships and communications that are open and unrestricted by any taboo issues.
Human rights imply an attempt to define and delineate inherent qualities.
Liberty bell stands for our civil liberties. The meaning will be different to each dreamer.
Ombudsperson characterizes one who has the ability to act as an intermediary; one who can investigate a complaint or suspicion.

see also
• Security *p. 192*
• Government *p. 254*

Intelligence & Security

Central Intelligence Agency See CIA.
CIA represents in-depth information. Depending on surrounding dreamscape factors, this may also reveal spying activity being done in the dreamer's life.
Civil defense portrays the protection of an individual's surrounding aspects. This symbol applies to personal preparedness.
Code blue warns of an extremely dangerous situation approaching.
Cold war warns against maintaining deep animosities or continuing underlying negative feelings.
Confidential file illustrates multiple secrets or hidden aspects.
Conspiracy warns of dangerous planning.
Dissident characterizes a disagreeing activist; one who strongly opposes an idea or perception.
Dossier typifies extensive "background" information.
Espionage advises of some type of pretension existing in one's life; ulterior motives; a separate agenda.
Eyes-only (clearance level) reveals information that is only available to the dreamer and no one else.
Gag order is a message to keep silent about something. Surrounding dreamscape details will clarify this.
Homeland security indicates measures taken to protect one's home (ideals and perspectives). However, if this is overdone, this symbol will point to a warning against being so overly protective that the rights of others have been compromised.
Hotline stands for an unbroken line of communication; the need to keep communications open at all times.
Identification card (ID) portrays that which one presents as an exterior self. Frequently this dream symbol will alter one's identity to reveal the real self.
Intelligence report offers the dreamer valuable information she/he has been needing.
Internal affairs stand for one's conscience.
Iron curtain won't relate to the former Russian situation but instead reveals one's voluntary separation of self from a life issue, denial, or escapism.
Men in black point directly to those holding huge secrets and devoting all their energies to keep them from becoming public; those with ulterior motives and secret agendas.
Military intelligence connotes ulterior motives for gaining information. This symbol may point to something in one's life that's a contradiction in terms.
National Guard pertains to a massive upheaval forthcoming in life.
Patriot Act suggests a loss of privacy and some associated rights.
Pentagon characterizes secretive dealings; ulterior motives.
Police come in dreams as an advisement to self-analyze one's actions and for needed introspection. Police can often be associated with one's higher self (self-policing).

Spy represents someone deceitful.

Propaganda signifies an attempt to indoctrinate others with one's personal beliefs. May indicate falsehoods.
Red-pencil signifies censorship.
Riot act defines a severe warning/chastisement. The dreamer will make the correct individualized association.
Secret may indicate a revelation for the dreamer.
Security risk stands for a plan or individual who carries a risk; untrustworthiness.
Shore patrol reflects one's inner spiritual guidance; conscience.
Smokey mirror hints at smoke and mirrors; an insubstantial element or trickery.
Spy indicates an untrustworthy individual.
Top secret connotes innermost thoughts and memories.
Watch list stands for individuals or events to keep aware of.
White House signifies perceived authority; a tendency to heavily rely on others who act as decision-making advisors.

Elections

Absentee ballot is usually suggestive of one's right to express an opinion.
Ballot stands for freedom of speech; ones right to make choices.
Campaign button signifies a show of one's attitude or opinion. May display a specific cause one has an affinity for.
Campaign fund is associated with the energies and/or resources that are kept for a special cause and/or goal.
Election connotes a firm decision.
Exit poll cautions against a desire to know what others think of something.
Majority illustrates the greater amount.
Majority rule applies to control held by those comprising the highest percentage of common belief or attitude, though it may not be the right belief or attitude.
Mandate is a symbol of a command or action that must be followed, usually ordered by self as a means of ensuring one stays on track.
Poll See survey (poll).
Primary caucus alludes to a gathering of opinions to discover a local, general attitude.
Primary election signifies efforts to pinpoint or solidify an attitude or direction.
Run (for office) See campaign.
Split ticket (voting) stands for a recognition of the best elements of multiple aspects; a tendency to be savvy enough to recognize the best qualities of people or a situation.
Voting machine defines the right to freely choose or make a personal decision.

Politics

County seat refers to an aspect of legal offices and a specific connection the dreamer has for one of these.

Green Party/Green Peace represents environmental concerns in one's life.

Gulag connotes a situation or relationship that forces another in some manner.

Forum See town hall/meeting.

Hammer and sickle relate to a common bond.

Home rule pertains to independence; a responsibility to self. This symbol may point to one's conscience.

Left-wing points to an open mind; tolerance; liberal perspectives; one who loves raising one's head to see what's outside the box or tends toward empathy for other's misfortune.

Master plan stands for big plans; a long-range plan. Indicates all elements associated with a specific goal have been taken into consideration.

Negotiations indicate a desire for compromise.

Party (political) represents a difference of philosophy.

Party line (political) stands for basic attitudes one doesn't veer from.

Quorum corresponds to an issue in a person's life that requires the cooperation or agreement of others.

Red tape reveals complications.

Regulations connote rules and limitations. May relate to guidelines one sets for self.

Repeal is representative of the act of voiding an action; revocation.

Rescind See repeal.

Right-wing means following a narrowly conservative perspective; fearful of attempting new endeavors or exploring innovative concepts; reluctant to think outside the box or have a willingness to even perceive what's out there; tending toward apathy for the unfortunates in life; self-centered.

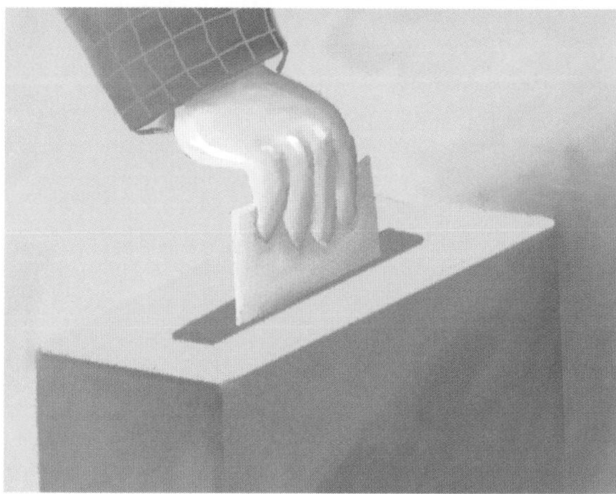

Secret ballot represents a conclusion one has come to oneself.

Secret ballot connotes a personal decision; inner thoughts.

Section Eight comes to the dreamer as a warning of undesirable character traits.

Spin See damage control.

Think tank advises one to spend time in deep contemplation or analysis.

Town hall/meeting alludes to a meeting place, more explicitly, a meeting that is needed.

Zoning commission applies to an attempt to control the activities of others.

Resistance & Rebellion

Anarchy warns of a lack of purpose or direction in an individual's life. May also indicate a need to rise up against adversity or injustice in one's life.

Backlash indicates a negative reaction.

Class action means action taken on behalf of others; someone ready to fight for the rights of others.

Dissident characterizes a disagreeing activist; one who strongly opposes an idea or perception.

Ecoterrorism/ist characterizes an action/individual that destroys the natural talents of oneself or others.

Hunger strike implies personal activism; a sympathizer.

Jailbreak defines an escape from a confining aspect in one's life.

Lie-in (protest) denotes efforts expended toward personal activism; a vehement protest.

Rebellion marks resistance; independent thought; activism.

Soapbox pertains to a personal need to sway or convince others of one's own perspective or attitude.

Taxation & Finance

Consumer price index refers to the increased cost of waiting to act—the additional price of indecision/ procrastination.

Death duty See inheritance tax.

Federal reserve system cautions of a situation that is slipping out of one's control.

National debt corresponds with a major obligation or responsibility in a person's life.

Surtax suggests a taxing situation, issue; more energy expended on an issue than an individual was prepared to give.

Systems of Government

Democracy characterizes a relationship, situation, or condition that benefits everyone; a tendency to focus concerns on the disadvantaged and middle class; empathy.

Dictator pinpoints a manipulative personality.

Federation portrays a unified group of individuals.

Feudalism warns of a domineering personality or situation.

Police state is an advisement to be more aware of that which is transpiring around oneself.

Foreign Affairs

Consulate represents a place of safety; where protection is provided.
Coup d'état denotes an overthrow of authority; a revolt of some type.
Customs (border) exemplifies a check time in one's life; a point in time when one needs to inspect paths and the manner they are traveled.
Deportation refers to the permanent physical removal of someone from one's life.
Diplomat characterizes an individual who is tactful.
Diplomatic immunity pertains to special benefits for those who use tactful methods of communication.
Diplomatic pouch stands for private and privileged information.
Dual citizenship suggests dual allegiance; loyalty to more than one individual or issue.
Embassy portrays some type of help or assistance for the dreamer.
Empire usually refers to a specific individual's extent of power or control.
Exile most often refers to a self-induced state of aloneness.
Expatriate signifies a full departure from a former ideology or loyalty.
Exports refer to those personal talents one gives to others; the sharing of one's abilities.
Foreign aid is assistance coming from an unexpected source.
Foreigner is associated with a different perspective or idea.
Foreign exchange pertains to the sharing of new ideas.
Foreign mission typifies the spiritual work one does outside the scope of one's own specific path.
Foreign policy will be unique to each dreamer in that it represents one's own personal perspective toward innovative or foreign ideas. This symbol may also point to a lack of understanding or ability to communicate with others.
Immigrant refers to a voluntary choice to dramatically change one's path and set of opportunities.
International law indicates common sense, logic.
International waters symbolize spiritual concepts that are so basic that everyone respects them with reflected behavior.
Nuclear-free zone represents a personal desire for harmony and peaceful conditions in one's life.
OPEC corresponds to a controlling power; an element or individual possessing the control.
Peace Corps relate to an opportunity to help others.
Protocol defines the right way to accomplish something; a correct sequence or method of going about an action.
Refugee characterizes a person who has experiential knowledge of a negative life element.
Summit conference stands for a serious need for an important communication; an advisement to generate a major discussion.
Superpower pertains to those with the most power and authority, but not necessarily possessing the proper ethics, morals, and spiritual qualities.
Third world represents impoverishment, usually related to one's character.
Trade agreement denotes an arrangement in which parties agree to a manner of interaction and the sharing of one another's talents.
Treaty relates to agreements that smooth ongoing relationships.

The U.S. Legislature

Balance of power implies a need to share responsibility and control; each individual requires her/his own portion that is answerable for.
Bill of rights means one's right to have rights. This is an important dreamscape fragment. Everyone has basic rights.
Blue book symbolizes the value of various spiritual concepts.
Camp David suggests a required pause needed in one's intellectual pursuits; a relief from responsibility.
Capitol Hill See Congress.
Caucus stands for a specialized meeting of selected people. May come as a suggestion that a meeting of some type is needed.
Congress represents a meeting of several people or groups for the purpose of a specific communication. This typifies a need for resolving differences between more than two or three people.
Constitution normally refers to perseverance; one's inner strength/fortitude. May also be associated with one's unique moral/ethical code.
Democrat See left-wing.
Executive session comes in a dream as an advisement to do some soul-searching.

Capitol Hill is a need for concord.

Fifth amendment represents a decision to keep personal matters a private affair.
Filibuster cautions of an obstruction to one's goals; a delay of time spent on an irrelevant issue.
Senate See Congress.
State of Union Address points to a general assessment of one's current condition and progress.
Statute generally signifies a specific law that may relate to ethical, moral, or spiritual aspects.
Steering committee may refer to one's own better judgment or it can relate to being coerced.
USDA (U.S. Department of Agriculture) may be representative of a protective measure; efforts put into an issue's close inspection for the purpose of ensuring that it's a positive aspect.

The People

Birthrate points to one's rate of progression toward new beginnings.

Census comes to the dreamer as a caution of the inability to exist anonymously.

Demographics advises of the wisdom of knowing those with whom one associates; having background information on an issue.

Denizen See inhabitant.

Focus group represents an unhealthy interest in what others think, an overconcern for the public's opinion—usually regarding one's appearance, behavior, or personal opinion/attitudes. This dream element points to a need for approval from other people in one's life.

Inhabitant implies the viability of a situation.

Mortality (rate) emphasizes a measure of viability. Recall surrounding dream detail to determine what this symbol referred to.

Mother tongue represents an advisement to return to one's own level of understanding. This denotes an attempt to learn that which is far too complex.

Native (indigenous) symbolizes one's right to something in one's life that may currently be denied.

Native American See American Indian.

People portray the more complex human components of dreamscapes. They are more diverse in meaning than any other image; therefore, the dreamer needs to recall multiple elements about the people presented to accurately analyze these human facets. Who was the person? Age? Was an occupation presented? What was the person wearing? Any jewelry? Did this person speak to the dreamer? If so, what was said? Refer to specific occupations, clothing, and physical characteristics for further clarification.

People represent the diversity of human facets of one's dreams.

Proletariat signifies the blue-collar workers. This symbol may point to one who does hard work to get somewhere.

Public domain applies to an aspect that is open to all, or not individually owned.

Public interest symbolizes an issue or element that is of general interest.

Public record is usually representative of information that's open to all; something that is not a secret or intended to be.

Public television symbolizes personal efforts expended toward a goal.

Public works pertains to general life benefits.

Social register illustrates those who are self-absorbed.

Survey (poll) portrays an interest in the opinion of others.

Tribespeople correspond to the universal unit of humankind.

Zero population growth actually denotes progress.

Legislation

Affirmative action connotes equality; action taken or required to affect a more balanced or positive change.

All-points bulletin warns one to be watchful for a negative element that's developing within one's immediate circle of friends and/or relations.

Amnesty symbolizes absolute forgiveness or a new measure of acceptance through tolerance.

Authorization is a symbol of permission granted; a legal right.

Back-to-basics denotes a need to return to the fundamentals.

Boilerplate (contractual) represents certain elements that cannot be avoided.

Council advises of the need to deliberate. This may even suggest self-examination.

Embargo implies the act of disassociation; a refusal to deal or communicate with another.

Legitimize illustrates an act that rectifies wrongdoings; something brought into balance once again.

Malpractice insurance points to the possibility of negligence; a preparedness against making a mistake.

Moratorium comes to the dreamer as an advisement to stop a certain behavior or cut out a specific element in his or her life. The surrounding related dream aspects will help to clarify what this dream element connects with.

Rosetta stone portrays a key to understanding a specific personal situation or issue.

see also
• Political Relationships *p. 125*
• Social Work *p. 252*

Property Law

Abandonment (of property) pertains to giving up one's interest in something.
Absolute assignment means giving something entirely over to another.
Absolute conveyance stands for washing of one's hands of an issue; giving something without conditions or expectations.
Absolute owner signifies one owning all interests in something.
Abstract of title warns one to double-check facts relating to the history or background of something.
Access rights (ingress and egress) connotes the rights to be involved in an issue.
Bill of sale represents a completed transaction in life.
Claim stands for possessiveness; a declaration of ownership.
Community property points to an idea/concept shared by many.
Copyholder represents the individual who has the sole right to an idea.
Copyright points to the originator of something; right to sole ownership.
Covenant (property) connotes restrictions devised and upheld by another. Can indicate bounds and restrictions related to one's home aspects.
Deed underscores one's right to something.
Easement (ingress/egress) denotes one's right to pass through another's space.
Eminent domain comes in dreams to remind us that others can easily steal away our most precious possessions through the means of legal manipulation.

Deed signifies a person's lawful authority over something.

Eviction notice comes as a serious advisement to get out of a situation.
Joint tenancy (title work) signifies equal ownership and rights of full inheritance. This would mean an idea, issue, or concept having equal rights of possession by the originators.

Welfare

Board of health is indicative of those who endeavor to maintain a state of healthfulness. This dream symbol will be related to those people who are associated with the dreamer or helpful individuals.
Entitlement program corresponds with additional assistance needed or given to a specific individual, group, or issue.
Food stamps emphasize the fact that everyone is entitled to emotional, mental, and spiritual nourishment.
Health department relates to an unhealthy aspect in one's life.
Health department violation refers to a negative (unhealthy) attitude or behavior that one is aware of.
Public assistance See welfare.
Public housing See welfare.
Social security relates to good intentions, but questionable planning.
Social service reflects humanitarian intentions.
Welfare applies to situations that may require the assistance or intervention of others.

Land grant exemplifies an open opportunity capable of fulfilling one's multiple goals.
Lease represents an extension of time.
Lemon law connotes a life aspect that has the capability to break one's stream of consistent troubles.
Lien represents a spiritual debt that needs to be paid before further advancement can be accomplished.
Mineral rights point to the rightful owner/person through which multiple blessings/benefits come.
Quitclaim deed may exclude an individual from further claim/ownership or it may actually include others depending on how the quitclaim read.
Real estate contract signifies the attainment of a goal.
Reassignment constitutes a new direction or purpose.
Release of lien points to a zero debt associated with an issue. Signifies one has paid one's dues regarding something.
Squatter's rights reveal an individual's right to be somewhere.
Tenancy in common represents a shared portion of an idea with no participant having a right to the whole of it.
Tenure signifies a well-deserved, lasting benefit or reward for efforts expended.
Variance (zoning) applies to an individual's right to be different or do something out of the ordinary.
Water rights come as an important dreamscape symbol verifying one's right to a spiritual belief.

Wills

Executrix points to an individual who has the right/ability to sort matters out and/or disburse benefits and reconcile debts.
Inheritance defines that which is handed down to another; what another has left behind for us to benefit from.
Legacy constitutes that which one leaves behind for others to benefit from or that which has been left for us by others.
Living will signifies an understanding of death or a futile situation.
Testatrix refers to a woman who has left a legacy.

Contracts & Covenants

Agreement represents an aspect that must be resolved.
Clause (in document) brings one's attention to something important; a reminder.
Contract portrays a bona fide agreement one must honor, even if the contract is with oneself in the way of a private resolution.
Covenant See agreement.
Fine print advises one to be particularly aware of details.

Fine print means pay attention.

Reveals the presence of extenuating aspects.
Small print See fine print.

Family Law

Adultery warns against taking something that cannot be yours. This symbol points to prevarications and betrayal.
Age of consent warns of being old enough to know better or take responsibility for one's actions; time to be culpable.
Alimony represents payments due. This may not always refer to financial issues. It may also point to a need to give more attention to one's life partner.
Annulment signifies the breaking of a relationship.
Banns (marriage) reveal an intent; an announcement.
Bigamy illustrates a lack of commitment; a disregard for others; a tendency toward self-importance.
Child support usually comes as an advisement to give more credence and support to one's child within.
Common-law marriage underscores the concept of living by the spirit of the law; having a mutual understanding of something; arrangements agreed without contractual formalities.
Custodial rights refers to something one is solely responsible for.
Death certificate refers to proof that something is finalized and no further activity is possible.
Decree signifies an authoritative statement; an order.
Divorce certificate points to proof that one has severed a relationship or perspective.
Marriage license suggests plans to commit to someone or something in the near future.
Paternity test warns against attempting to circumvent personal responsibility. Refers to validating ownership, possession, or rights.
Respondent signifies one who needs to address a problem, often a conflict.
Underage usually refers to being unprepared.

Miscellaneous

Abidance (compliance) represents a warning to follow the letter and spirit of the law.
Aboveboard means following the law or rules; honesty.
Affidavit refers to proof; verification.
Bill of lading pertains to the manner in which one holds to promises; how one delivers and follows through.
Binder (legal) stands for warranted promises or agreements.
Blight (urban) applies to negative elements that break down and erode advancement.
Blue-sky law is the preservation of one's efforts expended; prevention against backsliding.
Brief (legal) indicates facts presented in a concise manner.
Caveat emptor advises one to know issues; do homework and be knowledgeable regarding a specific aspect.
Citation (legal notice) stands for a commendation or reprimand from a higher authority.
County pinpoints a specific message for each dreamer.
Easement (conservation) stands for protecting/securing each aspect of one's progression before moving on.
Echelon refers to degrees or levels of importance; priority designations.
Escrow represents safeguards; protected or guaranteed elements.
Fire brigade suggests several individuals involved in trying to solve a problem or avert a potentially explosive situation.
Flag symbolizes loyalty to a cause.
Foreclosure forewarns of an upcoming failure or some aspect in the dreamer's life that will not be fulfilled.
Game laws denote the limits of one's predatory nature.
Gold seal stands for an official approval.
Grandfather clause pertains to an exemption of some type given.
Gun control warns of attempts to gain power or the upper hand over an issue.
Hierarchy represents stages of development or attainment in one's life.
Imprimatur warns against censorship; a barrier to one's freedom to choose for self.
Indenture suggests a need to perform a return service for another. This usually points to some form of debt.

see also
• Death *p. 118*
• Family *p. 126*

Miscellaneous (continued)

Informed consent (form) signifies proof of prior knowledge and one's agreement to it.
Injunction comes as a warning to stop destructive behavior.
Injustice defines a wrong conclusion or judgment made in one's life.
Law book comes in a dream as an advisement to check the legality/rightness of a particular attitude/behavior plan.
Lawsuit pertains to a demand for retribution; forcing justice or judgment.
Leading indicators come in a dreamscape to forewarn of certain situations or attitudes that are developing. Hints to what's approaching.
Legal aid implies everyone's inherent right to justice.
Legalese stands for a form of communication that one can't follow/understand without further explanations.
Legal holiday See specific holiday.
Legal pad indicates a need to make notes regarding a negative situation or chain of events in one's life.
Letter of intent signifies an insured or sealed promise; guaranteeing one's intention or an agreement.
License (any type) emphasizes an individual's credentials/permission/entitlement or legal right.
Lockdown characterizes confinement, usually for an individual's own safety.
Long arm reveals an individual or issue that has a long reach—it can affect many and have multiple ramifications.
Mail drop points to secrets or privy information.
Maritime law relates to the rules/concepts associated with an individual's particular religious/spiritual belief system.
Martial law emphasizes the importance of order in an individual's life.
Mason-Dixon line denotes a firm difference of opinion; a strong line one won't cross.
National Park Service refers to those who work to preserve inherent abilities/bounties.
No-fault comes as a message to discount blame or judgment.
Ordinance most often underscores a proper manner of behavior.
Patent Office stands for authoritative recognition.
Penal code always refers to karmic law.
Permission usually comes from one's higher self or other authoritative source to provide encouragement or motivation.
Permit reveals the rightness of a planned move or deed. Recall if the permit was being granted or denied. What was it for? Did the permit have a specific color?
Petition stands for a personal request. The key here is to recall who was petitioning whom and for what purpose.
Plea See petition.
Port authority represents one's right to advance into new path regions; one's right or readiness to pass through.
Power of attorney pertains to a shift of responsibility or culpability.
Private sector signifies minimum restrictions.

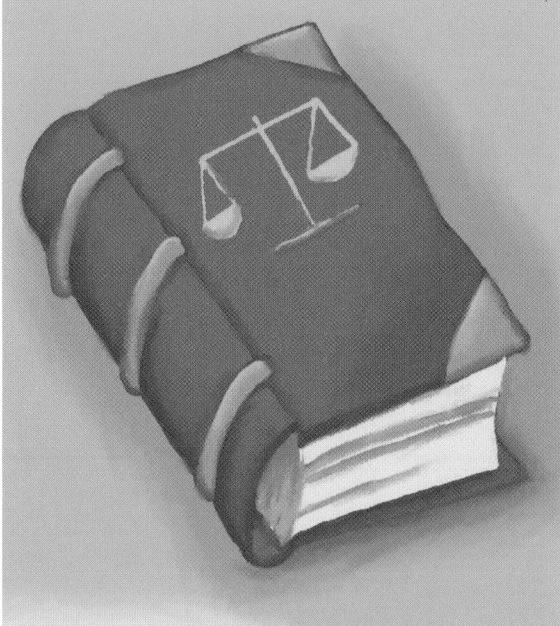
Law book reminds one to check the accuracy of something.

Pro-choice represents a decision that is not hindered by another's personal opinion; the personal freedom/right to make personal choices.
Pro-life alludes to a respect for life but not necessarily for rights.
Proviso connotes ulterior motives or special provisions.
Proxy pertains to a loss of input; a state of waning participation.
Reverter clause is usually representative of the knowledge that a plan has the possibility of needing to start from square one; leaving room for possibilities.
Right of first refusal is usually indicative of an individual who must be offered the first option to accept or reject something.
Selective service emphasizes a forced participation.
Settlement (agreement) stands for a need to negotiate and reconcile.
Special use permit (zoning) refers to a temporary or short-term activity.
Standard (flag) correlates to what one stands for or strongly supports. What type of flag was it? What did it represent to the dreamer?
Sue See lawsuit.
Tribunal pertains to self-judgment.
Trustee reveals a trusted individual.
Urban blight points to a situation that's degrading.
Waiver relates to a voluntary refusal; a decision to decline.
Warranty is a reference to validation.

Chapter 21

Faith & Religion

Distorted truth is the most common meaning for faith and religious symbols. They usually point to a belief distorted by a slanted perspective or biased opinion.

Texts & Rules

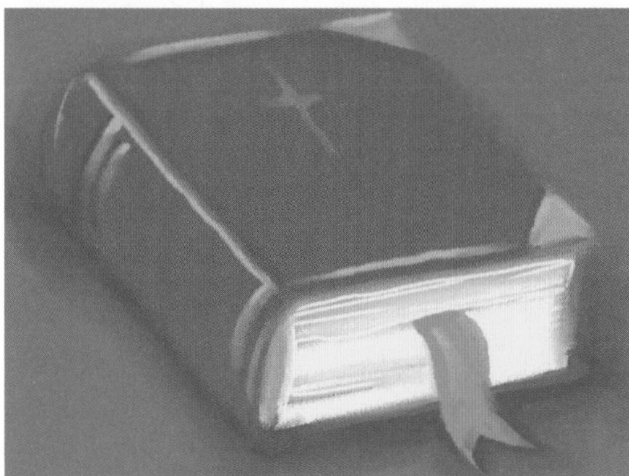

Bible represents the modification of language and ideas.

Bible portrays revised or altered words and concepts.
Book of the Dead signifies the fact that life goes on; a suggestion to have faith, fortitude.
Code of ethics suggests a specific standard of behavior.
Dean's list denotes intellectual accomplishments.
Genesis defines a major new beginning.
Good Book See Bible.
Gospel applies to a truth as perceived by a specific individual.
Hymnal denotes personal praise of the divine and our expressions of spiritual joy.
Illuminated text points to something important at which the dreamer needs to take a more serious look.
Litany suggests remembrance. It may warn against an unforgiving nature.
Liturgy cautions against spiritual formality.
Magnificat reminds one to be aware and appreciative of one's connection with the divine.
Proverb typifies an advisement or counsel. It will often be enlightening.
Psalm reflects inner spiritual thoughts. May indicate a contentedness.
Scripture See Bible.
Scroll (ancient) emphasizes solid truths.

Prayer

Prayer beads See rosary.
Prayer book represents a tendency to have spiritual expectations. It may also refer to a dependency on higher forces to accomplish one's goals.
Prayer shawl reflects spiritual humility and respect.
Prayer wheel warns of spiritual inattention; a tendency to place one's responsibility on the divine rather than recognizing and accepting one's own.
Rosary recommends a time to pray, more specifically, turn to one's spirituality.

Christianity

Advent denotes the beginning of something, the first signs of its entry into one's life.
Easter signifies victory; triumph over life's problems.
Ecumenical council stands for religious interference/control.
Epiphany pertains to a sudden enlightening event; a shuddering revelation. This most often is not spiritually related but is associated with a solution to a problem, the right attitude or perspective finally dawning, or some other brilliant inspiration that brings clarification.
Eucharist See Holy Communion.
Evensong symbolizes an appreciation for life's beauty and joys experienced each day; an expression of gratefulness; prayer of appreciation for one's blessings.
Excommunication represents judgment; spiritual judgment through arrogance.
Extreme unction is a forewarning of someone's probable death.
Gnostic is representative of intuitiveness.
Good Friday stands for shared grief; deep empathy.
Halloween illustrates personal revelations; insights into another's hidden character.
High holy days will usually signify a time of great importance for the dreamer, generally spiritual.
Holy Communion reflects what some believe to be their personal connection to a supreme being.
Holy day See high holy days. See specific holy day.
Last rites rarely is a forewarning of death. It usually enters dreams as a strong warning to make reconciliations.
Last Supper won't have anything to do with Christianity or Jesus, but will reveal the possibility of forthcoming tribulations to bravely face and overcome.
Latin mass represents an attraction/preference for religious traditions.
Laying on of hands represents good intentions.
Lent warns against setting aside an official or traditionally designated time for self-examination. This should be a daily exercise.
Palm Sunday defines an attitude of spiritual reverence.
Quakers stand for listening to one's inner voice or divine guidance/inspiration.
Religious ceremonies stand for man-made affectations and embellishments added to basic tenets.
Requiem comes to the dreamer as a forewarning of a dying or quickly declining situation, relationship, or other element in his or her life.
Sacrament is representative of any act that one believes will earn grace.
Sermon usually brings a personal message for each dreamer. What was the sermon about?
Shakers (sect) See Quakers.
Twelfth-day equates to an epiphany.
Vespers suggest the wisdom of evening reflection over one's day in order to analyze behavior and responses.

see also
• Feasts & Saints' Days *p. 349*
• Demonic *p. 367*

Christian Religious Figures

Abbess represents spiritual grace in leadership.
Abbot See abbess.
Acolyte is a symbol that warns of misplaced adoration of spiritual personalities.
Antichrist connotes an embodiment of negativity or evil.
Apostle means one who follows another's spiritual lead.
Atheist connotes those who would destroy spiritual beliefs.
Bishop applies to spiritual arrogance.
Cardinal (priest) See religious figure.
Chaplain signifies someone who will listen; a nonjudgmental individual.
Circuit rider (traveling cleric) advises one to utilize spirituality wherever one is.
Cleric See religious figure.
Deacon is usually indicative of an individual who has been spiritually helpful in one's life.
Dean characterizes intellectual authority or counsel.
Disciple characterizes an advocate. More specifically, it is a reference to a devoted supporter.
Evangelist is indicative of a zealous personality; someone who is strongly impassioned and may have a tendency toward coercion or guilt-tripping.
Friar See religious figure.
Heretic characterizes a diversion from popular belief systems. This may be a positive symbol in that it represents individuality; a freethinker.
Jesus freak is indicative of spiritual fanaticism; an intolerance of another's belief system.

Nun is indicative of the weaving of spiritual elements into one's everyday life.

Mendicant implies efforts expended for others.
Minister See religious figure.
Monk characterizes an individual who chooses to forgo materialism in lieu of devoting a life to spiritual good works/contemplation.
Mother superior (head nun) See religious figure.
Mystic (person) points to an overemphasis on the paranormal facets of spirituality and reality.
Neophyte See novice.
Novice reveals a lack of experiential or knowledgeable background; a beginner.
Nun represents the incorporation of spiritual facets throughout the fabric of one's daily life.
Padre See religious figure.
Parson See religious figure.
Pastor See religious figure.
Patron saint pertains to a guiding or protective ideal or motivational force.
Pieta symbolizes an internalized spirituality; deep emotional responses to one's spiritual beliefs.
Pontiff See pope.
Pope characterizes religious domination.
Postulant relates to determined intentions. This symbol may not necessarily have a spiritual connotation.
Preacher See religious figure.
Prelate See religious figure.
Priest(ess) See religious figure.
Prioress See religious figure.
Rector See religious figure.
Religious figure usually comes to draw attention to spiritual matters in one's life, not specific religious dogma.
Reverend See religious figure.
Saint usually reveals a desired quality, but may also warn against a perspective that one believes oneself to be a saint. May point to a tendency to look down one's nose on others.
Saint Christopher characterizes an individual who is capable and willing to carry another's burden or serve to uplift them during a stressful phase.
Vicar See religious figure.

New Testament Figures

Good Samaritan defines humanitarian acts.
Jesus represents a high spiritual messenger; one who sacrifices much for a goal.
John the Baptist emphasizes a forerunner; a messenger.
Judas (Iscariot) reveals misplaced trust; poor judgment.
Lazarus (biblical) exemplifies the technical capabilities of interdimensionality comprising true reality.
Magdalene (Mary) stands for a misunderstood personality. This dream symbol may be a reference to a false public opinion or impression of an individual. It may also equate to spiritual companionship and unconditional love in the dreamer's waking life.
Pilate (Pontius) exemplifies the fear of being bested and/or not liked. It may also refer to a fear of making decisions; concern about what others think of oneself.

Old Testament Figures

Adam (biblical) characterizes a weak personality; lack of self-control; easy manipulation. Also suggests a fear of reaching for more knowledge/ information.

Eve defines a counter to the theory of evolution. Represents a flaw in a generally accepted idea or perspective.

Goliath characterizes to the dreamer an individual or situation that must be overcome for advancement.

Herod the Great characterizes a fear of being bested. Refers to an obsession with self; a fear that someone else is perceived as being better/more admired.

Messiah corresponds with someone in the dreamer's life who will prevent his/her personal failure or loss of direction. Will point to someone who saves the day.

Methuselah relates to long-lasting.

Methuselah (biblical) applies to a great age; a time-tested aspect.

Moses (biblical) characterizes a messenger; one who has the capability of overcoming adversity through perseverance.

Noah (biblical) characterizes strong faith and behavior related to same.

Salome (biblical) characterizes one with ulterior motives.

Other Religious Figures

Fakir refers to one's inner strength.

Avatar is synonymous with spiritual arrogance.

Effigy warns of energies being misdirected in a negative way.

Fakir symbolizes the power within each of us.

Grand Lama characterizes high spiritual attainment.

Hierophant characterizes an enlightened individual; one who has the advanced development of knowledge coupled with wisdom.

High priestess characterizes one who has reached the attainment of knowledge coupled with wisdom.

Illuminati reveal individuals in one's life who are, in reality, unenlightened. Nobody should claim absolute enlightenment.

Magi apply to those who have attained spiritual knowledge and wisdom; spiritual awareness.

Magus portrays one who has attained high wisdom.

Maharishi constitutes a spiritual teacher, usually someone associated with the dreamer.

Mahatma defines a spiritually enlightened individual who lives beliefs.

Oracle usually reveals a forthcoming event in one's life. Yet this same symbol can also warn against being obsessed with the future or one's drive to know.

Prophet(ess) characterizes an astute and wise individual.

Rabbi See religious figure.

Sage (person) characterizes an individual possessing high wisdom gained through enlightenment.

Tin god signifies a perspective of self-importance.

Unbeliever may point to a skeptic or it may simply indicate someone who has yet to seriously look into an issue enough to be convinced.

Other Religions

Ancestor worship reminds us of the importance of learning from another's past experience or example.

Animalism symbolizes misplaced spiritual beliefs.

Animism represents the life force in all things; the fundamental essence.

Cult represents a group of individuals who have specific beliefs that are considered aberrant or dangerous. This dream symbol usually comes as a warning message regarding some associates of the dreamer in his or her waking life.

Indian Spirituality

Bodhisattva characterizes absolute selflessness.

Buddha characterizes highest spiritual attainment; enlightenment and the true wisdom that accompanies it.

Guru connotes spiritual arrogance; current spiritual fads.

Karma stands for making retribution. Also signifies behavioral balance.

Kundalini is representative of spiritual energy.

Swami See yogi.

Yogi usually implies spiritual showmanship.

Chinese & Japanese Spirituality

I Ching depicts a high interest in outcomes and the future. Therefore, it also represents a lack of acceptance for what is.

Koan symbolizes a need for contemplation; deeper analysis; the exercising of one's thought process.

Taoist indicates one who has a tendency to not interfere in things; one who lets life take its course without attempting to alter things.

Yin-yang reminds us of our duality; the female and male aspects within oneself.

Zen pertains to methods for attaining enlightenment, inner peace, and the activation of naturally inherent abilities.

see also
• Magic *p. 478*
• Ghosts & Spirits *p. 479*

Islam

Mecca is a dreamscape symbol that signifies to the dreamer a greatly desired goal or attainment.

Muezzin suggests a call to prayer.

Ramadan is representative of self-denial.

Judaism

Ark of the Covenant is a symbol that signifies our connective bond to the divine.

Essene represents to the dreamer a true visionary messenger who is quietly cognizant of the true aspects comprising reality, including all life interrelationships.

Hanukkah comes as a reminder for us to rekindle the light in our souls for our spiritual beliefs.

Kabala symbolizes the higher esoteric facets of spiritual truths.

Kaddish reminds us to remember our dead.

Kosher pertains to the proper manner or process.

Menorah reminds us of our beginnings; eternal spirits temporarily borrowing humanoid forms. Symbol may also come as an advisement to keep our inner lights shining in respect to blessings bestowed.

Mezuzah symbolizes an external sign of one's spiritual beliefs and the faith in the personal protection it has the potential to provide.

Old Testament comes as an advisement to readjust one's thinking on something. The dreamer will know what this issue is.

Passover signifies the protective elements of innocence or being guiltless.

Pharisee represents a spiritual hypocrite.

Phylactery pertains to a reminder of specific spiritual tenets. The dreamer will usually make individualized associations here.

Rosh Hashanah indicates a new beginning.

Sabbath See high holy days.

Synagogue reflects spiritual associations and the living practice of one's beliefs.

Tabernacle denotes sacredness or that which is perceived as such. Recall what was in the tabernacle. Where was it? What color was it? See specific color.

Talmud corresponds with right living according to a specific belief system.

Ten Commandments come to remind one of the simple basics of spiritual behavior.

Torah signifies an individual's high spiritual belief system. Refer to the condition and color of the dreamscape Torah. Was it protected or left exposed?

Wailing wall appears in dreams to stress the importance of showing one's feelings and expressing one's emotions or sensitivities.

Yom Kippur (Day of Atonement) comes to advise the dreamer that an apology, restitution, or resolution needs to be made.

Paganism

Shaman is a reference to one's spiritual skills.

Beltane equates to a springlike time frame in one's life, a time of purification and renewal.

Black mass denotes spiritual negativity; a destructive spiritual force.

Coven refers to a spiritually related group of people.

Druid represents esoteric spiritual aspects.

Heathen characterizes spirituality versus the dogmas of organized religions.

Pagan usually symbolizes the existence of a spiritual belief that differs from convention. This is not necessarily a negative connotation. Recall surrounding dreamscape details for further clarification.

Shaman characterizes the higher spiritual abilities and the associated sacredness.

Witch won't usually denote a negative connotation, for Wicca is a bona fide nature religion celebrating the seasons, spirituality felt in nature, and the natural gifts inherent in everyone. A witch most often represents an individual who recognizes and uses those natural abilities to help others.

Spirituality

Chakra symbolizes inner resources; reserves of energy.

Clairaudience will not necessarily be associated to a psychic skill but rather come in a dream to advise of a need to listen to someone more closely.

Clairvoyance comes as a suggestion to pay closer attention to insights, hunches, and inner intuitive feelings.

New Age equates to a blend of physics and spirituality. The symbol points to a realization and utilization of elements related to true reality.

Theosophy equates to a philosophical belief in the mystical connection between nature and spirituality; the inter-relationship of all living things; the web of life.

Religious Locations

Abbey symbolizes a need to regain one's spiritual sacredness toward beliefs.
Ashram cautions against spiritual reclusiveness.
Basilica warns against spiritual arrogance, believing one is more spiritually special or unique than another.
Bethlehem illustrates the beginnings of a new spiritual concept.
Calvary exemplifies personal sacrifices that may not be necessary.
Catacomb represents buried or hidden information. May point to buried memories.
Cathedral is a symbol of spiritual excesses; a grandiose spiritual attitude.
Chapel is an illustration of a temporary time of spiritual respite or peace.
Church indicates a type of spiritual connection and the quality of same. What was the church's condition? Size?
Churchyard defines spiritual inactivity; dormant spirituality; a seemingly dead spirituality.
Confessional signals a need for honesty. Suggests an untruth is preventing advancement and it's time to let it all out.
Convent pertains to voluntary spiritual isolation.
Eden connotes an unrealistic life perspective.
Gethsemane implies abandonment; betrayal.
Heaven stands for what one perceives as the ultimate state of being.
Hell may illustrate various conditions such as a great tribulation, extremely difficult situation, a dark and depressive state of mind, and so on.

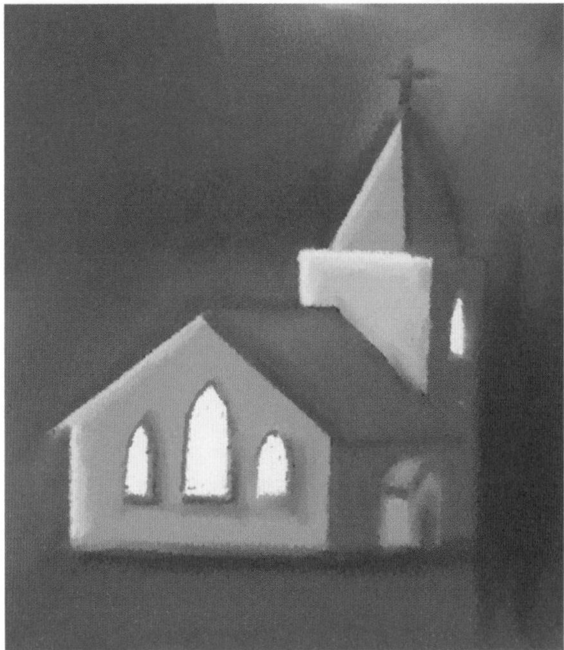

Church represents the state of one's spiritual beliefs.

Inner sanctum relates to a person's innermost thoughts and feelings, those that one needs to protect from being hurt/made public.
Limbo (religious dogma) connotes a state of inactivity; ineffectiveness; inaction. It may also pertain to a phase when one remains in neutral until opinions or perceptions are well formed.
Lourdes usually represents misinterpretation; false perception; illusion.
Mission (church) pertains to a specific work one needs to do. May point one in the right direction for one's life purpose.

Gods & Goddesses

God represents the highest authority. It may also be a reference to the ultimate goal in one's life.
Goddess signifies the feminine supreme being.
Golden calf warns of negative goals and misplaced priorities.
Mother Earth symbolizes one's natural blessings/bounties.
Mother god stands for a source of deep empathy and a giving nature.
Quetzalcoatl means a spiritual rebirth.
Sun goddess characterizes someone who is elated by feeling spiritually blessed. It may refer to the uplifting sense brought on by spiritual behavior.

Monastery pertains to privacy, especially in respect to one's spiritual beliefs.
Nirvana signifies a mental/emotional state of euphoria. This is not a positive dreamscape fragment, for it implies that the dreamer is living in a fantasy world and not within acceptance of daily reality. This usually indicates one living in one's own world.
Paradise relates to one's personal perspective of the perfect scenario, condition, or ultimate goal.
Priory See monastery.
Promised land most often applies to one's goals or the attainment of purpose.
Pulpit signifies preaching; telling others what to do and believe.
Purgatory reflects reparations; self-analysis and serious introspection followed by deeds that balance one's negative actions.
Rectory denotes spiritual arrogance. It may refer to the idea of one spiritually elevating oneself.
Sanctum See inner sanctum.
Shrine cautions against focusing on singular spiritual facets.
Sunday school signifies the deep insights gained from serious reflection and contemplation.
Tower of Babel warns of spiritual confusion; double-talk or excessive verbiage confusing spirituality's simplicity.
Vatican exemplifies a specific religious belief rather than a purely spiritual one.

see also
• Church Architecture *p. 311*
• Paranormal Tools *p. 480*

Religious Accoutrements

Ankh typifies enduring peace and spiritual knowledge.
Burning bush generally means epiphanies, but may also reveal one's deepening attitude of apathy.
Burnt offering signifies subjugation; attempts to appease or plead.
Calumet See peace pipe.
Canopic jar symbolizes preservation. Usually advises the dreamer of a need to recall or retain the memory of an event for the purpose of learning from it.
Ciborium is associated with a high respect for one's spiritual beliefs.
Crown of thorns connotes self-sacrifice; perhaps a masochistic personality.

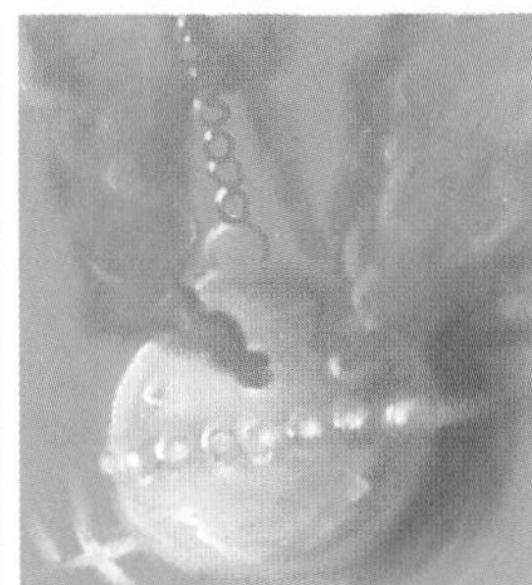

Incense may heighten spirituality.

Cross (crucifix) See crucifix.
Crucifix is an outward sign that marks one's self-sacrifices; a desire to display one's personal pains.
Elixir represents an imagined cure-all to life's problems.
Frankincense alludes to a biblical age past life.
Grail See Holy Grail.
Graven image See idol.
Halo illustrates spiritual enlightenment.
Holy Grail connotes a need for spiritual proof.
Holy water exemplifies a need for spiritual affectations to feel power behind one's beliefs; a lack of faith.
Icon forewarns against misplaced adoration.
Incense may represent a calmative or it can indicate spiritual embellishments. Surrounding dreamscape details will clarify which meaning was intended.
Missal See prayer book.
Myrrh defines spiritual insights and wisdom.
Revelation brings an insight; sudden understanding.
Sacred objects usually represent something one places faith in.
Sacristy corresponds with the sacred place within oneself.
Scapular (religious) reminds us to maintain personal protection. Alludes to the wisdom of watching your back.
Seven seals represent the stages of spiritual enlightenment.
Tree of life (design) represents the interrelatedness of all living things. This points to a need to realize that the individuality of others doesn't really make them separate, only unique. Also see tree hugger.
Unction See anointing.
Votive candle connotes spiritual comfort.

Church Furnishings

Altar denotes adoration. Watch this one.
Altar cloth serves the dreamer as a clarifying symbol for an altar. What's important here is to recall the condition, color, or designs of the cloth.
Altar rail represents respect for one's spiritual beliefs. Could also denote some type of barrier between a belief system and one's faith in same.
Church bells refer to a call to spirituality. May advise the use of greater spiritual behavior.
Footstool advises one to slow down as one travels one's life path. Perhaps one needs to assimilate deeper meanings of lessons being presented.
Gargoyle usually represents an attempt to protect one's spirituality. May refer to some type of distortion in one's life.
Hassock See footstool.
Luminaria represents spiritual celebration.
Monstrance depicts that which one reveres. This is a revealing symbol that will point out whether or not what one reveres is spiritually correct.
Pew won't necessarily have a religious connotation. It will usually symbolize a concept many sit and listen to or a place where same is done.
Shrine warns against focusing on singular spiritual facets.
Stained glass represents multifaceted elements creating a singular aspect. May denote differential perceptions of various individuals. What did the stained glass depict? Birds? Flowers? What type of design? What were the predominant colors?

Sacraments

Absolution means the shedding of self-guilt, probably a false one. Could point to a call for forgiveness or acceptance.
Atonement suggests reparation, reconciliation, or contriteness.
Baptism of fire stands for experiencing an ordeal before one thinks one is ready.
Exorcism characterizes a personally concerted effort to rid self of certain life aspects that don't necessarily have to be negatives.
Oath relates to promises that must be kept, even to oneself.
Offering represents one's good intentions.

Signs & Symbols

Celtic cross signifies an esoteric spiritual aspect.
Mandala is a sign to inspire or remind one of the beauty of spiritual expression (behavior).
Manitou represents a positive spiritual force.
Mantra portrays one's personal method of spiritual or psychological reinforcement.
Sign of the cross (gesture) often points to a silent prayer. May not refer to the literal act of praying, but rather being an outward expression of one's frustration or even hope.
Stigmata stands for a whiner; a persecution complex.
Swastika (configuration) may not stand for a highly negative element but rather for its original symbology, that of a religious sign of good luck or improved fortune.

Religious & Spiritual Activities

Act of God represents unpreventable situations. It may also point to a situation of blame-shifting by placing responsibility on an untouchable, absent source.

Anointing is indicative of a blessing. It may specifically refer to a higher recognition.

Beatification cautions against elevating others.

Benediction alludes to a spiritually sanctioned individual or deed.

Blasphemy corresponds with contempt.

Blessing portrays a recognition of sacredness.

Born-again usually signifies a renewed faith, not necessarily a religious one but simply a rekindled faith in something.

Canonize signifies spiritual conclusions based on personally devised criteria.

Catechism represents spiritual indoctrination.

Chant denotes a means to inner light and/or knowing.

Confirmation represents some type of verification.

Anointing is a depiction of approval from above.

Consecration is a recognition of sacredness or spirituality.

Creed defines one's basic spiritual beliefs. May point to personal perspectives.

Cross (making the sign of) exposes religious rather than spiritual faith.

Defrock cautions against doing something that isn't aligned with one's high ideals.

Defrocked signifies an attitude/perspective/behavior that is counter to one's professed belief.

Desecration signifies spiritual disrespect or apathy.

Exodus won't normally refer to a literal departure but rather equate to a flight from responsibility or a refusal to face reality.

Gift of tongues See glossolalia.

Glossolalia warns of unintelligible speech; a personal need to be noticed.

Godsend represents a blessing, a windfall, or possibly a manifested need.

Hail Mary (prayer) points to a last hope or last-ditch effort.

Hallow refers to an individualized idea of what is perceived as sacred.

Iconography exemplifies a call for extensive contemplation.

Orthodox connotes an adherence to strict basic beliefs or attitudes; firm convictions.

Passion play reveals a person's display of emotional dramatics; an exaggeration for the purpose of attention.

Prayer depicts a specific need or desire in one's life. Recall what the prayer's subject was. Who was the prayer directed to? Who was saying the words?

Prayer meeting advises of a state of spiritual weakness; a condition whereby one depends on the spiritual motivation and support of others.

Sandpainting illustrates spiritual healing knowledge.

Secularism indicates spiritual indifference. May point to activities or individuals having no correlation to spiritual aspects.

Speaking in tongues See glossolalia.

Angels

Angel refers to an angelic person.

Angel represents spiritual messages. May come to reveal angelic qualities that are associated with someone the dreamer knows.

Angel of death is most often a death premonition.

Archangel portrays critical spiritual messages from the highest source.

Cherub denotes young innocence. Can be a descriptive symbol for adult as well as a child.

Guardian angel portrays an individual's higher self; the inner voice heeded.

The Devil

Beelzebub See devil.

Deuce (devil) pertains to a situation that characterizes a perfect example of something bad. Epitomizes the worst of something.

Devil characterizes an individual or life aspect that is extremely negative and personally harmful.

Diablo See devil.

Evil may not refer to absolute negative aspects. It could be saying only that one believes or thinks a person, concept, or thing is evil.

Lucifer See devil.

Satan See devil.

see also
• Social, Political & Religious *p. 235*
• Peace *p. 357*

Religious & Spiritual Concepts

Abundance is synonymous with enough or more than enough of something.

Afterlife connotes a reassurance that no situation is hopeless, that there's light at the end of the tunnel. It reveals the uplifting fact that one can get past current problems.

Agnostic cautions against the tendency to demand proof of everything.

Apocalypse connotes a personal revelation. May possibly be associated with a personal conflict.

Armageddon alludes to a major conflict forthcoming (or expected) in one's life. May also refer to a great fear that is unwarranted.

Divine essence characterizes the idea of the Supreme Being and comes in dreams to either commend or advise.

Homage warns against giving this to anyone but the divine.

Immaculate assumption refers to the assumption (belief) that there is a God the Father and a God the Son without a God the Mother. This symbol refers to a huge misconception or assumption in one's life.

Immaculate conception most often attempts to reveal the accurate reality of this issue: immaculate in respect to being born without the stain of original sin. As a dreamscape fragment, this points to an innocent individual.

Judgment Day reminds us that all our life actions and thoughts will be one day reviewed and judged. This symbol comes to advise us to listen more to our conscience.

Last Judgment is a strong warning message. It implies there is little time left to bring balance into one's life.

Logos stands for the word of the supreme being.

Manna exemplifies spiritual nourishment.

Monasticism applies to a desire to lead a purely private life and forsake societal involvement and material trappings.

Monotheism points the way.

Olive branch naturally signifies a peace offering; a desire to end conflict and go forward.

Olive branch brings an end to strife.

Piety reveals an individual's spiritual state. The surrounding dream details will disclose whether or not this is a sincere state.

Pious See piety.

Rebirth (spiritual) does not imply a spiritual connotation, yet it signifies a renewal of some type, a new inspiration.

Sacred cow applies to misplaced priorities or to that which one personally perceives as being sacrosanct in one's life.

Second Coming symbolizes expectations made on how we think something will occur.

Soul defines one's vital and prime essence.

Supreme Being See divine essence.

True reality stands for all of the knowns and unknowns making up the totality of existence (of the what is).

Christmas

Caroler see Christmas carol.

Christmas defines a major spiritual awakening.

Christmas candle represents the light of one's spirituality. Was it burning? Was the wick broken or missing? How big was the candle?

Christmas card refers to spiritual greetings and messages.

Christmas carol indicates the sharing of spiritual joys with others.

Christmas ornaments imply one's spiritual beliefs need tidying up.

Christmas centerpiece (floral) represents spiritual talents and behavior.

Christmas club comes to the dreamer as a caution against the saving-up of spirituality for a special occasion.

Christmas gift is a dream fragment that is indicative of spiritual giving and sharing.

Christmas lights relate to one's shining spiritual light. They weren't broken, were they?

Christmas ornaments show up in a dreamscape to reveal the fact that someone is decorating spiritual beliefs with clutter.

Christmas stocking represents expectation of spiritual rewards.

Christmas tree is generally indicative of extraneous, unrelated aspects attached to spiritual beliefs.

Xmas See Christmas.

Yuletide See Christmas.

Chapter 22

History, Events, War & Weaponry

These symbols carry specific meanings associated with an individual's current behavior, perspective, or direction.

Timescale

Anachronism indicates something that is lacking chronology. Comes to reveal the fact that something's out of order.

Ancient history suggests elements that are irrelevant to a current situation.

Anniversary signifies important dates; a date to remember.

Annual (yearly) refers to an individual's tendency to repeat actions.

Archaic exposes an individual's outdated idea, belief system, or perspective.

Backlog relates to an aspect in life that's unfinished; something that requires attention.

Biannual applies to something happening twice.

Extinct indicates a life aspect that no longer exists. This dreamscape symbol usually comes as a warning to those who are attempting to hold onto something that has gone from their lives.

Foregone conclusion alludes to conclusions believed to be inevitable. However, this belief may not prove to be an actuality.

Forerunner refers to prerequisite research; something appearing before the main event.

Foresight usually advises of a need to increase one's awareness and perceptive abilities.

Future is most often a precognitive revelation.

Glitch indicates a temporary setback or problem.

Heyday points to a phase in one's life that is highly successful and pleasing.

Hindsight most often represents the lessons we're supposed to learn from bad choices or experiences.

Extinct cautions one to let go of something that is no longer in one's life.

Long run (time) means benefits reaped after an extended amount of time; a plan that will take a longer period of time to manifest its rewards.

Missing time may refer to forgetfulness/denial or it may be associated with the more important aspect of an abductee's implanted amnesia.

Outdated may not be a negative symbol, for it may apply to a long-held truth that few currently believe. Recall surrounding dream details for further clarification.

Out-of-date suggests one of two things. It may point to an outdated perspective or way of doing things, or it may advise that something has expired (therefore it is too late to do anything about it).

Overdue usually indicates procrastination. May also mean something is a long time in coming.

Passé implies that something is out-of-date, yet, depending on surrounding dream elements, this may reveal a personal opinion rather than actual fact.

Past sometimes serves as a past example or indicates something one should leave behind where it belongs.

Posthumous implies that which one leaves behind after one has gone. May not necessarily indicate a death but rather something that one leaves in one's wake.

Postseason corresponds to recent experiential events.

Prehistoric (settings/element) constitutes a long-standing aspect in one's life.

Primeval reflects a beginning or original element or idea.

Primordial symbolizes the first stage of development for a plan or its progression.

Quarterly applies to a specific proportion of time related to an aspect of the dreamer's everyday life.

Up-to-date refers to keeping one's finger on the pulse of events; keeping a close eye on a situation; maintaining full knowledge.

Ages

Age of Aquarius means a time of great change and major shifts in societal thought.

Age of Reason means old enough to understand.

Dark Ages (setting) See Middle Ages.

Golden age constitutes peace and/or prosperity.

Ice age represents an extensive span in one's life when spiritual matters are ignored or not held as a priority.

Iron Age represents strength.

Medieval usually denotes a lack of intellectual reasoning. It may also refer to a past-life experience, depending on surrounding details.

Middle Ages represent a time when one will begin to become more aware.

Millennium is a time marker that comes to dispel fear and anxiety.

Modern refers to a current time frame or method.

Neanderthal does not necessarily mean primitive but usually refers to a willful state of ignorance.

Stone Age connotes a backward or primitive idea, perspective, or manner of behavior.

see also
• Times of Day *p. 62*
• Months *p. 85*

Current Events

Accident cautions one to be watchful. May also point to a guiltless act.
Air show denotes an example being shown regarding the potential of thought process or reach for knowledge.
Auto show refers to a presentation of options available for one's lifestyle. This means elements such as diet, manner of living, behavior, and directional choices.
Bake-off represents the best possible outcome.
Bake sale represents efforts expended to help another.
Beauty pageant pertains to misplaced perception of beauty; an overemphasis on the physical attributes of an individual, especially women.
Boat show signifies the many types of options available for a personalized spiritual journey.
Boom (economic flourish) portrays a productive path.
Car show See auto show.
Catastrophe denotes major events in one's life that may end in a devastating manner.
Championship represents a final test/challenge.
Country Music Awards (CMA) refer to the rewards of simple joys in life.
Election day pinpoints a specific time to make a firm decision.
Inquest advises of a need to fully investigate some aspect in one's life. There is something yet to be revealed.
Motivational seminar may indicate low motivation. Recall what the seminar was motivating.
People's Choice Awards reveals public opinion; the attitude of the majority.
Rally defines a supportive attitude; a motivational force.
Sales rally refers to the gaining of motivation through others' support of a like goal.
Science fair points to innovative thinking; ingenuity; possibilities.
Semifinals show the stage of progression that has brought one close to the attainment of a goal.
Special Olympics stand for personal capabilities regardless of perceived handicaps.
Trade show stands for a display/presentation of the latest developments regarding a specific issue.
Two-minute warning is an attention-getting symbol that advises that one's time is nearly up to get something accomplished.
Weigh-in comes in dreams as an advisement to make a decision; express an opinion; to make a choice.
Workshop generally relates to a hobby or an individualized type of creativity used in an enjoyable manner. It points to the fact that some work can be done in a leisurely manner and actually be enjoyable. What type of workshop was it? Carpentry? Craft? Artsy?
World premiere relates to the initial introduction of an idea.
World Series pertains to competitive efforts applied to aspects unrelated to one's goal or life course.
World's Fair attempts to broaden one's perspective and reveal the existence of unlimited opportunities.

Recording Events

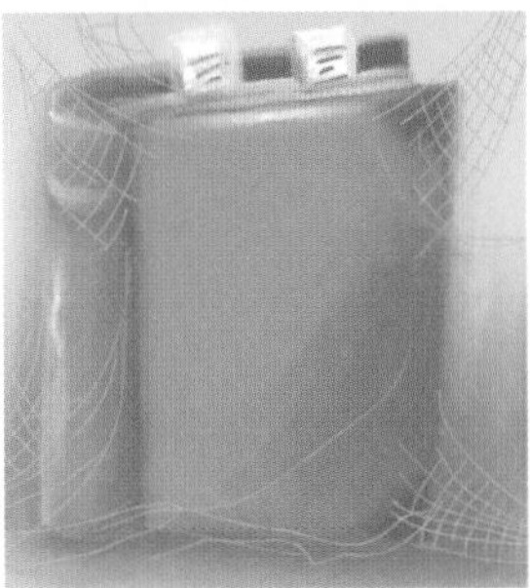

Archive reminds one of the past.

Anecdote denotes the need to learn more of an issue before making a decision or final judgment.
Annals (historic) refer to lessons learned from the past.
Archive denotes a repository of past events. This symbol may be a call to remember one's past.
Biography implies depth of personality; more to an individual than on the surface.
Cover story pertains to major news or information.
Daguerreotype advises of a special current meaning for past relationships; importance of old friends.
Deadline reminds one of the passing of time. May warn that time is running out. Often this symbol refers to the time restrictions one places on self.
First edition refers to the initial dissemination of specific information.
Good news pertains to an encouraging or motivational revelation.
Hard news represents important new information.
Headlines come as important messages. This will carry different meanings for each individual. Recall what the headlines were.
Herstory advises the dreamer to pay closer attention to a female's history. The dreamer will know who this female is.
Memoir comes as a prompting to record one's life events and remember same. By doing this, one usually has some type of revelation.
Moment of truth relates to a revelation or it indicates a need for introspection or open communication.
Newscast/flash almost always brings important information to light that is relevant to the individual dreamer.
News conference See press conference.
Oral tradition reminds us of the importance of preserving truths in life.
Out of print means that something is no longer readily available; a growing rarity.
Press conference signifies a revealing meeting; providing an explanation or making an announcement.
Press junket stands for efforts put into broadcasting information, usually regarding an issue with which one is personally associated.
Press release refers to an announcement of some type. This symbol usually comes to the dreamer as a revelation.
Red-letter marks a special event, individual, or idea; something to be remembered. Recall what the letter was related to.
Smear campaign comes to denote ruthlessness; slanderous activity.
Update stands for the presence of new information of which one must be aware; a change.

Leisure Events

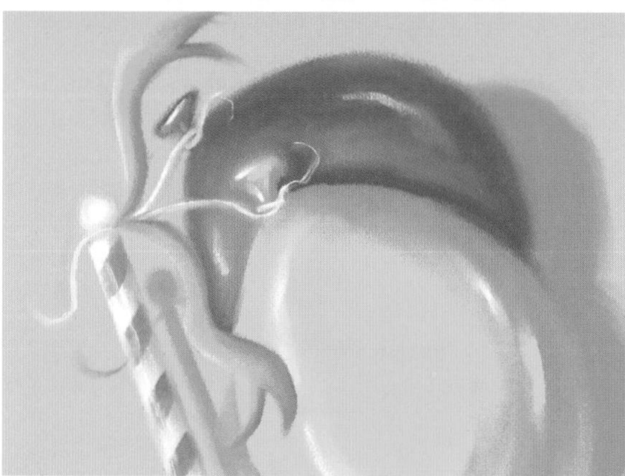

Carnival may suggest something that's not to be taken seriously.

Amateur night represents one's ability and willingness to hear others.
Birthday suggests a special reason to recall one's heritage (usually spiritual). May simply come as a reminder to celebrate one's recent steps toward new beginnings.
Burlesque means that something or someone is being mocked; a travesty.
Candid camera advises to remember that one is never alone, never unwatched.
Carnival defines a whimsical atmosphere or condition; a situation lacking seriousness; verging on the ridiculous. May warn of a dangerous hoodwinking situation.
County fair connotes wholesome pride in one's hard work and the sharing of the resulting products.
Ice show demonstrates the beauty of bringing out one's spiritual aspects and using them for the benefit of others.
Kentucky Derby represents a celebrated fast-paced competition in which many are interested.
Light show sheds light on that which one should give attention to or something one should avoid. This is a call to attention or a warning, depending on other clarifying dream details.
Pop quiz suggests a need to stay informed regarding a particular situation or issue.
Quiz show usually presents itself for the dreamer to gain a proper perspective of knowledge regarding a specific issue.
Regatta warns one against participating in spiritual competition.
Rodeo portrays an exhibition of one's power or control over others competing for control.
Silent auction signifies a situation where one is forced to pay a higher price (expend greater efforts) than necessary to ensure success or the attainment of a specific goal.
Talent show defines the ability that one perceives to be one's best talent.
Variety show connotes ideas that have been derived from multiple sources.

Celebrations

Extravaganza relates to fabulousness; going all out to present the biggest and best-ever display of something.
Fiesta alludes to a joyous inner celebration. What was the fiesta for? This gives greater clarity to the symbol.
Gala denotes a celebration; a joyous event or situation.
Gay Pride Day relates to individuality and everyone's right to celebrate the uniqueness of their beingness.
Junket signifies a self-serving act; selfishly gaining from ulterior motives of others.
Kwanzaa suggests a celebration of one's blessings.
Mardi Gras suggests it's time for one to openly express happiness or experience lighthearted freedom.
Masquerade illustrates deceit. Recall who one or someone one recognized was dressed as. This is usually a very revealing message.
Midway (carnival) denotes misplaced priorities; an inability to have a mature perspective of reality. This dreamscape symbol may point to ulterior motives or the possibility of being duped.
Oktoberfest relates to a reason to rejoice; a time to celebrate one's home, family, and closest friends. This is a revealing symbol that usually points out a positive element in an individual's life that may not be recognized for the benefits/blessings it brings.
Pageant refers to active acting out; a demonstration or showing of an idea.
Party (celebration) represents a reason for joy, perhaps an unrecognized blessing.
Procession symbolizes a chosen life path that follows many others.
Renaissance festival stands for the joy of celebrating new opportunities.
Rendezvous (of mountain men) stands for a joyful celebration of one's self-sufficiency.
Ticker-tape parade illustrates a major reason for celebration in one's life.
Women's Equality Day is a reminder that one needs to see every person as having equal rights/opportunities.

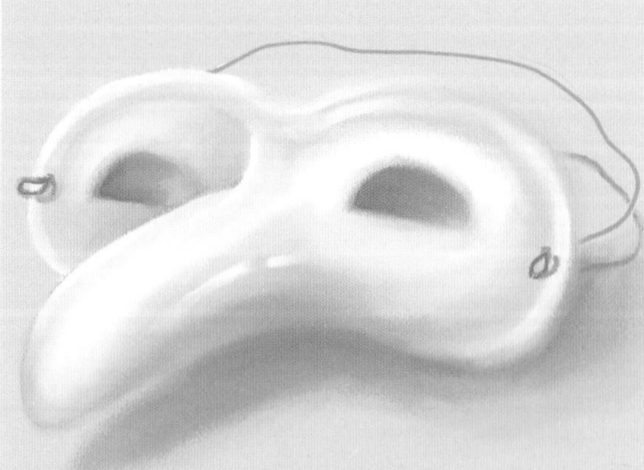

Masquerade symbolizes deception and can point to what is being hidden.

see also
• Theater & Entertainment *p. 220*
• Christianity *p. 336*

Parties

Block party characterizes a reminder to appreciate those around one.
Coming-out party represents an exposure of a particular element of oneself, usually individuality; a shedding of inferiority feelings.
Garden party shows joy taken in one's rewarding benefits brought through spiritual and humanitarian acts.
Sleepover See slumber party.
Slumber party represents trust. To invite someone to be present while asleep is an act of trust.
Surprise party stands for a wonderful unexpected blessing in one's life.

Social Events

All-nighter implies greater effort or attention given to an issue; greater effort or thought needs to be given to it.
Ball (gala) a celebrated event in one's life. Verifies one's recent steps taken.
Banquet suggests a generous situation; sharing.
Benefit (event) alludes to receiving or giving help through the aid of others.
Cotillion (formal ball) cautions against the need to be accepted or recognized.
Dinner dance suggests both the joyful and nourishing benefits of a healthful aspect.
Easter egg hunt marks a search for a more pleasing or acceptable reality.
Love-in refers to a lighthearted gathering of those sharing the same sense of freedom toward self-expression.
Reception (social) See receiving line.
Semiformal stands for a semiserious situation or issue, one needing greater than casual notice or attention.
Social (event) alludes to interaction with others.
Tea party (child's) represents immature or undeveloped social skills.

Sales

Clearance (sale) cautions of a last chance to accomplish something. May indicate a need to be rid of unnecessary attitudes or perspectives.
Fire sale suggests salvageable elements; still viable benefits.
Garage sale typifies the act of ridding oneself of extraneous aspects; setting priorities.
Rummage sale indicates an opportunity to obtain useful factors in life; opportunities.
Sale (reduced price) may represent a good deal or opportunity, yet it also may only appear to be so.
Sales promotion stands for enticements or incentives.
Yard sale denotes multiple opportunities; the chance of discovering a treasure among discards; seeing something of value where others don't.

Feasts & Saints' Days

All Fools' Day See April Fools' Day.
All Saints' Day appears in dreamscapes to remind us that goodness and perseverance, acceptance and tolerance, are qualities we must strive for.
Annunciation See announcement.
April Fools' Day reveals something foolish done by the dreamer or by an acquaintance of the dreamer.
Ash Wednesday applies to penance; a reminder of our physical mortality.
Candlemas Day comes to stress the importance of hope and perseverance.
Christening See baptism.
Feast days (saints') brings attention to a particular saint's attributes and advises the importance of utilizing those qualities in one's own life.
Festival represents a cause for celebration. Recall what type of festival it was.
Midsummer Eve stands for a time for celebration or the expression of joy. There are times in life when positive events come unrecognized and one needs to be more aware and appreciative of these small blessings.
New Year's Day stands for the first day of a new beginning, unless that particular day marks something of importance unique to the dreamer.
New Year's Eve connotes the approach of a whole new set of opportunities that are just around the corner.
Saint John's Eve See Midsummer Eve.
Saint Patrick's Day is a call for the dreamer to turn his or her attention to the spirit. Stands for a return to spiritual matters.
Saint Valentine's Day reminds one that love for others should be one's priority.
Valentine's Day stands for a celebration of those one has affection for. This symbol may come if one isn't expressing their feelings enough.

Valentine's Day may imply one needs to be more open in one's affections.

Memorial Days

Fourth of July means liberty.

Arbor Day calls for an outward display of spiritual attitudes. It may also refer to a celebration of same.
Armistice Day constitutes a conflict resolution in the dreamer's everyday life.
Cinco de Mayo refers to freedom; independence; victory.
Decoration Day See Memorial Day.
Earth Day is a symbol that comes as an advisement to bring one's perception or attitude back down to earth.
Father's Day alludes to the importance of giving recognition to the individual in the dreamer's life who is closely associated with fatherly confidence and advice.
Flag Day comes as a call for a show of loyalty.
Fourth of July denotes questionable independence. It may also refer to selective freedoms in the dreamer's life.
Grandparents' Day refers to an advisement to maintain respect and honor for those with great wisdom and experience.
Groundhog Day characterizes superstition in the dreamer's everyday life.
Independence Day See Fourth of July.
Labor Day celebrates one's accomplishments gained from personal efforts.
Martin Luther King Day reminds of the importance of tolerance and equality. Encourages celebration of the striving for rights.
May Day suggests a time of new birth celebration; rejoice in earth's blossoming gifts to humankind.
Memorial brings a special message for each dreamer. Who or what was the memorial for?
Memorial Day may pinpoint a specific time, event, or individual associated with the dreamer and may prompt one not to forget that facet of one's past. This symbol may also signify a need to give personal attention to courage.
Mother's Day pertains to honor and respect for the one who gave one a new beginning and nurtured us.
Pioneer days (celebration event) comes in dreams to remind one of the work it takes to get anywhere.
Presidents' Day comes as a reminder to honor those who have led many through both hard and good times.
Snow day refers to the joyful freedom and uplifting feeling spirituality can bring.
Thanksgiving Day reflects one's thankfulness or gratitude. Reminds one to count his or her daily blessings.
United Nations Day refers to a celebration of cooperation.
Veterans' Day reminds one to remember those who fought against adversity.

Armor & Injuries

Armor illustrates the dreamer's personal level of protection and self-preservation measures. Recall the armor's condition for greater clarity.
Armor plating means defensiveness. May point to tendency to be ready for a conflict.
Battery (injury) reveals a harmful situation or individual.
Collateral damage See roadkill.
Nosepiece relates to protective measures one uses as one advances along a chosen path.
Shield represents an individual's personal form of self-protection. This may include mental, emotional, or spiritual elements.

Artifacts

Doubloon refers to something of extreme value.
Megalith represents ancient truths that remain valid today.
Memento reminds one of what should be kept as important aspects in life.
Memorabilia defines a specific interest. May refer to a past life.
Mummy represents an unyielding personality; a lack of open-mindedness or tenacity.
Relic warns against having misplaced spiritual priorities.

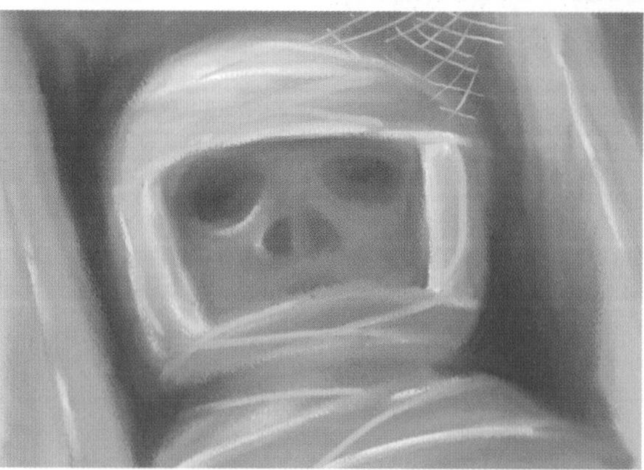

Mummy is a representation of an inflexible, small-minded attitude.

Tablet (ancient) suggests a true element of reality or a timeless truth.
Time capsule illustrates the main events and most important aspects of the dreamer's life. Recall what objects or artifacts were placed within the capsule.
Trilithon pertains to a doorway or entrance; an opportunity for ingress/egress.
Trilobite illustrates a time-tested spiritual concept. It may also refer to a solid truth.

see also
• Military Vehicles *p. 290*
• Religious & Spiritual Activities *p. 342*

War Arenas

Artillery range symbolizes mental exercises. Any game, puzzle, etc., that is routinely utilized to keep one's mental faculties sharp.

Battlefield points to the issue leading to conflict.

Battle station stands for one's perspective in an active disagreement or conflict.

Combat zone is directly associated with a particular issue, relationship, or type of behavior that's involved in some form of conflict for the dreamer.

Drop zone stands for the target perimeter of an issue one is in conflict over.

Ground zero represents a target for destruction. This is usually a serious message that warns an individual to cease zeroing in on someone or something with a destructive intent.

Gun room defines a personal supply of defensive methods used by the dreamer.

Home front refers to those issues closest to an individual, usually family and friends.

Military alludes to controlling factors in one's life.

Navy base connotes one's personal spiritual protective/defensive methods.

Navy yard suggests spiritual repair work that needs to be done.

Neutral ground/zone defines a phase, situation, or condition that is without opposing factors; a time or place allowing for peace regardless of differing attitudes.

Situation room represents a call to put efforts into resolving a conflict/disagreement.

War room represents a need to strategize.

Ceremonies

Baptism connotes a spiritual birth; a rebirth; perhaps a return to innocence.

Bar/Bat Mitzvah denotes the point of responsibility for self.

Celebration means a reason for rejoicing. Surrounding dreamscape will clarify the intent.

Ceremony implies a ritual; societal custom; specialized observance.

Ceremony (secret) See secret ceremony.

Coronation defines recognition from higher sources.

Marriage See wedding.

Pilgrimage symbolizes to the dreamer a necessary journey to gain a significant aspect associated with one's personal search.

Rendezvous is a dreamscape symbol that signifies a meeting.

Rite (ceremony) corresponds with a self-devised process; a fascination with ceremony.

Rite of passage portrays a transitional stage in one's life.

Ritual pertains to superfluous elements one believes are necessary.

Secret ceremony is a dreamscape symbol that is a representation of hidden elements to something. May indicate an ulterior motive.

Wedding usually doesn't relate to the ceremonial meaning but rather signifies a joining of some type, which will be clarified by the dream's surrounding details.

Stages of War

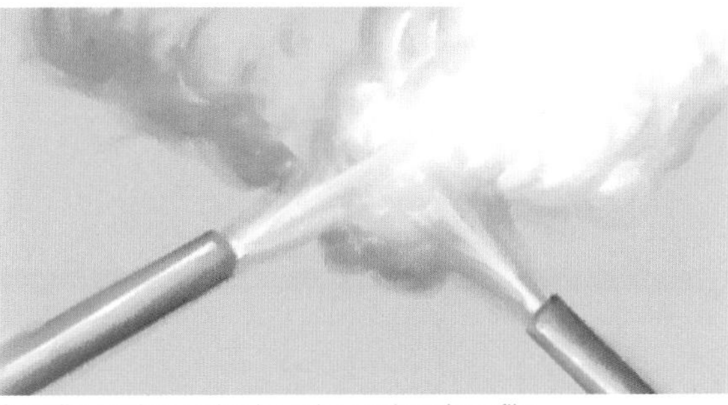

Crossfire cautions against becoming caught up in conflict.

Arms race points to an escalating conflict or disagreement in one's life.

Broadside indicates unexpected events; surprises in life that deeply affect one.

Call to arms stands for a time to move into action, to actively engage personal defenses.

Campaign illustrates an attempt to expend energies into a cause or goal.

Crossfire warns of being caught in the middle of a situation or relationship.

Forced march illustrates a life situation that needs focused attention yet shouldn't be forced into a conclusion.

Invasion warns of a multitude of invasive aspects entering one's life.

Line of fire warns the dreamer to remove oneself from the someone else's conflict; otherwise, he or she may get hurt.

Marching orders stands for a time for one to leave something behind; an end.

Outgunned connotes a failed attempt to better another. This may pertain to skills, intelligence, or accomplishment.

Postwar reflects a phase that follows a hard time or period of trial, conflict, or stress.

Red alert warns of an urgent situation; a highly hazardous time or destructive behavior.

Retreat (military) constitutes an unproductive time to go forward.

Sealed orders represents knowing what to do when the time comes.

Selective service emphasizes a forced participation.

Siege applies to an overwhelming inundation of something in one's life.

Skirmish implies a minor conflict.

Sortie refers to an attack that may be instigated by oneself.

Test ban signifies the cessation of an extremely dangerous practice/behavior.

Unarmed represents a nonthreatening issue or individual.

Vanguard represents a leader or the leading edge.

Warpath advises that one is proceeding along a course of action that has the strong probability of ending in an altercation.

Yellow alert (level) equates to a need for elevated awareness.

Zero hour represents the scheduled time to begin a plan or put an idea into motion.

Handheld Weapons

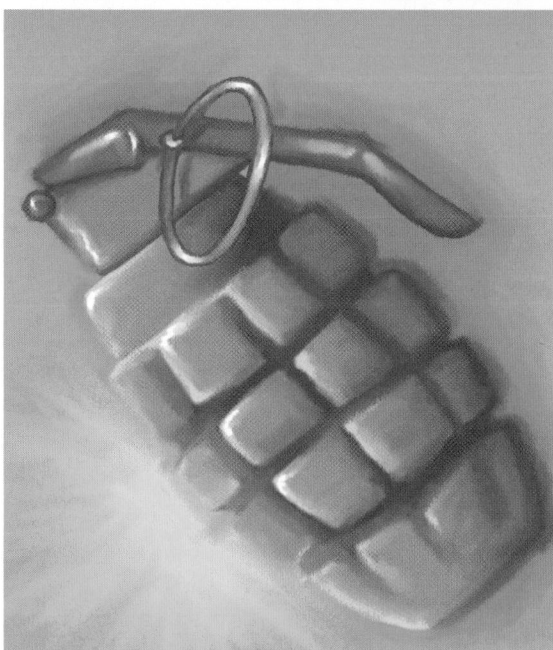

Grenade signifies the need to deal with a delicate situation.

Air gun signifies explosive thoughts or ideas. This dreamscape symbol carries a polarity interpretation. A negative meaning would be acting on sudden ideas before they're thought out. A positive meaning would refer to epiphanies.
Air rifle See air gun.
Assault rifle represents an aggressive personality, an individual who is always on the lookout and ready to pick a fight or argument.
Backup (gun) can refer to secondary protective measures. This dreamscape symbol also may warn of multiple life issues one is carrying around and stewing over.
Bazooka represents a person's inner power; personal resources in respect to defending oneself against various threatening aspects that arise in life.
Bowie knife See knife.
Carbine See gun.
Coup stick stands for the resulting benefits of bravery and courage.
Dagger represents harmful aspects in an individual's life. Frequently this dreamscape symbol indicates an associate or someone the dreamer knows.
Derringer exemplifies a source of hidden power.
Firearm See gun.
Grease gun points to behavior that makes progression or accomplishment easier.
Grenade signifies an aspect that has the capability of exploding if not carefully handled. It refers to a potentially explosive situation or relationship.
Gun warns of mental or emotional dysfunctions; erroneous attitudes or perceptions; potential for an emotional outburst or explosion. This dreamscape symbol may also point to an individual's protective measures.
Gunfire (hearing) comes as an advisement of a potentially dangerous situation close to the one doing the hearing.
Machine gun reveals a continual state of anger.
Peashooter represents a negative aspect (tool) that could cause harm to others. The surrounding dreamscape elements will clarify this meaning.
Pistol See gun.
Ray gun most often portrays one's own quality of self-protective measures. It may also denote one's spiritual effectiveness with others.
Revolver (weapon) See gun.
Rifle (weapon) See gun.
Riot gun characterizes an individual's effort to control a situation that's getting out of control.
Scattergun See shotgun.
Shotgun represents a life element that has the capability of causing multiple ramifications.
Smoking gun represents evidence; verification; a cause for suspicion.
Spear gun is a dreamscape symbol that relates to a desire to spear specific spiritual truths for the purpose of clear comprehension.
Squirt gun represents unexpected hits such as responses from other people that are uncharacteristic; surprising events.
Stiletto See dagger.
Stun gun may indicate the manifestation of an unexpected event that shocks, or this dreamscape symbol could signify a need for one to temporarily halt current efforts that are being applied to a particular issue or situation.
Switchblade exposes a tendency toward knee-jerk reactions.
Tranquilizer gun comes in dreams to symbolize a great need to calm a situation or particular individual in the dreamer's life.
Zip gun represents ineffective protective or defensive methods.

Specialized Weapons

Antiaircraft symbolizes the shooting down of one's thoughts or ideas.
Antiballistic missile represents one's immunity to the destructive ideas and thoughts of others.
Antitank typifies one's need for major defensive measures or protection against an aspect in life.
Artillery indicates one's level of mental acuity.
Gatling gun See machine gun.
Howitzer See cannon.
Laser gun advises of the wisdom to accurately target one's goal.

see also
• Accidental Injuries *p. 119*
• Enemies *p. 125*

Weapon Terminology

Hair trigger characterizes someone with a short temper.

Arms control advises of a need to rein in determination to actively pursue or exacerbate a currently ongoing conflict.

Ballistics usually refers to a test to prove guilt or innocence, but may also signify an extreme reaction to something as in going ballistic.

Cocked (position) indicates imbalance; a slanted aspect or perspective.

Double-barreled symbolizes twofold aspects to an issue; an element serving two purposes.

Gunshot (sound) represents an attention-getting element pointing to an emotional explosion or an imminent one.

Hair trigger stands for an explosive temperament.

Half-cocked (gun) means ill-prepared. May point out an anxiety to begin a conflict.

Logistics shows a need to give attention to planning detail.

Long-range represents something that will cause extended or multiple resulting effects.

Munition See ammunition.

Muzzle (gun barrel) pertains to aggressive communication.

One-shot underscores an opportunity that won't be repeated; the need to be successful the first time an attempt is made.

Potshot stands for an aggressive or cowardly retaliation.

Projectile portrays the entry of an unexpected element. Recall what was going through the air for clarity.

Salvo symbolizes a bombardment of some type that could elicit either a positive or negative response.

Shooting gallery (weapons) advises to give greater attention to one's personal protective or defensive measures.

Short-range suggests quick benefits, yet they may not be as desirable as those coming after a longer-range plan or greater efforts expended.

Target stands for a goal or focus of attention.

Top gun portrays the perfection of a skill.

Trigger (any type) indicates the singular element that has the capability to set off multiple responses or ramifications.

Weapon doesn't necessarily indicate a negative meaning, but usually applies to a preparedness to protect oneself from negative elements in one's life.

Defenses & Refuges

Armory applies to perseverance and inner strength.

Arsenal See armory.

Berlin Wall signifies the destructiveness of building walls to separate/segregate peoples. This dreamscape symbol emphasizes the rightness of tearing down those walls and becoming unified.

Berm represents support; protective aspects in an individual's life.

Besieged reflects an overwhelming situation.

Blockhouse applies to one's defenses.

Bombproof signifies a strong constitution; emotional strength.

Bomb shelter illustrates fear of disappointments; an individual's lack of faith.

Drawbridge alludes to self-generated barriers and their selective use.

Dugout implies a temporary withdrawal from some aspect in the dreamer's life.

Early warning system stands for an individual's inner awareness; their perceptual watchfulness.

Earth-bermed stands for a solid foundation that has to be monitored for a possible accumulation of outdated, destructive (mold) elements.

Berlin Wall denounces separation.

Fort symbolizes one's personal quality and strength of defense. Depending on surrounding dreamscape details, this symbol can mean one who is an introvert, who desires to remain safe within self, or it can refer to a need for self-protective measures.

Fortress See fort.

Foxhole See dugout.

Garrison See military post.

Moat constitutes spiritual distance; the use of spiritual beliefs as protective or defensive measures.

National Rifle Association (NRA) stands for one's rights to protect and defend oneself. This symbol may appear in the dreams of someone who is reluctant to stand up for her/his rights.

Rampart pertains to a means of self-protection.

Razor wire stands for one's defenses; a possible attempt to maintain distance.

Rear guard advises one to watch one's back and not leave self exposed.

Shellproof reflects a well-protected self; wise precautions set in place to prevent the entry of unwanted or negative elements; high awareness and discernment.

Smoke screen relates to defenses or deceptions. Recall the surrounding dream details.

Stronghold portrays one's personally protected defenses.

Trip wire warns of an attempt to foil another. It refers to a deception.

Chemical & Biological Weapons

Gas mask reminds one of the need for self-preservation.

Agent Orange represents an extremely destructive aspect in one's life. This being one that may appear beneficial at first but will later leave negative effects behind.

Biological weapons warn of an aggressively dangerous situation or individual; a contaminating element.

Chemical warfare applies to a manner of conflict resolution that causes debilitating or fatal effects.

Defoliant See Agent Orange; preemergent treatment.

Exfoliant (foliage) warns of an element capable of destroying any benefit to something.

Gas chamber advises to use discernment. Suggests increased awareness.

Gas mask cautions one to protect oneself from potentially harmful situations or relationships.

Germ warfare defines vicious and unconscionable retaliative responses.

Mustard gas warns against a highly dangerous aspect in one's life; a factor that could suffocate freedoms or beliefs.

Napalm denotes an explosive aspect in one's life.

Nerve gas connotes a desire to control others through emotional manipulation. Recall who possessed the gas or where it came from.

Airborne Weapons

Air raid signifies a warning to stop allowing others to change one's mind, attitudes, or thoughts on an issue.

Air strike connotes a warning for the dreamer to protect oneself from harmful ideas or belief systems. Advises fearlessness toward pointing out a bad idea.

Air terrorism warns against forced ideas or allowing others to change one's mind. The act of controlling another person's thoughts.

Bomb bay (compartment) represents aspects in one's life that are on the verge of exploding unless they are calmed or altered.

Bomber (aircraft) characterizes an unpredictable individual or situation.

Bombshell represents great disappointments. It may refer to shocking news.

Bombsight portrays destructive intentions.

Cruise missile warns of the destructive power of uncontrolled thoughts.

Enola Gay (Hiroshima bomber) refers to the possibility of a very bad choice being made in the offing, yet one has the chance to circumvent it.

Guided missile reveals a destructive intent. This dreamscape symbol may also point to a goal that one is intently focused on.

Homing device represents a need to get to the core of an issue.

ICBM (missile) represents a destructive force in a person's life.

Missile reveals a harmful negative aimed at one's experience. This could even be generated by oneself to another.

Warhead exposes a potentially explosive situation, relationship, or other type of element in one's life.

Offensive Positions

Command post most often indicates a center of authority or direction. Depending on related dreamscape elements, this symbol may point to oneself and be an advisement to take control of one's own decision/direction.

Counterattack indicates a retaliatory response.

Firepower represents one's level of emotional effectiveness on others.

Firing line illustrates a position of personal responsibility for an individual's emotional reactive control.

Front line represents the position of action or most exposure.

Full-bore refers to thoroughness; nothing held back; full steam ahead.

Military post indicates a domineering personality or situation.

Seaborne Weapons

Acoustic torpedo represents actions or intent to counter/nullify a specific falsehood.

Depth charge stands for a negative life aspect that will destroy one's spiritual foundation.

Destroyer (ship) warns of a life aspect that has the capability of destroying one's spirituality.

Flagship comes to advise of precedent-setting individuals or events.

Gunboat relates to dangerous spiritual attitudes or beliefs; spiritual beliefs or behavior that are headed for conflict, perhaps inner conflict.

Submarine comes as a warning against spiritual hypocrisy.

see also
• Aircraft *p. 301*
• Warships *p. 303*

Historical Weaponry

Battering ram connotes force applied. This symbol is most frequently a warning against the necessity of applying force to achieve desired results. This dreamscape symbol may also point to coercion.
Billy club exemplifies force; a forceful nature; ill-used power.
Blackjack (weapon) See billy club.
Brass knuckles stand for a severely aggressive or argumentative nature with intent to cause harm; prepared for a fight.
Broadsword See sword.
Cannon represents explosive aspects to one's life. May even be one's own personality.
Cannonball denotes the act of outraged explosions; acting in an uncontrollable manner.
Catapult refers to highly motivational aspects that serve to speed one forward or into action; an impetus.
Claymore See sword.
Coup stick stands for the resulting benefits of bravery and courage.
Crossbow alludes to that which leads straight to one's goals.
Cutlass See sword.
Double-edged sword See sword (double-edged).
Elephant gun signifies a potentially huge emotional explosion/conflict.
Flintlock See gun.
Harpoon stands for spiritual selectivity.
Javelin See spear.
Lance See spear.
Leister See spear.
Longbow pertains to directness; honesty.
Mace (club) represents aggressiveness.
Machete denotes a forcing of an individual's advancement or enlightenment.
Muzzle loader applies to antiquated communication methods; ineffective contacts.
Nightstick See billy club.
Powder (gun) See gunpowder.
Powder horn portrays a questionable attitude of being ready to enter an altercation or situation where conflict may be possible.
Rapier See sword.
Saber See sword.
Scabbard signifies the control of one's emotions.
Scimitar See sword.
Slingshot suggests inadequate measures of self-defense.
Spear refers to a method of obtaining a desired element or goal.
Straight arrow may portray an upright attitude or a closed mind, depending on the related dream details.
Sword (double-edged) stands for something that could backfire.
Sword connotes a self-defensive element; means of protecting one's position.
Tomahawk See hatchet.

Uniform

Bandoleer illustrates a warrior type of personal preparedness; strong defenses.
Cartridge clip (ammo) signifies one's preparedness to back up facts or means of defense.
Dog tag (military) denotes a friend's allegiance to another.
Holster corresponds with a life aspect that has the capability of providing some type of personal protection.
Mess kit symbolizes the tools that one uses in life to gain inner nourishment, knowledge, or a measure of forward progression.
Military cap represents regimentation. It may also suggest an inability to think for oneself.

Explosives

Atomic bomb exemplifies lack of compassion and a disregard for life. This symbol also signifies the danger in ignoring the smaller details in one's life. Smaller elements don't mean they're unimportant or can't carry power.
Blasting caps/powder See dynamite.
Bomb represents explosive situations or relationships; also disappointments; failures.
Bomb squad points to those who are skilled/capable of disarming a potentially explosive situation.
Car bomb points to a selectively destructive motivation.
Cluster bomb portrays a major outcome or effect that will create devastating effects on a wide variety of life aspects.
Dirty bomb refers to ulterior motives; an agenda that would negatively affect the most people.
Dive-bomb portrays an obsession with a specific goal or target.
Dynamite indicates an explosive aspect to something. May refer to a sudden revelation.
Explosive refers to a life aspect that has the potential of creating a devastating effect in one's life.

Bomb implies volatility and failure.

Fallout advises of forthcoming repercussions.
Fragmentation bomb forewarns of approaching fallout ramifications in one's life.
Incendiary (device) pertains to an explosive or fiery aspect in one's life.
Land mine reminds one to be aware of the pitfalls and setbacks hidden along one's life path or spiritual search.
Mine (explosive) reveals negative aspects along one's path.
Mine detector signifies an individual's inner sense or awareness to perceive upcoming troubles.
Minefield symbolizes a setup or condition of entrapment existing in one's path.
Molotov cocktail stands for a potentially explosive situation or attitude building.
Pipe bomb See bomb.
Plastic explosive See bomb.
Plastique See bomb.
Powder keg reveals a potentially explosive situation, relationship, or attitude.
Primer (explosive) reveals an element in an individual's life that has the potential to be one of the main ingredients of an explosive situation.
Smoke bomb warns of deceit.

Ancillary Equipment

Ammunition characterizes validations.
Bayonet illustrates a threatening position or situation.
Black powder stands for an element essential for an explosive situation to manifest.
Blank cartridge suggests a lack of power or effectiveness.
Bowstring (truss) signifies an individualized means of support; unusual support aid.
Buckshot pertains to solid facts of ammunition that backs up one's goal or claim.
Buckshot (rubber) means ineffectiveness; a threat with no backing; a warning.
Bullet pertains to the negative aspects of oneself that could injure others.
Bullet casing refers to spent or empty threats; emotional issues that have lost their explosive impact. This dreamscape symbol may also indicate something carrying the potential for leading to an explosive event.
Bullwhip implies an aggressively bullish nature; unyielding; demanding. May imply coercion.
Crosshairs advise of a need to readjust or alter one's sights on something. This symbol suggests that an individual isn't seeing something quite accurately or isn't focused on the true target.
Dumdum bullet defines powerful defenses; an awareness of one's protective preparedness and strength of same. On the opposite side of this coin, the dreamscape symbol can point to a powerfully deep-seated attitude that could be highly explosive.

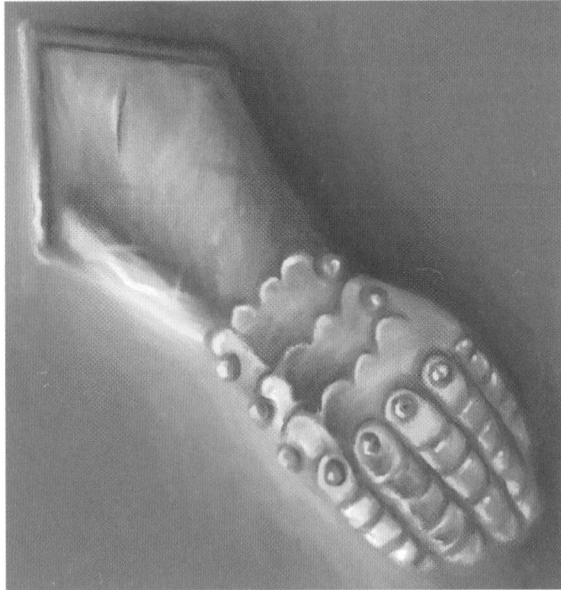

Gauntlet is indicative of the difficulties in one's life.

Field rations characterize the essential elements that are required to perform a specific job or achieve a particular goal.
Flak jacket See bulletproof vest.
Fuse (explosive) points to an amount of patience or acceptance. Recall length of fuse line for more clarity.
Gauntlet illustrates life's tribulations. These are frequently generated by oneself.
Gunpowder reveals a highly explosive aspect in an individual's life. This dreamscape element could refer to a relationship, situation, belief, or psychological state.
Gun rack stands for the possible ongoing conflicts or emotional explosions present in one's life. The key here is to recall if the rack was full or empty.
Ordnance (munitions) defines the tools or means that a person has available to defend or protect oneself in life.
Rifle scope See scope.
Rubber bullet See buckshot (rubber).
Shell (bullet) See ammunition.
Shot See ammunition.
Shoulder holster characterizes strong defensive or protective measures.
Shrapnel represents those aspects in an individual's life that leave permanent damage or reminders behind.
Silencer (gun) represents the quiet, silent negative forces that are capable of affecting those who don't maintain high personal awareness or become lax.
Silver bullet signifies a final solution; something that is capable of putting an end to a negative element.
Slug See bullet.
Tracer round (bullet) corresponds to an individual's intent to leave behind evidence of the source that affected something.

War-Related Conditions

AWOL is usually associated with denial; a flight from responsibility or reality; an inability to deal with an issue and deal with it.
Battle fatigue warns against continual struggles without taking time to reflect, meditate, gain inner peace.
Black ops signify covert or underlying agendas; secret activities.
Combat fatigue exemplifies the self-destructive effects of conflict.
Dishonorable discharge advises of grave admonishments from one's higher self.
Draft (conscription) warns of a forced attendance or attitude; coerced loyalty.
Honorable discharge is a commendation for efforts applied or accomplishments. Points to an ending.
Honorable mention constitutes a commendation from one's higher self.
MIA (missing in action) corresponds to one who has lost the way. This could also refer to apathy.
Walking wounded is a symbol of perseverance; forward-looking even after considerable tribulations.

see also
• Aggressors *p. 145*
• Passive Personalities *p. 147*

Warriors & Fighters

Confederate (soldier) is a characterization of southern attitudes or ideas.
Gladiator is a dreamscape symbol that advises of illogical reasoning for an individual's negative behavior.
Enemy informs the dreamer of negative aspects or associations in his or her life.
Firing squad characterizes an individual who could bring devastating ramifications. This dreamscape symbol may refer to a call to openly admit personal responsibility.
Foe See enemy.
Grand marshall characterizes one who has many followers.
Green beret refers to skill in handling oneself.
Guerrilla reveals a forceful activist; one who aggressively fights a resistance force.
Kamikaze characterizes a self-destructive personality.
Markswoman characterizes an individual who has the skill of being on target most of the time.
Military officer stands for arrogance. It may refer to a love of power.
Military police (MP) represents an active and correct conscience; the policing of oneself.
Militia refers to self-defense; personal, inner protective measures that one takes.
Minuteman chararacterizes an individual who can be depended on for support.
Mutineer illustrates rebellion or the need for some. The surrounding dreamscape details will clarify which meaning this symbol has for the dreamer.
Nazi exemplifies an individual who desires to have control over others; a megalomaniac who is apathetic to the rights of others.
Platoon represents a group of people with a like intent or purpose.
POW (prisoner of war) refers to one who has been drawn into a bad situation and is unable to get out of it.
Redcoat is one's adversary.
Warlord pertains to a recognized aggressive personality.
Weekend warrior suggests a temporary obligation.

Gladiator implies behaving badly for no good reason.

Peace

Amnesty is indicative of forgiveness or a new measure of acceptance through tolerance.
Clemency alludes to unconditional forgiveness.
Cultural exchange signifies an attempt to understand those who one perceives as being different from oneself.
Disarm refers to an action that neutralizes a negative aspect in one's life.
New Age equates to a blend of physics and spirituality. See page 339.
Pacifism represents a fear of conflict and signifies an individual's tendency to take the most peaceful and less troublesome path.
Peace offering connotes an attempt at reconciliation; an apology.
Peace pipe is a symbol that indicates harmonious intentions.
Peace sign is a symbol that demonstrates that a friendly and peaceful greeting is offered.

Wartime Activities

Active duty comes to advise the dreamer that the time has come to implement a plan or an idea. It's time to get into the action.
Act of war isn't usually associated with a literal war between countries but most often points to behavior inciting conflict.
Armor piercing (munitions) may stand for a chronically combative individual, but usually this symbol refers to the big guns, meaning major power or proof backing one's attitudes or issues.
Atrocities illustrate an absolute disregard for life.
Blowup depicts emotional explosions or a failed endeavor.
Duel advises of the strong possibility that an outcome or effect will turn out with severe consequences.
Marauding See raid.
Saber rattling signifies a threatening intent.
Shootout pertains to the resolving of a conflict. This dreamscape symbol won't necessarily infer that this is done in a negative manner.
Special forces represent specialized, intensive efforts applied to the accomplishment of a goal. Sometimes special forces directly relate to spiritual forces such as angels.
Squad represents a group of people who have a like interest.
Strike force refers to one's unfailing determination to reach a goal; a powerful motivation that sets an individual into decisive action.
Task force represents a need to combine efforts to be effective. This is usually in regard to a specific goal or problem.
Tour of duty represents a specific job/work one has promised (or needs) to perform.

Historical Events

Alamo indicates a final confrontation.

Armada pertains to a spiritually overbearing and manipulative personality.

Blitz shows an overwhelming aspect in one's life.

Chernobyl emphasizes the dangers of too little knowledge.

Civil War connotes an internal conflict within self regarding one's immediate surroundings.

Gold rush alludes to material desires; financial priorities.

Grand tour signifies a recognition of one's limitations.

Holocaust defines a monumentally devastating event.

Industrial Revolution pertains to a lack of self-reliance; a move that increases quantity and lessens quality.

Inquisition pertains to an invasion of privacy. Usually this will be a validating symbol for the dreamer.

Magna Carta represents a guarantee of one's basic rights.

Manhattan Project warns of a misuse of intelligence.

Marathon implies great efforts expended on an achievement.

Nine-Eleven (9-11 date) symbolizes a catastrophic event that shocks one to the bone.

Pearl Harbor a reminder to remain aware in life, not let one's guard down.

Prohibition represents the restrictions placed by others; suppression.

Revolution may not imply a violent military event but rather stand for a new way or concept. May point to activism or civil disobedience.

Witch-hunt exposes spiritual and moral immaturity and ignorance.

Woodstock (event) suggests free expression.

Wounded Knee (historical event) comes to remind us of the right/duty to stand up for one's rights.

Prohibition refers to limitations imposed on one's life by other people.

Miscellaneous

Battle cry exemplifies a need to generate greater courage.

Blockade exemplifies those blocks in life that are put in one's path by others. These can be overcome.

Carnage denotes dangerously negative aspects in a person's life that have the capability of causing far-reaching destruction.

Combat cautions of the wrong type of conflict resolution.

Confederate flag signifies a strong reluctance to let go.

Coup stands for a clever move; a strategic move that has been successfully executed; results from a masterful plan.

Crusades imply negative spiritual activism.

Fracas applies to a conflict.

Gun show represents choices for anger management or self-protection. May symbolize the variety of ways an emotional explosion may be forthcoming in the dreamer's life.

Holy war See crusades.

Massacre represents a grave misdeed done or forthcoming.

Media event defines a gravely important situation or issue needing one's attention.

New Year's resolution sets one up for disappointment and self-deprecating situations. This implies that a general plan is wise, but a solid resolution is not reasonable nor is a productive promise that one makes to oneself.

Confederate flag represents difficulty in giving something up.

Nuclear winter illustrates the devastating outcome of one's current behavior or path; a destruction of one's current condition and relationships.

Parade symbolizes a desire to be recognized. May indicate arrogance.

Riot signifies deep-seated discontent; demonstrative activism.

Terrorist attack denotes unexpected hostilities.

War portrays an ongoing conflict.

War bonnet reveals an intention to instigate or become involved in an altercation.

War cry signifies instigating acts and/or words.

War paint illustrates the intent to engage in some form of conflict.

Historical Sites

Historical site usually has some type of personal connection to the dreamer and this dreamscape symbol comes to reveal something important to the dreamer.

Historic preservation refers to an individual's need/desire to keep a past event or relationship from being altered in any way; a preservation of integrity.

Chapter 23

Popular Dream Characters

Although these elements may appear to be a bit of fantasy thrown into a dream, they are associated with an individual's character traits. They may also indicate a circuitous manner of reaching goals or gaining knowledge.

Roman Mythology

Brutus (Marcus Junius) forewarns against the self-destructing power that vindictiveness carries.
Diana is representative of women's wisdom; moonlight and its bright symbology of knowledge.
Fortuna characterizes a priority placed on material goods; a love of and a striving for riches.
Mercury characterizes a messenger in one's life.
Neptune See Poseidon.
Venus signifies deep affection.

British Mythology

Excalibur signifies something one has a singular right to.
King Arthur (of legend) signifies one's destiny.
Lady Godiva stands for going the extra mile for one's beliefs; giving of oneself for others.
Lady of the Lake characterizes an individual who holds the key to something; the keeper of the power or knowledge.
Merlin (of legend) characterizes the active manifestation of one's spiritual talents and its use for the benefit of others.
Round Table indicates an upcoming conference or the need for same.

Egyptian Mythology

Phoenix is something's purest form.

Anubis warns one to pay more attention to the ramifications of actions.
Cleopatra warns against using one's physical attributes in order to manipulate; ulterior motives; a personal agenda.
Criosphinx (ram-headed sphinx) characterizes inner strength through belief in convictions.
Hathor (Egyptian goddess) equates to the ideology of the mother goddess.
Isis portrays a bountiful aspect in one's life; moving mountains to achieve a goal; a willingness to do anything for one's love.
Ma'at (Egyptian goddess) stands for justice and righteousness.
Osiris characterizes renewal; a rebirth. This underscores the idea that all is not lost and the pieces can be picked up.
Phoenix is a representation of the quintessential example of a characteristic, ability, or attainment. May also emphasize a powerfully determined personality who bounces back and refuses to be defeated or blocked.
Sphinx comes as an advisement that one is close to discovering the totality (whole) of an issue.
Tutankhamen stands for the killing effects of jealousy, power, and greed.

Mythical & Mythological

Chimera characterizes self-delusion. It may refer specifically to something with no substance.
Cupid is indicative of the love in one's life.
Hero/heroine represents the characteristics of courage and perseverance.
Kokopelli characterizes an individual who easily compels others; one to whom others are drawn.
Legend (myth) relates to basic facts or underlying truths; referencing an actual event.
Lilith characterizes an independent and free-thinking woman.
Lorelei symbolizes false spiritual lures that one may encounter in one's life.
Mythical character will constitute a wide variety of interpretations. Refer to the specific character for help with the meaning of the dream symbol.
Philosopher's stone pertains to a magic potion or miracle one hopes will enter one's life in respect to bringing enlightenment or power.
Troll represents the skeptical, unbelievable concepts in one's life.
Viking characterizes one on a long spiritual journey.

Greek Mythological Creatures

Centaur depicts a balance of physical strength and intellectual capability.
Cyclops pertains to the lost aspects of reality; skepticism toward those ideas that one perceives as being far-reaching.
Gorgon characterizes those who are negative or make unproductive relationships.
Harpy suggests guidance upon death. This death may not be a physical one but may refer to elements such as a relationship or situational ending.
Hydra characterizes a persistent problem that has many varying aspects connected with it.
Medusa comes as a strong warning to straighten up one's thoughts before they become dangerous.
Minotaur suggests a demanding personality or situation.
Nymph symbolizes a person who takes great inner joy from being close to nature; one possessing multiple natural (nature) qualities.
Pan characterizes a call to return to nature and the appreciation of same.
Pegasus is representative of possibilities that are rarely considered.
Satyr characterizes a lack of self-control.

Cyclops portrays a cynical nature.

see also
• Books & Text *p. 218*
• Old Testament Figures *p. 338*

Greek Mythology

Achilles warns one of one's weak points. Can also indicate a lack of strength associated with specific aspects of a plan/idea that could ultimately turn out to be a recurring problem or area of concern.
Adonis warns against self-love. May also signify a false emphasis on external or surface characteristics.
Aphrodite means one who uses love for various ends. Makes love into a self-serving tool.
Apollo exemplifies male inner beauty, which is often self-denied.
Argonaut reflects one on an adventurous quest.
Artemis characterizes cleverness and resourcefulness.
Athena characterizes one who applies personal integrity to problem resolution. May also represent wisdom and/or a just personality.
Cassandra is associated with skepticism; one whom others don't believe.
Hades characterizes the dark forces (negative influences) and also may connote hell (an extremely difficult time).
Helen of Troy represents the factor that has caused great strife in one's life.
Hercules alludes to great strength. This could be strength of character, and the important revealing factor here is how this strength was used.
Hero defines great devotion and love.
Hesperides applies to the protection of an individual's spiritual values.
Hestia characterizes one who places a high priority on home and family life.
Icarus implies unawareness and the hazards it creates; unrealistic goals.
Lotus-eater reveals a spiritually unaware individual; one who has an inability to perceive reality; a lack of personal responsibility.
Muse characterizes a source of one's inspiration.
Narcissus warns against self-centeredness.

Trojan horse symbolizes acting without the knowledge of others.

Nemesis corresponds with guilt; karmic justice forthcoming for misdeeds done. This may also point to an ongoing irritation, anxiety, problem, or fear.
Nike symbolizes great inner strength; strong determination to carry something through to a successful conclusion.
Pandora characterizes a person who will eventually cause harm or bring negative elements into one's life.
Persephone reminds us to balance our spiritual and physical lives.
Poseidon most often signifies a spiritual application regarding one's life course, yet Poseidon may also represent earthly elements that are in turmoil and in conflict with one's spiritual beliefs.
Psyche characterizes one's soul.
Sappho stands for feminine camaraderie and confidences.
Sibyl characterizes an individual possessing strong prophetic abilities.
Trojan horse reveals stealth; deception; underhandedness. This symbol may also point to a manner of getting close to an issue or subject without the intention being broadcast or hinted at beforehand.
Zeus corresponds to a godhead; one of the supreme aspects of one's personal spirituality.

Legendary Creatures

Abominable snowman represents spiritual concepts that are not readily accepted in one's everyday life.
Bigfoot connotes aspects of reality that are not generally accepted.
Easter bunny characterizes an individual or specific life aspect that one believes will resolve difficulties.
Foo dog suggests one's personal defense mechanisms. May reveal that they need to be strengthened.
Golem pertains to misused spiritual abilities.
Green dragon reveals envious feelings one doesn't own up to.
Griffin characterizes strength and intelligence.
Kelpie signifies a playful, joyful spirituality.
Kraken portrays one's spiritual fears.
Leprechaun typifies wisdom. It may also refer to hidden spiritual development.
Leviathan relates to a great size or amount. The surrounding dreamscape details will clarify what this refers to.
Loch Ness monster stands for possibilities.
Mermaid reveals a state of spiritual confusion; indecision as to what the truth is; denial of reality.
Sasquatch See Bigfoot.
Unicorn is representative of real possibilities; the reaches of reality.
Werewolf pertains to a dysfunction that alternately varies behavior.

Fairies & Fairy Tales

Brownie See fairy.
Elf characterizes proof of something one is skeptical of or doubts. This symbol helps to eradicate doubt with proof.
Faerie See fairy.
Fairy is a representation of the intellect's far conceptual reach through reality.
Fairy godmother characterizes the reward of a brilliant spiritual revelation through one's personal efforts of reaching and stretching intellectual reason out past the imaginary limits of reality.
Fairy lamp signifies a suggestion to look at something with more delicacy. This means a need to pull back from an aggressive approach.
Fairyland equates to the delicate and nebulously fine spiritual aspects that can only be discovered by one who believes in possibilities.
Fairy ring characterizes concepts of true reality that cannot yet be proven through the currently known laws of physics. This particular dreamscape symbol refers to elements of life that are still misunderstood.
Fairy tale is a representation of hidden lessons that one still needs to learn to advance one's life path.
Gnome comes in a dream to warn of a need to guard one's beliefs or attitudes.
Goblin connotes a spiritual fear.
Pixie points to the presence of true reality's possibilities.
Sprite refers to possibilities.
Sylph is a characterization of spiritual grace.
Tooth fairy exemplifies a lack of reality in one's life; a belief that flattering speech will serve oneself.
Water sprite portrays the often unrecognized and unexpected elements of spiritual reality.
Wood nymph represents the undiscovered, hidden ways of nature.

Fairy symbolizes the expansion of knowledge beyond experience.

Fable & Folklore

Gingerbread house may refer to a tendency toward affectation.

Aesop is a representation of one who speaks the truth in a simplistic manner.
Fable symbolizes truths that are clothed in a story line or experience.
Folklore constitutes the preservation of the spirit of truths.
Gingerbread house warns of a self-induced perspective on one's personal life as being the epitome of sweet perfection. This dreamscape symbol may indicate a tendency to overdo the ornamentation in one's life (excessive affectations).
Golden Bough indicates a validation for one's readiness for advanced spiritual concepts and experiences in one's life.
Hansel and Gretel characterize loss of direction through misplaced trust; betrayal; placing trust in someone who has ulterior motives.
Lilliputian is a representation of something in life that is of little consequence or trivial. This dreamscape symbol may also reveal an individual's inferiority complex and lack of self-worth.

Heroes & Villains

Batman is a representation of overconfidence.
Bluebeard characterizes unspiritual behavior and lack of faith.
Boy Wonder is a depiction of high accomplishments gained from an early recognition of opportunities.
Hulk suggests an unrealistic belief in one's abilities. Warns against pushing oneself beyond limits.
Rambo symbolizes a desire or tendency for an individual to force solutions or closures through aggressive means.
Spiderman represents the use of personal talents and insights.

Rambo means a combative approach.

Wonder Woman characterizes a person who appears to be able to handle or accomplish anything. This dreamscape symbol emphasizes a woman's inner power and its unlimited potential.

see also
• Good Guys *p. 144*
• U.S. Sites *p. 374*

American Figures

Annie Oakley is one who is independent. Will refer to a self-sufficient woman.
Chaplin (Charlie) illustrates the importance of humor in life.
Cher characterizes a resilient personality; enduring talent.
Custer (George) characterizes the karmic results of bigotry and racism.
Einstein (Albert) characterizes the high responsibility of directing one's knowledge in appropriate manners; positive use of intelligence.
Franklin (Benjamin) illustrates diversified talents.
Garbo (Greta) characterizes solitude and a need for same.
Jackson (Andrew) epitomizes racism, genocide, and greed.
James (Jesse) portrays an individual who gains from the efforts of others; a lack of personal responsibility.
James (William) corresponds with deep thought.
Jefferson (Thomas) characterizes a striving for knowledge.
Judge Judy characterizes an individual who gets down to basic issues and doesn't beat around the bush; one who cuts to the chase.
Karloff (Boris) indicates a person the dreamer is uncomfortable with and somewhat fearful or skeptical of.
Kelly (Grace) represents hopes and dreams.
Kennedy (Jacqueline) signifies inner strength.
Kennedy (John F.) stands for wisdom behind leadership or power.
Kennedy (Robert F.) is an exemplification of tenacity.
King (Martin Luther Jr.) characterizes the courage to speak out against adversity and/or injustice.
Lewis (Meriwether) characterizes fortitude.
Lincoln (Abraham) represents integrity.
Mead (Margaret) pertains to knowledge gained through observation.
Michener (James) stands for in-depth research and background material.
Monroe (Marilyn) implies a draw toward physical aspects. This will usually indicate an overinterest in the physical facets of life that will result in an imbalanced character.
Parks (Rosa) represents the recognition and practicing of one's inherent rights and freedoms regardless of possible repercussions.
Pillsbury Doughboy characterizes personal contentedness; a satisfaction with oneself and one's position.
Pocahontas is a representation of intercession.

Abraham Lincoln suggests adherence to a code of strong moral values.

Pollyanna implies blind optimism. It may refer to an inability to accurately perceive reality.
Rand (Ayn) characterizes the importance of being objective in one's dealings with people.
Sawyer (Tom) characterizes a person who doesn't give logic and reason to the thought process.
Wright brothers characterize innovative thought. It may refer specifically to the concept of thinking outside the box.
Yankee Doodle characterizes loyalty.
Yosemite Sam is a representation of a rigid personality; one set in one's ways and resisting change.

Mythic Locations

Atlantis cautions against the negative or wrong use of high knowledge, power, or intelligence.
Avalon cautions one against the tendency to have utopian dreams and unrealistic life goals.
Camelot characterizes a paradisal society; the earthly utopian concept.
Elysian fields means an afterlife paradise, but in dreams it equates to an emotional state of high satisfaction (paradise) following an accomplishment having extended effects.
Fantasyland cautions of a need to return to reality.
Ivory tower stands for needed solitude; contemplative time. Rarely does this symbol refer to material riches or an arrogant attitude.
Lemuria See Atlantis.
Lower world (mythology) See underworld.
Never-never land represents a fear of growing up; an inability to face the world and the attending responsibilities of maturity.
Oz connotes a willful reluctance to face or accept reality.
Underworld stands for the hidden negative elements in one's life.
Utopia corresponds to an unrealistic goal or perspective of life.
Valhalla stands for heroic efforts and its benefits or rewards.
Wonderland usually indicates awareness and the marvels that one perceives, but this symbol can also represent wearing those rosy glasses that prevent one from seeing the whole of life.
Xanadu See Camelot.

Historical Personages & Characters

Blackbeard See pirate.
Columbus (Christopher) portrays misinterpretations; confusion; perceptual problems; possessiveness.
Conquistador connotes one who enjoys winning; having control over others.
Copernicus stands for an unshakable faith in one's idea or belief.
Curie (Marie) characterizes the application of intelligence; the instigating force behind discovery.
Darwin (Charles) alludes to evolution. This does not refer to biological aspects but rather emotional, perceptual, mental, or spiritual.
Diana (Lady Diana Spencer) See Princess Diana.
Fossey (Dian) defines one who strongly believes in convictions and has the fortitude and strength to fight for them; is fearless in the face of adversity.
Frank (Anne) characterizes strength of character in the face of adversity.
Freud (Sigmund) comes as a caution when conducting a self-examination of one's motives.
Gandhi (Mohandas Karamchand) characterizes living spirituality; fighting for spiritual principles.
Hippocrates characterizes an individual who can discern the difference between truth and superstition.
Historical figures hold a personal meaning for each dreamer. This meaning will usually be easily identified.
Hitler (Adolf) exemplifies the destructive effects of intensely negative forces; the result of manifested evil. This symbol mirrors the extreme apathy for all others wrought from total self-absorption.

Ebenezer Scrooge suggests one can improve oneself at any time of life.

Houdini (Harry) reveals an individual who impresses others through trickery or deception.
Joan of Arc characterizes what one can accomplish when one acts upon one's visions (inspirations).
Jung (Carl Gustav) portrays mental reaching to transcend current limitations.
Kant (Immanuel) illustrates one's ability.
Luther (Martin) represents the separation of the spiritual from the materialistic aspects in one's life.
Marie Antoinette characterizes insensitivity; arrogance; indulgence in excesses.
Mesmer (Franz) characterizes a person in one's life who has an ability to convince others of her or his viewpoint. This particular dream character also points to ulterior motives or manipulation.
Montezuma II represents an advisement to preserve one's higher ideals, ethnicity, or best qualities.
Newton (Isaac) pertains to the simplicity of true reality and the revealing messages nature has to teach.
Nightingale (Florence) exemplifies the power of determination and its resulting manifestations.
Pasteur (Louis) characterizes a person who is interested in the pure facts of an issue.
Pavlov (Ivan) exemplifies a conditioned response. It reminds that the reaction can be altered by understanding.
Picasso (Pablo) suggests a distorted perspective and/or confused thoughts.
Polo (Marco) characterizes an adventuresome discovery time; a period when one should strike out and experience one's unique path.
Ponce de León (Juan) represents a dysfunctional perception of reality and folly that results.
Princess Diana characterizes one having the inner strength to stand up for herself in the face of domineering factors.
Rasputin (Grigory Yefimovich) characterizes a manipulative personality; one who uses the impression of attained knowledge to control others and elevate oneself.
Robin Hood characterizes the courage to actively correct a wrong one observes being done; one who goes out on a limb to make a quiet difference; unconditional goodness without any form of publicity.
Scrooge (Ebenezer) reminds us that it's never too late to change for the better.
Teresa (Mother) characterizes a selfless personality; compassion; one who gives aid.
Tesla (Nikola) is a representation of a comprehension of a few elements comprising true reality.

Shakespearean Characters

Hamlet implies a surrounding of close associates; one's circle of friends.
Lothario characterizes a manipulative personality; ulterior motives; a deceiver.
Macbeth characterizes personal gain through serious misdeeds.
Puck relates to a mischievous personality.
Romeo and Juliet forewarn of an unproductive or doomed relationship.
Shylock is a representation of a self-serving individual who takes ruthless advantage of others.

see also
• Children *p. 127*
• The Devil *p. 342*

Children's & Nursery Rhyme Characters

Aladdin symbolizes one's wishes for easy access to one's goals; an easy way out. Advises to get motivated; get moving to accomplish goals oneself instead of just sitting around wishing for things to happen or suddenly manifest.

Ali Baba represents one who holds the key or answers to a particular problem in the dreamer's life.

Alice in Wonderland suggests an unrealistic life perspective. May possibly refer to an amazing phase of discovery.

Captain Hook portrays a devious personality.

Cinderella represents acceptance of one's situation; perseverance.

Genie characterizes false promises and hopes; empty visions of goals or desires quickly obtained. It may also refer to an unrealistic perspective on the part of the dreamer.

Golden goose represents an unlimited source of blessings or benefits.

Goldilocks connotes irresponsibility; a dependence on others.

Humpty-Dumpty characterizes a self-created (psychological) condition where one believes one cannot proceed without assistance.

Little Red Riding Hood is a representation of misplaced trust. It may specifically refer to misjudgment.

Long John Silver characterizes manipulative arrogance.

Mad Hatter characterizes one who has confusing thoughts; disassociative ideas; impulsive behavior.

Little Red Riding Hood signifies being wrong about something or someone.

Mother Goose pertains to immaturity.

Munchkin characterizes an animated personality; someone who has an exuberance for life.

Peter Pan pertains to the power of belief and faith. Emphasizes the importance of a childlike faith and open-mindedness.

Pied Piper characterizes a person who has a strong magnetic personality and can convince others of almost anything; the following of or susceptibility to these types.

Prince Charming pertains to an idealistic perception and overly optimistic goal; an unrealistic ideology; an illusionary persona.

Punch and Judy characterize a love/hate relationship.

Queen of Hearts comes in dreams to point out the importance of the emotional male yang being balanced by his own portion of female yin.

Seven Dwarfs stand for the six main energy forces within the body in association with one's activating spiritual development.

Sleeping Beauty won't normally be associated with a beautiful woman but rather the beautiful spirit and spiritual truths within everyone which not all acknowledge.

Snow White characterizes an innocent personality; naïveté.

Tinkerbell emphasizes the importance of having faith in one's potential.

Tin Man *(The Wizard of Oz)* suggests an appearance of ineffectiveness or insubstantial abilities to manage projects or carry through, yet this is a misconception of one's true character. A Tin Man will be someone who keeps his/her cool under fire and doesn't flaunt abilities or intellect.

Ugly Duckling pertains to misconceptions associated with first impressions; assumptions or judgments based solely on appearances.

Wizard of Oz comes to reveal a deception.

Demonic

Demon will always be a characterization of any aspect that plagues an individual's life or mind. Normally a negative connotation would be associated with a demon, but someone who is a procrastinator could be plagued by the subconscious nagging of the urgings to get moving.

Deuce (devil) pertains to a situation that characterizes a perfect example of something bad; the worst of something.

Devil characterizes an individual or life aspect that is extremely negative and personally harmful.

Fiend is a warning dreamscape symbol that most often will relate to someone with whom the dreamer is directly associated.

Lucifer See devil.

Fantasy & Science Fiction

Android means one without thought.

Android signifies a mindless personality or one incapable of thinking for oneself; one who finds safety in routine and fears variation from set ways.
Cyborg characterizes the natural blend of spirituality and physics that create reality.
Darth Vader characterizes an individual who misuses spirituality. May clearly refer to a spiritually dark individual.
Hobbit characterizes a gentle and peaceful personality.
Hobgoblin alludes to one's fears in everyday life.
Make-believe may refer to innocent daydreaming, or it may also indicate a particular psychological condition of living false illusions; an attempt to personally alter the truth to a fact or existing reality.
Science fiction denotes unrealistic attitudes or beliefs; an inability to understand true reality.
Star Wars refers to the ongoing conflict that takes place between good and evil and those who choose which side to fight on.
Time machine is an interesting dreamscape fragment, because it may specify a particular period in time the dreamer needs to give attention to or it may indicate, through a broken mechanism, that one needs to stay focused on the present.
Yoda characterizes the inner peace true wisdom brings.

Film & TV

A-Team represents the power of spiritual forces.
Bambi characterizes true innocence; naïveté.
Casper characterizes the demystification of reality.
Chicken Little characterizes paranoia; unnecessary fear.
Donald Duck indicates poor planning; one who always seems to have one's plans foiled.
Fantasia portrays the diversity of one's options for expressing spirituality.
Garfield pertains to self-absorption.
Goofy is a representation of someone who doesn't quite have it together but is a good person just the same.
Keystone Kops characterize a ridiculous legal aspect that holds no validity.
Kirk (Captain James T.) means one who has the courage to explore the far reaches of reality (go where no one has gone before). This portrays innovative thought, imagination, and thinking outside the box.
Lassie means a friend's loyalty.
Lone Ranger applies to a desire to work individually.
Mickey Mouse connotes acceptance of life's little irritations; an ability to utilize humor as a means of dealing with small problems.
Mighty Mouse cautions against misjudgments. Applies to an admonishment against forming solid opinions from first impressions or exterior appearances.
Pinocchio points to exaggerations or fabrications.
Popeye stands for belief in one's strength.
Road Runner denotes impetuosity. Advises one to give more thought before rushing forward.
Smokey the Bear symbolizes acute watchfulness.
Snoopy cautions against prying into the affairs of others.
Sorcerer's apprentice cautions against the desire to learn from misguided individuals.
Three Stooges expose a counterproductive relationship.

Horror

Frankenstein reveals inner demons.

Apparition means an important message.
Bogeyman characterizes those one fears in life.
Doctor Jekyll characterizes an individual's hidden aspects; the duality of an inner, true self and one's outward appearance. Also see Jekyll and Hyde.
Dracula characterizes an individual's infatuation with the overdramatized negative aspects of power. This dreamscape symbol may reveal a draining or tedious type of personality.
Frankenstein is a representation of self-created monsters in one's life; those out-of-control emotions or attitudes that require some kind of containment.
Gremlin pertains to a temporary problem or hitch in one's plans.
Imp characterizes a recurring irritation, possibly a person. This indicates a need to address the problem for proper closure.
Incubus warns against transferring aberrant psychological mechanisms to self-created (imagined) manifestations.
Jekyll and Hyde emphasizes a changeable personality; hypocrisy; vacillation. May point to someone who has a tendency to play both sides.
Monster will always stand for a fear one has.
Ogre stands for an inability to accept life; a poor self-image.
Vampire characterizes an individual who uses others for self-serving purposes; ulterior motives.
Zombie warns against the use of psychological manipulation for any reason.

see also
• Writing & Literature *p. 219*
• Television *p. 221*

Writers & Celebrities

Alcott (Louisa May) portrays a desire to reform repressive attitudes and perceptions.

Anthony (Susan B.) characterizes one who fights for one's rights, especially against gender-repressive abuses.

Barton (Clara) characterizes a great desire to provide others with basic comforts.

Bernhardt (Sarah) exposes overdramatized emotionality.

Cousteau (Jacques) signifies an in-depth spiritual search.

Dickens (Charles) is a dreamscape symbol that portrays old-fashioned morals that are still viable.

Dickinson (Emily) is a representation of the beauty of heartfelt expressions.

Hawthorne (Nathaniel) characterizes ethical and spiritual living.

Peale (Norman Vincent) is a symbol that reminds one to help oneself by stressing one's own inner power.

Poe (Edgar Allen) characterizes melancholy to a morbid range of ideas that stem from deep thought.

Rockwell (Norman) symbolizes the beauty of simplicity; seeing life without coloring it with personal attitudes.

Ross (Betsy Griscom) emphasizes the importance of symbolism. Stands for honorable service.

Shakespeare (William) is a symbol that reminds us of moral and ethical obligations and the behaviors leading to life tragedies.

Steinem (Gloria) symbolizes the realization of self-worth and unlimited potential.

Stowe (Harriet Beecher) represents human rights.

Thoreau (Henry David) reminds us to not lose sight of the beauty of the wisdom that nature freely displays.

Whitman (Walt) characterizes a gentle nature.

Miscellaneous Characters

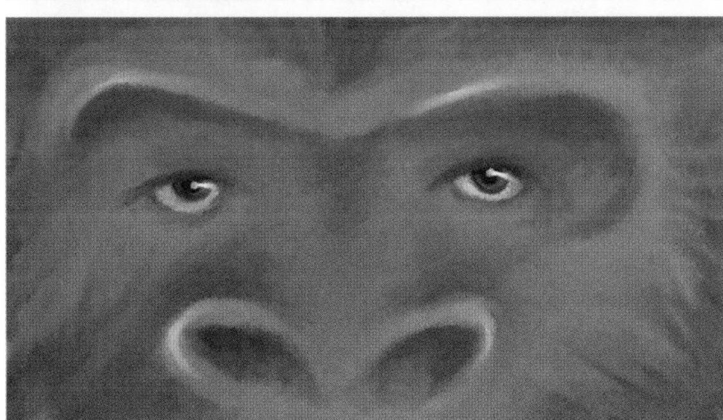

King Kong may indicate insuperable difficulties in one's life.

Bunyan (Paul) signifies the extent of one's potential.

Casanova (Giacomo Girolamo) characterizes a philanderer; a user; someone who has ulterior motives.

Centurion is a dreamscape symbol that characterizes an individual who is perpetually on guard.

Cossack is a representation of an individual who charges forth into action without having complete information beforehand.

Don Quixote characterizes an unrealistic optimism; a fear of facing negatives or accepting bad endings.

Godzilla is a dreamscape symbol that corresponds to fears; the fearsome events one is afraid to approach, experience, and get past.

Grim reaper comes in dreams as a warning of a potentially dangerous associate, situation, or course.

Gulliver characterizes an individual who has trouble dealing with personal adversity or trials.

Faust comes as a reminder that power and knowledge are nothing unless accompanied by the wisdom of the soul.

Flying Dutchman warns of spiritual imaginings.

Jack Frost characterizes one who could put a damper on spirituality.

Jane Doe signifies a repressed personality; one who doesn't express emotions or opinions; a fear of displaying independence.

John Doe See Jane Doe.

King Kong characterizes an overbearing personality; seemingly insurmountable problems.

King Solomon suggests great wealth. This dreamscape symbol may not refer to material riches but rather spiritual or moral wealth: a great amount of blessings.

Knight characterizes an advocate; a champion of a cause or another individual; one who stands up for another.

Mother Nature symbolizes plenty, bountiful gifts. This particular dreamscape symbol may also point to events outside an individual's personal control.

Sandman characterizes a need to rest one's mind.

Svengali reveals an individual who manipulates others for negative purposes and to their own ends.

Tar baby characterizes a situation from which one cannot extract oneself.

Tarzan characterizes an overblown perspective of oneself and one's abilities.

Christmas Characters

Kriss Kringle See Santa Claus.

Saint Nicholas See Santa Claus.

Santa Claus characterizes an overly optimistic personality; unrealistic expectations; good intentions.

Santa's elves symbolize those who would encourage unrealistic expectations or promote false hopes.

Chapter 24

Places

These diverse dream elements can carry a variety of meanings, which are most often associated with the primary underlying aspect of a specific life condition or situation. They also have the ability to point one in the right direction.

Continents, Countries & Regions

Africa represents uncluttered thoughts and ideas.
America See North America; South America.
Australia suggests congeniality. It may refer specifically to friendships.
Austria denotes an attention to detail; a tendency to strive for perfection.
Balkan States suggest a sense of being overburdened.
Belgium represents hospitality; a willingness to help others.
Canada relates to a diversity of inherent talents.
China (country) suggests the duality of fragile treasures and multiple mass-produced products. This refers to the fine, delicate elements in one's life being interspersed with common, unremarkable aspects.
Continent will direct the dreamer to an important aspect that's personally pertinent. Clarity will come when the specific continent name or country is shown. For general interpretations, see specific continents.
Country (foreign) will have a uniquely specific meaning for each dreamer.
Czechoslovakia suggests strong traditions and a personal sense of noble heritage.
Denmark symbolizes a tolerance or acceptance for another's unique individuality.
England represents a good friend. Also suggests a tendency to adhere to social mores.
Europe signifies diversity of ideas or perspectives or traditions.
Finland denotes a hardy character.

Iceland stands for strength of mind.

France refers to the inner strength to fight for one's rights/freedom.
Germany signifies fortitude and renewal.
Gold Coast is a representation of affluence as well as of those seeking to be associated with it.
Greece represents attained skills. It may also refer to philosophical ideas.
Hungary signifies pride in one's ethnic traditions; a strong character.
Iceland refers to largeness of character; self-reliance; fortitude.
India exemplifies a wealth of spiritual diversity.
Ireland is a dreamscape symbol that relates to undiscovered elements of reality; unproven aspects of reality; the range of reality's wide possibilities.
Israel represents holding onto one's rights with unyielding tenacity.
Italy refers to emotional expressiveness.
Japan suggests spiritual tranquility.
Malaysia suggests being underappreciated.
Mexico suggests a readiness for expressing emotions or opinions. This dreamscape symbol may come as an advisement to express oneself more openly, or it could be suggesting a need to hold one's tongue.
Mongolia stands for a stalwart and forthright character.
New Zealand suggests pastoral respite.
North America signifies perseverance and free expression of individuality.
North Korea currently represents suppression.
Norway stands for resilience; courage.
Philippines stand for hidden hazards.
Poland stands for a hearty character and a loyalty to one's traditions/roots.
Portugal refers to emotional expressiveness; an ease with which one can openly share feelings.
Russia symbolizes perseverance; a strong strength of character; eventual freedom to express individuality.
Saudi Arabia signifies power gained through wealth.
Scotland means proud heritage.
Sicily is a representation of deep familial bonds.
South America suggests there are hidden aspects to some bright-appearing benefits.
South Korea suggests a tenuous position/situation.
Spain is a symbol that suggests strong traditions.
Sweden represents a tolerance for another's individuality.
Switzerland suggests neutrality; a tendency to stay out of another's affairs. May also represent the presence of one's fine skill.
Tibet represents persecuted ancient spiritual traditions.
United Kingdom signifies an openness to possibilities.
Wales denotes good-heartedness; unpretentiousness.
West Indies refer to uncommon ideas; exotic or eccentric ideas/beliefs.

New York Sites

Broadway cautions against a tendency toward theatrics; a habit of overdramatizing; exaggerations.
Central Park portrays a means of respite within one's workday. May also refer to the positive and negative duality of life.
Coney Island See amusement park; hot dog.
Fifth Avenue is a representation of the uppity manner by which one presents oneself to others.
Manhattan is a representation of a wide range of diverse opportunities, yet they are costly to reach and maintain.
Park Avenue illustrates an egotistical personality; being out of touch with reality. It may also refer to misplaced priorities.
Rockefeller Center is a reference to cultural and/or extravagant events.
Seventh Avenue portrays one's outward affectations of aloofness.
Statue of Liberty emphasizes the ideal of equality and freedom.

see also
• Geographical Terms *p. 66*
• Travel Phobias *p. 158*

United States

Alabama stands for a staunch defense of traditional beliefs.
Alaska indicates one's untapped natural talents.
Arizona stands for the potential/power of inner strength.
Arkansas represents a tendency to have a difficult time understanding another's point of view; a type of stubbornness.
California represents the hope/expectation related to one's personal dream.
Colorado signifies the power of enduring fortitude.
Connecticut is a representation of foundational morals/ethics.
Delaware signifies individualism; liberty.
Florida signifies rewards following hard work; the upside after achievements/goals have been attained.
Georgia signifies a tendency toward a separatist type of independence.
Hawaii represents a protective attitude toward one's natural talents; deep respect for natural bounties/blessings.
Idaho represents pure objectivity; attitudes untouched by personal issues.
Illinois signifies tolerance; a live-and-let-live attitude.
Indiana signifies pacifism, a person's tendency to take a middle-of-the-road attitude.
Iowa stands for respect for the land; striving to nurture possibilities.
Kansas suggests the source of an issue—the meat of it.
Kentucky suggests efforts to contain one's impulsiveness; the wild streak in one's nature.
Louisiana suggests a person's uniquely uncommon characteristics and their celebration.

Hawaii refers to an appreciation of the good things that naturally exist in one's life.

Maine points to strong independence and fortitude; a strong character.
Maryland suggests separatist attitudes combined with qualities of perseverance.
Massachusetts signifies a strong sense of righteousness and a willingness to stand up for it.
Michigan suggests an abundance of fresh spiritual ideas/inspirations.
Minnesota signifies a hardiness of character.
Mississippi suggests a resistance to change.
Missouri signifies a tendency toward skepticism.
Montana refers to an abundance of wealth (natural talents and spiritual).
Nebraska suggests a stewardship of one's natural gifts and bounties.
Nevada signifies character and attitude extremes.
New Hampshire suggests a tolerance for the expression of individuality.
New Jersey refers to personal resourcefulness.
New Mexico signifies a pride of one's ethnicity/inherent traits.
New York stands for diversity; an acceptance of another's uniqueness.
North Carolina signifies the beauty of one's natural blessings and the need to recognize/appreciate them.
North Dakota represents one's roots and their traditions.
Ohio signifies quiet opinions; a tendency toward silent acceptance.
Oklahoma symbolizes a strong sense of self, not in a self-centered way, but a strong feel for one's individuality.
Oregon signifies spiritual abundance/fertility.
Pennsylvania symbolizes a new feeling of liberty or independence.
Rhode Island refers to a spiritual opportunity.
South Carolina stands for possibilities; the promise of hope.
South Dakota suggests one's homeland; home traditions.
Tennessee relates to joy felt for blessings.
Texas suggests an attitude of superiority; a sense of being a notch better; thinking too big instead of giving attention to smaller elements.
Utah suggests a tendency to have an attitude of spiritual superiority.
Vermont refers to an abundance of natural riches or blessings.
Virginia represents an appreciation of one's bounties or blessings; an abundance of opportunities to appreciate one's natural blessings.
Washington stands for spiritual abundance.
West Virginia refers to life's simplicities, its basics.
Wisconsin signifies a source of nutrients. These could relate to emotional, intellectual, or psychological needs.
Wyoming suggests civil liberties and their free expression.

U.S. Sites

Arlington National Cemetery represents honor, respect for those who have given the ultimate for others in their lives.
Beverly Hills corresponds with those who have the greatest responsibility and potential to help others; those with the means to help others.
Cambridge typifies the frequent negativity that may result from intelligence wrongly utilized.
Capitol defines the prime source of something.
Carnegie Hall pertains to high attainment and the recognition of same.
Chesapeake Bay refers to deeper spiritual conceptual connections.
Chinatown refers to the synergetic absorption of seemingly foreign aspects into one's belief system in one's everyday life.
Death Valley pertains to a particularly long-suffering stage in one's life.
District of Columbia suggests a need for awareness; one's conscience.
Golden Gate Bridge represents human potential, vision, and viable possibilities.
Haight-Ashbury characterizes an atmosphere that is conducive to freethinking.
Jamestown (Virginia) illustrates perseverance.
Las Vegas portrays indulgences; excesses; risks taken.
Library of Congress refers to a wealth of information; a source for further learning or research; the acknowledgment of an individual's sole right to claim ownership of an original idea.
Lincoln Memorial symbolizes all that one can be proud of in a particular people or in a specific nation.
Mackinac Bridge reveals the presence of a connecting option bridging a wide gap in one's life. This dreamscape symbol lets the dreamer know that the possibility for making this desired connection is available.
Mackinac Island stands for a return to more simple ways; a respite from life's hectic and complex world.
Mount Rushmore See Rushmore (Mount).
National monument most often brings an important message specific to the dreamer. Check for personal associations with the presented monument. See specific monument.
Niagara Falls connotes a powerful spiritual renewal.
Ozarks pertain to the basic necessities in life; a personality or lifestyle lacking extraneous elements; understanding and appreciating the value of simple basics.
Rushmore (Mount) warns against the invasion of another's sacredness; a disrespect for another person's spiritual belief.
Serpent Mound connotes personal verification. The dreamer will understand what this proof relates to. It will be different for everyone.
Silicon Valley represents the leading edge source for idea development.
Washington Monument represents basic rights.
Wedding chapel (Las Vegas) suggests a union made in haste with little forethought.
Wild West (setting) won't stand for wild as much as being free to travel one's chosen life course without red tape, restrictions, or limiting confinements.
Williamsburg comes to remind one of the laborious work that the simple life took and to advise one to appreciate how far one has come.
Yellowstone National Park pertains to nature's beauty and bounty reflected inside each of us if we'd only look within.
Yosemite National Park symbolizes the serenity that nature and its beauty has the potential of instilling.

Markets

Bazaar alludes to the vast array of learning sources and opportunities available.
Commissary See grocery store.
Farmer's market illustrates a nourishing opportunity. This nourishment is usually related to spiritual or corporal factors depending on other dreamscape elements.
Fish market defines the quality and extent of one's personal spiritual belief system. Recall the amount of fish available and their condition. What types were being offered?
Flea market alludes to opportunities, mostly unexpected ones.
Grocery store represents diet. Recall what was purchased for a better understanding of what this symbol is attempting to convey.
Market (shop) relates to available opportunities; choices.
Supermarket See market (shop).

World Heritage Sites

Blarney Stone denotes an individual's desire to be eloquent or persuasive.
Eiffel Tower is a dreamscape symbol that stands for a sign or reminder of a city's past achievement.
Forbidden City portrays a fear of knowledge and attending responsibility of same.
Great Pyramid is a reference to historical ignorance; lacking a true and clear comprehension of reality.
Great Sphinx is a symbol that relates to skepticism.
Great Wall of China is a symbol that warns of a deep rift in a relationship.
Lhasa pertains to high spiritual aspects; acquired deep spiritual wisdom.
Machu Picchu is a dreamscape symbol that characterizes ancient knowledge.
Sherwood Forest is a representation of a refuge or place of safety. It may specifically refer to respite for the dreamer from something.
Stonehenge connotes lost aspects of true reality.

see also
• International Buildings *p. 311*
• American Figures *p. 365*

Theater

Amphitheater indicates a clear view of events; a good comprehensive perspective.
Backstage means private life, attitude, or that which one does not publicly display.
Downstage points to an issue or element in life that requires closer attention.
Playhouse See theater.
Soundstage denotes a call to be aware of one's actions and words. Recall what type of set was presented. Was it a historical period set? Was it lit up or in darkness?
Stage connotes an opportunity or means of expressing oneself to a multitude of people.
Stage set See soundstage.
Theater constitutes a need to see more of what transpires around oneself.

Food Processing

Cannery means preservation. This dreamscape symbol usually advises the dreamer of a need to recall or retain the memory of an event for the purpose of learning from it to help advance his or her life's path.
Creamery symbolizes the dreamer's wholesome aspects that blend to create a richly cultural and rewarding life.
Meatpacking house illustrates the quality of foundational concepts of the basic ideas one ingests. Recall the condition of the place. Was it clean? Were there rodents or bugs? Did it smell badly?
Packinghouse See meatpacking house.
Slaughterhouse See meatpacking house.
Smokehouse is preservation.

Arts, Entertainment & Culture

Amusement park refers to a thrill-seeking personality. Is suggestive of an advisement for one to recognize value in the simple things.
Art gallery portrays the display or sharing of one's individualized expression. Also can point out what one admires in life.
Auditorium signifies a need for an audience.
Big top (circus) refers to the main event; where all the main action will take place.
Bullring characterizes a manipulative situation or condition; a setup.
Cinema See movie theater.
Circus indicates a laughable or ridiculous situation.
Cultural center refers to opportunities to learn more about others.
Dance hall pertains to an emotional outlet.
Gallery (art) represents qualities and life aspects one admires.
Library relates to a multitude of opportunities to extend one's knowledge.
Multiplex (movie theater) refers to multiple unrealistic perspectives.
Museum relates to antiquated concepts.
Natural history museum reflects a call to/desire for getting in touch with one's bonded relationship to all of life.
Opera house typifies a replay of events, indicating a need to better understand a recent situation. May also refer to a counterproductive element in one's life.
Park (grounds) constitutes a place or time of respite.
Penny arcade comes to remind us that we can afford to take a break or some amusement time, and it doesn't have to cost us much in the way of expended energy.
Petting zoo advises of a return to more basic, simplistic perspectives and appreciations.
Playground suggests childlike traits or attitudes.
Projection booth symbolizes the source of specific information.
Public library See library.
Racecourse exemplifies a designated course that one travels over and over. This advises one to set one's own course and take it at a steady pace.

Circus represents something that should not be taken seriously.

Racetrack usually alludes to the fast track.
Ring See circus.
Temple (site) represents a spiritual element in one's life.
Terrarium portrays a recognition and respect for one's natural abilities.
Theme park correlates to the manner in which one chooses to relax or find enjoyment.
Three-ring circus exemplifies a ridiculous situation or a confusing chain of events.
Tinseltown portrays a place that contains little of real value.
Valley of the Kings (Egypt) corresponds to undiscovered spiritual aspects of true reality.
Water park symbolizes taking joy in one's spirituality.
Wax museum depicts the mask that people present to others (even though it may seem to be an exact replica).
Zoo correlates to beautiful elements of individuality that are confined, perhaps by oneself.

Shops & Stores

Antique shop refers to where old tried-and-true ideas and ways can be found. But recall the condition of the dreamscape shop. If it was dusty, it means that antiquated thoughts or beliefs are being sold and represented as highly valuable.
Bakery most frequently stands for the ingestion of sweet and/or high-caloric foodstuffs. This is usually a warning symbol for the literal physical meaning. This may also refer to a source for generosity in a person's life.
Bargain basement suggests a wealth of opportunities. Recall the type of items that were featured.
Bookstore signifies research and a wealth of knowledge.
Boutique relates to specialty; specific aspects in life. What type of products were for sale in the dreamscape boutique? Recalling these will clarify the meaning.
Camera shop portrays the many and varied methods of preserving the truth or collecting facts. Could also indicate the options available for those intending to interfere in another's life.
Candy shop indicates the varied ways and methods that are available for experiencing life's small but meaningful joys.
Card shop cautions one to carefully choose how something is said. Advises to search for the right words.
Convenience store exemplifies a tendency to take shortcuts; quick measures taken.
Costume shop is a representation of opportunities to

Candy shop signifies many different ways of enjoying life's little pleasures.

understand others or experience another's persona.
Country store See general store.
Curio shop signifies a source providing many puzzling or interesting elements.
Department store connotes an aspect that offers a variety of opportunities.
Dime store See variety store.
General store connotes a variety of opportunities to choose from.
Gift shop illustrates opportunities for kindness.
Hardware store denotes hard work. May indicate a need for hard work applied to fixing up some aspect in one's life.
Head shop corresponds with a source that provides one with tools to escape from problems.
Health-food store represents a choice of multiple tools to maintain personal health. This may refer to mental or emotional health, depending on the surrounding dreamscape details.
Import shop portrays a multitude of opportunities to take advantage of valuable foreign ideas; being open to new experiences.
Jewelry store portrays exterior values that one may not necessarily hold within oneself.
Mall pertains to multiple opportunities available to one.
Millinery (shop) connotes a source for diversity of ideas.
Mini-mart stands for convenience; multiple opportunities showing up along one's path.
Mom-and-pop (store) represents a homelike atmosphere with associative attitudes of understanding and acceptance.
Redemption center (stamps/coupons) stands for an opportunity to restore one's inner peace; balancing out karmic aspects.
Registry (bridal) signifies a clear and definitive idea of what one wants in life. May reveal a specific character element.
Retail (store) applies to an opportunity. Recall the type for further clarification.
Rock shop correlates with natural talents and how they are utilized for the benefit of humankind.
Shop (retail) constitutes supply or opportunity. The type of shop will be the important element here.
Shopping center See mall.
Show window will usually be an attention-getting venue which literally shows what one needs or points to a solution. The key here isn't the window itself but whatever it featured.
Sporting goods store refers to tools and equipment for playing the game (getting along in life).
Store See shop.
Storefront pertains to a perception of the best opportunities that are currently available.
Strip mall suggests convenient opportunities.
Superstore portrays a chance to take advantage of a great range of opportunities.
Surplus store represents multiple opportunities.
Thrift shop relates to resourcefulness; effective management.
Trading post applies to a current need to be giving. This symbol comes when an individual isn't compromising.
Toy store portrays the child within. It often refers to childish behavior, perceptions, or fears. This symbol can also suggest methods adults utilize to toy with others.
Variety store represents good accessibility to a multitude of options.

see also
• Service Industries *p. 258*
• Store Personnel *p. 259*

Business & Industry

Advertising agency See Madison Avenue.

Back forty (land) signifies opportunities for further cultivation (development).

Chop shop emphasizes incorrect analysis; improper dismantling of conceptual ideas; fragmented conclusions.

Company town portrays group dependency.

Convention center relates to the meeting of like-minded people for the purpose of sharing information and learning.

Customer service desk implies a life aspect from which one can receive assistance or information.

Distillery is in reference to condensing conceptual ideas down to the basic facts or components; simplification.

Dump See landfill.

Employment agency directly suggests a change in the manner in which one works. This may not relate to one's type of employment but could pertain to how one goes about laboring along one's path.

Factory represents the manner in which one arranges or assembles path aspects that lead to goals.

Foundry alludes to the beginning stage when one is forming perspectives and initial plans.

Front office applies to responsibility or authority.

Headquarters is a representation of a central source regarding a specific idea.

Hostelry See hotel.

Hotel symbolizes a transition stage; a temporary condition.

Industrial park exemplifies a location where many energies are combining to generate specific outcomes.

Landfill reveals one's covered-up negative aspects.

Lot (land) represents one's chosen destiny. Recall surrounding dream details for further clarity.

Lumberyard connotes the current existence of dormant talents and abilities in an individual's life. This is a call to activate them.

Machine shop pertains to the creation of examples, models, or molds. Recall what condition the templates were in. What color? Shape?

Madison Avenue applies to advertising; a need to share or broadcast one's ideas.

Mail-order house will denote an opportunity source.

Mail room alludes to discernment in communicating ideas to the right people.

Metroplex implies a high concentration of societal involvement. May be indicating an advisement to give more attention to social servicing behavior.

Oil refinery comes as a message to refine one's crude qualities. One needs to soften or control insensitive expressiveness.

Parking garage/lot signifies the time or space one allots for ensuring a stable state or position.

Plant (industrial) refers to one's work efforts. This symbol may not imply one's awake-state place of employment but will rather apply to some other type of work the dreamer is involved in.

Plot (land) See lot.

Property See specific type.

Real estate office refers to a source of potential opportunities for obtaining a goal.

Receiving dock correlates to anticipation or expectation. Recall what was expected to arrive. What type of business was the dock associated with?

Repertory See repository.

Repository will correlate to a specific type of source within oneself; a personal store or reserve of strength, compassion, patience, etc.

Roadhouse See motel.

Saddlery represents aids available to assist one's life journey.

Service center will indicate a source capable of providing repairs or solutions.

Shipyard denotes preparations/intentions to embark on a spiritual journey, perhaps travel over new spiritual waters (new concepts).

Shotgun house not only stands for commonality, it represents a tendency or preference to be like everyone else; a lack of individuality.

Showplace symbolizes a presentation of perfection to others.

Showroom will display an array of specific opportunities for the dreamer. Recall what type of showroom it was.

Station (depot) See depot.

Stockroom will reveal what one should be retaining and reserving.

Storage connotes having reserves; preparedness.

Study See library.

Tank farm See storage.

Union hall corresponds with a desire to utilize one's talents and skills.

Waterworks connote the amount of spiritual talent a person uses.

Services

Barbershop implies a need to trim or restyle one's thoughts, attitudes, or belief systems.

Beauty shop illustrates an attempt to enhance appearances. May indicate the striving to maintain a false persona or raise one's self-esteem.

Box office implies that which attracts attention; a draw; popularity.

Hockshop See pawnshop.

Laundromat emphasizes some type of cleansing is required. Surrounding dreamscape details will usually clarify what this is.

Massage parlor may warn of ulterior motives or healthful benefits depending on the other dreamscape aspects.

Pawnshop represents sacrifices made.

Post office emphasizes a need to communicate with another. May refer to verbal or emotional expression.

Rental (equipment shop) signifies a source of opportunities to resolve temporary needs.

Shoe repair (shop) stands for a source for mending one's path difficulties; someone who can provide motivation and get one back on course.

Restaurants

Bed-and-breakfast stands for an easy or comfortable personality or situation; an individual who is at home anywhere. This dreamscape symbol also points out a home away from home and serves to underscore the fact that one doesn't have to be alone in life. On the same hand, this element identifies someone is open to the dreamer.
Bistro represents an informal relationship or atmosphere.
Bodega refers to sources of basic needs close to home. May be suggesting that the search for answers has been taken too far afield; answers are closer than one thought.
Cabaret See bistro.
Cafeteria represents a lack of choice; not realizing the wide scope of opportunities that are available.
Canteen means spiritual reserves; spiritual beliefs that one can always fall back on and gain encouragement from.
Chophouse See steak house.
Coffee shop exemplifies a rest period and the need to choose a specific manner for same.
Diner (eatery) represents aspects of nourishment that are recognized and used by many. This nourishment may be emotional or psychological.
Drive-thru (window) refers to convenience; a quick aid for accomplishing something.
Ice-cream parlor applies to opportunities to share one's spirituality.
Lunchroom implies a need to take time out from one's daily efforts to revitalize oneself.
Refectory corresponds to intellectual nourishment.
Restaurant reveals one's quality of diet. This diet may not refer to physical eating but rather what one fills her or his life with as far as beliefs, behavior, type of associates, and so on
Snack bar typifies choices.
Soup kitchen indicates a chance to nourish (help) others.
Steak house is a dreamscape symbol that signifies a source of encouragement or aspects that will act as an impetus for action.
Tavern relates to a perceived place or source of respite where an individual may receive support.
Tea garden indicates a source of healing strength, fortitude.
Teahouse signifies a small respite; a healthful break.
Tearoom See teahouse.
Truck stop characterizes a necessary resting phase along one's life path.

Mills

Flour mill See gristmill.
Gristmill corresponds to natural talents and the use of same.
Lumber mill relates to the shaping of opportunities.
Mill corresponds with a need to grind or break down something into more manageable or visible parts. This symbol advises one to look more closely at the parts that comprise the whole (situation).
Paper mill relates to the manner in which one processes information. Recall the type of paper being made. Was the mill's operation efficient? Did it require many workers or just a few?
Sawmill constitutes the act of personally identifying the basic factors of a problem.
Water mill See water-related buildings, p. 309.

Health

Hospital suggests renewed vigor.

Asylum warns of some type of craziness going on in one's life.
Birthing center reveals the atmosphere or surroundings that will provide opportunities for new beginnings.
Clinic (medical) refers to a factor in life that has the capability of providing assistance for minor problems.
Convalescent home illustrates a situation or life aspect that will serve as a healing factor.
Emergency room comes as a strong warning. Surrounding dreamscape will clarify this.
Emergi-center is a source of solutions to minor problems.
Fertility clinic reveals a need to understand why one isn't motivated to put energy into starting a new beginning.
Hospice portrays compassion.
Hospital comes as a rejuvenation advisement.
Hostel means a phase of respite for a beginning journey.
Infirmary See hospital.
Intensive Care Unit (ICU) is a warning to seek immediate help. This may be associated with mental, emotional, or physical aspects.
Maternity ward exemplifies a prime time to begin a new direction; fertile ground for nurturing new ideas.
Medical building emphasizes a need for some type of personal care or healing.
Mental hospital See psychiatric hospital.
Nursing home represents one's perspective toward those who are more experienced and have more knowledge. Recall the condition of the home. Who was residing there?
Operating room stands for the tools and conditions that are right for correcting a negative within oneself or another.
Post-op See recovery room.
Psychiatric hospital may represent a need for introspection; self-analysis.
Recovery room reflects a state of recovery from an emotional or damaging situational event. This is a sign that things will work out; one will recover.
Rehabilitation center advises one to change one's ways, or it may represent an intent to do so.
Rest area will naturally imply a much-needed rest from one's work or a stressful situation.
Rest home See nursing home.
Sanatorium illustrates a life element that is capable of providing a return to physical, emotional, or mental health.
Waiting room symbolizes expectations. Recall what type of room was presented. Was it a delivery room?

see also
• Sports *p. 263*
• Eating *p. 426*

Home

Back lot reveals a contrived exterior persona.
Backstreet usually implies the presence of clandestine behavior; private agendas.
Backwater warns of stagnant spiritual belief systems.
Backwoods portray pure spiritual talents.
Backyard alludes to one's rightful territory, perhaps cautioning one against sticking one's nose into other people's business.
Barnyard stands for down-home attitudes and/or relationships; an unaffected personality.
Downstairs represents a ground-floor or lower level element which must be experienced or covered before upward advancement can be achieved.
Gated community refers to one's guarded general surroundings; a tendency to be protective or defensive of one's friends. This symbol may also reveal an elitist attitude.
Homeland indicates a sense of one's roots; a strong identity.
Kibbutz refers to community involvement. This may not mean literally but rather is associated with a general attitude.
Motherland won't normally signify a birth country but will refer to one's nurturing when young; the moral training and sense of home comfort one remembers.
Neck of the woods See neighborhood.
Neighborhood refers to a cultural or economic indicator that will have a revealing effect on additional dream aspects. A neighborhood can expose one's inner attitudes or opinion, desires, or fears.
Old country pertains to long-held traditions and where one's heart might still lie. Also could point to the existence of certain underlying loyalties.
Outback See backcountry.
Refuge represents a protective force or situation.
Reservation (Native American) represents an advisement to relate or make associative connections between true reality and spiritual aspects. This symbol may also refer to the setting aside or confinement of issues one doesn't want to face or deal with.
Village usually represents a small, close-knit community. This symbol will normally refer to the composite grouping of one's friends and close associates.
Yard (back) See backyard.
Yard (front) implies that which lies in one's future. May also suggest what one presents to the public.

Farming

Hayloft signifies the tangible results of one's endeavors.

Dairy farm refers to a major aspect of one's life serving as a source to nourish the perspectives of oneself and others.
Farm denotes an atmosphere rich in character/spiritual nourishment and a back-to-basics perspective.
Farrowing house cautions against starting too many projects at the same time.
Feed store (ranch) stands for a desire to nourish and care for all life forms and the efforts expended toward achieving that goal.
Fish hatchery denotes a spiritual birthing; developing spiritual beliefs or ideas.
Hayloft pertains to the resulting evidence of one's efforts.
Paddock See corral.
Ranch signifies a domineering personality.
Sod farm is a representation of the transference or implanting of new ideas.
Turf farm See sod farm.
Vineyard exemplifies the fruit of one's efforts. Recall the condition of the dreamscape vineyard.

Sports, Pastimes & Leisure

Card room is a representation of a place of risk.
Casino See gambling casino.
Clubhouse symbolizes a desire to belong; a personal need for acceptance.
Day camp refers to the reservation of a portion of one's day for relaxation and mental rest.
Fitness center See health club.
Gambling casino relates to risks taken; a big opportunity with small odds of winning.
Health club/spa comes as an advisement of a need to shape up or restore some specific aspect of oneself.
Poolroom corresponds with a scheming atmosphere; plotting and planning. The key is to recall the condition of the room and those within it. Who was there? Do these elements lead to a determination of dirty dealings or healthy competition?
Resort typifies a strong advisement to obtain some needed rest; a need to get away from current stressors.
Ski resort signifies spiritual shallowness; the avoidance of higher concepts.
Solarium signifies the strong light that infuses a strong spiritual belief system.
Spa See health club.
Sports stadium applies to procrastination; a sit-and-watch attitude.
Yacht club denotes a particular desire to associate with only those who are perceived as being as spiritually elevated as oneself.

Public Places

Pumping station signifies a spur for action.

Arena symbolizes one's circle of relationships or activities.
Boomtown characterizes a productive life.
Borough refers to a specific area of concern in one's life.
City stands for a group density; being concentrated/saturated with many perspectives.
City hall represents a need to conduct oneself appropriately. Could also mean a difficult road ahead regarding a specific situation.
City room is associated with incoming information; news.
Civic center will be associated with cultural aspects. This will have a unique meaning for each dreamer depending on how elements in one's life relate to a cultural aspect.
Community center applies to the enjoyment of social contacts. May refer to a life element that is available to all.
Crisis center signifies a source for immediate help.
Downtown indicates the center or foundational basis of something. This symbol may be advising of a need to return to one's center.
Fire station refers to a preparedness for an emotional emergency; an immediate motivational need.
Ghost town corresponds to a tendency to live in the past; pining over what once was.
Information booth points to a need for more information. The whole story isn't known.
Inn connotes a resting place along one's life path.
Meetinghouse pertains to a coming together; shared ideas; a camaraderie.
Midtown represents a level phase in one's life where few ups and downs will be experienced.
Police station is a reference to restraints. This dreamscape symbol will suggest that someone is always watching you. Were you in the station? What were you doing? Were you the captain? In jail? Were you reporting a crime or being arrested?
Pound (animal) See animal shelter.
Public square represents neutral ground.
Pumping station refers to a source of motivation.
Senior center corresponds to an opportunity to learn from those who have gained experience and knowledge.
Sewage treatment plant signifies an attempt to salvage a bad situation; efforts expended to improve a bad situation.
Subdivision (residential) See suburb.
Suburb is a representation of an intermediate placement or position; a middle-of-the-road yet structured perspective.
Tank town will denote a seemingly unimportant location or stop along one's journey. The idea here is that appearances can be deceiving.
Uptown suggests an elitist area of perception/attitude.

Conflict & Military

Air-raid shelter means defensiveness toward attitudes and perspectives; strength of convictions.
Barracks suggests a lack of individuality. It may also refer to self-repression.
Base camp signifies our comfort zone—what one retreats to when rejuvenation or rest is required.
Boot camp applies to getting the basics of something.
Buffer zone signifies one's social distance or space separating oneself from others.
Checkpoint advises self-analysis.
Checkroom pertains to trust.
Concentration camp can signify forced attitudes, or it can come in a dream to advise of greater attention needed to an issue.
Control room refers to the source for pulling everything together and making things run smoothly.
Drop (location) relates to a specific locale associated in some way with the dreamer.
Field hospital cautions one to monitor oneself throughout the process of traveling life's more difficult path stages.
Hangar (plane) comes to advise one of the need for a time of contemplation; a rest period from research or expending great efforts.
Labor camp points to a situation in which one has made more work for oneself.
Nerve center signifies the source (hub) of one's motivational force. Depending on related dreamscape elements, this symbol may also point to one's sensitivities—the panel of buttons people can push.
Situation room represents a call to put efforts into resolving a conflict/disagreement.

see also
• Funereal Occupations *p. 247*
• Wartime Activities *p. 357*

Safe Places

Below deck corresponds to a protected place.
Booth connotes privacy; individuality.
Hideout may imply a need for sanctuary, or the act of running away from problems. Surrounding dreamscape details will clarify which meaning it has for the person.
Hidey-hole suggests secrets. If the compartment is for a person, the symbol is meant to relate to one hiding from something one should probably face.
Safe house clearly symbolizes a safe or secure place, situation, direction, or perspective.
Sanctuary emphasizes respite. It may indicate a place of peace. This symbol can refer to emotional, spiritual, or mental peace.

Places of Ill Repute

Bordello See house of ill repute.
Brothel See house of ill repute.
Cathouse See house of ill repute.
House of ill repute is a particular dreamscape element that refers specifically to a disregard for a negative element in one's life.
Red-light district comes in dreams as a symbol of a self-serving intention on the part of the dreamer.

Hedonistic Places

Bourbon Street pertains to a person's tendency to not take life seriously; a somewhat hedonistic perspective.
Country club represents social and recreational opportunities.
Hangout is a dreamscape symbol that stands for a place where one feels comfortable going for support.
Nightclub pertains to missed opportunities for gaining deeper understanding.
Nightspot See nightclub.
Open bar suggests benefits without cost.

Prison

Alcatraz See prison.
Jail reveals a state of self-confinement.
Penitentiary denotes an ultimate result or conclusion. This is a dream symbol that stems from one's higher self or conscience.
Pokey See jail.
Prison symbolizes self-imposed restrictions. The key element here is to recall what your role was, if any. Were you the prisoner or guard? Warden?

Frontiers

Backcountry alludes to simplicity. May also come as a sign pointing out the importance of something relevant in one's life that isn't readily visible or obvious.
Border represents some aspect in one's life that represents a dividing line.
Borderland exemplifies a fringe area in one's life or beliefs.
Cow town represents an unsophisticated setting or situation that relates best to the simple elements of life.
Old West (setting) signifies a secret wish for adventure in a less complicated world.
Provincial is a dreamscape element that implies an unsophisticated aspect or individual.
Settlement See colony.

Figures of Speech

Aboveground represents conventional standards that are held in society.
Breeding ground means a fertile condition or atmosphere; an atmosphere conducive to productivity or fruitfulness.
Hot spot is a representation of a place or situation that is intensely active, usually in a negative way.
Jumping-off place comes in dreams as a symbol that marks a beginning point.

Death

Burial ground See graveyard.
Cemetery See graveyard.
Crematorium connotes a finality; an aspect conclusion; an absolute closure.
Funeral home signifies a dying condition and a need to put it to rest.
Graveyard has ominous connotations. Most often advises of a condition or situation where the dreamer is treading on dangerous ground.
Morgue is a dreamscape symbol that connotes futility; a dead-end; an unproductive aspect to something.
Mortuary See funeral home.
Plot (cemetery) will most often come in dreams as a mortality reminder. This reminder is most often necessitated by an awake-state life of misdeeds or a lost course.

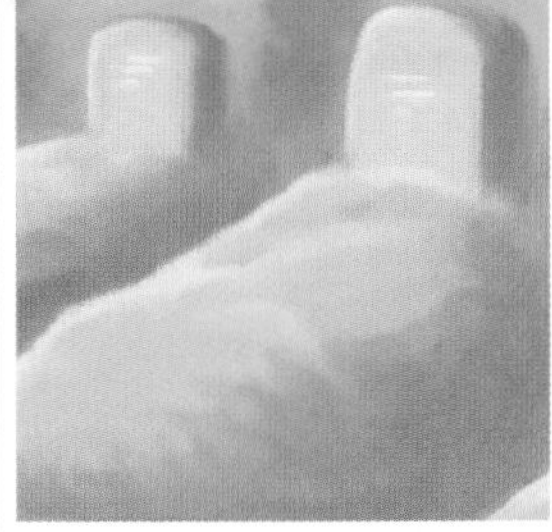

Cemetary plot reminds us of death.

Potter's field (burial place for paupers and strangers) advises of the wisdom of making a difference in life. This is not implying that one should make a name for oneself but leave behind something of value for others to benefit from. This symbol points out the fact that everyone should do something beneficial in life.

Directions & Placements

Above (direction) means a higher level.
Aground designates an off-course spiritual situation.
Askew refers to confusion in one's life; an off-balance perception or conclusion derived from incomplete information.
Back (directional placement) symbolizes background position. May caution one to either come forward or else stay in the background.
Back-to-back symbolizes the absence of a break between events or issues.
Backward (direction) connotes a reverse in one's direction. May represent a need or caution.
Behind (directional position) relates to a lower level, or it may point to the proper position one should be taking.
Behind (losing ground) suggests a quickened pace is required to catch up with matters. Perhaps more knowledge needs to be gained.
Below (directional position) stands for under or may be revealing the correct positional placement of something.
Beneath (directional position) usually reveals a hidden element not perceived.
Beside (directional placement) connotes an equal positioning aspect.
Between (directional placement) stands for the middle position.
Boreal (north) signifies a higher direction to one's path; elevated levels of study; higher attitudes and perspectives.
Bottom (directional placement) denotes foundation or beginning point.
Brink symbolizes the point at which a major decision or action will occur.
Center (position placement) defines a position that offers the widest variety of choices.
Clockwise pertains to advancements.
Crossways warns of a perspective or behavior that is counterproductive; more than misaligned, it's almost opposite from the truth of a matter.
Down (direction) represents a return to the basics; a fundamental level.
Faraway (perspective) indicates a life stage that is approaching a personal attitude of losing faith and motivation.

Aground suggests that one is having problems with one's spirituality.

Forward (direction) advises one to refrain from stopping one's path walk; of a need to continue going forward.
Front (position) denotes priority.
Kitty-cornered See crossways.
Left (directional position) characterizes diversification; a shift away from rigid, established perceptions or traditions.
Middle (position) points out neutrality. May imply a lack of opinion or decision-making ability.
Nadir (directional position) represents a beneath or under position. It may refer to a less advanced or developed aspect.
Over (direction) pertains to a need to pass or climb over a difficult element blocking one's path. This will call for determination.
Rear (position) brings a placement mark to some aspect in one's life. Each dreamer will make this specific association.
Right (direction/position) may represent a supportive role or point to ultraconservatism. Also see road signs for more directional interpretations.
Supine (position) relates to a time of rest, neutrality, or acceptance.
Tail (end) illustrates a position marking a last or final element.
Top (position) usually reflects an above or higher level.
Turning point denotes a realization, a crisis situation, or sudden epiphany which causes one to finally see the light.
Underneath (position) suggests hidden elements to an issue.
Underside suggests a need to look at all aspects (angles) of an issue, even those that are less obvious/visible.
Underwater pertains to a state of being submerged in spiritual issues.
Zenith (directional position) stands for the high point; fulfillment; reaching a goal.

Bars

Bar (liquor) See tavern.
Barroom relates to a place where emotional support or sympathy can sometimes be received.
Saloon portrays a state of unawareness. May also indicate a need to chill out and soothe one's stresses.
Speakeasy defines shared secrecy.
Taproom See barroom.
Tavern relates to a perceived place of respite.
Wet bar is a dreamscape symbol that represents an opportunity that arises to soften one's stress.

Chapter 25

House, Home & Garden

The house is a main dreamscape category. It directly relates to the mind, and home accessories provide a variety of clues associated with one's overall personality.

Accessories & Decor

Accessory (home decor) depicts the elements in one's life that contribute to personal perspectives.
Americana suggests a deep-seated sense of patriotism; a love of one's homeland.
Andiron symbolizes that which fires one into action; a life aspect that holds the fuel that, once ignited, flares up into action; the potential for action.
Antique corresponds to the value in old ideas or ways.
Artificial flowers See silk flowers.
Artificial houseplant See houseplant (artificial).
Ashtray represents important reminders to leave the past behind and move forward on life's path.
Beanbag pertains to the whole comprised of many equally important parts.
Carpet pertains to underlying characteristics of an individual's path.
Carpet pad is a symbol that pertains to a life aspect that softens one's path.
Cheval (mirror) typifies the need to see the totality of oneself. This would imply aspects that are being denied.
Chippendale (furniture) warns one against forcing beliefs and perceptions onto others.
Coffee-table book applies to something one openly shares with others.
Color scheme reveals a specific tone of something. This can refer to clothing, one's home decor, or an entire atmosphere/scene of a dream.
Decor See accessory (home decor).
Flypaper portrays personal awareness.
Fly swatter indicates an opportunity to personally deal with some of life's irritations or interferences.
Furnishings give clues to a dreamscape's atmosphere. How was a room furnished? Did it have a warm or cold feeling to it? Were there any period or ethnic decoration pieces?
Hanger (picture) See picture hanger.
Hot-water bag/bottle comes to advise one of a need to "warm up" emotionally.
Household effects (decor) reveal one's personality.
Houseplant (artificial) reveals a false behavior trait put on for appearances sake.
Indoor-outdoor (carpet) represents a need to balance or bring uniformity to personal aspects that one holds privately (within oneself) and displays publicly (without).
Jewelry box denotes one's collection of riches. Recall if they were more silver (spiritual aspects) or gold (material aspects).
Mosquito net refers to an awareness that offsets or deflects the minor irritations that can disrupt one's focused attention.
Plant (artificial) See houseplant (artificial).
Shaker (furniture style) stands for simplicity regarding an individual's needs.
Track lighting denotes a highlighted, featured subject/issue.
Vase reflects various personality characteristics that aren't always evident. The key here is to recall the condition, color, design, and so on.
Wall hanging will represent a multitude of meanings that will provide insight for the dreamer. Recall what the hanging was. What was it made of? What condition and color? Design? Was it straight or lopsided?
Wallpaper reflects personal characteristics. Recall the design, colors, and condition.
Wall-to-wall represents an abundance.
Welcome mat means congeniality; being open to new ideas.

Window Dressing

Blind (Venetian) indicates a habit of altering one's scope of perception; self-controlled views of life; choosing how much to see and understand.
Curtain means privacy; the time separating daily activities. This dreamscape symbol may refer to denials or secrecy.
Drapery See curtain.
Shade (window) pertains to privacy. This dream symbol may also be indicative of selective perception.
Tiebacks (curtains) stand for a desire to better understand something; wanting to have a better view of things.
Traverse rod denotes a means of keeping issues open or closed; the choice of doing the same.
Valance connotes a superficial idea.
Venetian blinds relate to selective perception; seeing only what one wants to admit to.
Window shade warns of a shaded perspective.

Soft Furnishings

Afghan See blanket.
Bearskin (blanket or rug) alludes to emotional warmth and security; an overbearing individual who has been neutralized.
Blanket signifies one who provides solace and support.
Bolster (pillow) signifies a need for support or to be bolstered up.
Buffalo robe denotes one's shield of inner strength.
Cushion denotes an aspect that softens or eases.
Dust ruffle signifies an attempt to keep extraneous elements from contaminating pure ideas/intentions.
Eiderdown See downy.
Kirman (Persian) emphasizes wisdom and a high interest in knowledge.
Mackinaw (blanket) denotes emotional warmth/comfort derived from camaraderie.
Pad See cushion.
Rug refers to how one covers something, relating to inner traits, character, or attitude.
Runner (rug) means an attempt to protect a part of one's path.
Sham (pillow) denotes an empty element; a cover story.

see also
• Doors *p. 316*
• Colors, Patterns & Fabric *pp. 414–423*

Furniture

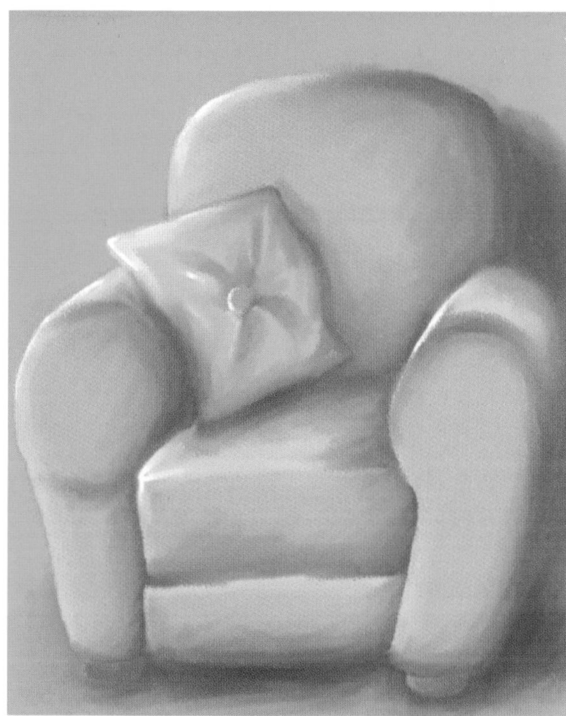
Armchair is a representation of time out to relax.

Adirondack chair refers to a respite time. May come as an advisement to take a break and enjoy the scenery.
Armchair indicates a rest period.
Barrel chair applies to personal mass. This warns of the tendency to carry around more weight than necessary. May refer to various aspects in life, not merely body weight.
Breakfront (furniture) signifies a crack in one's presented veneer; a break in one's affected presentation.
Captain's chair refers to a leadership position. Who was sitting in this chair? Was it empty?
Chair signifies a short or temporary rest period may be needed.
Chaise longue implies an attitude of nonchalance; indifference.
Cocktail table See coffee table.
Coffee table typifies an offering of comfort extended to others.
Daybed suggests the importance of pause times during one's day.
Drop leaf (table) suggests provisions made for expansion; realizing the possibility of needing to expand one's thinking or plans.
Easy chair implies a relaxed attitude.
End table suggests convenience; something close at hand.
Folding chair signifies a temporary situation, one in which one's position provides for the option of movement.
Footstool is a dream symbol that comes as an advisement to slow down as one's life path is traveled. Perhaps one needs to assimilate deeper meanings of lessons being presented.
Furniture alludes to one's character. Was it elaborate? Sparse? Spotless? Lived in?
Ladder-back (chair) indicates the need for a rest period before advancing further.
Lounge chair usually points out a lack of motivation.
Love seat signifies a situation or condition directly associated with two specific individuals. This symbol won't usually refer to love but will point to a close situational relationship with another.
Ottoman See footstool.
Pallet See bed.
Platform rocker suggests that this is a good time to feel secure in taking a well-deserved break or rest.
Potty-chair implies a need to retrain some negative aspect of oneself. Each dreamer will recognize what this refers to.
Recliner (chair) portrays acceptance. It may also represent indifference.
Rocker See rocking chair.
Rocking chair pertains to a well-deserved rest period in one's life.
Rolltop desk connotes a need to keep the specific aspects of one's life, work, or plans less public.
Secretary (furniture type) stands for business; things one needs to routinely take care of.
Side chair suggests a secondary position.
Sofa bed represents duality; multiple opportunities; something utilitarian.
Stool typifies an aid that assists one's advancement or progression. Depending on the type of stool, this could point to a small element providing temporary respite.
Swivel chair represents convenience; a means of efficient methodology.
Table pertains to an element of support and convenience.
Window seat suggests an opportunity to be aware of what's transpiring around one.
Wing chair applies to intellectual reaches; high insights.

Couches

Couch represents physical comfort; restfulness; leisure.
Davenport See couch.
Divan See couch.
Sofa See couch.
Settee See couch.
Slipcover represents an attempt/desire to improve an element in one's life. Depending on the related elements of the dream, this could be associated with one's perspective or aspects of behavior.

Kitchen

Breadboard refers to life aspects that support one's livelihood.

Bread box is the amount of energy put into one's livelihood.

Broiler characterizes the aspect in one's life that has the capability of bringing pressure or heat.

Butcher block (table) denotes negative aspects of one's life that others can gossip about or use negatively.

Coffee mill refers to an aspect that has the capability of energizing one.

Cookbook denotes the many opportunities and ways that serve to provide the formula to reach goals or help others.

Cookie jar connotes that which one reaches for; goals and aspirations.

Copperware is a warning. The dreamer will understand this by combining surrounding dreamscape fragments.

Countertop denotes work convenience.

Country kitchen denotes a large heart; emotional largess.

Creamer represents a life aspect that has the capability of providing deeper elements to one's life; deeper meaning; greater richness.

Crisper (fridge drawer) implies an attempt to preserve something; a desire to keep something new and fresh.

Double boiler indicates increased mental activity. Depending on surrounding dreamscape factors, this may refer to boiling emotions or situations.

Dripless (spout) stands for an element that safeguards against wastefulness.

Dutch oven denotes solid and sure methods of obtaining nourishment. This nourishment can be emotional, physical, mental, or spiritual.

Enamelware represents a simple, yet tried-and-true manner of accomplishing a goal or seeing something through to its conclusion.

Flask implies convenience. This would refer to a condition whereby an important factor to the dreamer is readily available; close at hand.

Flatware See specific utensil.

Garbage can connotes what one chooses to throw away. What was in the garbage can? Was it something that should not have been tossed away quite so lightly?

Ginger jar denotes a reserve of inner strength.

Graniteware See enamelware.

Griddle defines a hot situation or relationship. This advises of a need to take a neutral position in order to effect a cooling-down status.

Grill (cooking) alludes to a more productive way to accomplish something. This will be defined by the surrounding dreamscape details and will mean something different for each dreamer.

Hood (over stove) relates to a method of keeping ramifications to a minimum.

Hot plate advises of a need to keep up efforts regarding a specific situation or relationship.

Cookie jar denotes ambitions and targets.

Jug connotes common sense.

Mason jar relates a message to preserve something important in one's life.

Ovenproof relates to precautions taken while applying methods towards one's goals.

Pepper mill calls for finer perceptions or levels of awareness to be used.

Pie safe refers to an attempt to preserve what one has put effort into.

Pilot light stands for one's living spirit; one's true essence.

Porringer See bowl (utensil).

Pot holder suggests a controlled awareness in the face of heated issues or situations.

Pressure cooker corresponds to an extremely stressful situation, relationship, or element. May also advise one to retain more of the nutrients of the food eaten.

Salt shaker relates to a chance to cause an enhancement.

Speckleware See enamelware.

Stoneware symbolizes simplicity.

Summer kitchen denotes a desire to place oneself in a once-removed position; distancing oneself from the core of a heated situation, issue, or relationship.

Teakettle denotes a specified span of time before an idea or plan is ready to put into action.

Teaspoon portrays a small amount; a small or average measure of something.

Teflon stands for a protective shield. Relates to self-defense mechanisms.

Vat symbolizes a container of great size, meaning a large issue to contain in one's life.

see also
• Cooking *p. 170*
• Rooms in Private Homes *p. 315*

Crockery

Bowl (utensil) is a dreamscape symbol that indicates a pressing need for containment regarding an aspect in the dreamer's life.
Crockery See earthenware.
Cup symbolizes an individual's personal perspective on the quality and quantity of his or her life situation. Was the cup decorated? If so, how was it decorated? What was the cup made of? Was it filled or empty? With what?
Deep-dish illustrates an aspect in one's life that took some doing to create.
Dish refers to a presentation of something. What was on the dish? What color was the dish? What was its condition?
Earthenware (pottery) illustrates an awareness of reality; a down-to-earth state of being.
Mug is a dreamscape symbol that corresponds with someone possessing a particularly strong character. Recall if the mug had any words written on it. This will give further interpretation to the symbol.
Saucer is a symbol that relates to protective measures. It may also refer to something that is a means of containment.
Teacup is a dreamscape symbol that most often refers to a temporary situation, a situation that may tend to be overblown.
Teapot is a representation of a tool that can be used for creating or bringing about healing energies.

Cleaning

Broom cautions one to look past the surface; sweep away surface debris to get a clearer perception of what's beneath.
Broomstick refers to an aspect-in-hand that allows one to see past the surface.
Dry mop See dust mop.
Dust cloth stands for an element that will clear away extraneous aspects of an issue or attitude.
Dust mop stands for one's active efforts to keep one's path and purpose free of distractions.
Dustpan portrays the collecting and disposal of distracting factors. This means that one is focused on one's life path and refuses to be sidetracked.
Feather duster denotes the use of wisdom to make decisions; discerning intellect.
Housecleaning implies a need to get rid of extraneous aspects in life that only clutter one's progress or perspective.
Housework stands for the efforts that are expended to maintain a clean and comfortable home life.
Mop is a symbol that suggests a cleanup is required in one's life. This will refer to a uniquely individualized factor in each dreamer's life.
Oven cleaner will denote an attempt or desire to ensure one's methods are untainted.
Scrub brush is a dream symbol that indicates some form of cleansing is required.
Spring-cleaning symbolizes the energy put into keeping one's perspective clear of negative or opinionated aspects.

Cooking Utensils

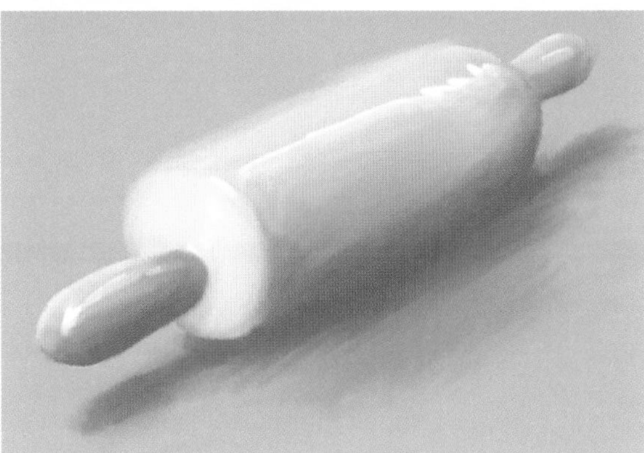

Rolling pin illustrates the unraveling of thoughts.

Bread mold suggests a possible need to change jobs or breathe freshness into the current one.
Bundt cake/pan signifies the little rewards in life that come in many forms and from various sources.
Cake pan refers to that which assists in achieving goals; a foundational tool.
Colander See strainer.
Cookie cutter stands for repetitiveness; a lack of variation, usually with respect to thought.
Cookie sheet is a symbol that refers to preparations for sharing a specific idea.
Cookware See specific utensil.
Cooling rack comes to suggest a cooling-down period.
Drip pan connotes a life facet that serves as a safeguard; a containment factor.
Frying pan is a symbol that relates to increased activity; a quickening of action.
Ladle signifies generosity; one who is always ready to pour out talents or abilities for the benefit of others.
Mortar and pestle is a dreamscape symbol that suggests one has a need to take something to a finer consistency; in other words, to look at the finer aspects of an issue.
Rolling pin represents a need to unroll concepts or ideas that one has balled up in his or her head.
Saucepan indicates a desire to affect surrounding elements in a personal manner.
Scoop (utensil) See ladle.
Screen (strainer) See strainer.
Sieve warns of an inability to manage personal containment; lacking self-control.
Skillet See frying pan.
Slotted spoon suggests a way to remain focused on the main issue and get rid of the extraneous elements.
Strainer implies the need to sift through something. It cautions the dreamer against arbitrarily taking everything in. In this sense, it advises one to be more discerning.
Tenderizer denotes an easing factor in one's life.
Vegetable steamer denotes the preserving of important elements in one's life.
Waffle iron represents a firm sense of neutrality.

Appliances

Alarm clock usually signifies that it's time to wake up and change ways.
Blender suggests mixing; warns against a separatist attitude toward various life aspects.
Carpet sweeper represents an attempt to keep the underlying characteristics of one's path clear of surface negatives.
Ceiling fan refers to a cooling period needed; a pause during advancement along one's path.
Deep freezer stands for a life aspect that has been set aside. Did the dreamscape reveal what was in the freezer?
Deep fryer connotes serious trouble.
Electric blanket See heating blanket.
Flatiron See iron (appliance).
Freezer implies that something needs to be put on ice for a time; a postponement or preservation is needed.
Hair dryer refers to a shielding of one's spirituality; reticence to talk about spiritual matters.
Heating blanket stands for emotional comfort.
Home entertainment center signifies personal methods of relaxation or information gathering sources.
Icebox See refrigerator.

Stove represents a way of finishing off a task.

Ice maker/machine symbolizes a frozen belief that there is but one way to the divine.
Iron (appliance) advises of a need to straighten out a relationship, perception, or situation in one's life.
Juicer refers to a life aspect that may produce a calming or easing effect.
Kettle advises of something brewing in one's life.
Laborsaving (device) may suggest a more efficient method of doing something. Surrounding dreamscape details will clarify this.
Microwave oven emphasizes an efficient and quick conclusion is needed.
Oven signals a method to gain completion or accomplishment. Recall oven's condition. Was it on? What was in it?
Percolator (coffee) indicates a state of brewing. Recall the situational presentation. Who was doing the brewing? Did the aroma have a disagreeable or a pleasant scent?
Refrigerator refers to a calming state. Advises one to cool off.
Rotisserie connotes a method of developing a plan or goal that ensures all aspects are given equal consideration.
Rug cleaner applies to an attempt to keep one's personal groundwork or foundational perspectives clear of negatively affecting elements.
Slow cooker denotes time taken to allow an issue to fully develop.
Socket (electrical) See outlet (electrical).
Stove denotes an opportunity to complete an aspect in one's life; a means to cook it (bring to fruition).
Toaster implies a forthcoming disagreement or disagreeable situation.
Urn (warming) pertains to the need to keep an aspect in your life warm (currently active).
Vacuum cleaner indicates that a cleanup is required. This may refer to a situation, relationship, or even some type of negative within oneself.
Wall plug See outlet (electrical).
Water purifier refers to an active attempt to filter the intake of spiritual elements; be spiritually discerning.
Water softener warns of attempting to soften spiritual truths. Cautions not to lessen the hard facts.

Dish-Washing

Dishcloth implies the clarity of something presented. Will usually mean that a cleanup is advised.
Dishpan pertains to one's habit of communicating clearly. It may also signify a pressing need to tie up loose ends.
Dishwasher is a tendency to let others clean up after one.
Dishwater denotes helpful aspects one utilizes to ensure clear communication.
Drain board (dishes) refers to an element that funnels unnecessary aspects away from the main issue.

Entertaining

Guest characterizes a temporary association.
Guest book comes in dreams to remind one to remember one's friends.
Guest list points to those one needs to include in something being planned.
Houseguest characterizes someone whom one allows to get close to one; the person one can let one's guard down in front of.
House party refers to openness; a willingness to let others in.
Housewarming denotes a desire to be liked.
Open house is a representation of a forthright personality; straightforwardness.

see also
• Drinking *p. 438*
• Meals *p. 440*

Wining & Dining

Bottle opener represents the key for quenching a specific type of thirst. The clue to clarified meaning is to recall if a certain type of bottle was displayed.
Breadbasket denotes a source of those life aspects that contribute to the quality and dependability of one's livelihood; that which holds elements of one's sustenance.
Coaster refers to protective measures; doing no damage.
Coffeepot illustrates a brewing situation and may indicate a percolating condition within oneself that advises of a rest.
Completer set (dinnerware, collectibles, etc.) denotes the whole of an issue. If one or more pieces were missing from this dreamscape element, then it means that one still doesn't have all the facts of associated aspects to an idea or situation.
Cruet represents specialized knowledge.
Crystal (glassware) implies displayed sophistication; a touch of social arrogance.
Cut glass signifies a finely faceted aspect in one's life.
Cutlery refers to sharpness; acuteness.
Demitasse (cup) pertains to the need for a small portion of motivation or energy to get one back on track. Suggests one needs nothing more than a little push.
Dessertspoon relates to special rewards.
Dinette set connotes informal or common aspects that are used to nourish one.
Dinnerware is a dream symbol that portrays one's personal perspective toward nourishing oneself.

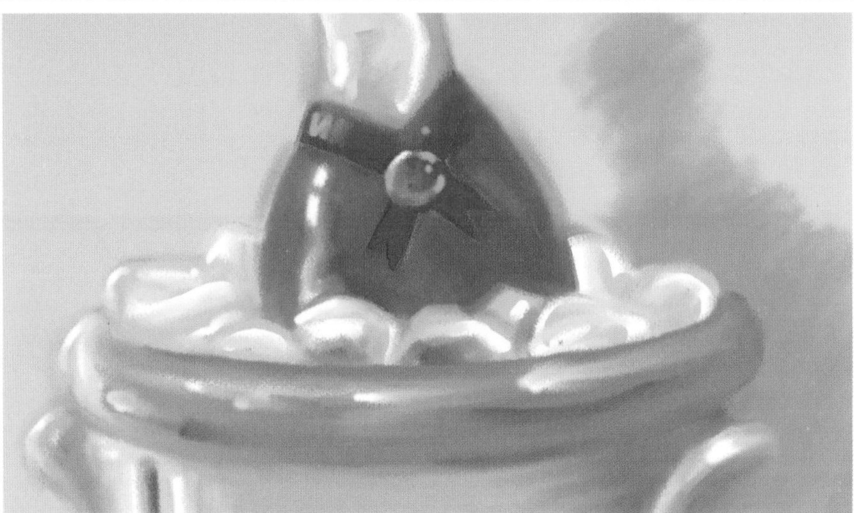

Ice bucket characterizes a tendency to refute one's true inner beliefs.

Finger bowl suggests an attempt to disassociate oneself from something in the dreamer's life; washing one's hands.
Fork (utensil) denotes a repressed personality.
Ice bucket portrays a frequency of denying one's personal spiritual aspects.
Lazy Susan is a representation of convenience.
Napkin (table) applies to one's personal level and quality of preparedness in life. Recall the color, fabric, and condition of the napkin to gain deeper meaning.
Place mat implies a mind for details.
Plate (dinner) connotes quality of nourishment in respect to one's personal attitude. This symbol refers to the specific attention given to the absorption of mental, emotional, or spiritual nourishment. Recall what type of plate was presented. Was it made of fine china, earthenware, or paper?
Platter (serving) connotes something easily obtained or attained.
Punch bowl denotes an aspect that has the potential to contain an unexpected element; a surprise factor.
Salver See serving tray.
Samovar See coffeepot.
Serving tray reflects order; efficiency.
Silver plate suggests a veneer of spiritual elements.
Silver spoon symbolizes a lack of experiential learning opportunities.
Silverware is a symbol that relates to utilitarian elements in one's life.
Swizzle stick pertains to a means of blending or coordinating various aspects.
Tablecloth being fabric will reveal multiple aspects. Recall the condition, type of fabric, design, and color.
Tablespoon denotes a larger measure than normal. In reference to some type of life aspect, it would indicate an ingredient of considerable importance.
Tableware See specific utensil.

Candlelight

Candle typifies that which can ignite one's spiritual or natural talents/abilities. May indicate hope.
Candleholder See candlestick.
Candlesnuffer means a tendency to reverse the effects of spiritual acts or "smother" the enlightening effects of another's spiritual deeds; cynicism; a lack of hope.
Candlestick connotes the quality of one's spiritual perception and manner of reception.
Tea light (candle) stands for a small, yet safe, illumination; a very good idea.

Nursery

Baby carriage represents undeveloped ideas and concepts that one carries around with one.

Baby monitor signifies an ongoing personal supervision of a newly accepted philosophy in one's life.

Bassinet is a dream symbol that means spiritual respite; a need to rest along one's newly begun path.

Cot refers to short periods of rest or pauses.

Crib (infant) exemplifies immaturity; an inability (or refusal) to face reality.

Flooring

Linoleum suggests a hardness to one's current life. The dreamer will recognize what this symbol refers to.

Slanted (floor) illustrates an adulterated aspect; a foundational concept/ideal that's affected by one's opinionated perspective.

Tile relates to versatility.

Vapor barrier is a dream symbol that stands for voluntary separation from spiritual matters; willful denial.

Lighting

Candelabra is a representation of an enlightening source that reaches out to illumine multiple life aspects.

Chandelier exemplifies the specialized light of ideas or thoughts that are outwardly displayed in a focused or attention-getting manner.

Dimmer switch may advise one to tone down an attitude of anxiety or excitement, or it may suggest adding energy and light to something in the dreamer's life.

Floor lamp suggests a light over one's shoulder, not in a spiritual context, but more for the purpose of seeing things more clearly.

Houselights portray one who has the attention of others.

Indirect lighting suggests a look at the entire picture (situation) instead of only focusing on the main issue.

Lamp connotes light required on an aspect of one's life. This symbol could refer to a relationship, an event or situation in one's life, or even to oneself.

Lamp shade emphasizes a need to tone down the light on something in one's life; control the light's direction; soften the brightness so it's not so harsh and perhaps blinding.

Light table points to an aspect in one's life that is capable of shedding light on issues or attitudes that are below the surface.

Mood lighting pertains to a ground-laying setup for a specific intention.

Sconce will symbolize a life aspect that has the ability to light one's way. Recall if it had a lit candle or bulb. Was it empty? Bright or dark?

Storage

Armoire alludes to hidden aspects of oneself.

Blanket chest See cedar chest.

Bookcase denotes broad-scope knowledge and suggests a need to study a variety of volumes. Was the dreamscape bookcase empty or full?

Bookshelf See bookcase.

Buffet See sideboard.

Bureau (furniture) See dresser.

Cabinet portrays that which is kept from the public eye.

Cedar chest reflects care given to the preservation of one's cherished memories.

Chest (cedar) See cedar chest.

Chest (of drawers) See dresser.

Chifforobe See dresser.

Clothes hanger is an advisement to let go of something one is clinging to or hanging on to. It is time to hang it up and move on.

Clothes rack suggests choices for expressing oneself.

Credenza symbolizes a superstitious nature; paranoia; a lack of trust.

Cupboard represents personal life aspects that nourish one.

Curio cabinet denotes a collection of high-interest issues. May indicate life puzzlements.

Drawer stands for organization.

Dresser signifies compartmentalized aspects of oneself.

Hanger (clothes) See clothes hanger.

Highboy corresponds to efficiency; a person's tendency to avoid wasting time on unnecessary steps.

Hutch (furniture) implies that which one displays publicly.

Lowboy exemplifies a multitude of extenuating factors existing just out of one's current perceptual view.

Sideboard stands for psychological elements that affect attitudes and opinions.

Silverware chest corresponds to a recognition and appreciation for the often unnoticed aids that one utilizes throughout life.

Tallboy See highboy.

Dresser stands for the categorization of aspects of one's character.

see also
• Babies *p. 103*
• Bathroom & Fittings *p. 314*

Bathroom

Basin See sink.

Bath mat refers to spiritual protection; personal safeguards one uses against the possibility of slipping spiritually.

Bathtub suggests a spiritual submersion is required. This would imply an individual who is fearful or has a reluctance to really get into his/her spiritual beliefs.

Bidet warns against incomplete hygiene.

Facecloth See washcloth.

Half bath denotes an alternative respite option.

Medicine chest will reveal what one needs to cure an ill, or it will display an excess that one is ingesting. Recall the surrounding dream details for further clarification.

Bathtub is someone disinclined to acknowledge his or her spiritual beliefs.

Shower curtain will expose one's inner negative character aspects. Recall if there were designs on this curtain. What color was it? Was the shower curtain dirty? Torn?

Shower head reflects an individual's strength of intention. Recall what type of shower head it was. Was it a water saver? Was it a massage type? Was it running? If so, was it a hard or gentle spray?

Sink refers to a life element capable of providing a cleansing opportunity.

Soap dish is a reminder that some element in one's life is in need of cleansing, usually one's hands.

Towel depicts a life aspect capable of absorption. This means an ability to lessen difficulties.

Towelette comes as a reminder to "keep it clean" regarding one's routine behavior. This "clean" refers to comments or other types of unintentional behavior that could be hurtful to someone else.

Washcloth represents a cleansing aspect.

Bedroom

Air bed comes in dreams as an advisement to sleep on it; that more thought-time is required before a decision should be made about something.

Air mattress denotes the need to sleep on it.

Bed cautions against overdoing; of a need for rest.

Bed board suggests a firm attitude or character.

Bedding (clothes or linens) portrays a condition of rest.

Bedpost symbolizes those aspects that support or lead to a resting period in one's life.

Bedspread portrays the type of rest one is receiving. Recall the color, design, and condition of the dreamscape spread. Was it a wild, geometric shape? Floral? In need of laundering? Torn? Was it the color of wake-up blaring red? Or a soothing color conducive to sleep?

Bedspring indicates the quality and/or variety of restful activities one utilizes.

Bedstead refers to aspects that support one's state of rest; the qualitative value of such rest.

Bed warmer suggests preparations for taking an intended respite from something.

Bunk bed relates to multilevel dreams: dreamscape fragments often have dual meanings for the dreamer.

Dressing table comes to point out the importance of taking a good look at ourselves once in awhile.

Feather bed suggests a down-to-earth perspective regarding one's personal attainment of wisdom.

Four-poster (bed) depicts night fears.

Hide-a-bed See Murphy bed.

Hollywood bed pertains to a lack of seriousness.

Linen (bedsheets) signifies one's moral/ethical behavior.

Litter (bed) is a symbol that implies laziness or a disinterest in physical comforts.

Mattress will reveal one's manner and quality of rest. Recall the condition and color of the dream mattress. Hard or soft? Lumpy? What size was it?

Mattress pad represents a personal interest in the quality of one's rest. Rejuvenation is important.

Murphy bed illustrates an efficient method; ingenuity.

Night-light represents a small measure of anxiety; a subconscious lack of self-confidence.

Nightstand/table comes to visually display an important item (aspect) one needs to further development or understanding.

Pillow pertains to a person's true temperament, state of mind, or level of reasoning. The key here is to recall what the pillow was made of, what color it was, the condition and its shape. Did the pillow have any design on it?

Sheet (bed) See bedding.

Sleigh bed (bed style) is a representation of a desire for one's spirit to reach/travel the heights of truth.

Spread See bedspread.

Trundle bed connotes the availability of accommodating a partner or assistant. This may imply a companion or some other type of close associate.

Vanity See dressing table.

Water bed is a symbol that comes to reveal a state of sleeping spirituality and advises one to wake up one's spiritual aspects and utilize them.

Heating

Ash can implies getting rid of one's materialistic trappings or extraneous life elements. This, of course, can also be pointing to belief systems, unrealistic goals, relationships, or business dealings.
Fire irons See andiron.
Fireplace denotes emotional warmth; heart warmth.
Fireplace screen stands for an attempt to keep damaging or negative elements from disrupting one's congenial or serene attitudes and feelings.
Gas burner pertains to personal responsibility regarding how potentially harmful aspects are utilized in a positive way.
Gas log refers to imitations in life; second-best options.
Hearth refers to a homey aspect; warmth and comfort.
Hearth rug implies measures used to protect one's personal feelings of comfort and privacy.
Heater represents an element that motivates.
Mantel pinpoints a person's priorities in life. Mantels are traditionally a place of distinction in the home and usually display items of pride or personal interest.
Potbelly stove denotes a companionable atmosphere; a time for reflection and introspection.
Radiator (heating unit) is associated with the emotional temperature of home life. Was the radiator broken? Cold? Steaming?
Room temperature would normally represent a comfortable attitude or atmosphere, yet the dreamer needs to recall if the room was cold or too warm to gain the intent here.
Scuttle See ash can.
Space heater is a symbol that constitutes a desire for personal comfort in respect to one's immediate surroundings. It also refers to a fear of being exposed to any disagreeable situations.

Potbelly stove represents a congenial time for thinking.

Bathing

Backsplash stands for an effort to keep spirituality from entering into issues that should remain separate.
Bathwater pertains to the quality of one's spiritual beliefs. Check the condition of this water. What color is it? Is it very dirty?
Bubble bath is a dreamscape symbol that warns against submerging oneself in negative situations, relationships, or beliefs.
Cold shower advises of a cooling-off period.
Foam (soap) See bubble bath.
Plug applies to voluntary holds or stoppages.
Soap is a symbol that advises one of a cleansing of some type that is needed.

Plumbing

Backflow warns of a backlash; possible retaliation or a boomerang effect.
Faucet implies the control one has in one's life. Usually this control is associated with spiritual aspects and implies control that is used to selectively turn one's spiritual behavior on and off.
Plunger represents a need to unclog something in one's life. Most often the dreamer will make this association and pinpoint what needs work.
Spigot See faucet.
Stopcock See faucet.

Leaks

Leak will indicate a loss of whatever the leak is associated with. Was the leak a slow drip or a flowing type? See below for some examples.
Alcoholic beverage container leak reveals an improvement in an individual's ability to face problems.
Gas leak (gasoline) points to reduced energy; dwindling motivation.
Gas leak (natural/propane) refers to a reduction of supportive elements that powered one's steadily advancing pace.
Hydraulic line leak means that one is doing something to make progress more difficult to achieve; someone is making life harder.
Milk carton leak could indicate a lessening of one's immaturity or losing some form of nourishment, which usually refers to emotional aspects of the dreamer's everyday life.
Oil leak points to increasing friction, usually associated with one's stress level. This symbol may mean friction between the dreamer and another person.
Toilet bowl leak pertains to something that the dreamer is doing in his or her waking life to hamper the natural release of stress.
Water leak is a dreamscape symbol that stands for a dwindling of spiritual attitudes or behavior.

see also
• Clothing *pp. 400–413*
• Tools *p. 444*

Tools

Brass tacks apply to the basic facts of an issue or situation; something of the utmost importance and its fundamentals.
Extension (cord) suggests a greater use of one's personal energies or efforts is needed.
Friction tape advises to smooth over a situation or relationship; for a need to protect a life aspect from sparking or causing a shocking incident.
Gimlet (tool) is a dreamscape symbol that indicates a personal need to bore into or penetrate something in one's life; search for deeper understanding.
Glass cutter represents a way to break through perceptual barriers or obstructions interfering with clear vision.
Glue gun refers to the tool that one can use to repair a broken relationship or situation.
Gouge See chisel.
Grapple (tool) indicates a struggle to hold onto something.
Grinder/grindstone advises of a need to apply greater effort.
Hacksaw alludes to difficult solutions.
Hammer warns of forced attitudes or beliefs.
Hand drill denotes extensive personal efforts expended for the purpose of getting to the bottom of an issue.
Hatchet pertains to a resentment; a desire to get even with someone; a retaliation; an irascible and disagreeable personality.
Hedge trimmers refer to an attempt to reshape one's path.
Miter box corresponds with a need for precision; exactness.
Nail (metal) represents a need for attachments; connections.
Nail gun is a dreamscape symbol that alludes to making quick and easy connections in one's everyday life.
Nail head will pertain to the basic aspect of an issue.
Needle-nose (pliers) See pliers (needle-nose).
Power mower See lawn mower (powered).
Power strip See extension (cord).
Putty knife illustrates a method or opportunity to correct a fault or negative element that exists in one's life.
Sledgehammer is a symbol that depicts forcefulness. It may refer specifically to a severe personality. It may also point out an aspect requiring extreme measures.
Socket set/wrench symbolizes resourceful utilization of problem-solving abilities.
Spatula refers to a personal life element that serves as a beneficial aid.
Stepladder is a dream symbol that signifies the careful taking of one step at a time for cautious life progression and advancement.
Step stool is a representation of a small, yet effective aid to progression.
String is a symbol that usually connotes an idea; the beginning formulation of a new concept or theory.
Tack (nail) pertains to a temporary attachment.
Tape See adhesive tape.
Tape measure advises the dreamer of a need to gauge limits, affects, responses, etc., before proceeding with a plan; an eye toward possible ramifications.
Thumbtack See tack (nail).
Tool is a dream element that symbolizes aids, opportunities, or methods for utilizing personal abilities.
Toolbox is a representation of a readiness to offer one's talents wherever or whenever they are needed.
Unplugged reveals a disconnection. This may refer to one's own rationale.
Workbench is a dreamscape symbol that indicates that personal efforts are needing to be expended.

Laundry

Bluing is a dream symbol that warns against spiritual arrogance; pretending more spirituality than possessing.
Clothes basket See hamper (clothes).
Clotheshorse is an individual obsessed with appearances.
Clothesline emphasizes the need for increased awareness. In some dreams, this symbol will suggest a need to air something, perhaps a grievance or grudge; get something out in the open.
Clothespin suggests an opportunity to air grievances or held-back opinions.
Detergent advises of a need to clean something in one's life. This will usually refer to one's outward presentation to others; the affectations used for public display.
Dryer (clothes) implies a need for more seriousness and maturity.
Fabric softener is a dream symbol that refers to a need to soften one's harsh or judgmental personality.
Hamper (clothes) suggests that which needs cleaning up in one's life.
Mangle (machine) denotes a need to iron out something in one's life.
Mudroom is a symbol that alludes to negative attitudes brought into the home.
Washing machine is a symbol that pertains to an aid that is capable of cleansing negative elements from one's life.

Maintenance

Gardening stands for attention in the way of nourishment and cultivation that is given to one's humanitarian and/or spiritual behavior. It may also refer to a cultivation of one's natural gifts.
Redecorating portrays a desire to change and start over; a fresh new beginning. It may more generally point to a change in attitude or perspective for the dreamer.
Renovation is an attempt to save or preserve some element in one's life.
Unfinished (furniture) shows opportunities to express one's own creativity and individuality.
Yard work stands for the personal efforts that are expended on improving one's surroundings; efforts toward nurturing and beautifying one's behavior.

Household Substances

Bottled gas See propane.
Charcoal starter (fluid) signifies the motivational force needed or applied to begin the process of working toward a positive resolution or outcome to a particular problem or difficult situation.
Glue pertains to a sticky situation, condition, or relationship. May also signify an element that is capable of repairing something.
Grout refers to the in-between elements; the connective aspects between main issues.
Paste (adhesive) indicates that there is a pressing need for temporary cohesiveness. This would imply the need to quickly make attempts at resolving a current problem or negative situation in one's life.
Primer (paint) portrays a protective or sealing element. Indicates the idea that the main issue is well protected before additional aspects are built on it. Also see base coat.
Putty (color/substance) is a dreamscape symbol that relates to a corrective aspect in one's life. Depending on associated dreamscape aspects, putty can also indicate an easily controlled individual.
Spot remover symbolizes an opportunity to remove a negative from one's life or resolve a conflict, perhaps make amends.
Starch constitutes firmness. This dreamscape symbol possesses duality and therefore may indicate that there is a need to be more firm in one's relationships, or it may reveal a method of behavior that is too firm.
Tar warns of an element or situation in one's life that has the potential of becoming permanent.
Thinner (solvent) is a dream symbol that signifies an attempt to make a plan or issue more workable.
Turpentine illustrates a life aspect that is capable of eradicating residual elements.

Waste

Garbage defines the useless aspects in one's life or those items one perceives as being useless. Recall if there were any specific items featured in the dreamscape garbage. There may have been items that shouldn't have been discarded.
Retention pond comes in dreams to reveal to the dreamer the importance of something one believes has no value.
Trash connotes the useless and extraneous elements in a person's life.
Trash can cautions one to throw out the life aspects that are useless; keep oneself unburdened.
Trash compactor refers to a pressing need to compress the negatives that are taking up too much space in our lives; to minimize and dispose of our negative attitudes.

Ornaments

Bric-a-brac is a representation of the unnecessary aspects with which one tends to clutter one's life.
Doily is a symbol that refers to the protective elements in one's life.
Figurine (statuette) comes as a warning message for the dreamer. This usually is a call to pay attention to what the figurine represents, perhaps for the individual dreamer.
Frame (picture) reveals an individual perception of what is framed in the dream. Recall its condition and color to help to clarify this dream fragment further.
Ornament will indicate the presence of an embellishment or extraneous aspect in one's life. May hint at a specific attitude.
Snow globe comes in dreams as a reminder that one should include spiritual aspects in one's everyday behavior. What scene was in the snow globe? Was the liquid clear or cloudy?
Snuffbox symbolizes a self-imposed need for a psychological aid.
Streamer correlates to an attention-getting message. It says, "Hey, look over here! Look at this!"
Tinsel is a dream symbol that illustrates glitter without substance; something that appears to have great appeal yet doesn't really stand up to its glitter.
Trimmings (festive) denote expanded benefits from a singular joyful blessing in one's life.

Household Safety

Domestic disturbance is a symbol that reveals a problem with a relationship.
Firebrick is a representation of an individual or situation that remains unaffected by another's emotional outbursts or tirades.
Firecracker is a dream symbol that indicates a means of channeling one's intense emotions in a controlled manner.
Fire escape indicates an individual's personal methods of avoiding or escaping from intense emotional situations or events.
Fire extinguisher suggests the existence of a specific method to calm another person's emotionalism.
Fire screen is a dreamscape symbol that connotes a means of emotional protection; methods whereby one guards oneself from personally displaying emotional outbursts or guards oneself from the tirades of others.
Smoke detector corresponds with one's inner awareness or insights that alert and warn of one that trouble is approaching in one's life.
Spill-proof is a symbol that refers to an idea or plan that has no chance of falling apart.
Storm cellar is a dream symbol that signifies an individual's personal methods of emotional defenses.

see also
• Horticulture *p. 42*
• Gardens *p. 43*

Garden & Exterior

Awning symbolizes temporary spiritual shelter; a temporary spiritual respite.

Bellpull is a symbol that denotes the knowledge and acceptance of possibly needing help through life.

Canopy See awning.

Cold frame stands for tough love; holding back on emotional warmth or compassion for the purpose of strengthening another.

Edger (lawn tool) cautions against attempting to control the natural order of things; wanting to always trim things to fit one's personal perspective of how it should look or be.

Hand mower denotes efforts to personally care for one's appreciated blessings.

Lawn chair represents an opportunity to gain blessings of leisure from nature; a chance to gain tranquility from easily accessible, natural sources.

Lawn edger implies a perfectionist; a tendency to attend to every loose end. May point out a perfectionist who can't stand anything being out of place.

Lawn mower (manual) characterizes an individual who expends greater efforts to avoid advancement (growth) than the work to attain it would take.

Lawn mower (powered) is a dream symbol that applies to someone who has an automatic reaction toward anything leading to one's personal growth and advancement; effortless denial.

Leaf blower comes as an advisement to give greater attention to one's inherent talents. This symbol refers to a nonchalant attitude bordering on apathy.

Rake may represent a tying up of loose ends in order to make a fresh start.

Leaf rake See rake (leaf).

Playhouse (child's) represents early formulation of interactive relationship.

Potting shed is a representation of a close bond with nature; an appreciation for one's natural gifts or talents.

Rake (garden) is a symbol that stands for working one's talents for the benefit of others; utilizing them.

Rake (leaf) implies a need to rake through a current situation or concept; to carefully inspect something. May also refer to the act of gathering up the last remnants of an issue for the purpose of clearing the way for new beginnings.

Sleeping porch represents an opportunity to gain insights when the mind is at rest.

Spreader (garden/lawn) is a symbol that relates to the dissemination of information or broadcast nurturing.

Toolshed points to a recognition of an individual's many opportunities to share talents.

Watering can symbolizes a personal effort to spiritually nourish or affect others.

Woodpile represents preparedness; personal effort expended.

Garden Accoutrements

Flowerpot signifies the conscious caring and personal cultivation of one's natural abilities and talents.

Gate pertains to that which must be passed through (or rather experienced) for one to advance along one's path.

Gatepost connotes a supporting factor that helps to mark specific events one must experience.

Gazing globe (garden) signifies an appreciation for nature's beauty and efforts to have it reflected in one's behavior.

Hammock cautions against laziness.

Hoe pertains to personal efforts applied to nurturing one's inherent talents.

Hose (water) reveals a willful direction of one's spiritual expressions.

Picket fence is efficiency; tending to live and process information in an orderly way.

Pot (any type) correlates with a container—refer to the specific type of pot presented.

Potsherd corresponds to a fact that provides partial validity to a specific concept, idea, or perspective; a fragment aspect of a single issue.

Split rail (fence) illustrates a self-devised personal perimeter; one's perceptual distance from others.

Sundial advises that now is the time to reconnect with one's personal spirituality.

Wicket See gate.

Types of Homes

Amenities denote positive benefits to a situation, relationship, or decision.
Bi-level indicates balance.
Billet cautions one to make accommodations for those who would provide protection or help.
Carport implies temporary shelter. Surrounding dream symbols will help to clarify.
Empty nest underscores the time frame allotted for oneself. This is not a self-serving message but rather comes as a sign of encouragement and motivation to rediscover the beautiful individuality of one's own inner essence.
Fleabag (lodging) cautions against misplaced trust.
Flophouse See fleabag.
Gated community refers to one's guarded general surroundings; a tendency to be protective or defensive of one's friends. This symbol may also reveal an elitist attitude.
Ghetto stands for tribulations to be overcome.
Group home suggests the advisability of working very closely with others. It may well be that success is dependent on doing so.
Habitat for Humanity signifies the unconditional sharing of one's talents.
Haven illustrates a life aspect within which one believes one is well protected. May refer to a place within oneself; a retreat within.
Hermitage stands for a place to gain needed respite, solitude, contemplation. Usually this symbol is advising a need to get back in touch with one's inner self and separate oneself from the current societal stressors.
Home base is a dream symbol that illustrates a personal operational base that one works from.
Homeless shelter is a dream symbol that represents a port in the storm; a hospitable respite when one is at wit's end during one's path walk.
Home office is a dream symbol that reflects the work one personally does. This symbol represents one's dedication to a purpose.
Hood (residential) See neighborhood.
Lodge refers to a safe haven.
Room and board corresponds to the two major necessities in life. Recall the dream's details for further information on this symbol.
Second-class (accommodations) exemplifies an alternative.
Showcase depicts what a person values; one's priorities. What was in the dreamscape showcase? Was the glass clear, clouded, or colored? Was the glass cracked?
Studio (apartment) stands for one with few needs.
Sublet exemplifies the absorption or sharing of another's perspective.
Suite (rooms) implies a temporary state of comfort.
Triplex will indicate an element consisting of three separate aspects.

Gated community means one is defensive about oneself or one's friends.

Parts of the House

Open window indicates a clear view of something. This will be understood to the individual dreamer.
Root cellar is the opportunity to preserve one's inner talents and bountiful gifts.
Storage connotes having reserves; preparedness.
Stovepipe connotes an exit route for negative elements in one's life.
Tank (utility) symbolizes the fact that one has the means to store something.
Threshold stands for a beginning point; being poised at the entrance.
Widow's walk (observational platform at top of a house) defines perpetual awareness. This dream symbol may also refer to a waiting period for the dreamer.

Inhabitants

Boarder (renter) is a symbol that refers to opportunities taken; temporary and short-term openings to utilize karma-balancing situations.
Homeless may not be the negative it appears to be. It may pertain to a journeyer, one who continually progresses along a life path.
Housebound refers to disinterest in issues unrelated to one's own, immediate surroundings.
Inhabitant implies viability of a situation.
Life tenant signifies a permanent relationship.
Renter (home) indicates a situation in which one has less responsibility.
Rent strike represents personal power and/or one's general effectiveness in one's everyday actions and situations.
Resident See inhabitant.
Tenant See renter.

see also
• Housing *p. 309*
• Furniture & Ornaments *p. 455*

Household Gadgetry

Appliance See specific type.

Electric razor connotes a personal urgency to shed certain thoughts or concepts.

Fuse box defines one's level of comprehension and readiness for higher knowledge. The number of good fuses clarifies this message.

Gasket is a symbol that alludes to a need to seal something; a finalization; a need to stop the leakage of something in the dreamer's life.

Guy wire is a representation of a supportive element in one's life; a balancing or reinforcing aspect.

Hibachi is a representation of the utilization of the right tool or method for accomplishing specific jobs.

Mixer (appliance) See blender; cement mixer.

Nutcracker will exemplify a need for resolutions and/or solutions.

Opener (device) is a dream symbol that points out an element in one's life that is capable of serving as an access tool used to accomplish a goal or desire.

Peeler (utensil) is a dream symbol that denotes a need to peel away the surface layer of an aspect in one's life that is lacking clarity or definition. Points to the existence of underlying layers to an issue.

Peg represents a marker; an indicator. May denote a natural connective element.

Peg-Board is a representation of a method of organization; an opportunity to sort things out and keep an eye on the most important elements of something.

Pestle connotes a life aspect that one has the opportunity to utilize for the purpose of clarifying or understanding a current puzzlement.

Pipe (conduit) corresponds with connecting aspects. It may refer specifically to an element that has the ability to relate one aspect to another.

Splash guard connotes defense mechanisms; methods of protecting oneself from negative elements.

Sprinkler is a symbol that signifies an attempt to inundate one's life with spiritual aspects; maintaining a spiritual priority with all things.

Squeegee connotes a need to gain clearer perceptions of a particular issue or situation.

Steam cleaner denotes spiritual motivations.

Steam iron relates to the utilization of spirituality to resolve problems.

Stopper is a symbol that correlates to containment; keeping something from getting away or escaping from one's control.

Sewing

Bias tape is a representation of efforts that one puts into making sure a plan doesn't unravel.

Darning needle symbolizes an opportunity to repair or make amends for something that one has done in one's life.

Pinking shears are a dreamscape symbol that signify an attempt to keep something in one's life from falling apart or unraveling.

Quilt is a dreamscape symbol that pertains to a personal manner of acceptance and inner comfort. The revealing factor in this case will be to recall if there was a particular design and color on the quilt that will help to further clarify the meaning of the dream.

Miscellaneous

Accommodation signifies compromise, perhaps a call to be more tolerant toward the people in one's life.

Addition (to home) stands for a desire to expand and/or improve one's sense of security and comfort zone. May also refer to a deeper appreciation of those closest to one.

Ajar is a symbol that indicates an out or opening left.

Alarm system (home) is a symbol that relates to an individual's home life. Is the home a safe haven? Or is it a place of continual unrest and discord?

Baseboard heat is a symbol that pertains to a rising level of intensified emotions that has the potential of having costly consequences.

Clutter defines a disorderly state. This dreamscape symbol usually refers to an individual's perspectives that need to be put in order.

Coal bin reveals the hidden negatives that one usually tries to conceal.

Fluff refers to a lack of substance.

Front burner is a dreamscape symbol that signifies a current situation that takes priority over others of less importance.

Home is a dream symbol that signifies one's place of comfort and security. More specifically, it is the place where one can shed affectations.

Home buyer is a representation of a desire to be settled; establish roots.

House brand is a dream symbol that connotes a tendency to stay with what one is accustomed to; a reluctance to expand one's experience or try new things.

Household word connotes a commonly held belief; easy recognition.

House-raising reveals a multitude of friends who are willing to help one build strong foundations or assist in expending energy to give aid.

Housewares refer to the basic necessities of life.

Indoors is a symbol that applies to the inner self; that which is private and rarely shown or expressed.

Inside See indoors.

Relocation most often foretells of an actual change of one's location.

Snooze alarm reveals the need for a small amount of additional rest.

Vaporizer comes in dreams to indicate a review of one's spiritual beliefs; a refresher endeavor. This dreamscape symbol may also point to a need for acceptance of spiritual ideas one seems skeptical or confused about.

Wicker pertains to ingenuity; resourcefulness.

Chapter 26

Clothing & Accessories

These two dream elements can be extremely eye-opening, as they both represent the manner in which individuals present themselves—the public persona, not necessarily the true, inner one.

Outerwear

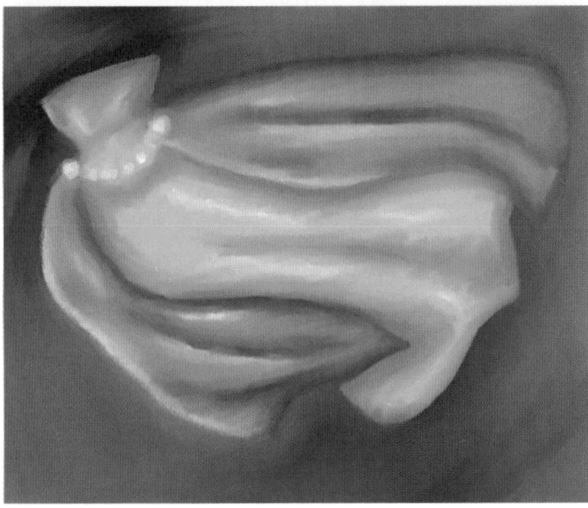

Cloak may signify a disguise or be used as protection from others.

All-weather (clothing) signifies qualities of attitude that serve in all situations, such as acceptance, patience, a sense of humor, and tolerance.
Anorak emphasizes one's personal methods of overall protection; shielding measures.
Blazer signifies that one has a casual attitude.
Bomber jacket suggests an untrustworthy character.
Burka refers to a shield one uses to distance oneself from others. May indicate an introverted or reclusive personality. Could expose one who hides in a shell.
Burnoose represents an ability to control stress.
Bush jacket characterizes an adventurous nature.
Caftan See burnoose.
Camouflage means hidden aspects; pretense. May point out an introverted personality who wishes to blend into the background and not be noticed.
Cape denotes temporary protective measures.
Capote See serape.
Car coat suggests a readiness for a short journey. May point to a phase of temporary diversion from one's path or goal.
Cloak See serape, burnoose, burka. May also have the additional interpretation of implying secretiveness.
Coat represents one's exterior presentation to the world; how one wants to be seen or what one uses to conceal the real self.
Coattail warns of the desire to let others lead; tendency to let others do the work in advance of oneself; advancing through the efforts of others instead of oneself.
Duster (coat) refers to actions taken to prevent extraneous factors from taking one's attention from the important aspects.
Greatcoat warns against distancing oneself from others.
Lap robe illustrates a desire to keep good relationships.
Mackinaw (coat) suggests personal security; confidence.
Mackintosh (fabric) denotes personal methods of protecting oneself from spiritual fads. It may refer to spiritual discrimination.
Overcoat exemplifies a personal state of self-protection. Will sometimes refer to a cover-up of some type.
Overshirt alludes to an altered mood; a preserving of the essence of oneself from others.
Parka connotes responsible reactions.
Peacoat suggests efforts to weather a spiritual crisis or conflict.
Pea jacket symbolizes efforts applied to spiritual aspects in one's life.
Poncho See serape.
Raincoat denotes a personal desire to insulate oneself from spiritual aspects in life.
Safari jacket denotes a predatory nature.
Serape symbolizes personal freedom; a unique life path.
Slicker See raincoat.
Snowsuit refers to an insulating effort to shield oneself from spiritual concepts or elements. May be resistance to blending spirituality with daily life.
Topcoat represents the final element applied to a situation; the finishing touch for completion.

Blouses & Shirts

Blouse represents a basic need; necessary aspect in one's life which often reflects one's level of emotional response—compassion vs. indifference, soft-hearted vs. dispassion.
Cuff (end of shirt) refers to that which protects one's mobility and tenacity.
Middy (blouse) suggests a beginning spiritual search; novice stage of spiritual knowledge.
Polo shirt suggests self-importance.
Shirt See blouse.
Shirttail relates to personal methods used to help others.

Skirts

Broomstick skirt suggests strong opinions kept to self.
Bustle (skirt type) means social haughtiness; being conscious of social status.
Hoopskirt signifies a tendency to distance oneself from other people. This would imply a greater than normal social distance.

Lapels

Lapel reveals one's quantitative ego. Here are a few examples:
Clownish lapel portrays immaturity.
Designer lapel signifies arrogance.
Narrow lapel shows one who rarely thinks of self.
No lapel denotes an absence of any egotistical aspects.
Wide lapel indicates a very large ego.

see also
• Ice & Snow *p. 61*
• Hands & Arms *p. 105*

Formal Attire

Ball gown reveals our right to celebrate recent steps or decisions in life. Recall the condition and style to determine if the symbol has a positive or negative meaning.
Black tie alludes to an extremely formal personality; a stuffy attitude; aloofness.
Business suit stands for an intent to be serious.
Crease (in dress pants) denotes one's level of perfection. Is the crease ironed in, or was it caused by wrinkles?
Dinner jacket See tuxedo.
Dress code denotes manipulation; placing restrictions on expressions of individuality.
Dress shoes come as a warning to stop trying to impress others—be yourself.
Evening gown refers to extravagance; a tendency to maintain efforts even when relaxing.
Formal attire stands for high-minded attitudes.
Robe (ceremonial) relates to a desire to present oneself in an aggrandized manner; a need to exaggerate self-importance.
Smoking jacket refers to pretensions.
Suit pertains to a formality; formal behavior.
Suspenders pertain to a supportive element that allows one to hold up under adversity.
Tie See necktie.
Tuxedo signifies a desire to present only one's best side.
Uniform signifies a specific intention or attention to a focused effort. Recall what the uniform represented. Waiter? Security guard? Police officer?
Vest indicates something close to one's heart and therefore protected. Also points out secretiveness or a desire for privacy.
White tie alludes to a formality.
Zoot suit signifies an overinflated self-image that is meant to project power.

Gloves

Gloves tend to represent personal service to others. Depending on the style and condition of the gloves in question, the dreamer can determine if this service is for oneself or for others and whether it is performed in a begrudging or purely humanitarian fashion.
Hand covering See specific type.
Kid glove is representative of gentle treatment. It may also signify an interaction in a specific environment needing a delicate approach.
Mitten is representative of a factor in one's life that is holding you back or is restrictive in some way; a limiting condition.
Muff connotes a tendency to avoid involvement.
Velvet glove reveals a congenial and gentle presentation that is covering the real characteristics of vindictiveness and ruthlessness.
White gloves warn against being a perfectionist; expecting too much; selectiveness; being nit-picky.

Knitwear

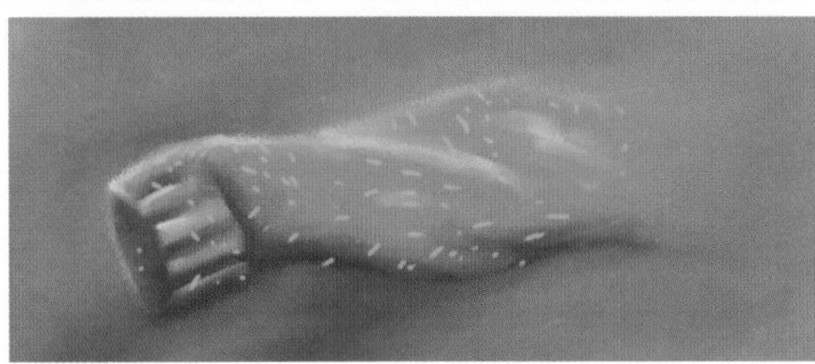

Sweater is an indication of a sympathetic nature.

Cable-knit (design) refers to interwoven ideas.
Cardigan is indicative of someone with an easygoing nature. It may also refer to maturity through experience.
Pullover suggests a deception; something that is pulled over one's eyes.
Shawl alludes to personal ideals, thoughts, and beliefs that are loosely concealed.
Sweater suggests warmth of character. Recall the style, texture, and color.
Turtleneck implies a reluctance to expose oneself; lacking self-confidence.

Neckwear

Bandanna is unclear thought; a tendency to cover same.
Bolo tie relates to attitudes that are not consistent; a changeable personality.
Bow tie alludes to an individual who is considered stuffy or straitlaced.
Button-down refers to the need to secure something in life.
Clerical collar points to a tendency to present oneself in a spiritual light.
Collar symbolizes an aspect that one considers burdensome; possible guilt.
Cravat applies to a desire to distinguish oneself from others.
High-necked (collar) represents constricted thoughts/attitudes.
Jabot represents speech and perceptual affectations; embellishments.
Mandarin collar denotes restrictions; chosen limitations.
Muffler recommends more communicative discretion.
Neckerchief is perseverance; extended personal efforts.
Necktie warns against choking off or smothering intellectual pursuits or inquisitiveness.
Ruff (collar) signifies an opinionated personality.
Scarf defines an open attitude toward new ideas.

Baby Clothing

Baby bonnet applies to a juvenile thought process.
Bib warns against sloppy talk from sloppy thought. Suggests a call to halt gossip. Cautions against thoughtless speech.
Bootie suggests immature steps taken; a new path that you or another might have entered upon with especially immature attitudes and expectations.

Hats

Beret pertains to a carefree, often eccentric, personality.
Black hat stands for a negative personality; the bad guy.
Bonnet characterizes old-fashioned ideas; often a prudish or overly simplistic attitude. May point to naïveté.
Bowler (hat) suggests a man's tendency toward primness, social propriety.
Chef's hat applies to the action of cooking up something.
Derby (hat) suggests outdated ideas; old-fashionedness.
Feather (in hat) signifies an accomplishment.
Fedora is a representation of underhandedness.
Fez connotes a thought process that is affected by specific perspectives or belief systems.
French beret See beret.
Haberdashery relates to the manner in which thoughts are displayed or covered up. Refer to specific hat type for more specific information.

Hat characterizes individual belief systems or thought processes.

Hard hat portrays strong opinions; a thought process that resists new ideas.
Hat corresponds with a way of thinking; personal inner thoughts. See specific type of hat for further information.
Hatband reveals added aspects to one's character.
Hockey helmet is representative of readiness for some kind of expected spiritual conflict in one's life. This indicates a situation where the individual has an almost fanatical spiritual attitude.
Homburg is usually considered to indicate hidden thoughts and perspectives.
Hood (headgear) signals a desire to keep thoughts and attitudes private. May warn of secrets or ulterior motives.
Miner's hat typifies light shed on ideas, concepts, or views.
Old-fashioned hats represent outdated ideas or attitudes that could be related to good old common sense, or ideas or attitudes that are behind the times.
Panama stands for a moderate perspective.
Pith helmet implies a tendency or desire to protect one's primal or elementary beliefs.
Silk hat implies a wish to seem successful; extravagance.
Slouch hat denotes a lazy mind; an unwillingness to apply mental energy.
Sombrero signifies withheld thoughts.
Stovepipe hat is representative of tall thoughts that are unexpressed or suppressed. It signifies a need to release or express oneself.
Straw hat represents confidence in perceptions and beliefs.
Tam-o'-shanter (hat) indicates perspectives affected by one's ethnicity.
Top hat cautions against intellectual arrogance.
Tricornered hat is representative of three-dimensional thinking. It also signifies thought that considers all aspects of a particular issue.
White hat reveals an individual who is on the right side or has the right attitude.

Caps

Baseball cap signifies informality.

Baseball cap usually points to a casual nature.
Bathing cap warns against a reluctance to approach spiritual concepts. It may reveal an actual situation of denial.
Beanie See skullcap.
Coonskin cap is a backward way of thinking.
Fool's cap relates to foolhardiness and associated outcomes.
Graduation cap emphasizes information gained through study rather than life experiences; learned perspectives vs. those gained through developed wisdom.
Havelock pertains to a lack of trust; an attempt to protect one's back.
Military cap represents regimentation; an inability to think for oneself.
Nurse's cap indicates one whose thought process is tightly woven with compassion and healing.
Skullcap corresponds to thoughts grounded in spiritual beliefs.
Sun visor See visor.
Swimming cap reveals an attempt to avoid spiritual issues.
Visor typifies an effort to see more clearly; see past the glare of an initial bright idea or something that seems too good to be true.
Watch cap is usually representative of awareness or watchfulness.
Yarmulke See skullcap.

see also
• Appearance *p. 90*
• Face *p. 92*

Style & Fit

Baggy clothing usually indicates a relaxed personality; one having a fair amount of general acceptance.

Cutaway clothing denotes openness; nothing to hide; forthrightness.

Henley (clothing style) suggests a casual character trait or an easygoing personality.

Ill-fitting clothing connotes a free spirit or one who is restricting thoughts.

Informal (dress) naturally is representative of a casual issue or attitude; congeniality.

Inside-out clothing suggests backward perspectives or a tendency to present a public persona that is opposite from one's private character.

Layered clothing doesn't refer to a homeless person, it indicates a preparedness for any eventuality; an eye on possibilities.

Loose clothing signifies an open mind; being open to new ideas.

Oversized reveals some kind of aspect in the dreamer's life that is too big for her/him at the present time. Connotes an issue or concept that one has not yet grown into.

Wrinkled clothing denotes a lack of concern for how others regard you.

Plus-size clothing reminds us that bigger or more isn't always better. Size can't be a gauge in estimating worth or potential.

Reversed clothing comes as a severe warning, and the dreamer needs to refer to the specific piece of clothing or element that was reversed in the dreamscape. Such an obvious reversal will generally indicate a serious dysfunctional aspect in one's life.

Reversible clothing usually signifies duality. It will refer to something that has a twofold purpose or effect.

Tattered relates to a worn-out or well-used element. May indicate high value.

Threadbare implies a worn-out aspect.

Tight clothing exposes self-imposed constrictions. It may refer to one's tendency to restrict oneself and set narrow limits.

Unfashionable clothing reveals the expression of one's individuality or uniqueness, probably associated with innovative thought that is considered to be well outside the box.

Wrinkled clothing implies indifference to opinion; self-confidence without having to show it.

Headdresses

Barrette is representative of thoughts that are caught up or that have been restrained.

Bridal veil may represent the presence of contradictions. Can indicate the preservation of one's secret past.

Coronet See crown.

Cowl pertains to protected thoughts. It may also be representative of an enigmatic personality.

Crown warns against egotism or setting one's sights on the goals of grandeur.

Diadem See crown.

Earmuff refers to a closed mind; hearing only what one wants to.

Feather headdress implies an arrogance for one's great intellect.

Feather (in hair) points to an epiphany; some type of bright idea or realization.

Headband warns against confining one's thoughts. Advises expanding and exploring new concepts; a need to express oneself.

Headdress reveals a uniquely specific and individualistic attachment. It may also correspond with a certain attitude or association.

Mantilla refers to an individual with highly developed emotional sensitivity.

Mantle (headgear) typifies a subconscious attempt to cloak one's inner feelings.

Tiara See crown.

Turban exposes twisted or convoluted thoughts.

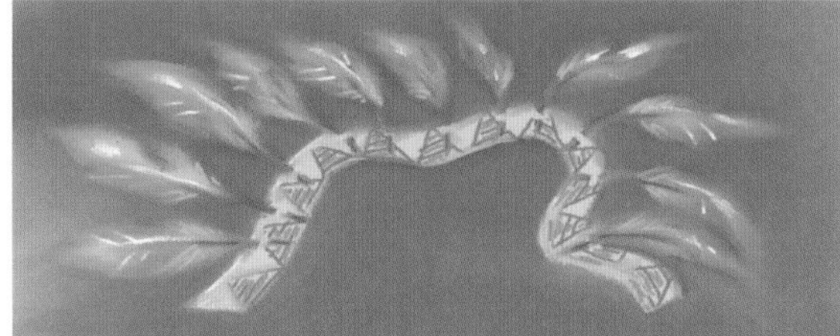

Feather headdress represents intellectual snobbery.

Leisure Attire

Hot pants symbolize impulsive behavior.

Blue jeans depict one who is comfortable and relaxed with one's spiritual beliefs.

Cargo pants represents the fact that one is prepared for the unexpected.

Casual wear suggests a relaxed attitude.

Combat fatigues indicate preparedness for conflict, ready for a fight.

Cutoffs (clothing style) refer to the preservation of a partially worn but still useable aspect.

Fatigues See combat fatigues.

High waters (pants) is representative of rapid growth in one's life, usually associated with progression.

Hip-huggers signify an expressiveness of individuality; a disregard for convention or criticism.

Hipster is representative of someone who always looks for the unconventional, new innovations or ideas that are coming from outside the box.

Hot pants suggest impatience; an inability to wait for the right time to actuate plans.

Informal (dress) naturally equates to a casual issue or attitude; being congenial.

Jeans connote a nonconformist. They may refer specifically to a relaxed personality—either the dreamer or someone else in his or her life.

Leisure attire connotes an informal situation or relationship.

Loungewear stands for a relaxed attitude; an easy-going personality.

Pedal pushers portray a personal preparation for work ahead.

Short shorts See hot pants.

Sportswear suggests an advisement to don an attitude of acceptance—good sportsmanship.

Sweatband represents an attempt to control one's efforts applied to a specific project or goal. It may also signify some kind of attempt to gain a greater measure of patience.

Sweat suit represents an intention of expending effort on an idea or project; a preparedness for forthcoming action.

Tank top suggests exposed behavior, as in having nothing to hide; out in the open.

Underwear & Night Attire

Bathrobe symbolizes how relaxed or comfortable one is with one's personal spiritual beliefs. Recall condition and type of dreamscape robe for more definitive clarity.

Bloomers suggest old-fashioned ideas, usually related to a prudish type of attitude.

Bobby socks imply an informal attitude; a casual personality.

Body stocking/suit pertains to a second skin one wears; being thick-skinned. Possibly represents a fear of being hurt.

Boxer shorts exemplify sexist perspectives; a sexually domineering attitude.

Bustier pertains to a tendency to reveal more than is necessary, usually to one's detriment.

Camisole depicts innocence.

Chemise See camisole.

Corsage (bodice) pertains to one's inner beauty that others perceive.

Corset See girdle.

Garter symbolizes the act of upholding something.

Girdle usually refers to that which surrounds one. This will indicate a separate aspect for each dreamer.

Housecoat See bathrobe.

Knee socks exemplify protective qualities of oneself.

Knickers relate to immaturity.

Lingerie See underwear.

Long johns illustrate preparedness.

Negligee See nightgown.

Nightgown denotes an appropriate preparedness for one's planned activity.

Pajamas See nightgown.

Pantyhose will apply to some type of feminine trait in respect to how a path is traveled. Surrounding dream details will make a clarifying association.

Petticoat See underwear.

Robe (bath) See bathrobe.

Sock See stocking.

Stocking pertains to covering one's footsteps.

Support hose means a personal recognition that one requires additional support as one travels through life.

Tights exemplify an ability to freely express oneself.

Trousseau signifies what one member of a partnership brings to the relationship.

Undershirt See underwear.

Underwear alludes to a covering up. It may refer to a fear of exposure.

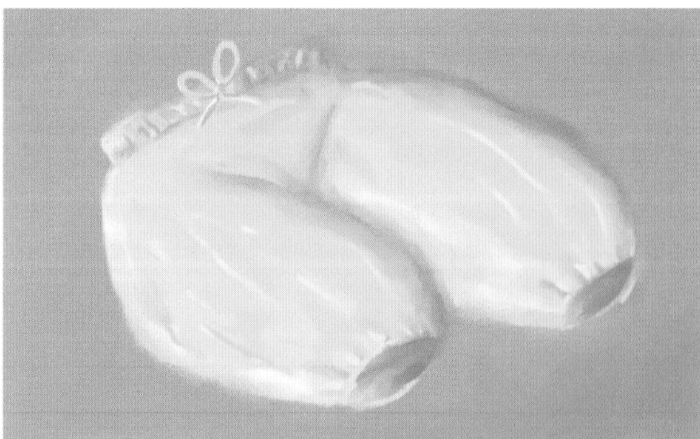

Bloomers signify outmoded thinking and sexual reticence.

see also
• Sleeping Disorders *p. 108*
• Ballet *p. 224*

Protective Wear

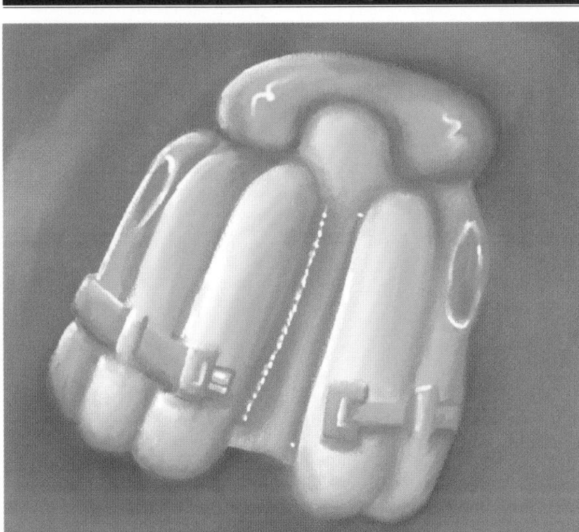

Life preserver refers to another opportunity to do something.

Apron alludes to self-protective measures.

Apron string refers to fear of or reluctance to let go of a protective situation or relationship; a connection restricting individuality or self-reliance.

Bulletproof vest exemplifies an emotionally devoid personality; a fear of being affected or affecting others; a measure against being emotionally hurt.

Chaps symbolize a need for temporary or short-term protection; a temporary situation that exists for increased awareness, watchfulness.

Coveralls denote protective measures related to one's place of work.

Diving suit implies spiritual insulation.

Flak jacket See bulletproof vest.

Gaiters (leg covering) refer to protective measures taken to insulate oneself while traversing a particularly difficult phase of one's path.

Gaiters (shoe covering) refer to protective measures taken along one's path.

Goggles are an attempt to better understand something.

Helmet connotes protected or hidden thoughts.

Jockstrap connotes a need for psychological counseling (support) in respect to one's sexually related attitudes.

Jodhpurs symbolize selective arrogance; a high attitude.

Lab coat signifies an analytical mind; attention to detail and research.

Leggings refer to self-protective measures one uses.

Leg warmers emphasize a personal concern and effort taken to ensure progression isn't hampered.

Life jacket See life preserver.

Life preserver corresponds with a second chance.

Overalls See coveralls.

Pinafore represents honesty and simplicity of character.

Pressure suit implies the application of a compensating or equalizing aspect to offset the effects of stress.

Radiation suit stands for a protective measure taken against potentially dangerous situations or negative elements that could prove to be toxic to one's mental, emotional, or physical well-being. It may also point to an insular personality.

Riding habit suggests an attitude of exaggerated self-worth when making a comparison between oneself and peers who are traveling the same path.

Ski mask relates to those with shallow thoughts and those who have a tendency to avoid deeper concepts.

Smock implies intentions to work; preparation to expend personal efforts.

Armor

Breastplate warns of a fear of being hurt. Indicates a lack of confidence in oneself or one's own defenses.

Chain mail denotes a lack of confidence in one's own protection; a personal fear of not being able to defend oneself.

Gauntlet (armored glove) relates to methods that prevent one being affected by the bad things in life. This may not be a particularly positive symbol because we become stronger and learn important lessons by being exposed to certain negatives that are in our path as we journey through life.

Mail (armor) illustrates the quality and strength of one's personal protective methods.

Beachwear

Bathing suit generally gives indications into one's personality or physical condition.

Beach bag stands for the elements of the spiritual beliefs we carry with us.

Bikini symbolizes a lack of inhibitions.

Sarong denotes simplicity.

Sundress suggests keeping an attitude/perspective befitting the occasion.

Ballet Wear

Ballet slippers may indicate a lack of seriousness; dancing through life. Also may refer to the graceful manner one utilizes to come to acceptance.

Leotard connotes perseverance; inner strength; a second skin.

Pointe shoe calls for a need to increase awareness and keep on your toes.

Toe shoes caution against a tendency to flit through life without setting one's feet firmly on the ground and not taking life seriously.

Tutu represents freedom to express inner joy.

Footwear

Boot symbolizes the outward quality and style of one's individual path walk.

Bootstrap refers to a path walked with strong determination; an aspect that serves as an impetus for perseverance.

Clog means that one's path is being traversed in a clumsy or difficult manner. This situation is correctable.

Cowboy boots represent precautionary measures taken to ensure a reasonably safe course.

Deck shoes denote a self-styled spiritual insulation; a voluntary separation from spiritual issues or concepts.

Designer shoes caution against walking a path designed or initiated by another. Each person needs to be his/her own path stylist.

Elevator shoes allude to a poor self-image; an attempt to present oneself in a brighter light or higher station; trying to appear taller or bigger than you are.

Footgear See specific types.

Footwear signifies the manner in which one's path is traveled. See specific footwear terms for more in-depth explanations.

Garden clogs represent a preparedness to nurture one's inherent, natural talents.

Go-go boots represent a path walked in an attention-seeking manner.

High heels caution against raising oneself above one's current level of development.

High-top (shoes) alludes to preparedness for one's walk through life.

House slippers See slippers.

Huarache See sandal.

Jackboot suggests a bully, one who is insensitive/manipulative/domineering.

Loafers (shoes) represent a lack of direction.

Moccasin illustrates a high level of awareness while cautiously progressing along one's life path.

Mukluks stand for efforts applied to the prevention of losing sight of one's spirituality.

Nurse shoes reveal one who willingly gives assistance to others while walking her/his personal life path.

High heels warn against trying to do more than one is capable of doing.

Old-fashioned shoes warn of an outdated way of reaching a goal; a path traveled via antiquated methods.

Old shoe stands for someone with a lot of experience at something.

Overshoes suggest an attempt to dissociate one's emotional responses from sensitive issues encountered along one's life path; a lack of bonding sensitivity with the earth.

Oxford (shoes) stands for immaturity; a desire to stay youthful and not be subjected to the responsibilities of adulthood.

Platform shoes suggest a desire to appear taller in the eyes of others; low self-esteem.

Saddle shoe marks a path walked conservatively, with practicality.

Sandal relates to a desire to walk close to the earth, yet the goal hasn't been attained yet.

Shoe shows how one's path is traveled. Refer to specific type.

Shoelace indicates the condition of one's manner of walking a life path. Was the lace untied? Dirty? Too tight? Broken?

Shoestring denotes meager resources.

Slippers denote a restful stage of one's path.

Snowshoes represent spiritual respect. They indicate one is softly treading through spiritual elements without being bogged down by them.

Spiked shoe symbolizes resentment of one's life problems or burdens.

Spur (boot) reveals aggressiveness; the use of improper motivational methods.

Squared toe (shoes) points to a rigid personality.

Stiletto heels indicate strength and/or formidable character behind a seemingly fragile individual.

Surgical shoe coverings represent a path walked in fear of being touched by any negatives.

Wing tip shoes suggest the donning of dapper airs.

Sporting Footwear

Golf shoes imply a path traveled in leisure; excessive complacency.

Hip boots See waders.

Running shoe denotes a need to get going with some aspect in life and may reveal a state of procrastination that needs to end.

Ski boots signify an intention to ignore spiritual issues.

Sneaker See tennis shoe.

Tennis shoe reflects a need to hold one's ground.

Track shoe means having a firm footing on one's path; determination.

Waders refer to a curious interest in spiritual matters yet hesitant to get the feet wet.

see also
• Legs & Feet *p. 105*
• Body Care *p. 116*

Bags & Baggage

Backpack implies the basic necessities pertinent to one's life.
Bag represents some type of interference in one's life.
Baggage means excesses in one's life; a carrying of unnecessary aspects, possibly referring to attitudes, beliefs, material possessions, etc.
Billfold See purse (handbag).
Carpetbag typifies self-interest; self-gain. May also mean highest priorities.
Carry-on bag points to attitudes or ideas that one believes are essentials.
Clutch bag/purse refers to aspects one holds close or dear.
Duffle bag is representative of a transition stage.
Fanny pack represents a tendency for one to keep personal issues close; reluctance to reveal too much about oneself.
Garment bag relates to protected characteristics or attitudes. It may refer to a part of us that is kept protected and hidden.
Gunnysack alludes to one's personal down-to-earth qualities.
Handbag See purse (handbag).
Haversack portrays a light traveler; one who recognizes the basics as opposed to excessive baggage.
Knapsack connotes flexibility; being free-spirited.
Luggage stands for extraneous aspects one carries about.
Pocketbook See purse (handbag).
Portmanteau See luggage.
Purse (handbag) illustrates an opportunity to utilize one's talents and abilities.
Rucksack See knapsack.
Sack See bag.
Satchel portrays that which we consider important enough to always carry with us, usually relating to basic ethics and beliefs.
Snap (fastener) represents a quick closure to an event or problem.

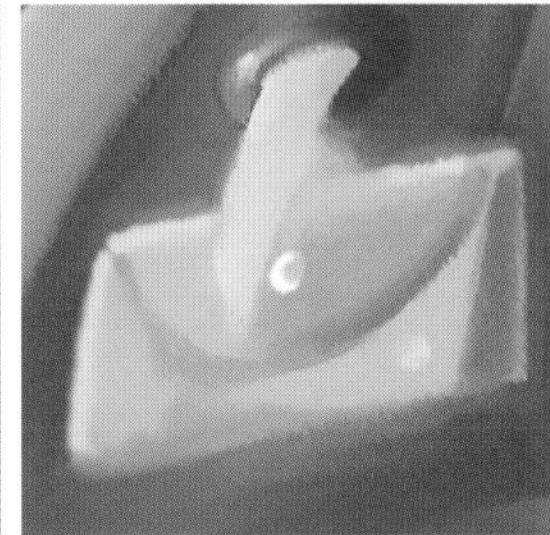
Purse represents using one's skills.

Tag See label.
Trunk (baggage) denotes heavy burdens; excesses that are perceived as valuable.
Vanity case portrays enhanced appearances.
Wallet See purse (handbag).
Ziplock (bag/closure) indicates a tight seal, even secrecy.

Fashion

Couture See fashion designer and haute couture.
Fashion designer warns against dictating another's lifestyle or manner of path progression.
Fashion plate warns against latching onto the latest popular attitudes or beliefs.
Fashion show signifies popular perspectives; what others are buying.
Haute couture warns against letting others dictate your style or method of expression; a loss of individuality.
High fashion See haute couture.
Runway (fashion show) stands for a method of displaying something. In some cases, a runway appearing as a dream symbol will reveal a tendency toward exhibitionism.

Belts & Buckles

Buckle portrays determination.
Belt symbolizes self-created restraints.
Belt buckle defines the excuse for one's self-restraint.
Cinch (belt) comes as an advisement to hold back on giving advice. Restraint is indicated.
Conch belt implies a desire to surround oneself with the more natural aspects of life.
Sash See belt.
Strap relates to a means of carrying something through life. May indicate a support or burden depending on the surrounding dreamscape details.

Cosmetics

Cologne See perfume.
Compact designates the act of smoothing over or covering up one's perceived faults.
Cosmetics denote those superficial aspects one utilizes to improve appearances. This usually refers to appearances other than physical ones.
Eyebrow pencil applies to aspects used to hide or reshape one's personal perspectives.
Eyeliner defines a tendency to emphasize perceptions by outlining them to others.
Eye shadow pertains to colored or enhanced perceptions.
Kohl See eyeliner.
Lipstick will denote inner personality traits. Was it a dark color or a light shade?
Makeup (cosmetics) may expose a false front one creates, or it may indicate a need to address opportunities to enhance one's self-image.
Mascara applies to an emphasis expressed or required.
Moisturizer (beauty product) refers to a need to express more compassion and overall sensitivity.
Nail enamel See nail polish.
Nail polish can reveal one's underlying personality or character. Recall depth of color and condition of polish.
Pomade (on hair) represents a fear of one's thoughts being affected or changed by others.
Powder (cosmetic) stands for a desire to put a matte finish on emotions. This means a person's intent to curb enthusiasm or tone down outward emotional displays/reactions.
Powder (talcum) See talcum powder.
Rouge suggests an intention to present a healthy state of well-being.

Beauty Aids

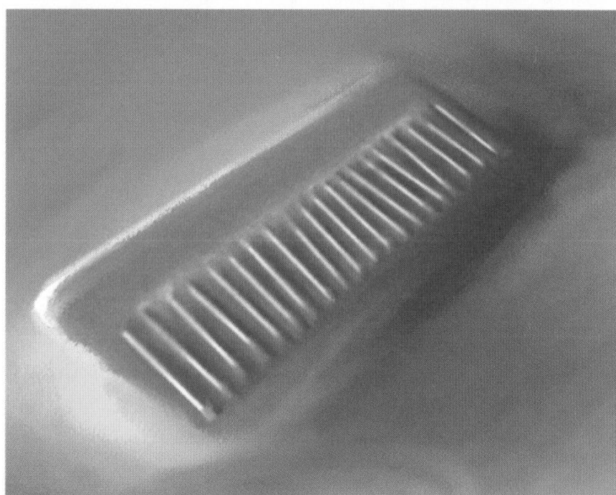

Comb implies need for mental clarity.

Clippers (hair) symbolize the trimming of life factors that affect one's attitudes.
Cold cream denotes a need for emotional softening.
Comb pertains to a need to straighten out one's thoughts.
Eyelash curler warns against willingly and purposely altering one's perceptions.
False eyelashes come to the dreamer as a warning of misplaced confidence placed in one's belief that one's attitudes and opinions are remaining private.
False nails represent a false sense of security. They may also point to shifting energy and responsibility to others.
Fine-toothed comb is a call to triple-check facts and conduct in-depth research.
Hairbrush advises of a need to clean out and untangle confused thoughts or ideas.
Kohl See eyeliner.
Lip balm relates to an attempt or desire to keep one's communications from being harsh.
Nailbrush refers to a need to change one's ways; clean up dirty methods and tactics.
Nail clippers illustrate an advisement to cut down and temper one's aggressive or rough behavioral tendencies.
Nail file comes as an advisement to smooth out one's rough edges in reference to dealing with others.
Nail scissors See nail clippers.
Orange stick (manicure) is a warning to clean up one's behavior; use more honest and straightforward methods.
Powder puff typifies a fragile nature or sensitive personality. May also refer to a prime or ideal situation or condition.
Puff See powder puff.
Razor stands for a delicate excising; careful removal of an unwanted element.
Razor blade emphasizes the cutting edge of something. Symbolizes life's multiple dualities.
Tweezers relate to a life element capable of extracting an irritating aspect from oneself or one's life.

Hairdressing

Hair curlers stand for a desire to alter or dress up an issue or attitude with softening elements.
Hairnet warns of a need to contain uncontrollable thoughts.
Hair pick stands for intensive thought—picking one's own brain; deep thinking/analysis/planning.
Hairpiece warns of a thought process that is partially false.
Hairpin applies to a method of controlling the odd thought.
Hair spray pertains to stiff thinking; unyielding attitudes.
Hairstyle See specific type.
Hat pin indicates a need to hold on to one's thoughts.
Mousse (hairdressing) warns against a lack of mental focus on important aspects.
Rinse (hair coloring) may relate to an intent to change a way of thinking or may reveal hidden perspectives and attitude.
Shampoo applies to the act of cleansing one's thoughts to get rid of negativity or extraneous elements.

Clothing-Related Phrases

Below the belt indicates retaliation and vindictiveness; unethical retribution.
Gussied up usually points to a desire to put one's best foot forward, but, depending on the related dreamscape elements, this may also point to an affected public image.
Hair shirt denotes self-reproach. It may also mean guilt.

National Dress

Burka is representative of a shield that one uses to distance oneself from others. It may indicate an introverted or reclusive personality. A burka could expose one who hides in a shell.
Dirndl is representative of simplicity in one's life.
Kilt implies that one takes great pride in one's ancestral heritage.
Kimono suggests servitude; inequality; suppression of opinion.
Lederhosen is representative of perseverance.
Muumuu relates to an individual with a carefree attitude. This could possibly refer to a tendency of a particular individual to hide behind appearances.
Obi (Japanese ceremonial sash) connotes personal encumbrances; superficial or extraneous beliefs, attitudes, or perspectives that are carried around.
Sari represents someone with an unaffected personality.
Toga pertains to an incomplete idea or concept.
Tunic See toga.

see also
• Gemstones *p. 74*
• Hair *p. 94*

Jewelry

Anklet shows the condition of one's own self-support system.
Bangle suggests individuality and the feeling of freedom to express it.
Bead signifies a small matter of importance. Although small, it's not a trivial matter.
Bezel represents the foundational support/motivation for one's shining, gemlike elements of spiritual behavior.
Bracelet connotes a subjugated situation or relationship.
Brooch connotes an attention-getting aspect or one who enjoys the attention of others.
Cameo signifies prominence; an aspect in one's life that's uniquely treasured or featured.
Choker represents voluntary self-restraint; the act of holding oneself back.
Coral indicates the visibility of one's spirituality; the outward expression of spiritual behavior.
Costume jewelry suggests an alternate way to improve appearances. May also point to a tendency to add extraneous elements to an issue.
Cuff link represents an arrogance toward one's work.
Diamond ring suggests a desire for a perfect relationship.
Earring pertains to the dressing up of what is heard; hearing and embellishing or exaggerating the statements heard.
Jewelry (excessive) implies an attention-demanding or self-aggrandizing personality.
Lapel pin will reveal a specific sympathy one has for a cause.
Locket corresponds to cherished relationships.
Necklace emphasizes a type of personal interest or attraction. May reveal inner traits.
Pectoral (necklace) suggests a representation of one's personal protective energy.
Pendant signifies something important. Recall if it had a gemstone. If so, what was the color, type, and clarity? Shape? Form? Silver or gold?
Regalia illustrates pretension.
Squash blossom (jewelry) pertains to inner strength.

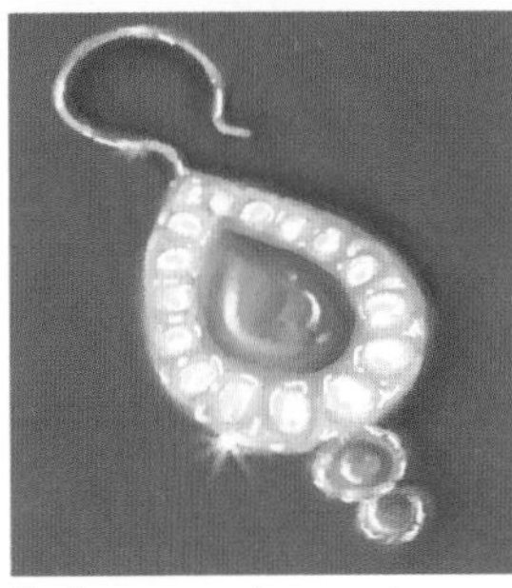
Earring means enhancement.

Stud (pin/earring) indicates an altered perspective.
Tie tack is representative of a hidden characteristic. Recall the style, color, design, or gemstone.
Trinket refers to personal value applied to a specific object.

Rings

Anniversary ring is meant to celebrate the time when a specific bond was forged with another person.
Antique ring signifies a very old bond or connection that one particularly cherishes.
Birthstone ring See birthstone.
Bridge ring symbolizes flashiness.
Broken ring reveals a broken bond with someone. More specifically, it may refer to a lost loyalty.
Celtic Knot ring represents one's complex interconnectedness with another person. This deeply involved relationship may be an underlying one that is not readily apparent.
Claddagh ring (Celtic) serves as a sign of one's open heart.
Cocktail ring suggests one's intent to be forever loyal to another.

Ring symbolizes a connection.

Designer ring reflects personal uniqueness.
Engagement ring refers to one's intent to be forever loyal to another.
Family crest ring indicates pride of both one's heritage and one's bloodline.
Friendship ring is representative of a close relationship with another person.
Graduation ring comes to the dreamer as a sign of the importance of his or her former accomplishment.
Infant ring suggests a special bond to a child. May refer to innocence.
Initial ring will refer to the initial of someone who is particularly important in the wearer's life.
Jump ring stands for a life element that is used for connective purposes.
Mother's ring symbolizes an appreciation of one's blessings.
Nose ring implies an in-your-face show of individuality.
Oversized gem usually denotes one's desire to be noticed.
Pinkie ring stands for an attempt to emphasize one's less obvious qualities; rounding out oneself.
Poison/potion ring (secret compartment) represents hidden emotions.
Promise ring indicates a show of intention to cherish a special relationship.
Religious ring points to one's devotion to a specific religious belief system.
Ring (generally) represents a bond of some type or gives a clue to character.
Shank too large is representative of the suggestion that the bond should now include other people.
Shank too small indicates one has outgrown a particular bond or loyalty.
Signet ring stands for a personal endorsement.
Super Bowl ring stands for a sign of a particularly important achievement.
Toe ring suggests a free spirit; an independent path.
Undersized gem indicates a protective attitude toward one's bond.
Wedding ring portrays a symbol of one's heartfelt bond of loyalty.

Miscellaneous

Accessory represents secondary or affecting aspects connected to a main issue.
Accoutrement connotes surrounding aspects of one's life that affect perspective.
Armband is representative of an outward show of emotions or attitudes.
Black clothing is representative of a forewarning of death. It may be physical, emotional, or spiritual.
Button advises of the need for an individual to have some kind of physical connection or link-up.
Buttonhole represents the openings that life presents to us for opportunities.
Clothing generally gives indications into one's personality or physical condition.
Costume represents some form of characterization. This may indicate one's alter ego or complete opposite personality. It could reveal one's true character or attributes one wears as a costume for the public at large.
Dance wear connotes an outward desire to express one's emotions.
Drag clothing generally refers to one's desire to understand another by walking in his or her shoes (that is, dressing alike), or it could also suggest a cover-up of one's true character.
Dress stands for feminine aspects.
Dress shields symbolize an attempt to present a cool image to others. In essence, it means that one never wants to let other people see one sweat.

Button suggests one needs to communicate or form a relationship with others.

Drip-dry suggests a natural method of letting things take their course.
Epaulet implies a haughty personality; pomposity; presumptuousness.
Fitting (clothing) denotes an attempt to keep one's public persona aligned with one's true character.
Frills stand for extraneous elements; added aspects that dress something up but don't add to its basic value.
Frock See smock.
Full dress relates to appropriateness in action and one's presentation.
Fur (clothing/coat) denotes a selfish personality.
Garb See specific clothing types.
Garment See specific type.
Granny dress signifies an unaffected personality; a confidence in one's genteel nature.
Hatbox is representative of altered or changeable perspectives; a tendency to switch attitudes.
Hat rack advises of the wisdom of hanging up presumptions for the purpose of being open and staying objective.
Head covering See specific type.
Hem stands for something that surrounds; something one is surrounded by.
Laces/lacing represents a means to secure a closure.
Laundry alludes to a specific item in one's life that needs cleaning up. Refer to specific clothing items for further clarification.
Laundry list comes as a reminder of things to accomplish and not forget about.
Menswear (clothing department) signifies characteristics of the male perspective, his choices of expression, the yang.

Monocle denotes a singular mental focus; an inability to open oneself to a wider scope or more availability to new ideas.
Pleat portrays rigid and sharply defined attitudes.
Pocket (clothing) suggests something owned and hidden; a possession.
Pouch See pocket (clothing).
Raiment See clothing.
Shoulder pads allude to false strength.
Snag (clothing) exposes an unexpected problem.
Sunglasses expose an altered perspective that is colored by personal opinions or psychological elements. Recall the color of the lens.
Unbuttoned won't imply sloppiness, but it will most often apply to a personal confidence or comfortable sense of self.
Underdressed is representative of a particular situation or issue that has been misperceived as a low priority.
Undressed represents honest intentions. Also see nakedness.
Unisex is something that is not gender specific, even a perspective.
Vestments stand for outward signs of one's position or belief.
Wardrobe reveals particulars regarding an individual's character. Recall the types and colors of the clothing.
Women's wear (clothing department) signifies the wide range of options a woman can choose from to express her individuality or attitude.
Zipper warns against a tendency to control situations. Pertains to an indiscriminate opening and closing of one's receptivity.

Chapter 27

Colors, Patterns & Fabric

These dreamscape aspects are associated with personality traits and interactive qualities. They expose true attitudes and often suggest a more efficient manner of progression or achievement.

Black to White

Black stands for mystery or negativity. It accompanies a premonition of a death.
Black-and-white means clarity; clear perception. It may also refer to the facts of a particular issue or situation.
Ebony See black.
Gray corresponds with the physical brain and the mind contained within. In some cases, this color may point directly to a lack of clarity; a gray area.
Ivory points to treasured or cherished elements.
Jet alludes to a deep mystery; high concepts; pessimism.
Off-white will indicate an affecting facet to something; something that is not quite pure or the whole truth.
Opal symbolizes truths from many sources.
Pearl gray represents dignity; classy character/behavior.
Putty relates to a corrective aspect in one's life. Depending on associated dreamscape aspects, putty can also indicate an easily controlled individual.
Sable portrays negativity; a dark mood.
White applies to purity and goodness; the positive aspects in life.

Shades of Brown

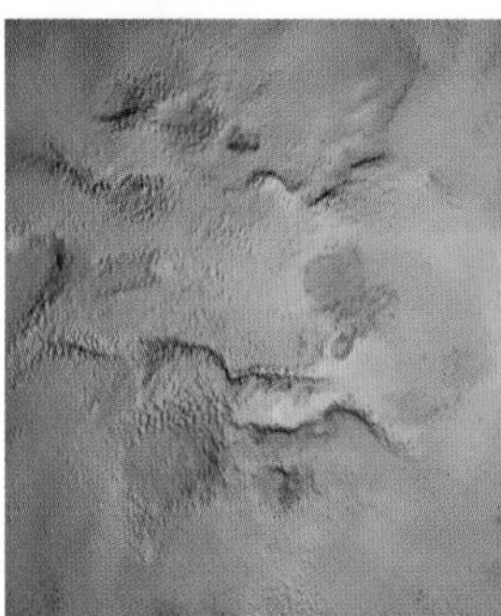

Earth tones show a practical nature.

Beige defines a neutral position; possible indecision; a blending into the background and not wishing to be noticed. Could indicate someone with an introverted personality.
Bisque reflects a lack of ambition. Specifically, it may refer to a loss of direction. May indicate neutrality.
Brindle signifies congeniality; an open perspective.
Brown symbolizes one's earthy aspects; life, attitude, and an emotional side rather than anything spiritual.
Buff suggests gentleness; a passive nature.
Cinnamon signifies an aspect that the dreamer perceives as being especially homey and companionable.
Earth tones represent a down-to-earth perspective or character; someone who is not impressed by societal dazzle.
Fallow symbolizes an unproductive condition or state.
Khaki implies a regimented personality.
Mahogany portrays an inner warmth of character.
Russet illustrates a rich, earthy perspective; an alignment with reality.
Sepia pertains to innocent ignorance; an undeveloped concept or perspective.
Tan See beige.
Taupe See beige.

Blues & Mauves

Azure denotes spiritual stretching in regard to thoughts extended past the knowns.
Baby blue is representative of a beginning development of spirituality; one's initial recognition of sensing an actual relationship with the divine.
Blue represents spirituality and spiritual aspects in life.
Cornflower blue usually signifies a gentleness, a dignity, to one's spirituality.
Delft blue stands for a fragile yet cherished attitude toward one's heritage.
Electric blue suggests a vivid and energetic expression of one's spirituality.
Indigo is representative of high spirituality.
Lavender portrays a gentle, comforting spiritual belief; spiritual wisdom and the peace it bestows.
Lilac represents spiritual purity.
Mauve implies a spiritual lightheartedness.
Midnight blue signifies mystery; an enigmatic personality or aspect.
Navy blue stands for rigid religious beliefs.
Peacock blue connotes a healing spiritual energy.
Periwinkle represents a fragile talent or inherent ability.
Purple constitutes attained spiritual wisdom and enlightenment.
Royal blue refers to a somewhat uppity/exclusive attitude toward one's spirituality. May indicate self-righteousness.
Royal purple usually indicates a genteel spirituality; one quietly cherished in a dignified manner.
Sapphire depicts a fragile spiritual nature.
Sky blue suggests clarity of understanding or presentation.
Turquoise defines spiritual health and well-being.
Violet alludes to a healing spiritual element.
Wedgwood blue suggests a dignified, gentle spirituality.

Yellow & Orange

Canary yellow usually stands for inner joy, but, depending on the surrounding elements, this symbol may reveal gossip or betrayal.
Citrine is representative of joyful spirituality.
Cream represents gentle joy; an inner peacefulness and acceptance of life.
Lemon constitutes bitterness or indicates a state of perpetual troubles.
Maize is representative of a lighthearted disposition; a tendency toward optimism.
Orange represents our physical and mental energies.
Saffron See orange.
Salmon warns against going against a spiritual current; a spiritual search that's somehow in error.
Sienna pertains to an earthiness to one's inner nature.
Tangerine refers to a positive life element that nourishes and refreshes.
Umber relates to earthiness; being natural.
Yellow stands for contentedness; inner peace.

see also
• Decorating Finishes *p. 316*
• Art & Images *p. 463*

Shades of Red

Auburn suggests a deeply impassioned sense of rationale; groundedness.
Blood red See maroon.
Brick red indicates a lack of empowerment, motivation, or energy; a sickly type of perseverance.
Carmine See maroon.
Cinnabar refers to emotional expressiveness; a zest for life.
Crimson suggests an old animosity. It may also refer to suppressed anger or some kind of resentment.
Fuchsia is representative of compassion, love, and humanistic expressions.
Garnet refers to intense emotions. (Although it is true that garnet can be a variety of colors, this interpretation corresponds to the more commonly known color of deep, dark red).
Magenta implies spiritual zeal.
Maroon relates to having spiritual depth; insights.
Oxblood refers to earthy emotions and personality traits.
Pink reveals some type of unrecognized weakness that can refer to one's mental or emotional state, physical aspect, or spiritual condition.

Brick red indicates feebleness.

Red may be representative of anger, a fast pace, or danger, depending on the symbol's related aspects as they appear in the dreamscape.
Rose portrays particularly strong admiration.
Ruby refers to life force; motivational energy and fortitude.
Scarlet See red.
Venetian red is representative of suppressed anger and possibly resentment.
Vermillion is usually associated with behavior or perspective that is tainted with a touch of negativity.

Green

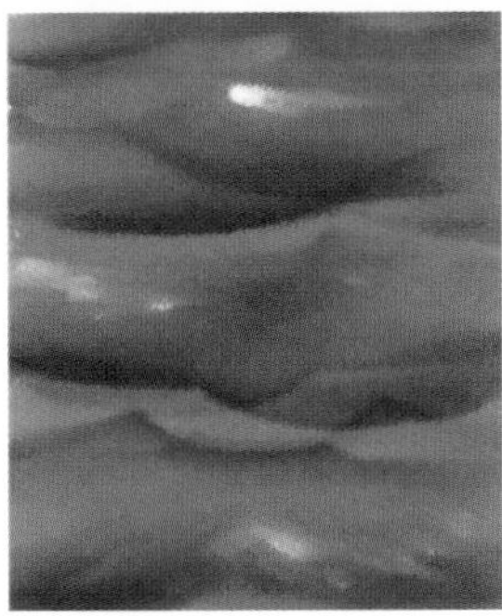

Sea green refers to spiritual acts.

Aquamarine pertains to the healing benefits of spiritual truths.
Bottle green usually stands for an individual's weakening energies.
Emerald signifies the presence and quality of one's specialized talent to heal others.
Green represents health and growth.
Hunter's green stands for fertile ground. It may also refer to someone's rich and bountiful natural talents.
Lime illustrates a negative emotion. More specifically, it can refer to bitterness.
Moss green is representative of an energetic personality or phase.
Olive green symbolizes one's waning natural talents. There's usually an underlying reason why one's inherent gifts or skills are beginning to lose their strength. This dream symbol will advise of the wisdom of spending time examining one's perspectives/outlook.
Peridot denotes a sunny disposition that serves as an uplifting and healing force for others.
Sea green refers to behavior touched with light spiritual tones.
Sorrel symbolizes an earthiness; naturalness.
Teal symbolizes spiritual beliefs interwoven in an individual's daily behavior.

Patterns & Textures

Coarse (texture) denotes harshness of character or behavior.
Design (pattern) portrays an array of specific meanings for each dreamer. For generalized interpretations, refer to the name of specific pattern types.
Downy (texture) naturally means a softness of some type. Depending on the related dream elements, this could be referring to a soft personality such as emotional sensitivity or having a tendency to give others a great measure of leeway, or it could be an advisement to toughen up.
Fractal pertains to one small aspect of the true reality.
Grainy (image/photo) marks an unclear viewpoint; an unclear perception or attitude. Recall what the photograph or image was of.
Majolica (pottery design) suggests celebratory gaiety.
Marquetry (pattern) denotes intricate details. It also means an attention to fine and complex concepts or situations; additionally, it can refer to an interconnecting of ideas or concepts.
Patterns (designs) indicate multiple characteristics, qualities, and methods through which behavior is expressed. Refer to specific pattern types in this dictionary for individual interpretation.
Pitted (texture) is representative of inner strength; tenacity; experience.
Queen's pattern (silverware, etc.) means a regal bearing without pretension.
Rough (texture) portrays an unfinished state; a need for refinement.
Sunburst (design) symbolizes the simplicity of the divine's truths.
Variegated (pattern) symbolizes a blend of ideas.

Geometric

Argyle implies well-defined perspectives.
Art deco symbolizes a particularly nonconformist or nonconforming attitude, idea, or behavior.
Butcher block denotes negative aspects of one's list that others can gossip about or use negatively.
Chevron implies strong goals.
Crosshatched suggests a well-thought-out idea; an analytical thought process.
Diagonal connotes an attitude, perspective, or path that is slanted.
Filigree means entanglements; complexities that were not foreseen by the dreamer.
Fluted usually denotes a gregarious personality. May also point out an idea that is open to interpretation.
Geometric See specific type.
Harlequin characterizes one who avoids responsibility; lacks a true view of reality and takes life too lightly.
Herringbone signifies order; symmetry.
Honeycomb refers to benefits gained through cooperation.
Mosaic symbolizes the many beautiful aspects that create a whole. This will have uniquely revealing meanings for some dreamers.
Parquetry defines richness in succinct wisdom.
Pinstripe typifies a thought process that finely vacillates between one's narrowly defined concepts.
Radial symmetry is generally representative of an outward radiation from a single source, usually an individual. Refers to the importance of giving or sharing one's inherent skills or talents.
Starburst is representative of illumination; intellectual enlightenment.
Stripe indicates duality; multiple perceptions of one element; unpredictability.
Waffle weave See honeycomb.
Zigzag defines a routinely altered course. May imply vacillating attitudes or perspectives.

Mosaic represents the combination of the best parts to form a unit.

Checks

Checker means continual duality expressed; someone with an ability to see both sides of a situation.
Glen plaid See checker.
Houndstooth signifies delusions; perceptive illusions.
Madras portrays a casual attitude or personality.
Plaid relates to knowledge from multiple sources.
Tartan See plaid.
Tattersall is multiple elements forming a single aspect.

Metallic

Copper represents intellectual brilliance coupled with an outgoing personality.
Gold denotes goodness.
Gunmetal symbolizes a reserved attitude toward spirituality.
Metallic denotes a lustrous appearance that may or may not reflect that which is inside or beneath.
Silver stands for the spiritual elements that exist for everyone.

Styles & Attributes

Art nouveau represents a flowing expression of individuality; the ease with which one displays her/his uniqueness.
Batik cautions against a tendency toward selective beliefs.
Fleur-de-lis connotes aloofness.
Homespun denotes simplicity of character and self-reliance. This dream symbol will usually indicate a personality without prevarications or ulterior motives.
Marbled suggests an ever-changing (evolving) pattern; an ability to integrate ideas.
Paisley signifies an element of true reality.
Psychedelic signifies an altered perspective.
Scallop applies to being grounded. This symbol refers to the tendency to return to one's center for the purpose of staying balanced and focused.
Squiggly portrays some kind of complexity in the dreamer's everyday life.
Swirl relates to a convoluted idea, plan, or perspective.
Tie-dyed reflects acceptance and implies nonchalance.
Wavy represents spirituality.
Whorled See swirl.

see also
• Metals *p. 75*
• Art Forms & Styles *p. 216*

Dots & Speckles

Dappled signifies an attitude or perspective that is not consistent.
Dot See polka dots.
Dotted swiss suggests uniformity; equality.
Flecked See speckled.
Glitter denotes a fascination.
Mottled denotes thought vacillation; indecision.
Piebald See spotted.
Polka dots corresponds to indecision.
Speckled denotes the existence of multiple elements.
Spotted portrays a hidden personality; vacillation.

Canvas & Sacking

Burlap symbolizes strength of character and the possession of an enduring constitution.
Gunny is representative of an unsophisticated personality; being warm but a little coarse.
Haircloth See horsehair (cloth).
Horsehair (cloth) refers to a sleek appearance, yet has a prickly response when rubbed the wrong way.
Jute means a rough type of inner strength.
Sackcloth is representative of self-imposed guilt. It also refers to the unnecessary punishment of oneself related to guilt.
Sailcloth correlates to endurance. It suggests the individual has a particularly strong constitution.

Woolen Fabrics

Angora represents a gentle and thoughtful personality.
Broadcloth represents a broad-scope perspective; being open to alternatives or varying opinions.
Broadloom See broadcloth.
Camel's hair indicates inner strength.
Cashmere connotes an individual's gentle nature.
Fleece means a comforting aspect but also may indicate fraudulence.
Flocking denotes the willful addition of emphasis or attention-getting elements to one's surroundings or means of communication.
Gabardine signifies a diligent work effort.
Jersey suggests a soft-hearted, soft-spoken personality.
Mohair emphasizes an irritating or heated situation.
Mouton reveals a deception.
Serge indicates an unyielding personality.
Shearling denotes warmth of character.
Virgin wool signifies an idea or life element that hasn't been affected by opinion or subjected aspects; originality.
Wool See shearling.
Worsted suggests a strong character yet emotionally warm and sensitive.

Woven Fabrics

Admiralty cloth (fabric) stands for maintaining control; keeping one's composure in the face of disappointment, surprises, or emergencies.
Canvas relates to a coarse yet strong personality.
Chambray denotes a dual purpose; twofold reason for doing something.
Tapestry (design/fabric) will usually illustrate a visual symbolizing an important message for the dreamer. Try to recall the details of the tapestry if it was a scene. Otherwise, this tapestry will signify that all interacting elements of a certain aspect should be given consideration.
Tweed denotes quiet, dignified intelligence/wisdom.
Twill suggests a coarseness to one's character or applies to a current attitude.

Satins & Silks

Satin indicates an individual who always looks on the bright side of life.

Alamode See silk.
Chiffon signifies those aspects that are easily seen through.
Grenadine refers to insubstantial thought; cursory thinking without in-depth consideration.
Grosgrain signifies a rough personality.
Moiré depicts a rough exterior personality; a lack of expressive sensitivity.
Organza reveals a hardened underlying personality.
Satin reveals an overly optimistic perspective. It may also refer to the soft sheen of one's character (as opposed to a need to be glossy).
Shantung denotes roughly disguised finesse.
Silk suggests an inner refinement; a delicate strength.
Taffeta will indicate a stiff personality who appears to be amenable.

Textured Fabrics

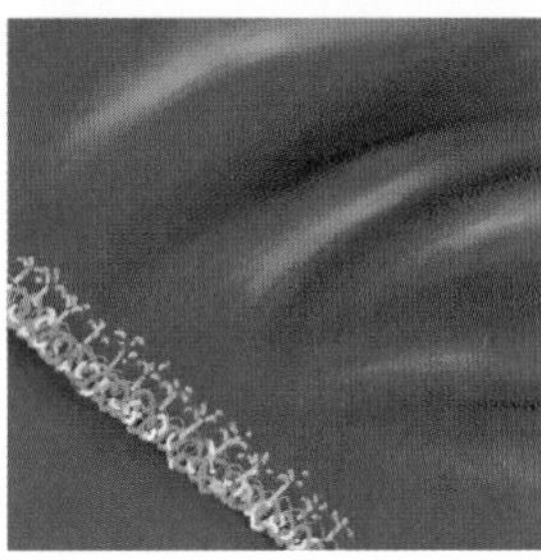

Brocade means kind and thoughtful.

Boucle pertains to a gentle, down-home individual who takes life in stride.
Brocade illustrates a way of life that's rich in compassion and possesses an emotional depth; a life of living spiritual beliefs.
Candlewick portrays the basis for one's moral, ethical, and spiritual motivation.
Chenille depicts old-fashioned ideas that remain valid throughout time.
Corduroy implies a rugged personality; being accepting of life's tougher experiences.
Crepe suggests a personality whose mental aberrations are easily perceived.
Damask exemplifies a rich and full experience.
Fuzzy most often refers to a soft touch; compassion and/or understanding.
Lamé typifies dream symbols pertaining to a flashy personality; a need to be noticed; a love of attention.
Moleskin alludes to a gentle and tolerant personality.
Poplin suggests a domineering personality.
Seersucker alludes to a lighthearted mood.
Shaggy (fabric) represents a disorderly thought process.
Velour symbolizes a warm, compassionate character. May also indicate a quiet dignity or wisdom.
Velvet denotes a soft and soothing situation, relationship, or state of mind; a very comfortable sense.

Synthetic Fabrics

Acetate symbolizes strength gained from an outside source. This points to an element (or individual) that provides support or encouragement.
Elastic denotes a giving or flexible relationship or situation.
Leatherette connotes an ability to forge ahead in the face of setbacks or problematic situations; being able to utilize substitutes; creativity.
Lycra See elastic.
Naugahyde See leatherette.
Nylon implies some form of disassociative personality trait; a personal desire to distance oneself from others or certain situations.

Vinyl means copying.

Polyester suggests a lack of originality; rarely expressed individualism; middle-of-the-road position or attitude.
Rayon applies to imitation. It can also refer to a synthetic aspect which has in itself no originality.
Rubber (material) alludes to an attitude, perspective, or other aspect in one's life that creates a cushioning or buffering effect.
Spandex See elastic.
Suede cloth is representative of a sympathetic nature. It is indicative of an individual who is true and gentle.
Synthetic (fabric) applies to an artificial aspect; an alternative or substitute.
Vinyl denotes an imitation.

Cottons & Linens

Cheesecloth is representative of an aspect that contributes to and serves to maintain wholesome attitudes; the straining of information; refined analysis.
Chino signifies a readiness on the part of the individual to expend energies.
Chintz defines an emotional or perceptual cover-up in one's life.
Cotton connotes a particularly unsophisticated self-image; a lack of expressive ego; a comfortable perspective of oneself.
Crinoline is representative of a particular stiffness to one's underlying character. It may also refer to a resentful acceptance of something.
Denim alludes to something that is long-lasting; an aspect that endures.
Dotted swiss suggests uniformity; equality.
Duck portrays a self-absorbed personality.
Egyptian cotton symbolizes the desirable character traits brought on by the inner beauty of fortitude and perseverance.
Irish linen pertains to the fragility of reality.
Lawn is representative of aloofness.
Linen usually indicates a rigid personality.
Marseille pertains to an emphasis needed. Recall what the raised area of the fabric was shaped like in the dream context.
Muslin indicates simplicity; homespun wisdom and common sense.
Ninon portrays a delicate aspect to one's personality. It refers to a specifically fragile sensitivity.
Oilcloth typically denotes a need for more healthful eating habits: not what one eats but rather the manner of eating. Generally, people eat on the go far too much and portions are far too large. People eat when upset or angry, and this is not good for their health.
Organdy portrays a stiff personality; insensitivity.
Oxford suggests a tailored perspective, one designed by personal attitudes; a subjective viewpoint.
Percale alludes to a preferred element, type, or quality.
Sateen implies a slick personality; cleverness.
Voile suggests the presence of fragile elements to one's character.
Zephyr cloth refers to optimism; looking on the bright side.

see also
• Animal Anatomy *p. 18*
• Needlework *p. 215*

Color Miscellany

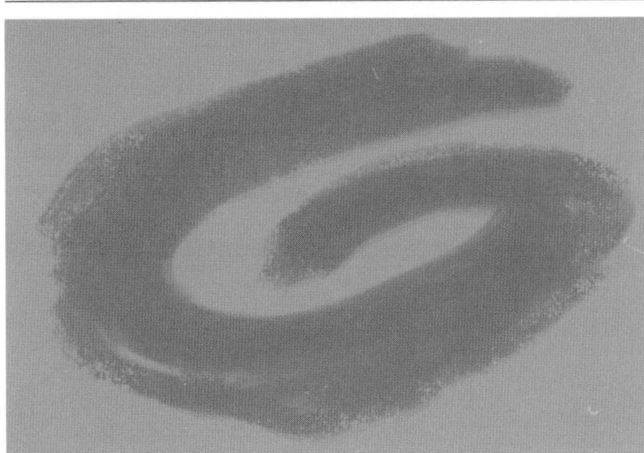

Clash of colors is an illustration of turmoil or muddled thinking.

Clash of colors indicates a conflict; mixed issues. It may also refer to a confused logic affecting situations or relationships in the everyday waking life of the dreamer.
Colorless stands for neutral; having no personal animation or unique expressiveness.
Color wheel is representative of the many choices that people have in their lives regarding their attitudes and their expressed behaviors. Recall if any of the colors were highlighted in the dream. These would be sending a particular advisement message.
Day-Glo (colors) will come as attention-getting markers to the dreamer. Recall what was colored in such an outstanding way.
Discolored signifies an emotion that has been altered by an outside factor.
Flannel usually relates to levelheadedness; being down-to-earth.
Fleck comes as an attention-seeking message for one to notice something outstanding in one's life.
Garish See gaudy.
Gaudy connotes a state of extremes; overemphasis.
Lightening (color) can refer to several aspects in one's life. It can be associated with hair lightening, which would be a call to lighten up on one's thoughts and attitudes, or it could refer to workload or behavior, which would be depicted by various activities such as repainting one's office or home walls with a lighter color.
Local color adds important clues to each individual's dream. Recall all the facets that were represented.
Monochromatic (one color throughout dream) indicates an overall perspective or personality aspect that "colors" one's life. Recall what color washed the dreamscape and then refer to the specific color involved.
Pastel (hue) implies a gentleness or soft quality that is associated with the specific color's individual interpretation. Refer to the specific color for further clarification of the dream symbol.
Pigment See specific color.
Polychromatic (multiple colors) corresponds to a Bohemian or eccentric personality; the freedom to openly express oneself.
Primary color corresponds to a basic or elemental aspect. This will correlate to the specific color presented in the dream. Refer to that color in this dream book.
Stonewashed suggests a lack of strong opinions; an on-the-fence type of perspective; an inability to take a firm stand.
Tint suggests an issue that's been altered by one's personal attitude/perspective. Recall what color the tint was to get a sharper interpretation.
Tricolored reveals three distinct elements belonging to an issue or situation.
Variegated (colors) symbolizes a blend of ideas.

Skins & Pelts

Buckskin refers to a soft-touch aspect to one's character.
Chamois (cloth) implies a soft nature.
Cowhide applies to the power of compassion.
Deerskin connotes some type of attachment to nature.
Ermine cautions against altering oneself for others. Advises of the wisdom of being oneself.
Leather reveals one's manner of interaction with others. The key is whether this dream leather was soft and supple or hard and brittle.
Leather (patent) See patent leather.
Patent leather depicts a personal need for attention.
Pigskin alludes to a tough attitude, situation, or perspective.
Sable portrays negativity; a dark mood.
Sharkskin relates to a spiritually unethical personality.
Sheepskin signifies warmth and comfort. It may refer to the need for an emotional response or support.
Snakeskin is representative of a swindler; someone with a shiftless personality.
Suede refers to a naturalness; no false affectations.

Lace

Chantilly lace signifies a special delicate touch to something.
Eyelet lace stands for simplicity yet is not to be equated with simple-mindedness.
Lace may denote an aloof or extremely particular personality, or it may allude to a sensitive and delicate nature. Recall other dream details for further clarification of this symbol.
Pointelle denotes a fragile-appearing personality, yet the individual may not be as delicate as initially assumed.
Tatting See lace.

Fabric Miscellany

Accordion pleat (fabric) suggests a flexible character.
Bridge cloth refers to preparations for a lighthearted debate or semiconflict.
Cloth See specific type.
Diaphanous (fabric) suggests a delicate life aspect.
Fabric is representative of a particular type of personality or varying traits. See specific fabric types.
Felt implies a softened attitude through the compression of comprehensive factors; acceptance by way of overlooking the more personally viewed.
Finespun refers to intricate and delicate details.
Frayed (clothing fabric) symbolizes wear and tear, usually associated with one's hardscrabble life which one has persevered through.
Fringe (on fabric) denotes a border; an aspect that is not well defined or encompassed within a specific conceptual framework.
Fuzz relates to a coating of some type being done; misrepresentation.
Gauze warns of an ineffective cover-up being done.
Gossamer See finespun.
Grass cloth will relate to spirituality associated with a specific life element. Was the grass cloth a wallpaper in one's home? Which room? Was it on an office wall? What type of office or business?

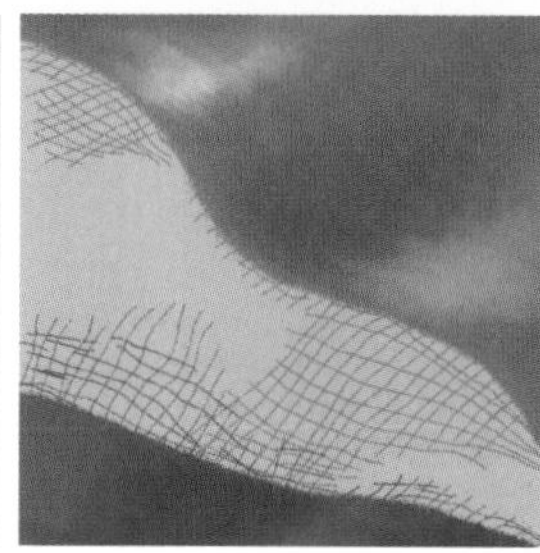

Frayed denotes the stresses of life.

Kapok denotes that which one uses to soften life difficulties.
Khaki (color/fabric) implies a regimented personality.
Linsey-woolsey usually indicates someone with a rigid personality. See also homespun.
Lint advises one to get actively involved in ridding oneself of stagnating extraneous life aspects such as attitudes, opinions, and narrow perspectives.
Maillot implies honesty; no hidden aspects.
Marquisette typifies a transparent personality or situation.
Nap (fabric) can suggest a directional move. Recall if the nap was straight up or slanted to the right or left.
Piping (on fabric) applies to an emphasis placed on a specific aspect of one's character. Recall surrounding dreamscape elements to determine which aspect this refers to.
Plush represents a pleasing or emotionally fulfilling element.
Puckered denotes a snag or problem associated with an element in one's life.
Ribbon symbolizes a positive element in one's life. Recall the fabric and color for more in-depth interpretation.
Ruffle depicts multiple secondary aspects to an attitude or perspective.
Run (in fabric) represents a flawed perspective or presentation of oneself.
Russet illustrates a rich, earthy perspective; an alignment with reality.
Scrim refers to an unclear perspective; someone with a foggy viewpoint.
See-through See transparent.
Selvage (of fabric) relates to something that will remain intact; will not come apart or undone.
Sheer (fabric) reveals a transparent personality.
Textile See fabric.
Tick (fabric) connotes a gentle and soft inner nature.
Transparent indicates a lack of deception or ulterior motive; open and honest relationships; nothing hidden.
Two-ply refers to a double-layered aspect or issue. Draws attention to a need to give attention to both aspects.
Velcro represents an easy, quick attachment. This may refer either to relationships or the acceptance of new ideas.
Webbing exemplifies interrelated aspects to a single element.

Woven & Patchwork

Basket weave denotes integrated ideas.
Crazy quilt indicates confusion or may mean that something in one's life is comprised of a particularly odd mixture of aspects.
Jacquard illustrates a complex situation or idea.
Patchwork comes to underscore the importance of variety in one's life. Pertains to multiple perceptive qualities.

Fabric Crafts

Card stock (paper) refers to an element that is meant to give greater endurance and strength to a communication or message.
Latticework stands for one's defenses that are not perceived by others.
Leatherwork exemplifies one's individualized, uniquely personal manner of relating to others.
Loom connotes multiple elements that are woven into a whole issue or aspect.
Maker's mark is a sign identifying the maker (originator) of something creative. This symbol will come as an advisement to be sure one knows the true source of a particular piece of information.
Matrix portrays an identified pattern to something in one's life.
Morocco (leather) signifies a gentle emotional expressiveness.
Swatch (cloth) portrays a sampling of one's hidden personality or inner character. Recall the type of cloth, design, and color.
Wringing (fabric) implies an effort to get the most out of a life element. What was being twisted? Color? Did it belong to anyone the dreamer relates to? If so, this points to anger or irritation directed to that individual.

Chapter 28

Food & Drink

Edibles connote some form of nourishment. This nourishment will most often be psychological or directly related to an individual's current emotional state of being.

Eating

À la carte symbolizes a caution to look at aspects individually instead of as a whole.
Antipasto represents variety, choices, and opportunities.
Appetizer signifies one's sources of personal motivation.
Box lunch applies to conservative attitudes; being frugal.
Breakfast connotes the quality of a new beginning.
Brunch depicts a starting point that begins in the middle. Suggests one go back to the beginning.
Buffet (meal) symbolizes the wide variety of opportunities open to us.
Canapé signifies attempts made; a time period of trying out various aspects; exploration; expanding one's experience.
Coffee break refers to a need to pause for the purpose of restoring one's energy.
Continental breakfast suggests a physiological need to lighten up one's stressful mornings.

Hors d'oeuvre indicates a taster of future events or activities.

Dinner connotes one's main source of nourishment.
Entrée symbolizes the main issue or concept.
Feast implies great satisfaction or personal pleasure.
Finger food denotes a casual or easy manner of gaining needed information.
High tea advises one to take time to settle down and contemplate or absorb that which has been experienced.
Hors d'oeuvre refers to a sampling or whetting the appetite for what's to come.
Leftovers advise one to utilize one's total potential.
Main course represents the central idea of an issue.
Munching advises one to chew information; mentally process information better.
Picnic corresponds to an enjoyable respite or a task completed with ease.
Potluck suggests the ability to make do with a variety of elements; an appreciation of what others have to offer.
Refreshments advises one to refresh oneself; a rejuvenation; a breather.
Savory signifies an appealing element in one's life.
Side dish will represent aspects that enhance a main element.
Slurping refers to the intake of information in an indiscriminate manner.
Smorgasbord will portray a variety of opportunities.
Snack implies rejuvenation or the reenergizing of oneself.
Supper is a symbol that pertains to a need to reenergize and nourish oneself.
Takeout (meal) comes as a suggestion to slow down and appreciate life's opportunity for important moments of leisure.
TV dinner usually stands for a relaxed, enjoyable manner of gaining information.

Diet

Appetite represents one's motivational state. Was the dreamscape appetite voracious or scant?
Butterball is a representation of excessiveness; an extraneous aspect; being overblown or fattened to the extreme.
Calorie alludes to an aspect that helps keep a balance for the dreamer.
Calorie chart illustrates opportunity options for balance in life.
Carb craze See fad diet.
Diet usually advises of a need to shed excessive aspects in one's life. This symbol may refer to attitudes, beliefs, negative emotions, superficial elements, and so on.
Dietetic (foods/drinks) represent aspects that help one in getting rid of the excessive or harmful facets of oneself.
Fad diet is a representation of reaching for popular attitudes instead of using plain logic and common sense.
Fast (food abstinence) usually stands for efforts to purify oneself; shed negatives.
Filling (food) depicts a main idea or issue.
Food is a dreamscape symbol that always connotes some type of nourishment. However, this nourishment rarely has a direct relation to the physical body.
Food fad is a symbol that suggests the acceptance of certain concepts because others are believing them.
Frozen food defines nourishing life aspects that are not being utilized or benefited from in any way.
Junk food is a symbol that warns the dreamer against putting energy into learning unimportant concepts, for they will not be fulfilling.
Macrobiotics comes in dreams to caution against extreme measures and advises one to temper the tendency to focus on one aspect. Suggests wide diversification.
Natural food (no additives) indicates a pure aspect; an aspect having no affecting factors, such as a basic idea or attitude.
Rich (food) is a dreamscape symbol that relates to bountiful benefits that carry multiple effects.

see also
- Eating & Drinking *p. 173*
- Cooking Utensils *p. 389*

Cook's Ingredients

Arrowroot defines an aspect that counters a harmful element in one's life.

Artificial coloring reveals false perspectives, ones purposely displayed to the public.

Artificial flavor reveals the presence of false attributes; imitation qualities.

Ascorbic acid relates to inner strength.

Baking powder signifies aspects in one's life that need to be blended or mixed with others.

Baking soda symbolizes a cleansing aspect in one's life.

Bicarbonate of soda See baking soda.

Bouillon cube is a symbol that pertains to aspects in one's life that bring clarity; clarity from a specific source.

Bread crumbs are a minuscule amount of something.

Brewer's yeast represents the source of innovative thought; brilliant thought and ideas; the power behind something; impetus.

Convenience food signifies a shortcut or time-saving procedure.

Corn flour stands for the benefits of inner strength/ fortitude; a natural acceptance and the benefits that grow from it.

Cornmeal typifies the versatile benefits of personal effort.

Cornstarch pertains to the personal enrichment one gains through personal efforts.

Flavoring represents the addition of personal perspectives to facts; making something more palatable to oneself.

Flavoring (artificial) See artificial flavor.

Flour advises of a need to increase one's efforts; one of the main basic elements of a plan or issue.

Food coloring See artificial coloring.

Gelatin implies cohesiveness; aspects that serve to bind.

Leaven See brewer's yeast.

Lemon oil stands for an attempt to cover up troubles (making something smell better); denial; diversionary tactics.

Orange oil stands for a source for cleaning and freshening our energies.

Pectin depicts a desire to solidify some aspect in one's life; a factor that has the potential to manifest a goal or plan.

Rice paper connotes a fragile facet in one's life. The surrounding dreamscape details will clarify what this association is.

Seasoning will indicate personal characteristics. Refer to specific type.

Self-rising flour suggests a resourceful individual; having knowledge and the associated wisdom; the perseverance to rise above adversity.

Stock (soup) is a dream symbol that relates to heartiness; rounded nourishment.

Suet stands for multifaceted utilization.

Thickener (additive) stands for an element that gives more substance to an issue, idea, or plan.

Tomato paste refers to a good idea that can be used in various forms to fit differing elements.

Yeast See brewer's yeast.

Flavors

Butterscotch implies something that has a rich flavor to it (spiritually or heartily wholesome).

Menthol connotes a fresh or refreshing aspect.

Mocha suggests a high quality; a richness.

Peppermint shows a cleansing or freshening of one's words; softer communication.

Spearmint signifies a refreshing idea or aspect to an element; insights.

Sugarcoating warns of an attempt to deceive; alter reality; be overly optimistic.

Tutti-frutti means irrationality.

Unseasoned will point to a raw life aspect that hasn't been spiced up or colored according to one's perspective or personal attitude; an objective aspect.

Vanilla indicates renewal.

Zesty points to motivation. It can refer specifically to a reenergizing element.

Dietary Essentials

Amino acid symbolizes aspects in life that are needed but may be lacking.

Carbohydrates relate to an essential element for balance in one's life.

Lysine (amino acid) represents a counter to a viral-like negative in one's life which could personally affect one's healthy perspective.

Protein symbolizes a necessary element in one's life. This is something other than food.

Vitamin corresponds to a specific nutrient. Recall the particulars associated with this dream symbol, for this message could imply that the dreamer needs more of this vitamin or is perhaps ingesting too much.

Cooking

Au naturel implies a tendency toward aspects that are natural, without trappings, decoration, or dressing. May also point to a lack of ulterior motives.

Batter means condition and quality of something before it is ready to be finalized.

Overdone reveals excess; extraneous aspects added.

Precooked refers to having a situation, idea, or other element well researched and prepared before presenting it to others.

Rare (undercooked) symbolizes an unfinished aspect; something that is not complete.

Raw usually stands for a basic, unaltered aspect in one's life; something in its natural state.

Recipe won't necessarily symbolically relate to the preparation of food but rather will refer to the proper steps and right elements associated with accomplishing a goal.

Underdone reveals a thought/situation needing further energy put into it before it can be fully realized.

Well-done (cooked) exemplifies a full conclusion or closure.

Fruits

Avocado may indicate a need to think more positively about life.

Apple typifies good health.
Apricot stands for a healing force that comes from within.
Avocado implies a soft-hearted personality with a tough skin. May also point to a need to lighten perspective toward a more optimistic attitude.
Banana symbolizes inner goodness. Sometimes seen only after other aspects have been peeled away.
Blackberry represents fruitful aspects of life that manifest through one's personal nature; the fruits of a spiritual life.
Black cherry represents an unusually sweet aspect; something uniquely pleasing.
Blueberry corresponds to the fruits of one's spirituality.
Boysenberry relates to the fruits of enduring life struggles.
Cantaloupe pertains to good beginnings.
Cherry means a sweet situation; prime aspects of something.
Citrus See specific type.
Coconut implies strength and nourishment can result from life's more difficult lessons.
Crab apple alludes to a tart personality; cantankerousness.
Currant refers to the little nourishing aspects that are abundant in our lives.
Date denotes versatility.
Dried fruit represents preserved talents; a move to extend the benefits of a good thing.
Elderberry symbolizes naturally occurring opportunities that are too frequently overlooked.
Fig refers to a triviality. Depending on related dreamscape aspects, a fig can point to inner nourishment for fortifying self-confidence.
Fruit most often points to the nourishing and beneficial effects of using one's talents for the benefit of others. Recall the condition of the dreamscape fruit for further clarification. See specific fruit.
Fruit cocktail constitutes a multitude of benefits.
Grape refers to multiple aspects, the fact that an issue holds many varying facets.
Grapefruit advises one to shed certain excesses in life.
Guava connotes bountiful spiritual talents.
Kumquat applies to small needs that are as important as seemingly greater ones.
Lemon constitutes bitterness or indicates a state of perpetual troubles.
Lime illustrates a negative emotion; bitterness.
Loganberry See blackberry.
Mandarin (orange) See tangerine.
Mango pertains to a hardened exterior personality covering a sweet inner sensitivity.
Maraschino cherry defines a desired goal; an attainment; the perfect effect or result of something strived for.
Melon symbolizes inner nourishment obtained through personal efforts.
Nectarine relates to a fresh idea or perspective.
Orange portrays the benefits of using inner energies or resources to help others.
Orange peel refers to personal efforts that have been expended to aid others.
Papaya connotes a need to calm emotions or anxiety.
Pawpaw stands for awareness of an aspect's subtleties.
Peach constitutes satisfaction; a desired element.
Pear represents duality.
Persimmon indicates a need to clarify resolutions and confoundments; an ongoing puzzlement.
Pineapple connotes a fresh aspect of an element in life.
Plum denotes an element of high quality as perceived by the dreamer. This may not necessarily be true.
Pomegranate refers to justice; wisdom; rectifying mistakes.
Prune refers to a distasteful or unappealing element.
Quince denotes an element in life that is effective only when brought into completion.
Raisin pertains to a nourishing benefit that manifested from part of another life element.
Raspberry depicts a distasteful or disagreeable element.
Rhubarb denotes a life aspect that contains dual elements.
Strawberry constitutes a congenial, cheerful nature.
Sultana pertains to expectation of deference; aloofness.
Tangerine refers to an element that nourishes and refreshes.
Watermelon portrays spiritual nutrients.
Watermelon seeds point to seeds of spirituality; aspects that may regenerate spiritual benefits or rewards.

Root Vegetables

Beet reflects intensity. Frequently indicates anger or deep embarrassment.
Carrot represents enticements; inducements.
Kohlrabi implies something in the dreamer's life that's difficult to sort out or understand.
Parsnip signifies neglected opportunities.
Potato symbolizes an essential or basic element in one's life; a basic nourishment.
Rutabaga See turnip.
Sweet potato symbolizes an agreeable element in one's life; an essential aspect that is very pleasing.
Turnip reflects a reversal; a changed attitude or decision.
Yam See sweet potato.

see also
• Crops *p. 44*
• Fruit & Nut Trees *p. 53*

Vegetables

Alfalfa denotes a need for nourishment.
Artichoke is a warning against accepting half-truths; concepts that are incomplete.
Asparagus comes as a reminder of our current physical beginnings; youth.
Bean represents one of many elements; a portion.
Broccoli signifies multilevel talents and their utilization.
Brussels sprouts indicate our little acts of goodness that nourish or encourage others.
Cabbage pertains to the rougher aspects directly affecting one's life.
Cauliflower alludes to bigness or generosity.
Celery denotes difficulties that require acceptance.
Cherry tomato connotes those little, often overlooked aspects in life that present us with a convenience or ease.
Chicory alludes to an aspect that serves as a substitute for the ones we believe will strengthen and motivate us; an alternate source of courage.
Collard greens See kale.
Cucumber pertains to possible difficulties forthcoming.
Eggplant implies ideas that incorporate spiritual aspects.
Endive connotes learning experiences that are somewhat bittersweet.
Green onion stands for a simple and readily available element used to counter a negative; a safeguard against being affected by negative aspects.
Green pepper represents a controlled temper; a cool thinker.
Indian corn connotes survivability; life-giving seed.
Kale represents a personal need of some type. The dreamer will usually know what need she/he has.
Leek represents a counterforce to negativity.
Lettuce represents the need to clear up a misunderstanding in one's life.
Morel See mushroom.
Mushroom represents a benefit resulting from a seemingly negative factor.
Onion points to an element in one's life that, although bringing tears, will end up being a healing factor.
Onion skin relates to fragile truths; healing factors.
Pumpkin represents playfulness; a wide range of expressions.
Pumpkin seed stands for an opportunity for one to express oneself.
Rabbit food See salad.
Radish signifies an emotionally volatile situation.
Romaine (lettuce) refers to a lighthearted, perhaps humorous, misunderstanding.
Salad indicates diversity. Recall the salad's condition. What type of foods comprised it?
Sauerkraut See cabbage.
Shallot See green onion.
Spinach refers to a nourishing life element; a beneficial aspect or opportunity.
Squash implies a source of energy.
Tomato implies an agreeable or attractive idea.
Vegetables stand for essential nutrients. See specific type.
Watercress suggests spiritual nourishment.
Zucchini indicates an unrealized benefit or positive element in one's life.

Grains & Cereals

Barley applies to essential elements in one's life.
Brown rice relates to wholeness; acceptance of the whole rather than choosing easier, softer aspects.
Bulgur signifies strength of character; a strong constitution.
Cereal stands for the basic, foundational beginnings of something. Recall whether it was hot (enthusiastic) or cold (blasé)?
Cob See corncob.
Corncob shows personal effort.
Cornflakes represents strongly motivated beginnings.
Corn kernel applies to the great significance of each small effort one makes.
Grain connotes life aspects that may bring emotional, mental, or spiritual nourishment.
Granola applies to inner nourishment of emotional, mental, or spiritual aspects.
Maize See corn.
Meal (grain) applies to the coarse lessons that provide nourishment.

Wheat portrays a type of sustenance.

Millet typifies a filler aspect; unimportant elements or issues on which one expends efforts, funds, or time.
Mush See porridge.
Oat See grain.
Oatmeal signifies a life aspect that comforts and nourishes.
Porridge signifies an enduring and nourishing life aspect.
Rice See grain.
Rye represents rejuvenation.
Wheat signifies some type of nourishing element in one's life. This usually refers to mental or emotional aspects.
Wheat germ suggests a highly potent nourishing aspect.
Whole grain refers to the entire aspect of a nourishing element.

Nuts

Almond (nut/oil) represents the need to avoid stress and/or give more attention to one's physical condition.
English walnut represents a richly nourishing aspect in one's life.
Filbert (nut) See hazelnut.
Hazelnut implies common sense.
Macadamia nut alludes to quality inner nourishment and deepened emotional receptivity in one's life.
Nut indicates a lack of logic and reason; in essence, someone who may be a literal nutcase.
Peanut will refer to the minor aspects of our life.
Peanut butter corresponds to a source of energy or motivation. May also reveal a sticky situation.
Pecan points to fulfillment following an achievement.
Pine nut stands for the fruits of one's inherent, natural abilities.

Spices

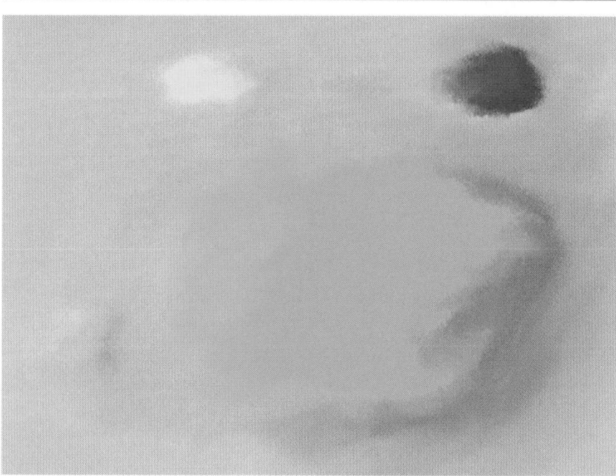

Spices encapsulate all human attributes and worldviews.

Allspice won't normally refer to a literal spice but rather that all elements of one's life should be spiced with acceptance for the things one cannot do anything about and also that one should use a smattering of a sense of humor sprinkled in one's behavior.
Black pepper refers to aspects to which the dreamer has a strong adverse reaction.
Cayenne pepper See red pepper.
Chili denotes situations or relationships that could develop into hot ones.
Chili powder illustrates one's personal ability to maintain control of situations.
Cinnamon signifies an aspect that the dreamer perceives as being especially homey and companionable.
Clove (spice) connotes a life aspect that one utilizes to make specific factors more appealing.
Curry powder refers to a particular slant used to spice something up.
Fenugreek defines an attitude that serves to aid acceptance.
Ginger depicts a life aspect that can be used to aid in obtaining personal acceptance and greater tolerance.
Hot pepper refers to an attraction and tolerance for touchy issues.
Jalapeño alludes to a spirited personality.
Mace (spice) See nutmeg.
Mull (spice) implies a maturity or more development is needed.
Nutmeg connotes an inherent, natural essence of self; an inborn ability.
Paprika See red pepper.
Pepper typifies a symbol that indicates a response is needed.
Peppercorn often points to a necessary communication forthcoming.
Poppy seeds stand for assumptions of guilt regarding an innocent party.
Red pepper stands for an issue warming up with the potential for becoming hot.
Spices represent personal qualities affecting aspects in one's life; one's unique perspective and how it affects behavior and experiences.

Sweeteners

Artificial sweetener points to an effort to be optimistic that isn't working well.
Blackstrap See molasses.
Brown sugar connotes a genuinely sweet personality; one whose true nature is without negative qualities.
Cane sugar See sugar.
Corn syrup See sugar.
Honey represents sweet benefits generated from one's efforts.
Maple syrup is a reminder to appreciate our needs that have been provided for in life.
Molasses defines a factor in one's life capable of providing needed energy or motivation.
Saccharin implies a tendency to be content with imitations.
Sugar may exemplify an energizing element, or it may allude to a highly desirable aspect in one's life; a sweet benefit or outcome.
Sugarhouse See maple syrup.
Sugar substitute See artificial sweetener.
Sweet (flavor) most often reflects a desirable element in one's life.
Sweetener indicates an attempt to make something more palatable or attractive.
Syrup portrays false sincerity; flattery; overdramatization.

Fats & Oils

Butter refers to the richness of a simple life and the unaffected perspectives that accompany it.
Corn oil defines the promise of beginning effort.
Fat See grease.
Grease warns of bribes and ulterior motives.
Lard indicates a heavy coating; cover-up or embellishment.
Margarine implies an effective substitute is available for the dreamer to use. This type of symbol will be personally recognized by each dreamer.
Oleo See margarine.
Olive oil applies to a positive, beneficial element in one's life.
Peanut oil refers to a rich source of nourishment which can imply mental, emotional, physical, or spiritual aspects.
Sesame seed oil alludes to a beneficial element in life.
Shortening connotes a required aspect of an element; a key ingredient.
Vegetable oil portrays a factor that contributes to the completion of something.

Preserves

Apple butter suggests attention given to healthful elements; an awareness of the more beneficial life aspects.
Jam (food) signifies a troubling situation.
Jelly See jam (food).
Marmalade See preserves.
Pickles See preserves.
Preserves reflect an individual's tendency to maintain fundamental elements of an aspect; not losing sight of all of an issue's various factors.

see also
• Herbs *p. 46*
• Mints *p. 47*

Condiments & Sauces

Applesauce denotes a pleasant blending of ideals.

Béarnaise sauce relates to a beneficial added element in one's life.

Chutney signifies an interesting mix of multiple elements, which is often a rich and beneficial one.

Condiment connotes an additional aspect one interjects to life; a dressing or spicing of something.

Dill pickle connotes a slight problem that is entering one's life.

Dressing (sauces) will correspond to one's tastes; how one makes life elements more to their liking.

Gravy represents an easy access to something.

Hot sauce implies a highly charged issue or attitude; a tendency toward spicing things up.

Ketchup applies to elaborations; a need to spice something up.

Marinara (sauce) implies a spicy aspect to a situation; the addition of an interesting facet.

Mayonnaise relates to the use of positive aspects to aid in attaining a nourishing aspect of a goal in life.

Pesto suggests some of the best aspects combined into one element.

Picanté (sauce) denotes a highly interesting (spicy) idea or event.

Pickle alludes to a difficulty that must be faced, accepted, or resolved.

Relish (condiment) refers to something that one savors.

Salad dressing/oil pertains to the personal manner in which one dresses up or enhances opportunities.

Salt exemplifies gregariousness and dependability.

Salt and pepper signifies duality; positive and negative elements.

Sauce signifies personal perspectives or character traits that alter basic elements.

Sweet-and-sour (sauce) marks an element containing the dual aspects of positive and negative factors; pleasing yet somewhat problematic aspects.

Tabasco represents a highly interesting subject; excitability.

Table salt See salt.

Tartar sauce symbolizes a personal perspective applied to a specific spiritual belief for the purpose of adding a more tasteful element.

Vinegar connotes a distasteful/bitter life aspect.

Food Waste

Kernel pertains to one's inner talents or abilities.

Peach pit stands for a healing element in one's life.

Peanut shells signify the use of all opportunities in life. Specifically, they refer to a full experiential awareness.

Pit See kernel; peach pit.

Pulp refers to leftover elements that still have some value.

Rind denotes that which harbors fruitful or bountiful aspects. This dreamscape fragment refers to the tough path or exterior that serves as the outlying regions of one's direction of fulfillment.

Legumes & Lentils

Bean sprouts caution against ignoring the importance of each part or aspect of a situation.

Kidney bean pertains to an intake of something that has the capability of cleansing or balancing oneself.

Legume See pea.

Lentils allude to time-tested aspects that emotionally or spiritually nourish.

Mung bean See bean sprouts.

Pea most often symbolizes a small amount of something. Recall what the pea was associated with in the dream.

Pinto bean connotes an essential element in one's life.

Soybean symbolizes a highly nourishing belief that is important for the dreamer.

Herbs

Basil corresponds to a light flavoring or hint. It may refer specifically to a suggestion.

Chive indicates positive factors that one intentionally adds to one's life.

Fennel connotes a need for emotional calming.

Garlic means personal defenses against negative aspects/forces.

Marjoram alludes to a delicate aspect; a fragile situation.

Parsley refers to unrecognized benefits and nourishing elements in life.

Potherb See specific herb.

Garlic symbolizes protection against damaging outside influences.

Meat

Bacon symbolizes one's job. It may refer simply to working.

Beef cautions one to ingest well-defined and developed concepts; against the acceptance of raw aspects.

Brisket denotes emotionally warming feelings.

Buffalo wings relate to attempts to intermix specific aspects that do not blend or will not coalesce.

Chicken denotes fear; a reluctance to face life.

Chicken liver points to a reluctance due to fears; possible inferiority complex or lack of faith in oneself.

Cold cuts represent aspects that provide immediate nourishment.

Drumstick refers to personal efforts leading to nourishment.

Filet mignon portrays some type of life aspect that is choice for the dreamer; a highly desirable aspect.

Bacon is simply a representation of one's profession or role in life.

Giblets refer to utilization; a message to make use of the whole aspect of something. This carries a specific interpretation for each dreamer.

Goose advises of a need for more seriousness in life.

Ham applies to theatrics; over-emotionalism; dramatics.

Jerky (meat) represents the nourishment from one's preserved convictions or ideologies.

Lamb refers to the divine.

Lean (meat) refers to an absence of extraneous elements. This may pertain to one's lifestyle or belief system.

Meat refers to solid basics; highly nourishing elements.

Mincemeat alludes to the destruction of something in one's life.

Mutton See lamb.

Offal pertains to waste aspects on which one shouldn't be expending efforts or attention.

Pork corresponds with one's efforts as they are applied to one's work.

Rasher See bacon.

Red meat in dreams will not specifically refer to food but rather a highly beneficial element; an aspect providing basic factors.

Roast (meat cut) relates to an issue or idea that one intends to develop.

Spareribs typify a need to get down to the bare bones of an issue.

Steak connotes high energy; a motivational factor.

Tripe denotes a worthless element; having no value.

Turkey refers to a hidden intelligence. It may refer to someone with quiet wisdom behind an unlikely exterior.

Veal pertains to a highly nourishing aspect in one's life.

Venison characterizes an unethical source from which nourishment is obtained.

Meat Dishes

Casserole typifies a situation or condition created by several aspects in one's life.

Chili con carne reminds us that we have the ability to control the heat of a situation.

Chili dog pertains to one's preference for involvement in spiced-up or particularly heated situations.

Goulash implies full-bodied nourishment, usually not in reference to food.

Gumbo refers to a sustaining, long-lasting nourishment.

Hash (food) relates to nourishment comprised of multiple factors.

Meat and potatoes connote a preference for the basics or prime factors of an issue.

Meatballs indicate irrationality; one losing sight of reason.

Meat loaf shows the combining of basic ideas or elements.

Pot roast signifies a complete aspect; the whole concept that has a nourishing potential.

Ragout See stew.

Sauerbraten See pot roast.

Shepherd's pie denotes simple, basic sustenance.

Steak tartare advises against willfully ingesting potentially harmful ideas; risky behavior.

Stew stands for anxiety; worry.

Meat Products

Blood sausage signifies the ingestion of a negative aspect.

Chipped beef stands for a tendency to criticize; nagging.

Frankfurter See hot dog.

Headcheese signifies the use of life elements having little nourishing value.

Kielbasa See sausage.

Knockwurst See sausage.

Liverwurst denotes a life factor that serves to energize or motivate others.

Pastrami exemplifies a condition, concept, or other element that elicits a more than mild emotional response.

Pemmican means personal energy or high wisdom.

Pepperoni refers to an interesting or personally provocative idea.

Prosciutto refers to an involvement in a personally interesting issue.

Salami depicts an interesting aspect to an issue.

Sausage denotes a concise concept; a situation or plan that has been given every conceivable consideration.

Spam (food) refers to a mix of secondary benefits.

Vienna sausage See hors d'oeuvres.

see also
• Livestock *p. 19*
• Marine Fish *p. 38*

Snacks & Nibbles

Animal cracker indicates a respect for life.

Bar (energy) means a recognition of those life elements that are capable of boosting one's perseverance.

Black olive suggests uniqueness; the more rare elements of life.

Bread and butter means one's livelihood; that which provides basic needs.

Corn chip signifies the small benefits/blessings one gains throughout daily life.

Corn dog pertains to the multiple benefits of efforts.

Dip (food) connotes a personal choice.

French toast relates to a life aspect that carries added benefits.

Fritter connotes a breaking-down process; a fragmenting.

Hash browns represent an important, basic factor in life.

Nacho connotes a wide range of personal expression.

Omelet connotes aspects connected to something with which the dreamer is directly associated. May signify a mixing up or blending of elements regarding a perspective, relationship, situation, event, etc.

Popcorn relates to a specific aspect of an idea; developed and full-blown elements.

Popcorn balls stand for a concept containing all its associative aspects.

Popper (appetizer) represents a taste for interesting ideas; a draw to adventurous experiences and opportunities.

Popper (popcorn) applies to a life element capable of developing ideas.

Potato chip portrays alternative forms of a basic need; various methods and manners of obtaining an essential aspect in one's life.

Potato skin relates to the most potent aspect of an issue; the place from which the greater number of benefits will be derived.

Pretzel refers to a twisted perception or thought process. This symbol may signify one's emotional or mental state and relate to a relationship, life situation, or even a specific belief system.

Saltine See cracker (food).

Scrambled eggs represent a mix of new ideas; a confused beginning.

Toast (bread) alludes to a difficult yet nourishing life element.

Trail mix (food) signifies an opportunity for rejuvenation.

Waffle depicts indecision; vacillation; evasiveness.

Potato chip depicts life's essentials.

Fish & Seafood

Brine shrimp show individual spiritual concepts or beliefs.

Calamari warns against the intake of too many spiritual concepts at one time.

Caviar means spiritual arrogance; a spiritually egotistical individual.

Prawn See shrimp.

Scampi See shrimp.

Seafood represents spiritual knowledge or nourishment. Recall the condition of the seafood. What type was it?

Shellfish relate to an attempt to absorb as many spiritual aspects as possible.

Shrimp symbolizes the absorption of refined spiritual aspects.

Shrimp cocktail shows a tendency to keep spiritual connotations throughout one's daily interactions.

Dairy Foods

Blue cheese stands for spiritual nourishment.

Cheese signifies those aspects of one's everyday life that are complete, full.

Cheese spread denotes a false impression (assumption) that an element has a wholeness or completeness; an element that's a lesser substitute for something greater.

Cottage cheese implies wholesome perspectives and attitudes.

Cream (dairy) portrays the quality of richness to one's life. This, of course, does not refer to monetary aspects.

Cream cheese illustrates a smoothly consistent and wholesome life aspect.

Curd shows rich rewards and nourishment through effort.

Dairy alludes to nourishment.

Egg implies the formation of new ideas; beginning perceptions.

Egg white defines the extraneous aspects of a situation, belief, or perception.

Egg yolk defines the basic foundation of an idea or perception.

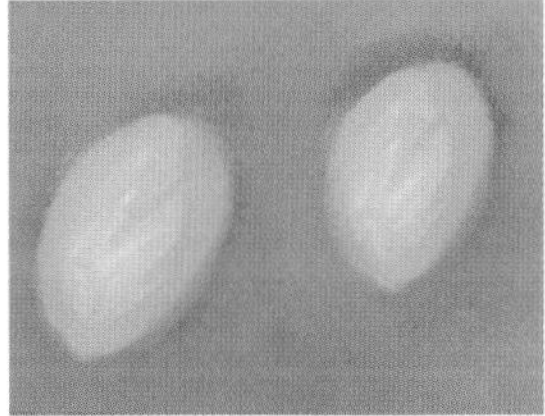

Egg indicates original thoughts.

Goat cheese represents a strong sense of purpose; a wholesome knowing of oneself.

Heavy cream signifies a blessing rich in extended benefits.

Mozzarella is an abundance of nourishing factors in one's life.

Ricotta (cheese) portrays a nourishing life aspect that creates recurring benefits.

Sour cream relates to the duality of having a best-case situation and yet of the situation possessing a problematic element.

Whipping cream refers to the frosting-on-the-cake type of meaning; unexpected benefits; additional benefits over and above what was expected or anticipated.

Yogurt relates to a type of healthful element in one's life.

Yolk (egg) See egg yolk.

Soup & Sandwiches

Alphabet soup advises of a mix of ideas; an aspect that has become confused by too many nonessential elements.
Bisque (soup) connotes a hearty constitution; a strong, earthy personality.
Bouillabaisse illustrates spiritual diversity; a broad base of spiritual concepts from which one can learn.
Bouillon (soup) stands for clarity in understanding.
Broth denotes clarity.
Chowder (clam) See clam chowder.
Clam chowder signifies rich and valued spiritual concepts that are utilized.
Club sandwich refers to multilayered or multifaceted aspects to a concept, situation, or perception one holds.
Consommé exemplifies the rewards and benefits of clear perspectives. Also see bouillon.
Duck soup means something easily accomplished.
Gazpacho suggests mental and emotional nourishment.
Hoagie See submarine sandwich.
Minestrone corresponds with diverse information or conglomerate issues.
Open-faced (sandwich) suggests a concentrated effort of awareness for information gained/about to be taken in.
Pea soup pertains to a cloudy view; an unclear perspective.
Sandwich constitutes a boxed-in feeling; a situation, relationship, or belief that creates a confining effect.
Soup represents a nourishing aspect generated from multiple elements.
Soup of the day signifies an offered choice.
Submarine sandwich reveals an unrecognized benefit in life.

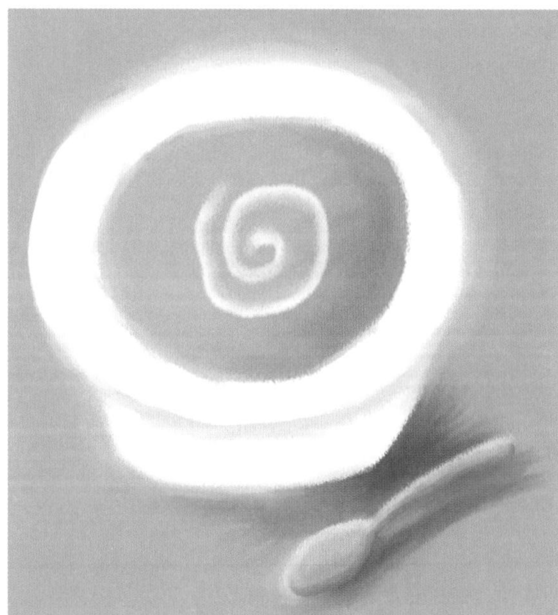

Pea soup connotes confused thinking regarding a certain situation.

Cookies & Crackers

Butter cookie represents a touch of sweetness to something in one's life; an unexpected blessing or pleasing element.
Butter cream See butter cookie.
Cookie pertains to life's small rewards.
Cracker (food) denotes small benefits or considerations.
Fortune cookie illustrates a desire for knowing one's future; anxiety over being the beneficiary of only good aspects in life.
Gingersnap typifies a calm that nourishes and restores one's emotional strength.
Graham cracker implies a positive experience bringing personal satisfaction.
Ladyfinger refers to a delicate or fragile situation.
Macaroon denotes a beneficial outcome generated by a rough time.
Soda cracker See cracker (food).
Tea cake indicates a light nourishing element in one's life.

Baked Goods

Bagel implies the ingestion or acceptance of a diversity of multicultural aspects.
Baguette (bread) pertains to life's basic necessities; the basics that sustain us.
Black bread signifies an element that provides robust nourishment.
Bread represents aspects that sustain us; necessities in life.
Bread stick represents the convenience or handy opportunities one often overlooks.
Brioche suggests light nourishment.
Brown bread typifies a down-home nature.
Corn bread represents nourishment through personal efforts.
Corn pone See corn bread.
Croissant defines beginnings rich in spiritual factors.
Crust alludes to the harder aspects of life that precede one's smoother and more palatable path.
Dough emphasizes the beginnings of specific aspects coming together; a period that precedes ultimate physical manifestation.
English muffin implies a start to a twofold purpose.
Flatbread See unleavened.
Kaiser roll suggests big issues that one attempts to take on or ingest.
Pumpernickel See rye.
Quick bread implies a quick fix to a problem that won't necessarily hold or suffice.
Scone portrays an essential piece of information.
Sourdough implies unlimited benefits stemming from a singular source.
Sourdough starter stands for an ongoing, regenerating wealth of benefits.
Starter (bread) See sourdough starter.
Unleavened implies that fundamental aspects have been unaffected by extraneous elements.

see also
• Digestion *p. 99*
• Eating & Drinking *p. 173*

Desserts & Puddings

Ambrosia warns that the quick and most appealing solutions are not always the right ones.
Apple pie signifies aspects one most closely identifies with as representing hearth and home. This almost always comes as a call to never lose sight of the importance of those closest to us.
Baklava depicts those sweeter life aspects that come quite naturally to one.
Banana split denotes one's inner goodness that is frequently enhanced by other expressions of one's talents.
Cheesecake suggests a rich reward; well-deserved outcomes.
Christmas pudding See plum pudding.
Cobbler symbolizes well-deserved rewards.
Compote suggests a mix of multiple benefits.
Cone See ice-cream cone.
Cruller (pastry) portrays an inflated and twisted perspective.
Custard alludes to the richly nourishing inner rewards of applying one's spirituality.
Dessert means the ingestion of something sweet after a meal. This is different from eating a sweet anytime. In this context, dessert refers to the rewards received in life for one's efforts applied to one's path; a rewarding benefit from the ingestion of new information or thought spent on an idea.
Ice cream indicates the intake of spiritual aspects that one doesn't externalize.
Ice-cream cone implies spiritual aspects carried around but not shared with others.
Ice-cream sandwich connotes spirituality that is hidden by physical or material aspects.
Jell-O implies anxiety; nervousness.
Mousse applies to superficial factors in one's life.
Parfait applies to a variety of spiritual concepts that are combined in a very confusing manner.
Pastry relates a perception of high value, something sweet. This would be associated with an individual's unique personal perspective and not necessarily be a true indication. Recall what the pastry was and what condition it was in. Was it dripping with honey? Was it stale? Underbaked? Coated with sugar? Refer to other types of pastry confections listed in this book.
Pastry shell refers to an unexpected and initially unrecognized benefit in one's life.
Patty shell See pastry shell.
Pie represents a benefit; the sweet fruit of an effort made.
Plum pudding signifies satisfaction, usually resulting from a success or accomplishment.
Pudding refers to an easy aspect.
Sherbet (frozen) applies to a desire to have fewer responsibilities in life.
Tart (pastry) See pie.
Topping represents the frosting-on-the-cake kind of symbology, thereby indicating a final element for a specific event or issue.
Turnover (pastry) implies a desirable benefit.

Cakes

Devil's food cake refers to pleasures one thinks one does not deserve.

Angel food cake signifies the ingestion of spiritual fluff.
Black Forest cake pertains to the richness of spiritual talents—the wealth of knowledge and potential; the dispelling of some spiritual mysteries.
Brownie pertains to those life aspects one views as personal treats.
Cake pertains to a goal or that which is strived for.
Coffee cake denotes nourishment through energizing pauses of respite.
Cream puff advises of something in the dreamer's life that's still in excellent condition. This usually comes to bolster feelings of inferiority or counter feelings of inadequacy.
Crumbles (confection topping) suggests the importance of the smallest element of an aspect; no element of something going to waste.
Cupcake signifies the generous giving of oneself.
Danish (pastry) means a benefit that manifests right after a decision is made.
Devil's food cake connotes rewards or joys one feels unworthy of receiving or enjoying; unjustified guilt.
Doughnut pertains to idle time.
Éclair relates to a lack of self-control.
Frosting may indicate a cover-up, or it may refer to an aspect that constitutes a final action that makes matters better or worse.
Fruitcake signifies a lack of logic and reason.
Gingerbread constitutes a nourishing factor that serves to settle temporary emotional upsets.
Icing See frosting.
Jelly roll connotes a frivolous, impassive personality.
Marble cake pertains to an achieved goal that will hold its strength and form for a long time.
Muffin represents small security factors in one's life.
Pound cake reflects a positive element that possesses a concentration of multiple benefits.
Shortbread/cake implies a source of energy.
Streusel signifies the topping (final touch) to something.
Wedding cake denotes celebratory sharing.

Candy & Confection

Bar (candy) relates to taking the time to recognize and enjoy the sweet aspects of life.
Bark See chocolate.
Bonbon See candy.
Breath mint reveals a need to freshen one's inner drive. Points to staleness.
Brittle See peanut brittle.
Bubble gum illustrates an arrogance in the face of negatives; a foolish attitude.
Candy pertains to the sweet aspects of life; the joys and blessings.
Candy apple signifies a negative element that neutralizes a positive one; nothing lost, nothing gained.
Candy cane points to the quality of familial relationships.
Caramel denotes the little joys in life that are worked for and savored for a time.
Caramel apple refers to a benefit carrying an extra measure of bonus. It can mean a sweet deal.
Carob identifies the substitutes that are available for us to utilize; alternatives. This applies to being innovative in respect to making do when first choices are not available.
Chocolate indicates questionable pleasures; temporary enjoyments that may bring negative effects.
Confection exemplifies an aspect perceived as sweet or desirable; little life aspects to which we treat ourselves.
Cotton candy refers to simple pleasures derived from life.
Easter egg portrays a colored or decorated perception.
Fudge applies to hedging; gray areas.
Glaze equates to the frosting on the cake; a final word, behavior, or event that tops everything that has gone before.

Candy represents life's pleasures.

Gum indicates a need to chew something over; a lack of understanding.
Gumball exemplifies a difficult concept, idea, or situation.
Gumdrop advises of a need to ponder something. This something is a temporary situation that only requires a bit more thought before it's resolved (dissolved).
Hard candy represents a lasting benefit. May indicate a particularly sweet idea one needs to mull over.
Honeycomb illustrates bountiful benefits or rewards.
Jelly beans refer to the small blessings in life one frequently overlooks.
Lemon drop signifies thought applied to a currently troublesome issue/situation.
Licorice connotes mobility; a motivational factor.
Lifesaver (candy) will literally make an implication of something needed to save a situation or reputation. It will denote a lifesaving aspect for the dreamer. Note the color.
Lollipop See sucker (candy).
Marzipan denotes an unrecognized benefit or reward; a positive aspect in disguise.
Meringue reveals a deceptive surface appearance or cover; a fluffy presentation or representation of a more serious issue.
Peanut brittle pertains to a temporarily difficult situation.
Penny candy points to the small enjoyments one can glean from life; the little things.
Petit four represents life's small aspects that serve as benefits or little treats (blessings).
Popsicle stands for personally altered spiritual perspectives that have been adjusted to one's specific taste.
Praline corresponds to a benefit that one perceives as being sweet and emotionally nourishing.
Red Hots (candy) stand for a motivational aspect.
Rock candy signifies an issue requiring deep contemplation or thorough analysis.
Sour ball connotes a distasteful situation that one voluntarily accepts and plans to carry through to its conclusion.
Spun sugar See cotton candy.
Sucker (candy) applies to an easily manipulated individual. Depending on other related aspects to the dream, this symbol can also point to a benefit that's long-lasting.
Taffy symbolizes difficulties in life; situations where one needs to pull oneself up and persevere.
Toffee typifies a difficult aspect to accept.
Truffle is personal comfort.
Wafer connotes an acceptable form or more utilitarian configuration of a specific life element with which one needs to be associated.

Cooking Techniques

Barbecue represents a burning thought or attitude.
Charbroil See barbecue.
Flambé connotes an intensely nutritional aspect. This will imply an emotional factor.
Poached is bringing something to fruition by gentle methods.
Preheat means groundwork.
Puree refers to discernment.
Sauté is the need for contemplation; deep thought.
Self-basting refers to an inner awareness to maintain smooth relationships.
Soft-boiled means unfinished.
Stir-fry advises the need to ensure an item is completed.
Stone-ground refers to a natural method of achieving ends.

Pancakes

Crepe (pancake) pertains to fragile beginnings.
Flapjack See pancake.
Griddle cake See pancake.
Hotcake See pancake.
Pancake implies that something has a flat quality. This will refer to a personal element in one's life, usually related to self-expression.

see also
• Mouth *p. 100*
• Continents, Countries & Regions *p. 372*

International Dishes

Chili beans indicate aspects that one sometimes adds to already-heated situations.
Chop suey warns of one's tendency to mix concepts; a habit of getting things wrong. Will advise one to listen harder and focus on the facts.
Dumpling signifies a nourishing aspect or one that relates to a sweet reward or benefit.
Egg roll stands for several individual aspects that are enveloped by a larger, all-encompassing one.
Enchilada typifies life aspects that serve to provide one or more of an individual's preferred methods of relaxation; a manner of experiencing enjoyment.
Fondue signifies warm emotional responses; congeniality.
French fry connotes shortcuts; life aspects that have time-saving qualities.
Hummus represents a simple benefit; a nutrient.
Irish stew symbolizes basic, foundational nourishment.
Lasagna represents a multilevel relationship or situation. Could also refer to some type of concept one is absorbing.
Macaroni See pasta.
Manicotti See pasta.
Noodle See pasta.
Pasta constitutes a substantial or basic element in one's life.
Pilaf (rice) denotes an essential or basic element in one's life.
Pizza indicates multiple opportunities forthcoming.
Primavera (food) pertains to multiple benefits.
Quiche refers to an unproductive effort; an insignificant aspect.
Refried beans stand for the suggestion to reanalyze something; look at it again.
Shish kebab alludes to multiple nourishing elements in life.
Soufflé reflects a delicate plan; the fragile execution of it.
Spaghetti exemplifies an ability to absorb complexities.
Tamale characterizes excitability; high emotions.
Tempura suggests an issue that's been covered up before being exposed/presented to others.
Yorkshire pudding refers to a lighter substitute for a heavier, more nourishing element.

Soufflé represents a flimsy project that is difficult to carry out.

Leftovers

Drippings relate to leftover aspects of something that could be useful in other ways at a later date.
Giblets refer to utilization. They tend to come to the dreamer as a warning message to make use of the whole aspect of something. This generally carries a specific meaning or interpretation for each individual dreamer.
Gristle constitutes a disbelief; skepticism; something hard to believe.
Peel See rind.
Pith stands for the elemental essence of something.
Shuck See husk.

Food Preservation

Additive designates something not of pure form. This symbol could also be pointing to a need to include surrounding factors when making decisions or formulating beliefs.
Dehydration (of food) indicates foresight. It may also refer to the preservation of blessings.
Freeze-dried is one of many dream symbols that implies a need to quickly preserve something in the dreamer's life.
Perishables will signify a situation or issue that needs immediate attention before it is no longer viable.

Taste & Smell

Acrid See bitter.
Aftertaste denotes secondary thoughts on an issue.
Bitter is something distasteful; something painful to take.
Food smell refers to the meaning of the specific food.
Mild signifies something that's readily accepted; palatable.
Rancid means an element in one's life has turned out bad.
Semisweet symbolizes a dual nature to something.
Sour indicates a distasteful situation to endure; a hard-to-take or hard-to-accept situation.
Tart See sour.

Hunger & Thirst

Famished cautions of an aspect in the dreamer's life that is being starved. The surrounding details in the dreamscape usually clarify what this means.
Hunger constitutes an inner need; a personal requirement that needs fulfillment before one can proceed along the pathway.
Pie-eyed indicates an intoxicated condition. This usually refers to a sober mental or emotional state rather than to a drunken state.
Ravenous denotes a seemingly insatiable interest in or desire for something.
Thirst means an inner need or void. Exposes a drive or desire.
Unquenchable See thirst.

Drink

Alcohol abuse denotes a need for one to face problems.
Alcoholic beverage symbolizes a need to relax.
Aperitifs refer to the lack of good nutrition.
Beverage is a life element that has the potential of fulfillment; quenching a thirst; satisfying an emptiness; some kind of refreshment.
Booze See alcoholic beverage.
Cappuccino connotes personal motivations that are enriched by generosity.
Cocoa portrays a life aspect that soothes.
Coffee stands for persevering energy; that which enriches one's motivations.

Tea represents a restorative force.

Coffee beans depict the freshness of renewed energy. It may refer to sparked motivation in one's life.
Coffee grounds signify the negative aspects one leaves behind after one has been reenergized.
Decaffeinated implies a lessening of one's motivation, energy, or interest.
Espresso illustrates rich and nourishing spiritual concepts; conceptual depth. Also suggests strengthened energies; reinforced motivation or perseverance in a particular situation.
Green tea represents a significant benefit.
Highball See alcoholic beverage.
Hooch See alcoholic beverage.
Hot toddy See alcoholic beverage.
Irish coffee exemplifies a life aspect that has the capability of providing balance.
Juice represents an easing factor in life.
Liqueur See alcoholic beverage.
Liquor See alcoholic beverage.
Mixed drink See alcoholic beverage.
Nightcap implies the existence of unresolved problems.
Posset See alcoholic beverage.
Punch (drink) suggests something unexpected; a surprising event.
Snifter implies an intention to ignore or divert awareness from responsibility or reality.
Sour mash suggests an easy-going personality.
Tea is representative of healing strength in one's life.

Milk

Acidophilus milk signifies the need to digest information better.
Buttermilk alludes to life's spiritually rich rewards.
Coconut milk characterizes a life aspect that provides rich lessons or rewards.
Condensed milk pertains to rich nourishment.
Evaporated milk signifies a life aspect that is capable of providing the dreamer with a highly concentrated dose of nourishment. This may be emotional, mental, physical, or spiritual.
Ice milk is representative of a refusal to gain spiritual nourishment; a reluctance to admit to that which one involuntarily gains.
Malted milk implies a needed nourishing aspect that has to be enhanced to make it palatable.
Milk connotes immaturity, or it may also apply to some type of essential nourishment. Recall the surrounding dream details to help to clarify this symbol.
Milk (chocolate) alludes to a sweetened perspective. It may specifically refer to a sugar-coating being done.
Milk (goat) points to a perspective cluttered with extraneous elements.
Milk (soy) refers to a perspective generated by self-serving aspects. It may also refer to the rich benefits to one's life that truth can bring.
Milk shake implies willful immaturity and the enjoyment of same.
Skim milk illustrates a nourishing aspect in life that could have been more beneficial.

Drinking

Bender exposes a desire to escape reality; a call to take responsibility or expand one's capacity for acceptance or tolerance.
Cider press reflects quality rest time; tranquility.
Draft (drawn liquid) implies one's act of drawing on inner reserves of energy; fortitude.
Drunken (state) warns of overindulgence; an escape from reality and one's responsibility to same.
Wineglass represents a specific new idea that has full potential.
Wine tasting is representative of the sampling of new ideas in one's life.

Beer & Cider

Apple cider See cider (apple).
Applejack See alcoholic beverage.
Beer See alcoholic beverage.
Bock beer symbolizes a strong constitution; strong beginnings.
Brew (beer) See alcoholic beverage.
Cider (apple) represents an aspect that contributes to one's time of respite or reflection.
Home brew denotes creativity and inventiveness; self-sufficiency.
Lager See alcoholic beverage.
Malt (ale) See alcoholic beverage.
Mead See alcoholic beverage.
Six-pack See alcoholic beverage.

see also
• Food & Drink Industry *p. 261*
• Bars *p. 382*

Wines, Spirits & Cocktails

Absinthe means a self-imposed bitterness in one's life.
Bourbon See alcoholic beverage.
Brandy See alcoholic beverage.
Cabernet See wine.
Chablis See wine.
Champagne See alcoholic beverage.
Chartreuse portrays an inner joy through healing.
Claret See wine.
Cocktail See alcoholic beverage.
Cold duck See alcoholic beverage.
Cordial See alcoholic beverage.
Corn whiskey See sour mash (drink).
Daiquiri See alcoholic beverage.
Eggnog symbolizes a rich or nourishing concept, plan, or idea.
Gimlet (drink) See alcoholic beverage.
Gin (drink) See alcoholic beverage.
Kava represents duality; positive and negative aspects of one thing.
Madeira See wine.
Margarita See alcoholic beverage.
Martini See alcoholic beverage.
Merlot See wine.
Mint julep See alcoholic beverage.
Moonshine See alcoholic beverage.
Muscatel See alcoholic beverage.
Piña colada See alcoholic beverage.
Pink lady See alcoholic beverage.
Port See wine.
Rosé See wine.
Rum See alcoholic beverage.
Sarsaparilla symbolizes innocence.
Schnapps See alcoholic beverage.
Screwdriver (drink type) See alcoholic beverage.
Sherry See wine.
Sloe gin See alcoholic beverage.
Swizzle See alcoholic beverage.
Whiskey See alcoholic beverage.
Wine denotes fully developed ideas; a healthy, full-bodied element in one's life.

Wine symbolizes well-rounded, flourishing concepts or components of life.

Mixers, Soft Drinks & Water

Orangeade symbolizes assistance one has rendered or accepted.

Bottled water (designer) signifies a general tendency to follow trends. This symbol will point to falling for false claims.
Club soda See soda water.
Cream soda illustrates a rewarding or beneficial aspect in one's life.
Ginger ale refers to a soothing factor; a calming aspect.
Grenadine typifies a personality smothered in false sweetness.
Ice-cream soda implies an effervescence to one's spirituality that is not demonstrated to others.
Ice water suggests the intake of spiritual concepts that are a blend of those that are understood and those that need contemplating. This is a good dreamscape fragment.
Limeade symbolizes the ingestion of a bitter aspect; having to accept a negative element.
Mineral water illustrates essentials in life; things that are basic and without extraneous facets.
Orangeade is representative of aid that one has given or received.
Pop (soda) See soft drink.
Root beer See soft drink.
Seltzer See soda water.
Soda See soft drink.
Soda fountain applies to available choices in life.
Soda pop See soft drink.
Soda water emphasizes spiritual elation.
Soft drink refers to a tasteful and personally satisfying element.
Sorbet See juice.

Abstinence

Abstinence suggests the need for one to stop doing something in life; self-control or self-denial.
Calorie counting signifies an effort to bring greater balance into one's life.
Carb counting is indicative of self-restraint.
12-step (AA program) is representative of courageous efforts to get one's life under control and for one to make improvements.

Fast Food

Burger See hamburger.
Fast food means nourishment: not necessarily unhealthy but certainly urgently needed.
Fish fry is taking care of things.
Food court represents a source of multiple opportunities for emotional nourishment.
Greasy spoon implies questionable aspects in one's life.
Hamburger is questionable nourishment; an aspect one depends on for support that may not be positive.
Hot dog refers to skill; having something covered.
Supersize (food portion) denotes a psychological need for abundance. This need stems from a need to ensure one has enough of something.

Utensils

Metate suggests a more basic or simpler way of accomplishing something.
Pan represents a tool available to bring something to fruition or completion in life.
Paring knife will suggest a need to pare down something in one's life. Associative dream aspects will usually pinpoint this issue.
Pasta fork is representative of a desire to stop an issue becoming a sticky one or prevent it becoming confusing by keeping all the elements separate.
Roasting pan stands for a method or opportunity to accomplish something or the vehicle through which it can be accomplished.
Soupspoon suggests an opportunity to help oneself to a beneficial resource.
Spoon typifies that which one spoons out to others or that which one takes in.

Meals

Blue plate (special) refers to one's specific spiritual foundation; a special element of that foundation or belief system.
Carryout refers to shortcuts.
Cookout See barbecue.
Haute cuisine implies extravagant methods of nourishment. It suggests one is reaching for nourishment that is highly regarded without realizing that the most beneficial nourishment comes from the simplest and most basic sources.
Meals-on-wheels represents the presence of people around you who are more than willing to give support.
Meal ticket reveals a dependency on others to provide for oneself.
Menu emphasizes one's multiple opportunities to gain inner nourishment.
Potlatch indicates an unconditional sharing of one's personal talents or gifts.
Square meal illustrates well-rounded nourishment; a fulfilling aspect.

Miscellaneous

Caffeine denotes motivational factors that serve as an impetus in life.
Corn-fed relates to inner strength; healthy perspectives.
Food bank represents inner strength; stored nourishment or energy.
Food chain advises one to do deeper thinking about how everything is interrelated or how one act of behavior can affect so many different elements.
Food service cautions against accepting any type of nourishment offered rather than choosing for oneself.
Fountain (drinking) signifies spiritual refreshment.
Freezer burn reveals a situation, idea, plan, or other personal element in one's life has been put on hold for too long.
Fruit basket signifies a gift of one's talents; a bountiful benefit received or given.
Greasy calls for increased watchfulness: an issue isn't as assured as assumed.
Grits connote unwilling acceptance.
Gruel reveals an unproductive factor; a false nourishment.
Harvest home signifies the inner joy felt when one helps others.
Hot potato points out an extremely touchy aspect that everyone would like to avoid.
Inedible warns of something that shouldn't be intellectually ingested; a concept that is negative; a preposterous idea.
Loaf (shape) usually implies a type of inner benefit or nourishment.
Morsel is representative of a small amount. This may appear to be a negative symbol, yet a morsel is still something that may be just a beginning.
Mouthful calls for a need for the mind to be focused when communicating with others. Saying a mouthful can sometimes be hazardous to one's health.
Mouthwatering alludes to a desire to be satisfied with a certain communication.
Near beer indicates a factor in one's life that verges on being negative; getting close to being a potentially destructive aspect.
Potable relates to an acceptable element in one's life which could refer to an idea, concept, action, plan, or direction.
Potpie connotes multiple benefits contained in one source; various elements contributing to a single nourishing source.
Produce (edibles) denote nourishing life elements. See specific type.
Small potatoes correspond to ineffectiveness or inconsequential aspects.
Sour grapes allude to denial.
Stale denotes a worn-out issue or attitude; a need to explore new concepts or to veer onto a new and different path.
Unripe reveals a situation or plan that needs more effort applied for further development.
Zwieback applies to an attitude of indifference to the difficulties one needs to face in life.

Chapter 29

Objects & Attributes

The inanimate objects in our dreams may seem somewhat inconsequential and not worth noting; however, they hold a prime placement by providing greater clarification to the overall meaning.

Tools

Adze represents personal energy expended on required work. Advises against the taking of shortcuts and various energy-saving methods.
Aerial ladder refers to the reaching for higher thought or loftier meanings to life.
Anvil indicates a need to reconfigure a life aspect. May be associated with the dreamer or someone the dreamer is acquainted with.
Auger cautions one to dig down for more information. May also point to the issue of one's emotions—to be more open and expressive.
Awl pertains to the presence of deceit; situations or relationships that are full of holes.
Ax warns of trouble ahead along one's path; an abrupt ending in the offing.
Ball cock cautions against not taking personal responsibility in the regulation of one's spiritual quest for the truth.
Bit (tool) corresponds to an effective aid in accomplishing a goal.
Bolt denotes strength of connections. This may relate to relationships or ideas.
Bolt cutter alludes to cutting strong ties.
Box cutter refers to a dislike for being boxed in. Also may point to an individual with a tendency to think outside the box.
Brush See specific type. Generally warns of a tendency to brush things aside; a habit of avoiding priorities or serious aspects. May point to a need to straighten out some type of confusion.
Caliper signifies a desire for perfection; accuracy. May come as an advisement to give greater attention to this.
Chisel refers to advancement by way of self-discovery; perseverance. Represents a life tool to use for taking one thing at a time.
Chuck (tool) See key.
Clamp (artery) points to a warning regarding one's physical condition.
Clamp (engine hose) refers to a need to seal off some type of destructive behavior.
Clamp (utility tool) comes as an advisement to become more serious; clamp down and straighten up.
Claw hammer indicates the duality of one's ability to secure something in life or take it apart.
Coupling (tool) stands for connecting elements.
Crimp (tool) symbolizes an attempt to shorten or pinch something into a shorter time frame.
Crowbar indicates a forced aspect.
Cutout (die) See die cut (model).
Deflector corresponds with one's protective measures.
Die cut (model) stands for the original from which replicas are formed. This symbol warns against a desire or tendency to imitate others. A die may also indicate a situation that cannot be altered.
Dolly (wheeled tool) represents a life aspect that serves as a support of help; a life factor that eases our way.
Drag (weighted implement) signifies the act of smoothing out; passing through life and leaving a smoother trail for those who follow the same path.
Dropper portrays a life aspect that serves to regulate the controlled measurement or quantity of something; a controlling aspect.
Funnel suggests a need to slow one's intake of knowledge in order to assimilate more. Indicates a need for better comprehension.
Gaff See hook.
Hand tools represent personal efforts geared to one's unique style of creativity.
Hook alludes to certainty; security; a secure aspect.
Ice ax connotes an attempt to chip away to regain one's formerly ignored spirituality.
Jack (tool) denotes a life aspect that has the capability of easing one's burdens or lifting some of the weight.
Jimmy See crowbar.
Joystick indicates controlling factors; an opportunity to be in control.
Level (tool) denotes stability and balance; a desire for same.
Lever corresponds with an advantage.
Mallet signifies a life aspect utilized for the purpose of getting something started; an instigating agent.
Meat hook denotes an aggressive nature; intrusiveness.
Miner's pick See pickax.
Monkey wrench usually warns of a disruptive aspect in one's life, perhaps even one's own behavior.
Oilcan signifies a means to lessen life irritations and rough relationships.
Oilstone See whetstone.
Pick (tool) corresponds to an aspect that allows one to get at something.
Pickax indicates a determination to understand (unearth) something; a desire to get to the bottom of an issue.
Pincers indicates a tight aspect in one's life. This may refer to another individual, relationship, business deal, personal situation, or belief. Recall who was using the pincers. What was being pinched?
Pipe cutter correlates to a precise move that results in a precision cut (severance). This is for the purpose of preparing oneself for a newly aligned connection.
Pipe threader represents an attempt to make a precise connection.
Pipe wrench illustrates the effort expended to maintain information integrity.
Plane (tool) illustrates a leveling out of something or a smoothing intent.
Pliers refer to a situation where one attempts to pry something out before it's ready to come naturally. This is a clear warning not to "force" things in life.
Pliers (needle-nose) stands for an attempt to grab hold of a fine detail.
Plumb (weight) represents a balancing or equalizing element; a straightening out.
Plumber's snake alludes to that which is capable of removing problematic elements.
Plumb line connotes an attempt to keep an element in one's life straight and true.

see also
• Construction *p. 311*
• Tools *p. 395*

Tools (continued)

Poker (tool) See andiron.
Prism refers to an individual advisement to view an element from all angles.
Quill stands for protective methods. It may refer to means of self-preservation.
Ramrod signifies a forcing action.
Rasp (file) indicates a need to smooth out something in one's life.
Ratchet (tool) signifies an opportunity to make adjustments in one's life.
Ream (tool) constitutes a need to clear out or broaden an aspect in one's life.
Router (tool) reveals a way through a current troublesome problem or difficulty.
Sandpaper See sander.
Saw represents the capability to cut through a problematic aspect in life.
Scissors denote a permanent separation. Recall their color. Were they used to cut something? If so, what was it?
Scraper reveals a need to clear away extraneous elements that cloud or cover basic aspects.
Screw (tool) usually refers to an injustice or bad deal.
Screwdriver signifies pressures in life. These may refer to self-induced pressures or problems. Recall who was holding the tool. Was it being used to unscrew something? This would mean a lessening of pressure.
Setscrew suggests an attempt to stabilize an issue/situation.
Sextant portrays a desire to understand one's personal relationship with spiritual elements in one's life.
Siphon denotes an advisement to rid oneself of extraneous spiritual elements.
Skewer is representative of a very dangerous or negative element about to appear in one's life. Recall what was on the skewer. Who was holding it?
Skid (tool) is representative of something that eases one's burden; something that serves to make advancement/movement easier.
Staple gun relates to a quick fix for something.
Strop advised of a need to sharpen one's perception.
Sump pump signifies a need to rid oneself of negative or erroneous spiritual beliefs or perceptions.
Tire iron See crowbar.
Tongs portray an aid in comprehension. They can mean something that provides greater understanding; a grasp on things.
Vise (tool) illustrates an advisement for the dreamer to get a firm grip on something. May also indicate building pressure or stress.
Whetstone is representative of a life element that will help to sharpen one's skills or understanding.
Wire brush exemplifies a heavy cleaning or the act of scraping away unwanted elements in one's life.
Wire cutters caution against severing a supportive element in one's life.
Wood splitter connotes an aid for maintaining one's preparedness.
Wrench warns against using force to accomplish a goal or closure.
Yardstick indicates a gauge of one's progression along one's life path.

Power Tools

Air hammer symbolizes nagging and harping. It may refer to a repetitive commenting on the same issue.
Band saw means cutting remarks or deeds within a relationship.
Blowtorch relates to a need to make either connections or separations in life. The surrounding dream elements will clarify which interpretation the symbol is intending.
Buzz saw See circular saw.
Chain saw represents the utilization of natural aspects to cut through problematic elements in life.
Circular saw expresses a need to quickly and cleanly cut through an aspect in one's life.
Coping saw stands for tools used to plan and carve out one's personally designed path.
Drill denotes thoroughness in aspects of learning.
Drill bit exemplifies the wide variety of learning tools that are available.
Drill press typifies those life aspects that improve the accuracy/efficiency of the learning process.
Jackhammer symbolizes an individual's hard shell; a need to break open the hardened barrier behind which one has hidden for too long.
Jaws of Life will correspond with a life aspect that can extricate one from a serious problem or situation.
Jigsaw denotes a need to cut corners; be clear about the shape of a situation.
Lathe relates to a life aspect that has the capability of accurately shaping or defining one's self-expression or goals.
Rotor (device) relates to a balanced perspective.
Rototiller stands for a cultivation of one's natural talents.
Sander (tool) applies to a life element that has the capability of smoothing over a rough aspect.
Voltmeter suggests a need to monitor one's energy output. This indicates a vacillation due to selective discrimination.
Winch implies an uplifting element in one's life that pulls us out of emotionally mired situations.

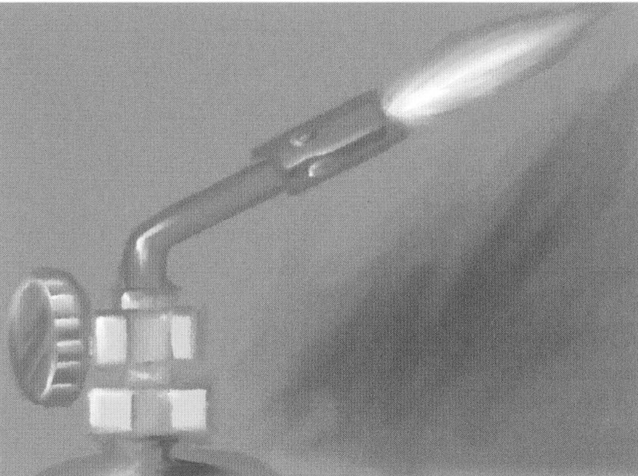

Blowtorch may indicate that the dreamer needs to detach from another.

Machinery

Air cleaner naturally stands for a need to clean (clear) the air. This symbol indicates the current presence of a misunderstanding or bad feelings.

Air conditioner represents cool or cold attitudes; insensitivity. May indicate a call to cool down a hot temper or angry attitude.

Air filter refers to the need to filter new ideas instead of letting them flood in and overwhelm. May also be indicating the opposite, that some issues are being altered by being run through one's personal perspective instead of being looked at in their entirety.

Aspirator warns of a need to clear out a congested mind, situation, or relationship.

Ball bearing connotes an easier, smoother method of operation.

Boiler (furnace) exemplifies hot situations or relationships in one's life.

Air conditioner suggests a bad atmosphere needs to be dealt with.

Buffing wheel stands for that which allows one to finalize goals.

Cog portrays a vitally important part of an aspect of one's life.

Coil may refer to the act of going in circles, or it may come to the dreamer to warn of the dangerous situation of coiling up as an internal spring, indicating inner tension and stress.

Hoist symbolizes a life factor that has the capability of uplifting the dreamer.

Mainspring relates to that which has the power; the energizing factor.

Manifold suggests the existence of multiple outlets or solutions.

Mechanical pertains to a lack of thought or personal input. This symbol could also stand for a lack of emotional responsiveness.

Piston represents the energy required to maintain momentum or keep something going.

Pulley indicates energy reserves; a supportive or assisting element.

Punch press defines a need to make a strong impression, stance, or statement.

Sewing machine is representative of a tool and/or opportunity that can be used to correct a severed situation or relationship that has fallen apart.

Vending machine refers to easy and convenient access to a want or need.

Farm & Garden Tools

Aerator connotes a need for less intense mental concentration applied to an issue.

Bale hook is an aid in handling heavy issues, such as understanding or patience.

Combine (machine) stands for several tasks being handled by a single aspect or solution.

Hay fork connotes a tool that helps us accomplish a goal.

Pitchfork See hay fork.

Posthole digger (tool) refers to one's intention to support or separate oneself from something/someone.

Pruning shears relate to a need to cut back on something; trim down excesses.

Scythe pertains to cutting through life's excesses or unnecessary aspects.

Shears See scissors.

Shovel connotes an individual's overindulgance. May refer to intake or output aspects.

Sickle pertains to an opportunity to rid oneself of extraneous aspects; cutting down on the unnecessary elements.

Spade See shovel.

Marine Equipment

Anchor comes to the individual dreamer as a warning to get spiritually grounded. Depending on the surrounding dreamscape factors, this symbol could also indicate a need to pull up the anchor and move away from a false conceptual belief system.

Ark is synonymous with compassion and generosity.

Diving bell alludes to a fear of losing one's grounded aspects during a personal spiritual search.

Gangplank indicates a way or path.

Moor See anchor.

Oar represents great personal efforts and suffering being endured while on one's spiritual path.

Paddle See oar.

Periscope advises one to give more attention to daily life rather than keeping self-immersed in spiritual matters. Spirituality needs to be interwoven in daily affairs in the way of one's ongoing behavior, not kept separate.

see also
• Ship's Anatomy *p. 304*
• Farming *p. 379*

General Equipment

Acetylene tank advises of a good situation in one's life that has the potential to turn explosive.
Apparatus (equipment) stands for life aspects that serve as tools or even opportunities one can utilize.
Balance wheel denotes a stabilizing aspect or influence.
Battery (cell) depicts reserve energy. This cautions against using up most of one's energy before something is accomplished.
Bellows indicate a requirement for more air; a need to remove oneself from some aspect in life that's suffocating.
Benchmark depicts an ultimate example or sample of something.
Chain means interconnected aspects; relevancy.
Counterweight represents an element that gives balance to an issue or situation.
Diffuser connotes a lessening of intensity; an aspect that serves to disperse effects rather than condense them; a softening element.
Drafting board advises one to sketch out plans. This would represent a certain need to do this before any actual action is taken.
Drawing board suggests plans, planning, or perhaps a need to refigure something.
Extension (ladder) comes as an advisement that one could be reaching higher.
Knee pad indicates planning; good preparations done, in other words, foresight.
Ladder denotes an opportunity for upward progression to be made.

Ladder stands for progress.

Locker relates to one's most private aspects.
Mat (pad) denotes an insulating quality or a means of protection.
Oil pan defines efficiency; an ability to cover all aspects of an issue.
Oxygen tank suggests one's anticipation of a suffocating situation or encounter; a preparation for an expected claustrophobic reaction.
Pellet stove defines an inefficient method of accomplishing something.
Pipeline symbolizes the connective link that runs from the past through the present to the future.
Range finder symbolizes one's personal priority to follow one's path; keeping an eye to the lay of the land before one.
Safety net suggests insecurity. It may specifically refer to a lack of self-confidence or a reluctance to take risks.
Sawhorse refers to a life aspect of the dreamer that has the capability of aiding efforts to resolve problems and carry out plans.
Tubing stands for extensions. It may also refer to some kind of a connecting element.

Agricultural Equipment

Branding iron is representative of possessiveness. It can also mean personal identification of something.
Bridle denotes a means of control.
Cart See wheelbarrow.
Cattle prod is representative of procrastination or a reluctance to go about one's business.
Chicken wire portrays how one fences oneself in when there is a lack of courage, faith, or perseverance.
Prod (device) comes in dreams as a life element that has the potential to serve as a motivational or energy-building impetus. Recall who was using the prod.
Quirt stands for a motivational factor in a particular situation.
Saddle defines personal control of one's journey through life. Recall the saddle's appearance. Was it plain? Heavily tooled? Worn or new?
Saddlebag denotes that which we carry with us on our life journey. Recall the bag's color and condition. Was it full? With what?
Saddle blanket typifies a symbol that gives an indication of what one's attitude is toward one's path.
Wheelbarrow stands for burdens shouldered. Recall what was in the dream wheelbarrow and who was pushing or using it.
Whip relates to a motivational source in one's life.
Yoke (crossbar) exemplifies a burden.

Weight

Deadweight comes to the dreamer as a caution of a need to unload the negative aspects he or she carries around that tend to slow down or prevent advancement or growth.
Heavy implies an intense or profound burden in one's life. The surrounding details will help to clarify which meaning is intended.
Lead weight equates to a heavy burden. This may refer to guilt or a current responsibility.
Sandbag warns of a spiritual withdrawal; an effort to keep the waters of one's spirituality back.
Top-heavy reveals the presence of an imbalanced state.
Weights pertain to burdens, some that have been willfully taken on.

Weapons

Arrow pertains to a swiftly traveled course one experiences in one's life.
Arrowhead illustrates the beginning of one's course.
Blowgun See blowpipe.
Blowpipe cautions against a dangerous individual or situation that has appeared in one's everyday life.
Flamethrower warns against directing uncontrolled emotions at others.

Quantity & Size

Allotment See ration.

Bottomless signifies a great depth to something or someone.

Brim depicts a full capacity; a life aspect that has been fully developed or explored. Was something full to the brim?

Compact (size) signifies something that's condensed; efficient; convenient.

Double-sized refers to twice the amount of something.

Empty connotes a lack or void.

Empty-handed brings the message of nothing given, nothing received.

Enlargement calls attention to something the dreamer needs to be made more aware of.

Exponent is additional elements associated with an issue.

Fragment See fraction.

Full (capacity) represents a condition that has reached its ultimate state.

Half (of something) implies more to be obtained; one doesn't have the all of it yet.

Half-and-half connotes a tempered situation or attitude.

Infinitesimal is a symbol that comes to remind us that everything, no matter how small it may seem, has importance in life—there's reason for its existence.

Infinity (sign) represents continuum, an ongoing situation, conceptual belief, or relationship. This refers to an element that will be present throughout one's life.

King-size denotes a revealed measurement or quantity of something in the dreamer's life. This usually points out the fact that this something is much larger than currently being perceived. Surrounding dreamscape details will clarify.

Lid (quantity) implies something that's within legal bounds.

Little (size) will denote a small amount of something but usually will also indicate greater importance.

Match (pair/likeness) suggests compatibility; equality.

Mote (size) corresponds to the presence or existence of something in one's life. This usually refers to an idea, belief, or emotion that is still alive.

Outnumbered implies that your plan, idea, or behavior is not shared by the majority. This is not necessarily a negative symbol. It may denote innovativeness and individuality.

Overfilled (glass/bowl) reveals one's inability to comprehend all that is taken in; much will be missed. This symbol is likened to the message of biting off more than one can chew.

Overloaded warns against taking on too much; approaching burnout.

Overstocked suggests that it's time to use one's talents to benefit others; time to share.

Overstuffed indicates a lack of acceptance; an inability to take one moment at a time.

Infinity represents something that will be with one for the whole of one's existence.

Pair may suggest duality, or it may imply a close connection between two elements in one's life.

Paltry may seem to suggest insignificance, but it usually indicates a personally held perspective of grandeur that is not being realized. This is a caution to lower one's inflated self-image.

Queen-size is representative of a larger than average portion of something.

Quota comes to the dreamer as a warning against attempting to force quantity rather than focusing on quality.

Ration comes in dreams to advise of a need to monitor one's use of a specific element. Suggests overextension or a need for moderation.

Roman numerals will give emphasis to the meaning of the number displayed. Refer to specific number for further clarification.

Smidgen stands for a very small amount of something; a trace.

Stack represents an amount of work to be done.

Trace (amount) indicates a hint of something; a subliminal presence.

Trifold reveals three separate aspects to something.

Triplicate reminds one that a specific piece of information needs to go to three separate individuals.

Twin-size is representative of singular. This usually points to the idea that one has to go it alone for a time or already is.

Unlimited points to endless potential/possibilities. The sky's the limit.

see also
• Design *p. 308*
• Styles & Attributes *p. 418*

Appearance

Adornment represents one's outward presentation of oneself; a public persona; an external enhancement.
Anomaly refers to a deviation from the norm of one's circles throughout life or of repeating the same mistakes.
Asymmetrical suggests a balance is required.
Blank refers to lack of thought or ideas.
Bulge pertains to a need to release something, usually pressure. May refer to emotions that are building up inside.
Cross-legged is representative of insecurities; of reluctance to share aspects of oneself.
Daintiness (mannerism) suggests fragile sensitivities; a need to get one's hands dirty or to toughen up.
Disjointed stands for a lack of continuity.
Disproportionate means unbalanced; perceptual irregularity.
Embellishment may not refer to exaggerations but rather to the addition of elements that better clarify, explain, or describe an issue.
Encroachment alludes to some type of infringement being done.
Extreme makeover is representative of a caution against trying to be something you're not; an advisement to like your own beingness; a warning to stop placing appearances at the top of your priority list.
Full-size reveals accurate proportions. This may indicate that the dreamer is either exaggerating or belittling something.
Glamorized warns against downplaying negative aspects.
High relief denotes an aspect in one's life that stands out and should be noticed or acted upon.
Inverted suggests to the dreamer a misinterpretation or misunderstanding; one has something backward or upside down.
Leaning (propensity) indicates a near-decision.
Linear stands for an alignment of some type. May possibly point to a time when no advancement is being made, usually for a reason.
Lopsided typifies a dream symbol that means slanted opinions or perceptions.
Miniature will usually refer to compact knowledge; a great amount of information or power located within an unexpected source.
Overrated pertains to an attempt to greatly enhance something.
Proportion comes as a symbol taking multiple forms and usually will reveal proper life priorities. Something may be out of balance in the dreamer's life.
Protrusion is representative of a loose end that needs to be handled.
Ravishing represents a highly attractive situation, idea, or individual.
Short connotes a concise element. May also indicate a need to expand some aspect in one's life.
Symmetry portrays balance.
Tilted represents to the dreamer a slanted perspective or foundational premise.

Designs & Shapes

Out of round is representative of something that has gone askew.

Clamshell warns of broken promises or secrets told. May indicate betrayal.
Crisscross relates to a return to some aspect in one's life.
Curlicue (design) suggests a flamboyant characteristic.
Dotted line suggests a need for an agreement. Indicates a time to own up to an attitude or participation in something.
Globe portrays earthly matters that need attention. Frequently this will imply a more broad-scope view of something.
Hexagram (star) signifies wisdom, particularly spiritual wisdom.
Hoop denotes a completed aspect; coming full circle into one's life.
Maltese cross indicates a specialized spiritual belief based on an ancient sect.
Nodule represents an irregularity. Recall surrounding dreamscape details for further clarity.
Out of round reveals something amiss; has become misshapen.
Pellet alludes to an element in one's life that contains multiple aspects.
Pinhole relates to an element without cohesive substance.
Ratio will illustrate priorities. Recall this symbol as accurately as possible, for it may suggest the proper ratio or it may have portrayed your current set of priorities.
Rosette (design) signifies a positive attitude/intention.
Round most often denotes completeness or coming full circle, but it is also a behavior that takes one in circles.
Saw-toothed implies an aggressive approach.
Segmented denotes a multi-faceted element in one's life.
Serpentine (configuration) denotes a winding life path.
Serrated See saw-toothed.
Slice will symbolize a fragment of a greater element in one's life; a sample or piece.
Sliver illustrates a fragment (negative element) that has the potential to pierce and become an irritant.
Sphere implies completion.
Spiral pertains to the interrelated aspects in one's life.
Square (configuration) denotes rigidness; narrow-mindedness.
Stencil denotes an example; a template to follow.
Wheel (design) represents completion; full circle; closure.

Condition

Cordoned alludes to an attempt at protective measures; an attempt at distancing.

Corrosion stands for the deterioration of something in one's life.

Corrugated refers to a time frame consisting of rough roads; difficulties ahead.

Creaky stands for something that's outmoded or has been ignored for too long.

Damp indicates the presence of an additional aspect to something in the dreamer's life.

Defective illustrates a flawed aspect in one's life. Surrounding dreamscape factors will usually clarify this for the dreamer.

Dense exemplifies thick or compact. This is usually meant to advise one to clear out or give air to some life aspect.

Dislocation connotes a conceptual or emotional lack of alignment.

Disorientation advises of one's lack of direction or place; confusion.

Dormant refers to underlying emotions or attitudes that affect behavior.

Double-edged signifies an aspect that has two interpretations or purposes.

Double-parked advises against being impulsive or hasty.

Double-spaced is a call to slow down and understand more; that clarity is needed.

Embedded refers to a hidden or absorbed element; camouflage.

Entrenched signifies a hunkered-down mode; full involvement.

Face-down (position) represents hidden aspects.

Flawed refers to shortcomings.

Foamy (consistency) refers to a life aspect that serves to soften or insulate.

Foolproof defines solidness; no possibility for error.

Frothy refers to mental, emotional, or spiritual confusion.

Full-blown defines something in the dreamer's life that cannot be developed or advanced beyond its present state.

Full-scale indicates total effort applied; strong determination.

Generic means all-inclusive; common; nonspecific. This would usually be a message to express one's individuality more often.

Half-baked signifies a premature aspect; an undeveloped idea or plan.

Half-mast reveals sorrow.

Hand-me-down refers to a highly useful aspect in one's life.

Hard (consistency) usually implies a difficult, unyielding, harsh, or insensitive aspect.

Hollow (space) illustrates a lack of depth; a shallow attitude or concept.

Immersion indicates a totality; a saturation; complete belief.

Imperfection may remind us that nothing is absolutely perfect in this world, or it could reveal an error in one's behavior, situation, or perspective. Recall surrounding dream details for further clarification.

Kink implies a problem or setback.

Knee-deep stands for a situation of being heavily involved.

Limp (flimsy) reveals a lack of inner strength; a defeatist.

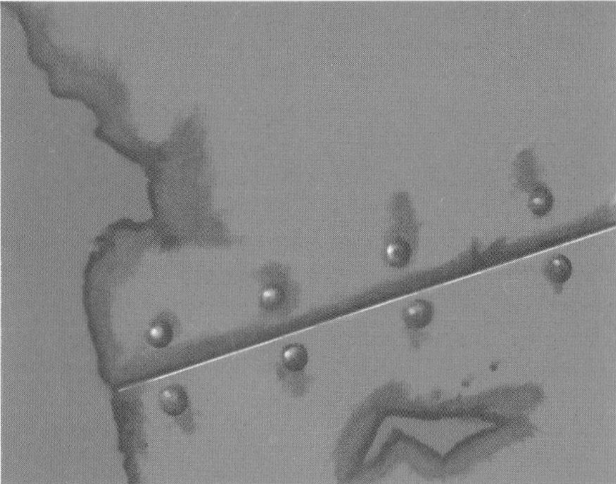

Corrosion represents the disintegration of an element of the dreamer's life.

Lodged implies a temporarily immovable situation; a time of inaction or neutrality.

Loose usually refers to extra room or leeway.

Lumpiness denotes multiple inconsistencies.

Makeshift reveals clear innovativeness; self-reliance.

Mashed exemplifies a destroyed factor in one's life; something that is not capable of being reconstituted.

Mess (condition) alludes to a state of near-total confusion. This most often refers to mental and emotional factors.

Mired pertains to the condition of being overwhelmed; bogged down.

Misfiled connotes a need for heightened awareness; concentrated attention required.

Mismatched reveals incompatibility; unsuitability.

Mutilated refers to something destroyed beyond recognition; the destruction of integrity.

Neutralized signifies a negation of power.

Nullified will pinpoint an unproductive aspect, thereby saving the dreamer time and effort expended on a path or purpose that is superficial and unproductive to a goal.

Off (position) defines a condition or state of affairs. This symbol may indicate a need to turn something on.

Off and on connotes a vacillation; an intermittent effort or attention.

On (position) symbolizes a current state of affairs regarding one's personal life. It may indicate a right on perspective, or it may warn of a need to turn an attitude or emotion off. Surrounding dreamscape factors will clarify which is intended.

Overbalanced connotes overcompensation.

Overexposure signifies redundancy; overkill; beating an issue to death.

Overgrazed reveals a situation or relationship that gave all it could. It's time to move on.

Overgrown will apply to a lack of interest or care given to a personal talent or inherent ability.

see also
• Creation *p. 172*
• Industry *p. 278*

Condition (continued)

Perforated will reveal an aspect in one's life that is not complete or is lacking continuity. May indicate a deception of some type.
Poached (stolen) applies to something obtained through ill-gotten methods.
Prefabricated indicates that certain elements of an issue or situation have been assembled in preparation for the composite completion.
Preshrunk alludes to a time-tested element.
Prewashed stands for a desire to maintain a state unaffected by impurities or foreign elements.
Pristine (condition) will usually denote an element that is well cared for, well preserved, or perhaps cherished.
Prorated pertains to equality; balance.
Ragged edge stands for something left unfinished in life.
Ramshackle illustrates something that's been poorly constructed, devised, or executed.
Retardation alludes to a comprehension inability, most often self-imposed.
Rickety (condition) warns of an unstable and/or precarious situation.
Saturated emphasizes a fullness or a level that has reached capacity. Recall what was saturated. What was the liquid? Water? Blood? Oil?
Scuffed defines wear; perseverance and fortitude.
Seepage exposes an insecure situation or piece of information. This symbol may also reveal the fact that some form of private information is leaking to another; possible betrayal.
Shallow signifies surface aspects; a lack of depth.
Shambles symbolize ruination; the destruction of something in one's life.
Shriveled denotes a loss of energy and vitality. This may be a positive sign, depending on the surrounding dream details.
Slipshod signifies poor quality; carelessness.
Smashed stands for a destroyed element.
Smoldering warns of a volatile situation; an explosive element ready to blow.
Sodden See soak.
Soggy See soak.
Somnolent See drowsy.
Spaciousness applies to unrecognized freedom for self-discovery.
Spoilage relates to inattention given a specific issue or life element.
Stipulation reveals a condition associated with something.
Stripped-down relates to the existence of essential elements only.
Submerged See immersion.
Substandard exposes behavior or qualities that do not meet acceptable levels.
Unfinished (condition/state) connotes a call to finish what was begun.
Uprooted pertains to a disconnection or disassociation. May refer to personal relationships or a plan, or it may connote an actual geographical relocation forthcoming.
Upside-down exposes a misconception or idea that isn't perceived correctly.

Paper & Packaging

Birthday gift relates to recognition of another's accomplishments in life.
Bow (ribbon) connotes finality; a finished aspect in one's life.
Box (container) warns of a boxed-in condition, situation, or relationship. Individuals can also box themselves in. May point to concepts and perspectives within the proverbial box and come as an advisement to think outside that box.
Bubble wrap suggests a protective measure; something needs special handling.
Bundle See package.
Butcher paper suggests attempts at concealment.
Candy wrapper represents recently experienced joys that shouldn't be so quickly forgotten.
Cardboard exemplifies insubstantial aspects in one's life; a superficial personality or relationship.
Carton refers to dual aspects; an aspect that contains some other aspect.
Confetti represents joyful celebration.
Fan (paper) suggests a gentle acceptance for a necessary heated-up phase.
Gift indicates an offering or an unexpected opportunity.
Manila paper depicts strong, firm communications.
Notebook suggests a need to recall details or keep a record of something.
Package applies to those material goods one perceives as being important in life. What was in the package? Was it gift-wrapped?
Packing (material) illustrates a need for protection. This implies that something in one's life needs to be handled in a delicate manner.
Pad (of paper) See notebook.
Paper usually refers to communication yet also has other interpretations depending on the specific type.
Papeterie represents mental organization; an efficient thought process.
Papier-mâché portrays what is done with information one receives. Recall what was formed from the paper—this will be the revealing element.
Papyrus corresponds with delicate information that requires careful discernment.
Parcel See package.
Parchment (paper) illustrates an authoritative message or source. Recall if the paper had writing on it.
Post-its (notes) stand for a need to remember something.
Present (gift) represents a benefit or offering. Recall what the gift was and who gave it.
Punch-out (paper) See cutout (paper).
Scratch pad See notebook.
Tissue paper represents a nonessential but pleasing added element to an issue.
Wastepaper reveals unnecessary elements in one's life. It's important to determine what these pieces of paper were.
Watermark denotes originality.
Wax paper connotes an airtight condition.
Wrapping paper denotes a hidden gift, a surprise, or perhaps a new idea soon to dawn or an enlightened attitude in the offing.

Quality

Absorbent signifies a need to take in something; a call for greater effort required for understanding.
All-purpose (product) will naturally point to an element in one's life that will serve multiple aspects.
Amorphous indicates an inability to bring thoughts together; indistinct thought; obscure perspective.
Best-case scenario stands for the best one can expect.
Borderline means a questionable aspect in one's life.
Colossus portrays something of great size.
Complementary will reveal an unexpected benefit.
Compressed indicates a lack of individuality.
Crisp connotes an aspect that's fresh yet fragile.
Custom-built indicates personalized attitudes; perception based on one's specialized database of knowledge.
Deep implies a considerable distance and will be associated with surrounding dreamscape elements.
Eclectic applies to the utilization of many varied aspects; using any available resource; the expression of one's unique totality.
Effervescent suggests high excitement over something.
Epic denotes an issue that is vastly detailed or complex.
Expansion signifies growth.
Expendable signifies a nonessential element.
Fireproof exemplifies a state or condition of being totally unaffected by another's intense emotional displays. This may also point to apathy.
Flushable suggests a disposable element; an advisement that something is safe to rid oneself of.
Fragile is a caution to tread lightly; handle something carefully.
Freestanding indicates independence; not needing supportive aspects.
Heavy-duty symbolizes strength, endurance.
Homegrown suggests an ability to make one's own way in life.
Homemade is representative of resourcefulness.
Imitation (objects) such as leather and fur convey a preferred aspect for one to utilize. However, if the object is something like food or original art pieces, then the message is to avoid these.
Indestructible advises of something in one's life that cannot be undone or gotten rid of; enduring strength and longevity.
Jagged edge implies a situation left with loose ends.
Knockoff stands for an attempt at imitation.
Lapsed refers to a voluntary omission of something from one's life.
Long (length) connotes a great measure of time or distance in association with a particular aspect in one's life.
Long-term emphasizes a commitment.
Low-level implies basics; a beginning phase.
Malleable symbolizes resiliency; someone with a flexible personality.
Misplaced alludes to there being a reason for temporarily being without something.
Murky denotes a lack of clarity; a confused issue or situation.
Nimbleness stands for tenacity; an ability to bounce back after a setback or after a disappointment.

Jagged edge indicates an aspect of life that still needs to be fully resolved.

Nonstick (surface) will symbolize an aspect in one's life that has the potential of easing one's way.
Novelty indicates a passing fancy; a temporary fad that usually pertains to a new and fascinating idea that proves to bare little substance when thoroughly analyzed.
Offbeat most often signifies thoughts/ideas that are considered outside the box.
Outgrowth alludes to a resulting effect or manifestation.
Paper-thin refers to weakness; having little substance.
Pliable may allude to acceptance or an easily manipulative personality. Recall surrounding dreamscape details for clarification.
Point (sharp end) suggests clarity.
Porous (surface/texture) correlates to gullibility; being easily manipulated.
Portable implies efficiency or convenience. May point to an idea or element that can be easily utilized in many areas.
Primo implies a most desired aspect; an excellent condition or situation.
Quick-set points to a speedy solidification of something; a final decision.
Rare (unique) portrays an uncommon element in life.
Ready-made may suggest a time-saving aspect, or it might advise of a need to devise something through one's own ideas or planning.
Receding alludes to a lessening or waning of something. If this was associated with water, the intent was associated with spirituality.

see also
• Characteristics *p. 138*
• Construction Features *p. 312*

Quality (continued)

Resonance denotes lasting strength.
Ripe refers to a matured situation, process, or other element ripe for development.
Roughcast illustrates a trail or experimental endeavor.
Rough cut pertains to a lack of finesse; something that is crude.
Rough-hewn reflects major efforts by one's own hands; a self-forged aspect.
Rustic exemplifies one's down-to-earth perspective and overall reasoning.
Scratch-proof portrays an aspect in one's life that is resistant to outside influence.
Seamless indicates an unbroken or complete element.
Sedentary is an advisement to expend greater efforts.
Self-sealing signifies an element that, by its very nature, will bring about closure.
Slack represents a waning of energy or motivation.
Slippery cautions one to watch one's step; be careful of one's footing.
Soft-core relates to a tempered approach to something.
Sparseness correlates to frugalness; lacking materialism.
Starkness portrays the bare elements of an issue.
Sterling portrays the highest quality for a specific characteristic or attitude.
Stiff portrays rigidness; an unyielding personality.
Stigma relates to a sign or mark revealing a specific quality or characteristic.
Styrofoam represents an insulating quality.
Suffused refers to thoroughness; something being interspersed throughout.
Tailor-made See custom-built.
Tame is representative of congeniality; neutrality or situational ease.
Taut can have opposing meanings depending on the dreamer's life situation. It can point to a situation/issue that is overextended or grossly belabored to the point of having no more elements to consider or explore. Or it can indicate that one still needs to deal with the slack (associated elements) of an issue. The latter refers to details remaining.
Tight See taut.
Top-shelf represents what one personally considers being the very best quality of a specific element; what one tends to reserve for special occasions or friends.
Transient (location/town) denotes a phase of one's path when an extra number of temporary contacts will be made.
Unbreakable most often refers to inner strength yet may relate to a relationship, agreement, or bond of some type.
Uncovered represents something that has been exposed or revealed.
Uncut stands for an element in its natural state.
Unfocused comes to advise of a need to center one's attention on the issue at hand. May indicate confusion or a lack of understanding.
Unglued is a call to regain composure; pull oneself together in order to better deal with or accept a situation.
Unhinged depicts a lack of control; loss of balance.
Unorganized implies a need to be methodical and efficient. Alludes to a disoriented thought process.
Unprepared suggests a lack of planning; no foresight.
Unsavory signifies a distasteful issue or situation.
Vintage (age designation) will stand for a specific time frame and perhaps represent outdated ideas. This symbol may also signify ideas confined to a specific attitude/perspective. Something can be vintage racist or McCarthyist.
Watered-down reveals waning spiritual strength or interest.
Water-repellent signifies a fear of being touched by spiritual aspects.
Watertight denotes spiritual confinement. The key here is to recall if the water (spiritual aspect) was kept out or retained.
Wispy represents an intuitive feeling; something one can't quite put a finger on.
Withered suggests a need for refreshing elements in one's life; a spiritual renewal or emotional uplift.

Feature

Backdrop warns against redesigning one's past or current reality.
Background illustrates underlying aspects in one's life that more attention should be given to.
Break (broken) points to the need to repair something in one's life. Surrounding dreamscape details should clarify what needs fixing.
Chink (gap) typifies faulty conclusions; a hole in one's perception or one's thought process.
Crack (hairline break) reveals the beginning sign of a possible failure; a hint that a problem is developing.
Cusp symbolizes crossroads or turning points in one's life.
Feature (main item) draws attention to an important life aspect that one may be overlooking or ignoring.
Foothold defines the attainment of a secure position.
Modifications exemplify an effort expended on improving something; alterations, usually for the better.
Offshoot exemplifies a resulting manifestation generated by something one has said or done; a ramification.
Seam (any type) denotes a joining element that may suggest a weak spot.
Shard exemplifies a hint, clue, or beginning insight; a fragment of an idea.
Split represents a breach or fragmentation; a separation of some type.
Tamperproof denotes a solid plan or idea.
Two-dimensional indicates a perspective lacking depth.
Two-edged connotes the duality of something having ramifications for oneself.
Waterproof pertains to spiritual apathy.

Heat & Fire

Back burner means something being kept on hold; that's not a top priority at this time.
Brush fire stands for a willful neglect or destruction of one's talents; a voluntary cessation of spiritual acts.
Extinguisher (fire) See fire extinguisher.
Fire alarm warns of dangers stemming from intense emotions.
Firebreak stands for stopgap methods one utilizes to control overemotional states.
Fire hose represents behavior or an element capable of stopping a situation from getting out of control.
Fire hydrant applies to an aid in calming emotionally distraught individuals or an emotionally intense situation
Fire line See firebreak.
Flammable (objects) implies a life aspect that has the potential to become explosive.
Hand warmer suggests a desire to stay prepared for hands-on work.
Heating pad advises of a need to reenergize oneself.
Heat-seeker will equate to a desire to have the latest gadgetry. Also points to someone who stays on top of issues; keeping current.
Hot water denotes a position of great difficulty.
Hydrant See fire hydrant.
Lighter means illuminating factors in life; motivators.
Lukewarm connotes a lack of enthusiasm.
Match (lighter) will indicate a potentially explosive aspect in one's life.
Overheated warns of a need to pull back and analyze something in a rational manner; emotions getting out of hand or getting the best of one.

Fire hose means action is curbed.

Puff (of smoke) alludes to the first indicator of forthcoming trouble with an aspect that surrounding dream elements will pinpoint.
Safety match illustrates a safeguard that prevents the use of potentially hazardous elements for the wrong purposes.
Soot exemplifies negative elements that have the capacity to contaminate oneself or one's life.
Spark may reflect inspiration, or it may warn of a dangerous situation, depending on the surrounding dreamscape details.
Tepid (temperature) signifies an attitude bordering on disinterest.
Tinder stands for a highly flammable aspect or situation; a volatile element.
Tinderbox points to a reasonably sizeable element in one's life that has the potential for igniting.
Watch fire comes to the dreamer as an attention-getting dream fragment. Recall the surrounding details for clarification. Location?

Ropes, Cords & Knots

Ball of twine alludes to the need to proceed cautiously. Closure for something can come easily if issues are handled slowly, otherwise entanglements will result.
Cord See rope.
Knot is a problem to untangle.
Lariat signifies an attempt to rope something in; to get a handle on it or secure it.
Lasso See lariat.
Lifeline signifies a life aspect that keeps one grounded; a facet that gives hope or acceptance.
Net alludes to entrapments; a method of catching another or not allowing anything to get by you.
Noose forewarns of harmful or disastrous outcomes if a current path is followed.
Restraints are representative of hindrances, usually self-made.
Retardant See restraints.
Rip cord constitutes a life-saving aspect in one's life.
Rope alludes to a helpful element in one's life; an aid.
Rope ladder See ladder.
Slipknot refers to an option for an out; alternative plans.
Square knot denotes a firm hold.
Tangled represents a complexity; a problematic situation; a lack of order.
Twine portrays a means of attaching, connecting, or tying something together; closure.

Solid Substances

Acetate (fabric/film) symbolizes strength gained from an outside source. This points to an element (or individual) that provides support and encouragement.
Grit illustrates irritations in life.
Mush (consistency) connotes unclear thoughts; confusion.
Powder (consistency) indicates a fine aspect. It may also represent a sifted element.
Residue alludes to that which is left behind; aftermaths. May refer to something left to attend to.
Wax typifies a pliable personality or plan.

Texture

Mash (pulpy mixture) represents an incomprehensible concept or situation.
Mushy (texture) points to inconsistency; an idea that's not based on firm elements; soft thinking.
Soft signifies gentleness.
Spongy (consistency) may imply resiliency, or it could indicate a lack of firm strength. Recall the dream's details for clarity.
Squishy (consistency) depicts indecision; a lack of solid opinions.
Stickiness pertains to a precarious situation or relationship.
Tacky (to the touch) implies a sticky situation or poor taste/quality.
Texture will portray a multitude of meanings. Refer to the specific type of texture.

see also
• Fire *p. 63*
• Liquid Actions *p. 166*

Furniture & Ornaments

Abstract (art) symbolizes confusion; skewed thinking.
Backrest depicts the necessary pauses along one's path.
Bar stool See high chair.
Bauble reflects an unimportant element; insignificance.
Birdcage stands for restrained thoughts; fear of extending one's thought process or doing further research. May also apply to emotional aspects.
Booster chair alludes to a need to see better on an issue. Better perspective is required.
Box spring relates to quality of rest times; quality of relaxation and a pause from the daily grind of life.
Confessional seat equates to confidentiality.
Crown jewel refers to one's greatest desire.
Diorama pertains to a visual example of something; a touchable and completely comprehensible presentation.
Footlocker will reveal one's personal priorities in life; keeping one's most important and basic elements close by.
Footrest advises of a need for a pause time; for a resting period from walking one's path; to reenergize oneself.
High chair represents an immaturity.
Library table suggests that more research/study is required.
Park bench stands for respite along the way; taking moments to appreciate what one has.
Pedestal comes as a warning against placing anything or anyone in a highly elevated position.
Plaque (decorative) will reveal an important element about someone. It will portray a little-known quality or characteristic.
Rack See shelf.
Sand chair reveals nonchalance bordering on apathy; a tendency to be completely comfortable with one's state of indecision.
Scepter indicates false authority, often spiritually related.
Scratching post signifies a need to deal with irritations so one can move on.
Sea chest portrays that which we carry with us on our spiritual search. This symbol could be revealing spiritual baggage or gems to hold onto. Surrounding dreamscape details will point to which was intended.
Shadow box (shelf) displays accumulated affectations and/or specific interests unique to the individual. What objects one places in a shadow box reveals much about one's character.
Shelf illustrates stored elements that may need to be set aside for a time. May reveal valuable aspects that need to be preserved.
Showpiece suggests an example of excellence.
Spittoon signifies a proper place for specific behavior.
Throne symbolizes a high position requiring respect and honor. This dream fragment may reflect the true level of an individual, or it may represent an arrogant perspective of oneself.
War chest signifies resources that have been reserved for a designated purpose.

Sticks & Supports

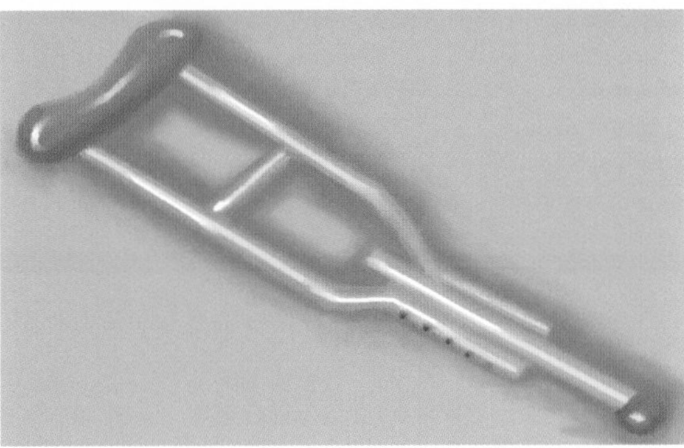

Crutch is representative of the need to be accountable for one's own actions.

Baton characterizes someone with an arrogant or egotistical personality.
Big stick denotes threats or a threatening situation or relationship. Could be associated with someone who feels insecure without it.
Cane See walking stick.
Crutch warns against the use of others as excuses for not taking personal responsibility. Acts as a message to stand on your own feet and utilize inner strength.
Mast See pole.
Pole (any type) pertains to a helpful aspect in one's life. The dreamer will make this personal association.
Prop may indicate a supportive factor or a type of personal crutch. Recall surrounding dreamscape details for clarification.
Reinforcement applies to extra support, strength, or endurance needed.
Ridgepole applies to an individual's personal shield or means of protective support.
Spike See stake (stick).
Staff (stave) See walking stick.
Stake (stick) denotes a marker or a support of some type.
Stick signifies an opportunity for self-expression that may be a positive or negative element depending on the dreamscape's related details.
Utility pole symbolizes a supportive element for communication or motivation depending on whether it was a telephone or power pole.
Walker (support) pertains to self-help methods serving one's progression.
Walking stick signifies a means of being independent.

Liquid Substances

Astringent signifies a severe personality. May relate to a need to calm one's ire.
Baby oil suggests protecting one's blossoming spirituality or new path.
Sealer See varnish.
Solution (liquid) will denote an answer stemming from multiple sources.
Varnish means a desire to finish an issue.

Arrangements

Alignment denotes the need to return to the course.
Alphabetical signifies order and priorities needed.
Bale stands for a need to open up. This may refer to one's thoughts, emotions, or finances.
Cluster connotes multiples of the same aspect, such as more than a couple adversaries or friends.
File (line) signifies a need to recognize one's place in life. This could indicate an arrogant personality or a call for more patience and acceptance.
Hodgepodge may have positive or negative interpretations. The negative intent would be a warning against believing in completely unrelated ideas that comprise a concept—in other words, inconsistencies and contradictions. The positive meaning would be an underscoring of one's accurate conceptual beliefs comprised of divergent aspects that interrelate.
Mock-up See model (prototype).
Model (prototype) portrays an intended plan.
Permutation See transmutation.
Prototype is representative of an initial sample of something that will follow; a model example.
Row (line) connotes the act of setting priorities and getting affairs or elements of an issue in line.
Sequential signifies a need to take one thing at a time.
Subdivided implies a need to break down an idea for the purpose of clarification or analysis.

Exercise & Sport

Back bend symbolizes energy expended to go the extra mile. In this sense, it may refer to an individual who has a tendency for going over and above what's necessary.
Base hit defines an action or a move that caused no negative ramifications in the individual dreamer's life.
Bobber (fishing) is usually representative of that which maintains the level of one's spiritual search or inquiry; holding one's spirituality at a steady level rather than raising it up or down depending on one's current mood or personal attitude.

Changes

Adjusting designates the need to make alterations, usually acceptance.
Alterations is representative of changes required.
Amendment is generally taken to mean that additions or changes are currently required in one's life.
Amends cautions one to make reparation.
Augmentation means an exaggeration; something added to the original.

Cleanliness

Bath salts bring a message to soften one's spiritual attitude.
Clean (anything) means attentiveness.
Clean sweep stands for an action that covered every single detail.
Debris signifies a need to clean up the remaining aspects of past actions.
Dirty usually means inattentiveness or lack of morals or ethics.
Grime reveals depression.
Immaculate (condition) usually denotes an exact perspective with nothing out of place or focus.
Saddle soap exemplifies care given to one's path; personal monitoring and maintenance of its quality.
Scum portrays that which lacks value. It also may refer to extraneous elements.
Smear (spot) relates to an undefined aspect; something compromised or less clear.
Smudge (spot) refers to a marred or contaminated element; an unclear issue.
Spotless can denote a too-perfect condition or state.
Stain (spot) will most often illustrate a negative element in one's life. Recall what was stained. What color was it? What caused the stain?
Streak (mark) symbolizes a touch of a different element contained in a specific aspect.
Tainted indicates some type of contamination. This may be an offensive behavior or idea that carries a negative element.
Tarnished illustrates an inner or inherent ability left unused.
Unsanitary implies a very unhealthy condition or situation in one's life.

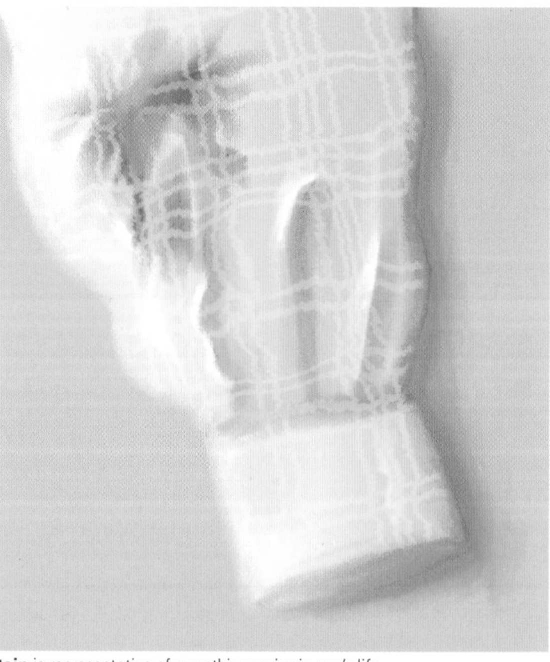

Stain is representative of something amiss in one's life.

see also
• Cleaning *p. 170*
• Luck *p. 199*

Personifications

Bar back characterizes one who can offer support.
Benchwarmer characterizes inaction yet preparedness for action.
Joker (card) is representative of humiliation.
Onlooker may exemplify those who watch. This may refer to one's higher self or conscience. Someone is always watching us.
Out-of-towner will most often point to someone who isn't familiar with a particular issue or concept.
Paper tiger stands for a false power; lacking authority or strength.
Pipe carrier symbolizes highly peaceful individuals. It may refer to those individuals who keep the sacredness of spirituality.

Movement & Location

Deceleration refers to a slowing down action. This dream symbol may also come as an actual advisement.
Decentralization calls for an admonition to stop being too focused, causing a myopic perspective. This dream symbol advises one to view things with a more opened eye, bringing a wider scope of information.
Disappearance illustrates an unexpected loss or departure.
Draft (pulling) signifies hard work; great efforts expended.
Dry run refers to practice; a need to test something out.
Juxtaposition advises of a need to compare different aspects. The surrounding dreamscape details will clarify what the dreamer needs to analyze in life.
Retrograde reflects a move downward and backward. This symbol usually advises one to go back to a former issue and perceive an element from a lower, closer angle.
Retrogression is representative of lost ground in respect to one's attained level of behavior, knowledge, or progression.
Vacation signifies the need to get away. This dream symbol may also denote a warning against being on vacation too long.

Charms

Amulet See charm.
Charm (object) exemplifies a lack of faith. It could also indicate someone with a superstitious personality.
Clover leaf (four leaves) See charm.
Curio exemplifies a life aspect that is of high interest to the dreamer.
Dream catcher signifies a desire to be shielded from the cause of one's fears. This isn't necessarily a good sign, because fears need to be faced and dealt with in order for them to stop being fears.
Keepsake applies to respect and honor felt for one's personal memories.

Beginning & Ending

Climax stands for the manifestation of long-sought goals; a dramatic or intense conclusion to something.
Closure doesn't mean forgive and forget, it means gaining acceptance and moving on.
Commencement means the beginning stage of applying what has been learned.
Conclusion refers to an ending.
Coup de grâce signifies an aspect that brings about finality; a fatal blow; an unexpected, shocking move.
Discontinued denotes a termination; no longer participating in an action.
Disintegration defines absolute finality.
Dismissal may stand for the shedding of a particular element of an issue, or it can point to denial, lack of acceptance.
Last (enduring) implies a perpetual state; something will remain unchanged.
Limit implies boundaries or restrictions.
Limitless relates to total freedom; permission to go or reach as far as possible.
Loose end corresponds to something left unfinished.
Resolution pertains to determination; a promise; a new rule.
Soluble connotes the capability and possibility of being ended or concluded.
Square one connotes the beginning point.
Termination will signify the end of something.
Walk-through (final inspection) refers to the last chance to make an objection to something in one's life.
Wreckage reveals a destructive end or conclusion.

Media

Art usually signifies creativity or a personal type of imaginative expression.
Art film represents experimental thought. This dream symbol is often presented to the dreamer to make him or her think deeper on a particular issue.
Cassette represents something important that the dreamer needs to hear.
Centerfold (magazine) depicts a position of prominence for the purpose of gaining the widest range of exposure and attention.
Classified ad serves as a guide for the dreamer. This specific dream symbol will lead one to that which is sought or else will indicate that which one needs to give to others to enhance their lives.
Comic book connotes a manner of escape from life; unrealistic perceptions; a hesitancy to face reality.
Indelible (ink) symbolizes that which cannot be altered, reversed, or undone.
Pinup won't necessarily indicate an erotic connotation but usually represents that which one admires or is attracted to in life. This dream symbol may also point to a distraction.
Poster will represent a message of some type. It may also reveal a personal interest or attraction.

Text & Books

Abstract (text) See summary.
Abstracting journal refers to the main points of various, specific issues; highlights.
Acceptance letter (received) denotes a go-ahead for one's plan. This go-ahead normally comes from one's conscience or higher self.
Addendum means something additional must be included in a situation or relationship. May reveal the presence of extenuating aspects associated with something.
Address book refers to the quality of friends and associates. Check its condition for greater clarity.
Admission ticket connotes one's right to participate in something.
Advertisement cautions one to look closer at a situation.
Almanac cautions one to check facts. Further research is needed.
Anthology indicates the variety of philosophies in which one believes.
Appendix (listing) signifies the need to do further research.
Article (written) signifies the need for further in-depth study.
Autobiography represents shared experiences; a willing opening up of oneself.
Baby book refers to a desire to remember all the phases of one's spiritual journey.
Black book is representative of secrecy.
Black border/edging (on letter) represents very bad news.
Black envelope usually portends a death of some type.
Blank book stands for a lack of ideas; having no clue as to what's going on; having no solutions.

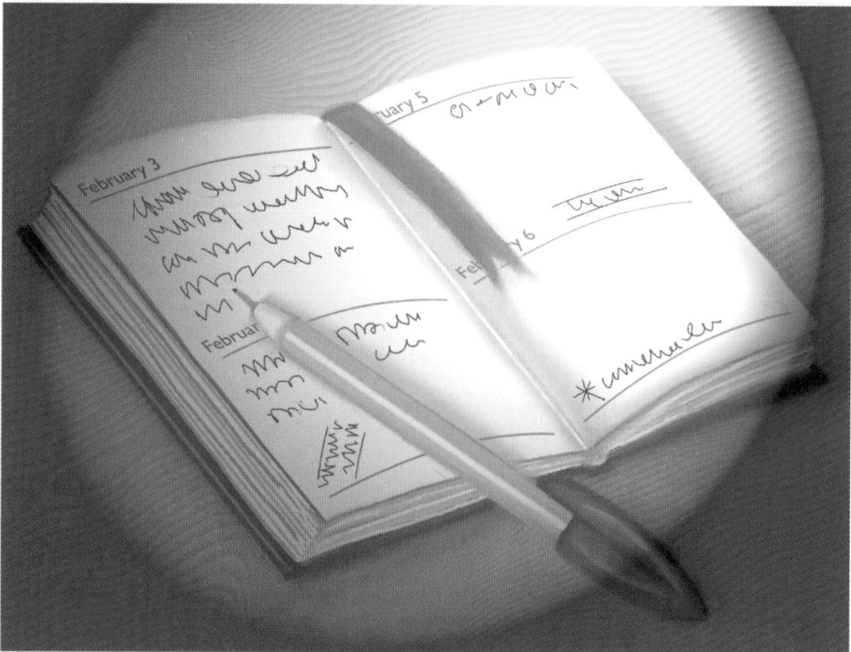

Diary is representative of the significance of one's memories of one's life.

Book cover/jacket refers to first impressions and reminds one not to make them the sole source of one's opinion.
Bookplate warns against an arrogance of knowledge; an intellectual possessiveness or aloofness.
Brochure indicates a hyped aspect; something that's portrayed in a glossy presentation.
Card catalog (library) alludes to order; an efficient and systematic way to maintain one's life.
Catalog illustrates the vast array of choices in life.
Certificate suggests a commendation for accomplishments or an official seal of legality. See specific type such as marriage license, divorce certificate, and death certificate.
Closed book suggests a person, situation, or concept that cannot be understood; something puzzling or too convoluted to analyze at this point.
Cover letter denotes an introduction or synopsis of a more detailed aspect.
Daybook advises of a need to be more time-efficient and attentive to responsibilities.
Dead letter advises the dreamer of certain failed communication attempts.
Diary connotes personal life accounts; the importance of remembering.
Dime novel alludes to unnecessary information; an intellectual waste of time.
Document (paper) signifies something recorded or official.
Draft (outline) connotes beginning plans.
Dream book signifies a source holding the keys to understanding and demystifying one's subconscious messages.
Dream dictionary stands for an opportunity to better understand oneself and one's life situations/relationships.
Dustcover (of book) is representative of measures that protect against an intrusion from negative or unnecessary aspects.
Dust jacket See dustcover.
Excerpt will refer to the sampling of an idea; getting an impression of what something is about.
Flyer See handbill.
Fly sheet See handbill.
Handbill represents the personal sharing of ideas; the tendency to broadcast one's thoughts, ideologies, or opinions.

see also
• Books & Text *p. 218*
• Buildings *p. 308*

Text & Books (continued)

Inscription comes as a warning or revealing message. Recall what was inscribed and what it was inscribed on in the dream context.

Journal may indicate a need to keep a journal, or it may reveal aspects happening in one's life that are being overlooked or not given enough attention to.

Label comes as a unique warning message for each dreamer. Recall what the label said.

Leaflet See brochure.

Letter implies correspondence needed. Frequently this will serve as a personal message for the dreamer.

Library card is representative of the easy availability of information without personal cost.

Library edition (book) will usually point to a popular title or subject, and the dream symbol may be pointing out an issue that is common knowledge.

Limited edition typifies something of higher value.

Log See journal; logbook.

Logbook advises of a need to keep a record of events.

Manual serves as a reference one relies on to double-check path progression. It may also refer to the need for analysis of one's direction.

Manuscript will most often connote an individual's private thoughts or detailed future plans. Recall who wrote the dream manuscript and what it was about. This can be an extremely revealing symbol about you or someone you know.

Old Farmer's Almanac stands for wisdom from nature; a natural, inherent wisdom.

Open book represents clarity; nothing hidden.

Pamphlet denotes information specific to the dreamer. Recall what type of pamphlet was presented. What did it say? What design, if any, was on it? What color was it? What condition was it in?

Postscript is representative of an afterthought and the need of the individual to express that afterthought.

Press run (book) reflects the extent to which a piece of information has been disseminated.

Query letter represents an initial presentation of an idea for the purpose of discovering another's possible interest.

Raffle ticket stands for a chance taken when an opportunity manifests. This dream symbol may also signify a goal that has very little potential for success.

Sealed book See closed book.

Season ticket represents planning ahead for the purpose of not missing elements of personal interest.

Summary will reveal a concise message that will mean something specific to the dreamer.

Voucher pertains to validation; reasons behind behavior.

White pages (phone book) denote the need to contact someone.

Yearbook alludes to a need to review or remember past relationships or experiences to facilitate learning from current life events.

Buildings & Structures

Awning symbolizes temporary spiritual shelter; a temporary spiritual respite.

Barricade means self-imposed blocks one places in the way of progress.

Barrier exemplifies a temporary pause for the dreamer. This may refer to various life aspects and won't necessarily imply an insurmountable obstacle.

Bench See specific type.

Birdbath is representative of the need for emotional or character cleansing. There's something in one's personality that needs attention or improvement.

Booby trap symbolizes a rigged situation or relationship; ulterior motives; a set-up.

Box seat means a high position; benefit of wealth or position.

Catwalk exemplifies ways to get around things; alternate routes. May also point to having a better perspective of things; an overall view.

Deadfall stands for unappreciated or unrecognized life aspects that serve to nourish. Points to positive aspects resulting from a seemingly negative event.

Deck (platform) represents improved perspectives; a better vantage point.

Drift fence See snow fence.

Drinking fountain indicates a source of basic nourishment. Recall its condition.

Duck blind is representative of a warning of deception; an ulterior motive; sneakiness.

Easement (power line) points to an acceptance of motivational elements.

Birdbath means a need to improve.

Floodgate pertains to personal controls that appropriately regulate one's spiritual intake.

Grillwork symbolizes effective defenses; protective measures that are strong without being able to be detected by others.

Guardrail refers to a life aspect that keeps one on course; protective measures applied to keeping one from overextending oneself or overstepping bounds.

Peephole indicates a hint associated with something the dreamer needs to know; a clue; insight.

Platform See stage.

Posthole pertains to preliminary preparations being done to apply supportive or separation efforts toward something. The purpose that the dream intends will usually be recognized by the dreamer.

Rail fence reflects the self-devised perimeters one sets.

Railing See handrail.

Turnstile cautions the dreamer to focus on a single aspect of something at a time; to slow his or her pace.

Glasses

Bifocal glasses See bifocals.
Bifocals indicate more than one perspective to any aspect; an ability to see both the surface and deeper levels.
Broken glasses denote an inability to adjust perspectives.
Contact lens See glasses (eye).
Cracked glasses indicate a fractured viewpoint.
Dirty glasses imply a perspective altered by negative attitudes.
Eyeglasses See glasses (eye).
Eyepiece See glasses (eye).
Foggy glasses refer to an unclear perspective.
Glasses (eye) refer to added aspects to one's sight (perceptual ability).
Granny glasses allude to a narrow view of things.
Greasy glasses signify perception altered by ulterior motives.
Heavily framed glasses denote a seriously obstructed perspective.
Lens signifies personal perception. The key is to recall the condition of the dream lens. Was it cracked? Clean or dirty? Was there coloration to it? If so, what color?

Sunglasses may indicate that the dreamer is an independent thinker.

Loupe suggests a need for closer inspection; deeper analysis is required.
Magnifying glass connotes closer inspection; deeper understanding.
Oversized glasses indicate a wide, comprehensive perspective.
Pitted glasses connote a perspective altered by hardships; cynicism.
Rimless glasses define an unobstructed view of things.
Rose-colored glasses apply to an overly optimistic perspective.
Safety glass(es) signifies a right perspective; a protected or guarded one.
Scope is representative of an in-depth look; closer attention to be given.
Scratched glasses are suggestive of a perspective that has been marred by personally damaging elements.
Scratch-resistant glasses indicate unaffected perspectives.
Shattered glasses pertain to fragmented perspectives.
Smeared glasses are representative of negative attitudes affecting the ability to clearly perceive.
Sunglasses denote a perspective resistant to popular opinion.
Thick glasses refer to major adjustments made to clearly perceive.
Tinted glasses portray a colored or slanted perspective.
Ultraviolet filter (lens) stands for a tendency/desire to keep spiritual elements out of daily issues.
Visual aids will denote life aspects that bring clarity to one's perception or one's comprehension.

Apparel & Accessories

Baby shoes signify baby steps one is taking along a path.
Back brace denotes a need for self-protective measures in respect to one's efforts expended. This dreamscape symbol may be pointing to the existence of a possibly harmful situation needing a "strong back" (endurance).
Badge signifies identity; a need to be identified or recognized. Sometimes will also mean a commendation of some type.
Bobby pin refers to keeping one's thoughts or attitudes in place instead of letting them become tangled or wildly windblown.
Cleat advises the dreamer of a need to get a better grip on one's path.
Dirty linen denotes misdeeds and the hidden facts of same.
Drawstring typifies personal choices and the presence of leeway in respect to how one follows up on those choices.
Half-slip pertains to something that's partially shielded. Usually refers to an aspect of one's personality.
Mask connotes hypocrisy. It may also reveal one's true character that is generally kept hidden.
Medal is a sign of encouragement or commendation from one's higher self or conscience.
Medallion stands for a self-confirming sign. It may refer to verification.
Medal of honor pertains to personal benefits; inner joy as a result of ethical or spiritual behavior.
Pom-pom (decoration) is representative of a cheerful personality. May refer to a reason to celebrate.
Veil emphasizes veiled thoughts; concealment of one's emotions or attitudes. May also point to a nebulous or cloudy idea or issue.

see also
• Eyes *p. 96*
• Jewelry *p. 411*

Containers

Barf bag will be associated with an awareness of a potential for experiencing a highly disagreeable situation.
Barrel means abundance.
Basket alludes to a need to gather more information.
Beaker applies to some aspect in the dreamer's life that needs precision blending.
Bell jar alludes to narrow-mindedness.
Bottle warns against keeping something bottled up inside.
Bucket denotes the retention of important spiritual truths. Recall the condition of the dreamscape bucket. Add to the interpretation the type of material it was made of. Was it dented? Did it have a hole? All these factors give added dimension toward clarity.
Bud vase signifies a personal pride and feeling of rightness in respect to one's new beginning.
Bushel indicates a large quantity of something. What was in the bushel?
Cache symbolizes the high value of one's hidden talents. This is most often a warning to stop stashing away one's abilities.
Caddy suggests a need to keep something in its proper place.
Can is a container. What the can contains determines the dream symbol's intent. See specific symbol entry words for a clearer meaning.
Canister (for food) represents basic necessities; the main ingredients that can be built on.
Carafe represents spiritual quality. What was the condition of the carafe? What did it contain?
Casket exemplifies life's precariousness; a reminder of our mortality.
Censer (incense vessel) stands for that which creates an affected atmosphere.
Chalice applies to one's spiritual aspects. This may not be a positive dream fragment, depending on the chalice's condition or color.
Coffer See cache.
Collection box See poor box.
Container suggests a need for containment. What was in the container? This symbol may also point to a need to release something that's been contained far too long.
Containment denotes a completely controlled situation; something that has no ability to spread or affect others, something that is no longer a problem. A resolution or solution has been found.
Cornucopia symbolizes one's inherent spiritual aspects and the wide variety of benefits resulting from the utilization of same.
Crate refers to one's desire to hide specific aspects of oneself.
Creel signifies one's personal tools for a spiritual search or involvement; what one spiritually reaps. Was the creel full or empty? What condition was it in?
Cuspidor See spittoon.
Cylinder (object) connotes a message. What color was it? Did it contain any writings?
Drop box stands for an element of convenience for transferring something out of one's hands.
Drum (container) See barrel.
Easter basket connotes optimism; hope for a positive outcome.
False bottom indicates incomplete conclusions; more to be discovered; possible secrets.
Grab bag advises one to be more discerning or selective.
Jar often represents that which one contains within oneself.
Jerrican relates to one's level of preparedness for life. Recall what the can contained. Or was it empty?
Keg See barrel.
Litterbag signifies orderly thought processes; recognition or discernment regarding the value of ideas.
Loving cup signifies one's token of affection/high esteem.
Pail signifies the amount of spirituality one uses in life. What was the pail made of? Was it full or empty? What quality was the content?
Pannier See basket.
Parfleche portrays basics. This alludes to an individual who sticks with basic necessities or bottom-line concepts.
Pipette signifies a careful method; efforts expended toward exactness.
Pitcher illustrates what one views as a source to quench a thirst or desire. The key is to recall what the pitcher held. Was it full or empty? Was someone holding it or pouring? What flowed from it? Color?
Poke (sack) See bag.
Quiver (arrow case) pertains to an intention to be well-prepared and focused on one's goals.
Rain barrel shows an awareness of and deep appreciation and respect for one's spiritual beliefs; a cherishing of one's every blessing.
Receptacle See container.
Shot glass points to a small amount of something ingested. Each dreamer relates to something different here.
Tankard refers to a great need for personal support/strength.
Urn (cremation) refers to the importance of remembering what has been learned by past experiences.
Wastebasket denotes that which is discarded. Recall what was in the wastebasket. Did it really belong there?

Wastebasket represents something that has been thrown away.

Household Items

Air freshener refers to a need to refresh an issue by revisiting it.

Atomizer means a cover-up.

Bandage indicates a healing is needed. It's time for an emotional wound to heal. May also point to a "temporary fix" requiring greater future attention.

Blow-dryer cautions against letting viable thoughts and ideas dry up.

Bobbin (sewing) pertains to the order of one's priorities; maintaining a smooth and untangled manner of operating; a first-things-first attitude.

Bone china is a fragile issue.

Bookend cautions one to stop studying a subject until deeper comprehension is attained.

Bookmark suggests a pause in studying or learning is needed. This would usually indicate a need for contemplation and assimilation of that which has already been learned.

Bootjack relates to a time to pause along one's path.

Bottlebrush advises one to keep clarity within oneself. Cautions one to clean out imperfect attitudes.

Box camera suggests old-fashioned attitudes; out-of-date perspectives.

Briquette stands for that which serves as an impetus; life aspects that light a fire and serve as motivation.

Butter churn connotes those aspects that create life's true and simple riches.

Calendar signifies time; a specific date. This dream fragment is usually presented as being important for the dreamer.

Can opener means the act of remembering or utilizing important life aspects.

Centerpiece signifies decorative appeal; attractiveness; that which creates an appealing atmosphere; the focus of attention.

Chamber pot connotes an aspect that is out of character or out of place in one's life.

Checklist advises increased awareness; attention given to details.

Clip (clasp) implies the act of holding something together.

Clippers (nails, dog) mean a need to trim down the riled attitude of a friend.

Clippers (nails, person) indicate an attempt to control one's negative aspects such as anger, aggressiveness, impulsiveness, and so on.

Cold pack (canning) represents unbiased information gathered followed by proper emotional expressiveness.

Comforter See quilt.

Compact disc (CD) symbolizes condensed information; acquiring a large block of knowledge in a short span of time.

Conversation piece symbolizes an aspect that draws attention or curiosity.

Cork (float) pertains to a resilient nature.

Cotton ball/batting suggests a softening of one's harsher character/behavioral traits.

Cracker (party favor) signifies inconsequential noise-making; an aspect that may appear serious yet proves to be innocuous.

Curler connotes one's attempt to figure something out.

Curling iron cautions against forcing conclusions; making attempts to understand complicated or high-minded concepts.

Drop cloth indicates preparedness; a safeguard; protective measure.

Extension (cord) suggests a greater use of one's personal energies and/or efforts; the dreamer could be doing more.

Ice bag See ice pack.

Ice scraper stands for a method or tool to bring about clearer perception. This symbol suggests a need for same.

Knitting needle warns of manipulation.

Can opener is a reference to the use of memory.

List advises of a need to remember details. Implies forgetfulness.

Loofah (sponge) indicates a need to perceive with greater depth.

Rag (cloth) relates to a remnant (leftover) factor in one's life that requires attention.

Ragbag refers to multiple fragments of a life aspect that needs to be taken care of, finished, or used for a secondary purpose.

Remnant usually denotes an unnecessary element associated with one's path or purpose, yet it could also refer to a loose end to which one needs to attend.

Safety pin refers to a secure manner of providing a temporary stopgap action.

Sealing wax defines privacy; confidentiality. Recall who was using the wax. What color was it? Was it impressed with a symbol or initial?

Shoe box correlates to the multiple personal methods used during one's progression in life; the various types of shoes worn. Recall any wording on the box.

Shoehorn implies a need to take larger steps toward one's path progression or life goal instead of always trying to stuff oneself into a confined path or manner of walking.

Shoe tree signifies an assortment of methods to use while walking through the varied phases of one's life path.

Staple (basics) pertains to basic ethics, humanitarian elements, and spiritual foundational aspects.

see also
• Accessories & Decor *p. 386*
• Appliances *p. 390*

Art & Images

Aerial photograph advises of one's need to broaden perspective; widen one's view to get an overall, more comprehensive understanding.
Album (photo) indicates the value of family, friends, and life experiences.
Bust (sculpture) represents an individual or ideal that's important for the dreamer's waking life.
Collage (art form) reminds us of life's diversity and the beauty of same. This dreamscape symbol usually calls for more acceptance on the dreamer's part.
Composite photograph will reveal one's multifaceted aspects.
Decal may advise the dreamer to pay attention to what the dream decal represented as a personal message, or it may indicate the dreamer's personal attitude about something. A decal symbol signifies the public expression of an attitude.
Decoy connotes imitation or diversion in one's life. Could be pointing to ulterior motives and personal agendas.
Diagram advises of the need for clarification before comprehension is attained.
Dry kiln advises of a need to absorb and fully comprehend that which one has attempted to learn; for a seasoning time.
Easel alludes to a life aspect that is capable of supporting one's future goals or plans.
Graffiti usually comes as a warning specific to the dreamer. Recall what the graffiti depicted.

Graffiti indicates action is necessary.

Graphics connote a need in the dreamer for further explanation. The dreamer will require a visual to completely understand something.
Inlay stands for the attitudes we accumulate in life and incorporate into our overall foundational perspectives.
Inset stands for an added element.
Kiln denotes personal energy applied to one's advancement.
Latent image reveals the presence of ulterior motives or attitudes.
Likeness applies to false appearance; something that appears like another.
Masterpiece is representative of excellence. It can also mean near perfection.
Scrapbook signifies a personal need to remember accomplishments or events of one's past. Was the scrapbook for a specific event or time? Was the scrapbook related to a particular individual?
Smiley face (image) usually comes in dreamscapes to remind us to be more lighthearted. More optimism is advised. Have a greater sense of humor.
Tagging See graffiti.

Kitchen & Cooking

Cauldron warns of a brewing situation, condition, or relationship.
Chafing dish exemplifies an aspect that requires constant attention; a need to prevent some aspect from getting cold.
China See ceramic.
Chopping block represents a dangerous path or result.
Chopsticks imply the utilization of an incorrect means to reach a specific end.
Cleaver symbolizes a life aspect that has the capability of severing something. The dreamer will know what this refers to.
Cooler is any factor that maintains a state of control or calm.
Cork (stopper) refers to control; restraint.
Corkscrew portrays deep involvement. May imply a twisted situation.
Cutting board refers to an attempt to be precise when excising something from one's life, behavior, or plans.
Disposal (garbage) advises of the wisdom of completely letting go of a closure's residual aspects.
Eggbeater (utensil) warns of attempting to form concepts from scrambled idea fragments.
Egg carton stands for the source of a multitude of new ideas. The key here is to recall the carton's condition and whether it was full or empty. Broken eggs inside?
Eggcup is an organized idea.
Egg timer advises of the wisdom to closely monitor a specific concept or situation.
Ice pick corresponds to personal energy put into chipping away at one's spiritual aspects that have been voluntarily hidden from view.
Lobster pot means a controlling factor that curbs a tendency to accept fad ideologies.
Lunch box represents something as simple as an advisement to cut financial corners, or it can indicate a temporary phase when one should be getting as much done as possible (working through lunch).
Measuring cup/spoon comes as an advisement to give attention to the importance of keeping the right balance of input into an issue. This means a balance of give and take, a balance of positive reinforcement and critical assessment.
Meat cleaver See cleaver.
Meat tenderizer alludes to a need to soften hard or tough facts one wants to believe; make them more palatable.
Milk glass alludes to an immature perspective.
Nutpick connotes efforts applied to absorbing nourishing life elements. May point to getting through to someone who's thought to be a hard nut to crack.
Place setting connotes an expected response or aspect.
Self-cleaning portrays a continual monitoring of one's motives and perspectives.
Twist tie denotes a means of closure that avails itself to future reopening if needed.
Warming pan refers to a life aspect that comforts.
Whisk broom suggests a need to routinely pick up after oneself. This refers to one's behavior and its effects.

Material

Ball of wax refers to a complete aspect of an issue encompassing all related elements.
Bisque (china) stands for something that has been left unfinished or is needing some refinement.
Board (wood) may refer to some type of building element or a kind of stiffness in one's character, attitude, or perspective; someone who is being unyielding.
Ceramic connotes the aspects in life that have a tendency to be more fragile, such as one's emotional sensitivity.
Cork (bark) stands for one's multilevel abilities.
Duckboard suggests protective measures in the way of maintaining an awareness of life elements touched by negatives.
Extract (a concentrate) illustrates basic aspects of an issue or idea.
Flotsam denotes erroneous spiritual concepts.
Hazardous waste warns of harmful aspects surrounding the dreamer. This will be different for everyone.
Jetsam exemplifies the extraneous aspects one needs to get rid of in life. It may also mean priorities.
Junk corresponds to the relativity of value.
Litter (refuse) pertains to mental or emotional confusion in one's life.
Lubricant indicates an irritated or rough situation or characteristic that requires smoothing to prevent further friction.
Lumber pertains to any type of tool or building aspect that serves as a driving force for one's advancement or path progression.
Padding corresponds to the effect of softening or easing something in life. It may also indicate an exaggeration depending on surrounding dreamscape details.
Particle board portrays multiple aspects of an issue.
Pipe dope refers to ensuring that one's connections to another are well sealed; a double-checking of thought processes that ensure certain ideas hold and are firmly in place.
Precut stands for an efficient manner of accomplishing a goal; having all the elements formulated and ready to fit together.
Rubbish See disposal.
Scrap will correspond with a single element in one's life that may or may not be currently relevant.
Scrap heap represents that which is of no value. Recall what was in the dreamscape heap.
Shavings (metal) represent the harsher aspects of oneself that have been shed.
Shavings (wood) stand for the formation of a personal method of using one's natural spiritual gifts.
Skein portrays the threads of a theory or situation.
Specimen will relate to a sample; an example.
Stuffing corresponds to a padding or filler element added to something; an extraneous aspect; exaggerations.
Trash See disposal.

Children & Toys

Ball (child's) suggests simplicity; ease of communicating ideas.
Balloon represents an exaggeration.
Beach ball refers to the lightheartedness of manifesting one's spirituality through daily behavior and interaction.
Blocks (toys) signify crude planning; simplistic activity.
Bundling board stands for a path shared with another, yet each remaining separate and free to have differing perspectives.
Butterfly net signifies one's intentions toward rejuvenating oneself; an intent to make self-improvements.

China doll is indicative of a female in one's life who is in a delicate state.

China doll means a woman with seemingly fragile qualities.
Collectible refers to highly valued aspects as viewed by the dreamer.
Collectibles are representative of the wide variety of life elements that one can be particularly drawn to or have an affinity for.
Coloring book suggests an opportunity to express one's personal perspective. May indicate a desire to alter or color things according to one's viewpoint. Recall what images were in the book.
Cornhusk doll signifies the end product of one's creative efforts.
Diaper exemplifies an effort to control something in one's life.
Doll characterizes a message to reevaluate relationship motives.
Dollhouse is a message to return to reality.
Kaleidoscope warns of distorted perceptions; vacillating attitudes.
Rattle (toy) is representative of something one amuses oneself with, and this usually indicates insignificance.

see also
• Children's Games *p. 206*
• Woven Fabrics *p. 419*

Office & Business

Attaché case stands for priority material regarding one's mission.
Bar chart symbolizes a quick gauge of how one is progressing.
Briefcase cautions one to have all facts together before making decisions or judgments.
Bulletin board pertains to messages; news; forms of communications.
Carbon copy suggests duplication. It may also mean a veering away from one's individuality.
Carbon paper stands for a life aspect that entices one away from individuality. This could be something like another's expression of ridicule, skepticism, etc.
Card (index) See index card.
Chart defines specific course perceptions. These may show what the dreamer has planned out or clarify what should be drawn up.
Charter (document) depicts a statement or record of one's purpose.
Check (bill) refers to one's valid debts.
Consignment stands for possible benefits gained from the actions of another.
Conversion chart (measurements) is representative of options having equal value in one's life.
Copies connote multiples of the same thing. This usually denotes an advisement to repeat some positive aspect. May also point out redundancy.
Copy relates to a duplicate or imitation.

Pushpin means one must take note.

Corkboard connotes some kind of acceptance; a venue of information or display.
Date book represents a reminder for important scheduled events in one's life.
Disclaimer points to an effort to avoid culpability or responsibility.
Disclosure statement stands for honesty; a chance to recognize/reveal any known negatives related to an issue.
Docket See date book.
Folder usually represents information.
Fountain pen suggests quality of writing. What was or was about to be written with the pen? Who was picking it up or using it?
Index card indicates a need for organization.
Inventory comes as an advisement to take stock of one's life.
Lapboard corresponds with efficient work habits; keeping the process convenient.
Legend (symbol code) will usually reveal a key to solving some life problem. This could provide an inspirational idea.
Letterhead connotes a message that points out importance for the dreamer. What did the dreamscape letterhead say? Was the lettering a specific color? Style of type?
Paper trail exemplifies evidence one leaves behind.
Paperweight means a need to retain important information.
Pointer (any type) will call one's attention to something important in one's life.
Pushpin will usually point to a need to make note of something; keep something on the front burner or in a convenient place where one will be reminded of it.
Replica See copy.
Reproduction stands for an imitation; a copy.
Rubber band emphasizes the extension or stretched limit of an issue or perspective.
Rubber stamp comes as a personal message that warns, advises, or commends. Recall what the stamp said for further clarity.
Staple (fastener) typifies a connective aspect.
Stationery symbolizes a need to communicate with another. May reveal the quality or attitude of that communication. Recall type of stationery. Color? Style?
Sticker (gummed) will present a personal message for each dreamer depending on what the sticker symbolized or said.
Tear sheet corresponds to evidence; verification.
Uptrend stands for initial signs of an improving situation. May point to increased acceptance or optimism; an upward tendency.

Tobacco & Smoking

Cheroot See cigar.
Cigar denotes absorption of specialized ideas or concepts.
Cigar box alludes to the manner by which one holds specific ideas or concepts.
Cigarette pertains to absorption of well-defined ideas.
Cigarette butt relates to ideas that have been used up; ideas that are old and no longer viable.
Cigarette case signifies the practice of holding onto certain ideas until one is ready to look at them.
Cigarette filter cautions against the acceptance of ideas only after they've been run through the filter of one's personal attitudes and perspectives.
Cigarette holder warns against keeping a distance from well-defined ideas.
Cigar tube denotes a desire to keep certain ideas fresh and new.
Humidor reveals a negative factor that depletes an individual or atmosphere of spiritual qualities. This symbol stands for something that adds or preserves spiritual aspects.
Meerschaum (pipe) illustrates an analytical mind; reason and wisdom.

Personal Effects

Back scratcher is representative of an opportunity to become involved in a mutually synergistic relationship. It may also point to an element that one receives benefits or payback from.
Card (to verify identity) comes in dreams to mean a verification of one's identity and right to participate in a specific activity or be in a certain place. This symbol may be a call to examine one's behavior in respect to being true to oneself—not pretending to be someone one is not. The symbol may also appear as a warning message to underscore the fact that someone is venturing into areas that are either not their concern or not within their right to be involved.
Collection denotes a personal possessiveness.
Dental pick relates to self-analysis because of negatives that one has spoken.
Ditty bag is representative of emergency measures of preparedness for possible life events.
Earplug warns of a closed mind. This dream symbol means that one is not even hearing what one wants to.
Emery board See nail file.
Hair pick alludes to the straightening out of tangled thoughts or confusion.
Handkerchief is representative of preparedness.
Kerchief See handkerchief.
Kit means having all the parts comprising a whole.
Marker (token) represents an asset owned.
Paraphernalia connotes personal possessions that are unique or important to an individual.
Sachet connotes a cover-up being done; a replacement scent or aspect being utilized.
Safety razor See razor.
Shaver See razor.
Shaving cream denotes an element that helps to soothe an abrasive situation or relationship.
Stamp (label) will reveal a personal message for each dreamer. Recall what was stamped on what object.
Token symbolizes a sign or indication.

Mirrors

Broken mirror means that one is not being seen as a complete individual.

Broken mirror (piece[s] missing) stands for an incomplete picture of oneself. This means that one is looking only at certain attributes or faults rather than seeing the whole person.
Ceiling mirror signifies a tendency to have to look up to see oneself, giving a diminutive perception.
Clouded mirror implies a lack of clear perception of oneself.
Colored mirror denotes a colored perception. Refer to the specific color for further clarification.
Compact mirror refers to a minimized viewpoint and may indicate a sense of inferiority.
Cracked mirror typifies a faulty self-image.
Floor-to-ceiling mirror indicates a clear viewpoint of one's wholeness.
Foggy mirror means an unclear, indistinct self-impression; no clear understanding of oneself.
Looking glass See mirror.
Magnifying mirror represents an egotistical view of oneself.
Mirror means self-perception; a call for self-examination.
Pitted mirror relates to irregularities with one's self-image.
Rearview mirror signifies a perception of oneself as judged from hindsight. This may be a deprecating perspective.
Reflection comes in dreams to suggest one reflects on an important factor in one's life.
Reflection in window glass pertains to sudden insights into one's true personality.
Reflection pool refers to spiritual contemplation.
Reflector will be a guiding indicator.
Slanted mirror suggests a biased viewpoint.
Warped mirror implies an unbalanced perspective.
Wavy mirror points to indecision about oneself; a vacillating perception.

Adhesives

Adhesive signifies a strong attachment. May point to a stuck condition.
Adhesive tape denotes the need to bring a connectedness into life. May indicate scattered thoughts, perspectives or conditions that require cohesiveness.
Masking tape pertains to an attention to detail. It may also mean an ability to keep differing aspects separate.
Rubber cement See adhesive.
Self-adhesive relates to a cohesive aspect that can come only from oneself.
Self-stick relates to an element having cohesiveness by its very nature.
Tear strip is representative of easy access.

Sound & Music

Bell is a call for increased awareness. May indicate a call to duty or responsibility.
Cowbell calls for the expression of compassion.
Ground noise See humming.
Guitar pick is representative of a need to express oneself very carefully.
Horn (fog) See foghorn.
Reverberation is representative of dissemination.
Sleigh bells refer to a carefree, nonchalant attitude where a more serious attitude should be given.
Whistle most often typifies an attention-getting sound. Recall the surrounding details of the dream for further clarification.
Wind chimes symbolize comforting thoughts; perhaps a gentle calling.

see also
• Time Miscellaneous *p. 86*
• Musical Styles *p. 225*

Stores & Shopping

Bar code relates information that is systematically hidden. It might also refer to the concealed costs of an item.
Cart (shopping) See shopping cart.
Case goods are representative of a need to keep something protected or advises of the wisdom of putting something away.
Coupon illustrates life aspects that save time, energy, or money.
Courtesy card signifies the little amenities in life; small conveniences.
Merchandise suggests choices available. The type of merchandise will bring a different message to each dreamer.
Purse strings symbolize one's assets that are tightly controlled. These don't need to refer to monetary assets but could represent humanitarian or personal talents. Could point to a tendency toward stinginess.
Shopping bag implies expectation; an intent to obtain a need or desire. Were any emblems or words on the bag? What color was it?
Shopping cart stands for high expectations.
Shopping list calls attention to one's need to not forget important elements of an issue or situation. This symbol won't usually stand for things one needs to buy.

Clocks & Time

Clock always calls the dreamer's attention to a warning of time.
Clock radio indicates an acceptance of one's responsibility for something or someone.
Counterclockwise is often representative of an aspect that goes against the grain; an unexpected event; a reversal; going backward.
Deferment suggests a postponement or permanent release from responsibility. In some cases, this symbol will point to procrastination.
Delayed will usually be presented in a dream to remind us that timing is important and that delays are sometimes for the best.
Dial (sun) See sundial.
Double-booked is usually a call to slow down: one's schedule is too full.
Double time indicates a need to make up for lost time.
Pendulum stands for the swinging momentum of life; the ups and downs that can be expected.
Retroactive exemplifies an aspect in one's life that is currently affected by one's past.
Watch See clock.
Watchband may reveal how time is personally perceived. Recall what material the band was made of. Gold? Gemstones? Leather or vinyl? What was the color or design?
Watch chain stands for efficiency; punctuality.

Hardware & Parts

Carpet tack signifies efforts expended on maintaining the integrity of one's path or journey.
C-clamp applies to a need to hold something together until it can maintain its own position. This usually refers to a relationship in the dreamer's waking life.
Cotter pin symbolizes simple solutions and/or tools for making connections and securing them.
Dead bolt is representative of attention to security. This may imply protection from others in respect to the exposure of one's hidden activities, thoughts, or perceptions; a desire to keep an aspect of one's life secure.
Dial portrays an indication of level or quantity. This may refer to several aspects and will be clarified by surrounding dreamscape facets.
Dowel suggests a specific connective aspect.
Eye hook implies secured perceptions; those that one is unwilling to alter.
Hinge alludes to probabilities.
Knob illustrates a means of controlling something; self-motivation.
Link corresponds with a connective factor in one's life. This will directly refer to a specific aspect in the dreamer's life.
Nozzle pertains to one's personal mode of delivery; how one interacts with others. Recall the condition of the nozzle and if it was working properly. What was coming out of it? Was this substance hazardous? Was it clear? What color was it?

Nuts and bolts indicate the core elements of a particular problem.

Nuts and bolts signify the basics of an issue.
Pedal (device) applies to an opportunity to advance or increase motivation.
Pin (fastener) implies a need for temporary restorative or corrective measures to be taken.
Rivet exemplifies a secured aspect.
Roach clip illustrates resourcefulness; a tendency to utilize every element of something.
Rung (any type) depicts a connective aspect.
Spare parts connote preparedness; resourcefulness.
Toggle bolt stands for a strong issue; one that will hold up under scrutiny.
U-bolt represents a strong support.
Washer (seal) connotes a sealing effort; an attempt to confine.
Wing nut is representative of intellectual leverage.

Postal Service

Card (greeting) reveals emotions and/or attitudes. Also see greeting card.
Envelope signifies a communication. What color was it? Who was it from? To whom? Was it empty?
Express delivery/mail advises one to instigate a communication as soon as possible.
Greeting card will portray a specific sentiment depending on the type of card it was. This message will carry a different interpretation for everyone.
Junk mail means insignificance.
Mail (postal) connotes communication forthcoming or needing to be sent.
Mailbox is representative of communication.
Mail call advises of a forthcoming message or communication.
Mailer See envelope.
Mailing tube stands for a desire/effort to keep something in good condition and maintain its integrity.
Mail-order catalog relates to multiple opportunities that are readily available and easy to take advantage of.
Mail pouch/packet stands for many different communications needing to be made.
Next-day delivery reveals an urgent document or communication.
Postage stamp is representative of the value of various communications. Recall what the stamp was on. To whom was the letter addressed? Was the stamp from a foreign country?
Postcard connotes a brief message or communication.
Postmark will pinpoint a specific date that will be important to the dreamer.
Stamp (postage) See postage stamp.
Stamp collection constitutes a recognition of a specific aspect's value.

Mailbox means social contact.

Logos & Brand Names

Brand name pertains to general knowledge; that which is generally recognizable.
Made in USA (label) See union label.
Monogram represents important initials that will have a specific meaning for each dreamer. Many times a monogram will turn out to be an acronym. Recall what the letters were.
Name brand usually indicates a preferred choice for the dreamer. It may also signify a brand to avoid, depending on how it's presented.
Service mark is an attempt to define one's purpose.

Communication & Relationships

Ball club will represent those to whom one shows support.
Blue box refers to unethical communications; stealthy dealings.
Bucket brigade is the sharing of spiritual truths toward a common goal, usually to extinguish a negative element.
Contribution means one's personal input.
Cortege alludes to an individual's personal surrounding of associates or assistants.
Counterpart characterizes a clonelike aspect of something or someone; a complementing factor of same.
Dead heat warns against obsessive competition.
Deadlock means an impasse; a no-win situation, plan, or relationship.
Dedication symbolizes an expression of respect and honor.
Discrimination usually points to intolerance; a lack of acceptance.
Disobedience will usually point to an expression of one's individuality.
Disorderly conduct can refer to one's right to express objections like the symbol of civil disobedience, or it can be an advisement to get a better handle on one's behavior.
Dissent stands for an objection or disagreement and one's right to express it.
Doting warns against an overbearing, smothering behavior.
Engagement (wedding) See betrothal.
Example most often comes from one's higher self as a communication to the conscious aspect of the dreamer.
Executive order will usually be a message from one's conscience or higher self.
Eyeservice indicates a lack of integrity and personal responsibility; one can't be trusted unless being watched.
Face off is representative of a confrontation.
Face-to-face stands for the wisdom of having a physical encounter to communicate instead of through the many electronic faceless methods.
Foot in door naturally represents the first step in a new direction or entry into a new situation.
Glazed (look) may indicate confusion, a lack of understanding, or a shocked reaction.
Golden rule signifies ethical and moral behavior.
Good old boy See old-boy network.
Guidelines will signify behavioral perimeters.
Hint is almost always a clue for the dreamer. These should be recalled.
Hoodwinked reveals a deception.
Interrogation points to a need to examine one's own motives or attitudes.
Joke will usually reveal something important for the dreamer, frequently about oneself.
Kneehole (space) denotes an accommodating situation or relationship.
Last-call return stands for a desire or need to return to a conversation. It may also refer to the fact that an issue isn't over.

see also
• Trade *p. 169*
• Messengers & Communication *p. 259*

Communication & Relationships (continued)

Mix-up reveals a lack of adequate communication.

Mockery indicates a feeling of humiliation. May indicate personal embarrassment.

Model (example) points to a quality that's considered the ideal.

Monotone signifies inexpressiveness. It calls for more outward expression of feelings.

Mother wit symbolizes age-old, dependable wisdom.

Oration will reveal an important aspect for the dreamer. Will emphasize something the dreamer has been wanting to know.

Outranked will usually underscore one's rightness that has externally been overridden by another who is perceived as being more knowledgeable or experienced. This symbol comes as a personal verification message.

Overruled will come as a guiding message from one's higher self or even one's own conscience.

Parley defines an attempt to negotiate a peaceful resolution.

Parody See sarcasm.

Parting shot implies a last word or the expressing of one's final say on something.

Presentation relates to the exposure or disclosure of something. The dreamer will make the right association as related to his/her life.

Proclamation will usually reveal a disclosure of some type.

Promise illustrates a personal responsibility to carry something through.

Pronouncement See proclamation.

Rebuttal refers to a defense of one's personal opinion or attitude.

Reciprocation may refer to retaliation or compensation, depending on associated dream elements.

Recommendation stands for a suggestion. In order to discover if this is a positive or negative symbol, recall what was recommended. For whom and why?

Repartee will reveal an individual's true or hidden thoughts.

Repudiation indicates some type of denial or condemnation.

Requisition pertains to a personal request, often a prayer, for the necessary elements to accomplish a goal or purpose.

Restitution is representative of compensation. It can also imply reparation.

Retaliation denotes vindictiveness; reprisal.

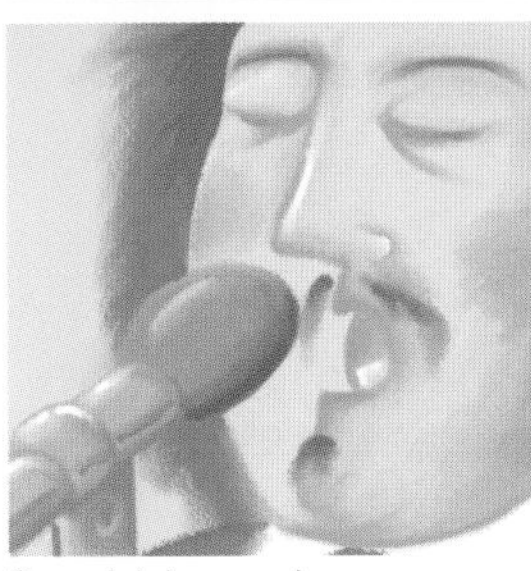

Speech brings a unique message.

Retraction won't necessarily refer to one's words but usually suggests a need to pull back or pull something in, such as an unproductive behavioral aspect like being too forward, being tactless, giving incorrect advice, interference, and so on.

Rhetorical question poses possibilities and impels self-analysis.

Riddle constitutes a self-devised complexity.

Room service won't normally represent servitude but rather the things one can accomplish through simple communication (by lifting up the phone).

Roughshod signifies harsh control of others.

Segregation may not imply a racial matter but rather is a symbol that usually advises us to keep diverse issues separate from one another. This dream symbol would imply that the dreamer has been mixing concepts or issues.

Speech portrays a specific message for each dreamer depending on what was said to whom.

Stranglehold connotes a state of being manipulated, forced, or controlled.

Subversion pertains to an attempt to undermine a plan or individual.

Validation points to approval or acknowledgment; assured fact.

Verbal abuse naturally refers to hurtful comments made from an insensitive personality.

Welcome wagon implies one's state of acceptance by others.

Word of honor denotes integrity related to promises.

Flags, Signs & Symbols

Banner denotes a means of getting attention. Try to recall what the banner said to gain greater clarity.

Check (mark) is representative of aspects that one urgently needs to attend to.

Emblem comes as a message for the dreamer. It usually attempts to call attention to whatever the emblem represents, for this will have a specific meaning to each dreamer.

Embossed is a symbol of emphasis on something. It comes to draw attention.

Flagpole is representative of opportunities to prove one's loyalties.

High voltage (sign) warns of a dangerous situation. May signify the high probability for an upcoming explosive confrontation.

Pennant (small flag) applies to identity or loyalties. Recall what the pennant represented. What was the color? The condition?

Placard will usually come as a specific message for each dreamer. Recall what the placard said. Did it have colors? Was a name written on it? Was it embellished with a particular design?

Red cross emphasizes assistance; immediate help in an emergency situation.

Red flag naturally reveals a warning. Perhaps it's time to stop some type of behavior or give up a plan.

Seal (emblem) will reveal a specific meaning to each dreamer depending on what the emblem was.

White flag connotes a peaceful resolution; a capitulation; an end to conflict.

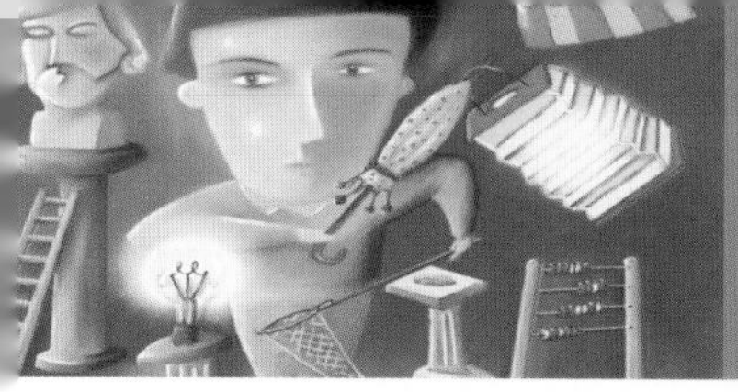

Events & Experiences

Debut refers to the time to introduce something or to bring something out into the open. It usually points to an attitude or underlying conflict that has been brewing.

Discovery signifies a perceptual discernment.

Discrepancy connotes an inconsistency; a question of credibility.

Distress sale points to the ongoing value of imperfections. It cautions against discounting the value of something just because it's not in mint condition.

Errand reminds us of the importance of attending to responsibilities, however small.

Excavation suggests a need for the dreamer to dig deeper into an issue that requires further understanding or that needs to be exposed.

Excursion refers to a leisurely side trip taken to learn more about the lay of the land surrounding one's path.

Expedition typifies a dreamscape symbol that defines a search or quest.

Feat designates a great step that is forthcoming and will be successfully achieved. This symbol comes as encouragement for one who is anxious about accomplishing this deed.

Implosion reveals an inner fragmentation beginning. This is a warning that indicates a self-destructive course is being set and will be devastating if the withheld negatives are not externalized by facing or openly expressing them.

Inauguration underscores one's official beginning of something.

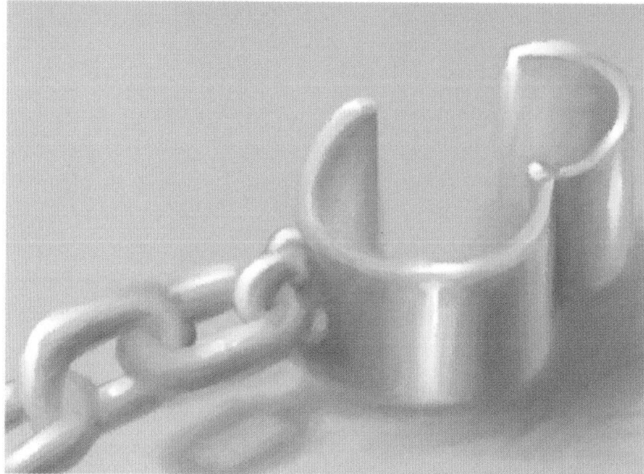

Liberation often indicates the need for one to free oneself from something.

Infiltration warns of a negative aspect in one's life.

Initiation marks a beginning of something one will relate to.

Interception connotes an interference in one's life. Surrounding dreamscape details will clarify this.

Introduction advises of a need for new relationships or concepts in one's life.

Irradiation signifies an altered aspect.

Liberation defines a state of freedom; release from limitations. Often one needs to liberate oneself.

Meltdown reveals an absolute failure or collapse of something in one's life.

Nomination will reveal the best qualified person; the person of choice.

No-show emphasizes a reluctance to participate. Recall associative dream details to pinpoint what this refers to.

Osmosis emphasizes understanding; comprehension.

Outsmarted implies one didn't consider all aspects of an issue or situation. This is actually an experiential learning symbol.

Overindulgence is representative of an excessiveness.

Oversight points to something that's been left out; a vital detail has been forgotten.

Overthrown implies a missed goal; reaching too far.

Overturned may indicate a need to reverse a decision or choice, or it could suggest that one give closer inspection to something—leave nothing unturned.

Pelted stands for an inundation of something in one's life; an overwhelming element.

Pinprick represents an attention-getting message. The surrounding dreamscape elements will usually clarify this for the dreamer.

Practical application refers to putting knowledge or experience into action.

Prostration may refer to a reverential attitude, or it may imply a submission.

Pulsation exemplifies steadiness; dependability; a continuum.

Rear-ended indicates an unexpected event; an attack that comes from behind.

Reclamation most often signifies a need to take back one's self-control and/or individuality; to reclaim oneself and one's inherent rights to choose or make personal decisions.

Reconnaissance warns of a need to thoroughly look something over and be aware of all aspects of it before proceeding.

Reinstated stands for an acceptance of something that was previously discounted.

Relinquished portrays a life element one is advised to give up. Most often this suggests acceptance and moving forward.

Restoration See renovation.

Retreat (respite) stands for a suggested rest. Contemplation is called for.

Showdown represents the time for confrontation or resolution.

Simulation will denote a reproduction or practice effort.

Spot test stands for preliminary work done or efforts expended toward discovering a method to resolve a conflict or remove a negative from one's life.

Tailgate picnic suggests convenience for camaraderie. This is an advisement to take advantage of it.

Temper tantrum warns against being selfish; a lack of acceptance.

Vigil implies perseverance.

Waylaid suggests a pause or temporary halt to one's life progression.

Whistle-stop emphasizes a message; a need to stop and pay attention to an existing situation.

see also
• Chemicals & Gases *p. 282*
• Lighting *p. 392*

Lights, Lamps & Illumination

Beacon means a source of enlightenment that will further spiritual development or understanding; a light to be guided by.

Blinker (light) attempts to bring one to attention; a warning.

Broken lightbulb signifies a temporary lull in one's ability to see clearly; a short period of puzzlement or confusion.

Bulb (light) applies to a new awareness; solutions; bright ideas. Unless the bulb was burned out or broken, then the opposite meaning applies. If the dreamscape bulb was too big for the socket, then it points to grandiose ideas.

Dim advises of a situation that lacks clarity or any sharp definition.

Direct lighting will point to a specific life element that's highlighted to attract one's attention to it.

Flare See flashlight.

Flasher (warning light) comes as some type of warning that will be clarified by surrounding dreamscape details. What was the flasher light associated with? Was it night or day?

Flashlight advises of a need to better illuminate a specific aspect in one's life. More light (knowledge) needs to be gained.

Floodlight applies to an acute awareness.

Hazard light refers to one's personal ability to sense dangerous situations; forewarning insights.

Hurricane lamp connotes one's preparedness for properly absorbing spiritual concepts in one's everyday life.

Idiot light will usually reveal some type of guidance for the dreamer.

Illumination reveals some important factor to which the dreamer should pay particular attention. This is a very important message.

Lantern refers to more light being required on an issue or situation.

Lightbulb stands for a new thought; inspiration; sudden awareness.

Low beam (light) usually calls for the need of more light on a subject. Greater perspective is required for an accurate view.

Mercury-vapor lamp calls for special illumination that is required on a particular subject. The dreamer will make this association.

Penlight represents a personally responsible state of awareness for the dreamer.

Quartz lamp See mercury-vapor lamp.

Roman candle See fireworks.

Searchlight See flashlight.

Strobe light signifies an attempt to alter reality or see it under a different light.

Ultraviolet lamp symbolizes an aid to nourish one's personal growth.

Wick stands for that which generates a type of illumination; a source of revealing information; possibly high insights.

Sensory Input

Double take advises of the need to take a second look at something.

Fumes are representative of harmful situations generated from one's lack of controlled response.

Joss stick See incense.

Mesmerized warns of a lack of awareness that is usually a conscious move to avoid personal responsibility for one's beliefs or path.

Musty indicates a need for fresh air (getting away from stale ideas).

Overview stands for a good perception of the multiple aspects of an issue/situation.

Pungent symbolizes effectiveness; strong impression.

Tasteless is a reference to inappropriateness, disinterest, or lack of desire.

Vibration signifies an insight or indication.

Chemicals

Aerosol cans warn of being under pressure too much.

Concoction connotes a mix of personal perceptions.

Mace spray signifies one's personal defenses against external negative forces or influences.

Pepper spray See mace spray.

Repellent (chemical) refers to the use of negative behavior to maintain social distance.

Coverings

Aluminum foil is representative of a warning regarding food that one ingests. Perhaps a change in one's diet is required, or maybe a change in perspective (ideas).

Beach umbrella signifies a good perspective of spiritual beliefs; one who is not enamored with nor blinded by the glare of outlandish claims.

Enamel represents a condition of heavy coating; a thick veneer to one's outward presentation.

Foil See aluminum foil.

Hull (casing) represents a hard personality veneer.

Lens cover advises of a state of blindness; perceptual aberrations.

Lid (cover) applies to a limit marker; a cap on quantity.

Liner See lining.

Lining signifies an insulating or protective shield.

Netting (mosquito) constitutes some form of protective measure; an insurance-type aspect.

Parasol connotes a frivolous spiritual attitude or belief system.

Sheath represents a cover of some type.

Shrink-wrap represents an attempt to preserve some aspect in one's life.

Tinfoil See aluminum foil.

Umbrella constitutes skepticism and a willful insulation from spiritual issues.

Veneer is representative of a false exterior. It may refer to a self-designed presentation of oneself.

Abstract

Affirmation means confidence in one's belief system or perspective.

Aftereffect will point to a secondary reaction setting in after the first reaction has had time to settle.

Aftermath usually means the consequences of something and comes as a premonition type of symbol.

Anathema reveals an issue or individual to avoid.

Applications refer to one's need to apply oneself.

Approval warns against one requiring this in order to feel self-worth or have faith in belief systems.

Backup (plan) denotes one's reserves; contingencies.

Brass ring symbolizes an aspect that suggests a strong possibility to have the ability to realize goals; something that may manifest one's dreams or goals; goals that are in reach.

Cancellation advises against going through with something.

Catharsis advises of the need to release emotions; a closure is required.

Complication means entanglement. This may even refer to one's own thought process.

Confinement advises of an inability to proceed. Marks a time frame when a pause or delay is required. There is also another meaning for this symbol, and that is a warning that one is confining oneself in some way or holding oneself back.

Consequence doesn't always imply negativity but may only indicate the result of something else.

Contingency means possible alternate plans.

Contradiction alludes to discrepancies in one's life. It cautions one to examine oneself and one's dealings.

Danger of any kind clearly means just that. The surrounding dreamscape elements will help to pinpoint the source.

Dazed connotes a non-receptive state of mind; unclear thoughts.

Dazzled warns against being blinded by amazement; perceptual abnormalities; being affected by seemingly spectacular aspects.

Decision denotes the need to give serious thought to something; time to stop vacillating or procrastinating.

Derelict (remiss) warns against neglecting responsibilities.

Deterrent points the way to avoid an undesirable situation.

Dichotomy is representative of opposing attitudes regarding one idea; a seeming contradiction.

Dispensation comes as a grave warning for those who believe they are above the law.

Divergence means a veering from one's normal or customary character, attitude, or path.

Double duty represents the multiple uses brought about by a single effort.

Futile reveals an unproductive situation, relationship, or effort.

Galvanized stands for motivation; an electrifying spur forward or into awareness.

Gimmick warns against using methods of trickery or manipulation.

Good faith represents trust.

Heads up represents an advisement to be watchful and aware; a forewarning.

Incomprehensible refers to an issue that one is not yet ready to address.

Huddled indicates a fear of self; lack of self-confidence and responsibility.

Illogical (aspect) indicates confusion or illogical thought present in the waking state.

Improvisation relates to an ability to cope; a quick wit.

Incomprehensible indicates a concept or situation one isn't prepared enough to tackle.

Ineligibility advises of one's lack of readiness.

Inescapable reminds one to face reality.

Inference implies forthcoming innuendos; possible new insight.

Innovation stands for independent thought; perhaps visionary thinking.

Integration rarely refers to ethnicity but rather comes as an advisement to combine diverse aspects. This indicates that the dreamer was missing something or not including all possible factors associated with an issue or concept.

Knack refers to a talent or skill.

Latent symbolizes the hidden aspects of oneself; those emotions or attitudes that are not openly expressed to others.

Lather applies to confusion; possible frustration or anger.

Loophole implies a conniving nature.

Low-key symbolizes a private individual; humility; one who tends to keep out of the public eye; a possible introvert.

Low profile See low-key.

Mainstream illustrates a widely accepted idea; beliefs held by the majority; commonality.

Margin stands for limitations; staying within specified, defined perimeters.

see also
• Attitudes *p. 136*
• Characteristics *p. 138*

Abstract (continued)

Marginal denotes a questionable factor in one's life.
Mat (tangle) signifies confusion.
Matchless constitutes a lack of energy or motivation; an inability to incite interest.
Mercy comes as a message to use same. This is a call for compassion or empathy.
Mesh suggests a need to be more congenial or compatible.
Methodical connotes efficiency; organization skills.
Middle-of-the-road applies to indecision; fear of taking a stand.
Misconception advises of an idea or attitude held in error. This is a wonderful message symbol that keeps the dreamer on track.
Multiple-choice refers to the many opportunities available.
Mundane points out the balancing factors in life; a necessary counter to high spiritual levels.
Naïveté characterizes an innocent or uninformed person.
Old guard suggests a great reluctance to alter attitudes or perspectives.
Old hand characterizes gained experience.
Old hat connotes an old-fashioned idea; something that has been around for a long time and is generally well known.
Old school is representative of strong, traditional perspectives that aren't currently applicable.
One-handed refers to the success of one's personal efforts. This suggests something done with ease.
One-sided illustrates a biased presentation or perspective.
Open-and-shut refers to a simple or basic aspect that has no complexities associated with it.
Open-end connotes a life aspect having no limits or restrictions; great potential or possibilities.
Outlet exemplifies an opportunity to release negative or retained aspects that restrict one's freedom or health.
Out of step usually points to individuality and the gumption to resist coercion to get in step with the crowd.
Out of sync represents a current attitude that causes a shift away from being aligned with a relationship, issue, or situation.
Out-of-the-way usually means that one needs to go out of one's way to gain an important lesson or discover a solution/key to something.
Overblown alludes to an exaggeration.
Overkill alludes to an exaggeration; an excessive amount of attention or effort applied to something in one's life.
Oxymoron will reveal a contradiction specific to the dreamer.
Pampered pertains to actions that retard one's growth.
Paradigm See example.
Paradox reveals a situation or concept that appears contradictory.
Pipe dream won't have to denote a fantasy or impossible goal but usually defines a high aspiration that has a high probability of attainment if one's path is carefully traveled.
Pitfall stands for a major setback or dangerous course leading to great difficulty.
Platitude illustrates a lack of original thought; superficial responses.
Point (advice) symbolizes suggestions from one's higher self.
Point (bottom line/crux) reveals the essential idea or basic premise.
Point (purpose) connotes a need to focus on the reason for something.
Point of view See perspective.
Preferential (treatment) refers to partiality. The key here is to determine who gave this treatment and why it was given.
Prejudice applies to a biased opinion or perspective.
Premeditated correlates to a life aspect that has been well thought out.
Premise pertains to a theory or idea one has.
Pretext suggests an ulterior motive; a hidden agenda.
Probability signifies the presence of an alternative element or course.
Rationale implies a precise reason or excuse for one's behavior. Recall the surrounding dreamscape elements for further clarification.
Reassurance comes as a verification or message of encouragement.
Repetition may indicate the act of repeating one's mistakes, or it may stand for a need to repeat things until the right lessons are learned.
Requirement defines a necessary quality, skill, or perspective one must possess in order to accomplish a select goal.
Reverie suggests an advisement to deeply contemplate an element in the dreamer's life. This individualized element will be readily recognized.
Rudimentary correlates to elemental aspects; the beginning stage or basic idea.
Scheme naturally indicates a plan, but one needs to recall the details to determine if it was for productive and positive purposes.
Self-help (resources) constitutes a desire to improve oneself. Recall what type of self-help sources were shown.
Sensationalism cautions one to readjust priorities.
Speculation warns against making assumptions.
Stumbling block denotes a temporary setback.
Substitution is representative of an alternative.
Sufferance suggests gentle acceptance; forbearance.
Supplement implies the need for an extra element.
Surrogate See substitution.
Two-fisted signifies great strength behind resolve.
Two-handed reveals an element weighty enough to require both hands (extra energy). May also point to an element fragile enough to require added awareness or caution in handling it.
Unconditional represents a lack of strings being attached; a true unrestricted element.
Undecided suggests a need to give more thought and analysis to an issue.
Violation implies a message from one's conscience.

Knives & Blades

Blade See knife.

Boning knife warns of a threatening aspect directed toward one's foundational attitudes or beliefs.

Butcher knife is representative of a cutting-up or chopping-at situation. It may also refer to an aspect used to cut down someone or something.

Deboning knife denotes an aspect in one's life that could remove one's support system. It may refer perhaps to an attitude or decision.

Drawknife is representative of personal efforts that have been applied to something.

Incision symbolizes a need to release a negative attitude or emotion.

Knife reveals a cutting off from some specific element in life.

Penknife See pocketknife.

Pocketknife pertains to experience and the lessons gained.

Locks & Keys

Padlock is indicative of items that one keeps secret.

Church key See bottle opener.

Combination lock denotes the various methods of opening something up or solving problems.

Key denotes a solution to a problematic situation or an inspiration.

Keyhole suggests an opportunity in life. May point to a clue; a small insight.

Key ring refers to an effort to keep an important life aspect from being lost.

Lock emphasizes a secure aspect. Depending on the surrounding dreamscape details, this symbol may reveal a need to unlock something.

Lock pick implies a desire to unlock something; solve a problem. Was the lock your own?

Master key See passkey.

Padlock represents hidden elements; aspects one keeps hidden.

Passkey is representative of advancement opportunities in one's life; elements that provide key solutions or simply inspirations.

Miscellaneous

Amalgam warns of an element in one's life that affects one's communication skills in a negative manner and could end up causing harm down the road.

Artifact denotes validating aspects in one's life.

Automat signifies quick fixes; shortcuts to accessibility.

Backlist applies to something that endures.

Bait denotes enticements. This is a warning dream symbol.

Blooper suggests that one laughs at one's mistakes.

Boomerang cautions one to watch for aspects that will come back at or turn on oneself.

Box top represents something that needs opening in one's life. What kind of box is the dream presenting? Are there words on it?

Bubble means negative aspects in life; a possible indication of one's insulating efforts—keeping oneself in a bubble.

Chalk line denotes level-headedness; straight and true.

Corn tassel refers to the multiple energies associated with spiritual nourishment.

Cross section advises of the wisdom of looking within something, usually oneself.

Death trap warns of an extremely dangerous life situation.

Disneyfication reveals a tendency to put an unrealistic spin on situations.

Ducking stool advises of unjust and unwarranted conclusions; assumptions and false judgments.

Idiot box refers to that which wastes intellectual potential.

Imprint connotes that which has gone before; a sign of one's passing. This doesn't necessarily have to be the imprint of a foot.

Inhibitor suggests a blocking aspect in one's life. This blocking may be voluntarily achieved through denial or even acceptance.

Jig (lure) connotes an unfair advantage.

Manhole is representative of the self-generated setbacks and pitfalls one has experienced in one's life.

Mistake will almost always be representative of the presence of an error one has made in life. It usually comes as a good sign to reveal a misstep in thought and can be corrected.

Murphy's Law implies a pessimistic outlook.

Odds and ends symbolize remnant aspects that need to be attended to.

Panic button represents high anxiety or an extreme state of confusion. It's time to do something.

Pull tab depicts an element that has the capability of making it easy to begin or open something.

Salt lick constitutes an attempt to provide others with what they need.

Track (evidence) illustrates a sign of one's passing.

Transmission means pacing oneself.

Ventilation applies to an attempt to maintain fresh ideas; a method of preventing staleness.

Weir symbolizes a spiritual trap; perhaps control or manipulation.

Chapter 30

Bizarre, Unusual & Abstract

Although these dreamscape elements may appear to be meaningless, they reveal possibilities and may literally indicate an unusual situation or condition. Frequently, bizarre and unusual dream aspects will point the dreamer to a solution for a current awake-state problem.

Mind Bogglers

Enigma defines confoundments. These may be solvable, depending on the effort applied to contemplating them.
Flying pig suggests a belief that something has a no chance of becoming reality.
Hologram means a false perception of reality.
Mind-boggling implies a lack of comprehension; an inability to understand.
Miracle corresponds to the normal working of true reality.
Pandora's box (Greek mythology) defines a harmful situation that should be avoided. This dream symbol may also refer to an individual or issue.
Quantum leap defines a major advancement regarding one's path progression or conceptual knowledge.

Metaphysical States

Ad hoc symbolizes an active single-mindedness; being focused on one issue.
Alpha and omega define the most important aspect of an issue or concept. A clear view of the beginnings and endings.
Altered state (mind/reality) will usually reveal a skewed perception but may also indicate a journey through any of the parallel dimensional aspects of true reality.
Chaos represents disorder of some kind; confusion.
Ethereal denotes spiritual or true reality aspects that are associated with one's life.
Havoc pertains to total confusion, usually one's thought process.
Immortality corresponds with the eternal life of one's spirit.
Indefinable pertains to higher aspects of reality that one has no established terms to correspond with. Sometimes this symbol can refer to that which overwhelms one.
Invisible (being) may denote an actual out-of-body experience, or it may indicate that one isn't being effective or is possibly being ignored.
Kismet means destiny.
Metamorphosis suggests a complete change. This could refer to a situation, relationship, belief, or an aspect within oneself, such as perspective or attitude.
Obsolescence refers to outdated information, attitudes, or manner of doing something.
Occult means hidden or little-understood aspects. Therefore, this symbol will refer to something in one's life that needs to be looked at harder and given deeper contemplative time.
Regression indicates a backward direction. Recall the dream's surrounding details for more clarity.
Reincarnation comes in a dream to remind one of a new beginning and an opportunity to advance oneself in one's life.
Transmutation depicts some type of transformation needed or currently happening.

Magic

Black magic warns against obtaining personal goals through the use of negativity.
Cabal refers to schemers that in some way affect the dreamer's life.
Magic may refer to an illusion or to something in one's life that is difficult to understand.
Magic bullet illustrates a solid solution.
Magic carpet is representative of a quick and secure method of enhancing or speeding the attainment of one's personal goal.
Magic lantern denotes a need to examine something further; take a closer look at something.
Magic mirror signifies one's true reflection of one's inner self.
Magic shop advises of multiple methods of trickery and illusion for unscrupulous people to use; methods of deceit.
Magic square verifies one's ideas or conclusions.

Witch's brew means a potent mix.

Magic tricks usually refer to ulterior motives; manipulative behavior.
Scrying (glass/mirror) stands for an effort/desire to perceive more clearly.
White magic stands for one's gifts used to benefit others.
Witch ball signifies a protective element that is used for the purpose of repelling negative elements.
Witchery denotes behavior that's not fully understood; unconventional behavior.
Witch's brew applies to a blend of various effective elements.

Harnessing Metaphysical Energies

Bermuda triangle means spiritual fluctuations.
Circle (ceremonial) may expose the putting on of another's path through fantasized means for the purpose of self-aggrandizement.
Crop circle characterizes skepticism in the face of facts.
Dream catcher signifies a desire to be shielded from the cause of one's fears. This isn't necessarily a good sign, because fears need to be faced and dealt with in order for them to stop being fears.
Feng shui stands for a desire to achieve harmony through another's idea of it instead of making adjustments according to how one feels about one's own rearrangement ideas.
Ley line portrays a field or course of flowing energy and refers to a path lit with high energy and good probabilities for success.
Twilight zone reflects experiences that one has difficulty accepting.
White noise warns of a loss of focus, concentration; being distracted by irrelevant aspects.
Wind chimes symbolize comforting thoughts; perhaps a gentle calling.

see also
• Metaphysical Phobias *p. 159*
• Divinatory Professions *p. 245*

Metaphysical Abilities

Autohypnosis denotes the need to go within to learn more about oneself; changes have to start with oneself.

Automatic writing refers to one's conscience; one's higher self.

Autosuggestion stands for self-taught methods. May point to acceptance.

Clairvoyance means one should pay closer attention to insights and hunches.

Déjà vu pertains to the manifestation of past precognitive or dream experiences; a repeat experience.

Dream analysis symbolizes an attempt to understand the clues, messages, and insights our subconscious or higher self holds.

Dream walker characterizes a spiritually wise individual whose quiet behavior reflects acceptance.

Extrasensory perception (ESP) is a misnomer, because there is nothing extra about it. However, if one has this event in a dreamscape it usually will be an attempt to normalize this talent or related event for the dreamer; demystify.

Futurist reveals someone who has an eye for long-range planning or ramifications.

Futuristic (scene) usually corresponds with an individual's unique vision or conceived idea of the future. May also be presented as a visual of one's fears.

Hallucination may be an insight into true reality or may warn against conscious imagining that one believes as fact.

Handwriting on wall reveals a message; forewarning.

Incantation typifies one's need for spiritual trappings.

Lucid dreaming represents the awareness of a situation and ability to interact with it or have some control.

Macabre relates to some personally unspeakable deed or situation; an appalling and abhorrent act or personality

Mental telepathy See telepathy.

Mind reading See telepathy.

Out-of-body presented in a dreamscape usually corresponds with a true experiential event. It also may reveal a need to look at something from a different perspective.

Paranormal (events/abilities) reveals inherent talents or elements of true reality.

Posthypnotic suggestion warns of a vulnerable state; being easily influenced or manipulated.

Precognition underscores an awake-state natural ability.

Prediction may, in fact, come as an actual event. Usually it reveals an outcome associated with the dreamer's current course in life.

Premonition is heightened awareness; an insightful impression.

Presage relates to a strong personal insight.

Prophecy stands for a forethought; an inspiration; a foreknowledge.

Psychokinesis stands for repressed emotional energy.

Psychometry is representative of a heightened receptivity to others.

Quantum meditation is indicative of slipping into and participating in the various multidimensional, near-parallel realms of true reality.

Reincarnation comes in a dream to remind one of a new beginning and an opportunity to advance oneself.

Second sight See clairvoyance.

Telepathy signifies insights; a subtle knowing.

Virtual meditation is representative of meditation that takes one's consciousness into the realms of true reality where one interacts with others.

Ghosts & Spirits

Banshee warns of death. This may forewarn of a spiritual, emotional, or actual physical demise.

Doppelgänger comes to the dreamer as a warning against imaginary or self-created fears.

Exorcism characterizes a personally concerted effort to rid oneself of certain life aspects that don't necessarily have to be negatives.

Ghost indicates a fear of spiritual matters. This dream symbol may also refer to recurring episodes of guilt.

Ghost Dancer characterizes a strong spiritual belief. It may also refer to one's faith in the power of one's spiritual strength.

Ghost Dance shirt denotes spiritual protection and one's powerful belief in it.

Ghost story implies a possibility; a subject to contemplate.

Haunting corresponds to self-generated fear. May indicate guilt from past behavior.

Jack-o'-lantern reveals one's perspective on life. Recall how it was carved. Sad? Angry? Fearful? Scary?

Kachina (doll/image) corresponds to our ancestral teachers; the star-born ones.

Mirror image usually personifies an alter ego. It may also refer to one's hidden self, the private persona.

Phantom may represent one's fears, or it may present a spiritual message. Recall surrounding dreamscape details for clarity.

Philadelphia Experiment emphasizes elements of true reality that are currently doubted; issues generating skepticism.

Poltergeist represents misunderstood spiritual concepts and their resulting self-generated fears.

Revenant characterizes a return of someone long absent from one's life.

Séance exposes misplaced spiritual priorities.

Shade See ghost.

Specter See ghost.

Spook See ghost.

Spooked implies timidity; a fearful nature.

Wraith can sometimes be a forewarning of one's death, but usually it represents one's unhealthy obsession with dying. This symbol may also be associated with fear of the death of a relationship, career, goal, or close friend.

Curses & Enchantments

Abracadabra See charm.
Amulet See charm.
Bewitched warns against allowing anyone to capture one's free will; a lack of individuality, thought, or control over one's life. This dreamscape element may also point to an unrealistic perspective; being overly enamored with something or someone.
Bugaboo implies the subject of one's worst fear; a continual problem or irritation.
Charm (object) exemplifies a lack of faith. May indicate a superstitious personality.
Curse (spell) See spell.
Enchanted emphasizes acute vibrational perception.
Evil eye makes one's personal fears known to the conscious mind. Reveals a superstitious nature.
Fetish See charm.
Hex (sign) typifies a method one uses to maintain spiritual protection.
Hoodoo will most often signify a questionable or extremely unusual way of doing something; an unconventional method. See voodoo.
Jinx constitutes an excuse. This implies a situation where one refuses to admit responsibility; using a scapegoat.
Juju warns of a psychological aberration, particularly regarding the effects others have on you. This suggests a need to believe in oneself.
Maligning reveals a slanderous personality; malicious defamation of another.
Mojo stands for one's inner power; the magic combination of enchanting elements; charisma and charm.
Mumbo jumbo pertains to illogical and irrational thought.
Necromancy may signify interdimensional communication. It also refers to ease of multilevel communication or perception.
Palladium constitutes a personal safeguard; an element of personal protection.
Potion is representative of a positive or negative element that one has to accept in life. Recall the surrounding dreamscape details to determine if this was a good or bad aspect that one has to be aware of and either accept or reject.
Spell (incantation) may not be a negative dream element but usually comes as a behavioral advisement.
Voodoo reflects spiritual misunderstanding.

Fancy Dress

Clown suit is representative of immaturity. It may also mean false/forced happiness.
Dracula cape warns of delving into the dark side of esoteric aspects.
Elf shoes signify a path traveled with an intellectual awareness of reality's true nature. Points to an understanding and acceptance of possibilities.
Loincloth represents a basic need.

Personifications

Beautiful people warn against equating glamor or high-class social standing with a priority to strive for or envy.
Buccaneer characterizes those who may threaten or harm another's spiritual beliefs.
Geronimo characterizes one's familial protective qualities.
Medicine woman characterizes one who has the knowledge and skill to heal.
Mentalist reveals deception.
Warlock is imagined power.
Witch won't usually denote a negative connotation, for Wicca is a bona fide nature religion celebrating the seasons, spirituality felt in nature, and the natural gifts inherent in everyone. A witch most often represents an individual who recognizes and uses those natural abilities to help others.
Wizard refers to arrogant intelligence, often an alleged or contrived intelligence.

Paranormal Tools

Adhesive represents the need to connect with someone or to bring a situation together.
Aladdin's lamp means having the source of great potential in one's hands but also needing the wisdom to use it properly.
Almanac warns one to check facts. Further research is needed.
Assortment usually reveals available options.
Aura portrays one's spiritual condition.
Byword emphasizes a particular message. Recall what this byword was, how it was used, and by whom.
Crystal ball cautions against impatience to know the future and/or the use of unnecessary perceptive tools. May mean lack of faith; anxiety.
Divining rod See dowsing rod.
Dowsing rod applies to a spiritual talent or opportunity.
Dream book signifies a source holding the keys to understanding and demystifying one's subconscious messages.
Dream dictionary stands for an opportunity to better understand oneself and one's life situations/relationships.
Ectoplasm denotes a misplaced focus on spiritualism. May also point to a nebulous element in one's life; something that can't quite be pinned down and identified.
Esoterica represents conceptual aspects in one's life that require deeper contemplation.
Horoscope warns against a tendency to be led through life by what others say.
Kirlian photography illustrates one's field of energy. Was it bright and strong? Weak?
Mescal button See peyote.
Mucilage See adhesive.
Ouija board comes as a severe warning to look within for answers instead of turning to a dependency on others.
Peyote connotes the sacred aspects of personal spiritual attainment.
Planchette represents a tool for the subconscious.
Rune symbolizes a personal revelation; a key or solution.
Water witch See dowsing rod.

see also
• Religious Accoutrements *p. 341*
• Charms *p. 457*

Characterizations

Behemoth symbolizes an aspect in one's life that is mammoth; perhaps overwhelming; too big to handle alone.
Blob stands for something that's undefined; nebulous; vague.
Faux (false) points to an imitation; a replication. This symbol carries polarity. The positive intent would be associated with imitations that save lives, such as those of fur coats. The negative intent would be related to an advisement to stop presenting false fronts (acting two-faced).
Microcosm signifies a small example or replica of a larger comparable.
Nuance is representative of a subtle suggestion. It may also refer to a fear of openly expressing an opinion or personal attitude; an innuendo.
Phony naturally means a false element. It may also refer to an imitation or deception.

Carnival

Absurdity connotes an outrageous or ridiculous situation, belief, or perception.
Bearded lady points to an anomaly in one's life; someone the dreamer needs to pay more attention to.
Bed of nails refers to a hard and difficult life phase.
Carousel is representative of a path that is going in circles and will prove to be unproductive for the dreamer.
Chamber of horrors points to one's subconscious fears; extreme anxiety.
Freak show comes to remind us that compassion and intellectual understanding bring acceptance for that which is different.
Grotesque reveals a distorted perspective out of touch with reality.
Hocus-pocus usually suggests trickery or an attempt to deceive.
Illusion will usually reveal a falsehood believed by the dreamer in the waking state.
Juggler characterizes efficiency; organization.
Kewpie doll represents unrealistic expectations.
Kiddie ride alludes to immature aspects.
Marionette is likened to a person who lacks personal responsibility or thought; having no expression of individuality; lacking self-confidence.
Medicine show reveals false cures or solutions.
Mutant/mutation will indicate an altered perspective or character.
Optical illusion points out an element in life that is not perceived with accuracy; a false view. This symbol reveals the fact that things are not as they appear.
Palmistry typifies irrationality; a lack of acceptance.
Razzle-dazzle points to an overly dramatic attempt to impress, perhaps for the purpose of concealment.
Ruse applies to a cleverly devised scheme; perhaps an ulterior motive.
Snake oil pertains to a lack of value; something useless.

Metaphors

Bandwagon warns against the inclination to follow others or fad ideas. May point to a penchant for grandstanding or lobbying.
Bells and whistles connote a life element that's full of extra benefits. Depending on the related dreamscape aspects, this symbol could also reveal a tendency to want more than is necessary.
Brainchild characterizes the birth of a brilliant idea.
Brownie point cautions against the expectation of praise; doing good for the purpose of gaining praise or reward.
Can of worms means troubling aspects; problems; an issue that will be troublesome if pursued.
Cloud nine signifies a state of elation.
Cut-and-dried means having no questions about something; an aspect that is clear and factual.
Elbow room implies a need for greater personal space from others; more distance is required.
Fail-safe illustrates one's self-preservation aspects. This may refer to emotions, mental faculties, spiritual factors, or one's physical immune system.
Field day signifies a state of great enjoyment or opportunity; a time of high activity.
Full swing represents an issue, plan, or situation that's well underway.
Off-the-rack/shelf alludes to something that is easily accessible.
Off-the-record signifies a secret or information that is not for general information.
Pet peeve advises of a need to gain acceptance in life.
Plan B denotes a second choice; the necessity of having to fall back on the alternate plan.
Point-blank emphasizes an in-your-face immediate and direct element one needs to deal with; no beating around that bush.
Rain check connotes postponements; promises to fulfill at a later date; perhaps procrastination. What was the dream rain check for? Who was giving it to whom?
Reality check comes to advise of the need to get real; take off the rose-colored glasses.

Elbow room indicates that one is feeling cramped by the presence of others.

Formal Belief Systems

Custom connotes traditionally accepted practices.

Harassment denotes a lack of acceptance; hanging on to irritations; a refusal to let go and let things be.

Hard line denotes a firm position or belief.

Malpractice refers to impropriety or negligence.

Precept indicates a spiritual, ethical, or moral law.

Prerogative depicts a right or personally sanctioned authority to engage in an activity or follow a course.

Mental States & Conditions

Arcane pertains to the ability to understand complex concepts. Depending on dreamscape factors, this symbol may come as a caution to shed outdated thought.

Deflation relates to a loss of motivation or a need to go back and begin something over again. May also advise of a need to place less importance on something.

Digression warns of not staying mentally focused; a tendency to easily get off track.

Disappointment warns against having expectations.

Distraction emphasizes the fact that the dreamer is allowing diversions to interfere with advancement or focusing attention on one's purpose.

Evasiveness cautions against avoiding reality or responsibility.

Exhaustion pretty much explains itself. It reveals one's state of overdoing, perhaps beating one's head against a wall and needing to pursue an alternative course of action or perspective.

Expectation warns against being impatient and calls for acceptance.

False pretense advises of a deception or manipulation.

Fathomless advises of concepts that are far over one's head.

Fearless may allude to carelessness; a lack of giving due respect to dangerous life aspects.

Folly indicates a lack of reasoning and logic; impulsiveness; recklessness.

Forsaken refers to a life aspect that must be given up. This may also indicate a self-generated psychological ploy for sympathy or attention if it refers directly to the dreamer's beingness.

Haphazard advises of a fragmented mind; a lack of orderly thought.

Letdown signifies a disappointment. Advises against expectations.

Off-the-cuff refers to spontaneity; instinctual reactions; impulsiveness.

Overwhelmed may refer to lack of acceptance of a forced knowledge one isn't ready to comprehend.

Procrastination implies an inability to motivate oneself, or it may imply the existence of inner fears.

Self-analysis reminds us to recheck our motives, perspectives, and behavior for personal affectations.

Representations

Deletion suggests a missing or removed aspect in one's life.

Disbursement means sharing one's talents; the expending of personal efforts to aid others.

Easement exemplifies a passage opportunity; a way to something.

Energy audit is a call to assess one's use of personal energy. This implies a change in disbursement is required.

Exceptions come in dreams to remind us that life is diverse and not everything neatly fits into a general rule.

Exemption may equate to some form of immunity from responsibility or culpability.

Exhibition emphasizes one's general perceptions; what one is aware of looking at.

Exposition stands for a display of available options or improved ways of doing things. This symbol will come to encourage a dreamer who previously thought she/he had exhausted all options.

Fact of life connotes an event or life aspect that one cannot avoid facing.

Omission will reveal an important message for the dreamer. It will pinpoint an aspect that has been left out of one's perspective or conclusion.

Prerequisite indicates a necessary element one needs to obtain before proceeding.

Project (venture) will usually be representative of or actually depict a preferred course of action for the dreamer; illustrate what one should be working on.

Provocation emphasizes a need to gain greater acceptance.

Reaction time will reveal one's level of awareness and resulting responses.

Slow-release See timed-release.

Solution (resolution) will come as a key message and be specific to each dreamer.

Timed-release points to a need to pace oneself. It may also refer to a need to experience something or spread out the initialization of a plan over time; spread out one's efforts and not expend them on one life element.

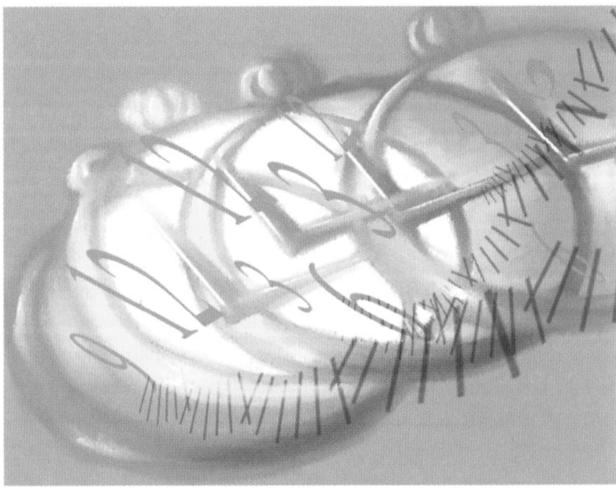

Timed-release indicates that one should not rush into something.

see also
• Thought Processes & Intelligence *p. 130*
• Texts & Rules *p. 336*

Objects

Dust bunny stands for an accumulation of extraneous life aspects that are interfering with and affecting the more important elements; a buildup of irritations.
Eyeball (out of head) advises of watchers around one.
Forbidden fruit stands for those truths of reality that exist for our discovery, but we're fearful of admitting knowledge of them.
Megalith pertains to ancient truths that remain valid today.
Melting pot usually advises of the negative situation caused by blurring or stirring or confusing concepts or issues.
Menhir See megalith.
Microbe will correspond with something that has entered one's life unnoticed. Other dream fragments will clarify whether or not this is a positive facet.
Microorganism See microbe.
Pentagram indicates the little things in life that one can't quite figure out; the forever how and why questions we find ourselves wondering about.
Photoreceptor symbolizes a strong personal desire to expand one's knowledge; a thirst for truth.
Smudge pot/stick reflects preservation; the clearing out of negativity.

Views & Interpretations

Continuity denotes a state of absolute coherence; a perceptual manner that contains no distorting aspects.
Counterculture defines something considered a turn from the norm; visible expressions of individuality different from those of the majority.
Culture shock represents a need to return to reality and have the acceptance or inner strength to face problems.
Desegregation represents an integration of perceptions, attitudes, or concepts. Usually this is an advisory message.
Distortion depicts a perspective made unclear by slanted personal attitudes.
Endless defines a condition or aspect that has no limit or is immortal, boundless.
Future shock defines a fear or lack of acceptance for one's path direction.
Linear perspective reveals a false perspective of time and distance. This indicates that the dreamer fears a goal will take a long time to achieve.
Manifest destiny constitutes an attitude of racial superiority.
Mirage connotes illusions; misperceptions; delusional behavior.
Murphy's Law implies a pessimistic outlook.
Nonsense may not be nonsense in a dream. It frequently represents something the dreamer has not sorted out and may reveal solutions.
Off-the-wall represents shocking, totally unexpected, and perhaps irrational behavior.
Subculture suggests a differing perspective.
Warped warns of a distorted perspective, attitude, emotion, or belief.

Events & Experiences

Coincidence connotes destined connections.
Correlation symbolizes interconnecting aspects.
Crisis means an unexpected disturbing event that one must face and overcome.
Demonstration is a symbol that usually brings a visually explanatory message for the dreamer. It may show how to accomplish something.
Destruction typifies any life aspect that causes great harm. What was destroyed by whom?
Drudgery is a dream aspect that comes to remind us that all our efforts are worthwhile, no matter how tedious or boring.
End (of something) clearly means just that. As simple as this interpretation is, it can relate to just about anything in the dreamer's life and the surrounding details will help to clarify this.
Equilibrium equates to balance. This may refer to mental, emotional, physical, or spiritual aspects for the dreamer.
Extension (more time) refers to a deadline reprieve; more time allotted.
Fiasco advises of a situation or relationship that will have so many negative aspects that it will go wrong from the time of its inception.
Finale means a conclusion; a dramatic ending.
Force majeure signifies an unavoidable cause of failure.
Groundbreaking refers to an effort to discover hidden aspects. For some dreamers this may indicate a beginning.
Hiatus constitutes a break in one's work; a rest period.

Practical joke refers to something that dissipates tension in one's life.

Mind-expanding relates to an experience or learning event that results in greater understanding or new revelations.
Monotony suggests expansion of one's horizons or goals.
Mystery will correspond to a puzzlement in one's waking life and will usually contain demystifying factors.
Practical joke applies to a stress-releasing event. Recall whether or not this joke was harmful. Who was the instigator? Who was the victim? What was the response?
Predicament will suggest a dilemma or entanglement. This dream may present a potential solution.
Preliminary suggests initial research is required.
Prelude portrays an event or situation that precedes the main element.
Procedure most often reveals an efficient course or direction.
Rapture (event) constitutes a belief that one will be saved from something.
Reprieve signifies a temporary suspension of a problematic or distressful situation.
Upheaval constitutes a major disturbance to one's routine; a disturbing event/issue.

Harmony & Disharmony

Controversy applies to a difference of opinion. This may even imply a self-generated factor whereby an individual's actions don't match expressed attitudes.
Explanations come to clarify a specific aspect for the individual dreamer.
Expletive denotes emphasis placed on something to which the dreamer will personally relate.
Exploitation reveals deception or manipulation being done.
Gentleman's/lady's agreement characterizes decency; a kind of integrity.
Honeymoon indicates a harmonious, loyal relationship; a unique bond that has been forged.
Leading question stands for behavior intended to discover information.
Liaison indicates a connecting aspect. Surrounding dreamscape details will clarify this.
Lineage stands for an alignment of some type. Surrounding dreamscape details will clarify this for the dreamer.
Referral signifies personal assistance and being directed to its source.

Retribution may mean agreement.

Retribution is representative of atonement. May also indicate retaliation, depending on the dreamscape's surrounding aspects.
Silent treatment won't necessarily be a negative symbol but rather a method of making others think for themselves.
Tactics stand for methods of behavior.
Time-sharing represents cooperation; the harmonic sharing of a mutually beneficial aspect.
Truce constitutes a desire to resolve relationship difficulties.
Tryst is representative of a secretive meeting.
Vendetta stands for discord associated with revenge and blame.

Miscellaneous

Bedtime story is representative of restful and peaceful thoughts before one retires to bed. It refers to those thoughts that are on one's mind just before sleep takes over. This dreamscape element may be suggesting that less stressful thoughts be entertained before one should attempt to sleep.
Dragon is representative of one's self-generated fears in one's life.
Stench reveals the presence of a serious negative element in one's life.
Stink See stench.

Alerts & Warnings

Black flag See Jolly Roger. May also warn of a need to stop a type of behavior.
Crossbones denote severe consequences; a deadly idea, attitude, behavior, or relationship.
Definition spelled out in a dream will clearly come as an important personal message for the dreamer. Pay close attention to these.
Expulsion forewarns of disastrous results coming if one doesn't alter one's current behavior.
Extrication advises of a need to remove oneself from a harmful situation, relationship, or belief system.
Fallacy comes as a caution to check the facts of something in one's life.
Forewarning almost always comes to reveal a near-future event/ramification/outcome.
Free-floating cautions of spiritual indecision.
Harbinger is representative of a forerunner; something that comes first.
Hunch portrays personal insights; psychic impressions. Recall what the hunch was, because this will be an important message.
Jolly Roger (flag) warns of a dangerous aspect in one's life. This could relate to a situation, relationship, or even oneself. Because the Jolly Roger (skull & crossbones) is commonly associated with a pirate ship, this symbol is most often connected to a spiritual aspect.
Marker (sign) will usually designate a personal message for each dreamer.
Misdemeanor will warn of an offense one did. This type of symbol is in direct relation to one's conscience.
Omen comes as a sign. Recall surrounding dreamscape details to determine whether or not this is a positive or negative indication. Generally, an omen is commonly perceived as a bad sign, but that's certainly not all-inclusive of the term.
Point of no return clearly signifies a point in one's life where there is no turning back; no chance to alter or correct events.
Portent will be a clear sign that forewarns of the potential for danger or a disruptive element of one's life course.
Preamble will define an introductory element that precedes an event or situation; a forewarning.
Precaution is representative of heightened awareness; an attention given to probabilities; preparedness.
Prognosis will reveal a probable outcome.
Revival comes as a warning to revitalize an element in one's life. Advises of a need to be reinspired, reenergized, or motivated.
Revoked is a suggestion to rescind or correct something in one's life.
Tardiness cautions against procrastination. Suggests the possibility that one's actions or response will be too late.
Tommyknocker implies a serious warning. It may be a forewarning of a dangerous situation or element.
Ultimatum is representative of a last-resort choice.

Index

A

Index

Index

Index

Index

Index

Index

Index

Index

Index

Index

Index

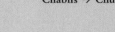

Index

Index

Index

Index

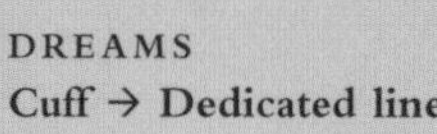

Index

Index

Index

Index

E

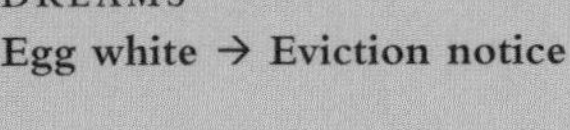

Index

Index

Index

Index

Index

Index

G

Index

Index

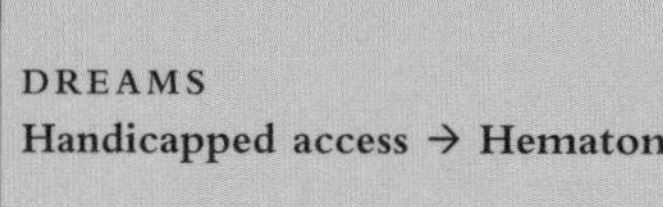

Index

Index

Index

Index

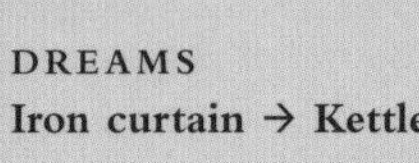

Index

Index

L

Index

Index

M

Index

Index

Index

Index

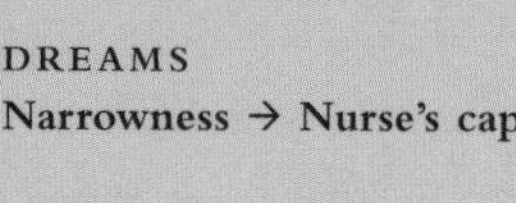

Index

Index

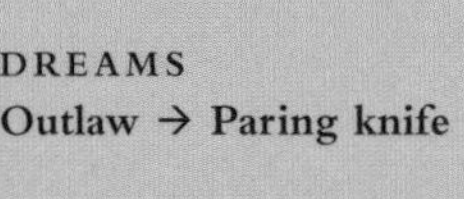

Index

P

Index

Index

Index

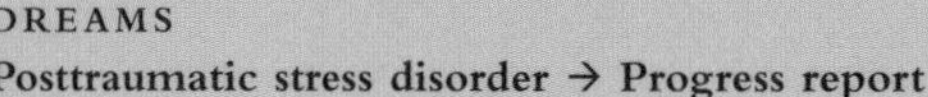

Index

Index

Q

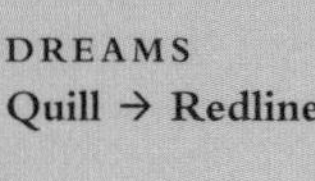

Index

Index

Index

S

Index

Index

Index

Index

Index

Index

Index

Index

Index

Index

Index

Index

Index

W

Index

Index

Thunder Bay Press
An imprint of the Advantage Publishers Group
5880 Oberlin Drive, San Diego, CA 92121-4794
www.thunderbaybooks.com

ISBN-13: 978-1-59223-577-3
ISBN-10: 1-59223-577-8

Library of Congress Cataloging-in-Publication Data

Summer Rain, Mary, 1945-
20,000 dreams : discover the real meaning of your dream life / Mary Summer Rain ; illustrated by Ivan Hissey.
p. cm.
Includes index.
ISBN 1-59223-577-8
1. Dream interpretation. 2. Symbolism (Psychology) I. Title: Twenty thousand dreams. II. Title.

BF1091.S817 2006
54.6'3--dc21

2005055968

Printed in China
1 2 3 4 5 10 09 08 07 06

This book was conceived, designed, and produced by
IXOS PRESS LIMITED
The Old Candlemakers, West Street,
Lewes, East Sussex BN7 2NZ, U.K.

Publisher: David Alexander
Creative Director: Peter Bridgewater
Art Director: Sarah Howerd
Commissioning Editor: Mark Truman
Designer: Richard Constable
Illustrator: Ivan Hissey